Exhibit 8. New Single-Family Home Prices: 1964–Present

Period	Median					U.S. Average	
	United States	Northeast	Midwest	South	West	Houses Actually Sold	Constant-Quality House[1,2]
Annual Data							
1964	18,900	20,300	19,400	16,700	20,400	20,500	34,900
1965	20,000	21,500	21,600	17,500	21,600	21,500	35,600
1966	21,400	23,500	23,200	18,200	23,200	23,300	37,100
1967	22,700	25,400	25,100	19,400	24,100	24,600	38,100
1968	24,700	27,700	27,400	21,500	25,100	26,600	40,100
1969	25,600	31,600	27,600	22,800	25,300	27,900	43,200
1970	23,400	30,300	24,400	20,300	24,000	26,600	44,400
1971	25,200	30,600	27,200	22,500	25,500	28,300	46,800
1972	27,600	31,400	29,300	25,800	27,500	30,500	49,800
1973	32,500	37,100	32,900	30,900	32,400	35,500	54,200
1974	35,900	40,100	36,100	34,500	35,800	38,900	59,200
1975	39,300	44,000	39,600	37,300	40,600	42,600	65,500
1976	44,200	47,300	44,800	40,500	47,200	48,000	71,200
1977	48,800	51,600	51,500	44,100	53,500	54,200	80,200
1978	55,700	58,100	59,200	50,300	61,300	62,500	91,900
1979	62,900	65,500	63,900	57,300	69,600	71,800	104,900
1980	64,600	69,500	63,400	59,600	72,300	76,400	115,600
1981	68,900	76,000	65,900	64,400	77,800	83,000	124,700
1982	69,300	78,200	68,900	66,100	75,000	83,900	127,600
1983	75,300	82,200	79,500	70,900	80,100	89,800	130,300
1984	79,900	88,600	85,400	72,000	87,300	97,600	135,600
1985	84,300	103,300	80,300	75,000	92,600	100,800	137,300
1986	92,000	125,000	88,300	80,200	95,700	111,900	142,600
1987	104,500	140,000	95,000	88,000	111,000	127,200	150,300
1988	112,500	149,000	101,600	92,000	126,500	138,300	156,000
1989	120,000	159,600	108,800	96,400	139,000	148,800	162,200
1990	122,900	159,000	107,900	99,000	147,500	149,800	165,300
1991	120,000	155,900	110,000	100,000	141,100	147,200	167,400
1992	121,500	169,000	115,600	105,500	130,400	144,100	169,800
1993	126,500	162,600	125,000	115,000	135,000	147,700	176,300
1994	130,000	169,000	132,900	116,900	140,400	154,500	186,800
1995	133,900	180,000	134,000	124,500	141,000	158,700	191,000
1996	140,000	186,000	138,000	126,200	153,900	166,400	195,900
1997	146,000	190,000	149,900	129,600	160,000	176,200	200,500
1998	152,500	200,000	157,500	135,800	163,500	181,900	205,500
1999	161,000	210,500	164,000	145,900	173,700	195,600	216,200
2000	169,000	227,400	169,700	148,000	196,400	207,000	224,600
2001	175,200	246,400	172,600	155,400	213,600	213,200	231,300
2002	187,600	264,300	178,000	163,400	238,500	228,700	241,900
2003	195,000	264,500	184,300	168,100	260,900	246,300	255,300
2004	221,000	315,800	205,000	181,100	283,100	274,500	275,600
2005	240,900	343,800	216,900	197,300	332,600	297,000	297,000
2006	246,500	346,000	213,500	208,200	337,700	305,900	311,100
2007	247,900	320,200	208,600	217,700	330,900	313,600	311,600
2008	232,100	343,600	198,900	203,700	294,800	292,600	295,500
2009	216,700	302,500	189,200	194,800	263,700	270,900	282,400
2010	221,800	329,900	197,700	196,800	259,300	272,900	282,200
2011	227,200	322,800	203,300	211,400	256,000	267,900	280,100
Quarterly Data							
2011							
Q2	228,100	289,100	211,600	209,900	259,200	267,600	280,700
Q3	223,500	324,100	195,400	210,300	251,400	263,000	276,200
Q4	221,100	322,800	209,800	201,200	252,000	259,700	279,200
2012							
Q1	238,400	305,400	223,100	217,300	272,300	278,000	279,200
Q2	235,300	367,700	224,100	206,000	255,000	280,300	282,700

[1] The components of a constant-quality house reflect the kinds of new single-family homes sold in 2005. The average price of a constant-quality house is derived from a set of statistical models relating sales price to selected standard physical characteristics of new single-family homes sold in 2005.

[2] Effective with the December 2007 New Residential Sales Release in January 2008, the Census Bureau began publishing the Constant Quality (Laspeyres) Price Index with 2005 as the base year. (The previous base year was 1996.) "Constant-Quality House" data are computed for this table from price indexes published by the Census Bureau.

Sources: Census Bureau, Department of Commerce; Office of Policy Development and Research, Department of Housing and Urban Development
http://www.census.gov/const/quarterly_sales.pdf (see table Q6)

REAL ESTATE
FINANCE

Theory and Practice

Seventh Edition

Terrence M. Clauretie
Professor Emeritus, University of Nevada, Las Vegas

G. Stacy Sirmans
Florida State University

United States

Real Estate Finance: Theory and Practice, Seventh Edition

Terrence M. Clauretie and G. Stacy Sirmans

Executive Editor: Sara Glassmeyer

Developmental Editor: Arlin Kauffmann

Rights Acquisition Director: Audrey Pettengill

Rights Acquisition Specialist, Text and Image: Amber Hosea

Senior Manufacturing Planner: Charlene Taylor

Art and Cover Direction, Production Management, and Composition: PreMediaGlobal

Cover & Internal Images: © Antony Edwards/ Getty Images, © fotog/Getty Images

For product information and technology assistance, contact us at
www.oncourselearning.com

Library of Congress Control Number: 2013935511

ISBN-13: 978-1-285-18137-0

ISBN-10: 1-285-18137-9

OnCourse Learning
7577 Central Parke Blvd. Suite 100
Mason, OH 45040
USA

Visit our corporate website at **www.oncourselearning.com**

Printed in the United States of America
1 2 3 4 5 6 7 17 16 15 14 13

To Patty, Sean and Kevin
TMC

To Elaine, Stace, Candace, and Berkeley
GSS

A Special Dedication To James R. Webb
1947–2009

A Special Dedication To Nasser Daneshvary
1950–2012

BRIEF CONTENTS

PART 4 SPECIAL TOPICS IN REAL ESTATE FINANCE 523

CONTENTS

6　Alternative Mortgage Instruments 102

7　Federal Regulation of Financial Institutions Related to the Mortgage Market 143

PREFACE

Goals and Foundation of the Text

Although the institutions, regulations, and structure of the real estate finance market will continue to change, the historical details and lessons from which economic behavior takes place will not. As a means to teach these lessons, we want to provide a real estate finance textbook that is based on sound economic and finance principles. A foundation of theory will allow you to understand the structure of the real estate finance market as it changes throughout your lifetime.

The title of this textbook, Real Estate Finance: Theory and Practice, suggests that the material covered here reflects a blend of theory and practice. In fact, our goal is to apply the theoretical aspects of financial economics to explain how real estate financial institutions and markets have evolved to their present state, and why they take the form they do. To promote a greater understanding of how real estate financial markets work, we present material based on a foundation of economic and finance theories and assist readers in putting those theories into practice.

Even with this emphasis on economic and financial theory, we do not neglect the descriptive approach that is necessary to understand the structure of real estate finance markets. You will gain an understanding of major institutions and the roles they play. You will learn about major federal legislation that impacts real estate finance, particularly the residential area. You will also learn how law shapes and affects the form of the real estate finance market.

Special Features

- Each chapter begins with Learning Objectives designed to help you focus on the chapter's key concepts.
- Summaries, Key Terms, and Web Sites complete the chapters to further develop what you have read.
- Review Questions and Problems are included at the end of each chapter to help you review the material and alert you to areas that may need more study.
- A website link providing tables and financial data worksheets to aid in understanding financial relationships and solve end-of-chapter exercises is provided.
- An excel file named ALLFILES.xls used for simulations of financial analysis situations is provided. Chapters 11, 15, 18 and 19 include many end of chapter problems where the ALLFILES.xls problems can be used. The excel file can be found at **www.oncourselearning.com**.
- A complete Instructor's Manual is available. It includes chapter summaries, a test bank of questions and answers by chapter, and lecture handouts. This manual is also available online at **www.oncourselearning.com**.

Topic Coverage

The textbook is divided into four parts. Part 1 deals with financial markets in general, finance theory, and the application of finance theory to real estate. Here, we lay down the foundation for understanding how financial markets operate. We discuss the primary tools of financial analysis and show, in general, how they apply to real estate. Part 1 of the text is designed to give the student a basic understanding of finance theory as it applies to real estate and mortgage markets.

Part 2 discusses issues related to residential real estate finance and focuses on the latest changes in the industry. After developing the history of real estate, we investigate alternative mortgage instruments and the effect of terms of financing on property. Next, we look at federal housing policies and their impact on the residential real estate market, along with the government takeover of Fannie Mae and Freddie Mac and the U.S. Treasury Department's Troubled Asset Relief Program (TARP). Two chapters are devoted to the secondary mortgage market, one to a description of this market and one to issues related to the valuation of securities created in the secondary mortgage market and credit default swaps. We complete the second part of the textbook with three chapters on residential loan underwriting, loan processing and origination, and mortgage insurance.

Part 3 deals with commercial real estate finance. We present issues concerning the use of debt (leverage) in financing properties, the impact of tax laws on financing commercial properties, and sources of commercial real estate financing. In this section we also discuss various methods of financing commercial properties, including equity participation loans and sale lease-back agreements.

Part 4 addresses special topics such as real estate in a portfolio context, material related to lender legal liability, ethics and fraud in real estate finance, and agency problems in real estate finance.

Finally, we would like to continually develop this textbook and make it better with each edition. If you have any comments or would like to make suggestions that would improve it for future editions, please write us at: Terrence M. Clauretie, or G. Stacy Sirmans, c/o Real Estate Executive Editor, OnCourse Learning, 7577 Central Parke Blvd, Ste 100., Mason, OH 45040. Also feel free to e-mail Terrence M. Clauretie at mike.clauretie@unlv.edu.

New to This Edition

Additional changes to the seventh edition include the following:

Chapter 2 – New Figure 2-2 graph on Inflation/T-Bill Yield: 1961-2010; updated Figure 2-4

Chapter 3 – Updated Figure 3-4 Chicago Mercantile Exchange House Price Index for Las Vegas, NV and Los Angeles, CA 1987–2012

Chapter 4 – Edited to make more readable and the history has been brought up-to-date.

Chapter 5 –Strictly focused on fixed-rate mortgages. Edited to make more readable and brought up to date.

Chapter 6 – Edited chapter to make more readable; deleted the calculator keystroke illustrations. Revised the reverse mortgage example.

Chapter 7 – New Chapter on Federal Regulation of Financial Institutions Related to the Mortgage Market

Chapter 8 – New topic on Regulation Z and The DODD-Frank Act

Chapter 9 – Updated Appendix

Chapter 10 – New table on Ginnie Mae Financial Highlights—Fiscal Years, 2009–2011

Chapter 11 – New topic on Cash Flows with Default Losses; new Tables added on Cash flows from a hypothetical CMO with defaults and Cash flows from a CMO where the assumed default losses are increased; new Appendix on Mortgage Derivatives and Structured Finance

Chapters 12, 13, 14 – edited chapters to make them more readable. Made any needed updates for FHA and VA loans and private mortgage insurance.

Chapter 15 – edited to make more readable; added some discussion; revised the cash flow tables.

Chapter 16 – edited to make more reader friendly; revised discussion on income tax changes and made any needed updates.

Chapter 17 – updated to include more recent data on sources of funds, especially CMBS's

Chapter 19 – rewrote sections to make easier to read and updated information where necessary.

Chapter 20 – revised to make easier to read; revised REIT requirements; updated REIT data; updated information on corporations and REITs.

Chapter 21 – edited to make more reader friendly; added a number of new studies and citations.

About the Authors

Terrence M. Clauretie received his Ph.D. in Economics from Washington State University. He is currently a professor of Real Estate Finance at UNLV. To date, he has authored three texts and 85 articles in academic and professional journals. He is a fellow of the Homer Hoyt Advanced Studies Institute, and also a former adjunct professor of the National Association of Corporate Real Estate Executives.

G. Stacy Sirmans is Chairman of the Department of Risk Management/ Insurance, Real Estate, and Legal Studies at Florida State University. He is also the Kenneth G. Bacheller Professor of Real Estate and the Research Director of the Center for Real Estate Education and Research at FSU. He has published extensively in the real estate and finance areas on a variety of topics and his work has appeared in journals such as the *Journal of Financial and Quantitative Analysis*, the *Journal of Real Estate Finance and Economics*, and the *Journal of Real Estate Research*. His research has appeared in various media outlets such as the Wall Street Journal, Money Magazine, Business Week, USA Today, Kiplinger Magazine, New York Times, L.A. Times, Chicago Tribune, Miami Herald, and a number of other major news outlets. Prior to FSU, Dr. Sirmans served on the faculties of Emory University and Clemson University. He also served as a Visiting Scholar to the Federal Home Loan Bank Board in Washington, DC. He is currently President-Elect of the American Real Estate Society and he serves on the editorial boards of the *Journal of Real Estate Finance and Economics, Journal of Real Estate Research, Journal of Housing Research, Journal of Real Estate Literature*, and *Seniors Housing and Care Journal*. He earned his Ph.D. from the University of Georgia.

Acknowledgements

The authors would like to thank the following people for their invaluable feedback and guidance with this edition:

Darren A. Prum, University of Nevada, Las Vegas

Eric Blazer, Millersville University

Richard Cohen, University of Alaska, Ar Anchorage

Karen Gibler, Georgia State University

Anthony Grady, Saint Augustine University

David Harrison, Texas Tech University

Karen Eilers Lahey, The University of Akron

Keith Munsell, Boston University

Milena Petrova, Syracuse University

Tracey Seslen, University of Southern California

Carlos Slawson, Louisiana State University

Malcolm Tennant, Access Reverse Mortgage, St. Petersburg, Florida

Charles Tu, University of San Diego

Finance and Real Estate

*T*he three chapters in Part 1 of this book set the stage
for applying financial economics to real estate. Here,
the text discusses the nature of finance and economics and describes financial markets with reference to those
institutions that play a role in real estate finance. It also
looks at money, credit, and interest rates. Interest rates, as
you may expect, play an integral role in real estate finance.
The determination of both the general level of interest rates
and those on particular debt securities is presented. Finally, in
this part we present the major finance concepts and principles and show how they apply to real estate markets.

REAL ESTATE FINANCE: AN OVERVIEW

LEARNING OBJECTIVES

After reading this chapter, you should understand the relationship between finance and real estate. You also should understand how financial markets work in terms of the flow of funds from those with credit to lend to those with a demand for borrowed funds. You also will learn which major financial institutions direct the flow of funds.

INTRODUCTION

Each chapter in this textbook tackles a different subject in real estate finance. The text is by no means exhaustive. In fact, it is quite modest in its coverage. Be aware that when you have completed this course, your knowledge of real estate finance will be greater than it is now but still lacking in many respects. You can gain additional knowledge of real estate finance from more in-depth study of the various subjects in this textbook, as well as from real-world experiences. If your professional goals direct you to the world of real estate finance, expect to gain much knowledge through your day-to-day experiences. With this in mind, you will nonetheless need to get as much from this book as possible. To accomplish this, you need to begin by understanding the framework of real estate finance—what real estate finance is and the environment within which it takes place. Chapter by chapter, you will learn about individual real estate finance topics. As each topic is introduced, we will attempt to place it in the framework of general finance models. You should understand that real estate finance subjects are applications of more general finance principles. We tend to focus as much on finance principles and concepts as on descriptions of real estate finance institutions. The application of general finance principles to real estate is discussed in detail in Chapter 3. For now, we discuss what real estate finance is all about.

The Nature of Real Estate Finance

The nature of real estate finance can be framed by three questions:

1. What is finance?
2. What is real estate finance?
3. What is the environment of real estate finance?

What Is Finance?

Finance is the study of the process, institutions, markets, and instruments used to transfer money and credit between individuals, businesses, and governments. Finance is applied economics. Economics is the study of the allocation of resources for the purpose of producing goods and services for various members of society. Finance is the study of how the flow of money and credit facilitates that production and allocation. Although finance can be seen as a segment of the more general field of economics, there are differences in the focus of the two fields of study. This is not to say that finance is different or unrelated to economics; it is not. It does have a different focus, however, and utilizes certain concepts more than the traditional study of economics. The focus of finance differs from that of economics in several ways.

If you have had a course in economics and one in finance, you can appreciate how the two subjects differ in their approaches. First, in the theory of the firm, for example, microeconomics focuses on the profit maximizing assumption. Policies of the firm are geared toward maximizing profits within the constraints of the structure of the industry. In finance, at least managerial finance, the focus is on maximizing the value of equity interest of owners. This involves a lot more than maximizing the profits of the firm. In fact, a myopic view of maximizing profits could lead to less than a maximization of the value of the firm's equity position. Thus, finance is concerned with issues such as the character of securities (debt or equity) issued by the firm to finance assets. Seldom, if ever, in a microeconomics course does one consider the character of the securities issued by firms.

Second, the focus of finance is more on the intertemporal transfer of funds between individuals. This is another way of saying that finance considers the time value of money and the implications for interest rates on the time value of money and financing decisions. Finance is concerned with the valuation of assets, and the valuation process explicitly considers the timing of the cash flows associated with the ownership of an asset.

Third—and this is also related to the valuation of an asset—finance focuses on cash flows, not profits. Cash flows are important because they can be either reinvested in other income-earning assets, or they can reduce expense-costing liabilities. Again, microeconomics focuses on profits.

Finally, the study of finance makes extensive use of the concept of risk. **Risk** is the possibility (and associated probabilities) that the actual result (return on investment, for example) will differ from the expected outcome. Finance considers the effect of risk on the valuation (the cash flows) of an asset. It also analyzes the risk–return trade-off, the general principle that states that investors require additional expected returns for taking on additional risk.

These are just several ways in which the focus of the study of finance differs from that of economics. Again, finance can be considered a subfield of economics. Yet, most agree, the focus of finance is different from that of economics.

What Is Real Estate Finance?

There are several subdisciplines within finance including the following:

- Managerial or corporate finance
- Investment and securities (including real estate) analysis and portfolio theory
- Financial institutions and financial services
- Personal finance
- Insurance and risk management
- Real estate finance

Each of the subdisciplines deals with a different area of finance. Real estate finance is a very broad category and includes the study of the institutions, markets, and instruments used to transfer money and credit for the purpose of developing or acquiring real property. Real property, in turn, is the rights, powers, and privileges associated with the use of real estate. Real estate is land and all fixed and immovable improvements on it. Real estate finance would include, but not be limited to, a study of the following:

- Owner-occupied residential property
- Rental residential property
- Terms of residential property leases
- Appraisal of residential properties
- Loans (mortgages) on residential properties
- Sales and exchange of residential properties
- Economics of brokerage of residential properties
- Markets for exchange of residential mortgages
- Valuation of residential mortgages
- Commercial properties, including urban office buildings, suburban office buildings, hotels/motels, retirement communities, recreation facilities, mini-warehouses, warehouses, apartment complexes, industrial facilities, and retail trade facilities
- Loans on commercial properties
- Markets for the exchange of commercial property loans
- Valuation of loans on commercial properties
- Appraisal of commercial properties
- Investment in commercial properties
- Portfolios of real estate investments
- Real estate taxation issues
- Law and real estate lending

Since real property includes not only real estate but all of the rights and privileges of the use of real estate that can be transferred, the study of real estate finance does not have a narrow focus.

What Is the Environment of Real Estate Finance?

Financial instruments are used to transfer money and credit for the purpose of developing and acquiring real property. The institutions that create and purchase those instruments and the markets within which they are transferred constitute the environment of real estate finance. In essence, the environment is the financial system of the United States. This portion of the financial system is not insignificant. Table 1-1 shows the stock of fixed assets in 2010 and 2011. Private, nonresidential structures

TABLE 1–1

Current-Cost Net Stock of Fixed Assets and Consumer Durable Goods (billions of dollars; year-end estimates)

		2010	2011
1	Private fixed assets	34,388.3	35,193.2
2	Nonresidential structures	11,188.8	11,688.4
	Office	1,624.5	1,670.6
	Shopping	623.1	644.9
	Warehouse	383.1	396.2
3	Residential	17,393.1	17,510.0
	1–4 unit	11,952.3	12,013.4
	5 or more units	1,701.6	1,630.1
	Manufactured	215.8	217.1

Source: Bureau of Economic Analysis.

consist primarily of what is termed commercial real estate (office buildings, shopping centers, industrial properties, and so on). In 2011 the U.S. Bureau of Economic Analysis estimated the total value of this category at $11.7 trillion. The value of private residential structures (single-family houses and apartment complexes) is estimated to be $17.5 trillion. Therefore, ignoring government structures, the total value of private real estate in 2011 was approximately $29.2 trillion.

In considering the economy as a whole, there is an identity called the **savings-investment cycle**. The identity indicates that, by definition, the amount of savings equals the total amount invested. Table 1-2 shows the gross savings and investment in the United States for 2012. Savings are identified by three groups: individuals (personal), businesses, and government. In 2012 the federal government's savings were negative (deficit spending). In 2012 about 24 percent of total savings came from individuals. Businesses saved $714.2 billion in undistributed profits (retained earnings). The total savings of $1,983.4 billion resulted in an equal amount of "investment" (accounting for a statistical discrepancy of $46.1 billion). This does not mean investment by purchasing stocks and bonds but rather investment in the sense of new plant construction, equipment, and real property.

The financial marketplace is the system whereby savings are transferred from what are termed surplus income units to what are termed deficit income units. The best way to understand the process is to consider a simple example. If an individual has more income than consumption, he or she is a surplus income unit and adds to the amount of savings. On the other hand, a corporation that needs to construct a manufacturing facility and does not have sufficient revenue above expenses to meet the cost will have to borrow funds. This deficit income firm may issue a bond. If the bond is purchased by the income surplus unit, a small

TABLE 1–2

Saving and Investment, 2012 (second quarter on an annual basis, billions of dollars)

1	Gross saving	1,983.4
2	Net private saving	1,187.1
3	Personal saving	472.9
4	Undistributed corporate profits with inventory valuation and capital consumption adjustments	714.2
5	Government	−1,207.1
6	Gross domestic investment	2,029.5
7	Households	426.0
8	Business	1,627.0
9	Government	471.4
10	Statistical discrepancy	46.1

Source: Bureau of Economic Analysis.

portion of the national savings–investment cycle is completed. Of course, this is a very simple example.

The actual process involves sophisticated markets and institutions that facilitate the closing of the cycle.

Figure 1-1 illustrates a simple **flow of funds** in the savings–investment cycle. This is the environment of real estate finance. On the left side of the figure are the surplus income units with funds to lend. On the right side are the deficit income units with a need to borrow credit. Surplus and deficit income units are broken down into three categories: individuals (households), businesses, and governments. Both surplus and deficit income units exist within each category, but some categories will be dominated by one type. Recently, for example, the federal government has been a deficit income unit (but some state governments are surplus income units).

Excess funds flow from the surplus income to the deficit income units either directly or through intermediaries. Direct financing takes place when the surplus income unit advances funds directly to the deficit income unit. The transaction usually involves a surplus unit purchasing the security (a bond, for example) issued by the deficit unit. Brokers may facilitate the transaction but are not necessary in many cases. **Financial intermediaries** are financial institutions that channel funds from the surplus income units to the deficit income units. Intermediaries provide special services (discussed in Chapter 3) under the theory of financial intermediation. Of special interest to real estate finance are the activities of the secondary mortgage market. Here, intermediaries purchase residential and commercial mortgages from other intermediaries or from brokers that deal with surplus income units. They purchase the mortgages with funds raised through the sale of securities

FIGURE 1-1   **Flow of Funds in the Savings–Investment Cycle**

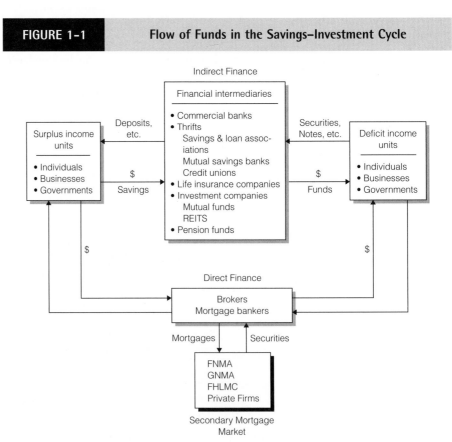

Source: © 2014 OnCourse Learning

that they create. As an example, a secondary mortgage market agency will sell a security to a surplus income unit through a broker and use the proceeds of the sale to purchase a mortgage from a deficit income unit, again through a broker.

A CLOSER LOOK AT FINANCIAL INTERMEDIARIES AND FINANCIAL MARKETS

The intermediaries shown in Figure 1-1 vary in purpose and form but fulfill the same function—facilitating the flow of funds in the financial system. Intermediaries perform several functions, discussed in detail in Chapter 3. In short, because of their special position in the financial market, they take on (for a fee) several risks or offer services associated with lending. First, they provide liquidity to savers (for example, checking accounts). Second, they borrow short and lend long, exposing themselves to adverse (upward) movements in interest rates. Third, they can evaluate the credit risks of borrowers. Because of this ability to evaluate credit risk, they are in a good position to take on the risk that a borrower may default on a loan.

Government regulation and supervision of some of the financial intermediaries are discussed in detail in Chapter 7. As you will see a rather large and complex system has developed to regulate and supervise financial intermediaries, both at the federal and state level. Let's consider briefly the principal financial intermediaries.

Commercial Banks

Commercial banks accept demand deposits (checking accounts) and time deposits (savings accounts and certificates of deposit). They also may borrow funds from other sources. Together these funds are advanced to individuals, businesses, and the government. Commercial banks are supervised by the Federal Reserve System. Their deposits are insured by the Federal Deposit Insurance Corporation (FDIC). They are an important source of commercial real estate loans, especially loans for the acquisition, development, and construction (ADC loans) of real estate projects. They are also a source of residential loans.

Thrift Institutions

Thrift institutions include savings and loan associations, mutual savings banks, and credit unions. They are called thrifts because they are a major depository of individuals' savings. Prior to the early 1980s, they were prohibited from accepting demand deposits. They could accept only time deposits. Now, they can compete with commercial banks for demand deposits. The distinction between savings and loan associations and mutual savings banks is in the form of ownership. The mutual savings bank form of ownership (a cooperative as opposed to a stock company) must be approved by state law. A dozen or so states allow this form of ownership. There is little practical distinction between them, however. They share the same trade association, the U.S. Savings and Loan League, and are supervised by the same government agency, the Office of Thrift Supervision (formally the Federal Home Loan Bank Board). Their deposits are insured by the FDIC. (Prior to 1990, their deposits were insured by the Federal Savings and Loan Insurance Corporation [FSLIC].) Credit unions are restricted by their charters to serving members of a designated affiliation, such as employees of a corporation, government unit, or other entity. They are supervised by the **National Credit Union Administration** (NCUA), and their deposits are federally insured by the National Credit Union Share Insurance Fund. At one time, thrifts were the largest single source of residential mortgage credit. Now, the secondary mortgage market has supplanted thrifts as the major source of such funds. Prior to 1982, thrifts were restricted in their investment activities. Savings and loans, in particular, were directed to invest in residential mortgages. Deregulation of thrifts beginning in 1982 allowed them to broaden their investments to include more commercial real estate investments.

Investment Companies

Investment companies pool the funds of many savers and invest the funds in a portfolio of assets. Many companies invest only in stocks, and some of these specialize only in growth stocks, income stocks, or stock of companies in certain industries. Some investment companies, called real estate investment trusts (REITs), specialize in real estate properties or mortgages on real estate properties. Others invest in mortgage-type securities such as Government National Mortgage Association (GNMA) bonds.

Insurance Companies

Insurance companies, especially life insurance companies, receive periodic or lump-sum payments from individuals or organizations in return for a promise to make future payments if certain events occur. They have a need to invest these funds to build a reserve until the event occurs, at which time there will be a claim. Since they have a long investment horizon, life insurance companies invest in many commercial real estate properties.

Pension Funds

Private **pension funds** pool the contributions of employees and invest the funds just as insurance companies do. They need to build a reserve to meet the retirement needs of the contributors. Currently, they invest modestly in commercial real estate properties. It is expected, however, that their investment in real estate will increase in the future.

Direct Financing

Much of the flow of funds in the savings–investment cycle takes place without the use of intermediaries. Surplus income units advance funds directly to deficit income units with the aid of brokers that facilitate the transaction. Thus, when an individual purchases a bond directly from the federal government or when a home seller grants a note to the home buyer, **direct financing** takes place. Often a broker may be involved, as is the case with the purchase of most corporate securities.

Secondary Mortgage Market

Of particular interest to those involved in real estate finance is the role of the **secondary mortgage market** agencies and firms. These agencies and firms include the Federal National Mortgage Association (FNMA), the GNMA, the Federal Home Loan Mortgage Corporation (FHLMC), recently the Federal Home Loan Bank Board, and many private firms. They obtain funds by issuing securities (often through brokers) called mortgage-related securities (MRSs). They then use the funds to purchase mortgages. The cash flow stream from the mortgages is used to service the interest payments on the MRSs. Let's distinguish between secondary and primary markets and look at the importance of secondary markets to the efficient flow of funds in the financial system.

Primary and Secondary Markets

You are undoubtedly aware of the exchanges, such as the New York Bond Exchange and the New York Stock Exchange. Existing securities are bought and sold on these exchanges. On these exchanges, the owners of the securities did not originate or create them. When a security is created and sold for the first time by a deficit income unit, that transaction takes place in the **primary market**. Secondary mortgage market agencies and firms are classified as such because they purchase (and sell) mortgages that have been previously originated by other lenders. That is, they themselves do not originate the mortgage to the borrowing household. When a mortgage is originated by a lender to a household, this takes place in the primary market. New securities are created in the primary market, and any subsequent sale of the security takes place in the **secondary market**.

Secondary markets are helpful, if not necessary, to the success of primary markets. A large and active secondary market makes securities more liquid. A buyer of a security in the primary market will be concerned if it is difficult to resell the security. Investors do not like securities that are not easily sold (not liquid). The reduction in marketability (or liquidity) risk due to a large and efficient secondary market leads to a reduction in the yield required by investors in the primary market. But a reduction in the investor's required yield also translates into a lower interest cost for borrowers. In this way, secondary markets lower the costs of completing the savings–investment, or flow of funds, cycle.

Money and Capital Markets

Financial markets can be divided into two categories: money markets and capital markets. Both involve the flow of funds between users and suppliers of credit. **Money markets** deal in short-term securities (maturities of 1 year or less), and **capital markets** deal in long-term securities (over 1 year in maturity). Many organizations deal in both markets. The federal government, for example, issues both short-term Treasury bills and long-term Treasury bonds to finance its deficits. Corporations finance their assets with long-term bonds and equity but have an occasional need for short-term financing. When they do, they borrow for the short term from commercial banks or issue commercial paper. Most real estate financing takes place in the capital markets. Mortgages are long-term securities. The exception would be the need for short-term ADC loans that are refinanced with long-term permanent loans when the real estate project is complete.

ORGANIZATION OF THE BOOK

The remainder of this book is organized as follows. Chapters 2 and 3 complete Part 1. Chapter 2 deals with the determination of interest rates. The interest rate is the "price" of credit, and an understanding of how interest rates are determined is essential to understanding the real estate finance market. Chapter 3 outlines some of the fundamental principles of finance and indicates how these can be applied to real estate. They include asset valuation, leverage and capital structure, option valuation, the theory of financial intermediation, portfolio theory, efficient market theory, and agency theory. These basic finance principles are applied wherever possible throughout the remainder of the book.

The 11 chapters in Part 2 deal with residential real estate finance. Chapter 4 outlines the history of residential finance until World War II, then breaks the postwar era into decades and shows the evolution of the residential real estate market to its current market structure. Chapter 5 shows the mechanics of the fixed-rate amortizing mortgage, which became the normal vehicle for residential mortgage financing in the 1930s. Chapter 6 examines alternative mortgage instruments—mortgages other than the standard fixed-rate 30-year loan. Alternative mortgages include the adjustable-rate mortgage, graduated payment mortgage, and reverse mortgage. Chapter 6 also illustrates the mortgage refinancing process. Chapter 7 discusses the federal regulation of mortgage lenders. Chapters 8 and 9 discuss federal policies on residential housing. Federal laws related to four issues are considered: housing affordability, market efficiency, competition in the housing finance market, and equity (fairness).

The next two chapters are designed to acquaint you with the secondary mortgage market. Chapter 10 presents the structure of the secondary mortgage market and includes a description of the major secondary mortgage market agencies and the MRSs that they create. Chapter 11 follows with a discussion on the cash flows and valuation of those MRSs. Chapter 12 focuses on risk management by lenders, especially the minimization of default risk. It discusses standard borrower qualification and loan underwriting procedures. Chapter 13 describes the steps in the loan origination and processing procedures, including the real estate appraisal process. It also presents a summary of the activities of mortgage bankers. Finally, Chapter 14 closes the section on residential finance with a discussion of government and private mortgage insurance programs and foreclosure laws.

Part 3 is concerned with commercial real estate finance. Chapter 15 looks at the theoretical aspects of leverage and capital structure, including the discounted cash flow process used in property valuation. The federal income taxation of commercial, income-producing real estate is presented in Chapter 16. The chapter also explains the alternative methods of taxation such as tax-deferred exchange and installment sale financing. Chapter 17 briefly describes the sources of funds for commercial real estate acquisition and development. It also provides a description of the increasing role of capital markets in the financing of commercial real estate, including the use of commercial mortgage-based securities to finance commercial real estate activity. The next three chapters discuss several different finance arrangements. Chapter 18 provides a description of acquisition, development, and construction financing. Chapter 19 looks at various permanent loan arrangements, including equity participation loans and sale-leaseback arrangements. The last chapter of this section, Chapter 20, discusses the various forms of ownership of commercial real estate, including investment vehicles such as real estate investment trusts and real estate limited partnerships.

Part 4 completes the book with a presentation of related finance topics. Chapter 21 examines portfolio considerations for large investors (typically referred to as institutional investors) in commercial real estate. Chapter 22 discusses ethics in real estate finance with a focus on liability, fraud, and agency problems. As mentioned, throughout the book we focus on the application of finance principles to real estate.

Key Terms

Capital markets	National Credit Union Administration
Commercial banks	Pension funds
Direct financing	Primary market
Finance	Risk
Financial intermediaries	Savings-investment cycle
Flow of funds	Secondary market
Insurance companies	Secondary mortgage market
Investment companies	Thrift institutions
Money markets	

Review Questions

1-1. a. Define the study of finance.

b. How is the focus of finance different from the field of traditional economics?

1-2. a. Define real estate finance.

b. What real estate–related topics are of concern to real estate finance?

1-3. What does the flow of funds cycle show?

1-4. List five types of financial intermediaries and give a brief description of each.

1-5. a. Distinguish between primary and secondary markets.

b. Give an example of each.

1-6. a. Distinguish between money and capital markets.

b. In which of these markets does most real estate financing take place? Why?

Web Sites

http://www.fdic.gov/
FDIC data on commercial banks and savings and loans

http://www.real-jobs.com
Career interests in real estate and potential employers

http://www.census.gov
Data on the employment and job market

http://www.commerce.gov/
Department of Commerce Web site with data on the GNP and its accounts

http://research.stlouisfed.org/fred2/
Data on all aspects of the economy including the money supply and interest rates

http://www.ffiec.gov
Site for the Federal Financial Institutions Examination Council. This council oversees such government agencies as the Federal Deposit Insurance Corporation, the Comptroller of the Currency, and the Consumer Finance Protection Bureau

http://www.economagic.com
More than 100,000 data files on economic time series, many with charts.

http://www.bea.gov
Data on national income accounts

http://consumerfinance.gov
Information on rules and regulations pertaining to consumer mortgage lending

MONEY, CREDIT, AND THE DETERMINATION OF INTEREST RATES

LEARNING OBJECTIVES

When you have finished this chapter, you should understand how the supply and demand for money and credit affect (and are affected by) the economy and, in turn, affect the general level of interest rates. The level and volatility of interest rates have a great effect on real estate activity, as you will see in later chapters. Interest rates affect the demand for mortgages and housing; an increase in rates reduces the affordability of housing. Rate increases also affect the timing and value of the cash flows associated with mortgages and other real estate securities. As an example, if interest rates fall, many homeowners will refinance their existing mortgages, shortening their maturity. You also should understand how yields on individual debt instruments are determined. Finally, you should understand why, at any point in time, securities of different maturities may have different yields and what this difference may imply about how financial markets view changes in interest rates in the future.

INTRODUCTION

In this chapter we explore the determination of interest rates. We begin with a discussion of the relationship between the economy and interest rates. We are interested in the manner in which the general level of interest rates is determined. We often hear about the periodic changes in interest rates in the financial markets. It is this "general" level of rates that is the focus of the first part of this chapter. We then explore the determination of interest rates on specific, individual debt securities. We discover those security-specific characteristics that determine interest rate or yield (the terms *interest rate* and *yield* are used interchangeably in this chapter). Finally, we expose what current interest rates may indicate about the future direction of interest rate changes.

THE GENERAL LEVEL OF INTEREST RATES

To understand how various forces interplay to determine the level of interest rates in the economy, it is helpful to begin by assuming that only one type of credit instrument exists. In actuality, there are hundreds of different credit instruments. Each has its own interest rate (yield) that reflects not only the general economy but also the various elements of risk particular to the issuer. In this section, we focus on the general level of interest rates and not individual rates that are affected by the peculiar risk characteristics of different credit instruments. To do this, it is useful to assume that there is only one type of credit market instrument in the economy. For the purpose of this simplified model, we will consider a bond.[1]

Assume that the bond is riskless in all respects. The issuer will meet all interest and principal payments with certainty, and the instruments can be sold instantly for cash at a stated price. Finally, assume there is no expectation of inflation (or deflation) at any time in the future. The price of the bond is inversely related to, and determined by, the market-required yield. If the bond promises to pay $1 per year into perpetuity (no repayment of principal ever) and the market yield is 10 percent, then its price will be $10. The $1 annual payment will yield 10 percent on the $10 investment ($1/$10 = 0.1). If the required market yield is 12.5 percent, then the bond will sell for $8, the $1 payment being 12.5 percent of the investment ($1/0.125 = $8). Note that the market value of the bonds can be defined in terms of either their price or their yield.

Figure 2-1 shows the supply and demand for the bonds in terms of either concept. Panel A represents the market in terms of the price and Panel B in terms of the yield. Panel A is the conventional graph with an upward-sloping supply curve and a downward-sloping demand curve. As the price increases, suppliers (those demanding credit) will desire to place more bonds in the market. This makes sense since higher bond prices reflect a lower yield or interest cost to the issuer. Lower prices (higher yields) lead to an increase in the quantity demanded. The intersection of the curves establishes the equilibrium price. The curves are reversed in Panel B because the yield, measured on the vertical axis, is the inverse of the price.

What might be the value of the equilibrium rate of interest in this simple model? It is difficult to say because the assumptions employed to demonstrate this market are never fully met in the real world. No such rate has ever been observed. The closest approximation is the market for Treasury securities in a no- or low-inflation time period, such as during the 1930s or the early 1950s. At those times, Treasuries yielded approximately 2 to 3 percent annually. Investors in Treasuries

| FIGURE 2-1 | Supply and Demand for Bonds |

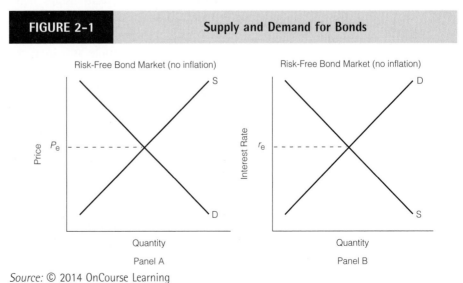

Panel A

Panel B

Source: © 2014 OnCourse Learning

during these periods could expect a 3 percent yield with no deterioration in return due to inflation. For that reason the yield is referred to as the real rate of interest. The real rate of interest is the equilibrium rate on riskless bonds in a noninflationary environment.

Once consideration is made for risk, the possibility of inflation, or other factors, the supply and demand curves in Figure 2-1 will shift. Although the figure implies a rather simplistic determination of interest rates, a large number of real-world factors determine the position of the curves and, thus, the rate of interest on specific securities. Those factors are considered next, beginning with a discussion of inflation.

MONEY, THE ECONOMY, AND INFLATION

In this section, we outline a transition mechanism of money and interest rates that operates somewhat as follows:

money supply → economy → inflation → inflationary expectations →
credit markets → interest rates

This money–inflation–interest rate mechanism has been studied and outlined for decades. One of the economists who explored these relationships was Irving Fisher, an early twentieth-century American economist.

The Equation of Exchange

Fisher is known for developing the **equation of exchange**.[2]

$$MV = PT$$ (Equation 2-1)

where, for a given period of time, for example, 1 year, M represents the money supply, V its **velocity of circulation**, P the general price level, and T the volume of trade. The velocity of circulation is the average number of times \$1 turns over in 1 year. It is the total annual dollar transactions divided by the supply of money.

The equation holds by a definition of the terms. The left side is the product of a stock (M) and a flow (V) and represents the total amount spent on goods and services. The right side is also the product of a stock (P) and a flow (T) and represents the total amount received from the sale of goods and services. It is true by definition since what is spent in the economy during a year equals what is received. The value of the equation lies in the assumptions that are made about the behavior of, and the relationships between, the variables. Fisher's statistical studies indicated that the velocity of money was fairly stable and changed only gradually over long periods of time. Also, for a fully employed economy, the volume of trade can expand only at a modest rate, constrained by the amount and growth of real resources. This view leaves the money supply and the price level positively related (by the equation) and free to take on values of an unlimited range. Furthermore, the price level becomes the passive variable in the model, determined by changes in the money supply.

Consider some possible values for the variables in the equation on a year-to-year basis. If the volume of trade can increase only with the growth in real resources (historically about 2 to 3 percent annually), then growth in the supply of money in excess of this rate will cause the price level to rise. Given the stability of the velocity of money and the constraint on the growth rate of the volume of trade, the rate of the growth in prices (inflation) should be 2 or 3 percent below the rate of growth of the money supply. The greater the rate of growth in money, the greater the rate of inflation. This **monetary theory of inflation** is well known and generally accepted by many economists, Milton Friedman[3] among the foremost.

It is evident that, for a fully employed economy, the limit on growth in the real volume of trade is determined by growth in real resources. The velocity of money is stable, Friedman says, because it depends on the demand for real money (the demand to hold real money balances by the public), which is determined primarily by slowly changing institutional factors. Therefore, money supply and prices are linked, he says. Evidence also suggests that the direction of causation runs from money to prices. That is, increases in the supply of money lead to subsequent changes in the level of prices. There is no evidence to suggest that an increase in prices is followed by a subsequent change in the supply of money. In summary, theory and evidence give strong support to the proposition that inflation is a monetary phenomenon, resulting from an increase in the money supply in excess of the increase in goods and services.

The Fisher Equation

The rate of inflation plays an important role in the determination of market interest rates. In another work, Fisher developed a well-known equation bearing his name.[4] This is not to be confused with the equation of exchange he developed earlier. The **Fisher equation** completes the final portion of the money–inflation–interest rate mechanism. Generally, economists agree that inflation, especially if it is consistent year after year, creates expectations of future inflation. The **adaptations model of inflationary expectations** postulates that credit market participants adapt their expectations of near-term future inflation on the basis of the most recent experience.

Fisher begins with the **real rate of interest**, observing that it is a rate that would exist on default-free bonds, which are at no risk that the principal will not be repaid, in a noninflationary environment. Investors expect to be better off in a real sense as a result of their saving and investing. By investing $100 at the real rate, they would receive, for example, $103 at the end of 1 year. In the absence of inflation, they are 3 percent wealthier in real terms. However, if during the year unexpected inflation of 5 percent occurred, then the real purchasing power of the $103 end-of-year wealth would be only about $98 ($103/1.05). Investors who expect 5 percent annual inflation in the future would require approximately an 8 percent yield to offset the rise in general prices ($108/1.05 – $103).

Moreover, borrowers who anticipate the same inflation rate expect to repay the principal with depreciated dollars. They are willing to pay the higher nominal rate. In this fashion, inflationary expectations become incorporated in nominal interest rates. The Fisher equation expresses this relationship as

$$I = r + p \qquad \text{(Equation 2-2)}$$

where I is the equilibrium nominal rate of interest observed in the credit market, r is the real rate of interest, and p is the expected inflation over the maturity of the bond. For our example, 8% = 3% + 5%. You now can see why it is difficult to observe the real rate of interest. Although the nominal rate is observed in the market, a precise measure of inflationary expectations cannot be observed, only estimated. If one views the money–inflation–interest rate mechanism from beginning to end, the line of causation runs from money to the economy to inflation to inflationary expectations to credit markets to interest rates. Furthermore, consistent and substantial increases in the money supply at one end create higher market rates of interest at the other. The experience of the 1960s and 1970s, when rapid increases in the money supply were associated with very high market interest rates (peaking in 1981 after several years of very loose monetary policy), is an excellent example of the mechanism in action. Figure 2-2 shows the relationship between

| FIGURE 2-2 | Inflation/T-Bill Yield: 1961–2010 |

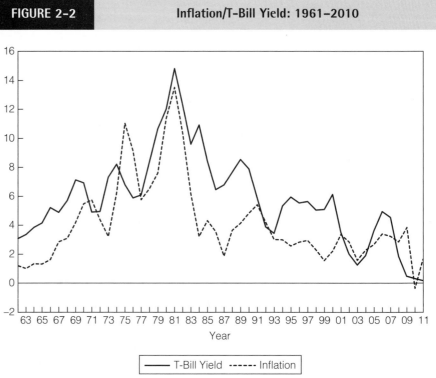

Source: © 2014 OnCourse Learning

the 1-year Treasury bill (T-bill) rate and the rate of inflation in the previous year for each year from 1961 through 2010. For example, in 1980 the rate on 1-year T-bills was approximately 13 percent. The figures show that the inflation rate the year before was also about 13 percent. The nearly coincident lines indicate a very close correlation between interest rates and the year-earlier level of inflation. It is dramatic evidence of the link between inflation and interest rates.

The Gibson Paradox

Despite the evidence in support of the money–inflation–interest rate mechanism, not all economists agree that increases in the growth rate of money will necessarily result in higher nominal interest rates. They argue that an increase in the money supply will lead to an increase in the demand for bonds as well as for goods and services. This results in upward pressure on bond prices, forcing interest rates down. This is called the *liquidity effect* and was well accepted by Keynesian economists of the postwar era (1940s to 1960s). Curiously, Keynes himself noted a series of articles written in *Bankers Magazine* by A.H. Gibson.[5] The articles noted and emphasized the close positive correlation over more than a century between the interest yield on bonds and the wholesale price index in England. Gibson noted the same relationship as in Figure 2-2. Keynes thought the relationship to be more than coincidence and believed that a general model could be developed to explain it. In other words, Keynes himself did not accept the liquidity effect without reservations. It turns out the Fisher equation is a model that explains the relationship.

Those who were convinced that increases in the supply of money should depress interest rates concentrated only on one element of the entire mechanism. They explained the impact of money on the demand for goods and services (inflation) and on the demand for bonds but ignored the further effects of inflation and inflationary expectations on credit markets. These effects are discussed next.

Liquidity, Income, and Price-Anticipation Effects

An increase in the supply of money can have three effects on credit markets: liquidity, income, and price-anticipation effects. The **liquidity effect**, recognized by Keynesian economists, refers to the initial short-run effect of an increase in the money supply on interest rates. An increase in the supply of money will cause individuals to possess excess cash, which will lead them to readjust their portfolios by purchasing more bonds. The increase in the demand for bonds will depress interest rates. This is only a short-term effect. Eventually, the increase in money also will spill over into a greater demand for goods and services, creating an increase in national income.

The **income effect** comes into play when the higher level of income causes an increase in the demand for credit (supply of bonds). Businesses will demand more credit (issue bonds) to expand their plants and equipment to meet the increased demand for their products. Households will increase their demand for credit to purchase durable goods such as houses, autos, and appliances. The increase in the demand for credit by both sectors will place upward pressure on the level of interest rates. Finally, the **price-anticipation effect**, captured in the Fisher equation, reflects the decrease in the supply of credit (at current rates) as a result of future expected inflation.

The three effects are summarized and demonstrated in Figure 2-3. The supply and demand curves, S and D, duplicate those from Panel A in Figure 2-1, the initial curves for a riskless bond in a noninflationary environment. They establish the real rate of interest in terms of price at P_1. The vertical axis measures the price of the bond. Recall that an increase in the price represents a fall in interest rates and vice versa. The liquidity effect is demonstrated by an increase in the demand for bonds from D to D′. Bond prices (interest rates) rise (fall) initially to P_2. As the increase in the supply of money causes an increase in income, businesses and households demand more credit—that is, they supply additional bonds. The shift

| FIGURE 2-3 | Supply and Demand for Bonds |

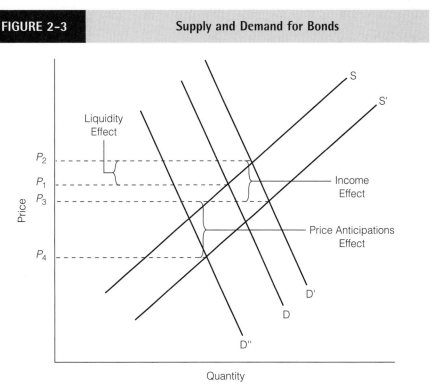

Source: © 2014 OnCourse Learning

of the supply curve to the right from S to S′ lowers the price of bonds to P_3; interest rates are now rising. Finally, market participants who expect inflation to occur in the future reduce their supply of credit (demand for bonds) from D′ to D″. The final equilibrium price P_4 is lower than the initial price, indicating that market rates have risen from their initial level.

THE DETERMINATION OF INTEREST RATES ON SPECIFIC CREDIT MARKET INSTRUMENTS

U.S. Treasury bonds are generally considered to be free of default risk (the risk that the bond issuer will be unable to make interest or principal payments). In addition, short-term Treasuries (say a year or less in maturity) are free of maturity risk (see the section on maturity risk). As a result about the only consideration by investors is the expected rate of inflation. Although the expected rate of inflation is not possible to observe directly and can change, sometimes dramatically, over a short period of time, the long-run relationship between inflation and short-term Treasuries as depicted in Figure 2-2 will be approximately accurate and the Fisher equation will be relevant in establishing yields on Treasury obligations.

Table 2-1 shows a selection of yields on various Treasury and non-Treasury securities. The difference in the yields reflects different risk characteristics of the securities. Risk characteristics include default, callability, maturity, and marketability, and tax effects.

Default Risk

Default risk is the risk that the bond issuer will be unable to pay the interest and principal on the obligation. Rating agencies such as Standard & Poor's and Moody's investigate the financial strength of corporations and municipalities that issue bonds. A description of the ratings of these agencies is presented in Table 2-2. Since a lower rating reflects a greater possibility of default, the yield on lower-rated bonds will be greater than that on higher-rated bonds. Also, virtually all corporate bonds have some default risk. Thus, the Ford Motor Co. bonds that mature in 2018, for example, carry a higher yield than the 10-year Treasuries.

Callability Risk

Callability risk refers to the possibility that an issuer of a bond may call it (demand to buy it back) prior to maturity for an amount equal to or near its face (principal amount) value. Noncallable bonds cannot be called prior to maturity. The investor in a noncallable bond benefits if market interest rates fall below the rate offered on

TABLE 2-1

Yields on Selected Bonds, September 17, 2012

BOND	YIELD TO MATURITY
1-year T-bills	0.17
2-year Treasury notes	0.26
10-year Treasury notes	1.87
GNMA 6s	3.86
Municipal Aaa-rated 5-year bonds	1.08
Municipal Aaa-rated 25-year bonds	3.24
Municipal Baa-rated 25-year bonds	5.43
Ford Motor Co., 2018	4.08
Ford Motor Co., 2047	7.13

Source: © 2014 OnCourse Learning

TABLE 2-2
Description of Agency Ratings

MOODY'S	STANDARD & POOR'S	QUALITY INDICATION
Aaa	AAA	Highest quality
Aa	AA	High quality
A	A	Upper-medium grade
Baa	BBB	Medium grade
Ba	BB	Contains speculative elements
B	B	Outright speculative
Caa	ccc & CC	Default definitely possible
Ca	C	Default, only partial recovery likely
C	DDD-D	Default, little recovery likely

Source: © 2014 OnCourse Learning

these bonds. The bondholder will be entitled to receive the higher coupon rates until maturity. The market value of a noncallable bond with a coupon rate in excess of the market rate will be above its face value. If market rates for bonds of equivalent risk are 10 percent, the market value of a noncallable bond with a coupon rate of 14 percent ($140 annual coupon payment on a $1,000 face-value bond) will be about $1,200. When issued, an equivalent bond that is callable will have a lower value, or higher yield, because of the likelihood that the issuer will take advantage of its right to call the bond at near its face value ($1,000). The issuer will likely finance the call by issuing new bonds at a lower interest rate.

The premium for callability risk can be seen in the yields of the Government National Mortgage Association (GNMA) securities. These bonds are described in greater detail in Chapters 10 and 11. Essentially, they are securities backed by a pool of mortgages. The mortgages have a coupon rate that is 0.5 percent greater than the rate on the bonds. That is, if the mortgagor (homeowner) is paying 7 percent on his or her mortgage the GNMA bond investor receives a 6.5 percent coupon rate. If a homeowner decides to prepay his or her mortgage prior to maturity, the entire principal is passed through to the GNMA bondholder and no further interest payments on this amount will be forthcoming. The homeowner has issued a callable bond (mortgage) and is likely to exercise the call option if market rates fall below that on the mortgage. Homeowners will refinance (call) their mortgage at the lower interest rate. Since GNMA bondholders do not benefit from an increase in value should rates fall, they are exposed to callability risk. The GNMA 6s in Table 2-1 had a current coupon yield (6 percent) above the yield on 10-year Treasury bonds (3.78 percent). Since they have callability risk, they are priced lower in the market and have a higher (3.86 percent is greater than 1.87 percent) yield to maturity. The higher yield is not due to default risk since the mortgages backing GNMA bonds are all Federal Housing Administration (FHA) or Veterans Affairs (VA) insured. In addition, GNMA, an agency within the Department of Housing and Urban Development, guarantees the timely payment of interest and principal to the bondholders. Therefore, the higher yield must be due to callability risk.

Maturity Risk

Maturity risk refers to the risk associated with bonds with longer maturities. There are actually two related risks here. First, the values of bonds with longer maturities change more than those with shorter maturities when interest rates change. This is called **interest rate risk**. Appendix 4-A in Chapter 4 shows how changes in interest rates affect the value of bonds with various maturities. Longer-term bonds have more interest rate risk because they have longer lives over which it is possible for market rates to change. Also, purchasing power risk increases with maturity. **Purchasing power risk** is the risk that inflation will erode the value of the principal amount of the bond. Other things being equal, longer-term bonds will be priced lower to yield more than shorter-term bonds. This yield difference is exemplified, in part, by the difference in the yield on the 10-year Treasury and the 1-year Treasury. It is also evident in the yield difference between the two Ford Motor Co. bonds, one maturing in 2018 and the other in 2047.

Income Tax Considerations

There is a class of bonds called municipal bonds. This class includes bonds issued by government jurisdictions other than the federal government. Municipal bonds are issued by the various states (and possessions), counties, municipalities, and other non-federal government organizations. The interest from these bonds is tax-free at the federal level (but not the state level for investors in other states). The tax-free nature of the interest payments means that investors will accept a much lower return on these bonds. Consider an investor in the 40 percent tax bracket. The investor can purchase a taxable bond that has a 9 percent taxable yield. After tax the investor retains 5.4 percent. The investor would accept a 5.4 percent yield on a comparable municipal bond (comparable in terms of risk). Equation 2-3 demonstrates this relationship:

$$MY = TY(1-T) \qquad \text{(Equation 2-3)}$$

In Equation 2-3, MY is the yield on a municipal bond, TY is the taxable yield on a comparable nonmunicipal bond, and T is the investor's tax rate.

Marketability Risk or Liquidity Risk

Marketability risk refers to the risk that the bond may not trade in a large, organized (liquid) market. The inability to sell the security quickly for cash for its intrinsic value will cause investors to require a yield premium. Although not represented in Table 2-1, such securities exist. Examples would include the bonds issued by very small municipalities or small companies. If all of the noninflationary risks are combined into the notion of a risk premium k, the following equation will describe the return on a particular security:

$$I = r + p + k \qquad \text{(Equation 2-4)}$$

where I is the nominal rate, r the real rate, p the expected inflation rate, and k represents other risk factors specific to the security.

THE YIELD CURVE AND FUTURE INTEREST RATES

The yield spread between the 10- and 1-year Treasuries in Table 2-1 is 1.70 percent. Why does this difference exist? There is no difference in the default, callability, or marketability risk between the instruments. In fact, Table 2-3 shows that different maturity Treasuries in September, 2012 had different yields, increasing as maturity lengthened. However, the difference in yield among securities may be more than justified by maturity risk alone. Figure 2-4 demonstrates visually the relationship between the maturity of the various Treasury obligations and their yields from Table 2-3. It is called a **yield curve**. A yield curve is a line that relates maturity and yield on bonds of the same grade at a point in time. The yield curve on a given date does not always appear as it does in Figure 2-4. Examples of other yield curves are shown in Figure 2-5. You may wonder why the yield curve is not

TABLE 2-3
Yields on Treasuries, September 17, 2012

MATURITY	YIELD TO MATURITY
3-month	0.11
1-year	0.18
2-year	0.27
3-year	0.35
5-year	0.72
7-year	1.23
10-year	1.88
20-year	2.68
30-year	3.09

Source: © 2014 OnCourse Learning

FIGURE 2-4	**Yield Curve**

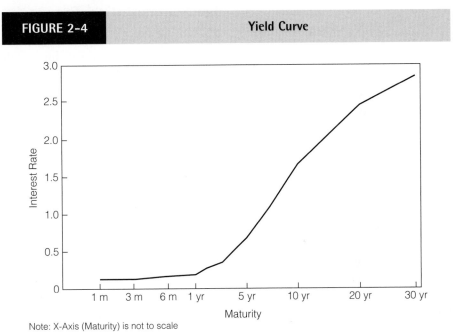

Note: X-Axis (Maturity) is not to scale

Source: © 2014 OnCourse Learning

FIGURE 2-5	**Examples of Yield Curves**

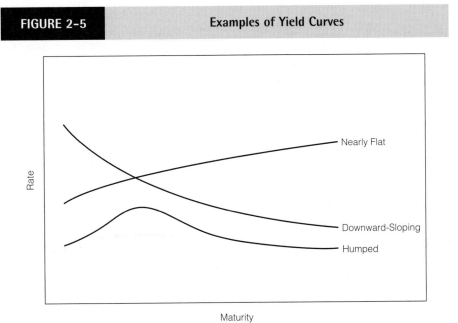

Source: © 2014 OnCourse Learning

flat or why there is such a variety of curves at different times. Three principal theories are responsible for the shape of the yield curve, and this is where we see that the shape of the yield curve may be different from what one would expect from maturity risk alone.

Liquidity Premium Theory

According to the **liquidity premium theory**, long-term rates tend to be higher than short-term rates because a premium must be paid to investors who are reluctant to tie up their funds for long periods of time.

If there is a liquidity premium, it is likely to be small and certainly does not explain the situations in which long-term rates occasionally fall below shorter-term rates. A more general explanation is required.

Market Segmentation Theory

The **market segmentation theory** suggests that there are two (or more) markets for securities of different maturities. Just as there are two markets for apples and oranges, each with their own equilibrium price, so it is with security markets, according to this theory. Different markets may exist because some institutional investors may have different needs for short- versus long-term bonds.

Pension funds, for example, may demand long-term investments only, while commercial banks may prefer shorter-term securities. Populated by different participants, the markets will have different equilibrium interest rates. This theory makes the heroic assumption that investors will not change their preference for securities as a result of yield discrepancies. This is unlikely. If an investor who prefers a short-term investment notices a higher yield on a long-term security, he or she will have an incentive to shift to the longer-term security. As long as it can be sold in a liquid market (Treasuries, for example), he or she can sell it at any time, effectively causing its maturity to meet his or her particular needs. Note that this investor may not shift to the longer-term security if he or she expects interest rates to rise by the time he or she intends to sell it in the market. An increase in interest rates would result in a decline in its value, possibly resulting in a loss. In the absence of any expectation of a change in interest rates, there is no reason to expect that investors would segment themselves in one end of the maturity spectrum and ignore superior returns in the other end. Segmentation may occur if there are expectations of changing interest rates, however. A third explanation of the yield curve is that higher yields will be necessary to attract investors to a maturity segment of the market if they have certain expectations of interest rate changes.

Expectations Theory

To understand the **expectations theory**, consider the yields in Table 2-3. Let us begin by analyzing two yields, a 1-year and a 2-year Treasury, 0.18 and 0.27 percent, respectively. These two rates were the observed equilibrium yields in September, 2012. Since they were equilibrium rates, the supply and demand for these two securities were equal. There was no desire for investors to shift from one to the other and cause the equilibrium rates to shift.

Consider an investor with a 2-year investment horizon and $1 to invest. In September, 2012 the investor has (at least) two choices. One is to purchase a 2-year Treasury priced to yield 0.27 percent compounded annually. The other is to purchase a 1-year Treasury priced to yield 0.18 percent and to roll it over in September, 2013 into another 1-year Treasury at a rate to be determined in the market at that time. With an initial investment of $1, his or her wealth in September 2014 under each alternative will be

Choice 1 $\$1(1.0027)^2$

Choice 2 $\$1(1.0018) \times (1 + r_1)$

where r equals the 1-year rate of interest established in the market in September, 2013.

Since both the 1-year and 2-year security markets are in equilibrium in September, 2012 investors must view the choices as identical. They are indifferent to them because they expect the same wealth position in September, 2014, regardless of which choice is pursued. Therefore, investors must feel that

$$\$1(1.0027)^2 = \$1(1.0018)(1 + r_1)$$

or

$$(1 + r_1) = \frac{(1.0027)^2}{(1.0018)} = 1.0036$$

To be indifferent between the two choices, investors in September, 2012 must expect that the 1-year rate to be established in the market in September, 2013 will be 0.36 percent. They expect interest rates to rise. Investors will receive the same 2-year return if they invest in a 2-year bond at a rate of 0.27 percent annually or a 1-year bond at 0.18 percent followed by rolling the investment over to another year at 0.36 percent.

This same logic can be used to compute r_2, the 1-year yield investors expect 2 years in the future (September 2014 through September 2015, in this example). Since the 3-year yield in Table 2-3 is 0.35 percent, the following equation is used:

$$\$1(1.0027)^2(1 + r_2) = \$1(1.0035)^3$$

$$(1 + r_2) = \frac{(1.0035)^3}{(1.0027)^2} = 1.0051$$

$$r_2 = 0.51\%$$

Investors believe that in September 2014 rates will rise slightly in the third year over the second.

At times, the longer-term yields have been below the short-term yields. It is not unusual to observe a 1-year rate above those of a 2-year rate, for example. In such cases, it can be shown that investors expect that rates will fall in the future.

The expectations hypothesis explains a wide range of yield curves with varying slopes. Generally, upward-sloping curves indicate that market participants expect rates to rise in the future, and downward-sloping curves indicate expectations of falling rates.

Summary

Economic conditions, including actual inflation and inflationary expectations, establish the general level of interest rates. In the absence of inflationary expectation, the risk-free rate would equal the real rate. For a risk-free bond, the nominal rate can be described with the Fisher equation, by which inflationary expectations are added to the real rate to provide the nominal rate. Risk characteristics of individual issues cause the nominal rate on their securities to be larger by those risk factors. Specific and different risk factors of individual securities include default, maturity, callability, and marketability (liquidity).

The yield curve shows the yield on securities of varying maturity. It incorporates the market expectation of future interest rates. An upward-sloping curve signals expectations of rising rates, and a downward-sloping curve indicates falling rates.

Key Terms

Adaptations model of inflationary expectations

Callability risk

Default risk

Equation of exchange

Expectations theory

Fisher equation

Income effect

Interest rate risk

Liquidity effect

Liquidity premium theory

Market segmentation theory

Marketability risk

Maturity risk

Monetary theory of inflation

Price-anticipation effect

Purchasing power risk

Real rate of interest

Velocity of circulation

Yield curve

Review Questions

2-1. a. What is the real rate of interest?
       b. Give two reasons why the actual yield on a corporate bond would be greater than the real rate of interest.

2-2. a. What is the equation of exchange?
       b. How can the equation of exchange be used to explain the monetary theory of inflation?

2-3. a. What is the Gibson paradox?
       b. What is the Fisher equation?
       c. What is the relationship between these two concepts?

2-4. List and explain the types of risk associated with specific securities.

2-5. a. What is the yield curve?
       b. Give three explanations why long-term and short-term Treasuries would have different yields on the same date.

2-6. Presently, a 1-year Treasury yields 7.8 percent and a 2-year Treasury yields 9 percent.
       a. What does this say about market expectations of the 1-year Treasury rate that will be observed 1 year from now?
       b. Will it be higher or lower than the present 1-year rate?
       c. Give an estimate of its value.

2-7. What does it mean when we say that mortgages (or pass-through securities backed by mortgages) are callable?

Problems

2-1. Provide the missing data, assuming that the Fisher equation is accurate.

CASE	REAL INTEREST RATE (%)	NOMINAL INTEREST RATE (%)	EXPECTED INFLATION (%)
A	3	8	
B	3		3
C	3	6	

2-2. Provide the missing data, assuming the equation of exchange is accurate.

CASE	SUPPLY MONEY ($)	INDEX OF VELOCITY	REAL PRICE LEVEL	TRANSACTIONS	GNP
A	1,000B	4	8	500B	
B	1,000B	10			5,000B
C		5	10	900B	
D		5		800B	4,000B

2-3. Assume the current money supply is $1,000B and that the velocity of circulation is 5. Real transactions are $500 billion and the price level index is 10. Next year, the Federal Reserve is expected to increase the money supply to $1,200B and real transactions are expected to increase by $50 billion. If the velocity of money remains constant, what will be the rate of inflation if the equation of exchange holds each year?

2-4. Determine the price of a bond that promises to pay $10 annually in perpetuity for the following interest rates.

INTEREST RATE (%)	PRICE
8	—
9	—
12	—
14	—

2-5. Provide the missing data in the following table.

CASE	RISK-FREE RATE (%)	NOMINAL RATE (%)	MATURITY RISK PREMIUM (%)	CALLABILITY RISK PREMIUM (%)	DEFAULT RISK PREMIUM (%)
A	3.0	9.0	2.0	1.0	
B	3.0		2.0	2.0	2.5
C	2.5	8.5	1.0	2.0	
D		14.0	2.0	1.5	4.0

2-6. a. Given the following yields on risk-free Treasury securities, determine the 1-year expected rate for the period January 1, 2007, to December 31, 2007 (current date January 1, 2005).

MATURITY DATE	RATE (%)
December 31, 2005	2
December 31, 2006	3
December 31, 2007	4

b. What is the expected 1-year rate for the period January 1, 2006, to December 31, 2006?

2-7.   Assume an investor is in the 30 percent tax bracket and can invest in nonmunicipal bonds that have a yield of 8 percent. What rate of return would the investor require on a comparable (risk) municipal bond?

Notes

1. In the most general sense, a mortgage is a bond.
2. Irving Fisher. *The Purchasing Power of Money.* New York: The Macmillan Company, 1922.
3. Milton Friedman. *Studies in the Quantity Theory of Money.* Chicago: University of Chicago Press, 1956.
4. Irving Fisher. *The Theory of Interest.* New York: The Macmillan Company, 1930.
5. John Maynard Keynes. *A Treatise on Money.* Vol. 2. New York: The Macmillan Company, 1930, p. 198.

Web Sites

http://www.interest.com
Information on mortgage rates

http://www.hsh.com/
Graphs of historical interest rates

http://www.mortgagemag.com
Latest mortgage news

http://www.nationalmortgagenews.com/
Latest national mortgage news

http://www.treasury.gov/resource-center/data-chart-center/interest-rates/Pages/TextView.aspx?data=yield
Management/interest rate/yield. Each day the yield curve is posted on this site.

http://www.treasury.gov
Current and historical yield curves

FINANCE THEORY AND REAL ESTATE

LEARNING OBJECTIVES

After reading this chapter, you should understand how basic finance principles can be applied to real estate. An overview of several finance principles is presented, including asset valuation, the theory of leverage and optimal capital structure, option valuation, the theory of financial intermediation, portfolio theory, efficient market theory, and agency theory. In-depth analyses of the applications of these principles to real estate are presented throughout the text. After reading this chapter, you should see how finance principles can be applied to a wide variety of real estate topics.

INTRODUCTION

Many principles of financial analysis have been developed within the framework of corporate managerial finance and corporate securities markets. But these same principles can be and are applied in practice to real estate–related subjects. Therefore, in addition to describing the institutions, laws, and markets for real property and real property securities, we will show how finance principles also can be applied to these areas. That is, we seek to integrate finance theory with a description of real estate institutions and markets. We begin with one of the more fundamental finance concepts: asset valuation.

ASSET VALUATION

Asset valuation is concerned with those principles that maximize the wealth of the investor. An asset provides cash flows over time to its owner. The valuation of the asset depends on the expected amount, timing, and risk associated with the cash flows. These elements are all included in the **discounted cash flow (DCF) model** of valuation in this equation:

$$\text{PRESENT VALUE} = \sum_{i=1}^{n} \frac{CF_i}{(1+r)^i} \qquad \text{(Equation 3-1)}$$

In this equation, *CF* stands for periodic cash flows, *r* is the appropriate discount rate, and *n* is the number of cash flows.

The formula applies to any asset capable of providing cash flows to its owner. In real estate, those assets include equity positions, such as land and buildings, mortgages collateralized by real estate, securities backed by pools of mortgages (pass-through, mortgage-backed bonds), options to purchase real estate, stock in corporations that invest in real estate equity and mortgages (real estate investment trusts), rights to the servicing income from a portfolio of mortgages, and many others.

Since each asset can be valued in terms of the amount, timing, and risk of the cash flows, there are four elements in the equation: (1) the (present) value, (2) the amount of the cash flows, (3) the time period in which or over which the cash flows occur, and (4) the discount rate. Given any three of the four elements in this basic valuation equation, the fourth can be computed. Furthermore, different situations in real estate finance call for determining each of the four elements.

Amount of After-Tax Cash Flows

Each asset provides its owner with an expected cash flow. For valuation purposes, the relevant amount is the after-tax cash flows. Because of the tax shelter characteristics of real estate, actual cash flows are often different from the (accounting) income generated by the asset. Net operating income (NOI) is determined by subtracting the actual "out-of-pocket" expenses of operating the real estate asset from the revenues. Operating expenses will include building and grounds maintenance, utilities, insurance, and property taxes. Federal and state income taxes will be based on the NOI, less depreciation, and represent a cash outflow. Depreciation, however, is a noncash expense and, although it is a deduction for the purpose of determining taxable income, it is not a cash outflow. Also, cash flows result from the future sale of the property after the payoff of any mortgage balance and payment of capital gains (loss) taxes. Why do we focus on after-tax cash flows as opposed to NOI (or accounting profits) in determining value? Because cash flows not only recognize profits, they go further to indicate the amount of cash, on a periodic basis, that is available to the owner of the asset to increase his wealth. Although the taxable income on an investment may be negative, indicating a loss, the cash flow available to the owner may be positive. The owner has the opportunity to reinvest this cash flow and obtain a market rate of return. In fact, if this income and after-tax cash flow relationship were to prevail in each year of the life of the investment, the reinvested cash flows would continue to accumulate. Although the original investment would show annual accounting losses, the investor's wealth would be substantial. It is the asset's cash flows that determine the rate at which the investor's wealth accumulates and thus the value of the asset. The difference between NOI and cash flows is reflected in the practice of many industrial firms that use two alternative accounting practices for income reporting and for tax purposes. In accounting for ending inventory, for example, one method called first-in-first-out (FIFO) may maximize reported earnings, whereas an alternative method called last-in-first-out (LIFO) will reduce earnings and, thus, taxes. This practice recognizes that the added cash flows from minimizing taxes allow for a greater accumulation of wealth, since the cash flows can be reinvested in other corporate investments.

Timing of Cash Flows

The timing of cash flows simply refers to the idea that, other things being equal, the sooner a cash flow is received, the greater its present value. This is so because the sooner it is received, the sooner it can be employed to increase interest-earning assets or reduce interest-costing liabilities, both of which will increase the owner's wealth. This principle is recognized in the DCF model by the fact that the later in the life of the asset that a cash flow is received, the larger is the discount factor $[(1 + r)^i]$ that is applied. Also, as seen in the Appendix 4-B of Chapter 4, values of assets with early cash flows change less when market interest rates change than do other assets.

Risk of Cash Flows

The concept of **risk** involves the recognition that probabilities can be assigned to alternative (possible) future cash flows. If a probability of 100 percent can be assigned to a future cash flow, there is no risk. The common example of a risk-free investment is that of a Treasury bill for which there is no possibility of default. Most other investments pose at least some possibility that the actual cash flow will differ from the expected cash flow. When probabilities cannot be assigned to these possibilities, uncertainty is said to exist. When probabilities can be assigned, risk is said to exist. Thus, risk exists when there is the possibility that the actual cash flows will differ from those expected (for any reason), and probabilities can be assigned to those possibilities. All assets involve risk, especially real estate–related assets. Consider the risk of the following real estate assets.

Commercial Project

The cash flows of a commercial project, such as a hotel, apartment complex, or office building, will depend on a large number of elements, all subject to risk. These include the actual revenues and a multitude of expenses. The revenues, in turn, will depend on many other risk factors, such as the state of the local and national economy, amount of competition, expertise of the property management, and so forth. The terminal cash flow, the amount received by the investor when the asset is sold or otherwise disposed of, is also subject to risk. It will depend on the projected cash flows at that time, which are all subject to risk. The value of the real estate asset will be more sensitive to some of these variables than to others. Nonetheless, all represent elements of risk in the sense that their actual amounts may differ from the expected amounts.

Real Estate Limited Partnerships

Many people invest in real estate through **real estate limited partnerships (RELPs)**. These are discussed in more detail in Chapter 20. Limited partnerships are partnerships that provide limited liability to the partner–investors, just as corporate stock does. This form of investment involves no management of or decision making about the underlying real estate asset, but gives the investor a right to receive some of the cash flows associated with the real estate, such as tax benefits and appreciation in value. As an example, a partnership may be formed with many partner–investors pooling their funds to purchase a hotel. The partners would receive cash flows from the investment after the expenses of forming and operating the partnership. Thus, in addition to the risk of the cash flows of the real estate, the RELP investor incurs other risks. Risk may be associated with the actual cash flow taken by the general partner for operating the partnership. There is also the risk of the value of the partnership interest on resale. Since there is no organized, liquid marketplace for RELPs, substantial liquidity or marketability risk may exist for these investments.

Real Estate Investment Trusts

Some investors invest in real estate through **real estate investment trusts (REITs)**. These are also discussed in Chapter 20. This form of investment consists of purchasing stock in a corporation that in turn purchases real estate properties (equity

REIT), mortgages on real estate properties (mortgage REIT), or a combination (hybrid REIT). As long as the corporation meets certain Internal Revenue Service (IRS) regulations, it can pass the cash flows of the real estate along to the stockholders without incurring a tax liability at the corporate level. The stockholder in the REIT incurs the same risk as the underlying real estate asset, in addition to the operating risk of the REIT and liquidity risks associated with the resale of the REIT stock. (The stock of large REITs, however, is exchanged on the major stock exchanges.)

Residential Mortgage

Consider a lender of a residential mortgage. The amount and timing of the payments are spelled out in the note as part of the contract between the lender and the mortgagor. Yet, the possibility remains that the amount and timing of the cash flows may differ from that outlined in the note or even that expected by the lender. The mortgagor could be delinquent in some payments or, worse, default on the mortgage. If the latter occurs, the lender will be forced to foreclose on the property and will have to liquidate the REO (real estate owned). The precise value at liquidation is unknown and also subject to risk. In the case where the property has positive equity and there is no delinquency, the mortgagor may prepay the loan because he or she desires to sell the property or refinance the loan at a lower interest rate. Thus, the timing and amount of the cash flows are subject to risk, despite the terms of the note indicating the amount and dates of the payment.

Mortgage-Backed Securities

The same risk associated with individual mortgages applies to securities backed by pools of mortgages, especially if those securities are of the pass-through type (see Chapter 10). An investor who purchases $100,000 in a mortgage-backed security (MBS) will "own" a small (prorated) portion of several hundred mortgages. He or she will receive a prorated share of all monthly principal and interest payments, as if he or she were the original lender. The investor also will receive a prorated share of any mortgages that are prepaid in a given month. The investor faces the same prepayment risk as the originator of a loan who would hold it in a portfolio. Because MBSs represent large pools of mortgages, the portfolio effect may reduce the risk, such as a default, associated with individual mortgages. However, systematic risks, such as a substantial decline in market rates that would lead to accelerated prepayments, would not be diversified away. In fact, prepayment assumptions are such an important element in the valuation of MBSs that the research staffs of large institutional investors expend great effort to identify those variables that affect prepayments and the manner in which they do so—that is, their functional relationship. Investors also wish to identify MBSs that may have greater or lesser prepayment rates than average. If they can be successful in doing so and still purchase the security at the average value for all such securities, they may reap excess returns. A lot of research has been devoted to establishing the prepayment risk associated with MBSs. Finally, note that 2008 was a particularly risky year for MBS investors. Because of the large number of defaults (especially subprime loans) on the underlying mortgages many MBSs lost much or all of their value. In late 2008 the federal government had to "take over" Freddie Mac and Fannie Mae so as to guarantee their bonds (MBSs) against default. Investors in the MBSs of private conduits were not so lucky. We look at the mortgage crisis of 2008 in much more detail in Chapter 10.

Collateralized Mortgage Obligations

Collateralized mortgage obligations (CMOs), discussed in Chapter 10, are similar to MBSs, except the timing of the cash flows associated with the underlying mortgages (that serve as collateral) have been "rearranged" to serve the needs of various types of investors. Precisely because many investors do not like the risk associated with MBSs, financial institutions have created CMOs. As with an MBS, the underlying collateral is a pool of residential mortgages. An investor can purchase various "tranches" in the CMO. A tranche promises bond-like payments on certain dates. The originator of the CMO estimates the payment and prepayment behavior of the underlying mortgages and constructs the tranches accordingly. All payments and prepayments from the entire pool of mortgages may go to the first tranche until it is paid off with known payments on known dates. (Any excess prepayments are invested for payment to later tranches, and any shortfalls are made up from the originator's funds.) Although this arrangement makes the payments of the first tranches more certain, it increases the risk associated with the later, or "residual," tranches.

Commercial Mortgage-Backed Securities

Commercial mortgage-backed securities (CMBSs) are similar to residential MSSs except, as one would imagine, these bonds are backed by mortgages on commercial properties such as office buildings and shopping centers. This, of course, invites a whole new set of risk considerations not present in their residential counterparts. A bond backed by a commercial mortgage inherits some risk associated with the mortgage. In turn, the commercial mortgage inherits risk from the property financed with the mortgage. For this reason CMBSs are often rated by agencies such as Moody's and Standard & Poor's. These rating agencies will analyze the risk of the bonds by looking at a myriad of factors including the local economy, the supply and demand for commercial real estate, the loan-to-value ratio, and so forth. Needless to say, the risk of a CMBS is related to the risk of the property ultimately backing it up.

Interest-Only and Principal-Only Securities (IOS and POS)

From a pool of mortgages, it is possible to sell rights to receive principal payments only or rights to receive interest payments only (see Chapter 11). These two cash flows will behave differently when, for example, market interest rates change. If market rates rise, mortgagors will tend to prepay less often. The owner of the **principal-only securities (POS)** will receive the same total payments as he or she otherwise would, but they now will be stretched over a longer period of time. This factor, and the fact that (discount) rates have risen, will lower the value of the POS. On the other hand, because interest is paid on any outstanding principal, the owner of the **interest-only securities (IOS)** now will receive a larger stream of payments than he or she otherwise would have. The value of the IOS will, therefore, rise. Thus, the size and the timing of the cash flows associated with IOS and POS are subject to risk and will behave differently from each other in response to a change in market rates.

Servicing Rights

Continuing with the residential loan example, the value of the **servicing rights** (see Chapter 11) to mortgages depends on expected cash flows, which are subject to risk. Servicing rights arise when an originator of a portfolio of mortgages sells that portfolio to an investor, perhaps on the secondary mortgage market, but continues to service the loans for a fee. The originator will collect the monthly payment, send out delinquency notices, collect delinquent penalty payments, and so forth. He or she will forward the payments to the new owner in return for a portion of the payment. For example, 0.25 percent of the loan balance would be a reasonable fee. The originator's after-tax cash flow is composed of this fee, less any operating expenses and taxes associated with servicing the loans. These cash flows have value and can be sold. That is, many originators will, subsequent to the sale of the mortgages, also sell the servicing rights. The value is determined with reference to the size and timing of the flows in relation to the risk. The major risk comes through prepayments that, should they accelerate, would eliminate the remaining servicing fees associated with the prepaid loans. A decline in market rates will cause the value of servicing rights to decline.

Role of Risk in Valuation

The importance of considering risk in a real estate investment lies in the determination of the discount rate to employ in the DCF model. A basic principle of finance requires that the greater the perceived risk, the greater the required rate of return (discount rate) of an investment. Unfortunately, there are no formulas by which one can translate a given level of risk of a real estate investment into a proper discount rate. The returns on an individual real estate project cannot easily be related to the marketplace (as can be done with common stock) to determine systematic risk, for example. In the stock market the capital asset pricing model (CAPM) can be utilized to suggest a discount rate for equity. With the CAPM the risk-free rate, the return on the market, and the stock's systematic risk are employed to suggest a proper equity discount rate.

Such convenient formulas are not available to real estate analysts, but general guidelines can be followed. One example is that the discount rate associated with the equity portion of a real estate investment should be higher than the rate associated with the debt on the project. The risk of the debt is less since the debtor stands first to receive any cash flows after operating expenses and usually will have a lien on the property should there be a default. Since debt holders presumably estimate their risk in calculating their required rate on debt, an upward adjustment is justified for the risk of equity cash flows. Some well-known problems are associated with using risk-adjusted discount rates.[1] Even if subjective in nature, however, the principle remains that the greater the perceived risk, the greater should be the appropriate discount rate.

THE THEORY OF FINANCIAL LEVERAGE AND OPTIMAL CAPITAL STRUCTURE

Financial leverage is the concept of using debt to finance an investment project. The two primary sources of capital for financing any project are debt and equity. Real estate projects are most often financed with a mix of these two. Financial leverage can best be illustrated by examining the relationship between the overall return on the project and the return on the equity. For example, say that a particular real estate asset provides a 12 percent return. That is, the annual after-tax cash flow is 12 percent of the cost of the asset. If the asset is financed with all equity, the return to the equity investor is equal to the overall return on the asset, 12 percent. If, however, debt can be obtained at a favorable rate (less than 12 percent) it can be used to enhance the return to the equity. A portion of an asset that yields 12 percent is financed by lower-cost debt, the difference flowing through to the equity holder. This means that favorable financial leverage will result in an equity yield greater than 12 percent. The amount of debt used and the cost of the debt will determine the extent to which the equity yield is increased. The process of incurring debt at a cost less than the return on the investment is positive (favorable) financial leverage. Negative (unfavorable) financial leverage occurs when the cost of borrowing exceeds the return on the investment. This would result in a decline in the return on the equity. Thus, financial leverage creates financial risk if there is some chance that the cost of the debt may exceed the return to the investment. This risk usually is created by variability in either the return on the investment or the cost of the debt or both. The effect of financial leverage on equity yield is illustrated in later chapters.

Leverage and Value

The value of the equity position of the investor increases, to a point, with the use of **leverage**. As seen, the basic principle that drives the process is that the investor can borrow at a rate less than the return on the asset. One reason why debt financing may carry a smaller cost for reasonable levels of loan-to-value ratios is the perceived degree of risk associated with debt payments. Lenders are given preference before equity holders to receive cash flows in the form of interest payments because of their legal position. Additionally, with the exception of default, the amount of the payments is not subject to risk, as is the case with equity that represents a claim on the residual cash flows.

Irrelevance of Capital Structure

The proposition offered by Modigliani and Miller is that, in a world without taxes, rearranging the cash flows of a corporation due to different proportions of debt and equity cannot create value.[2] They offer as proof the ability of an equity holder to use homemade leverage (borrow personally) to purchase the stock in an all-equity firm. After paying interest on the personal indebtedness, the residual cash flows are identical to those that would occur had the firm issued the debt. Since the replication of the cash flows does not depend on the firm issuing the debt, the **capital structure** of the firm itself does not create or enhance value. That is, although value may be created by sorting the cash flows of a firm into debt and equity returns (because of, for instance, different risk preferences of investors), there is no need for the division to be done at the firm level. It can be done at the personal level. The question becomes, if Modigliani and Miller are correct about the valuation of the firm, can value be created through the use of leverage in real estate projects? The answer is yes, as we will demonstrate with an example.

Assume that an investor owned a 100 percent equity position in an office building and desired to use leverage to increase value. Following Modigliani and Miller, the division of the cash flows into debt and equity components can be done either by leveraging the property or borrowing personally. Assume that a lender advances funds to the property owner personally. The owner pledges to make loan payments from the cash flows of the property. It would appear that the lender stands to receive the same cash flow, regardless of whether the loan was collateralized by the real estate or advanced to the property owner personally. In such a case, however, the property owner would now be in a position to borrow additional funds from a second lender by pledging the property as a loan, leaving the first lender in a subordinated and much more risky position. To prevent just such an occurrence, the first lender would demand that the loan be collateralized by the property. In this fashion, the leverage is forced to be applied at the property, and not the personal, level. Because leverage cannot be created as cheaply anywhere else, leverage can add value.

OPTIONS AND
REAL ESTATE
FINANCE

Definition of Options

Options are rights. The owner of an option has a right, but not an obligation, to purchase (call option) or sell (**put** option) an asset at a predetermined price (strike price) from or to another individual on or before a given date (exercise date). The student may be most familiar with stock options, the right to buy or sell common stock at a given price. Options have intrinsic value and market value, the latter generally being greater than the former. The intrinsic value is the excess of the current price of the asset over the strike price for a call or the excess of the strike price over the current market price for a put.

An option that gives the holder the right to buy a share of stock at a strike price of $50 has an intrinsic value of $6, if the current market price is $56 and transaction costs are ignored. This is so because the holder can exercise his or her right and immediately resell the stock in the market. However, this action is unlikely. The value of all call options (without dividends) and some put options is greater unexercised at any time prior to the expiration date. This is another way of saying that the value of the option will be greater than its intrinsic value. Additionally, options with no intrinsic value will nonetheless have some positive market value because of their nature as a right and not an obligation.

Consider the above call option where the market price of the stock is $45. The option has no intrinsic value. The value on the expiration date will be positive only if the market price rises above $50 and will be equal to the differential. Figure 3-1 shows a probability distribution of the market value of the stock on two dates: 3 months in the future and 6 months in the future. The shaded areas of the two curves represent the portions where the market value will exceed the strike price on each date. The probability distribution which represents the market values for a date 6 months in the future is more dispersed than that for 3 months in the future. The reason lies in the behavior of market values that change over time. Through time, stock prices follow a pattern that has a large random component, due to the unpredictable manner in which information arrives at the marketplace. The longer the time period over which prices can move, the greater the cumulative effect of the random components. Put another way, the distribution of tomorrow's possible market values is more constrained than the distribution a year

FIGURE 3-1	Probability Distribution of Stock Prices

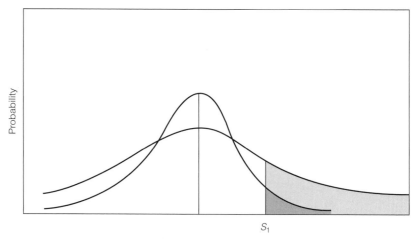

Source: © 2014 OnCourse Learning

from now. Furthermore, the greater the volatility of price movements, the wider will be the probability distribution of prices on any given date. In other words, you also can view the two distributions in Figure 3-1 as that of the prices of two different stocks on the same date, the wider distribution representing the more volatile stock. Figure 3-1 shows that the greater portion of the 6-month probability distribution lies above the strike price S_1. Thus, there is a greater chance that the market value will exceed the strike price by a larger amount in 6 months versus 3 months. If the exercise date of the option is in 6 months, as opposed to 3 months, the current value of the option will be greater. Thus, two important determinants of an option's value are the time to expiration of the option and the volatility in the value of the underlying security.

In addition to options on common stock, there are also traded options on debt instruments such as Treasury securities or MBSs. The value of debt securities fluctuates as a result of several factors, the most important being the change in market interest rates. The values of debt securities move inversely to changes in interest rates. Furthermore, for a given change in the market rate, the magnitude of a change in the value of a debt security is dependent on its duration (similar to maturity). Translating from our discussion of options on equities, this means that an option on a debt security will have a greater value the longer the duration of the security and the more volatile interest rates are expected to be (during the term of exercise). As the volatility in interest rates increases and is extrapolated into the future, the value of options pertaining to real estate–related debt increases.

Examples of Options in Real Estate Finance

With the exception of options on MBSs, there are no standardized option contracts that are traded on an organized exchange. This does not mean that options in real estate are limited to those on MBSs. Various real estate contracts grant valuable options to one or both parties to the transaction. Consider the following real estate–related transactions.

Residential Mortgage

When a homeowner obtains a mortgage with a lien on a residence, he or she also has contracted for some options. A **prepayment** or **call option** gives the homeowner the right to prepay the current balance on the mortgage at any time prior to its maturity. Since prepayment penalties (payments required to prepay prior to maturity) are rare in residential mortgages, being prohibited by law in some states and by the Federal Housing Administration (FHA) or Veterans Administration (VA) on insured loans, they are viewed by lenders as a provision that would place them at a competitive disadvantage. The mortgagor has essentially issued a callable bond. That is, he or she has issued a note (in return for current cash to purchase the residence) that allows to call the mortgage at any time prior to maturity. The strike price is the balance of the mortgage at the time it is called (prepaid). The value of the remaining payments at the time of call is a function of the market rate of interest on mortgages of like risk at the time of the call. If the market rate of interest falls so that the value of the remaining payments increases, the mortgagor is likely to call the note since its strike price (balance) is less than its value (to the lender).

Figure 3-2 shows the value of two securities with identical contract rates—one a noncallable bond, the other a callable mortgage—as a function of the market rate of interest. At very high market rates, both obligations are valued identically and below their face value. As interest rates decrease, the values of both obligations

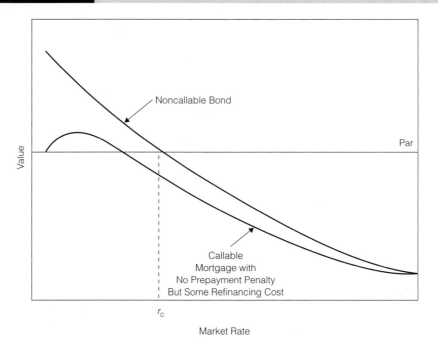

FIGURE 3-2   **Value of Mortgages**

Noncallable Bond

Par

Value

Callable
Mortgage with
No Prepayment Penalty
But Some Refinancing Cost

r_c

Market Rate

Source: © 2014 OnCourse Learning

rise. As the interest rate approaches the coupon rate, the value of the mortgage increases less than the value of the noncallable bond, reflecting the increased probability of prepayment. In the case where the market rate is slightly below the contract (coupon) rate, both obligations will have a value slightly above the face value. Mortgagors are unlikely to prepay their mortgage on the basis of very small differences in rates. As the market rate falls further, the likelihood of prepayment increases and, at some point, becomes so great that the value of the mortgage is equal to its balance. The value of the noncallable bond continues to increase as the market rate continues to fall below the contract rate. The difference between the two curves is the value of the call option on the mortgagor. This difference will widen if the market anticipates an increased volatility of interest rate. That is, if expected volatility increases, the two curves will be redrawn with a larger gap between them.

The mortgagor has another option as well—the put option. The mortgage is secured by a lien on the residence. In the event of default (nonpayment of any contractual obligation, primarily, but not restricted to, the principal and interest), the lender can foreclose on the property and liquidate it to satisfy the obligation. If the situation is such that the lender has no recourse to the personal assets of the mortgagor (as would be the case in a state that has enacted such a prohibition or if the mortgagor has little or no other assets), then the only remedy is to access the market value of the property. In the case where the market value of the property falls below the balance of the loan (negative equity), the mortgagor has a put option that has intrinsic worth. That is, the mortgagor in putting (selling) the property to the lender in satisfaction of the loan obligation exercises a put option at a strike price (value of the property) less than the value of the obligation (loan balance). Now, the mortgagor may not choose to exercise the option in this situation. A person may believe that the property could have a greater value in the future and continue to make the monthly payments. Of course, if an unavoidable event such as involuntary unemployment, a divorce, or a move to another residence occurs, this would precipitate the exercise of the default put option. In essence, the unavoidable event moves the exercise date to the present.

Options on Commercial Properties

The same default option pertains to commercial properties financed in part by debt. In the event the development does not work out as planned and the market value of the property falls below the indebtedness, the owner will put (sell) the property to the lender. In contrast to residential debt, there may be some slight differences in the exercise of the option. If the property is suffering a net operating loss, the owner will be quicker to put the property to the lender rather than hold the put option. The lender also may require contractual provisions that reduce the value of such a put option, such as a personal note that allows the lender to attach assets other than the property used to secure the debt. The lender also may require a larger down payment than is typically required for residential properties. This reduces the probability that the value of the property will fall below the loan balance and, thus, reduces the value of the put option.

Options on House Prices

Currently the **Chicago Mercantile Exchange** (CME Group) offers futures and options on **house price indices** (S&P/**Case-Shiller indices**) for 20 major metropolitan areas.[3] Each index is calculated on what is called the repeat sales pricing technique. This technique compares the price of a sample of houses sold in the latest month to their prices when sold at an earlier time. Some observations are discarded if the current price appears to be an outlier (perhaps indicating, for example, that major renovations were made in the property between sales). The indices use a base value of 100.00 for the year 2000. The indices are designed to allow those with an investment interest in housing (developers, builders, mortgage insurers, home supply business, and so forth) to hedge their risks. They would hedge their risk of a market decline, for example, by buying puts or selling futures on the index.

The value of a futures or options contract is $250 times the current index value. If, for example, the current index value for Los Angeles is 211.44 then the contract price will be $250 \times 211.44 = \$52,860$. The values of futures contracts move in "ticks" which is 0.2 of an index point or $250 \times 0.2 = \$50.00$ per contract. Twice daily, investors' positions are "marked-to-market," which means their accounts are credited with gains and debited with losses. Figure 3-3 provides more detail about the contract specifications.

Figure 3-4 shows the value of two indices from January 1987 through June 2012. The indices show both the periodic advances and declines of the two housing markets as well as their collapse beginning in mid-2006 for each market.

Explicit Options

Finally, there are explicit option contracts that are entered into routinely, often in relation to the purchase of raw (undeveloped) land. A developer may wish to secure the right to purchase land while completing a development package, including arranging the financing of the project. Purchasing an option to buy land at a given price in the future allows the developer to do this. The price of the option generally will be small relative to the purchase price. A developer may pay $40,000 for the right to purchase a parcel of land for $2 million any time within the next 9 months. The value of the option to the developer may well be worth its price. Should land values escalate over the period of exercise, the option will be valuable. If the value of the land in question rises to $2.2 million by the last day of the exercise period, the option will be worth $200,000. If prices fall

FIGURE 3-3	Contract Specifications

Contract Specifications

	Futures	**Options on Futures**
Ticker Symbol	Composite **CUS**. Boston **BOS**. Chicago **CHI**, Denver **DEN**, Las Vegas **LAV**, Los Angeles **LAX**, Miami **MIA**, New York **NYM**, San Diego **SDG**, San Francisco **SFR**, Washington, DC **WDC**	
Contract Size	Each contract shall be valued at $250 times the CSI Index, e.g., if the value of the index for Los Angeles was reported at 267.74, the contract value equates to $66,936 (= 250 × 267.74)	One futures contract
Minimum Price Fluctuation (Tick)	Minimum price fluctuation or "tick" shall be 0.20 index points ($50.00)	Minimum price fluctuation or "tick" shall be 0.10 index points ($25.00)
Trading Hours All Times Listed in Central Time (CT)	Offered exclusively on the CME Globex electronic trading platform on Sundays through Thursdays, 5:00 p.m.–2:00 p.m. (CT) the next day	Traded Via open outcry in GSCI pit Mondays through Fridays, 8:00 a.m.–2:00 p.m. (CT)
Contract Months	Contract months extending out 18 months in the future shall be listed on a quarterly cycle in the contact months of February, May, August, and November; contract months extending out 19 to 36 months into the future shall be listed on a bi-annual schedule in the contract months of May and November; and contract months extending out 37 months to 60 months into the future shall be listed on an annual schedule in the contract month of November	
Cash Index Release Schedule	8:00 a.m. CT (9:00 a.m. EST) on the last Tuesday of every calendar month. For example, the March 2006 index values will be released on May 30, 2006. These index values will reflect transactions recorded over a 3-month period January 2006 to March 2006	
Last Trading Day	Trading in expiring contract ceases at 2:00 p.m. CT (3:00 p.m. EST) on the business day preceding the index release day for the contract month	
Composite Index Weights	Boston 7.4122%; Chicago 8.8868%; Denver 3.6825%; Las Vegas 1.4802%; Los Angeles 21.1620%; Miami 4.9862%; New York 27.2390%; San Diego 5.5134%; San Francisco 11.7879%; Washington, DC 7.8500%	
Cash Settlement	Cash settled on the day the CSI Indices are released. For example, the May 2006 LAX contract will settle to the March 2006 CSI Los Angeles Index scheduled for release on May 30, 2006	European-style, exercised into the associated futures contract
Strike Prices	NA	At 5 index point intervals above and below previous day's close in underlying futures
Calendar Spreads	Calendar spreads for all to regions and the composite	NA
Regional Spreads	All possible pairs of regions/composite for each contract month	NA
Position Limits	5,000 contracts	

[1] Strikes at 1 index point intervals will be listed on demand.

S&P/Case-Shiller Home Price Indices Futures and Options

Source: © 2014 OnCourse Learning

significantly, the option holder can buy the property in the market at a lower price, losing the option premium. Of course, in an efficient market the option should be priced at an amount that reflects, among other factors, the volatility of land values in the area.

THE THEORY OF FINANCIAL INTERMEDIATION

As the word *intermediary* suggests, financial institutions "stand between" the suppliers and users of credit. The most common **financial intermediaries** are commercial banks, savings and loan associations, mutual savings banks, and life insurance companies. The common understanding is that an intermediary, such as

| FIGURE 3-4 | Case-Shiller Home Price Index for Las Vegas, NV, and Los Angeles, CA, 1997–2012 |

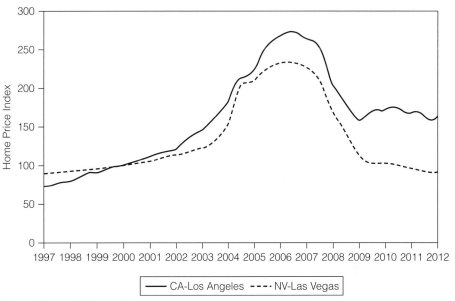

Source: © 2014 OnCourse Learning

a depository institution, receives credit from suppliers when it issues a liability (deposit). It lends the credit, creating an asset for itself, at a higher rate of interest than it provides on the deposit. The margin between the two rates is expected to cover the costs of operations and provide a normal return to the capital invested in the institution by stockholders. As we will see below, this scenario is often difficult for financial intermediaries to achieve. For now, let us focus on this simple notion of an intermediary.

Given that this is a simplified version of what intermediaries do, you may ask why they exist. It appears that suppliers and users of credit could deal with each other directly and eliminate (share) the margin charged by the intermediary. In fact, this is done quite often when investors purchase corporate, municipal, Treasury, and other securities directly from the issuer. Money market funds have been established to aid the small investor in this process of direct lending. Yet, intermediaries continue to exist. If this is so, they must provide an economic service. In a competitive economy, consumers will not pay for a service they can provide for themselves without cost. In fact, intermediaries perform several valuable economic functions. To understand them, consider a direct loan from you to your neighbor so that he or she may purchase a house. Here you are the mortgagee, and you and your neighbor have bypassed the intermediary. An alternative is to deposit your funds in an intermediary institution, which would then advance a loan to your neighbor. From your perspective, are there reasons for which the latter arrangement would be superior to the former? Several reasons are evident.

Liquidity Risk. When a deposit is made in a financial intermediary, the depositor receives a liquid asset. The deposit can be made in the most liquid of all assets, a transaction or demand deposit on which the depositor can write checks. It can also be made in the form of very short-term deposits with maturity dates of generally less than 1 year. Contrast this liquidity with a direct loan in the form of a mortgage to your neighbor.

Credit Evaluation and Risk Management. Intermediaries may have a superior knowledge of the credit risks associated with either the mortgagor or the property being mortgaged. They are also aware of various measures for reducing risk. The intermediary will place various covenants in a mortgage to reduce risk. Examples are the escrow requirements for property taxes and hazard insurance, provisions for penalties for delinquent payments, and so forth. Intermediaries also reduce risk through diversification—that is, through holding many mortgages. In short, financial intermediaries often have better credit evaluation and risk reduction procedures than do most individuals.

Interest Rate Risk. Mortgages generally have long maturities. Fixed-rate mortgages specify a contract rate of interest that will remain unchanged over their life. Accordingly, they are subject to **interest rate risk**. This risk is increased by the prepayment option held by the mortgagor. By issuing short-term deposits and investing in long-term, fixed-rate mortgages, intermediaries transfer interest rate risk to their stockholders, noteholders, or deposit insurer (Federal Deposit Insurance Corporation, FDIC). To the extent that intermediaries do not properly judge interest rate risk, they will fail to obtain a sufficient margin between the rate they pay on deposits and the rate they charge on long-term, fixed-rate mortgages. As we will see in Chapter 5, it is apparent that this has caused some intermediaries great difficulties in past years.

Many savings and loan associations have reduced their exposure to interest rate risk by either issuing adjustable-rate mortgages (ARMs) or selling off their fixed-rate mortgages while retaining the servicing fees. The former approach has narrowed the spread between the rate they pay on deposits and the rate they receive on their assets, the yield on ARMs being less than that on fixed-rate loans. The narrowing reflects the reduced risk. The latter approach allows an institution to focus on the first two functions: providing liquidity and credit evaluation and risk reduction. Notice that where the need for liquidity or credit evaluation is unnecessary, as with investment in short-term Treasury securities, the role of intermediaries is nonexistent. The function is taken over by nonintermediaries, such as money market funds. Because lack of liquidity and credit evaluation is a problem with investment in real estate securities such as mortgages, financial intermediaries will continue to be involved in real estate finance.

PORTFOLIO THEORY

As with an individual asset, a portfolio of several assets has an expected return and expected risk (as measured by the variance in returns). **Portfolio theory** says that when assets are combined to form a portfolio, the expected return on the portfolio will be equal to an average of the expected returns on the individual assets, weighted by the relative amount of each asset included in the portfolio. This should be no surprise. The same cannot be said about the risk, however. The risk of the portfolio is not equal to a weighted average of the risk of the individual assets because risk is a measure of the extent to which the actual returns of an asset can differ from the expected returns, as measured by their probabilities. Risk refers to the random component of returns over time. Portfolio construction exploits the random element in the returns of individual assets by combining several assets whose returns are less than perfectly positively correlated (move in exact synchronization, up and down) with each other. In fact, if the returns of two assets are random yet perfectly negatively correlated (move in the opposite direction), it is possible for the return on a portfolio to be constructed with no risk at all—that is, the returns will be certain.

In short, portfolio construction allows a reduction in the risk of the portfolio over that present in individual assets, without a sacrifice in expected returns. Furthermore, if the transaction costs required to establish a portfolio of a given size are identical to the total transaction costs on the individual assets (which is likely), then the risk reduction available through portfolio construction can be achieved without additional cost.

Several studies have demonstrated the benefits of diversification through portfolio construction of real estate assets. The benefits occur when properties of different types (hotels, warehouses, office buildings, farmland) and/or different geographical regions are combined. The greatest reduction in risk is through geographical diversification, where regions are defined in terms of their economy (manufacturing, mineral extraction, and so on). Today, large institutional investors such as life insurance companies and pension funds employ staffs of analysts to select real estate investments that meet portfolio requirements of risk reduction and return retention.

EFFICIENT MARKET THEORY

The term **efficient market** refers to the notion that an asset trades in a market where its value reflects all available information about that asset. The asset is priced "efficiently" in the sense that no one individual is able to trade on the basis of information available to all other market participants and, in the process, make excess returns. The term *excess returns* is important. The concept of an efficient market does not preclude an individual from making normal returns (a return for effort) in seeking out and effectively analyzing information available to the market. An investor cannot make returns in excess of normal returns by employing information that is available to everyone. The two concepts—that the price of an asset includes all available information and that no one can make returns in excess of normal by trading in an efficient market—are essentially identical. To make excess returns, a trader would have to have information that the asset is mispriced. But if the trader has that information, and it is available to all market participants, then the asset would not be mispriced.

Market efficiency can be discussed in terms of the type of information that is available about assets. **Weak form** market efficiency exists where the price of the asset completely reflects its historical prices (including the present price), so that knowledge of only those historical prices provides a trader no advantage over other market participants in earning an excess return. **Semi-strong form** market efficiency exists when the price of the asset reflects not only past price behavior but any other publicly available information. **Strong form** market efficiency exists when the current price reflects all information, whether public or private (inside information).

The conditions that lead to market efficiency in any form include the existence of many investors (market participants), uniform and widespread information, no market restrictions, no transaction costs, and investor preferences that value greater returns and less risk. The large organized stock markets come closest to meeting the requirements of an efficient market. It is no surprise then that numerous studies have shown stock markets to be efficient. Virtually no study has demonstrated a scheme whereby past price behavior alone can be used to make excess returns above transaction costs in the stock market. Any such scheme, on discovery, would be so quickly exploited by market participants as to obviate its usefulness for this purpose. That is, the scheme would represent new information that would be made available quickly to all market participants, and market prices would quickly reflect this new information.

Many studies also have shown that market prices of stocks quickly react to new information that affects their value. Unless action is taken within minutes of new information, excess returns cannot be made. It is not surprising that some studies have demonstrated that markets are not efficient with regard to nonpublic (inside) information. Inside knowledge can be used to make excess returns, although, even here, the time frame within which an investor must act is very limited.

As markets for assets lose the qualities of an efficient market, the ability to make excess returns by acquiring and trading on information, especially nonpublic information, increases. Markets tend to be less efficient when they are dominated by a few large investors, involve assets that are traded infrequently, and have large transaction and information costs. This latter description may apply to some real estate markets. Although some studies have demonstrated that real estate markets are efficient in terms of past price information (weak efficiency), there is less evidence that this is so for other types of information. For example, information that may affect the value of real estate may not be widely disseminated, including knowledge about proposed changes in zoning laws and regulations, road improvements, the availability of public utilities, other nearby developments, and so forth. Most analysts agree that real estate markets do not enjoy the efficiency of more liquid markets dominated by many participants.

AGENCY THEORY

Agency theory and agency problems deal with the relationship between principals and agents. An **agent** is someone who is retained by another (principal) to conduct activities for the latter's benefit. Agency problems are situations where the agent has an incentive to act in his or her own behalf to the detriment of the principal. These situations give rise to **agency costs**. These are costs born by the principal to minimize or prevent agency problems and include monitoring, bonding, and structuring costs. These costs take various forms, but all are intended to prevent the agent from placing his goals ahead of the principal's. **Monitoring costs** are outlays for audits and other control procedures. An out-of-town owner of a property may hire a manager to operate the property. The manager (agent) should have the goal of minimizing expenses, maximizing rental revenues, keeping the property in good condition, and so forth.[4] The owner will incur costs to monitor the operations of the manager, including auditing the books and inspecting the property. The owner should inspect the property to make sure that maintenance costs incurred, per the books of the property, are actually used to keep the property in good condition.

Bonding costs are payments made to third parties to ensure the honest behavior of agents. The bonding company contracts to reimburse the principal for any dishonest behavior of agents. In the above example, if the manager were paying invoices for the maintenance of the property to a repair firm owned by his brother-in-law and the repairs were not actually made, then the dishonest act would be subject to reimbursement by the bonding company.

Structuring costs involve compensation to agents to ensure performance consistent with the interest of the principal. In the above example, the owner of the property may enter into a contract with the manager whereby the latter would receive a portion of any operating profits from the property. This gives the manager an incentive to reduce unnecessary expenses and to keep the property in good operating condition to attract tenants.

There are many other examples of agency relationships and agency costs in real estate. The owner of a mall may enter into a lease where revenues received by a tenant over and above a certain amount are shared between the two parties. This gives the mall management an incentive to draw customers to the mall through various promotions. A mortgagee will require that property tax and hazard insurance be escrowed since the property serves as collateral for the loan. The mortgagee of a commercial property will expend effort to make sure that the owner does not encumber the property with other loans. This is done by recording the first mortgage with the county clerk. An agent employed to sell a property will be paid on the basis of a percentage of the sales price. This provides an incentive for the agent to obtain a buyer willing to pay the highest possible price.[5] Or, a lender making a construction loan to a developer will hire a voucher-control agent. The agent will make sure that any loan disbursements are paid to the contractors who build the structure that serves as collateral. Otherwise, if funds are diverted elsewhere, the unpaid contractors will put a lien on the property that will supersede that of the lender. Consider that, in a foreclosure of a residential property, the lender may not have an incentive to expend effort to make repairs on the property because any losses (including those caused by a decline in value) may be insured through a private mortgage insurer. To avoid this possibility, private mortgage insurers provide by contract that repairs to the property must be made before a claim can be submitted; furthermore, repair expenses cannot be made part of the claim. This provision ensures that the property is kept in as good condition as possible, maximizing its liquidation value.

Next, consider the subprime mortgage melt-down of 2006 through 2009. Subprime refers to a loan that is made to a borrower with less than an adequate credit rating. A great portion of the problem arose from agency problems. Over the last few decades, the secondary mortgage market has become more and more important. Large numbers of mortgage bankers and mortgage brokers came into the mortgage origination business. These brokers specialized in originating loans either as an agent for a large lender or for sale in the secondary mortgage market. They had, essentially, no risk position in these mortgages (risk of default, for example) once they were transferred to a lender or a secondary mortgage market conduit. Yet, these mortgage brokers received fees for originating the mortgages. Often, they would receive a **yield-spread-premium (YSP)**. A YSP occurs where the interest rate on the mortgage is above that in the market at the time of origination. A broker may, for example, originate a 9 percent loan when the market rate is 7 percent. The mortgage, when sold, will yield a premium (a $250,000 loan may sell for $265,000), which the broker receives. Mortgage brokers have an incentive to originate as many loans as possible. For several years prior to 2008, mortgage brokers offered loans that had low interest rates (and interest-only payments) for the first year or so (sometimes shorter) to induce borrowers to take out a loan they may otherwise not be able to afford. The loans would have their interest rate re-set after a short period to a rate well above the market rate. When house prices fell in 2006 through 2010 and the interest rate on the loans re-set, many borrowers defaulted. The losses were absorbed by the ultimate lender or investors in the secondary mortgage market. The incentive to originate loans was so great that some mortgage brokers required no documentation (no-doc loans) regarding the borrowers income. There were also cases where the mortgage broker would fabricate the income of the borrower. In such cases, agency problem brokers made large fees and commissions on loans they originated but passed the default risk on to others.

Finally, consider the situation of the homeowner who has retained the services of a real estate agent to sell his or her property. The homeowner will sign a listing contract with an expiration date. As the contract nears its expiration date (with no sale in sight) the real estate agent will have two options: increase his or her effort to sell the property (perhaps by bringing more buyers to visit the property) or convince the homeowner to reduce the asking price in hopes of generating a sale. These two options have different implications regarding the final selling price. The first option will likely generate a higher price while the second will have the opposite effect. Clauretie and Daneshvary[6] investigated the relationship between selling price and the time to expiration of listing contracts for a sample of 24,100 properties sold in Clark County, Nevada. They found that property prices were lower if the property is sold near the end of the listing contract. The evidence, they suggest, is that the price reduction effort of the real estate agent dominates the agent–effort effect. This behavior may not be in the interest of the homeowner.

In conclusion, agency problems exist in many real estate activities and transactions. Agency costs are incurred by the principal to minimize activity on the part of the agent that serves the latter's interest at the expense of the former.

Summary

The principles of finance that have commonly been applied to an analysis of corporation finance and corporate debt and equity securities can easily be applied to real estate and securities collateralized by real estate. The principles of asset valuation apply to real estate, mortgages, and other real state-related securities such as MBSs. Leverage, whereby debt is used to increase the value of equity contributions, is especially relevant to real estate investments. Options—some explicit, others not so obvious—exist in many areas. Real estate finance historically has been intricately tied to our financial institutions. The theory of financial intermediation is important for understanding the role, success, and failures of intermediaries such as thrifts. Real estate assets can be combined by themselves, or with other assets, in portfolios that reduce risk. Large institutional investors, such as pension funds and life insurance companies, explore their risk-reducing opportunities when they invest in real estate. The uniqueness of real estate properties and lack of widespread knowledge of all relevant facts allow for some inefficiencies. There is evidence that this leads to excess returns for some real estate investors. Finally, agency problems and the costs of monitoring agents are also present in real estate. Contracts and an intricate system of laws address client–agency problems.

Key Terms

Agency costs

Agency theory

Agent

Asset valuation

Bonding costs

Call

Capital structure

Case-Shiller Home indices

Cash flows

Chicago Mercantile Exchange

Collateralized mortgage obligations (CMOs)

Commercial mortgage-backed securities (CMBSs)

Discounted cash flow (DCF) model

Efficient market

Financial intermediary

House price indices

Interest rate risk

Interest-only securities

Leverage

Monitoring costs

Options

Portfolio theory

Principal-only securities

Prepayment or call option

Put

Real estate investment trusts (REITs)

Real estate limited partnerships (RELPs)

Risk

Semi-strong form

Servicing rights

Strong form

Structuring costs

Weak form

Yield-spread-premium

Review Questions

3-1. What are the four terms of the discounted cash flow (DCF) model?

3-2. Differentiate between income and cash flows.

3-3. Why does the DCF model focus on cash flows and not income?

3-4. a. Define risk.
b. Which term in the DCF model reflects risk?

3-5. a. Provide several examples of real estate assets that involve risk.
b. Explain the source of the risk.

3-6. a. Define leverage.
b. Explain how leverage can be used to increase the value of equity in a real estate investment.

3-7. Discuss the concept of optimal capital structure as it pertains to real estate investments.

3-8. a. Define options.
b. Give several examples of options in real estate.

3-9. List three "services" provided by financial intermediaries.

3-10. Explain how financial intermediaries can be exposed to interest rate risk.

3-11. Define an "efficient market."

3-12. Explain why a stock market, such as the New York Stock Exchange, is more efficient than some real estate markets.

3-13. a. Define agency costs.
b. Give several examples of agency costs in real estate.

3-14. If you were a large homebuilder in a major metropolitan area how might you hedge your risk that the market for your houses might crash?

3-15. Explain how agency costs contributed to the subprime meltdown from 2006 through 2009.

Notes

1. For example, the discounted cash flow model implies that the riskiness of cash flows increases at a compound rate over time since the adjustment to the discount rate for risk is compounded by raising the term $(11r)$ to the ith power. This is unlikely to be true in reality.

2. Franco Modigliani and Merton Miller. The cost of capital, corporation finance, and the theory of investment. *American Economic Review* 48 (1958), 261–297.

3. The 20 cities are Phoenix; Los Angeles; San Diego; San Francisco; Denver; Washington, DC; Miami; Tampa; Atlanta; Chicago; Boston; Detroit; Minneapolis; Charlotte; Las Vegas; New York; Cleveland; Portland; Dallas; and Seattle.

4. Sidney Rosenberg and John Corgel. Agency costs in property management contracts. *AREUEA Journal* 18 (Summer 1990), 184–201. The authors found expenses of managed properties to be 6 percent greater when the property management was unrelated to the property owner's company.

5. Thomas S. Zorn and James E. Larson. The incentive effect of flat-fee and percentage commission for real estate brokers. *AREUEA Journal* 14 (Spring 1986), 27–41. The authors found that percentage-fee incentives in broker's contracts are superior to a flat-fee structure to obtain higher prices for sellers of real estate.

6. Terrence M. Clauretie and Nasser Daneshvary. Principal-agent conflict and broker effort near listing contract expiration: the case of residential properties. *Journal of Real Estate Finance and Economics* 37 (2008), 147–161.

Web Site

www.cme.com/housing
CME Web site

Residential Real Estate Finance

*P*art 2 focuses on residential real estate finance. The main object of study is the one- to four-family (but typically one-family) residential mortgage. Multifamily property (apartments) finance is considered commercial financing and is not discussed in Part 2. Included in this section is a discussion of federal policies and laws related to residential finance, financing terms and their effect on property prices, the structure of the secondary mortgage market, and the pricing of mortgage-related securities. Risk management also is discussed. Here we talk about borrower and property qualification and mortgage insurance—both private and government (FHA/VA).

RESIDENTIAL MORTGAGE FINANCING IN THE UNITED STATES

LEARNING OBJECTIVES

After reading this chapter, you should have an understanding of how residential mortgage lending evolved from the earliest of times through World War II. The early history sets the stage for the modern system of residential finance as we know it. Also, this chapter will give you an understanding of the major forces that have changed and shaped the mortgage market since the end of World War II. You should understand how forces in the economic environment, especially inflationary factors, resulted in changes in both the types of institutions writing mortgages and the types of mortgages available. This chapter also outlines how federal government policies aided or hindered the transition. Understanding the development of residential mortgage lending through time will allow you to more fully appreciate the structure of the present system.

INTRODUCTION

At its core, real estate finance involves the transferring of funds from a lender to a borrower, typically for the purpose of buying or improving real property. As with any arm's-length agreement, mutual benefits are derived by the parties to the contract. Furthermore, since the transaction usually involves the movement of funds over time from one party to another, the agreement inherently involves risk to one or both parties. This is unlike a transaction where, for example, goods are exchanged for cash with no future commitment by either party. Various measures have been invented, developed, and employed to minimize the risk of real estate lending. Additionally, legal institutions have promulgated rules and laws that have affected the risks involved by defining the rights and duties of the parties. Loan risks are minimized when mortgages are made to creditworthy borrowers for a fraction of the value of the property and when the lender is able to quickly secure possession of the collateralized property in case of default. The timing and the right to possession of the collateral by the lender are very important to minimize risk.

PRE-AMERICAN DEVELOPMENTS

Roman Law

Many aspects of U.S. and Western law can be traced to the Roman Empire. Roman real property law went through several stages. Initially the instrument used in real estate loans was termed the **fiducia**, from the Latin word for *trust* or *confidence*. Ironically, it apparently did not mean that the lender had trust or confidence in the borrower since this instrument provided for legal title and possession of the property to be held by the lender. If the obligation of the borrower under the terms of the loan was met, then the *fiducia* called for a reconveyance of the title and possession to the original owner (borrower). This arrangement apparently became awkward, and the **pigus** was developed. Under this instrument, there was no transfer of the title. The land was "pawned," so to speak, with the title and possession remaining with the borrower. However, the rights of the lender were well-protected. Under this arrangement, the lender had the right to take title and possession of the property under a "suspicion of the probability of default" by the borrower. Later, the **hypotheca**, which means *pledge*, was developed. This instrument was similar to the *pigus* except that the lender could take possession of the property only in the event of an actual default.

German Influence

As the Roman Empire began to wane, German customs took hold in Europe. German law recognized the concept of a **gage**, a deposit made in promise of the fulfillment of an agreement. Often a borrower would physically deliver portable property as a gage, as would be done today at a pawn shop. In such a case, it was termed a "live" gage. When the collateral for the loan was real property, this arrangement was impossible. The gage in this case stipulated that in the event of default, the lender could take possession of the property but could not look beyond that gage for relief. That is, the borrower had the option of fulfilling the obligation or putting the property to the lender, a put option.

English Developments

The French introduced the Germanic gage system to England after William the Conqueror's invasion in 1066. For loans involving real property where there could be no physical transfer of the pledged property, it was termed a "dead" gage. Since the French word for "dead" is *mort*, it was appropriately termed a *mort gage*, or *mortgage*. Lending in England in the Middle Ages was complicated by the prohibition of interest by the church. Charging interest for a loan was termed **usury** and thought to be sinful. The basis of the prohibition, as indicated by the writings of church scholars such as St. Thomas Aquinas, was "natural law." Thomas Aquinas relied heavily on Aristotelian philosophy, which sought guidance in "natural law," or what seemed natural. It was natural in an agrarian economy for land to produce food, for animals to produce offspring, and so forth. But it was not natural for money to reproduce, and hence came the judgment that charging interest was unnatural and sinful.

Thomas Aquinas was quick to point out, however, that an interest charge could be justified under some circumstances, such as in the case where the lender suffered harm by virtue of the loan. By stretching the definition, harm could be defined as a lost opportunity. In any event, lenders, in order not to run afoul of the church's prohibition, would lend funds not for interest but so that the lender would have the right to possess and reap the benefits of a portion of the land securing the loan. In these early times, if there was a default, the lender had the right to take possession of the entire land and had no obligation to give the borrower anything in return. As the common law developed, borrowers were able to invoke the intervention of the Chancery Court during the reign of Queen Elizabeth I (1558–1603) on the basis of unfairness. The Chancery Court ruled that this was unduly harsh, especially where the debt was small and the borrower had only temporary financial difficulties. Borrowers could petition the court, stating how they intended to pay the debt. The court began to allow the borrower to redeem the property (after the default) on payment of the delinquent amounts. This was termed the **equitable right of redemption**.

This right, in the eyes of the lender, was soon abused. Borrowers could redeem their property long after the actual default. In effect, they had a call option on the real estate with an exercise price equal to the amount of the delinquent payments. Furthermore, the exercise period was unlimited. Lenders sought and received a provision for foreclosure whereby after a certain period of time the borrower was prevented (foreclosed) from redeeming the property in the fashion described. The exercise period of the option was reduced.

Today we experience the remnants of this system. In all states a mortgagor can redeem his property by paying delinquent amounts, including any legal and other expenses, up to the point of actual foreclosure. This is the equitable right of redemption. Additionally, some states, by statute, grant an additional period of time during which the mortgagor can redeem the property. This is called a **statutory right of redemption**.

AMERICAN RESIDENTIAL FINANCE: EARLY AMERICAN HISTORY THROUGH THE DEPRESSION YEARS

During the years following the American Revolution, there was little need for real estate lending. In rural areas, most families lived on small farms that were kept in the family and passed down from generation to generation. The need to finance the sale of these small properties was rare or nonexistent. This remained, for the most part, until after the Civil War. Occasionally, a "building society" would be formed in an urban area to garner sufficient funds for the organizers to purchase their residences. Once such funds had been accumulated, the society would cease to solicit additional funds. The first such building society was the Oxford Provident Building Association, formed in Philadelphia, in 1831. The "dices" that were collected from the members were not considered deposits or liabilities but rather shares of equity. At first the shareholder was not entitled to a fixed "dividend," or even to redeem the shares on demand. Later, many of the building societies began to provide for liquidation at face value. This change moved the societies away from being stockownership corporations toward being thrifts as we know them today. By the time of the Civil War, there were only a handful of such societies.

The post–Civil War westward expansion required that the sale of new farms be financed. The funds required to finance these sales were, for the most part, in the hands of large Eastern institutional investors. It was during this time that the mortgage banker became prominent. Mortgage bankers were specialists who would originate mortgages in the expanding West for their investor correspondents in the East. The typical farm mortgage at this time was a short-term loan (usually 5 years) with only interest paid semiannually. A loan that has interest-only payments is called **nonamortizing**, which means none of the principal is included in any of the payments. The principal balance of these loans is never reduced. For this reason, the loans usually covered only 40 to 50 percent of the value of the property. On maturity the loan would be refinanced at a new rate of interest for a small origination fee, say, 1 percent of the loan's balance.

Mortgage bankers dominated the small-farm mortgage market because few savings and loans existed until the latter part of the 1800s. Commercial banks were also not active in this market. Under the National Banking System (1863–1913), federally chartered banks were prohibited from making real estate loans. This would be changed in 1913 with the establishment of the Federal Reserve System whereby banks were authorized to originate 5-year loans with a maximum of a 50 percent loan-to-value ratio. State banks that were allowed to issue real estate loans also originated short-term, nonamortizing loans.

It is interesting to note that the type of loan originated in this era was very similar to what today would be considered a 5-year adjustable-rate mortgage (ARM). By keeping the maturity short, lenders minimized their interest rate risk. If market rates rose subsequent to origination, the lender would be faced with, at most, only a few years of below-market returns. Some default risk was associated with this type of loan, however. Since it was nonamortizing, there was a greater likelihood that the value of the property might slip below the balance of the loan. This was particularly true for properties with second and third mortgages. The default risk associated with such loans became apparent in the late 1920s and early 1930s during America's pre-Depression and Depression years. Huge numbers of borrowers were forced to default on their loans.

During the early 1920s, **building and loan associations** experienced their most rapid growth. Associations grew from 5,356 with $571 million in total assets in 1900 to 11,777 with $8.8 billion in assets in 1930. During this time, the associations gradually changed the rules on dividends and retirement of shares to compete with commercial banks; this represented essentially a circumvention of the laws that restricted entry into banking. For example, some associations issued "shares" with a definite "interest" (dividend) rate maturing at specific dates. They were analogous to certificates of deposit. Other shares could be redeemed on short notice at par and without a penalty. The growth of associations at this time also was aided by federal income tax regulations that exempted the associations from tax as long as they loaned their funds to members for home building.

During the early 1920s, property values rose rapidly as the money supply grew at a historically rapid rate. Lenders were not restrained in advancing funds to purchase high-priced properties. Then, with the collapse of the banking system in the early 1930s, the money supply plummeted. Declining property prices followed, leading to a record number of defaults and further eroding the capital position of lenders.

The default risk of the short-term nonamortizing loan popular at the time can be demonstrated by analyzing the performance of such loans during the 1920s and 1930s. Saulnier discusses the loan histories of the largest 24 insurance companies during this period.[1] From 1920 through 1924, only 24.4 percent of the loans originated by this group of lenders were **fully amortized**, meaning that by the end of the payment stream the debt would be reduced to zero. During this time the foreclosure rate was 5.3 percent of all loans—15 percent on the nonamortizing loans and only 2.8 percent on the amortizing loans. From 1930 through 1934, the worst part of the Great Depression, foreclosure rates rose to 21.1 percent overall—28.1 percent on nonamortizing loans and 17.8 percent on amortizing loans. During the entire decade of the 1920s, the foreclosure rate was 21 percent on loans of 4 years or less maturity and 13.5 percent on 10- to 14-year maturity loans. Clearly, for this particular set of loans, the shorter nonamortizing mortgages experienced greater foreclosure rates.

This experience led to a change in the type of mortgages originated by all lenders. The changes made by the life insurance companies used in the Saulnier study exemplify those changes. Although only 24 percent of the loans originated from 1920 through 1924 were fully amortized and 79 percent had a maturity of less than 9 years, by 1930 to 1934, 31.5 percent were fully amortized, and the proportion with a maturity of less than 9 years dropped to 66 percent. During the 1940–1946 period, 94 percent of all loans originated by life insurance companies were fully amortized, and only 3 percent had a maturity of less than 9 years. The dramatic drop in the proportion of short-term, nonamortizing loans in the latter period also reflects the laws and agencies established by the federal government during the Depression to support the mortgage market.

The collapse of the economy from 1929 through 1933 threw the real estate lending market into disarray. After the 1929 crash, property values fell to about half the 1928 level. The dramatic drop in personal income led to large-scale delinquencies on mortgage loans. As a result, lenders, particularly depository institutions such as thrifts, were caught in the middle. They were not receiving their periodic payments on the loans, and foreclosures offered no remedy due to the drop in property values. Depositors withdrew large sums of cash to meet their living expenses. Between 1931 and 1934, net withdrawals from savings and loan institutions amounted to $1.84 billion, about one-third of their 1930 deposit level. By 1935, one-fifth of all mortgage loans resulted in real estate owned (REO) for the thrifts. Many states passed legislation enacting moratoriums on foreclosures. Following Iowa's lead in passing legislation in February 1933, 26 additional states passed such moratorium legislation.

Generally intended to last for only a few years, some moratoriums lasted well into the 1940s.

The chaotic situation led the federal government to enact programs or agencies to aid the real estate lending market. There were six such programs in all.

1. The **Reconstruction Finance Corporation (RFC)**, established in early 1932, used government credit to lend $114 million to savings and loan associations and $290 million to mortgage loan companies from its beginning through October 1937. The loans helped the thrifts survive their liquidity crisis.

2. The **Federal Home Loan Bank System (FHLBS)** was established by the Federal Home Loan Bank Act in July 1932. The act established 12 Federal Home Loan Banks, which in turn chartered federal institutions and accepted qualified state institutions as members. Through the sale of bonds and a line of credit to the U.S. Treasury, the system lent more than $200 million to thrifts from 1932 through 1937.

3. The **Home Owners Loan Corporation (HOLC)** was established by the Home Owners Loan Act in June 1933 to help distressed homeowners by refinancing their short-term rollover loans into 15-year amortizing mortgages at restricted interest rates. It was authorized to issue up to $4.75 billion in 4 percent notes guaranteed by the government. Through the end of 1936, it loaned more than $3 billion to homeowners with mortgages held by thrifts, commercial banks, and mortgage companies. It also lent money directly to the mortgagor for up to 80 percent of the value of the property. It ended its lending in 1936.

4. The **Federal Savings and Loan Insurance Corporation (FSLIC)** was established by the National Housing Act in 1934. FSLIC, similar to the **Federal Deposit Insurance Corporation (FDIC)** for commercial banks, was established to insure the deposits at thrifts. The agency charged thrifts a small premium for the insurance and used these funds to pay depositors' claims of failed institutions. Government backing gave the agency credibility. The FSLIC was merged with the FDIC in 1989 by a thrift reform act.

5. The **Federal Housing Administration (FHA)**, also established by the National Housing Act, insured mortgages against default. The agency would charge an insurance premium to the mortgagor to cover the cost of expected claims. Again, government backing established credibility for this insurance provider. The FHA would insure loans up to 80 percent of the value of one- to four-family properties as long as they were long-term, amortizing loans. This loan program acted to lower default risk by imposing interest rate ceilings, loan limits, and loan-to-value ratios. It also required appraisals and first-mortgage positions. At first the term was for 15 years, but later 20-, 25-, and 30-year loans were instituted. Lenders, burned by the high default rates on short-term loans during the Depression, were quick to make loans with the new insurance provisions.

   Conventional (nongovernment-insured) loans also took on the characteristics of the long-term FHA loan. By making the maturity longer, lenders exchanged default risk for interest rate risk. This exchange would not become apparent for a few decades. When it did, it caused thrifts great problems. As one can imagine, in a volatile interest rate environment, the interest rate risk on a long-term mortgage with a prepayment option is very great.

6. The **Federal National Mortgage Association (FNMA or Fannie Mae)** was established in 1938 to purchase FHA-insured mortgages. It raised its funds by borrowing from the Treasury and selling shares in the association to the financial institutions with which it did business. Its main purpose was to aid the acceptance of FHA-insured loans by establishing a market for these loans. As interest rates rose, the value of some FHA loans fell. The FNMA would purchase them at face value, thus providing lenders with additional funds to originate mortgages. FNMA would sell the loans when interest rates dropped. Temporary losses were covered by its line of credit to the U.S. Treasury. FNMA was eventually given status as a private company in the late 1960s. By the 1990s FNMA was a major secondary mortgage market agency. The current operations of this agency are discussed in Chapter 10.

MODERN RESIDENTIAL FINANCE (POST–WORLD WAR II)

Toward the end of World War II, the Veteran's Administration (VA) was given authority through the Servicemen's Readjustment Act of 1944 to develop a mortgage insurance program similar to that of the FHA. The VA could guarantee up to $2,000 of home mortgage debt for a qualified veteran. The initial contract interest rate was 4 percent and the VA had the authority to set a maximum interest rate until 1992 when Congress eliminated rate caps.

Since World War II, some noticeable trends have been noted in the amount and holders of mortgage debt. During the 1950s, savings and loan associations enjoyed the greatest growth in mortgage lending. They increased their holdings nearly 16 percent annually to raise their share of the total from 19 to 29 percent. The growth came at the expense of a decline in the share held by commercial banks and individuals and resulted primarily from savings and loan associations being granted favorable tax status for investing in residential mortgages. They continued to increase their share of the market in later decades as well.

After 1950, commercial banks initially lost ground but later recovered their share of mortgage lending. By the 1980s, their share was the same as it was in 1950. Although there was no trend in the share held by individuals, there was some fluctuation due primarily to the interest rate cycle.

When interest rates are relatively high, borrowers tend to hold onto existing mortgages. If they are holding relatively low-cost financing, they have little incentive to repay the debt. Also, it is more difficult for individuals to sell property when interest rates are high. Therefore, they often finance all or part of the sale themselves. The sellers become mortgage holders. These loans, termed **purchase money mortgages**, owner-carrybacks, or owner-seconds, are usually short-term loans with balloon payments. The increase in the share held by individuals in the 1980s partially reflects the very high interest rates of the late 1970s.

The most notable trend is that of the share held by federal and related agencies. Several federal agencies were active in the 1970s and 1980s in raising funds for residential finance. They enjoyed the backing (credit) of the federal government and were successful in attracting funds to residential financing via the secondary mortgage market. They were especially successful during periods of high and volatile interest rates. Many lenders that in earlier times held loans in their own portfolios began to avoid interest rate risk by selling off loans that they originated to the federal agencies. In addition, the agencies were given broadened powers by the government to expand the secondary mortgage market. Legislation was passed to eliminate taxation at the entity level. The government believed it was important for the secondary market to provide funds for the housing market during periods of high interest rates. By 1990 the agencies were so successful and such large players in the market that they could virtually dictate the terms, conditions, and underwriting criteria of mortgage instruments offered in the marketplace. If terms of the loans did not conform (conforming loans) with the requirements of the federal agencies, they would not be available for sale or purchase in the secondary market.

The expansion of the secondary mortgage market accelerated in the early 1990s. Although the amount of mortgage debt held by savings institutions fell nearly 3 percent annually from 1990 to 1996, the share held by federally related agencies rose by 10 percent annually during this same period. By 1998, 59 percent of single-family mortgage debt and 33 percent of multifamily mortgage debt was securitized by federal agencies. A decade-by-decade review of the postwar mortgage market follows.

THE 1950S: A DECADE OF STABILITY

In 1950, one-half of all mortgage debt (residential and commercial) was held by depository institutions. By 1960, the ratio had risen to 56 percent. Because of the widespread acceptance of the 30-year, fixed-rate mortgage (FRM), these institutions were particularly vulnerable to interest rate risk. The risk occurs when there is a large difference between the maturity of an institution's assets and liabilities. This is called a **maturity mismatch**. Even if most mortgages are prepaid prior to their 30-year maturity, their expected "life" is still measured in years—several years. Most deposits have maturities of less than 1 year; some are payable on demand.

To appreciate the severe problems associated with the maturity mismatch problem that appeared later in the 1970s and 1980s, consider a typical thrift of the 1950s. It would originate and hold in its portfolio mortgages yielding close to 5 percent. At the time, it would pay 3.5 percent on short-term deposits. The spread would cover operating expenses and provide for a return on the capital invested in the thrift. Consider what would happen if market interest rates rose so that depositors required a higher rate, say, 6 percent. Furthermore, assume that there are no regulatory restrictions on the rate the thrift can pay on deposits. As the 3.5 percent deposits matured, they would be rolled over at the 6 percent rate. The yield on new mortgages would also be higher, say, 7 percent. This would discourage holders of the old 5 percent mortgages from prepaying them. If the 5 percent loans were assumable—as all FHA, VA, and many conventional loans were during this decade—then they would likely be passed on to the new buyers of any properties that were sold. In summary, the rise in rates would result in an increase in the thrifts' expenses with little change in their revenues.

With a continuation of this trend, the thrift's net worth could become negative. The thrift cannot escape the problems caused by the rise in rates by selling its low-rate loans since their value in the market is significantly less than their balance or the amount of deposit liabilities. The thrift may prefer to retain the loans rather than incur a loss on their sale that would be recorded in their year-end income statement. Once the problem created by the maturity mismatch and the rise in interest rates has occurred, the thrift is "locked in" and must hope for a fall in rates to extricate itself from insolvency.

The maturity mismatch problem is exacerbated by the general lack of prepayment penalties on mortgages. If the profits of a thrift decline when market rates rise, one would expect the reverse when they fall. Recall, however, that borrowers have a valuable prepayment option. With no penalties, they can refinance existing loans at lower rates should rates fall. They incur some refinancing costs, such as appraisal fees and loan origination fees, but the present value of the interest savings derived from the refinance could easily exceed these costs. Thus, when rates fall, the thrifts pay less to retain deposits but also earn less on their long-term assets. Should rates rise, subsequently the maturity mismatch problem recurs. The problem is not only one of rising interest rates but one of volatile interest rates. Lenders who originate long-term, FRMs without prepayment penalties grant borrowers valuable options. Recall that such options increase in value when interest rates become more volatile.

Maturity mismatch turned out not to be much of a problem in the 1950s for two reasons. First, the annual inflation rate was low and stable, around 2 percent. This translated into low and stable interest rates. From 1950 through 1958, the 3-month Treasury rate was 3.27 percent at its highest (1957) and was as low as 0.95 percent (1954). There was never any pressure for deposit rates to rise above the yield on mortgages. Second, Regulation Q, issued by the Federal Reserve Board in the 1930s, placed a limit on the rate commercial banks could pay on deposits. Limits on savings and loan deposit rates would not begin until 1966 when the Federal Home Loan Bank Board (FLBB) set the maximum rate that thrifts could pay on savings deposits at 0.25 percent over the commercial bank ceiling. At the time, thrifts were not allowed to issue demand deposits. The Interest Rate Adjustment Act of 1966 authorized the 0.25 percent advantage over banks to compensate for this competitive disadvantage. During the 1950s, the limit on the rates that banks were allowed to offer was intended to preserve their profitability and solvency. Left to compete, they would drive the rate up to whatever the market rate would be, increasing their expenses but not, in the aggregate, attracting more total savings. Of course, if the market rate for deposits was below the Regulation Q ceiling, then it would be nonbinding.

In summary, although the structure of the mortgage market was such as to have potential for serious problems for banks and thrifts, the stable inflation and interest rate environment of the 1950s suppressed any evidence of such problems. It would not remain hidden; hinted at in the 1960s, it emerged as a major concern in the 1970s and led to a restructuring of the mortgage market in the 1980s.

THE 1960S: CREEPING INFLATION, DISINTERMEDIATION, AND THE RISE OF THE SECONDARY MORTGAGE MARKET

The rate of inflation accelerated during the 1960s, partially as a result of the expanded war effort in Vietnam. The 1.5 percent inflation rate in 1960 was quadrupled in 1969 when it reached 6.1 percent. Interest rates reacted accordingly, incorporating inflationary expectations. The 3-year Treasury yield rose gradually from 3.98 percent in 1960 to 7.02 percent in 1969. Short-term rates occasionally rose above the Regulation Q restricted rate offered on bank deposits.

Owners of large deposits began to withdraw their funds and invest in Treasuries. With the development of bond funds, even small savers could take advantage of attractive Treasury yields.[2] The withdrawal of funds from the intermediaries under these circumstances was termed **disintermediation**. Although the regulatory agencies raised the Regulation Q limits when market rates rose enough to cause significant disintermediation, their actions were often delayed. In the meantime, the withdrawal of deposits from banks and thrifts led to a reduction in funds available for mortgage lending.

Figure 4-1 demonstrates this point. Data on Regulation Q ceiling rates, short-term Treasury yields, the net increase in deposits at savings institutions, and new mortgage lending clearly show the relationship between interest rates, disintermediation, and the mortgage market. As long as market rates were below or only slightly above the Regulation Q limit, disintermediation was not a problem and the regulation served its purpose of preserving the profitability of financial institutions. When market rates rose moderately above the limit, however, depositors withdrew their funds from the thrifts, which in turn cut back on mortgage lending.

Unlike the business and government sectors, a prospective homeowner was unable to directly finance his or her purchase. In simple terms, he or she was unable to issue a bond (mortgage) in any market to obtain the funds necessary to purchase a residence. Intermediation worked best in the mortgage market for the

FIGURE 4-1	Regulation Q Maximum Rates, Market Yields, and Net S & L Deposits

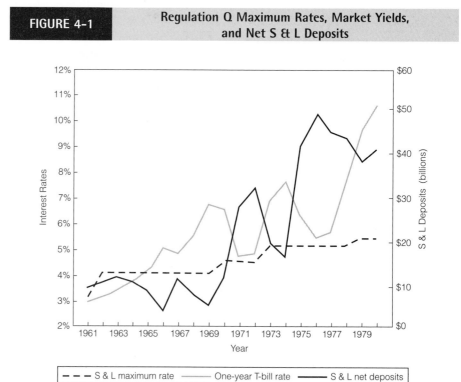

Source: © 2014 OnCourse Learning

reasons suggested in Chapter 3. The business and government sectors could issue bonds in the market directly to investors, avoiding the intermediation process. Since home buyers were restricted to the intermediaries for loans, they found funds tight whenever the intermediaries experienced an outflow of funds. It was not until the development of the secondary mortgage market that home buyers could finance directly their purchases through the issuance of a bond, so to speak (GNMA bonds are discussed in Chapters 10 and 11). It was ironic that the federal government could compete for and divert funds to its own use through direct financing (issuing bonds to the public) at the time it directed financial institutions to limit the rate they could offer on deposits.

The greatest disintermediations of the decade occurred during the 1966 "credit crunch" and again in 1969. In the third quarter of 1966, short-term Treasuries had a yield of 5.38 percent while thrifts paid 4 percent on time deposits. In that quarter there was a $726 million outflow of funds from thrifts. This compares to an average inflow of $2.2 billion per quarter for the previous 4 years.

Because of the manner in which it was financed, housing became particularly vulnerable to cyclical movements in interest rates. The bulk of residential loans were made by depository institutions that suffered a maturity mismatch problem in their capital structure and an unreliable supply of funds that resulted from restrictions on deposit rates. Regulation Q limits would continue through the 1970s. The standard FRM with its tilt (affordability) problem would continue to dominate all forms of residential loans through the early to mid-1970s. But the cyclical nature of the housing market had already evidenced itself in the 1960s and made it clear that residential financing needed help in the form of a well-developed secondary market for mortgages.

An additional problem faced by borrowers was the difficulty in comparing the effective costs of loans due to the nonstandardized methods of computing interest. To address this problem, in 1968 Congress passed the Truth in Lending Act to assure a meaningful disclosure of credit terms and costs. This would allow borrowers to better "shop" for mortgages and avoid abusive lending practices.

A **secondary mortgage market** is one in which securities are bought and sold subsequent to their initial origination. It is a market where existing securities are traded. Up until the 1960s, there was limited activity in the secondary market for mortgages. Most lenders were also investors. They held the loans they originated in their own portfolio.

As we discussed in Chapter 1, a secondary market for any security is important for several reasons. First, it increases liquidity. The initial investors in securities (lenders) prefer to originate loans that can be resold quickly and without loss of their intrinsic value. Without a large, organized secondary market, this is unlikely. With no secondary market, lenders will charge for lack of liquidity by requiring a higher rate (offering a lower price) on the loans they originate and must hold in their portfolio.

Second, a secondary market reduces the interest rate risk associated with the maturity mismatch problem. Lenders can continue to exploit their expertise as originators and sell off the loans to other investors. These investors, in turn, avoid the mismatch problem because they need not rely on short-term deposits as a source of funds. They can issue long-term bonds to finance their mortgage purchases. The long-term bonds will not be subject to either fluctuations in short-term rates or Regulation Q restrictions. Alternatively, secondary market investors can finance the purchase of mortgages by issuing bonds that essentially pass through the monthly interest and principal payments of the mortgages to the bondholder. In this manner, the ultimate bondholder becomes the lender.

That bondholder may be in a better position to absorb interest rate risk than the thrift.

Third, an organized secondary market can aid the smooth flow of funds from capital-rich areas to capital-deficient areas. Excess funds from the more stable Northeast may be used to satisfy the needs of borrowers in rapidly growing areas of the country such as the Southwest. This would tend to equalize interest rates between the various regions of the country.

At this time two new federal mortgage agencies were created to expand the secondary market. In 1968 the Housing and Urban Development Act established the Government National Mortgage Association (GNMA, commonly called Ginnie Mae). In the process it also privatized the FNMA, or Fannie Mae, that was created during the 1930s. The second new agency, the Federal Home Loan Mortgage Corporation (FHLMC, or Freddie Mac), was created in 1970. Both agencies are discussed in detail in Chapter 10. Briefly, GNMA guarantees (but does not actually issue) bonds of the pass-through type as long as the mortgages backing them are government underwritten (FHA or VA). A pass-through channels each principal and interest payment from the homeowner through to the bondholder. The FHLMC issues various types of bonds, including long-term bonds, to raise funds to purchase conventional mortgages.

Because of the activity of GNMA in the 1960s, the share of all mortgage debt held by federal agencies or in pools (which is what GNMAs are) rose to 8 percent from 6 percent in 1960 and 4 percent in 1950. The major expansion of secondary market activity was yet to come, however. As we will see, the share held by agencies and pools would rise to about 47 percent by 1996.

The disintermediation of the late 1960s slowed the growth of thrift participation in the mortgage market. The 16 percent annual growth in the volume of mortgage holdings of savings and loans that characterized the 1950s slowed to 9.6 percent in the 1960s. The disintermediation was also a hint of more severe problems to come in the 1970s, when inflation would accelerate even more. The regulatory authorities felt that they could not eliminate Regulation Q for fear that rapidly rising rates on deposits would result in mass insolvency for thrifts with large portfolios of low-rate mortgages. Yet with Regulation Q in place, the disintermediation problems would accelerate.

THE 1970s: PROBLEMS OF THE FIXED-RATE MORTGAGE IN AN INFLATIONARY ENVIRONMENT

The decade of the 1970s began with a 6 percent rate of inflation and ended in 1979 with prices rising at 13.3 percent annually. Moreover, the volatility in the annual rate of inflation increased significantly. The 1979 rate was the highest inflation rate of the decade, but it had been as low as 3.4 percent in 1972. This resulted in a wide fluctuation in the conventional mortgage rate from around 7.25 percent in 1972 to 13.75 percent in 1980. The high-inflation environment caused both supply (thrifts) and demand (affordability) problems for the mortgage market during this decade. It was clear by mid-decade that the standard fixed-rate, 30-year, amortizing loan, and the thrift industry were in trouble. Yet up to that point, the housing market had relied almost exclusively on that type of loan and on financial intermediaries to supply it.

Demand Problems

The problems of the FRM in an inflationary environment may be summarized as follows. First, inflation creates expectations of future inflation and, through the Fisher equation (see Chapter 2), a rise in long-term interest rates. The home buyer faces a higher rate and a higher payment for a given value of a house. Second, if inflation actually occurs as expected, there is no increase in the real cost of housing over the term of the loan. The real cost is increased in the early part of the loan and decreased in the later part. This **"tilt" effect** causes an affordability problem for the home buyer. The lender charges a premium in the interest rate to compensate for future inflation. Home buyers must make their initial payments out of an income that has yet to benefit (rise) from the future inflation.

The examples in Table 4-1 demonstrate this tilt effect on housing affordability. In these examples, it is assumed that the borrower's income will rise at an annual rate of 2 percent (for productivity) plus the rate of inflation. In other words, real income grows at 2 percent. It is also assumed that the contract rate on the loan is equal to the real rate (3 percent) plus the rate of inflation. The contract rate establishes the constant dollar payment. For example, annual inflation in case B is expected to be 2 percent, the borrower's income will grow at 4 percent, and the contract rate on the loan will be 5 percent. The last column for each case is the important column. It shows the real payment divided by the real income of the borrower over the course of the 30-year loan.

In year 5 of case B, inflation would have reduced the real value of the $429.45 payment to $388.97 ($429.45/(1.02)^3$), while the borrower's monthly income would have risen to $3,650, or $3,312 in real terms. The real-payment-to-real-income ratio is 11.74 percent ($388.97/$3,312). In each case, the tilt effect occurs; the real-payment-to-real-income ratio is greater in the first year of the loan and declines throughout its life. The magnitude of the tilt effect increases as expected inflation rises. The affordability problem caused by inflation and the FRM is evident. Although the real cost of housing over the 30-year period is identical, in each case a greater portion of that cost is redistributed to the front end of the loan as inflation increases. By the late 1970s inflation had risen to historically high levels. Interest rates responded and housing affordability plummeted.

TABLE 4–1

Effect of Inflation of Real Payment of Fixed-Rate Mortgage

$80,000, 30-year mortgage; $3,000/month initial income				
	YEAR	**MONTHLY PAYMENT ($)**	**REAL PAYMENT ($)**	**PAYMENT/ INCOME (%)**
Case A: 0% inflation; 3% interest rate	1	335.36	335.36	10.96
	5	335.36	335.36	10.12
	10	335.36	335.36	9.17
	20	335.36	335.36	7.52
	30	335.36	335.36	6.17
Case B: 2% inflation; 5% interest rate	1	429.45	421.03	13.76
	5	429.45	388.97	11.74
	10	429.45	352.30	9.60
	20	429.45	289.01	6.40
	30	429.45	237.09	4.36
Case C: 8% inflation; 11% interest rate	1	761.86	705.42	23.05
	5	761.86	518.51	15.65
	10	761.86	352.89	9.65
	20	761.86	163.45	3.67
	30	761.86	75.71	1.39

Source: © 2014 OnCourse Learning

The lender includes the expected inflation premium in the contract rate; however, there is no guarantee that the actual rate of inflation over the life of the loan will equal the expected rate. The real cost of housing will be different from the expected cost as well. If inflation turns out to be much greater than expected, the homeowner will face a lower real cost, and the lender will incur a reduction in the real rate-of-return on the loan. The reverse will be true if inflation is lower than expected. Thus, uncertainty about future inflation adds another problem to the workability of the long-term, FRM. As inflation accelerated in the late 1970s and its variability was magnified, there was increased incentive for the market to develop mortgage loans that eliminated tilt and inflation uncertainty problems.

Supply Problems

The supply problems of the standard, FRM in an inflationary environment stem from the maturity mismatch structure of financial intermediaries and the use of Regulation Q. During the early part of the 1970s, the yield curve was upward sloping. Lenders who saw profit opportunities in the spread and originated a large volume of FRMs may have failed to consider the implications of the yield curve. Recall from Chapter 2 that an upward-sloping curve is indicative of expectations that market rates will rise. Maturity mismatch and rising rates can combine to produce long-term losses or a savings outflow if deposit rates are restricted, which is exactly what occurred.

By 1979, the rate on 3-month Treasuries had risen to 10.04 percent. Disintermediation became such a problem that the regulatory agencies allowed the deposit rate to rise to 5.5 percent. But even at this rate, thrifts still experienced disintermediation.

Introduction of Alternative Mortgage Instruments

The demand and supply problems created by the long-term, FRM in an inflationary environment led to a rethinking of the type of residential loan that would serve the needs of the housing sector. Many new mortgage designs were suggested. Some solved the tilt problem, others the interest rate risk problem, and still others both. These **alternative mortgage instruments (AMIs)** are discussed at length in Chapter 6. The more popular AMIs are briefly described here.

The graduated-payment mortgage (GPM) was introduced to solve the tilt problem. Different versions were employed, but the main concept was to reduce the initial payment below, and raise the later payment above that which would be required to amortize the standard fixed-rate loan. The contract rate would be fixed.

One problem with the GPM was its provision for negative amortization in its early years. **Negative amortization** occurs when the loan balance grows rather than declines over time. The rising balance could exceed the value of the property at some point, raising the risk of default. The GPM did not gain wide acceptance until the FHA insured these loans.

Another problem of the GPM is one shared with the FRM: that of unanticipated changes in the inflation rate. The contract rate on a GPM is set at the beginning of the loan, so that increases in the actual rate of inflation over the expected rate would lower the real cost to the borrower and lower the real return for the lender.

The **shared appreciation mortgage (SAM)** was designed to solve the affordability problem. With this loan the lender would offer a contract rate below the market rate in return for a share of the appreciation of the property at a specified later date or when sold, whichever occurs first. Assuming that the collateralized property would appreciate in value at a rate equivalent to general inflation, the share of appreciation received by the lender would be a function of the actual inflation rate, not an expected rate. By tying the yield on the loan, *ex post*, to the actual rate of inflation, the problem of unanticipated changes in the inflation rate was avoided.

The maturity mismatch problem is one of interest rate risk. Recall that with interest rate risk, as the market rate rises, the value of the asset declines, especially fixed-income assets such as FRMs. The most popular AMI developed to alleviate this problem was the ARM. The ARM allows the lender to shift some or all of the interest rate risk to the borrower. In its most simple terms, the ARM provided for a periodic adjustment of the contract rate to reflect more closely the market rate. The maturity of the loan is effectively the length of time selected between adjustments, for example, 1 year. Initially, adjustment terms ranged from 6 months to 5 years. Eventually, the market settled on the 1-year adjustment period as the most popular term. ARMs are usually amortized over 30 years, so that default risk is not as much an issue as with GPMs. Thus, regardless of the periodic interest rate adjustments, the ARM will fully amortize to a zero balance over 30 years.

A lender with a portfolio of 1-year ARMs and liabilities consisting of 1-year deposits would have no maturity mismatch and no interest rate risk. Most borrowers were not willing to accept a complete transfer of the interest rate risk to themselves. As a result, lenders retained some of the risk by agreeing to limits (caps) on the periodic change in the contract rate or on the maximum rate over the life of the loan.

Because some of the interest rate risk has been shifted to the borrower and the fact that the periodic adjustments effectively create a series of short-term loans, the initial contract rate on an ARM is less than that on an FRM of the same maturity. One way to compare FRMs and ARMs is to think of the FRM as one 30-year loan whereas a 1-year adjustable ARM is a series of 30 1-year loans. This alleviated the affordability problem in a high-interest rate era but did not completely eliminate it. There is evidence to suggest that borrowers prefer ARMs when interest rates are high because of increased affordability.

One proposed AMI was designed to alleviate both supply and demand problems. The **price level adjusted mortgage (PLAM)** provides for an initial contract rate equal to the real rate. Recall that the nominal rate is the sum of the real rate and the inflation rate. Thus, this contract rate would be less than what is normally observed. The low monthly payment that results helps solve the tilt and affordability problem. Each year thereafter, the balance of the loan and, thus, the payment would be adjusted to reflect changes in inflation. The annual adjustment would be that year's actual rate of inflation multiplied by the ending loan balance. If no inflation occurred, there would be no adjustment, and the lender would receive the real rate of return. The PLAM loan has complicated features that are difficult for the average homeowner to understand. Perhaps for this reason, it never gained popularity. In 1990 the FHA began to explore the possibility of insuring PLAMS but, to date, has not done so.

Continued Growth of the Secondary Market

The activities of the federally related agencies (Fannie Mae, Ginnie Mae, and Freddie Mac) continued to grow in scope and importance in the 1970s. By 1980 these agencies held (or guaranteed the debt backed by mortgages) slightly more than one-fifth of all mortgage debt outstanding. Lenders were beginning to realize the risk of holding loans in their own portfolios. The prepayment option granted in the typical mortgage magnified this risk. In addition, there was the assumability option. All FHA and VA loans and some conventional loans were written to be "assumable." Under an assumption the buyer "assumes" the responsibility of making payments on the existing loan. The assumability option has intrinsic value whenever the current market rate exceeds the contract rate on the mortgage. The seller of the house can pass the low-rate loan to the buyer, capturing its value in terms of a higher selling price for the property. The seller-mortgagor and buyer benefit at the expense of the lender, who continues to carry a low-rate loan in a period of high market rates. The assumability option combined with the prepayment option cause interest rate risk to be very burdensome for thrifts when interest rate volatility is high.

The high and volatile interest rates of the late 1970s convinced many lenders to shift the interest rate risk to organizations and investors that were better prepared to handle it. They did this by selling the mortgages that they originated to the secondary market (FNMA, FHLMC, GNMA).

THE 1980s: DEREGULATION, THE GROWTH OF ALTERNATIVE MORTGAGE INSTRUMENTS, AND THE THRIFT CRISES

From the passage of the **Depository Institutions Deregulation and Monetary Control Act (MCA)** of 1980 to the passage of the Financial Institution Reform, Recovery, and Enforcement Act (FIRREA) of 1989, this decade witnessed the greatest changes in the residential finance market since the 1930s. The changes resulted primarily from the interest rate risk that traditional mortgage lenders faced in the inflationary environment of the early part of the 1980s.

Widespread Savings and Loan Failures

The 1980s witnessed more problems with the solvency of savings and loan associations than did any other period in history. The problems were caused by a combination of the structure of the industry, regulation, legislation, the economy (especially interest rate volatility during this period), and some dishonest and incompetent management.[4]

The spread between the rate received on new mortgages and that paid on deposits narrowed by more than a percentage point from 3.49 in 1979 to 2.39 in 1987. The rate paid to depositors rose to very high levels in the early to mid-1980s as a result of competition and the removal of Regulation Q limits. Although rates on new mortgage loans rose, they did not keep pace with those paid on deposits, causing the spread to narrow. Additionally, the yield on the total mortgage portfolio of savings and loans lagged below that on new mortgages, due to the slowing of prepayments on existing loans originated earlier at low rates.

The profit squeeze caused by the narrowing of the rate spread was also tightened by an increase in the operating expense ratio. The scenario of **thrift failures** in this decade is fascinating and can be outlined as follows.

Pre-1982—Regulatory Restriction of Competition and Risk-Taking. Depository Institutions Deregulation and Monetary Control Act of 1980. Prior to the 1980s, the regulatory agencies acted to limit thrift competition and risk-taking by placing ceilings on deposit rates (right-hand side of the balance sheet) and mandating that thrift assets be held primarily in the form of residential mortgages (left-hand side of the balance sheet). The Depository Institutions Deregulation Committee (established by the Monetary Control Act of 1980) removed rate ceilings on some designated deposits, and in 1982, thrifts were allowed to offer a money market deposit account with a competitive rate. In January 1983 other rate ceilings were removed.

Gradually during the early 1980s, deposits subject to ceilings became a smaller fraction of the total. But thrift assets remained primarily long-term, residential mortgages or mortgage-backed securities. The maturity mismatch problems surfaced during this period of rising interest rates. As interest expenses increased dramatically, interest revenue rose modestly, producing losses in 1981 and 1982. The maturity mismatch problem caused widespread losses for thrifts.

Thrift losses during this time led regulators to take action. In late 1981, the **Federal Home Loan Bank Board (FHLBB)** and the FSLIC created an instrument called the income capital certificate (ICC). Troubled thrifts were allowed to sell a certificate to the FSLIC of which the intent was to repurchase the certificates when the weak thrifts became profitable. The institution could add the amount of the certificate to its net worth. This allowed the FSLIC to avoid closing institutions with negative net worth.

1982—Competition and Incentives for Risk-Taking Introduced; the Garn–St. Germain Act. The **Garn–St. Germain Act** hastened the removal of limits on deposit rates, expanded the types of assets in which thrifts could invest, and instituted measures to alleviate, or "hide," the problem of insolvent thrifts. Among other things, the act (1) authorized a savings account to compete with money market funds; (2) preempted state restrictions on due-on-sale clause enforcement; (3) called for the savings account interest differential between banks and thrifts to be phased out by 1984; (4) provided FSLIC and FDIC assistance; (5) allowed thrifts to diversify beyond fixed-rate residential mortgages and invest in commercial, agricultural, and consumer loans, as well as real estate development projects; (6) allowed bank holding companies to acquire thrifts across state lines. These provisions were intended to reduce the maturity mismatch problem, with its attendant interest rate risk, and avoid the cost of resolution of troubled thrifts.

Although the act appeared to accomplish its two main goals, the results were short-lived and created longer-term problems. Thrifts were allowed to invest in shorter term, but more risky, assets. Many did and, in the process, substituted default risk for **interest rate risk**. The system created incentives for risk-taking by thrifts.

1982–1985—Incentives for Risk-Taking and FSLIC Forbearance. The equity position in a stock form of savings and loan (or any corporation, for that matter) is similar to holding a put option on the firm's assets. If the firm does well, any excess operating cash flows after debt holders are paid belong to the stockholders. If the firm suffers operating losses, the value of the equity position declines. At the point where the equity (net worth) becomes negative, the value of the debt exceeds the value of the assets and stockholders can "put" the firm's assets to the debt holders in satisfaction of the debt. For savings and loan associations the debt holders are, for the most part, either insured depositors of the institution or the FHLBB. For insolvent thrifts the stockholders have an incentive to take on very risky investments. Since the debt holders are insured against losses by the Treasury-backed FSLIC, the stockholders have an option to put the assets of insolvent thrifts to the taxpayers.

The undertaking of risky investments by insolvent thrifts was aided by FSLIC **forbearance** by allowing troubled institutions to continue to undertake risky investments and by allowing accounting practices that were at variance with **generally accepted accounting principles (GAAP)**.

Regulatory Accounting Principles versus Generally Accepted Accounting Principles. Prior to the FIRREA (discussed in the following), federal regulators allowed thrifts to operate in a manner different from rules imposed on nonfinancial businesses by GAAP. Under these **regulatory accounting principles (RAP)** thrifts' income and/or net worth were generally overstated. RAP was at variance with GAAP in several ways: (1) allowing origination fees to be included in income, (2) not requiring assets to be marked-to-market, (3) revising procedures to acquire troubled thrifts through mergers, and (4) the method of reporting gains and losses on the sale of assets. Under RAP, securities such as stocks could be recorded at cost, whereas GAAP required that they be recorded at market value and the loss recorded as a deduction in net worth.

1985–1988—The "Zombie" Theory of the Spread of Thrift Failures.

Thrifts that were insolvent but were allowed to continue operating were known as "zombies." Ed Kane describes the **"zombie" theory of thrift failure** as follows: The intention of a zombie thrift is to grow out of its problem by taking on high-risk investments. If the investments work out, the thrift survives and becomes profitable. If they do not, the thrift has nothing to lose since the stockholders presently have no positive net worth. Since its debt (deposits) is insured by the FSLIC, the creditors have no incentive to take control away from the stockholders. Thus, despite its negative net worth, the thrift continues to operate, taking on high-risk investments.[5]

1989—The Bush Initiative and the Financial Institutions Reform, Recovery, and Enforcement Act.

On February 6, 1989, President George H.W. Bush announced a plan to resolve the growing thrift crisis by restructuring the regulation of the savings and loan industry, improving supervisory controls to prevent abuses, increasing the financial strength of the FSLIC, increasing penalties for fraud, creating a new corporation to handle the closing of insolvent thrifts, and begin placing these institutions under the control of the government in an orderly manner. The initiative was passed by Congress in August 1989 as the **Financial Institutions Reform, Recovery, and Enforcement Act (FIRREA)**. FIRREA replaced the FSLIC with the **Resolution Trust Corporation (RTC)** and placed it under the control of the FDIC. The RTC was given 7 years to dispose of assets acquired when the FSLIC took over failed thrifts.

The act changed the FHLBB to the **Office of Thrift Supervision (OTS)** and placed it within the Department of the Treasury. The act established a set of capital requirements, including one that is risk-based. A risk-based capital requirement is one that requires the thrift to have more capital (net worth) if its assets are in higher risk classes.

These rule changes are outlined in Table 4-2. The new rules prohibited investments in some types of assets. Thrifts could not invest in junk bonds—bonds rated below the top four ratings—or in direct-equity investments, either securities or real estate. Thrifts were given until July 1, 1994, to divest themselves of these types of investments. They could, however, invest up to 3 percent of their assets in service companies (subsidiaries) that could hold such investments.

Because of several weaknesses, the act failed to alter substantially the situation that led to the crisis in the first place. For example, the act allowed the continuation of insurance for large deposits ($100,000) and higher-risk institutions continued to pay the same flat insurance premium as institutions with lower-risk assets. In fact, the risk-based capital requirements encouraged thrifts to return to low-risk (default) mortgages, which exposed them once again to interest rate risk. Additionally, the act failed to establish a mandatory closure level of capital. One weakness of the preact regulatory environment was the failure to close (or require recapitalization of) thrifts as their net worth shrank.

TABLE 4-2
FIRREA Mandated Changes in Thrift Investments

	OLD RULES	NEW RULES
QTIs	60% tangible assets[a]	65% of portfolio assets[b]
Assets included in QTIs:	Residential loans, FHLBB stocks, CDs of other S&Ls. Investments in RELPs, others	1. Primary QTIs (55%); residential loans, home equity loans, mortgage-backed securities, obligations of FDIC, RTC, and FSLIC resolution fund, stock of FNMA, FHLMC and FHLB
		2. Secondary QTIs (15%); 50% of residential loans originated and sold within 90 days, 200% of acquisition development and construction loans for low-priced homes, 200% of residential, church and nursing home loans in low-income neighborhoods, and consumer and education loans (10%)
Commercial real estate loans	40% of tangible assets	400% of capital[c]
Prohibited investments	None	Junk bonds, direct equity investments in securities and real property[d]

[a]*Total assets less goodwill.*

[b]*Total assets less goodwill less value of property used in business less liquid assets. Original requirement of 70% was reduced to 65% by banking reform legislation in 1991.*

[c]*No divestiture required.*

[d]*Divestiture required.*

Source: © 2014 OnCourse Learning

Post–FIRREA Regulatory Structure of the Mortgage Market

Figure 4-2 outlines the changes in the regulatory structure of the mortgage market that resulted from FIRREA. The effects of the changes can be summarized as follows.

Federal Asset Disposition Association. This agency was established prior to FIRREA to dispose of properties owned by thrifts as a result of foreclosures. It was liquidated by the new RTC.

Federal Deposit Insurance Corporation. This agency took over the supervision of state-chartered thrifts from the FHLBB and became the guarantor of the Savings Association Insurance Fund (SAIF). It also manages the RTC.

Federal Housing Finance Board. This agency was established to oversee the 12 Federal Home Loan Banks as a result of the dissolution of the FHLBB. This board oversees the advances of the federal home loan banks to member savings and loans.

Home Loan Bank Board. Abolished by FIRREA, its employees were allocated to the FDIC, RTC, OTS, and the Federal Housing Finance Board.

Federal Savings and Loan Insurance Corporation (FSLIC). Also abolished by FIRREA, its insurance activities were transferred to FDIC and OTS.

Office of Thrift Supervision. This agency took over the duties and powers of the FHLBB and its chairman. Under the supervision of the Treasury Department, it establishes capital requirements for savings and loans. By FIRREA mandate, those capital requirements can be no less stringent than those for national banks.

Resolution Trust Corporation. Its role was to liquidate and dispose of former FSLIC-insured institutions that were placed into conservatorship in the 3 years

FIGURE 4–2	FIRREA-Mandated Changes in Regulation of Mortgage Market

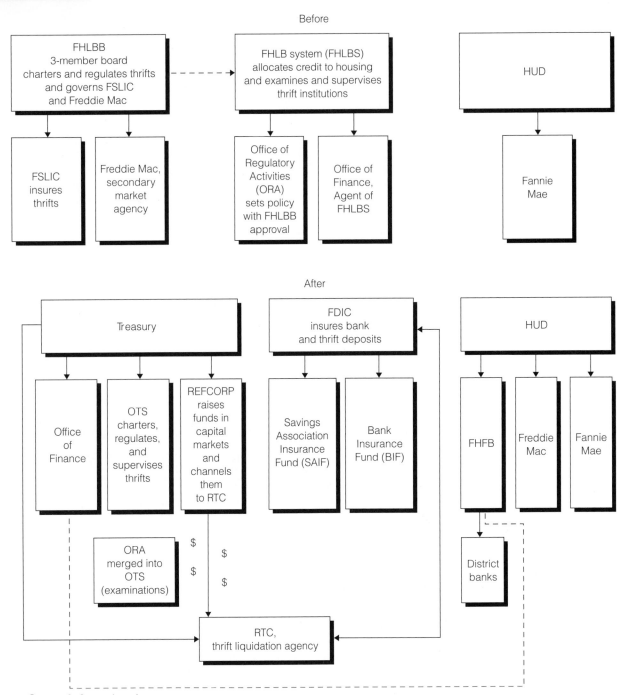

Source: © 2014 OnCourse Learning

after January 1, 1989. The RTC established a real estate asset division that identified properties of significant cultural, recreational, or scientific value. A 1993 study by Forgey, Goebel, and Rutherford provides a look at the disposition of properties by the RTC for the period August 1989 through June 1992.[6] The top five states by number of RTC sales were Texas, Florida, Arizona, Louisiana, and Colorado, respectively, while the top five types of property by number of sales were single-family homes, condominiums, residential developed land, duplexes, and residential unimproved land, respectively.

Federal Home Loan Mortgage Corporation (Freddie Mac). This secondary market agency was given a new, independent board of directors and encouraged to expand its purchases of mortgages to include those provided to low- and moderate-income families.

Risk-Based Capital Guidelines. One of the more important provisions of FIRREA was the requirement that thrifts have sufficient capital to absorb risks associated with their assets. Because of federal insurance, depositors will not pressure financial institutions to either invest in less risky assets or obtain sufficient stockholder equity, as would be required by the private marketplace. FIRREA regulations in this area are intended to substitute for market pressures. Table 4-3 shows the present risk-based capital guidelines for thrifts and banks.

TABLE 4-3

Risk-Based Capital Guidelines; December 1992

	NATIONAL BANKS (%)	SAVINGS ASSOCIATION (%)
Minimum ratio of capital to risk-weighted assets Risk weights	8	8[a]
Cash	0	0
U.S. Treasuries and securities guaranteed by the U.S. Treasury (except mortgage securities)	0	0
FHA-insured, VA-guaranteed mortgage loans	20	20
Qualifying mortgage loans secured by one- to four-family homes	50 (if conservatively valued)[b]	50 (if original LTV £80% or backed by approved MI)[c]
Qualifying multifamily mortgage loans (existing property, 5–36 units, LTV £80%, 80% occupancy over preceding year)	100	50
Delinquent loans (90 days or more) one- to four-family residential	100	100
Other	100	200
Ginnie Mae securities	0	0
Freddie Mac and Fannie Mae mortgage securities	20	20
High-quality nonagency mortgage securities[d] backed by agency securities	20	20
backed by nonagency securities or mortgage loans	50 or 100	20
Other mortgage securities backed by qualifying	50	50
mortgage loans by nonqualifying loans	100	100
Stripped mortgage securities	100	100[a]
Residual mortgage securities	100	100[a]
Retained subordinated class of mortgage securities	Same as underlying collateral, but capital required against transaction	Same as for banks[c]
Goodwill	100[e]	100 for qualifying supervisory goodwill not excluded for assets base[f]
Real estate owned	100	200

(Continued)

TABLE 4-3
(Continued)

	NATIONAL BANKS (%)	SAVINGS ASSOCIATION (%)
Minimum ratio of capital to risk-weighted assets Risk weights	8	8[a]
Equity investments (equity securities, investments in real property, investments in subsidiaries)	100	100 for amount not excluded from assets; all equity investments except certain subsidiaries must be phased out of asset base over 5 years
Nonresidential construction loans and land loans with LTVs above 80%	100	100, but part above 80% LTV excluded from asset base immediately
Standard risk category for all other assets, including nonqualifying one- to four-family mortgage loans, nonqualifying multifamily mortgage loans, customer and commercial loans	100	100

[a]Denotes items that are likely to change once the interest rate component is adopted.

[b]Regulation does not define "conservatively valued."

[c]Denotes items that may have different capital requirements under OTS's forthcoming optional "marginal capital calculation" for mortgage-related assets.

[d]OTS defines these as investment-grade securities (assigned to one of the two highest rated categories by a nationally recognized rating agency) backed by first-lien residential mortgage loans. OTS includes mortgage-backed bonds in this category, but OCC does not.

[e]Most goodwill is excluded from the asset base and deducted from capital.

[f]Nonsupervisory goodwill must be immediately excluded from asset base and thus deducted from capital. Qualifying supervisory goodwill is phased out over 5 years.

Source: © 2014 OnCourse Learning

THE 1990s: DOMINANCE OF THE SECONDARY MORTGAGE MARKET

The 1990s and the early 2000s saw the government-sponsored enterprises (GNMA, FNMA, FHLMC) and the secondary mortgage begin to dominate the mortgage market. Mortgage bankers gained an increasing share of originations and the percentage of residential loans that become securitized increased rapidly during this period. (Securitized means that entities in the secondary mortgage market issue securities or bonds and use the funds to purchase mortgages.) Mortgage bankers, of course, originate loans exclusively for sale in the secondary market. In 1990 mortgage bankers originated 34 percent of all residential loans compared to 64 percent by depository institutions. By 1997 mortgage bankers originated 57 percent of all loans.

The increased share of originations by mortgage bankers led to a similar increase in loans that were securitized in the secondary mortgage market. Whereas 42 percent of all outstanding residential loans were securitized in 1990, that percentage increased to 60 percent by 2002. Fannie Mae and Freddie Mac are the two major participants in mortgage securitization. In 2003 Fannie Mae held about $181 billion in mortgages in its portfolio and had about $1.58 trillion in outstanding mortgage-backed securities. This accounted for about 26 percent of the residential mortgage market. At the same time, Freddie Mac had about $36 billion in mortgages and $1.06 trillion in outstanding securities. This comprised about 17 percent of all residential mortgages.

Increased securitization by nature requires standardization. Both residential and commercial loans must be standardized to achieve marketability in the secondary mortgage market. Thus loan documents and evaluation processes are standardized across transactions. This provides less room for borrowers to negotiate loan terms that meet their specific needs. However, standardization should provide greater market efficiency in both mortgage pricing and mortgage processing.

Mortgage lending also became more national in scope. The Internet helped lift the restriction of mortgage lending being a local market and created new expansion possibilities for mortgage lenders. In some cases, the entire lending process from application to closing can be accomplished on-line. The World Wide Web also provided additional shopping and comparison opportunities for mortgage borrowers.

The 1990s experienced very low mortgage interest rates. Low inflation and other factors provided a market of interest rates comparable to several decades before. This produced greater housing affordability and substantial growth in house prices in some areas. This also produced a refinancing "craze" that started in 1993 and continued into the 2000s. To be competitive, some lenders began offering no-fee loans advertised sometimes as "no closing costs, no money down" options. However, for most of these loans, lenders charged higher interest rates. In some other options, the lender would wrap the fees into the new loan balance and finance them over the mortgage term.

Risk-Based Guidelines Expanded to Cover Interest Rate Risk

On June 30, 1995, the board of governors of the Federal Reserve System approved two measures related to the supervisory treatment of interest rate risk. They established guidelines to incorporate interest rate risk under Section 305 of the Federal Deposit Insurance Corporation Improvement Act. Section 305 of the act requires banking regulators to revise risk-based capital standards to include provisions for interest rate risk. In 1995 the board instituted a two-step approach to implementing the capital standards. The first step revises the capital standards to explicitly account for a bank's exposure to a decline in economic value as a result of a change in interest rates. The rule encourages regulators to utilize a new supervisory measurement process that focuses on a bank's economic value exposure, historical earnings performance, and exposure to interest rate movements. The second step is a rule that establishes an explicit minimum capital charge for interest rate risk that is based on the level of a bank's measured interest rate risk exposure. The supervisory measurement process includes a measure of a bank's underlying economic value and how that value would change in response to changes in interest rates. The bank's economic value is defined as the present value of its assets less the present value of its liabilities plus the net present value of its off-balance sheet instruments. The model then estimates a change in the net position as a result of a 200-basis point change in interest rates. In short, the interest rate risk guidelines explicitly account for the maturity mismatch problem in assessing adequate capital for banks.

THE 2000S: A PERIOD OF EXTREMES

The refinancing frenzy of the 1990s was followed by the housing market craze of the 2000s. At the end of the 1990s investors began moving funds out of financial assets into real estate based on its perceived reliability. Investors "discovered" housing and began including it in their list of "speculative" investments. This created an exuberance in the housing market that resulted in rapidly increasing house prices. Based on the Standard & Poor/Case-Shiller Home Price Index, house prices on a national level rose by 28 percent from 2000 to 2002. By 2004, house prices had risen 63 percent from their 2000 level and by 2006 prices on a national level were up an average of 87 percent from their 2000 level. In 2007, however, prices dropped by about 10 percent from 2006 and by the end of first quarter 2008, house prices had dropped by about 15 percent from their 2006 high. By the end of 2008, customer traffic and sales had hit record lows at the major homebuilders. The financial meltdown triggered a wave of contract cancellations as buyers worried about an already weak market.

By the end of 2007, gauges of house prices were showing prices falling sharply across most of the United States. Inventories of unsold homes remained high and were expected to increase as more and more foreclosed homes came on the market. Some major real estate markets were also seeing rising foreclosures on condominiums and bankruptcies on entire condo projects. Over the period 2003 to 2006, the number of new condominium units increased 145 percent.

By 2007, a weakening economy and rising mortgage delinquencies threatened to create a dangerous spiral as decreasing house prices and tighter credit began to adversely affect consumer behavior. In addition, leading homebuilders began posting losses much greater than expected. A number of the nation's small and midsize home builders were experiencing financial trouble. As the housing slump deepened in 2007 and housing inventories increased, home sellers became creative. Disguised discounts made it harder to tell exactly a home's true selling price. Incentives that may have artificially inflated or distorted prices ranged from free cars to cash rebates.

By 2007, with falling home prices, borrowers were showing a willingness to walk away from these speculative investments and the accompanying mortgage debt. Up through the 1990s, most homeowners had enough equity in their homes such that voluntary foreclosure was not a consideration. However, with falling house prices wiping out investors' equity, borrowers became increasingly willing to suffer lower credit ratings and default on their mortgages. This was a departure from past behavior of borrowers who tended to walk away only as a last resort. Just an investors played a big role in pushing up house prices during the housing boom, they accounted for a bigger proportionate share of loan defaults. By 2007 and early 2008 investors found themselves caught in a changing market as house prices fell and lenders tightened standards. In many cases, investors found their plans to either sell the house or refinance thwarted. In addition, many investors found themselves facing sometimes severe prepayment penalties when they considered refinancing their current loan. As a result, the subprime market began to disappear and more affluent borrowers turned to "private-money mortgages." These are high-cost loans originated in a market where there is very little tracking of statistics.

The housing market bust in 2007 created turmoil and resulted in a deluge of mortgage defaults, of which the subprime mortgage market played a key role. The fallout from the subprime debacle in the mid-2000s was best evidenced by the collapse of Countrywide, the nation's largest mortgage lender. It was taken over by Bank of America. The failure of Countrywide was viewed as a major risk to the

U.S. economy since, at that point in time, it serviced about one of every six loans in the country. This was followed in 2008 by the collapse of several Wall Street investment firms and a "takeover" of Fannie Mae and Freddie Mac by the federal government. The latter was at least partly a result of Fannie Mae's and Freddie Mac's movement into the subprime mortgage market between 2004 and 2007, with total GSE exposure exceeding $1 trillion. This action stimulated the growth of the subprime mortgage market and increased the GSE's risk exposure in terms of default. Acting within their implicit federal government (which subsequently became explicit), Fannie Mae and Freddie Mac had access to substantial capital at reduced rates. Under the guise of being committed to "affordable housing," these two entities became the largest buyers of subprime mortgages. Following the revelation in 2004 that their accounting practices had been fraudulent, Fannie Mae and Freddie Mac were anxious to prove their dedication to promoting home ownership. Noting that not all subprime mortgages are bad loans, nevertheless, starting in 2003 the quality of subprime loans declined, moving from the standard long-term, fixed loan with a reasonable down payment to low down payment, low initial interest rate adjustable loans.

Efforts to reform Fannie Mae and Freddie Mac over the 2000s decade fell on deaf ears in Congress until 2008 when the accumulation of toxic mortgage debt became overwhelming. On Sunday, September 7, 2008, Treasury Secretary Henry Paulson announced plans to take control of the troubled mortgage giants Fannie Mae and Freddie Mac. The companies' chief executives were ousted and a $200 billion infusion of capital was provided to restore the financial health of the firms. The firms went into conservatorship with management control given to their regulator, the Federal Housing Finance Agency. In return for the infusion of capital, the U.S. Treasury received $1 billion of preferred stock in each company. A special worry was the $5 trillion of Fannie Mae- and Freddie Mac-issued debt and mortgage-backed securities held by central banks and other worldwide investors. Under the takeover plan, the Treasury announced it would buy at least $5 billion of new mortgage-backed securities issued by the two entities. Both Fannie Mae and Freddie Mac were exposed to some of the mortgage market's most troubled participants, such as Countrywide Financial Corp.

Regulators were criticized for failing to prevent the reckless lending practices that fueled the credit crisis. By the end of 2008, at least twenty-five banks had failed and regulators were worried that another 200 banks could be at risk of collapsing.

To help distressed homeowners, in early 2009, Fannie Mae was considering a test program of preapproving short sales of homes. In a distress home "short sale," the lender agrees to accept the selling price of the house rather than the greater loan balance and the borrower is forgiven the difference. In early 2009 Fannie Mae began running pilot projects to streamline the short sale process by establishing the loss that Fannie Mae would be willing to take even before a buyer for the house is found. Borrowers favor short sales because they help preserve their credit histories by providing an exit from the mortgage. Lenders sometimes are willing to do short sales because it saves having to take possession of the property and market it, although a loss is still taken.

Also in early 2009, the U.S. Congress was considering a bill designed to aid homeowners currently in Chapter 13 bankruptcy renegotiate their mortgages. This type of restructuring is referred to as a "cram-down" and would let judges set new repayment terms for mortgage borrowers. This legislation is designed to give homeowners more leverage with lenders in negotiating mortgage restructuring. At the beginning of 2009, it was estimated by Moody's economy.com that nearly 10 million homeowners were struggling with their mortgage payments.

Further anxiety was created when Standard & Poor's downgraded a large number of residential mortgage securities. By 2007 the ratings agencies such as Standard & Poor's, Moody's Investor's Service, and Fitch Ratings were coming under fire for their generally favorable and sometimes top ratings on subprime mortgages. As is typical, over this period underwriters, creating security issues, worked closely with rating companies to garner the best rating possible to make the securities marketable. As of the end of 2007, Wall Street had built a global market for more than $2 trillion in mortgage securities. The prevailing logic at the time was twofold: that U.S. house prices would never fall dramatically nation-wide and that borrowers would be faithful to their mortgages. This, however, proved to be faulty. As house prices fell and homeowners defaulted on mortgages at ever-increasing rates, the pain and panic was felt worldwide. The circumstances have been compared to the mortgage crisis of the 1980s.

Credit markets eased slightly after the financial crisis intensified at the end of summer 2008 when the U.S. government moved to take stakes in major banks. However, lending remained constrained in nearly all market sectors. But, by the end of 2008, the damage caused by the lengthy financial crisis began to overwhelm some borrowers and industries. Retailers and auto makers, for example, experienced decreasing revenues because of reduced consumer spending. Also, while some banks that had received capital infusions such as Citigroup Inc. and Bank of America Corporation were seeing some increase in consumer confidence, others such as JPMorgan Chase & Co. still faced investor worry and lack of confidence. To avoid a major meltdown, by the end of 2008 federal regulators were pushing financial institutions to lend more to boost the economy.

By the end of 2008 at least 200 institutions had received taxpayer capital through the U.S. Treasury Department's Troubled Asset Relief Program (TARP). TARP was proposed in late September 2008 as a $700 billion bailout fund. It was touted as necessary jumpstart for lending to offset the slowdown by banks trying to reduce risk and conserve capital. However, the initial indications were that lending did not increase with TARP. While encouraging increased lending, regulators have, however, warned banks against loosening credit too much.

The accumulation of toxic mortgage debt that poisoned the global financial system and led to the greatest financial crisis since the Great Depression of the 1930s was thought by some to be the result of the aggressive buying of subprime and Alt-A mortgages and mortgage-backed securities by Fannie Mae and Freddie Mac. Some observers felt that there was undue pressure by Congress to support affordable housing and this resulted in Fannie Mae and Freddie Mac becoming the largest buyers of subprime and Alt-A mortgages between 2004 and 2007 (over $1 trillion). From 2003 to 2006, as the percentage of subprime loan originations rose from 8 to 20 percent of total mortgage originations, the quality of these loans steadily declined. Efforts by some in Congress in 2005 to rein in Fannie Mae and Freddie Mac activities failed.

A major positive result of the housing boom was the increase in the homeownership rate for the nation's households. The homeownership rate peaked at 69.2 percent in 2004. By the end of 2007, the homeownership rate had fallen to 68.2 percent. However, this still exceeded the relatively constant homeownership rate of 64 percent from 1970 through the early 1990s. In 2012 the homeownership rate was 65.4 percent, the lowest since 1997. Although homeownership rates have been relatively constant, by 2012 homeowners' equity in their homes had fallen to a post–World War II low.

The end of the 2000s decade found housing prices starting to rebound. In addition, home mortgage rates were at an all-time low. The average rate on a

30-year FRM was less than 4 percent. Low rates plus improving housing market conditions along with government policy allowed some borrowers to pursue loan refinancing and modifications as an alternative to foreclosure.

Although mortgage foreclosure rates leveled off in 2011, they remained a persistent problem for the housing market due, among other things, to ARM resets. The top states for foreclosures after the housing market collapse were California, Florida, Texas, and Michigan. By the end of 2012, there was a small drop in foreclosures nationwide, accounting for a little more than 3 percent of the housing market. For perspective, data provider CoreLogic was showing 57,000 completed foreclosures in September 2012 down from 83,000 for September 2011. In contrast, before the collapse of the housing market foreclosures average 21,000 per month between 2000 and 2006. Since the housing market collapse, there have been almost 4 million completed foreclosures across the United States. Although foreclosures in the late 2000s were rampant, the downward trend in foreclosures was interpreted as an improvement in the housing market.

Summary

The government mortgage market programs of the Depression years were established for a twofold purpose. One was to provide liquidity to lenders through direct loans and insuring deposits. Another was the promotion of a long-term, amortizing instrument through default insurance and a secondary market for such loans. The government was successful on both counts. Through these agencies and the establishment of insurance guaranteed by the VA in 1947, the postwar residential finance system was in place. America entered this new era with the following:

- a well-established system of thrifts, insured by the government and able to provide the services of intermediaries;
- a long-term, fixed-rate, amortizing mortgage as the principal (virtually only) type of loan; and
- an economy characterized by stable inflation and interest rates.

The residential mortgage and housing market went through some dramatic structural changes from the end of World War II through the early 1990s. The standard, fixed-rate loan that dominated the marketplace at the end of the war was joined by a host of AMIs in the 1980s. The most popular alternative evolved to be the ARM. The FHA-insured GPM made modest gains in acceptability. Other AMIs, such as SAMs and PLAMs, were relegated to a small segment of the market.

The role of the major lenders also shifted. Thrifts lost ground to the mortgage bankers in the share of total originations as the federal government provided greater support for the development of the secondary mortgage market. Developed in the late 1960s and early 1970s, the secondary mortgage market exploded in the 1980s until by 1990 it was so large and pervasive that it could dictate the types and terms of mortgages that would be originated in the primary market. Loans that do not conform to secondary market requirements cannot be sold into the secondary market and must be retained in the lender's portfolio.

The regulatory structure was also changed, primarily because of the large-scale failure of the savings and loans in the 1980s. The FSLIC was replaced by the

RTC and housed within the FDIC. The FHLBB was replaced by the OTS and placed within the Department of the Treasury. This reorganization separated the former supervisory agency from the former insurance fund.

Many of these changes were the result of the high inflation rates in the 1970s and early 1980s. High inflation caused interest rates to rise rapidly. In turn, the standard, fixed-rate loan became a weak instrument, exposing thrifts to significant interest rate risk. Interest rate risk led to losses, which led to speculation and risky lending behavior. This, in turn, led to widespread failure of thrifts. Although mismanagement and fraud added to the thrift failures, the root cause was the combination of the economic system and a lax regulatory system. The 1990s saw the rapid development of the secondary mortgage market as mortgage bankers became the dominant originators, and by 1997, for the first time in history, the majority of mortgage loans were securitized. The early to mid-2000s saw a housing boom in which house prices soared and mortgage financing was easily obtainable through a variety of options, some of them very risky for borrowers. The housing market collapsed in the mid-2000s with a significant drop in house prices and increased mortgage default. At the end of the 2000s decade, the housing market was still recovering.

Key Terms

Alternative mortgage instruments (AMIs)

Building and loan associations

Depository Institutions Deregulation and Monetary Control Act (MCA)

Equitable right of redemption

Federal Deposit Insurance Corporation (FDIC)

Federal Home Loan Bank Board (FHLBB)

Federal Home Loan Bank System (FHLBS)

Federal Housing Administration (FHA)

Federal National Mortgage Association (FNMA or Fannie Mae)

Federal Savings and Loan Insurance Corporation (FSLIC)

Financial Institutions Reform, Recovery, and Enforcement Act (FIRREA)

Fiducia

Forbearance

Fully amortized

Gage

Garn-St. Germain Act

Generally accepted accounting principles (GAAP)

Home Owners Loan Corporation (HOLC)

Hypotheca

Interest rate risk

Maturity mismatch

Negative amortization

Nonamortizing

Office of Thrift Supervision (OTS)

Pigus

Price level adjusted mortgage (PLAM)

Purchase money mortgages

Reconstruction Finance Corporation (RFC)

Regulatory accounting principles (RAP)

Resolution Trust Corporation (RTC)

Secondary mortgage market

Statutory right of redemption

Thrift failures

"Tilt" effect

Usury

"Zombie" theory of thrift failure

Review Questions

4-1. Summarize the historical use of property as collateral for a loan to finance its purchase.

4-2. What was the major difference between the *fiducia*, the *pigus*, and the *hypotheca* in Roman law?

4-3. a. Define an equitable right of redemption.
b. What is the origin of the equitable right of redemption?

4-4. Explain why mortgage bankers were popular in the post–Civil War era.

4-5. a. What were the characteristics of mortgages in the latter half of the nineteenth century?
b. Explain why they minimized interest rate risk for the lender.

4-6. Outline the causes of the high default rate on mortgages during the 1930s Depression.

4-7. How did federal programs support the mortgage and housing market in the 1930s Depression?

4-8. What was the purpose of the following agencies: (a) FSLIC, (b) FHA, and (c) FNMA?

4-9. Explain how the mortgage market of the 1940s differed from that of the 1920s.

4-10. Discuss the major changes in the residential finance market from 1950 to the 1990s with regard to
a. the types of mortgage lenders.
b. the types of mortgage loans.
c. the role of the federal government, including legislation.

4-11. Fully explain the concept of interest rate risk as it relates to thrift asset-liability maturity mismatch.

4-12. Explain why increased interest rate volatility increases interest rate risk of the type indicated in Question 4-11.

4-13. Identify the problems created by Regulation Q during the 1960s and 1970s.

4-14. Define disintermediation and explain why it caused severe disruptions in the housing market.

4-15. Indicate three benefits of a well-organized secondary market for mortgages.

4-16. a. Identify the supply problems of a standard, fixed-rate mortgage in an inflationary environment.
b. Identify the demand problems of a standard, fixed-rate mortgage in an inflationary environment.

4-17. What are the major changes in the regulation of financial institutions that were brought about by the Depository Institutions and Monetary Control Act of 1980 and the Garn-St. Germain Act of 1982?

4-18. Outline the critical issues on each side of the "battle" for enforcement of the due on-sale clause in the late 1970s and early 1980s.

4-19. Explain how borrowers attempted to circumvent the enforcement of the due-on-sale clause.

4-20. Indicate the major reasons for widespread failure of savings and loans in the 1980s. Include a discussion of (a) FSLIC forbearance, (b) regulatory additions to net worth, and (c) RAP versus GAAP accounting.

4-21.   Explain the "zombie" theory of savings and loan failure as outlined by Professor Kane.

4-22.   What provisions of FIRREA addressed the causes of the savings and loan failures?

4-23.   What are some of the weaknesses of FIRREA?

4-24.   How did FIRREA change the regulatory structure of the mortgage market in terms of (a) the regulators and (b) the rules and regulations?

4-25.   a. What are risk-based capital guidelines?
         b. Give an example of current risk-based capital guidelines for thrifts.

Problems

4-1.   Determine the Period 1 and Period 2 market net worth of the following savings and loans:

PERIOD 1		PERIOD 2	
Assets		Assets	
30-year mortgages,		30-year mortgages,	
9% coupon	$50,000,000	9% coupon	
Building and land	$5,000,000	Building and land	$5,000,000
Liabilities		Liabilities	
1-year CDs at		1-year CDs at	
1-year market rate	$50,000,000	1-year market rate	$50,000,000
Equity		Equity	
1-year market rate 7%		1-year market rate 7%	
30-year market rate 1%		30-year market rate 10%	

4-2.   Determine the required net worth, or capital, of the thrift (based on the following selected assets) under the indicated risk-based capital guidelines (not necessarily real-world guidelines).

ASSET	RISK WEIGHT	BOOK VALUE
Treasuries	0%	$1,000,000
Residential mortgages	25	3,000,000
Commercial mortgages	50	2,000,000
GNMAs	20	3,500,000
REO	250	800,000

Notes

1. Raymond J. Saulnier. *Urban Mortgage Lending by Life Insurance Companies.* New York: National Bureau of Economic Research, 1950. During this time, insurance companies held about one-sixth of all residential mortgage debt outstanding.

2. The first money market fund, the Reserve Fund, was organized in November 1971.

3. In fact, a study by Hendershott and Schultz shows that, after building a substantial capital base in the 1970s, the FHA single-family mortgage insurance fund lost roughly $10 billion in the 1980s. Negative equity, unemployment, and loan size were seen to be significant determinants of default. See Patric

H. Hendershott and William R. Schultz. Equity and nonequity determinants of FHA single-family mortgage foreclosures in the 1980s. *Journal of the American Real Estate and Urban Economics Association* 21 (Winter 1993), 405–430.

4. Creative financing also included such loans as wraparound loans, buydowns, zero interest rate financing, and other nontraditional loans.

5. A savings and loan is defined as a failure when there is a resolution by the FSLIC through (1) liquidation, (2) merger with another financial institution with the aid of the FSLIC, or (3) merger as the result of supervisory action.

6. Edward Kane. The unending deposit insurance mess. *Science* 246 (October 1989), 451–456.

Web Sites

http://www.freddiemac.com
Information on the Federal Home Loan Mortgage Corporation

http://www.fdic.gov/bank/index.html
FDIC data on commercial banks and savings and loan associations

http://fisher.osu.edu/departments/finance/research/publications/
Topics of general interest to finance students

http://www.occ.treas.gov/
Information on regulation of thrifts by the Office of the Comptroller of the Currency

http://www.fhfa.gov
Federal Housing Finance Board; one of the largest sets of available historical mortgage rates by property type and loan type

http://www.hud.gov/offices/hsg/ramh/res/resp0222.cfm
Access to HUD rulings that affect mortgage brokers

http://www.fanniemae.com
Fannie Mae Home Page

http://www.heritage.org/research/economy/bg2127.cfm
Subprime mortgage market

APPENDIX 4-A   The Era of Creative Financing

Although creative financing in mortgage lending has a long history, the early-mid 1980s ushered in a new period of creative financing. A mortgage originated with a financial institution is generally written at current market terms (interest rate, maturity, etc.). This is typically referred to as market financing. **Creative financing** refers to financing terms different from market financing, or "nonmarket financing." These favorable financing terms can create a transfer of wealth from the lender to the borrower. For example, a mortgage at a contract rate of 6 percent when the market rate is 10 percent, other factors constant, would have value to the borrower. The advantageous financing affects the value of the property because it is "attached" to the property (remember the definition of a mortgage).

Suppose that the borrower of the 6 percent mortgage wanted to sell the house to which the mortgage is attached. The borrower/seller may offer the buyer the option of buying the house and taking over the payments on the existing mortgage.

That would be in lieu of the buyer originating a new mortgage. Since the new mortgage would be written at the current market rate (10 percent), the existing loan at 6 percent would have value by virtue of being below-market. The buyer and seller could negotiate a price to be paid for the favorable financing and this amount would be included in the negotiated price of the house. Thus, the financing has affected the value of the property.

Creative financing was popular in the sale of raw or agricultural land shortly after federal law established separate tax rates for ordinary income and capital gains (1930s and 1940s). Sellers of land realized that they could get a price greater than the market value of the property if they were willing to finance the sale themselves at a below-market interest rate.[1] Within this process, the seller would realize higher capital gains on the sale but would receive lower interest income (taxed as ordinary income). In 1986 tax laws eliminated the distinction between ordinary income and capital gains.

Under the conditions of the late 1970s and early 1980s, there were several ways to originate nonmarket financing. The following provides a discussion of these methods.

Government-Underwritten Loans

One form of creative financing was related to government-underwritten loans (FHA, VA). FHA and VA tried to minimize default risk by keeping the borrower's payments as low as possible. Thus, until the late 1980s, they set a maximum (ceiling) rate of interest on loans that they insured. The rate was referred to as a "pegged" rate because it was set by the Secretary of HUD. As long as the market rate on conventional loans was equal to or below the pegged rate, the terms of each type could be identical and borrowers and lenders would be indifferent between conventional and FHA/VA loans. If the agencies were slow to respond, however, rising market rates could exceed the ceiling. Lenders would prefer to originate conventional loans with their higher yield unless they could raise the yield on the government underwritten loans above the ceiling rate. They did this by charging discount points.

When market rates were substantially higher than the ceiling rates, as was the case in the early 1980s, FHA and VA loans were attractive to borrowers who were prevented from paying more than one point. Any points needed to equalize the rates were usually collected from the seller of the house who, in turn, required a higher selling price. A buyer of a property financed with an FHA/VA loan makes a lower payment than if it were financed with a conventional loan since the contract rate is lower. Because of this, the buyer should be willing to pay discount points. However, the FHA/VA prohibited the buyer from paying more than one point. The seller of the property would be willing to sell to an FHA/VA-financed buyer only if points are captured in the selling price. Thus the value of the below-market interest rate is ultimately incorporated into the transactions price of the property.

Assumable Loans

For much of their history (up to the late 1980s) FHA and VA loans were assumable because they could not contain a due-on-sale clause. At the same time, some conventional loans lacked a due-on-sale clause and the clause was found to be unenforceable in others (until 1982). The **assumable loan** is attached to the property, just as a physical characteristic such as a pool, fireplace, or garage. The sale price of a house should reflect any "value" of the assumable loan. If the assumable loan has a below-market interest rate, a buyer of a property could pay more than for an identical property without an assumable loan and have the same

TABLE 4-1A

Value of a Low-Rate Assumable Loan 1982

Assumable loan	
Originated	1972
Remaining term	20 Years
Payment	$419.53
Rate	7.5%
Original balance	$60,000
1982 balance	$52,077
Alternative new conventional loan	
Term	20 Years
Balance	$52,077
Rate	15%
Payment	$685.74
Payment savings	$266.21
Present value of payment savings	$20,217

monthly payments. Also, the actual "value" of the assumable loan may be less than the present value of the payment savings.

Suppose, per Table 4-1A, a purchaser of a property attached by an assumable loan would be provided with $52,077 in financing but the rate on this amount would be considerably under current rates: 7.5 percent versus 15 percent. By assuming the loan, the buyer saves $266.21 per month over alternative financing at market rates. Since the assumable loan has value, the buyer would be willing to pay more for the house than she would if there were no assumable loan. Stated differently, given two identical houses, one with the assumable loan in this example and one with no assumable loan, the former would demand a higher price in the market. The assumable loan has value, just as any other amenity, and its value will be reflected in the price.

INTEREST RATE RISK INCREASES: VALUE OF ASSUMPTION OPTION BECOMES AN ISSUE

To appreciate the problems faced by lenders, we will first discuss the value of the assumability option in assumable mortgages. The value of this option was an issue in the early 1980s. Lenders sought to eliminate its value for conventional mortgages by inserting and enforcing the **due-on-sale clause** in mortgages or deeds-of-trust.[2] The due-on-sale clause stipulates that, if the property to which the mortgage is attached is sold, the balance of the mortgage is due and payable in full. Lenders inserted this clause more frequently as interest rates rose during the 1970s. By the 1990s, virtually all conventional mortgages had this clause.

Remember that value is created for the assumability option when the contract rate on the existing loan is less than the current market rate. This transfer of wealth from the lender to the borrower was so great at times in the 1980s that borrowers maneuvered to capture its value even for loans that had the due-on-sale clause. This was done primarily by devising ways to keep the existing payments on the low-rate loan in place. Borrowers fought in two ways—by attempting to conceal the sale from the lender and by litigating in court. For example, rather than selling the property outright, the seller may enter into a long-term lease, giving the lessee the option to buy at the end of the lease for an agreed amount.

Another way that borrowers kept the existing loan in place was by using a land sales contract or contract for deed. Here, the seller promises to deliver the deed to the property at some future time. The buyer, in consideration for this promise, agrees to make monthly payments for the period of the contract. Title to the property remains in the hands of the seller, who continues to make the payments on the original loan to the lender.

Still another method to circumvent the clause was to transfer the property into a trust for the owner's benefit. Instead of the property being sold, the beneficial use of the property would be transferred.

Sellers and buyers of residential properties also sought to preserve the value of low-rate loans through litigation. Lenders had gradually increased their use of the clause in trust deeds. The trust deed would also indicate the types of actions that would trigger the clause. As borrowers sought additional ways to avoid the exercise of the clause, more conditions were included in the deeds. The three most popular actions that would trigger the clause include a sale, lease, or further encumbrance of the property.

These maneuvers led to several test cases, the most famous of which was the *Wellenkamp* decision in California (1978). To understand the arguments in this case, one should review pre-Wellenkamp litigation in that state.

Wellenkamp Case

At first the courts viewed the due-on-sale clause as a restraint on the free transfer of property rights. Although an early case allowed a "reasonable" enforcement of the clause (*Coast Bank v. Minderhout*, 1964, 61 C2d 311), most cases did not allow for its enforcement unless there was a deleterious impact on the security for the loan. At the time it was not much of an issue because market rates and contract rates were nearly identical. In the late 1960s, the situation changed, and the court held that it was reasonable for the clause to be enforced for the purpose of portfolio restructuring (*Cherry v. Home Savings and Loan Association*, 1969, 276 CA2d 574). However, the California State Supreme Court reversed this thinking and ruled that economic considerations other than security impairment could not be used to justify enforcement of the clause (*LaSala v. American Savings and Loan Association*, 1971, 5 CA3d 865).

In 1974 the California courts once again rejected profit or portfolio considerations as a justification for enforcing the due-on-sale clause (*Tucker v. Lassen Savings and Loan Association*, 1974, 12 C3d 629). In this case, a land sales contract had triggered the clause.

Up to this time, no case involved a regular sale of the property as a trigger for enforcement of the clause. It was not certain how the courts would rule in such a case. However, in 1978 in the *Wellenkamp* case, they followed their previous decisions and rejected the automatic use of the clause in a regular sale where there was no impairment of the lender's security interest (*Wellenkamp v. Bank of America*, 1978, 21 C3d 943).

Federal Regulators and the Assumability Issue

Federal regulators such as the Federal Home Loan Bank Board (FHLBB, now the Office of Thrift Supervision) were concerned about the profitability of their member associations at this time. They could not keep the interest cost of funds artificially low (through Regulation Q) forever. Money market funds provided small savers with alternatives, and disintermediation was a constant threat. They saw the need for members to be able to raise the yield on their mortgage portfolio when properties with low-rate loans were sold. They directed their members to enforce the due-on-sale clause. As a result, a California case made it to the Supreme Court of the United States in June 1982. The U.S. Supreme Court agreed with the FHLBB and allowed the automatic enforcement of the clause for all federally chartered thrifts (*Fidelity Federal Savings and Loan Association v. de le Cuesta*, 1982, 458 U.S. 141). Here, the Court indicated that the regulator's requirement to assure the solvency of the nation's thrifts overrode the individual borrower's right to transfer the property with the original financing.

The stakes involved in the above litigation were not insignificant. With very high interest rates in the late 1970s and early 1980s, thrifts stood to lose (and borrowers gain) large sums through the inability to enforce the due-on-sale clause on conventional mortgages. In California alone, the wealth transfer resulting from the *Wellenkamp* decision was substantial. By comparing the financial statements and the turnover of conventional mortgages of state and federally chartered savings and loans from 1978 through 1981, Larry Ozanne was able to estimate the magnitude of the wealth transfer.[3] Ozanne estimated the net income of the state associations in California was between $58 and $170 million less in 1981 than it would have been had they been able to enforce the due-on-sale clause.

Wraparound Loans

A wraparound loan is a way to obtain additional financing while keeping an existing loan in place. The wrap is a junior mortgage that "wraps" around an existing loan. The amount of the wrap would equal the balance of the existing loan plus whatever additional amount of funds is loaned. The wrap borrower acknowledges (by virtue of the wrapping) the existence of the original loan but accepts no liability for this loan. The original borrower who is now the wrap lender remains liable for making the payments on the original loan. Sometimes the wrap lender may be a third party who has assumed responsibility for the original mortgage. Thus the buyer who is the wrap borrower accepts the property "subject to" the existing mortgage. The process would proceed as thus: The wrap borrower would make the wrap mortgage payment to the wrap lender, who in turn would make the payment on the original loan.

Although this process is complex, there are incentives for using this financing structure. Essentially the wrap loan provides additional funds to the borrower above the amount of the existing mortgage. So why not just take a second mortgage for that amount? The answer lies in the advantages to both the borrower and lender. The wrap can allow the borrower to obtain financing at a lower cost than the average cost of his or her first and second mortgages. For the wrap lender, it is an opportunity to leverage off the existing mortgage and enhance the return to the wrap loan.

Because the wrap borrower is not responsible for the payments on the original loan, procedures should be put in place to ensure that these payments are made. One way to accomplish this is to require the payments to be made through an escrow arrangement. In fact, all payments could be made through the escrow agent such that all parties are provided some protection.

A seller wishing to do a wrap should seek approval of the arrangement from the original lender. Problems may arise when a wrap is used with an existing mortgage that is not assumable. The sale of the property could trigger the due-on-sale clause in the original mortgage. An assumable mortgage allows a wrap to be done by a third party. This may be an individual or a financial institution. For example, a bank may assume the existing loan from the original lender and become a wrap lender to the buyer of the property.

Because of the leverage effect, it may be possible for the lender to write a wrap loan at a rate less than market yet still earn an effective yield greater than the market rate. To illustrate, suppose that you want to purchase a property for $150,000 and you can make a $20,000 down payment. The property has an existing mortgage that can be wrapped. This loan is a fixed-rate loan at 7 percent, monthly payments. The loan had an original balance of $110,000 and has 20 years left on its original 30-year term. The current market rate for a new fixed-rate loan is 10.5 percent for 20 years. The seller will give you a wrap loan for the purchase price at 8.75 percent, monthly payments.

The variable of interest is the effective yield for the wrap lender. This will be affected by the structure of the wrap loan. Let's assume that, to make the payments more affordable for the wrap borrower, the wrap loan is amortized for 30 years with a balloon at the end of 20 years. Thus, this wrap will be simultaneous term, partially amortized since the 20-year term is the same as the remaining term for the existing loan. However, the wrap loan will not be completely amortized over this period.

First, the payments on the respective loans can be calculated:

EXISTING LOAN	WRAP LOAN
$PMT_E = \$110,000\ (MC_{7\%,30}) = \$731.83$	$PMT_W = \$130,000\ (MC_{8.75\%,30}) = \$1,022.71$
$BAL_{10} = \$94,394$	$BAL_{20} = \$81,604$

To calculate the effective yield for the wrap lender, we have to determine his or her equity investment. First, a total of $130,000 is being provided by the wrap lender. However, he or she has a debt source of funds in the amount of the existing loan balance, $94,394. Thus, the wrap lender is investing only $35,606 of his or her own equity funds. The return on these funds is the difference in the monthly payments of the two loans, $290.88. Remember that the wrap lender will collect the payment on the wrap loan and make the payment on the existing loan. Also, in this structure the wrap lender will collect the balance of the wrap loan at the end of 20 years. The equation to determine his or her effective yield on these funds is

$$\$35,606 = \$290.88(PVIFA_{i\%/12,240}) + \$81,604(PVIF_{i\%/12,240})$$

Solving for the interest rate gives an effective yield of 11.48 percent. Thus, the wrap lender can provide below-market financing to the lender while simultaneously earning a yield greater than the market rate.

There are other ways to structure a wrap loan. A **simultaneous term, fully amortized wrap** loan would be written for a term equal to the remaining term on the existing loan, and both would be fully amortized over this period. The wrap loan could be an **extended term wrap**. In this case, the wrap loan would be written for a longer term than the remaining term on the existing loan, and both loans would be fully amortized. For the period after which the existing loan is repaid, the wrap lender would lose the leverage effect since he or she is collecting the wrap payments, but there is no payment on the existing loan to provide financial leverage. One could even write a **shorter term wrap**, in which the wrap loan would be amortized for a shorter term than the remaining term on the existing loan. This presents a problem for the wrap lender since the wrap loan is repaid before the existing loan is fully amortized. Since the wrap borrower would likely demand clear title once the wrap loan is repaid, the wrap lender would be required to repay the existing loan over the period of the wrap loan. This could be accomplished in a number of ways including (1) The payments on the existing loan could be increased so that it fully amortizes over the shorter wrap loan term; or (2) a balloon payment could be made on the existing loan at the end of the wrap term.

Buydown Financing

A **buydown mortgage** is a fixed-rate mortgage in which the seller prepays some of the loan interest to "buy down" the interest rate for the buyer/borrower for some period. This type of financing becomes more popular in periods of high interest rates (such as the early 1980s). The seller is usually a builder seeking to promote home sales in a slow market. The buydown allows the borrower to acquire cheaper financing in the early life of the loan. A typical buydown transaction is as follows: The prepaid interest buys down the borrower's interest rate by 300 basis points, 200 basis points, and 100 basis points over the first 3 years of loan life, respectively. Suppose the contract rate on the loan is 10 percent. This buydown would give the borrower interest rates of 7, 8, and 9 percent, respectively, over the first 3 years. These lower rates would be reflected in a lower payment for the borrower. In the fourth year, the payment reverts to normal since the contract rate is now being charged.

The good news with a buydown is that the lower initial payments may allow the buyer/borrower to qualify for the loan when he or she otherwise might have problems. The bad news is that, as with other types of favorable financing, the seller will likely attempt to capture the value of the buydown into the price of the property.

To illustrate the buydown process, suppose that a borrower takes a mortgage for $100,000 at 10 percent for 30 years, monthly payments. The seller has agreed to buy down the interest rate for the first 3 years to 7, 8, and 9 percent, respectively. In the fourth year, the loan rate reverts to the normal contract rate of 10 percent.

The payment under the normal 10 percent rate is $877.57. The monthly payments for the first 3 years and thereafter would be

$$\text{Year 1}: \$100,000 \, (MC_{7\%,30\%}) = \$100,000(0.0066530) = \$665.30$$
$$\text{Year 2}: \$100,000 \, (MC_{8\%,30}) = \$100,000(0.0073376) = \$733.76$$
$$\text{Year 3}: \$100,000 \, (MC_{9\%,30}) = \$100,000(0.0080462) = \$804.62$$
$$\text{Year 4--30}: \$100,000 \, (MC_{10\%,30}) = \$100,000(0.0087757) = \$877.57$$

The buydown fee paid by the seller at the outset is the present value of the payment shortage over the buydown period. This would be

$$
\begin{aligned}
\text{Buydown fee} = \text{PV of shortage} = &\ \$877.57 - \$665.30(PVIFA_{10\%/12,12}) \\
&+ \$877.57 - \$733.76(PVIFA_{10\%12,12})(PVIF_{10\%12,12}) \\
&+ \$877.57 - \$804.62(PVIFA_{10\%12,12})(PVIF_{10\%12,24}) \\
= &\ \$212.27(11.374508) \\
&+ \$143.81(11.374508)(0.905212) \\
&+ \$72.95(11.374508)(0.819409) \\
= &\ \$2,414.47 + \$1,480.72 + \$679.92 \\
= &\ \$4,575.11
\end{aligned}
$$

The effective cost of the loan for the borrower can be calculated as

$$
\begin{aligned}
\$100,000 = &\ \$665.30(PVIFA_{i\%/12,12}) \\
&+ \$733.76(PVIFA_{i\%/12,12})(PVIF_{i\%/12,12}) \\
&+ \$804.62(PVIFA_{i\%/12,12})(PVIF_{i\%/12,24}) \\
&+ \$877.57(PVIFA_{i\%/12,324})(PVIFA_{i\%/12,36}) \\
i = &\ 9.47\%
\end{aligned}
$$

Owner Financing

During periods of high interest rates, sellers often found it difficult to obtain what they believed to be the value of their property. Other sellers with assumable loans, as in the preceding example, had built up substantial equity in their property. They wanted to capture the added value of the assumable loan in the property price. To do so, they had to find a buyer with a sufficient down payment to assume the loan.

In some cases the down payment could be sizable. When no buyers with sufficient cash could be located, sellers would often extend owner financing at below-market rates under a land contract. With a land contract, the buyer makes payments under the terms of a contract to purchase the property at a later time, say, 4 or 5 years. The value of the house is increased if the payments under the contract are lower than those that would exist with a conventionally financed purchase. If the agreement involved a wrap around, the seller would continue to make the low-interest payments under the existing low-rate loan during the period of the land contract. The arrangement benefits both parties because the buyer obtains the use of the property with low payments for several years while the seller obtains a higher price for the property. Both gain at the expense of the lender, who continues to carry the old low-rate loan. The value of owner financing was often limited by the fact that the seller carryback had a short term, say, 3 or 5 years, with a balloon payment.

Key Terms

Assumable loan

Buydown mortgage

Creative financing

Extended term wrap

Shorter term wrap

Simultaneous term, fully amortized wrap

Review Questions

4A-1. List and describe three different types of "advantageous financing."

4A-2. What is meant by capitalizing advantageous financing into the price of the property?

4A-3. Why might one expect that the cash-equivalent value of an assumable loan would not be fully capitalized into house prices?

4A-4. Summarize the empirical findings on the issue of the capitalization of creative financing into house prices.

4A-5. What are the implications of creative financing for appraisal practices?

4A-6. Explain how land contracts are used as a form of creative financing.

Problems

4A-1. Determine the value of the following assumable loan (value of the payment savings): Original balance $67,000

Contract rate 8%

Market rate 12%

Remaining term 18 years

Original term 30 years

4A-2. Determine the cash-equivalent value of the above loan 1 year later if the market rate falls to 10 percent.

4A-3. A developer is offering a buydown in order to sell a property. With a market rate of 12 percent, she is willing to buy the rate down for the first 2 years to 8 and 10 percent, respectively. If $80,000 is borrowed on a 30-year term with monthly payments, what is the buydown fee?

4A-4. Smith wants to buy a property for $120,000, but he has no money to make a down payment. Jones, the seller, is willing to do a wrap for the purchase price with an existing monthly payment mortgage having a fixed rate of 8 percent. This existing loan had an original balance of $100,000 and has 20 years remaining on its original 30-year term. The current market rate is 12 percent on 20-year mortgages. Jones is willing to write the wrap loan at a 10 percent interest rate.

a. What is the effective equity yield for Jones if the wrap is written for the remaining term of the existing mortgage and both are held to maturity?

b. Suppose that, in order to lower the payments on the wrap loan, the amortization period is extended to 30 years. Now what is the effective equity yield for the wrap lender?

c. Assume the conditions in part b except that a balloon payment is required on the wrap loan at the end maturity of the existing loan. What is the effective equity yield for the wrap lender?

d. Assume the conditions in part a except that the wrap loan is written for 12 years. What is the effective equity yield for the wrap lender assuming a balloon payment is required on the original loan? What is the effective equity yield for the wrap lender assuming increased amortization on the original loan to equalize the maturity of the wrap loan?

Notes

1. As an example, the payment on a 30-year loan for $100,000 at 10 percent is the same as that on a $115,307 loan at 8 percent.

2. A deed-of-trust is an instrument that places title to the property with a trustee (third party) until the loan is fully paid. These concepts are discussed in Chapter 12.

3. Larry Ozanne. The financial stakes in due-on-sale: The case of California's state-chartered savings and loans. *AREUEA Journal* 12(4) (Winter 1984), 473–494.

FIXED-RATE MORTGAGE MECHANICS

LEARNING OBJECTIVES

In this chapter you will come to understand the mechanics and terms of the standard fixed-rate mortgage (FRM). You will become familiar with basic mortgage math and the process of calculating the effective cost of a mortgage. This process follows the basic concepts of discounted cash flow analysis, which are presented in Appendix A of this chapter.

MECHANICS OF THE FIXED-RATE MORTGAGE

One of the most enduring products of the Depression era is the 30-year, fixed-rate, fully amortizing mortgage and has dominated the mortgage market since the 1930s. Currently, mortgage lenders also typically offer a 15-year fixed-rate mortgage (FRM). To understand the mechanics of mortgages, we begin with the FRM by showing how to calculate payments, amortization, outstanding balances, and the effective cost of the loan. The background will be invaluable for understanding much of the remainder of the residential finance section of this book. A financial calculator will be very useful in this section.

The Mortgage Payment

Recall from the time value of money analysis that the present value interest factor for an annuity (PVIFA) is

$$\text{PVIFA} = \frac{(1+i)^n - 1}{i(1+i)^n} \qquad \text{(Equation 5-1)}$$

where i equals the interest rate and n equals the number of payments. If the payment amount is known, it can be multiplied by the PVIFA to determine the present value of the annuity such that

$$\text{Present value of annuity} = \text{payment} \times \text{PVIFA}_{i,n}$$

Now, if the present value of the annuity is known (along with the interest rate and number of payments), the above equation can be rearranged to solve for the payment such that

$$\text{payment} = \frac{\text{Present value of annuity}}{\text{PVIFA}_{i,n}}$$

This can be written alternatively as

$$\text{Payment} = \text{Present value of annuity} \times \text{mortgage constant}$$

where the mortgage constant is the reciprocal of the PVIFA and can be written as

$$MC_{i,n} = \frac{i(1+i)^n}{(1+i)^n - 1} \qquad \text{(Equation 5-2)}$$

The **mortgage constant** calculates the payment per dollar borrowed at a given interest rate and term. The mortgage constant calculates the amount of payment required to amortize $1 at a certain interest rate and a given number of payments. The mortgage constant multiplied by the amount borrowed yields the payment. Note that **mortgage payments** are structured as an ordinary annuity, which means that the payments fall at the end of each period.

For example, suppose that you borrow $100,000 at 10 percent for 30 years, annual payments. The yearly payment required to repay principal and interest would be

$$\text{Annual Payment} = \$100{,}000(MC_{i,n}) = \$100{,}000 \left[\frac{0.01(1.10)^{30}}{(1.10)^{30} - 1} \right] a$$
$$= \$100{,}000(0.1060742) = \$10{,}607.42$$

It is common for mortgages to be repaid monthly; thus the payment must be adjusted to reflect monthly amortization. The mortgage constant would be written as

$$\text{Mortage Constant } (MC_{i,n}) = \left[\frac{i/12(1+i/12)^{12n}}{(1+i/12)^{12n} - 1} \right]$$

Using the monthly mortgage constant, the monthly payment to satisfy principal and interest is $877.57. This is calculated as

$$\text{Monthly Payment} = \$100{,}000(MC_{10,30}) = \$100{,}000 \left[\frac{0.00833(1.008333)^{360}}{(1.008333)^{360} - 1} \right] = \$877.57$$

Note that even though the mortgage contract terms (contract interest rate, term) are typically expressed on an annualized basis, the interest rate and term must be adjusted to reflect monthly amortization when the payment is calculated. That is, the interest rate is divided by 12 and the term has been multiplied by 12. The interest rate and term must always be measured in the same units (yearly, monthly, etc.).

Amortization of the Mortgage

The above calculation provides the payment required to fully repay the mortgage over its specified term since each payment contains a portion of principal repayment. This means that each consecutive payment will reduce the balance of the mortgage such that, when all payments are made, the mortgage balance is zero. In other words, the payback of the mortgage is included in the monthly payment. Thus, each payment is the sum of two components: interest and principal repayment. Although the total payment remains constant, the two components do not remain a constant proportion of the payment. The early payments will be

TABLE 5–1

Monthly Amortization Schedule for $100,000 Loan at 10% for 30 Years

	PAYMENT ($)	BEGINNING BALANCE ($)	INTEREST ($)	PRINCIPAL REPAYMENT ($)	ENDING BALANCE ($)
1	877.57	100,000	833.33	44.24	99,956
2	877.57	99,956	832.96	44.61	99,911
3	877.57	99,911	832.59	44.98	99,866
4	877.57	99,866	832.22	45.35	99,821
5	877.57	99,821	831.84	45.73	99,775
6	877.57	99,775	831.46	46.11	99,729
—	—	—	—	—	—
—	—	—	—	—	—
—	—	—	—	—	—
355	877.57	5,115	42.63	834.94	4,280
356	877.57	4,280	35.67	841.90	3,438
357	877.57	3,438	28.65	844.92	2,589
358	877.57	2,589	21.58	855.99	1,733
359	877.57	1,733	14.44	863.13	870
360	857.57	870	7.25	870.32	0

Balances are rounded to the nearest dollar.

Source: © 2014 OnCourse Learning

comprised primarily of interest with very little of the payment going to principal reduction. With each payment, the interest proportion decreases (because the principal balance is decreasing) and the principal repayment proportion increases. Over the total payments, the sum of the individual principal repayments will equal the original amount borrowed.

Table 5-1 shows the allocation between interest and principal repayment for the first 6 months and the last 6 months for our example. As seen, the amount of interest paid for a given month is greatest in month 1 and declines for each consecutive month. The portion of the payment that is principal repayment behaves just the opposite. The smallest proportion of principal repayment is found in the payment for month 1. The amortization of the mortgage is a form of forced saving since it requires the borrower to replace debt with equity. With each payment the borrower is contributing additional equity to the property.

Because only the interest portion of the mortgage payment is tax deductible and since interest is a declining portion of the monthly payment, the after-tax cost of the mortgage is increasing over time. For example, note from Table 5-1 that interest in month 1 is $833.33 with principal repayment of $44.24. For a borrower in a 25 percent marginal tax bracket, the after-tax cost of the payment is $669.24 (44.24 + (833.33(1 − 0.25))). However, the after-tax cost of the 360th payment is much higher at $875.76 (870.32 + (7.25(1 − 0.25))).

The Outstanding Balance of the Mortgage

As the **amortization schedule** in Table 5-1 shows, the amount owed on the mortgage declines with each payment. Thus, after each payment, the mortgage will have some **outstanding balance**. The balance remaining after a given payment is the *present value of the remaining stream of payments discounted at the contract interest rate.* For our example, the outstanding balance at the end of 6 months is

$$\text{Outstanding balance} = \$877.57(\text{PVIFA}_{10/12,354})$$
$$= \$877.57(113.64)$$
$$= \$99,729$$

Factors Affecting the Contract Interest Rate

The contract interest rate in a mortgage is important because it is the rate on which the payment and amortization of the loan are based. This contract interest rate on the mortgage can be affected by a number of factors. For example, an increase in the loan amount, loan term, and/or the lock-in period can increase the contract rate. On the other hand, a higher down payment, paying more discount points, or having higher quality credit will generally reduce the contract rate.

The Effective Cost of the Mortgage

The **effective cost** of the mortgage is the borrower's actual percentage cost of borrowing and can be different from the contract interest rate. The effective cost of the loan is affected by loan fees charged by the lender. In the absence of loan fees, the effective cost of the loan is equal to the contract interest rate. Any closing costs classified as additional finance charges are loan fees and affect the cost of the loan. Loan fees are charged by the lender to cover expenses incurred in loan processing and preparing the loan documents. It is common for an **origination fee** to appear on the closing statement. Other items typically classified as finance charges that can affect the cost of the loan include (1) lender inspection fee, (2) assumption fee, (3) underwriting fee, (4) Veteran's Administration (VA) funding fee/Federal Housing Administration (FHA) Mortgage Insurance Premium (MIP), (5) tax service fee, (6) document preparation fee, (7) flood certification fee, (8) prepaid interest, and (9) mortgage insurance premium (first year).

The lender may also "discount" the mortgage, that is, charge the borrower **discount points**. A point is equal to 1 percent of the loan amount and is a cash charge paid by the borrower to the lender at the time of loan origination. In effect, lenders allow borrowers to "buy down" their contract interest rate by paying points. Remember that the contract rate is the rate on which the mortgage payment is based. Thus a borrower can trade off an initial cash charge for a lower monthly payment. The payment of points has the effect of raising the effective cost of the loan.

The lender must disclose to the borrower the effective cost of the loan. Along with other items, Truth-in-Lending laws require the lender to disclose the **annual percentage rate (APR)** of the loan. The APR is the effective cost of the loan assuming that it is held to maturity. This disclosure foils those lenders who may try to hide fees and upfront costs behind low advertised contract rates.

Calculating the APR

The charging of discount points has the effect of increasing the borrower's cost of the loan by reducing the amount of funds actually acquired by the borrower. Consider our previous example with a loan amount of $100,000 at 10 percent for 30 years and a monthly payment of $877.57. If no points or loan fees are charged, the APR on the loan will be the contract rate of 10 percent. However, with points or fees, the APR rises above 10 percent. This can be illustrated by considering an equation of which the left side gives the amount of funds effectively received by the borrower (face amount minus the points/fees) and the right side gives the amount that the borrower repays. The following examples help to clarify.

Loan APR with No Points or Fees

To calculate the APR of the loan (LAPR) the following equation can be used:

$$\text{Contract amount of loan} - \text{points/fees} = \text{pmt}\,(\text{PVIFA}_{i,n})$$

The left side of the equation is the face (contract) amount of the loan minus the points and fees. PVIFA is the present value interest factor for an annuity. In our example the contract loan amount is $100,000 with no points or fees. The payment is $877.57 and the term is 360 payments. The unknown variable in the equation is the interest rate (i). Thus the equation can be written as

$$\$100,000 - 0 = \$877.57 \, (\text{PVAIF}_{i,360})$$

Solving for i yields an interest rate of 0.8333 percent monthly, which annualizes to an APR of 10 percent (0.8333% × 12).

APR with Two Discount Points

With two discount points the equation would be written as

$$\$100,000 - 2000 = \$877.57 \, (\text{PVAIF}_{i,360})$$

This equation shows that the amount of funds actually acquired by the borrower is $98,000. However, the payment stream is based on the face value of the loan; thus, the borrower repays 360 payments of $877.57. Solving for i yields an APR of 10.24 percent. A rough rule of thumb is that one point will raise the APR by about one-eighth of a percent.

Effective Cost and Early Repayment

Since the typical mortgage is not held for its entire life, an additional consideration for the borrower is the effective cost of the loan (in percentage terms) under a shortened holding period. If a loan does not have any financing costs (such as discount points), the effective cost under any holding period is equal to the contract rate. Once financing costs are introduced, however, the holding period becomes critical. As will be illustrated later, when financing costs are present, the effective cost of the loan will be sensitive to the holding period. That is, a loan with two points, for example, will have a different effective cost under two different holding periods.

An understanding of this raises questions about how mortgages are priced, that is, how lenders set the trade-off between contract rates and discount points. Avery, Beeson, and Sniderman in a 1996 study[1] examined an aspect of this by looking at the relationship between the mortgage rates advertised by lenders and the behavior of borrowers. Specifically, they examined how the quality and number of applicants vary in response to short-run fluctuations in lender rates. They found that lower advertised rates attract more and better-quality applicants. They also found that the low-rate lenders tend to be mortgage banks and mortgage subsidiaries of commercial banks and savings and loans institutions (S&Ls) that sell off a larger portion of the loans they originate.

Because most mortgages are not held to maturity, it is important to understand how a shortened holding period will affect the interest cost. For now, we also will assume that there is no prepayment penalty on the mortgage. To illustrate with our previous example, suppose that the loan is prepaid at the end of 5 years. This means that the payment stream for the borrower is the monthly payment for 60 periods plus the outstanding balance at the end of the fifth year. The effective cost with no points or fees would be calculated as

$$\$100,000 - 0 = \$877.57 \, (\text{PVAIF}_{i,60}) + \$96,574 \, (\text{PVIF}_{i,60})$$

where the balance of the mortgage at the end of year 5 is

$$\text{Bal}_{EOY5} = \$877.57 \times \text{PVIFA}_{10/12,300}$$
$$= \$96,574$$

PVIF is the present value interest factor of $1. Note that in deriving the outstanding balance the mortgage constant reflects an interest rate and term adjusted to monthly compounding.

Solving the above equation for the internal rate of return yields an i of 10 percent. This shows that with no discount points or loan fees the holding period does not affect the effective cost (yield) of the loan.

If points or loan fees are present, the effective cost over the holding period will be a function of the time the mortgage is held. If we use our example of two points being charged and assume that the mortgage is held for 5 years, the effective cost (yield) is calculated as

$$\$100,000 - \$2000 = \$877.57 \, (\text{PVAIF}_{i,60}) + \$96,574(\text{PVIF}_{i,60})$$

The effective cost is 10.52 percent. Holding other factors constant, the shorter the holding period, the higher the effective cost of the loan. In general, the shorter the expected holding period, the less willing the borrower is to pay points due to the effect on the cost of the loan.

The Effective Cost of Prepayment Penalties

Some mortgages assess a penalty to the borrower for repaying a mortgage before maturity. The penalty may be stated as a percentage of the outstanding balance at the point of prepayment or as some other yield maintenance provision. The mortgage may have a specified window of time in which the penalty can be assessed. For example, a mortgage may call for a prepayment penalty if the loan is repaid within the first 10 years. The **prepayment penalty** has the effect of increasing the cost of the loan. Using our previous example, suppose the mortgage has no points or fees, but it does have a prepayment penalty of 5 percent if the loan is repaid within the first 10 years. The effect on the cost of the loan if it is repaid at the end of year 5 would be

$$\$100,000 = \$877.57 \, (\text{PVAIF}_{i,60}) + \$96,574(1.05)(\text{PVIF}_{i,60})$$

The prepayment penalty increases the effective cost from 10 to 10.74 percent.

Some lenders offer a **prepayment protection mortgage (PPM)**. This type of mortgage, which was prominent in the 1940s, faded in the 1970s when high market rates made refinancing unattractive and the mortgage market became more standardized with the emergence of the secondary mortgage market. The use of PPMs continued to fade in the early 1980s. The decreasing rates of the late 1980s and 1990s, however, renewed borrower interest in refinancing and raised concerns by lenders and/or investors in prepayment protection. Primarily, lenders and investors were seeing their returns eroded by borrowers replacing older, higher interest rate loans with new, lower rate mortgages.

The PPM differs from the standard mortgage in that the borrower gives up the right to prepay the mortgage without penalty in exchange for a lower interest rate. This provision does not preclude prepayment; it simply attaches a cost to it. The cost may be assessed in different ways. For example, Freddie Mac has two PPM structures that apply to both fixed-rate and adjustable-rate mortgages. One method restricts prepayment for the first 3 years of life and charges a penalty of 2 percent of the outstanding loan balance. The other provision has a 5-year restriction and charges a penalty of 6 months' interest on the remaining balance. The penalty applies only to refinancing and is not triggered by loan repayment resulting from sale of the property.

Some mortgage lenders offer programs whereby borrowers can reduce their contract rate by accepting a prepayment penalty. The rate is generally reduced by about one-quarter (say, from 8 to 7.75 percent). The homeowner can typically sell the property or pay down the mortgage by as much as 20 percent during the first 5 years without a penalty.

The 15-Year Fixed-Rate Mortgage

In today's mortgage market, lenders offer a variety of loan choices, particularly relative to loan term, which has ranged from 10 to 30 years. A common alternative to the 30-year, FRM offered by most lenders is the 15-year mortgage. This loan provides for full amortization of the loan over a 15-year term rather than 30 years. This loan's major appeal is the significantly less interest paid over the life of the loan. The major drawback is a higher monthly payment.

From our previous example, a loan was made for $100,000 at 10 percent for 30 years, producing a monthly payment of $877.57. Switching to a 15-year term holding everything constant produces a monthly payment of $1,074.61. Reducing the term by half increases the payment by $197.04 each month; however, over the life of the loan total interest is $93,430 compared to $215,925 with the 30-year term. Thus the borrower pays $122,495 less total interest over the shorter term. One additional note: In a normal economic period with an upward sloping yield curve, the 15-year loan should be priced less (in terms of the interest rate) than the 30-year loan. This could make the shorter term even more appealing to borrowers.

The 40-Year Fixed-Rate Mortgage

The run-up in house prices between 2000 and 2005 created an affordability problem. House prices increased much faster than household incomes. As a result, the typical household could afford less and less housing. To help alleviate this problem, lenders began offering mortgages with longer maturities such as the 40-year mortgage. The longer amortization period lowers the monthly payment and makes the mortgage more affordable. Following our example, suppose the $100,000 loan at 10 percent is amortized for 40 years. The monthly payment would be $849.15.

Interest-Only, Fixed-Rate Mortgage

Some lenders offer FRMs that are interest-only. This means that, for some initial period, the monthly payment is interest-only and contains no amortization of the loan principal. This type of loan is appealing primarily to borrowers with high opportunity costs or other investment opportunities. Lenders generally limit the loan-to-value ratio of this type of loan to a maximum of 95 percent and restrict the financing to one-unit primary residences, excluding manufactured homes and cooperatives. There are two typical structures for the interest-only fixed-rate loan. One is a 30-year loan with an initial 10-year interest-only period followed by a 20-year fully amortizing period. The second option is a 30-year loan with an initial 15-year interest-only period followed by a 15-year fully amortizing period.

Suppose that our previous example is written as a 10/20 interest-only, fixed-rate loan for $100,000 at 10 percent for 30 years. For the first 10 years the monthly payment is interest-only at $833.33. Afterward, the payment for the remaining 20-year term is $965.02. This payment allows the loan to be fully amortized over this remaining 20-year term.

Balloon/Reset Fixed-Rate Mortgage

Some borrowers desiring a lower beginning contract rate but still preferring a FRM may opt for a balloon/reset mortgage. This is a FRM that provides a 30-year amortization but balloons, that is, it becomes due and payable over a shorter term. This means that the mortgage is only partially amortized over its stated term and there is some remaining loan balance that must be paid. Typically these loans are written to balloon in 5 or 7 years. Some loans offer an option to reset the rate and extend the mortgage for the full 30 years. Freddie Mac has a secondary market program to buy balloon mortgages but only those with reset provisions.

Suppose our previous example is written as a 5/25 balloon mortgage for $100,000 at 8 percent. The loan has an amortization of 30 years, producing a monthly payment of $733.76 for the first 5 years. The loan balloons at the end of year 5 with a balance of $95,070. The borrower has the option to reset the rate and reamortize the loan at 11 percent. Doing this, the borrower's payment is now $931.79 for the remaining 25 years.

Biweekly Mortgage Amortization

Some borrowers for budgeting reasons prefer to make mortgage payments biweekly (a payment every 2 weeks). Some lenders offer this alternative, which creates a mortgage with biweekly amortization as opposed to monthly amortization. To illustrate, take our earlier example of borrowing $100,000 at 10 percent for 30 years. With monthly amortization, the payment is $877.57. With biweekly amortization the payment is

$$\text{Pmt} = \$100,000 \ (MC_{10/26,780}) = \$404.89$$

Note that the biweekly payment is not the monthly payment divided in half. This is because amortization is done biweekly versus monthly. Also note that no substantial interest savings is gained by opting for the biweekly payments. With monthly amortization the borrower pays 360 payments of $877.57, totaling $315,925. Total interest paid is $215,925. With the biweekly amortization, the borrower pays 780 payments of $404.89, totaling $315,814. Of this total, $215,814 is interest.

Saving Interest with Early Repayment

With our earlier example of $100,000 at 10 percent for 30 years, in monthly payments, the borrower pays total interest of $215,925 if the loan is held to full amortization. Some borrowers may wish to reduce this total expense by making early repayments of principal. For example, suppose that immediately after originating the loan the borrower decides to make one extra payment per year. To minimize inconvenience, the borrower divides the monthly payment by 12 and adds this amount to the regular payment. Thus, instead of paying $877.57 each month the borrower pays $950.70 ($877.57 + $73.13). Since the lender cannot collect interest in advance (each payment pays the accrued interest for the previous month), the extra payment amount is posted to the principal. This acts to speed up the amortization of the loan. Also, since the lender cannot collect interest on any principal amount that has been repaid, less interest is associated with each payment going forward.

What effect does this have on the mortgage? First, let's calculate the number of payments required to amortize the loan with the $950.70 payment:

$$\$100,000 = \$950.70(PVAF_{10/12,n})$$
$$n = 252.02 \text{ payments or } 21 \text{ years}$$

This shows that the borrower can fully amortize the loan with 252.02 payments of $950.70. Under this scheme the borrower pays total interest of $139,595 (($950.70 × 252.02) − $100,000). Total interest paid under the normal scheme is $215,925; thus the borrower pays $76,330 less interest by making one extra payment per year.

Fixed-Rate Mortgages and Interest Rate Risk

Recall that interest rate risk is the risk of loss due to changes in market interest rates. Fixed-income assets are especially susceptible to interest rate risk due to the fixed nature of their income streams. Fixed-rate, fixed-payment mortgages are fixed-income assets. Thus, their market values will change inversely with market rate changes. That is, as market rates rise, the value of the mortgage will decline. As we discuss later, this factor caused major problems for mortgage lenders in the 1980s. The effect on the FRM of a change in market rates can be illustrated using our previous example. A lender originates a mortgage for $100,000 at 10 percent for 30 years in monthly payments. This yields a monthly payment of $877.57. Suppose that 5 years later the market rate is 12 percent on 25-year FRMs. The outstanding balance (face value) of this mortgage is $96,574 (as shown previously). However, the market value of this loan is

$$\text{Market value} = \$877.57/MC_{12,25} = \$83,322$$

The loan would be discounted at the higher market rate to reflect current market conditions and thus the market value of the loan is significantly less than the face value. This loss in value occurs whether the lender holds the loan in its portfolio or sells it in the secondary market. A more in-depth analysis of the relationship of interest rate risk with maturity and duration is presented in Appendix B of this chapter.

Summary

The mechanics of the fixed-rate, fixed-payment mortgage include calculation of the payment, the outstanding balance, the amortization schedule, and the effective cost. The APR is the effective cost of the loan if it is held to maturity. Calculations show that the holding period is critical in determining the effective cost of the loan if the loan is discounted or has a prepayment penalty. Fixed-rate mortgages are inversely affected by changes in market interest rates.

Key Terms

Amortization schedule
Annual percentage rate (APR)
Discount points
Effective cost
Mortgage constant
Mortgage payments

Origination fee
Outstanding balance
Prepayment penalty
Prepayment protection mortgage (PPM)

Problems

5-1.   John takes a fully amortizing mortgage for $80,000 at 10 percent interest for 30 years, monthly payments. What will be his monthly payment?

5-2. Dave wants to buy a house. To do so, he must incur a mortgage. A local lender has determined that Dave can afford a monthly payment of $600, principal and interest. If the current interest rate on 30-year, fixed-rate mortgages is 9.50 percent, what is the maximum amount of mortgage that Dave could qualify for?

5-3. Mike qualifies to borrow $120,000 on a mortgage at 9 percent for 30 years, monthly payments.
a. What is his monthly payment?
b. How much interest does Mike pay in the first month of the loan?
c. How much interest does he pay in the first year of the mortgage?
d. If he decides to repay the mortgage at the end of year 3, what is the outstanding balance at that time?
e. How much total interest does he pay over this 3-year period?

5-4. You borrow $75,000 for 30 years with monthly amortization, and your payment is $590.03. What interest rate is being charged?

5-5. You want to purchase a house that has an asking price of $125,000. You can get a loan for 80 percent of the bank's appraised value at 9.50 percent for 30 years, monthly payments. The appraiser values the house at 95 percent of the asking price.
a. What will be your monthly payment if you take the loan?
b. What would be the balance of the mortgage after 5 years?
c. Set up a 5-year amortization schedule showing total annual mortgage payments, total interest, and principal paid annually, and the balance at the end of each year. (Do not set up a monthly amortization schedule to answer this problem.)

5-6. Local lenders are offering the following terms for 30-year, fixed-rate mortgages. If your objective is to minimize the cost of borrowing, which alternative do you prefer?

CONTRACT INTEREST RATE (%)	DISCOUNT POINTS
8.25	2.75
8.50	2.00
8.75	1.00

a. Assume monthly payments and that the mortgage is held to its maturity. What is the effective cost (APR) of each alternative?
b. Assume monthly payments and a holding period of 5 years. What is the effective cost of each alternative?
c. Assume that each mortgage has a 3 percent prepayment penalty. What is the effective cost of each alternative?

5-7. Determine the monthly payment for the following mortgages of $90,000 each.

MORTGAGE	INTEREST RATE (%)	MATURITY (IN MONTHS)	PAYMENT
A	10	360	___
B	11	300	___
C	9	300	___
D	8	260	___

Residential Real Estate Finance

5-8.   Determine the yield-to-maturity at origination for the following mortgages.

MORTGAGE	MONTHLY PAYMENT ($)	MATURITY (IN MONTHS)	AMOUNT AT ORIGINATION ($)	YIELD-TO-MATURITY
A	500	360	50,000	——
B	600	360	65,000	——
C	550	260	62,000	——
D	550	300	60,000	——

5-9.   How long would it take to pay off the following mortgages? (*Hint*: *Never* is a possible answer.)

MORTGAGE	PAYMENT ($)	COUPON RATE (%)	INITIAL LOAN ($)	MATURITY
A	400	10.0	45,000	——
B	800	10.5	75,000	——
C	600	11.0	62,000	——
D	550	11.0	60,000	——

5-10.   Determine the discount points necessary to provide a yield-to-maturity of 10 percent for the following mortgages with 30-year maturities.

MORTGAGE	MONTHLY PAYMENT ($)	COUPON RATE	AMOUNT AT ORIGINATION ($)	DISCOUNT POINTS (IN $)
A	$800	N/A	100,000	——
B	900	N/A	110,000	——
C	950	N/A	125,000	——
D	700	N/A	110,000	——

5-11.   Determine the balance of the following 30-year mortgages at the end of the fifth year. (*Hint*: The balance of a standard fixed-rate mortgage at any time is equal to the present value of the remaining payments discounted by the rate on the mortgage.)

MORTGAGE	ORIGINAL AMOUNT ($)	CONTRACT RATE (%)	BALANCE
A	100,000	10	——
B	90,000	8	——
C	80,000	12	——

5-12.   Suppose that a lender offers you a 15-year, monthly payment mortgage for $120,000 at 6 percent with two discount points.
a. Calculate your monthly payment.
b. What is the APR on this loan?
c. What is the effective cost if the loan is repaid at the end of year 8?

5-13.   To buy your dream home you use a 10/20 interest-only, fixed-rate mortgage. The loan has monthly payments and is for $110,000 at 7.50 percent. The lender charges you two discount points.
a. What is your payment for the initial interest-only period?
b. What is your payment over the 20-year amortization period?
c. What is the APR on the loan?
d. What is the effective cost of the loan if it is repaid 6 years after the interest-only period?

5-14.   You are 12 years into your fixed-rate mortgage, which is a 7-year balloon/reset with monthly payments over a 30-year amortization. Your original amount was $90,000 at an initial rate of 6 percent. At

refinancing, the rate was reset to 8 percent. At closing, your financing costs were 3 percent.
a. What was your initial payment?
b. What is your payment after the reset?
c. What is the APR of this loan?
d. What is the effective cost of the loan if you repay it today?

Note

1. Robert B. Avery, Patricia E. Beeson, and Mark S. Sniderman. Posted rates and mortgage lending activity. *Journal of Real Estate Finance and Economics* 13 (1996), 11–26.

Web Sites

http://www.timevalue.com/products/tcalc-financial-calculators/overview.aspx
Time value of money calculator

http://www.hsh.com
Current mortgage information, rates, ARM indexes, etc.

http://www.coldwellbanker.com
Coldwell Banker online

http://www.realtor.org
National Association of REALTORS®

http://federalreserve.gov/regulations/regref.htm#Z
Federal Reserve Regulation Z, which includes APR

http://www.fhfb.gov
Federal Housing Finance Board for loan market shares

https://www.fanniemae.com/singlefamily/mortgage-products
Fannie Mae different types of loan products

http://www.bankrate.com
Mortgage rates, mortgage analysis, mortgage calculator

http://www.quickenloans.com
Mortgage rates, mortgage calculator

http://zillow.com
Mortgage rates, mortgage calculator

http://freddiemac.com
Mortgage market surveys

APPENDIX 5-A   Elements of the Discounted Cash Flow Model of Valuation

The discounted cash flow (DCF) model is expressed by the equation:

$$PV = \sum_{i=1}^{n} \frac{CF_i}{(1+r)^i} \qquad \text{(Equation 5A-1)}$$

where PV stands for present value, CF is the amount of the cash flows, r is the discount rate, and n represents the number of periods over which the cash flows are received. Information on three of the terms is sufficient to determine the value of the fourth. Interestingly, different problems in real estate finance may call for solving one of the particular terms in the basic equation. A simple example is the determination of the payment on a standard mortgage, given the amount of the loan PV, the maturity n, and the lender's interest charge r. Although financial tables are available, calculations are easily performed using a standard financial calculator that has at least four keys representing the terms in the equation (PV, PMT, %, n). Let's begin by considering the familiar 30-year, fixed-rate mortgage discussed in this chapter.

Case A In this first case, assume that the mortgagor desires to borrow $90,000 (PV). The lender offers a 30-year (360 monthly payments, n) loan with a contract rate of 10 percent (%). This is sufficient information to compute the required monthly payment (PMT) in the following equation: After inputting 90,000 for PV, 360 for n, and 10/12 for %, the calculator will compute the payment, PMT, and display the solution: $789.81. In this case, we solved for the payment. Now, let's look at a situation where the objective is to find a present value.

$$\$90{,}000 = \frac{PMT}{(1 + 0.008333)^1} + \frac{PMT}{(1 + 0.008333)^2} + \cdots + \frac{PMT}{(1 + 0.008333)^{360}}$$

Case B Assume in the above example that the mortgagor decides he or she cannot afford such a high payment and has only $650 available for the monthly principal and interest payment. He or she wants to know how much he or she can borrow. There is sufficient information to determine the amount from the following equation: Again, we have three of the four necessary elements.

After inputting 650 for PMT, 360 for n, and 10/12 for %, the solution would be displayed as $74,068. Next, let's consider a case where the missing element is the interest rate r.

$$\text{Amount} = \frac{650}{(1 + 0.008333)^1} + \frac{650}{(1 + 0.008333)^2} + \cdots + \frac{650}{(1 + 0.008333)^{360}}$$

Case C After arranging for the above loan, the mortgagor is informed by the lender that there is a 2 percent discount applicable to this loan (two points charged). In this case, the mortgagor will receive only 98 percent of the $74,000 loan, or $72,587. The payment, however, remains $650 per month. This raises the effective interest rate on the loan. The federal Truth-in-Lending law (see Chapter 8) will require the lender to restate the actual rate as the annual percentage rate (APR). The lender can compute the APR and inform the mortgagor of the rate by solving the following equation for r:

$$\$72{,}587 = \frac{650}{(1 + r)^1} + \frac{650}{(1 + r)^2} + \cdots + \frac{650}{(1 + r)^{360}}$$

Inputting 72,587 for the present value, 650 for PMT, and 360 for n will result in an APR of 0.0853 per month, or 10.25 percent annually. The use of the discount points has raised the effective interest cost on the loan by 0.25 percent annually. Larger discounts will result in higher effective yields. A final example looks at determining the term n of a loan given the other three terms.

Case D Here, assume that there are no discount points (Case B). The mortgagor desires to borrow the $74,068 and is willing to pay a 10 percent annual interest cost but desires to reduce the payment to $640. This can be accomplished by extending the term of the loan beyond 360 months. We can solve for n in the following equation:

$$\$74{,}068 = \frac{640}{(1.008333)^1} + \frac{640}{(1 + 0.008333)^2} + \cdots + \frac{640}{(1 + 0.008333)^n}$$

Inputting 74,068 for the present value, 10/12 for %, and 640 for PMT, the solution for n appears as 402. The loan will be amortized in 33.5 years.

To summarize, three of the four terms of the DCF model are required to solve for the fourth. As long as three terms are known, the fourth can be solved. Although financial tables can be used for this purpose, they can be cumbersome. Today most real estate students and professionals become quite adept at solving financial problems with the use of an inexpensive financial calculator. We suggest you acquire one if you have not already done so. It will be quite useful for solving problems in this and the remaining chapters. Also, note that situations in real estate finance will call for solving different terms of the basic valuation model.

APPENDIX 5-B   Maturity, Duration, and the Interest Rate Risk of Mortgages

The discounted cash flow (DCF) model tells us that the value of a mortgage, or any debt instrument, is determined by discounting the expected future payments to the present:

$$\text{Value} = \frac{\text{PMT}}{(1 + r)^1} + \frac{\text{PMT}}{(1 + r)^2} + \cdots + \frac{\text{PMT}}{(1 + r)^n} \qquad \textbf{(Equation 5B-1)}$$

If the payments (PMT) are fixed, then a change in the discount rate will alter the value. Thus, when market rates of interest change, so do the values of debt instruments. As interest (discount) rates rise, the value of the obligations falls.

Consider two mortgages originated today, both for the same balance and at the same rate of interest but with two different maturities.

	BALANCE ($)	ANNUAL RATE (%)	MATURITY (YEARS)	MONTHLY PAYMENT ($)
Mortgage A	100,000	12	30	1,028.61
Mortgage B	100,000	12	15	1,200.17

Each payment stream when discounted at 1 percent monthly has a value of $100,000. Assume that the day after origination (tomorrow) market rates rise to 14 percent annually. The values of each mortgage will be reduced. According to Equation 5A-1, the two values will be $86,812 and $90,120 for mortgages A and B, respectively. The standard explanation for the difference in the degree of loss is the difference in maturity. When interest rates rise, holders of existing debt have a claim to payments that are lower than would exist on the same size of new debt. The longer those payments are stretched out, the lower their value. Stated differently, the holder of mortgage B receives larger payments earlier than the holder of mortgage A. Mortgage B holder has the opportunity to reinvest those payments at the higher market rate. By year 15, mortgage B is completely paid off and all funds are reinvested at the higher rate. But now consider the following "mortgages."

	BALANCE ($)	ANNUAL RATE (%)	MATURITY (YEARS)	MONTHLY PAYMENT ($)	PAYMENT AT MATURITY ($)
Mortgage A	100,000	12	30	1,028.61	0
Mortgage B	100,000	12	30	1,301.00	100,000
Mortgage C	100,000	12	30	0	3,594,964

Mortgage A is a typical amortizing mortgage. Mortgage B is an interest-only mortgage with a repayment of principal at maturity. The payments act as those of a typical corporate bond. Mortgage C has no intermediate payments. Interest is accrued and the total is paid at maturity, the same as a zero coupon bond. The DCF equations for these mortgages (A, B, C) appear as follows:

$$A \quad \$100,000 = \frac{\$1,028.61}{(1.01)^1} + \frac{\$1,028.61}{(1.01)^2} + \cdots + \frac{\$1,028.61}{(1.01)^{360}}$$

$$B \quad \$100,000 = \frac{\$1,000}{(1.01)^1} + \frac{\$1,000}{(1.01)^2} + \cdots + \frac{\$1,000}{(1.01)^{360}} + \frac{\$100,000}{(1.01)^{360}}$$

$$C \quad \$100,000 = \frac{\$3,594,964}{(1.01)^{360}}$$

Following the previous example, if interest rates rise to 14 percent tomorrow, then the values of the three mortgages will be as follows:

$$A = \$86,812$$
$$B = \$85,933$$
$$C = \$55,235$$

Although the mortgages all had the same maturity (30 years), the decline in value as a result of the increase in interest rates was not identical. The explanation lies in the timing and amount of the cash flows. As in the previous example, the mortgages that have large and early intermediate payments decline less in value. The holder of mortgage C has no intermediate cash flows whatsoever to reinvest at the higher (14 percent) rate. The holder of mortgage A has the benefit of receiving some principal with each payment. The amortized portion of the payment can be reinvested at the higher rates along with the interest payments.

The difference in the change in values of the mortgages lies in the difference in the extent to which the cash flows of the mortgages are "pushed" back toward their maturities. A measure of the extent to which the cash flows are pushed back is called the **duration**. Although each of the three mortgages in our example has the same maturity, they have different durations. The duration of a debt instrument is a measure of the average time prior to the receipt of the cash flows. More accurately, it is the weighted average of the lengths of time prior to the receipt of the cash flows using the relative present values of the cash flows as the weights. The formula for duration is as follows:

$$D = \frac{\sum t \times CF_t/(1 + r)^t}{\sum CF/(1 + r)^t} \qquad \text{(Equation 5B–2)}$$

An example is provided in Table 5B-1.

Note that the values in the numerator are weighted by t, the period in which the cash flow occurs.

$$A = \quad 7.9$$
$$B = \quad 8.4$$
$$C = 30.0$$

The percentage change in the price of debt instrument as a result of a change in interest rates can be determined by

$$\frac{\Delta p}{p} - D \times \frac{\Delta r}{(1+r)}$$ (Equation 5B-3)

For the three mortgages we have

$$A = -14\% = -7.9 \times \frac{0.02}{1.12}$$

$$B = -15\% = -8.4 \times \frac{0.02}{1.12}$$

$$C = -45\% = -30.0 \times \frac{0.02}{1.12}$$

In summary, the change in the price of a debt instrument as a result of a change in market rates of interest is a function of its duration. Duration is closely allied to maturity. Longer maturity bonds will have longer durations. But, the duration of a bond will be less than its maturity (except for zero-coupon bonds, which have the same duration as maturity). Because duration and maturity are closely related, a common misconception is that a bond's maturity determines the extent to which its value changes as a result of a change in interest rates. To be precise, price changes are determined by duration.

TABLE 5B-1

Computation of Duration of Bond

COUPON, 8%; FACE VALUE, $1,000; PAYMENT, SEMIANNUAL; MATURITY, 7 YEARS; MARKET RATE, 9%.			
1	2	3	4
PERIOD	SEMIANNUAL CASH FLOW (CF)	$CF/(1+r)^t$ (PRESENT VALUE OF COLUMN 2, IN $)	$t \times CF(1+r)^t$ (COLUMN 1 × COLUMN 3, IN $)
1	40	38.28	38.28
2	40	36.63	73.26
3	40	35.05	105.16
4	40	33.54	134.17
5	40	32.10	160.49
6	40	30.72	184.29
7	40	29.39	205.75
8	40	28.13	225.02
9	40	26.92	242.25
10	40	25.76	257.57
11	40	24.65	271.13
12	40	23.59	283.04
13	40	22.57	293.42
14	1040	561.57	7,862.00
TOTAL		948.89	10,335.83

Duration = 10,335.83/948.89 = 10.89 periods.

Comments: Total value of column 3 (denominator for duration formula) is also the value of the bond. Duration is 10.89 periods, or 5.44 years, less the maturity of 7 years.

ALTERNATIVE MORTGAGE INSTRUMENTS

LEARNING OBJECTIVES

Alternative mortgage instruments (AMIs) are mortgages other than the standard fixed-rate, fully amortizing loan. After reading this chapter, you should understand the basics of several types of AMIs. The basics of AMIs include the determination of standard mortgage terms such as the interest rate, payment, discount points, term of the loan, and so forth. You should understand not only how the terms are determined but how they are interrelated. Finally, you should understand how the characteristics of various AMIs solve the problems of a fixed-rate mortgage (FRM) in an inflationary environment.

INTRODUCTION

In previous chapters, we saw how the inflationary environment of the 1970s and 1980s created problems for the standard fixed-rate mortgage. Supply problems were related to the asset-liability maturity mismatch of traditional mortgage lenders. Thrifts held short-term liabilities (deposits) and originated long-term assets (mortgages). Inflation created expectations of continued inflation that in turn caused the nominal interest rates on thrift deposits to rise. Mortgage prepayments slowed with rising rates, and the thrifts were saddled with relatively low-rate mortgages. In short, mortgage lenders were paying more on borrowed funds than they were earning on invested funds. This scenario, which exemplifies the interest rate risk of fixed-rate mortgages, turned profits into losses.[1]

Demand problems were related to borrower affordability. Rising interest rates on mortgages caused the payment to increase beyond the affordability range of many potential homeowners. The "tilt" problem caused the "real" payment to be extraordinarily high at the beginning of the fixed-rate mortgage and lower at the end. Thus the attractiveness of AMIs increased from both a supply and demand perspective. Both lenders and borrowers saw AMIs as a vehicle for achieving market transactions. In addition, lenders saw AMIs as a means by which to shift all or at least some of the interest rate risk from themselves to borrowers.

Beginning in the mid-2000s affordability again became a problem but this time it was caused by a house price/household income imbalance as a result of rapidly rising home prices relative to more-slowly increasing incomes. Fixed-rate mortgages became unaffordable not because of high interest rates as in the 1980s, but from exceedingly high house prices. Borrowers found various AMIs attractive because of the increased affordability that they provided. Lenders found AMIs attractive since this type of financing, in many instances, was the only means by which a borrower could qualify for a loan.

We will discuss AMIs first from the standpoint of supply problems, then from that of demand problems.

PROBLEMS OF SUPPLY: INTEREST RATE RISK AND THE ADJUSTABLE-RATE MORTGAGE

The most popular AMI designed to solve the problem of interest rate risk is the adjustable-rate mortgage (ARM), originally called the variable-rate mortgage. Another is the price level adjusted mortgage, which is discussed later in the chapter. We will treat the ARM in detail here.

A simple example of interest rate risk may be useful. Suppose that a borrower takes a mortgage of $100,000 at 10 percent for 30 years, monthly payments. The monthly payment is $877.57. Since lenders typically write loans at the market rate of interest because of competition, we assume that 10 percent is the prevailing market rate when the loan is originated. Now, suppose that one second after the loan is originated the market rate rises to 12 percent. If this loan is fixed-rate, then the lender must bear all the interest rate risk. With a fixed contract rate the payment is fixed at $877.57. Since this payment stream now must be discounted at 12 percent, the value of the loan drops to $85,316. Thus an asset for which the lender just paid $100,000 is now worth $14,684 less. However if the lender had the power to adjust the contract rate on the loan to the market rate (in this case from 10 percent to 12 percent), the value of the asset is maintained ($100,000 in this example). The increase in the contract rate would most likely be reflected by increasing the loan payment.

The basic concept behind the **adjustable-rate mortgage (ARM)** is to allow the contract interest rate on the loan to move with the market rate. This provision reduces the interest rate risk faced by the lender in an increasing interest rate environment by shifting it to the borrower. At first, one might conclude that an ARM is no less risky than an FRM because it allows the interest rate on the loan to fall as well as rise. Recall, however, that with an FRM the borrower is protected against interest rate increases and can refinance when rates fall. Thus, for the lender the ARM significantly reduces interest rate risk because it is preferable to an FRM when interest rates rise yet no worse when they fall. Because they face less interest rate risk with ARMs, lenders require a lower return. And, because borrowers are accepting interest rate risk, they require the loan to be priced accordingly with a lower contract rate.

Borrowers have proven reluctant to absorb all of the risk associated with rising rates. As a result, nearly all ARMs have provisions that limit the amount by which the rate can increase, usually periodically and over the term of the mortgage. All ARMs share a number of characteristics. They have (1) a lower initial interest rate than FRMs, (2) a rate that in some fashion is tied to the market (an index) so as to measure movement, and (3) provisions for limiting the amount by which the rate or payments can change. We first will describe the characteristics of typical ARMs. Then we will provide an example of how the payments and loan balances of ARMs behave as a result of changes in the market rate. Finally, we will discuss the pricing of ARMs. Pricing refers to how lenders set the different terms of the ARMs in relation to each other. For example, if the lender agrees to a very strict limit on the periodic change in the interest rate, he may require a higher initial rate than otherwise. Alternatively, he may keep the rate low but raise the amount of discount points. The trade-off of terms is referred to as the pricing of ARMs. The pricing of the ARM is important because it ultimately determines the yield for the lender and the cost for the borrower of the loan.

Some of the terms on ARMs are a result of secondary mortgage market requirements. For example, the secondary market is less likely to buy ARMs that may experience negative amortization. Lenders are thus less likely to write loans under terms where this may occur.

Description of ARMs

An ARM can be described by a number of different features. These include the frequency of rate change, index, margin, interest rate caps, payment caps, caps on negative amortization, initial period discount (teaser), and convertibility. ARMs are written with 30-year maturities. Regulations allow the term to be extended by one-third.

One provision of an ARM is the **frequency of rate change**—how frequently the lender can adjust the contract rate on the loan. When ARMs were first developed, rate adjustment periods ranged from one month to 5 years. Typical adjustment periods were 6 months, 1 year, 3 years, or 5 years. To minimize interest rate risk lenders, of course, would prefer ARMs that adjusted instantaneously to changes in the market rate. This is impractical, however, so lenders have settled on only a few alternative adjustment periods. The longer the time between adjustments, the greater the interest rate risk assumed by the lender.

Over time, as the terms of ARMs became more uniform, the market gravitated to the 1-year adjustable ARM as a standard. Although other adjustment periods can be found, today most ARMs adjust once a year. This means that the contract rate is adjusted once a year, and this adjustment is usually reflected in a change in the monthly payment. However, in recent years lenders have become more willing to postpone the first payment adjustment until as far as 7 to 10 years into the future. For example, a lender may offer a hybrid ARM such as a 7/1 ARM. This loan locks in an initial interest rate for 7 years and adjusts annually thereafter. Hybrid ARMs are usually 3/1, 5/1, 7/1, or 10/1 where the initial lock-in period is 3, 5, 7, or 10 years after which they become 1-year adjustables.

The **index** represents the market rate and provides the basis for adjustment to the interest rate on the ARM. The contract rate on the ARM will not equal the index but rather will equal the value of the index plus a fixed "add-on" or margin. Changes in the contract rate on the ARM are typically the result of a change in the value of the index. In general, the index must be (1) beyond manipulation by the lender, (2) not excessively volatile, (3) an established index, and (4) acceptable to the borrower.

The index will be either a rate on a Treasury obligation (bill or bond) or some measure of the cost of funds to the lender. If the index is the yield on a Treasury obligation, the rate will be selected on a Treasury with a maturity corresponding to the frequency of adjustment on the ARM. If the ARM adjusts to the market rate every year, then the index will be the yield on a 1-year Treasury bill. If the rate on the ARM changes only every 3 years, then the index will be a 3-year Treasury note yield. These are referred to as **Constant Maturity Treasury (CMT) Indexes.** Another index is the **London Interbank Offered Rate (LIBOR).** The LIBOR reflects the rate most major international banks charge each other for large loans. Freddie

Mac purchases LIBOR ARMs based on the 1-year LIBOR index, which has historically closely tracked the 1-year CMT index.

If the index is based on the lender's cost of funds **(Cost of Funds Index, COFI)**, it will be equal to some recent (regional) rate paid on savings deposits as determined by a federal regulatory agency. The **11th District Cost of Funds Index** is a typical standard that tracks what the average deposit rate costs banks. The 11th District refers to the western region of the Federal Home Loan Bank System. A large proportion of ARMs written in California is tied to this index. The funds used as a basis for the calculation of the 11th District Cost of Funds Index are the liabilities of the financial institutions within that district. These include money on deposit, advances from the Federal Home Loan Bank, and all other borrowed funds. The cost of these funds is the interest paid on these funds.

When the ARM is adjusted, the lender determines the value of the index and adds a markup called the margin. Some lenders use the value of the index at a point in time while others use a "moving average" of a number of weekly values. For example, a lender adjusting a 6-month ARM may average the weekly values of the index over the last 6 months.

The **margin** is an amount, in basis points, added to the index to arrive at the loan's contract rate. For example, if the index value is 6 percent and the margin is 150 basis points, the rate on the loan will be 7.5 percent (until the next adjustment). The margin is stated in the mortgage contract and cannot change over the life of the loan. Thus, changes in the contract rate on the ARM are a result of movements in the index and not changes in the margin. Most margins will range from 150 to 275 basis points.

Most ARMs have two types of **interest rate caps: periodic adjustment rate cap** (or **rate cap**) and **life-of-loan rate cap.** The former places a limit on how much the contract rate can change from one period to the next. The latter establishes a ceiling that the contract rate can never exceed. The life-of-loan cap (life cap) is usually stated as a number of percentage points over the initial rate. If the initial rate on an ARM is 6 percent and the lifetime cap is 6 percentage points, the maximum contract rate over the life of the loan will be 12 percent.

The periodic adjustment cap is usually set at either 1 or 2 percent. Other things held constant, the smaller (tighter) the adjustment cap, the greater the interest rate risk exposure to the lender. A 2 percent adjustment cap on a 1-year ARM means that the rate can increase by no more than 2 percent (200 basis points) in 1 year. If the market rate has risen by 3 percentage points, the lender will not receive the market return. Adjustment caps may also establish a floor of the same size. A 2 percent adjustment cap means that the contract rate on the loan cannot increase or decrease by more than 200 basis points on the adjustment date. A loan that has a 2 percent periodic cap and a 6 percent lifetime cap will usually be advertised as having 2/6 caps.

Most hybrid ARMs have an additional interest rate cap called the "first adjustment cap" that applies to the first adjustment at the end of the fixed-rate period. Thereafter, the state periodic cap will apply. Loans with first adjustment caps may be expressed as having a 2/2/6 cap structure. This means no more than a 200 basis point change to the existing rate at the first adjustment. After that, the regular 2/6 cap structure would apply. Be careful to note that lenders offer a variety of cap structures such as 6/2/6 or 5/2/5 and that this can affect the initial contract rate offered on the loan.

In general, the lender cannot charge a contract rate greater than index plus the margin. However, the adjustment cap means that the lender cannot charge this amount if he or she is constrained by the cap. Thus the contract rate for any given period will be either (1) the index plus the margin or (2) the previous period's contract rate plus the adjustment cap. An exception to this is if the rate is being adjusted downward. The lender will usually reserve the right to adjust the rate down the same as it was adjusted upward (i.e., based on the periodic cap). For example, suppose that the current contract rate is 8 percent and the loan has a 200 basis point periodic cap. Even though the new index plus the margin calculation may yield 5 percent, the rate would only be adjusted downward to 6 percent because of the periodic cap.

Negative amortization is an increase in the loan balance from one period to the next and is a result of payments that are less than the full amount of the interest charge. Since negative amortization represents a default risk, lenders may limit the amount of negative amortization that can occur on as ARM. ARMs that simultaneously adjust the contract rate and the payment and have no optional payment cap will not have negative amortization. The usual limit is 125 percent of the original loan amount. Thus, the balance on a $100,000 loan will not be allowed to exceed $125,000 through negative amortization. There are two scenarios under which negative amortization can occur: when the loan has a payment cap or when the interest rate is adjusted more frequently than the payment. The payment cap (which is not a real constraint) allows the borrower to make a lower payment than the one that reflects the rate being charged. The lender will add the difference in the payments to the mortgage balance at the end of the adjustment period. Likewise, if the interest rate is adjusted upward more frequently than the payment, the incremental interest is added to the mortgage balance. Both or either of these may result in the borrower owing a higher mortgage balance at the end of a given period than at the beginning.

To attract borrowers, lenders sometimes offer an **initial-period discount,** an initial contract rate on the loan that is less than the index plus the margin at that time. If, for example, the index is 8 percent and the margin 150 basis points, the **fully indexed rate** on the loan should be 9.5 percent. The lender may offer a rate, for the initial period only, of 8.5 percent. The initial-period discount is sometimes referred to as a **teaser rate.**

Some ARMs are written to be **convertible.** This means that, within a given window of time, the ARM can be converted to a fixed-rate mortgage. A nominal conversion fee is charged and the mortgage is generally converted at an interest rate slightly above market.

An ARM also may have some other features that are common to other types of loans. They may be assumable at the option of the lender, have a prepayment penalty, or have up-front discount and origination points.

ARM EXAMPLE

The best way to understand the fundamentals of ARM construction and pricing is to consider an example. First, let's assume that the loan is tied to the Treasury Rate index and that the future index values are as indicated in Table 6-1. Next, Table 6-2 describes the characteristics of the ARM. For simplicity, the index (and thus the contract rate) is held constant for months 61 through 360. The initial monthly payment for the first year is calculated as

$$PTM_1 = \text{Loan Amount}\left[\frac{i(1+i)^n - 1}{(1+i)^n - 1}\right]$$
$$PTM_1 = \$100,000(MC_{5.25/12,360})$$
$$PTM_1 = \$100,000(0.005522)$$
$$PTM_1 = \$552.20$$

At the end of the first year when it's adjustment time, the lender makes two calculations: (1) the contract interest rate for the next period (year 2) and

TABLE 6-1

Future Interest Indexes and Contract Rates for Adjustable-Rate Mortgage Example

MONTH	1-YEAR ARM	
	INDEX	CONTRACT RATE %
1	4.75	5.25
13	7.00	7.25
25	8.00	9.25
37	8.50	11.00
49	6.75	9.25
61	8.50	11.00

Source: © 2014 OnCourse Learning

TABLE 6-2

Information for Adjustable-Rate Mortgage Example

Loan amount	$100,000
Term (monthly payments)	30 years
Adjustment period	1 year
Margin	2.50
Initial contract rate (teaser rate)	5.25
Discount points	2.00
Periodic cap	2.00
Lifetime cap	6.00

Source: © 2014 OnCourse Learning

(2) the outstanding balance of the loan at the end of the first year. The index plus the margin (7 + 2.5) equals 9.50 percent. However, the previous rate plus the periodic cap (5.25 + 2) equals 7.25 percent. The maximum rate that the lender can charge is 7.25 percent and this loan is not fully indexed. Fully indexed means that the borrower is paying a contract rate equal to the index plus the margin. This loan is not fully indexed because the rate hits the cap first. Note that the interest rate cap is a real constraint because the lender cannot hold the borrower liable for the lost interest due to the less than fully indexed rate. In other words, the lender has only partially shifted the interest rate risk to the borrower.

To determine the payment for the second year, the lender must also know the amount to be financed, that is, the loan's outstanding balance at the end of the first year. This is calculated as

$$\text{Outstanding Balance} = \text{Payment}(\text{PVAIF}_{5.25/12,348})$$
$$= \$552.20\ (178.54)$$
$$= \$98,590$$

The new information needed to determine the new payment is now known: the new contract rate is 7.50 percent and the amount to be financed is $98,590. The new payment is

$$\text{PMT}_2 = \$98,590\ (\text{MC}_{7.25/12,348})$$
$$= \$679.13$$

This process is repeated for each adjustment. The loan is structured such that, although the payment may increase in some periods and decrease in others, the loan will fully amortize over the contract period of 30 years.

The payments over the first 5 years are shown in Table 6-3. The loan balances are given in Table 6-4. Note that the outstanding balance of the loan at the end of a given year is calculated using the contract rate for that period.

TABLE 6-3

Payment Summary for ARM Example

MONTH	PMT
1	$552.20
13	679.13
25	813.63
37	935.83
49	815.60
61	933.43

Source: © 2014 OnCourse Learning

TABLE 6-4

Loan Balance for ARM Example

END OF MONTH	OUTSTANDING BALANCE
0	$100,000
12	98,590
24	97,554
36	96,168
48	96,168
60	95,237

Source: © 2014 OnCourse Learning

Comparison of ARM Performance

Lenders are interested in how various ARMs will perform financially over different interest rate scenarios. If lenders trade off the various terms in proper balance, there should be no difference in performance across the loans. For example, tighter interest rate caps may be offset by a greater margin or a higher beginning contract rate.

There are several ways to measure the investment performance of loans. A typical method is to calculate the effective cost (yield for the lender) using the internal rate of return (IRR) calculation. This is the same method as was used for the fixed-rate mortgage, but it is complicated by the fact that only the initial interest rate is known. On an ex ante basis, one may calculate the effective cost on most likely, worst-case, and best-case scenarios. On an ex post basis, the analysis is easier since the interest rates and payments are known. For our example, two effective cost calculations, the APR and the effective cost under a 5-year holding period, are shown in Table 6-5. Remember from Table 6-1 that the index is assumed to remain constant after the fifth year. Since the loan has a fully indexed contract rate at this point, the contract rate and the payment will remain constant for the remaining term of the loan.

In a rising-interest-rate scenario, the effective cost (yield) will be greatest for ARMs that are uncapped, allow for frequent rate changes, have large margins, and do not have large initial-period discounts.

TABLE 6-5

Effective Costs of ARM Example

APR	5-YEAR HOLDING PERIOD
9.93%	8.67%

Source: © 2014 OnCourse Learning

For illustration, let's compute the effective cost (yield) for our example assuming prepayment at the end of the fifth year. The equation is written as

$$\text{Present Value of Loan} = PMT_1/(1 + IRR) + PMT_2/(1 + IRP)^2 + PMT_3/(1 + IRR)^3$$
$$+ PMT_4/(1 + IRR)^4 + PMT_5/(1 + IRR)^5 + \cdots$$
$$+ PMT_{60}/(1 + IRR)^{60} + \text{Balance}_{60}/(1 + IRR)^{60}$$

(Equation 6-1)

where PMT is the monthly payment and Balance$_{60}$ is the outstanding balance of the loan at the end of the sixtieth payment (end of the fifth year). The equation would be

$$\$98,000 = \$552.20 \, (PVAI \, F_{i\%/12,12})$$
$$+ \$679.13 \, (PVAIF_{i\%/12,12}) \, (PVIF_{i\%/12,12})$$
$$+ \$813.63 \, (PVAIF_{i\%/12,12}) \, (PVIF_{i\%/12,24})$$
$$+ \$935.83 \, (PVAIF_{i\%/12,12}) \, (PVIF_{i\%/12,36})$$
$$+ \$815.60 \, (PVAIF_{i\%/12,12}) \, (PVIF_{i\%/12,48})$$
$$+ \$95,237 \, (PVIF_{i\%/12,60})$$

This equation can be solved for i either by using a financial calculator or by an iterative process of trial and error. Using the financial calculator, the cash flow mode is required since the payments are different each year. For our example, the effective cost over a 5-year holding period is 8.67 percent, as shown in Table 6-5.

The APR of the loan can also be calculated. Assuming that the payment for the sixth year remains constant for the remaining term of the loan, the equation would be

$$\$98,000 = \$552.20 \, (PVAI \, F_{i\%/12,12})$$
$$+ \$679.13 \, (PVAIF_{i\%/12,12}) \, (PVIF_{i\%/12,12})$$
$$+ \$813.63 \, (PVAIF_{i\%/12,12}) \, (PVIF_{i\%/12,24})$$
$$+ \$935.83 \, (PVAIF_{i\%/12,12}) \, (PVIF_{i\%/12,36})$$
$$+ \$815.60 \, (PVAIF_{i\%/12,12}) \, (PVIF_{i\%/12,48})$$
$$+ \$933.43 \, (PVIF_{i\%/12,300}) \, (PVIF_{i\%12,60})$$

The APR of this loan is 9.93 percent.

OTHER VARIATIONS OF ADJUSTABLE-RATE MORTGAGES

At some points in time (such as the mid-2000s) lenders have offered some variations of the ARM other than the standard ARM. The following are some examples.

The Interest-Only ARM

With an interest-only ARM, the payment for the initial period is only interest with no repayment of principal. After the initial period the loan becomes fully amortizing for the remaining term. Typical loan structures are 3/1, 5/1, 7/1, and 10/1. A 3/1 interest-only ARM means that the payment is interest-only for the first 3 years. Typically the contract rate is fixed for the interest-only period. After the interest-only period, the ARM becomes a fully amortizing, 1-year adjustable for the next 27 years. During the amortization period, these loans are typically 1-year Treasury security or LIBOR-indexed ARMs with 2/6 interest rate caps.

To illustrate, suppose that a lender offers a 3/1 interest-only ARM with an initial contract rate of 5 percent and a contract rate in year 4 of 6.50 percent. Borrowing $100,000 over a 30-year term would produce a monthly payment of $416.67 for the first 3 years and a monthly payment in the fourth year of

$655.55. If the contract rate stays constant at 6.50 percent for the remaining 27-year term, this payment will fully amortize the loan over its term.

The Option ARM

The option ARM gives the borrower the flexibility of making one of several payments each month. The optional payments include a "minimum" payment, an interest-only payment, and a fully amortizing 30-year payment. Some option ARMs also allow for a fully amortizing 15-year payment. Option ARMs generally have a low introductory contract rate. With the minimum payment option, the payment amount may not be enough to pay all the interest that is being charged. The unpaid interest will be added to the principal balance of the loan, resulting in negative amortization. The interest-only payment allows the borrower to avoid deferred interest but there is no repayment of principal. Also, the interest-only payment is generally not allowed if it is less than the minimum payment. The interest-only payment may change every month as the contract rate changes. If the borrower wishes to have loan amortization, he/she can choose to make the fully amortizing payment.

The option ARM contract typically restricts the minimum payment from increasing more than 7.50 percent from year to year. This may produce the major risk of making the minimum payment: "payment shock" resulting from a sharp increase in the payment. This may happen in two ways. First, every 5 or 10 years the payment must be recast to become fully amortizing. The payment increases to the amount that will fully amortize the loan over its remaining term at the current interest rate. The second way is the restriction on negative amortization. The loan balance cannot exceed a negative amortization maximum, which is usually 110 percent to 125 percent of the original loan balance. Once the loan balance reaches the maximum, the payment immediately increases to the fully amortizing level.

The option ARM would be most attractive to the borrower who expects to own the property for a short time and prefers flexibility in the monthly payment. Also, because of its low initial rate and payments, borrowers can usually qualify for a larger loan amount.

The Alt-A Loan

The Alt-A mortgage is an "alternative documentation loan" or a "no doc loan" and is subject to different approval standards than traditional loans. With an Alt-A loan the borrower may not provide income verification or documentation of assets; thus, approval is based primarily on the borrower's credit score. Obviously these loans do not fall into the "conforming" mortgage category. Characteristics that may cause this include (1) reduced borrower income and asset documentation, (2) debt-to-income ratios that exceed allowable limits, (3) a less-than-stellar credit history, and (4) loan-to-value ratios that exceed established maximums.

During the mortgage crisis of 2007 and 2008, Alt-A loans drew special attention because of their characteristics. The lack of necessary proof or documentation that would ordinarily be required to write a conforming loan invited borrower fraud in terms of factors such as overstating income. The use of Alt-A loans was popular with investors buying nonowner-occupied properties and this increased the likelihood of default.

Flexible Payment ARMs

A flexible payment ARM (FPARM) is an ARM that allows borrowers to make very low mortgage payments initially with the expectation that these will increase over time. FPARMs are complicated, so the borrower must be careful to understand the risks. For example, a major drawback is the possibility of "payment shock," which is a dramatic increase in the monthly payment. The primary appeal of the FPARM is the low payment in the early years. The borrower may be facing affordability problems or may have alternative uses for the funds such as other investments or home improvements.

The initial contract rate on the FPARM is a teaser that may be as low as 1.25 percent but it applies only to the first month. In the second month the rate increases to the fully-indexed rate. The contract rate adjusts monthly with no limit on the size of interest rate changes except a maximum over the life of the loan. One consolation is that most FPARMs use the COFI, which adjusts slowly to market changes.

Payment changes on an FPARM are more complicated than those on a typical ARM. The minimum initial payment is calculated as the interest rate in the first month and will increase by 7.50 percent per year. Although the interest rate changes in the second month, the initial payment holds for the year. In following years each minimum payment is 7.50 percent higher than the minimum payment in the preceding year. There are two exceptions to this 7.50 percent rule. First, the loan must be recast every 5 years to be fully amortizing; in other words, the payment is increased to the amount that will repay the loan over the remaining term at the current interest rate. Second, the loan balance cannot exceed a negative amortization maximum. After the first interest rate adjustment the minimum payment is normally not sufficient to cover the interest due and the excess is added to the mortgage balance. Negative amortization maximums on FPARMs usually range from 110 to 125 percent of the original loan balance. When the loan balance reaches the maximum, the payment is automatically increased to the fully amortizing level. Either of these provisions can result in payment shock. This is especially true for loans that have very low initial rates and high margins.

Pricing Adjustable-Rate Mortgages

Pricing of ARMs refers to the effect on the value of an ARM of changing one or more of its terms. If the introduction of a term, such as a cap on the rate change, causes the lender more interest rate risk, this will lower the value of the ARM. To compensate, the lender will have to charge discount points or, alternatively, add some basis points to the margin. The trade-off in terms, an attempt to maintain a certain "value" for the ARM, is referred to as the pricing of the ARM terms. To understand how ARMs are priced, first consider a "perfect" ARM, one that completely eliminates interest rate risk for the lender. Such a theoretical ARM would have an index that changed with the market rate and reflected, at all times, the interest cost of funds to the lender. The lender would set a margin sufficient to cover operating expenses and provide a return to capital invested in the institution. There would be no caps at all on the loan, and its rate would change simultaneously with the index. With this perfect ARM, the lender would be completely hedged against interest rate risk. The opposite extreme would be a completely bound ARM. Once the rate was established, zero caps on the interest rate would prevent any change at all. Such a bound ARM would be essentially a fixed-rate mortgage, but with an ARM rate of interest—a bad deal for lenders. For the purpose of our discussion, a bound ARM is a hypothetical reference loan. No lender would originate an essentially fixed-rate loan with a lower ARM rate of interest. Between these two extremes lie ARMs that are actually originated by lenders. They have rate caps, life-of-loan caps, payment caps, and initial period discounts. They do not adjust instantaneously with an index, but only periodically. The longer the period of adjustment, the greater the interest rate risk. Now, a perfect

ARM would always be valued at par, a value equal to 100 percent of its balance. A perfect ARM might look as follows. It would have a rate tied to an index that reflects the lender's cost of funds. (Assume that index is currently 7 percent.) Next, the lender would establish the margin necessary to cover operating costs, say, 200 basis points. The rate on the loan would be 9 percent. At future dates, it would always be valued at the amount of its balance.

The introduction of restrictive terms would lower its value. If the lender adds a 2 percent rate cap, the value may fall to 0.975 percent of par, for example. The 2.5 percent discount is the price of the cap. To restore value, the lender would have to charge 2.5 discount points at origination. Alternatively, the lender could add 25 basis points to the margin. In this case, the present value of the additional basis points over the expected life of the loan would equal the 2.5 discount points. How did we decide that the "price" of a 2 percent cap was 2.5 discount points at origination or 25 basis points added to the margin? The answer lies in pricing. Pricing methods are the subject of numerous research studies. Although their methodologies have varied, these studies have yielded similar results in terms of establishing the pricing of various ARM terms.

One method uses **historical replication.** By constructing a theoretically perfect ARM and then tracing the movements of an actual index over some historical period, this method can replicate the ARM's cash flows. The present value of the cash flows is then calculated. The process is then repeated with one term changed. For example, a 1 percent rate cap may be added. If the present value of the cash flows of the capped ARM is less than that of the perfect ARM, then a determination is made concerning the discount points or the addition to the margin that would be necessary to equate the present values of the two loans.

Another methodology uses a simulation of interest rates rather than actual rates over an historical period (which may not be repeated). With a **simulation model,** the cash flows of a perfect ARM are traced by allowing a random movement in the index. The change in the index from one period to the next may be taken from a normal probability distribution. If the mean of the distribution of rate changes is positive, then rates will drift up over time, and vice versa. If the distribution of rate changes is given a large variance (or standard deviation), then rates will fluctuate more widely around the trend. In this manner the cash flows of the perfect ARM may be generated thousands of times and an average found. The same process is then used for an ARM that is capped or has an initial period discount. Various discounts are applied to the capped ARM so as to create the same present value as the perfect ARM. Assumptions that are made concerning the trend and volatility of interest rates will have a dramatic effect on pricing relationships. The results of numerous pricing studies reveal the following approximate prices for various terms.

Adjustment Caps and Periods. Figure 6-1 shows the relationship between the size of rate caps, the adjustment period, and the value of an ARM. Here, interest volatility is assumed to be about normal (15 percent standard deviation in annual rate). If there were no interest rate volatility, then all the ARMs would be priced at par because there would be no interest rate risk. If the periodic rate cap is zero, the ARM is completely bound, and if it has a contract rate equal to that of a perfect ARM, it will have a value somewhere below par—0.982, for example. As the size of the cap increases, so will the value of the ARM (interest rate risk is reduced). The longer the adjustment period, the lower the value of the ARM for any given rate cap. None of the ARMs shown has a value of par (100 percent) because none are perfect—that is, they all have some lag in the adjustment to the index.

| FIGURE 6-1 | Periodic Rate Caps, Reset Frequency, and Loan Value |

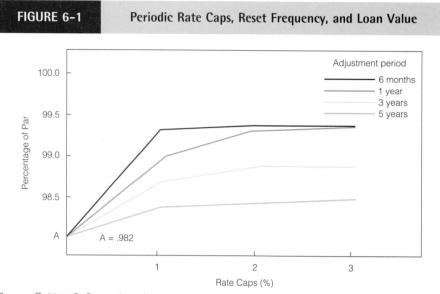

Source: © 2014 OnCourse Learning

Initial-Period Discount (Teaser Rate). Figure 6-2 prices initial-period discounts, or teaser rates.[2] Assuming a 7 percent index and 200 basis point margin, the fully indexed rate is 9 percent. Interest rate volatility is again assumed to be normal in this example. The solid line represents the value of a completely bound ARM. It reaches its maximum value when there is no initial-period discount. (For consistency, we place its value with no discount (9 percent) at the initial value in Figure 6-1.) The dashed line represents the value of an ARM with a 2 percent cap. For deep initial-period discounts, the cap may prevent the loan from becoming fully indexed on the first or early anniversary dates. For small teaser discounts, the value quickly approaches that of a perfect ARM.

| FIGURE 6-2 | Teaser Rates and Loan Values |

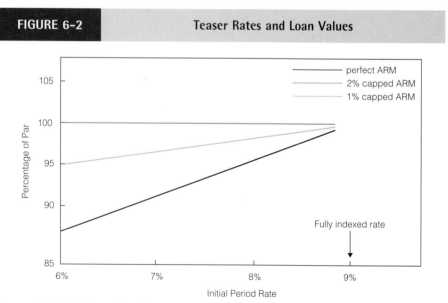

Source: © 2014 OnCourse Learning

FIGURE 6-3   **Life-of-Loan Caps and Loan Value**

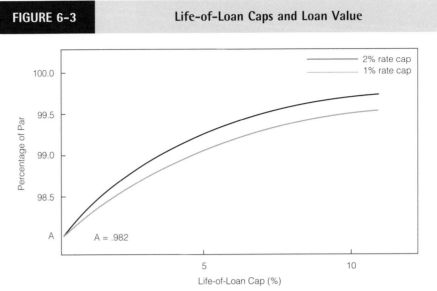

Source: © 2014 OnCourse Learning

Life-of-Loan Caps. Figure 6-3 shows the value of an ARM with various life caps but with no rate adjustment caps (rates are free to fluctuate). With a zero lifetime cap the ARM is again bound and has the same value as an FRM in the previous figures. As the life of the loan cap increases, the value increases and approaches par for very large caps.

Margin. An increase in the margin, other things being equal, will raise the value of an ARM. Figure 6-4 shows the value of the perfect ARM in our example reaching 100 percent of par when the margin equals 200 basis points. Research has indicated that the value of an ARM increases about 1 percent for every 25 to 30 basis points added to the margin.

FIGURE 6-4   **Margin and Loan Value, Perfect ARM**

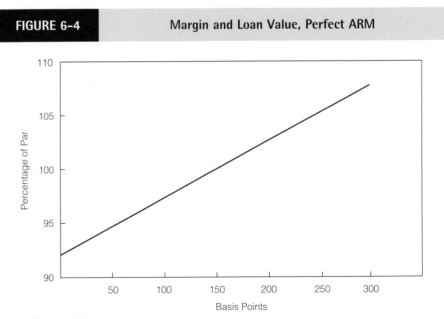

Source: © 2014 OnCourse Learning

Interest Rate Volatility and Trend. The expectations of borrowers and lenders concerning the direction and volatility of future interest rates also will affect the pricing of ARMs. Interest rate volatility adds value to the borrower's refinance option on a fixed-rate loan, lowering its value to the lender. Also, if interest rates are expected to rise in the future, the value of an ARM will rise relative to a fixed-rate loan. Figure 6-5 shows the value of a bound ARM (FRM), an ARM with a 2 percent rate cap, and a perfect ARM—all as functions of expected interest rate volatility. Again, if we assume that the normal level of volatility is represented by 15 percent per annum standard deviation, a bound ARM will have a value of approximately 0.982. Point A corresponds with the same points in Figures 6-1 and 6-3. A perfect ARM will be valued at par, regardless of the volatility of interest rates; it adjusts instantaneously to rate changes. The 2 percent capped ARM occupies an intermediary position between the perfect ARM and the bound ARM.

Figure 6-6 shows the values of the same three loans as a function of the average rate of interest subsequent to origination. If rates rise, the value of the bound ARM will fall the greatest, the perfect ARM not at all. For index rates above 7 percent, the difference in the curves represents the value to the lender from originating an ARM over a fixed-rate loan. For levels of the index below 7 percent, the values of the bound ARM and the capped ARM will rise above the perfect ARM. The capped ARM experiences a smaller increase in value, reflecting the fact that the ARM will adjust to the lower rates only within the tolerance of the 2 percent cap. The rate on the bound ARM will not adjust to the lower index. Note, however, that because of the ability to refinance a loan, the bound ARM's value eventually returns to par at sufficiently low interest rates. That is, if the index falls significantly, borrowers will refinance their bound ARM. In summary, research has predicted what has been illustrated in the preceding figures.

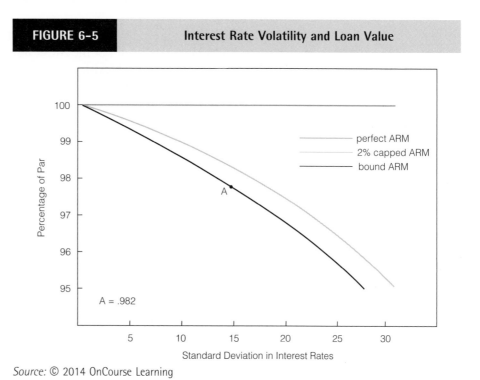

| FIGURE 6-5 | Interest Rate Volatility and Loan Value |

Source: © 2014 OnCourse Learning

FIGURE 6-6   Value of Various ARMs

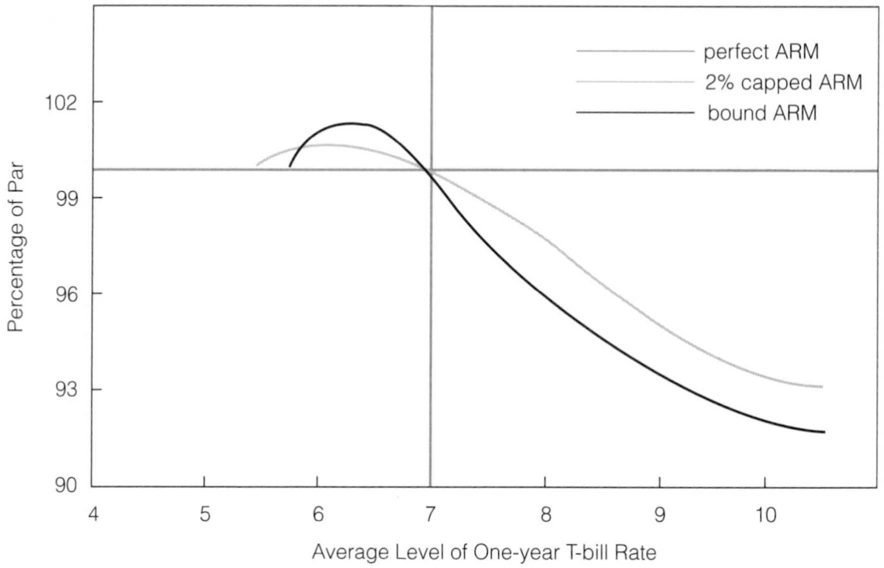

Source: © 2014 OnCourse Learning

Specifically, for normal expectations of interest rate volatility, the following will hold true:

- In exchange for tighter rate caps and less frequent rate adjustments, lenders will require either added discount points or a larger margin. For a 2 percent cap and a 1-year adjustment, the discount will lie in the range of 1 discount point.

- In exchange for an initial-period discount on the rate, lenders will require an addition to the margin or discount points. For a 2 percent rate-capped ARM, a 1 percent break on the initial rate may require approximately 2 discount points.

- Lenders require a discount to provide a life-of-loan cap. The discount will depend on whether or not the ARM also has a rate cap. The additional discount is slight if the ARM has a rate cap. This is so because the rate cap lessens the likelihood that the life cap would become binding in the near future. Without a rate cap, the addition of a 5 percent life cap likely costs between 1 and 1.5 discount points.

- Other things being equal, an addition of 25 to 30 basis points to the margin adds about 1 percent to the value of the loan. A lender can charge 1 less point by adding 25 to 30 basis points.

- Expectations that interest rates will rise or become more volatile will lead lenders to charge greater discounts on fixed-rate loans or strictly bound ARMs.

There is an almost limitless number of combinations of ARM terms. With eight or nine terms to play with, lenders could conceive of virtually endless permutations of ARM loans. Lenders have experimented with many combinations of terms over the years, seeking to find loans that would appeal to borrowers, yet provide interest rate protection. In fact, a 1994 study by Sa-Aadu and Shilling[3] estimated a model of ARM choice over a full set of alternative ARM contracts and found that borrowers perceive a broad array of ARMs as equivalent. They argue that it makes little sense for lenders to offer a wide variety of ARMs that are perceived as being the same.

The secondary market agencies have used computer simulation programs to arrange the various terms and construct ARMs that they thought would protect them from interest rate risk. They defined the terms of ARMs they would purchase and to a great degree forced them on lenders who originated loans primarily for sale. As a result of this process, many types of ARMs became almost nonexistent, such as the 5-year adjustable. As more and more combinations of terms became less popular, the market gravitated to only a few different types. Today, the most popular ARM is the 1-year adjustable tied to a 1-year Treasury index. Yet, even for this standardized loan, terms such as the number of discount points will vary, depending on expectations concerning the trend and volatility of interest rates. Such expectations not only have a dramatic effect on the terms of successful ARMs but also affect the share of total loans represented by ARMs.

Problems in ARM Calculations

Evidence shows that lenders sometimes make errors when ARM adjustments are made. Generally, adjustment errors seem to be unintentional and correctable. Most errors appear to stem from sloppy or faulty procedures, calculation errors, and/or faulty computer software. As Elledge, Fletcher, and Norris[4] point out, errors are most likely to occur during four events: (1) loan origination, (2) the initial entry of the loan data into the system, (3) the loan adjustment date, and (4) the times of changes in the system. Some causes of errors they cite are (1) mistakes in the original loan setup process, (2) lack of agreement of terms disclosed to the borrower and the terms in the note and rider, (3) selection of the wrong index or index value, (4) selection of the index on the wrong date, (5) failure to make any adjustment in some years (or ever), and (6) incorrect allocation of payment between interest and principal.

Since the loan document is viewed as a contract, lenders must correct any errors that result in overcharges to borrowers and refund any overpayments. On the other hand, undercharges cannot be collected by lenders from borrowers.

FRM–ARM Spread

The rate of interest on an ARM is typically 1 to 3 percentage points below that on a fixed-rate loan. The reason is simple. Lenders accept a lower rate for shifting a portion of the interest rate risk to borrowers. The more risk they can shift to borrowers through loose rate caps and frequent adjustment periods, the lower will be the rate relative to that on a fixed-rate loan. At any particular time the FRM-ARM rate spread will depend on several factors. Two of the most important are the market's expectations of the trend and volatility in interest rates. We saw in Chapter 2 that the yield curve can be used as a simple forecasting tool for future interest rates. When the yield curve is upward sloping and interest rates have recently been volatile, lenders will offer larger discounts on ARMs and the FRM—ARM spread will widen. When the yield curve is flat, the spread will narrow. On occasion, the yield curve has been downward sloping, suggesting that interest rates may fall. In this case, lenders have less incentive to offer ARMs and the spread has nearly disappeared. Generally, however, borrowers can expect to get a 1 to 3 percent break on the ARM rate over the FRM rate.

The demand for ARMs is affected by two primary factors: (1) the level of market interest rates in general and (2) the spread between the prices of FRMs and ARMs. Higher market rates in general reduce the affordability of FRMs and make ARMs more appealing. Likewise, the greater the differential between the rate on FRMs and the rate on ARMs (since it is lower), the greater the demand for ARMs.

PROBLEMS OF DEMAND: THE TILT EFFECT AND THE GRADUATED PAYMENT MORTGAGE

The **tilt effect** occurs when expectations of future inflation cause interest rates to rise. Lenders then charge a higher rate on newly originated loans to compensate for expected inflation, preserving a real rate of return. The higher rate, in turn, causes payments on a standard, fixed-rate loan to increase. Since the FRM is an annuity, all payments are raised uniformly. The real (inflation-adjusted) size of the initial payment can be substantially greater than the latter payments. That is, in terms of buying power, a $1,000 monthly payment today is much greater than a $1,000 payment 10, 20, or 30 years from today.

Although the income of the borrower is expected to increase over the term of the loan, because of the inflationary expectation the borrower must make the initial payments out of current income, not future income. This results in very burdensome payments at the start of the loan and easy payments at the end. Consider that 30 years ago, a $110 payment would have represented about 25 percent of the head of household's income. That sort of payment was common on mortgages at that time.

The principal AMI designed to offset the tilt effect is the **graduated-payment mortgage (GPM).** The concept of the GPM is rather simple. The payments on a fixed-rate loan are rearranged to be lower at the beginning of the loan and higher at the end. The payment pattern is designed to track the income of the borrower as it is affected by inflation. The rate on the loan is not changed, just the pattern of payments. Generally, the payments are constant for a year and then increased in each successive year. For some GPMs the payments are scheduled to increase for only several years before leveling off for the remainder of the mortgage term. Because the interest rate on a GPM is approximately that on a level-payment FRM, the initial smaller payment may be insufficient to meet all of the interest obligation. Any residual is added to the balance of the loan, resulting in negative amortization for about the first half of the term.

GPM EXAMPLE

Let's say that the rate on a level-payment FRM is 12 percent and that, for simplicity, payments are made annually. With no discount points, the equation for a $100,000 loan appears as follows:

$$\$100,000 = \frac{12,414}{(1+0.12)^1} + \frac{12,414}{(1+0.12)^2} + \cdots + \frac{12,414}{(1+0.12)^{30}} \quad \text{(Equation 6-2)}$$

To convert this loan to a GPM with payments rising by 7.5 percent for the first 5 years and fixed thereafter, the payments must be restructured. The initial payment must be chosen such that each of the five succeeding payments is 7.5 percent greater than the preceding, the remaining payments for 24 years are equal to that of the sixth year, and the above equation is maintained. The following payment schedule is the result:

$$\$100,000 = \frac{791.40}{(1.01)^1} + \cdots + \frac{850.72}{(1.01)^{13}} + \cdots + \frac{91453}{(1.01)^{25}} + \cdots + \frac{983.12}{(1.01)^{37}} + \cdots$$
$$+ \frac{1,056.85}{(1.01)^{49}} + \cdots + \frac{1,136.11}{(1.01)^{61}} + \cdots + \frac{1,136.11}{(1.01)^{360}}$$

The amortization schedule for this loan appears in Table 6-6. Note that negative amortization occurs through the first 5 years. The payment on the GPM is insufficient to meet the interest charges during this period. The payment does not even equal that for a standard level-payment mortgage until approximately the fourth or fifth year of the loan. For example, the interest charge on a $100,000 loan at

TABLE 6-6

Amortization Schedule of GPM Loan $100,000, 12%, Initial Monthly Payment = $791.37

YEAR	BEGINNING BALANCE	INTEREST	PAYMENT	ENDING BALANCE[a]
1	$100,000	$12,142[b]	$ 9,496[c]	$102,646
2	102,646	12,439	10,209	104,875
3	104,874	12,677	10,974	106,577
4	106,577	12,845	11,797	107,625
5	107,625	12,928	12,682	107,871
6	107,871	12,905	13,633	107,143
7	107,143	12,813	13,633	106,323
.	.	.	.	.
.	.	.	.	.
.	.	.	.	.
30	13,812	179	13,633	0

[a]*Beginning balance + interest − payment = ending balance.*
[b]*Although the interest rate is 12% per annum, the interest cost is slightly higher than $12,000 because of the negative amortization in the initial months.*
[c]*12 × $791.37.*

Source: © 2014 OnCourse Learning

12 percent is approximately $12,000 for the first year. Yet the 12 payments of $791.40 add up to only $9,496. The difference, $2,504, is added to the loan balance. Payments exceed the interest charge only at the end of the fifth year.

A method for solving for the initial monthly payment (the remaining payments are tied to the first payment by the pre-established growth rate) is presented in Appendix 6-A. The computations can be somewhat involved, so standard tables have been developed to ease the problem of determining the initial payment. Table 6-7 is an example of such a table. The factors in the table are multiplied by the amount of the loan balance to arrive at the initial payment. Note that the entry for a 12 percent loan with a 7.5 percent growth in payments for 5 years is 0.007914, or $791.40, for a $100,000 loan.

The most popular GPMs are insured by the FHA. At one time, the FHA had two GPM programs, 245a and 245b. The 245a program set the initial loan-to-value ratio such that the negative amortization would not exceed 97 percent of the initial appraised value of the property. The 245b program was more liberal; under this program negative amortization could bring the loan balance to 113 percent of the property value. The 245b program was terminated in October 1987

TABLE 6-7

Factors to Compute Monthly Payment in First Year of GPM[a]

GROWTH RATE FOR FIRST 5 YEARS	INTEREST RATE						
	9	9.5	10	10.5	11	11.5	12
0.050	0.006671	0.006986	0.007305	0.007631	0.007961	0.008296	0.008635
0.075	0.006079	0.006372	0.006670	0.006971	0.007283	0.007596	0.007914
0.010	0.005543	0.005816	0.006094	0.006377	0.000666	0.006958	0.007255

[a]*First payment = Factor × loan balance.*

Source: © 2014 OnCourse Learning

because of its default risk. Even though the GPM solves the tilt problem, it has some shortcomings and has not gained widespread acceptance.

The benefits of the GPM are simple. By partially eliminating the tilt effect (most GPMs have constant payments after the first 6 years, not throughout the life of the loan), borrowers can qualify for a larger loan than with a level-payment mortgage. Housing becomes more affordable. Also, the increase in payments each year corresponds with the expected increase in the borrower's income. There are three main problems with the GPM, however: negative amortization, interest rate risk, and inflexible payment schedules.

The most obvious problem of the GPM is the default risk associated with negative amortization. In our example, negative amortization reached 107.8 percent of the loan balance in year 5. Assuming no appreciation in housing prices (or a decline, as was the case in some regions of the country during the 1980s), the original loan-to-value ratio would have to be as small as 92.5 percent to avoid negative equity and the likelihood of default. For this reason the FHA 245a program required a larger down payment than for fixed-rate loans, usually about 10 percent. Although the GPM is designed to solve the affordability problem associated with the tilt effect, it creates another affordability problem in terms of the larger down payment required to mitigate default risk.

A second problem of the GPM involves interest rate risk. Although it is common to speak of interest rate risk as related to the maturity of a debt obligation, it is actually related to its effective maturity, or duration. The reader is referred to Appendix 4-B for a discussion of duration, maturity, and interest rate risk. Recall that duration is related to the maturity of a debt obligation but is not quite the same thing. Generally, the longer the maturity, the longer the duration. The two are related because duration measures the extent to which the payment pattern of a debt obligation is pushed back in time. However, large intermediate payments shorten duration (but not maturity) and lower interest rate risk by allowing the lender to reinvest those payments at current interest rates. A standard mortgage includes some amortization of the principal in its payments and thus has a shorter duration than, say, a corporate bond of equal maturity but with interest-only payments. The latter, in turn, has a shorter duration than a zero-coupon bond. A zero-coupon bond has no intermediate payments at all; its only payment is at maturity. In that case, duration and maturity are the same.

The following examples are intended to clarify the relationship between maturity and duration:

DEBT	MATURITY	DURATION
1-year ARM	1 year	10.8 months
30-year FRM	30 years	7.7 to 8.5 years
GPM	30 years	11 to 12 years
Zero-coupon bond	30 years	30 years

In any event, it is the duration of a debt instrument that determines its interest rate risk. But since duration and maturity are closely related, it is common to speak of interest rate risk as being determined by maturity.

The negative amortization on a GPM lengthens its duration over that of a level-payment loan of equal maturity. This increases its interest rate risk. Simply put, if rates rise subsequent to the origination of a GPM, the lender is placed in the position of having a loan with a growing balance financed at an old, low rate.

Lenders will seek compensation for this risk through a slightly higher rate of interest (the FHA insures against default risk, not interest rate risk) than that on the level-payment loan. This factor partially defeats the affordability advantage of the GPM. Higher down payments (to control for default risk) and higher initial yields (to compensate for interest rate risk) have combined to offset some of the affordability advantage of the GPM.

Another problem with the GPM is the inflexibility of its payment schedule. Although graduated, it is graduated for only several years and for a predetermined set amount. There is no guarantee that the borrower's income will increase in relation to the schedule of payments. One finds it difficult to imagine that a borrower's income will rise by 7.5 percent annually for 6 years and level off for the remaining 24 years. As presently structured, GPMs become standard, fixed-rate loans after the first 6 years. A GPM can be designed such that the payments increase throughout the life of the loan. This would involve an even smaller first year's payment and greater negative amortization until approximately 12 or so years into the life of the loan. It would also increase the loan's duration, further raising interest rate risk for the lender. But there is still no guarantee that borrower's income will increase so as to track the predetermined schedule of payments. Another problem with the GPM involves the treatment of interest expense for tax purposes. The tax ramifications of AMIs are discussed later in this chapter.

SIMULTANEOUSLY SOLVING THE PROBLEMS OF SUPPLY AND DEMAND: THE PRICE LEVEL ADJUSTED MORTGAGE

One AMI, the **price level adjusted mortgage (PLAM),** solves both the tilt and the interest rate risk problems of an FRM.[5] The lender desires to earn a real rate-of-return on a loan and also be compensated for any erosion due to inflation. This is the reason that lenders add an expected inflation premium to the real rate when setting the rate on a standard loan. Unfortunately, this creates a tilt problem. It also does not guarantee that the lender will be protected from erosion due to unexpected inflation. The lender is subject to risk associated with unexpected increases in inflation and market rates of interest.

The PLAM solves these problems by separating the return to the lender into two components: the real return and compensation for inflation. With the PLAM, the inflation component is determined after the inflation has occurred and is equal to the exact amount of the inflation. The contract rate on the PLAM is the real rate, approximately 3 percent. Annually, the balance of the loan is adjusted for the amount of the previous year's rate of inflation. For instance, a lender makes a $100,000 loan, and in the first year the rate of inflation is 6 percent. Under the PLAM, the lender would receive a 9 percent return in the first year—3 percent as the contract rate of interest and a 6 percent increase in the balance of the loan. If there were no inflation at all in the first year, there would be no upward adjustment of the loan balance. The lender would receive only the real rate-of-return, 3 percent, but that would be sufficient in the absence of inflation.

The low contract rate makes the loan more affordable for the borrower. Because inflation need not be anticipated with the PLAM, there is no tilt effect. The borrower only pays the inflation premium through an upward adjustment of the balance after the inflation has occurred. Presumably, the increase in the borrower's income will have approximated the rate of inflation. The only drawback of the PLAM (besides its complexity) is the provision for negative amortization. The negative amortization occurs through the adjustment of the balance for recent inflation.

PLAM EXAMPLE

To understand how a PLAM works, consider Table 6-8. For purposes of illustration, we assume that the inflation rate is 4 percent for the first 3 years, 6 percent for years 4 through 6, and 5 percent for the remainder of the loan. The initial contract rate is the real rate, 3 percent. Each year the beginning balance is amortized over the remaining life of the loan at the real rate. The PLAM behaves as follows:

- **Year 1.** In the first year, the payment is established by amortizing the $100,000 loan over 30 years at 3 percent. The payment is substantially less than that on a standard loan amortized at 9 percent—$5,102 versus $9,734. In the absence of inflation, the ending balance would be $97,898. The actual ending balance is adjusted upward by 4 percent ($101,814 = $97,898 × 1.04).

- **Year 2.** This payment is set by amortizing the adjusted balance ($101,814) over 29 years at 3 percent. Since the ending balance from the first year was adjusted upward by 4 percent, the payment in the second year will be 4 percent greater than in the first year—$5,306 versus $5,102. Recall that it is amortized at the same rate, 3 percent. If the borrower's income has kept pace with inflation, there will be no increase in the real payment. The ending balance in the absence of inflation would be $99,562. This is adjusted upward by the inflation during the second year, 4 percent, so that the adjusted ending balance is $103,545.

TABLE 6-8

Price Level Adjusted Mortgage Examples[a]

YEAR	BEGINNING BALANCE	INTEREST (3%)	PAYMENTS	ENDING BALANCE BEFORE ADJUSTMENT	ENDING BALANCE AFTER ADJUSTMENT
1	$100,000	$3,000	$5,102	$97,898	$101,814
2	101,814	3,054	5,306	99,562	143,0545
3	103,545	3,106	5,518	101,133	105,178
4	105,178	3,155	5,739	102,595	102,59510
5	108,750	3,263	6,083	105,930	112,285
6	112,285	3,369	6,448	109,206	115,758
7	115,758	3,473	6,835	112,395	118,015
.	.	.	.	.	.
.	.	.	.	.	.
.	.	.	.	.	.
.	.	.	.	.	.
14	126,629	3,799	9,618	120,810	126,851
.	.	.	.	.	.
.	.	.	.	.	.
.	.	.	.	.	.
.	.	.	.	.	.
.	.	.	.	.	.
28	53,864	1,616	19,043	36,438	38,259
29	38,259	1,148	19,995	19,412	20,383
30	20,383	611	20,994	0	0

Inflation rate: 4% Years 1–3, 6% Years 4–6, 5% Years 7–30.

[a]*Loan amount = $ 100,000; Real rate = 3%.*

Source: © 2014 OnCourse Learning

- *Year 5.* Skipping to the fifth year, the beginning balance is $108,750. Amortized at 3 percent the payment rises to $6,083. This is a 6 percent increase from the previous year, reflecting the 6 percent inflation in year 4. Negative amortization continues.

- *Remaining Years.* Continued inflation causes the loan balance to increase for several years. In this example it reaches a peak in the fourteenth year. The reason the balance does not continue to grow beyond the fourteenth year is that with each successive year the balance is amortized over a shorter remaining term. For short terms, a large proportion of the payment represents amortization. In the fourteenth year, only $3,799 of the $9,618 payment is interest; the rest is principal reduction. Eventually, this large amount of amortization exceeds the adjustment of the balance for inflation. The payments in the last few years of the loan appear very high. The last payment, nearly $21,000, is four times greater than the first. This will not be a burden if the borrower's income has kept up with inflation. The last payment is greater than the first by a compounded growth factor of about 5 percent annually over the 30 years.

- *The Effective Cost.* Calculating the effective cost of the PLAM is an IRR process similar to that shown earlier for the ARM. Using our example from Table 6-8, let's calculate the effective cost for a 5-year holding period. The equation would be

$$\$100{,}000 = \$5{,}102/(1 + \text{IRR}) + \$5{,}306/(1 + \text{IRR})^2 + \$5{,}518/(1 + \text{IRR})^3$$
$$+ \$5{,}739/(1 + \text{IRR})^4 + \$6{,}083/(1 + \text{IRR})^5$$
$$+ 112{,}285/(1 + \text{IRR}/(1 + \text{IRR})^5$$

(Equation 6-3)

The PLAM is an ideal loan for solving both the demand and supply problems of the fixed-rate mortgage in an inflationary environment. By tying the return to inflation after it has occurred, lenders need not include inflationary expectations in the contract rate. Neither do lenders have to correctly estimate future inflation. The inflation component of the return is determined on an annual basis as the inflation occurs and is exactly equal to the amount of inflation. The PLAM is not a popular AMI for several reasons, however.

The PLAM has several drawbacks that explain its relative obscurity in the mortgage market. First, it is a relatively complex instrument and one that is rather difficult to explain to borrowers. Second, even with moderate inflation, the upward adjustment in the loan balance in the early years creates negative amortization. The PLAM's negative amortization is greater and occurs for a longer time than that of a typical GPM. Even with the moderate inflation in our example, the loan balance reaches 127 percent of the original balance. With such negative amortization, default risk becomes a concern if equity in the property is eroded. Also, payments increase as a result of inflation. If a borrower's income fails to keep up with inflation, payment-to-income ratios above a stress level can result.

There is some difference of opinion on the default risk of PLAMs. Proponents of the PLAM argue that any inflation that drives the negative amortization of the loan also will increase the value of the property. If the two increase in proportion, there should always be positive equity. Also, as previously indicated, there should be no payment shock, as the income of the borrower also will increase with inflation. McCulloch argues that since 1920 the experience in the United States has been that nominal incomes and house prices keep up with inflation.[6] He claims that the payment-to-income ratio over the life of a PLAM will likely be much more stable than that on an ARM. The reason is that when unexpected inflation occurs, the balance of the loan is adjusted after the inflation so as to compensate the lender. With an ARM the lender raises the interest rate on the loan at the anniversary date for all remaining payments. This reintroduces the tilt problem all over again. Manchester tracked the payment-to-income ratios on a hypothetical FRM, ARM, and PLAM originated in 1967.[7] Through 1982 the after-tax payment-to-income ratios on the FRM and ARM fell steadily, from 15.5 and 14.1 percent to 5.8 and 7.6 percent, respectively. The after-tax, payment-to-income ratio on the PLAM remained nearly constant over this time, falling only slightly from 13.6 to 12.6.

With regard to negative amortization, Pesando and Turnbull indicate that the major risk of PLAMs comes from the difference in regional house appreciation rates.[8] Looking at the prices of houses in several Canadian cities, they conclude that there are substantial differences in the rate of home price appreciation by region. Lenders that originate PLAMs for which the negative amortization is tied to a national inflation rate may find that houses in localized areas may not appreciate as rapidly (or may even fall) as the national average. They found, for example, that based on historical differences in regional house appreciation rates, there would be an 11 percent chance that the loan-to-value ratio of a house in Vancouver would exceed 100 percent 5 years after financing with a PLAM. The same probability would be 21 percent in Toronto and 40.5 percent in Mississauga.

Regional variation in the growth in property prices is also characteristic of the U.S. economy. Consider that between 1983 and 1988, home prices rose by 22.9 percent in the South and 81.2 percent in the Northeast, according to figures from the National Association of REALTORS®. During this time, average home prices rose by only 7.5 percent in Texas, and between 1985 and 1987 they fell by more than 5 percent in that state.

The variance in local house price appreciation around national trends clearly indicates that localized default problems could crop up due to failures in regional economies. This regional risk is likely one of the reasons lenders have not embraced the PLAM, especially in the absence of any provision for default insurance.

Another problem with the PLAM is that it does not quite solve the maturity mismatch problem. At the beginning of the year a lender may offer 8 percent on 1-year deposits. If inflation that year turns out to be only 2 percent, then the rate-of-return on PLAM mortgages will only be 5 percent, less than the interest expense. That is, although the PLAM eliminates the need to accurately predict inflation from the standpoint of the lender's assets, it does not do the same from the standpoint of deposit liabilities. Lenders that originate substantial amounts of PLAMs may have to issue deposits for which the rate is also tied to inflation after the fact. Such price level adjusted deposits (PLADs) would allow the lender to originate mortgages without any risk of predicting future inflation. Whether depositors of thrifts could be persuaded to accept PLADs is another question. Later, we indicate that the PLAM also suffers from an unfavorable income tax treatment of the borrower's interest expense.

THE DUAL INDEX MORTGAGE

Some countries have developed other mortgage variations to account for changes in market interest rates and interest rate risk. An example is the **dual index mortgage (DIM)** that uses more than one index to make adjustments. From the standpoint of the lender, the DIM is very similar to the ARM in that the interest rate is adjusted periodically in response to changes in market rates. From the standpoint of the borrower, however, the DIM is not comparable to the ARM. For example, the borrower's initial payment may be low based on a low interest rate but the rate due the lender may be some higher rate. The difference is made up through negative amortization, which may be experienced several years before the mortgage balance begins to decline. Over the loan term the payment will be adjusted in response to changes in an index of wages and salaries. Having the borrower's payment tied to a wage and salary index while the lender's income is tied to an interest rate index creates the dual index mortgage.

The anticipation for this type of loan is that, at some point, the borrower's payment will be sufficient to pay interest and principal. However, if wages and salaries don't keep up with inflation, the payment may not increase enough to accomplish this. This would result in an outstanding balance at the end of the loan term. In some cases lenders assume the risk associated with this whereas in others they seek insurance protection. For example, in Mexico where this type of mortgage is used to battle high inflation, insurance is provided to lenders by the Mexican government.

Other AMIs include the shared appreciation mortgage, the reverse annuity mortgage, and the pledged account mortgage, also called the flexible loan insurance program.

OTHER ALTERNATIVE MORTGAGE INSTRUMENTS

Shared Appreciation Mortgage

The high interest rates of the late 1970s and early 1980s provided the motivation for the **shared appreciation mortgage (SAM),** first offered by Advance Mortgage Corporation in 1980. Savings and loans were given permission by the Federal Home Loan Board to offer SAMs in 1982.

The shared appreciation mortgage works similarly to the PLAM, except that it has no annual readjustments of the loan balance and the monthly payment. The lender establishes an initial low rate on the loan and collects for the inflation premium in a lump sum later. The payment consists of a portion of the appreciation in the value of the house. The amount of the appreciation is determined when the property is sold or by appraisal on a predetermined date (say, in 10 years), whichever occurs first. By lowering the initial rate (and payment), the SAM relieves the affordability problem of standard loans. It also provides some diversification benefits for the borrower. Instead of having the majority of wealth tied up in a residence, the borrower can spin off the right to a portion of the property's appreciation in return for reduced payments. The payment savings then can be invested in other nonresidential assets.

One task facing the lender is pricing the SAM. Pricing entails the simultaneous determination of the reduction in the initial interest rate and the share of the appreciation of the property. The lender must decide what share in appreciation will compensate for the reduced interest rate on the loan. The greater the reduction in the rate, the larger the required share of appreciation. The trade-off must be such that the expected return on the SAM equals that on a standard loan. The required share will depend on a number of factors, including the lender's tax bracket, the loan-to-value ratio, the reduction in the interest rate, the rate on a standard loan, and expected inflation in housing values.[9] If the lender is in the 30 percent tax bracket and the nominal rate of interest is 10 percent, for instance, the after-tax nominal rate is 7 percent. If the nominal rate is 10 percent, then inflation expectations could reasonably approximate 7 percent.

Assuming that the after-tax, nominal interest rate equals the expected house price appreciation rate, the model can be stated as

$$\alpha = \frac{v \cdot \beta}{1 - t} \qquad \text{(Equation 6-4)}$$

where α is the share of appreciation, ϑ is the loan-to-value ratio, β is the reduction in the initial interest rate, and $(1 - t)$ represents 1 minus the lender's tax bracket.

As an example, if the loan-to-value ratio is 0.9 and there is a one-third reduction in the interest rate on the loan and the lender's tax bracket is 25 percent, then the share of appreciation is

$$0.4 = \frac{0.9 \times 0.33}{0.75}$$

The formula makes intuitive sense. A larger loan-to-value ratio means that the lender is putting up more funds on a given house. The funds are advanced at a reduced rate. With larger loan-to-value ratios, the lender is putting up a greater portion of the funds required to acquire the property and thus will demand a greater portion of the appreciation of the asset. An increase in the loan-to-value ratio from 80 percent to 90 percent requires a 12.5 percent increase in the share. Also, the greater the reduction in the interest rate, the larger the required share.

There are several considerations not included in the share-determination formula. First, if the expected rate of housing inflation rises above the after-tax nominal rate, then the required share will be reduced. Second, for lenders the SAM is a better hedge against inflation than an FRM. With an FRM the lender loses with increases in inflation but does not gain with a decrease (because of the prepayment option). With the SAM the loss from unanticipated inflation is mitigated by sharing in house appreciation. For borrowers the SAM is a hedge against the possibility that the price of the house will not rise as rapidly as general house prices. It also has diversification benefits discussed previously.

There are some shortcomings of the SAM that have prevented it from becoming a popular AMI. First, the determination of the amount of appreciation can be difficult and will depend on many factors. Second, there is the risk that individual property prices may not appreciate as fast as general housing prices. The Community Reinvestment Act (discussed in Chapter 9) likely will preclude lenders from setting different terms on SAMs to reflect neighborhood risk. Third, there is the risk that the borrower, who has given up a share of the property appreciation, will not have an incentive to maintain the property. Also, the question of improvements may complicate the determination of the appreciation. If the homeowner adds, say, a pool at a cost of $15,000, the property's value may rise by only $9,000. There may arise a dispute between the lender and borrower as to which additional value is pertinent.

Finally, there are problems with the tax treatment of the interest expense, as outlined later in the chapter.

REVERSE MORTGAGE

This type of mortgage was approved by the Federal Home Loan Bank Board (FHLBB) for member thrifts in January 1979. As the name implies, it acts in reverse of a regular mortgage. With a regular mortgage the borrower receives a large cash inflow (loan) in the present and makes monthly payments (cash outflows) over the life of the loan. With a **reverse mortgage** the borrower receives a series of monthly payments and, at the end of the loan, makes a large cash repayment. Whereas a typical mortgage is "falling debt, rising equity" because of the amortization, a reverse mortgage is described as "rising debt, falling equity" because of the accruing debt. In both types of loans, the house serves as collateral and its value will exceed the amount of the loan. Reverse mortgages are designed so that the borrower never owes more than the value of the house. In essence, a reverse mortgage is a means by which retired homeowners can take equity out of their owner-occupied residences.

Since reverse mortgage loans are nonrecourse, the debt is limited to the net proceeds from the sale of the house. The amount the borrower owes is the sum of all the loan advances plus all the interest that is accrued. If, however, the loan balance increases to equal or exceed the value of the collateralized home, the total debt is limited by the value of the home. The borrower can never owe more than the home is worth at the time of repayment. A reverse mortgage is due and payable when the last surviving borrower dies, sells the home, or permanently moves from the home. A permanent move means that the borrower has not occupied the home for at least 1 continuous year. Repayment can also be required by failure to pay property taxes, improper maintenance, or failure to maintain homeowners insurance.

In 1988, the Federal Housing Administration collaborated with AARP in designing a reverse mortgage program called the Home Equity Conversion Mortgage (HECM). The FHA program requires that the borrowers be at least 62 years old and receive counseling, usually done by telephone. The home must be owner-occupied with no existing mortgage (or an amount such that the reverse mortgage proceeds are used to pay it off). Various housing units qualify for reverse mortgages including single-family homes, one to four-unit properties, townhouses, condominiums, and some manufactured housing. The maximum value considered in the formula for the purpose of calculating the amount a homeowner is eligible to borrow is currently $625,500. Homes above this value are still eligible but approval falls outside the normal guidelines.

The FHA HECM is the most widely available reverse mortgage program. Reverse mortgages are also offered by some states, local governments, and other "proprietary" (private) lenders. Most private lenders have ceased offering their reverse mortgage products due to concern over residual home value. Reverse mortgages may have contract interest rates that are fixed or that adjust with LIBOR. Typical margins range between 2 percent and 3 percent and FHA-insured HECM's have a 10% lifetime interest rate adjustment cap. The loan amount depends on the age of the borrower, the current interest rate, and the value of the home.

In most cases the cost of originating the HECM is financed into the loan. These fees may include an origination fee, third-party costs (appraisal, inspection, etc.), and a mortgage insurance premium (MIP). The MIP is in two parts: an upfront fee, and a percentage annually on the outstanding balance. The MIP guarantees that should the total debt exceed the value of the home at the time the loan is repaid there is no liability (beyond the value of the home) to the borrower nor the estate.

Reverse mortgages are designed primarily for homeowners age 62 & over with home equity of 30 to 40% or more on their current residence. Whether or not to remain in a home is a major life decision for most elderly homeowners. Reverse mortgages provide the option to do so by providing funds for medical expenses, home improvements, or supplementing Social Security. Mayer and Simons estimate that 6 million U.S. households could benefit from the use of a reverse mortgage.[10] A study by VanderHart shows that this decision is influenced by financial and demographic factors such as income, wealth, home equity, marital status, and health.[11] Social Security and Medicare benefits are not affected by reverse mortgages

TABLE 6-9
Reverse Mortgage Example

YEAR	BEGINNING BALANCE	INTEREST FOR THE YEAR	YEAR-END PAYMENT	ENDING BALANCE TO BORROWER
1	$25,000[a]	$1,250	$12,323.11[b]	$38,573.11[c]
2	$38,573.11	$1,928.65	$12,323.11	$52,824.87
3	$52,824.87	$2,641.24	$12,323.11	$67,789.22
4	$67,789.22	$3,389.46	$12,323.11	$83,501.79
5	$83,501.79	$4,175.09	$12,323.11	$100,000

[a]*Total advances ($15,000 + $10,000)*
[b]*Payment calculated as: $68,092.96 – FV; 5 I/YR; 5 N*
[c]*Ending Balance = Beginning Balance + Interest + Payment*
Source: © 2014 OnCourse Learning

but Supplemental Security Income (SSI) and Medicaid can be. Loan advances are generally not taxable (although some annuity advances may be partially taxable) and interest charged is not tax deductible until it is actually paid.

The terms of reverse mortgages are flexible enough to create several different types. There are various ways to structure a reverse mortgage: (1) an immediate cash advance, (2) a credit line account that the borrower may draw on as needed, (3) a monthly cash advance, or (4) some combination of the preceding. A fixed payment, fixed-term loan provides for a fixed payment for a certain length of time, usually 10 years. If the property is sold or the owner dies prior to the 10-year term, the loan is paid off from the proceeds of the sale of the property. If the owner is still living in the house at the end of 10 years and repayment is required, often, another reverse mortgage can be taken out to refinance the existing one, if there has been some appreciation in the property's value.

Table 6-9 illustrates the reverse mortgage payment scheme. Suppose that the borrower takes a $100,000, 5-year reverse mortgage at 5 percent, annual payments. The borrower will take an advance to pay off an existing mortgage balance of $15,000 and the borrower wants to take an advance of $10,000 to make repairs. The table shows that the borrower's annual payments (received at the end of each year) would be $12,323.11. Remember that the payments are constructed such that the borrower owes exactly $100,000 at the end of the loan term. Since the advance amounts (totaling $25,000) will begin accruing interest immediately at 5 percent, $31,907.04 is the amount that will be owed at the end of the fifth year. The remainder is $68,092.96 ($100,000 – $31,907.04), upon which the annual payment will be based.

A fixed-payment, lifetime reverse mortgage is designed to eliminate mortality risk. This is particularly worrisome for some retirees. Many fear that if they outlive the term of the reverse mortgage, their payments will experience financial hardship. The lender will buy a deferred life annuity from a life insurance company with a portion of the loan. The deferred life annuity will begin payments to the homeowner at the end of the loan.

This form of transaction takes the mortality risk out of a reverse mortgage. The lender does not assume the mortality risk but shifts it to an insurance company that is able to diversify the risk. But, as Boehm and Ehrhardt point out, reverse mortgages have exceptionally high interest rate risk.[12] Also, movements in interest rates contribute to prepayment risk. Klein and Sirmans show that prepayment is most sensitive to marital status, age of the borrower, and term of the loan.[13] In addition, Miceli and Sirmans show that lenders must protect themselves against the risk of undermaintenance by the borrower.[14]

PLEDGED ACCOUNT MORTGAGE

A **pledged-account mortgage,** also referred to as a **flexible loan insurance program (FLIP),** is a loan arrangement that creates graduated payments for the borrower. The arrangement combines a deposit with the lender and a standard, fixed-rate loan to create a graduated-payment structure. Rather than use the funds in the deposit as a down payment (and thereby lower the amount of the standard loan), the borrower uses interest payments and a reduction in the principal of the deposit to supplement payments on the fixed-rate loan. The deposit will be pledged along with the house as collateral for the loan. An example will clarify how this loan arrangement works.

Assume the buyer desires to purchase a $110,000 house and has $30,000 in cash. Instead of financing the acquisition with an $80,000 loan, the buyer makes a down payment of only $10,000, places $20,000 in a pledged account, and borrows $100,000. Assume the interest rate on the loan is 10 percent, while the rate earned on the deposit is 7.5 percent. The monthly payment required to amortize a $100,000 loan over 30 years at 10 percent is $877.57, or $10,531 annually. Also assume the borrower wants payments to increase at 7.5 percent annually for the first 6 years. The arrangement can be structured as indicated in Table 6-10.

In the first year the buyer makes a $4,746 payment on the loan. The difference ($10,531 − $4,746) is made up of a principal and interest contribution from the pledged account. In the following year the borrower makes a $5,102 payment. This is 7.5 percent larger than the first year's payment and, again, the difference is made up from contributions from the pledged account. Because some principal is being used up, the pledged account is being exhausted. In the seventh year the borrower's payments are up to $7,324, and the deposit is exhausted. After the seventh year the borrower makes the full payment, $10,531, necessary to amortize the loan.

Had the borrower made a $30,000 down payment and financed $80,000, the monthly payment would have been $702.06, or $8,425 annually. The

TABLE 6-10

Pledged Account or FLIP Mortgage[a]

YEAR	BEGINNING DEPOSIT BALANCE	REDUCTION IN PRINCIPAL	BUYER'S INTEREST	ENDING PAYMENT	TOTAL	BALANCE
1	$20,000	$4,285	$1,500[b]	$ 4,746	$10,531[c]	$17,215[d]
2	17,215	4,138	1,291	5,102[e]	10,531	14,369
3	14,369	3,969	1,078	5,485	10,531	11,478
4	11,478	3,774	861	5,896	10,531	8,564
5	8,564	3,550	642	6,338	10,531	5,656
6	5,656	3,293	424	6,813	10,531	2,787
7	2,787	2,997	209	7,324	10,531	0
8–30	0	0	0	10,531	10,531	0

[a]$100,000 loan, 10%; $20,000 deposit, 9.5% payments increase at 7.5% annually.
[b]7.5% of beginning balance.
[c]12 × 877.57.
[d]Beginning balance plus interest less principal reduction.
[e]Previous payment × 1.075.

Source: © 2014 OnCourse Learning

pledged-account arrangement, like a graduated payment mortgage, causes the initial payments to be below, and the later payments to be above, those on an $80,000 standard FRM. For the borrower the main advantage of the pledged-account arrangement is the lower initial payments and their effect on affordability. The lender may be in a slightly greater default risk position with this arrangement than with an $80,000 loan (down payment of $30,000). Although the account is pledged as collateral, it is quickly exhausted. As with a GPM, the arrangement provides for negative amortization. As the account is exhausted, the loan-to-value ratio increases. As long as the property price does not fall, however, there will always be positive equity.

One disadvantage to the borrower is the larger total finance charges that result. The present value (discounted at the mortgage rate, 10 percent) of the total payments under the pledged-account loan is $76,224. Add to this the $10,000 down payment and the $20,000 deposit (which is exhausted), and the total cost in terms of present value is $106,224. The present value of the payments on an $80,000 loan plus a $20,000 down payment is $100,000. The larger finance cost associated with the pledged account loan results from the fact that payments made on the loan financed at 10 percent are made from an account that earns only 7.5 percent. As long as the borrower makes less on the pledged account than is charged on the mortgage, the pledged-account arrangement will result in overall higher finance charges. If the borrower could earn a rate on the deposit equal to that charged on the mortgage, the result would be a wash—no higher or lower total finance charges, just a rearrangement of the payment pattern.

In an efficient market one would expect that the loan arrangement will grant neither net benefits nor costs to the borrower or lender. The higher default risk faced by the lender is offset by the larger yield on the loan (resulting from the low-cost pledged account). If there were no greater default risk, one would expect that lenders would either reduce the rate on the mortgage or offer higher rates on the pledged account, until the total cost on a pledged-account loan would equal that on a standard loan with a larger down payment.

Home Equity Loans

Home equity loans are typically revolving credit lines in which the borrower's home serves as collateral. Loans generally have specific credit limits based on the borrower's equity. Once the loan is approved, the borrower can draw any amount up to the credit limit at any time, although some plans require a minimum draw. The borrower is usually required to make at least a minimum payment based on the amount owed. The minimum payment is based on some agreed on amortization period. Home equity loans are used for a variety of purposes including home improvements, new cars, vacations, college education, and so on.

Historically, lenders would not approve second mortgages where the combined loan-to-value ratio exceeded 80 percent of the house value. Over time lenders have relaxed these restrictions and today a homeowner may be able to borrow up to 125 percent of the value of the home. Other changes that have occurred are the number and type of home equity loans and a relaxing of credit standards. Loans that were previously available only to borrowers with excellent credit are now accessible to borrowers with less than perfect credit records, albeit with interest rate pricing differences.

The interest rate charged on a home equity loan is based primarily on the total loan-to-value ratio and loan size. The interest rate is usually variable, based on the prime rate and may have a maximum (and minimum) cap. Some loans have minimum payments that are interest-only, whereas others have minimum payments that include amortization. Some lenders offer teaser rates for some initial time period, usually 3 to 6 months. Also, some lenders offer to pay the closing costs associated with the home equity loan. This offer may be tied to the interest rate charged or to a minimum draw of funds at closing.

ALTERNATIVE MORTGAGE INSTRUMENTS AND THE TAX DEDUCIBILITY OF INTEREST PAYMENTS

The relative attractiveness to both lenders and borrowers of AMIs is especially affected by the tax treatment of the interest deduction on these loans. The amount and timing of the deduction depend on the type of mortgage instrument, whether a standard loan or an AMI. With a standard loan all interest payments are taxed as income to the lender and deductions by the borrower. With some AMIs this symmetry may not hold because borrowers, being cash-basis taxpayers, may not fully use interest deductions, while lenders, being accrual-basis taxpayers, must include all interest charges in income.

As an example, consider the GPM. In the initial years the interest expense will be greater than the payment, leading to negative amortization. The borrower cannot deduct the excess of the interest charge over the amount of the payment. The deduction is deferred until positive amortization begins.[15] Thus, although the initial payments are less on a GPM, so are the interest deductions. The lender, on the other hand, must include all of the interest charge in income even though the cash inflow is less.

Negative amortization also characterizes the PLAM. The adjustment for inflation is considered a finance charge, but since it is added to the loan balance and is not a cash payment, the borrower cannot make a deduction for tax purposes. As with the GPM, the lender must include all of the interest charge, including the adjustment for inflation, in interest income.

Under the SAM the lender offers a low rate of interest in exchange for a share of the appreciation in the property. For a very low initial rate, the share of the appreciation will be large. The initial payments on the SAM will provide for few tax benefits. The shared appreciation portion of the interest charge is deductible, but only when paid and for owner-occupied properties.[16] There will be a large deduction when the property is either sold or appraised. If the borrower finances the share of the appreciation (interest) from the same lender, the tax deduction will be disallowed. In this case, it will have to be amortized over the life of the new loan.[17] For SAM loans the interest deduction can be large, late, and in some cases, not fully used. From the standpoint of the lender, the SAM loan is not so onerous. Interest income is reported only to the extent of actual cash payments. As the property appreciates, the lender is obtaining a rate of return but does not have to make any tax payments until the property is sold or appraised. This is similar to the increase in value of a capital asset. The increase in value is not taxed until the asset is sold.

The tax treatment of AMIs might create some sort of clientele effect since some AMIs actually may be advantageous for some types of borrowers. Young borrowers in a low tax bracket may have insufficient itemizations to take advantage of tax deductions. GPMs and PLAMs may be well suited for these types of borrowers. The deferred tax deductions allow these borrowers to "store up" tax benefits until a time when they are more valuable.

In summary, the tax treatment of AMIs will distort the amount and timing of their after-tax payments. The value of each can be determined by discounting the after-tax cash flows by the after-tax discount rate. Because of the asymmetry of the tax treatment of interest expense for the borrower and interest revenue for the lender, the relative values of AMIs may diverge. It is likely that the tax treatment of negatively amortizing loans has added to their costs and their relative obscurity in the marketplace.

Alternative mortgage instruments emerged partially as a result of interest rate risk faced by lenders. One consequence of interest rate risk was that as rates rose, borrowers had an incentive to retain their loans and not pay them off. However, as rates fell, borrowers, facing no prepayment penalty, had an incentive to refinance at the lower rate. We now take up the economics of refinancing from the standpoint of the borrower.

MORTGAGE REFINANCING

The menu of AMIs also must be considered by the mortgage borrower in a mortgage refinancing decision. Although there may be no plans to sell the property to which the mortgage is attached, the borrower may have an incentive to trade an existing mortgage for a new one. For example, in periods of declining mortgage rates, homeowners often will refinance to a lower rate to take advantage of the resulting payment savings. Another borrower may refinance and borrow more than the amount currently owed to take out equity (maybe to send a child to college). An owner of an income-producing property may refinance to improve cash flow by lowering financing costs. A clear example is the "rush to refinance" that occurred in 1993 when mortgage rates were at their lowest point in two decades. Some borrowers refinanced their mortgages from fixed rate to fixed rate, fixed rate to adjustable rate or vice versa, adjustable to adjustable, or some other alternative.

The refinancing decision can be viewed as a net present value decision. If refinancing were a frictionless (i.e., costless) transaction, borrowers would refinance with any decrease in the interest rate. Since it is not costless, however, borrowers will refinance when they are confident that the benefits will outweigh the costs. A paper by Dickinson and Heuson shows that the refinancing decision is quite complicated with a number of factors being considered. These include interest rate movements, transactions costs, changes in borrower income and house value, personal financial opportunities, and the prepayment option embedded in the mortgage.[18] Yang and Maris show that information asymmetry makes it more difficult for the lender to price the refinancing.[19] An example of information asymmetry is the fact that the borrower may have more information about how long he or she will hold the mortgage than does the lender.

REFINANCING OWNER OCCUPIED RESIDENTIAL PROPERTY

To make an effective refinancing decision, one must compare the terms on the existing mortgage with those on the new financing. Recall that the general terms of the mortgage will be the amount owed, the contract interest rate, the maturity, discount points, and so on. In deciding whether to refinance, one compares the cost of refinancing to the benefits. The costs of refinancing would include the costs of getting out of the existing mortgage (maybe a prepayment penalty) plus the costs of acquiring the new mortgage (origination fee, discount points, etc.). The present value of this total cost is compared to the present value of the payment savings. If the benefit outweighs the cost, the borrower would refinance.

In making the refinancing decision, there are some factors that are known to the borrower related to the existing mortgage contract. These include the borrower's current contract rate, current payment, current remaining term, and the current outstanding balance. In structuring the refinancing, the borrower must make several assumptions. These include: (1) what will be the amount of the new loan (for example, the payoff of the existing loan, the payoff plus financing costs on the new loan, the payoff plus financing costs of new loan plus some equity extraction)? (2) What will be the term of the new loan (for example, equal to the remaining term of the existing loan, longer than the remaining term of the existing loan, or shorter than the remaining term of the existing loan)? (3) What will be the holding period of the financing (equal to or shorter than the term of the mortgage)?

Refinancing for the Remaining Term. For example, suppose that a borrower took a 30-year, fixed-rate mortgage for $100,000 at a 10 percent contract rate, monthly payments. This loan has a prepayment penalty of 3 percent of the outstanding balance if repaid within the first 8 years of life. After 5 years the contract rate on 25-year, fixed-rate mortgages is 7.5 percent. The attraction of the lower rate would cause the borrower to consider refinancing. A quick analysis shows the borrower's current position:

$$\text{Current payment} = \$877.57$$
$$\text{Payoff of existing loan} = \text{Outstanding balance} + \text{Prepayment penalty}$$
$$= \$96,574 + 2,897$$
$$= \$99,471$$

Obtaining a new 25-year, fixed-rate mortgage will cost the borrower 4 percent in financing costs. This includes a 1-point origination fee, 2 discount points, and 1 percent other costs (an appraisal, survey, etc.). Thus, the financing costs on the new loan are $3,979 ($99,471 × 0.04). This is a total cost of $6,876.

Refinancing the payoff for 25 years at the lower 7.50 percent rate results in a payment of $735.08. By refinancing the borrower has a monthly payment savings of $142.49. Since the refinancing decision is essentially an investment decision, all values would be set to present value terms using the borrower's opportunity cost of capital of 7.50 percent. Assuming that the borrower plans to hold the mortgage for its full term, the present value of the payment savings is $19,282. Comparing this with the financing cost of $3,979 produces a positive net present value of $15,303. Thus, the borrower would refinance. This calculation can be shown as:

$$\text{NPV} = \$142.49 \ (\text{PVAIF}_{7.5/12,300}) - \$3,979 = \$19,281 - \$3,979 = \$15,302$$

Refinancing for a Longer Term. The earlier calculation assumes that the borrower refinances for a term equal to the remaining term of the existing loan. But suppose the borrower refinances with a new loan of traditional maturity, that is, 30 years. For simplicity, assume that the new contract rate is still 7.50 percent. The borrower still has the same payoff of the existing loan and has financing costs on the new loan of $3,979. The borrower's new monthly payment is now $695.52 ($99,471 at 7.5 percent for 30 years). Assuming that the borrower plans to hold the new mortgage for the full term, the net present value of refinancing for the borrower is now:

$$\text{NPV} = \$182.05 \ (\text{PVAIF}_{7.5/12,300}) - \$695.52(\text{PVAIF}_{7.5/12,60}) \ (\text{PVI F}_{7.5/12,300}) - \$3,979$$
$$= \$24,635 - \$5,354 - \$3,979 = \$15,302$$

Refinancing for a Shorter Term. On the other hand, suppose that the borrower wants to refinance to a 15-year mortgage. Again, assume that the contract rate on the new loan is 7.50 percent. The payment on the new loan is $922.11, which is $44.54 more than the payment on the existing loan. However, the benefit is that the borrower is relieved of the payments on the existing loan. Assuming the borrower holds the new loan for the full 15 years, the net present value is now:

$$\text{NPV} = -\$44.54 \ (\text{PVAIF}_{7.5/12,180}) + \$877.57 \ (\text{PVAIF}_{7.5/12,}) \ (\text{PVIF}_{7.}) - \$3,979$$
$$= -\$4,805 + \$24,086 - \$3,979$$
$$= \$15,302$$

Financing the Financing Costs. Loan amortization and property value appreciation may allow the borrower to finance the financing costs into the new loan. This means that the borrower has no out-of-pocket expense for the new loan. The amount the borrower needs is equal to the payoff of the existing loan plus the financing costs of the new loan, which totals $103,616 ($99,471 + $4,145). At 7.50 percent over 25 years, the new payment is $765.71. The borrower has no outlay up front and has a monthly savings of $111.86. The present value of this savings at a 7.50 percent opportunity cost is $15,136.

Financing the Financing Costs and Extending the Term. The borrower may finance the financing costs into a traditional 30-year mortgage. In this case, the monthly payment is $724.50 ($103,616 at 7.5 percent for 30 years). Now the borrower has no up-front outlay and has a savings of $153.07 for 25 years. However, the borrower also has to make the payment on the new loan for the last 5 years. The net present value is now:

$$\text{NPV} = \$153.07 \ (\text{PVAIF}_{7.5/12,300}) - \$724.50 \ (\text{PVAIF}_{7.5/12,60}) \ (\text{PVIF}_{7.5/12,300})$$
$$= \$20,713 - \$5,577$$
$$= \$15,136$$

Shortening the Holding Period. An important consideration is the length of time the borrower plans to hold the mortgage. The previous calculations assume that the borrower plans to hold the financing (whether new or existing) for its entire term. The analysis would be revised somewhat if the borrower has a planned holding period of less than the maturity of the debt. Let's first look at our original refinancing scenario. Suppose that, when considering refinancing, the borrower knows that the mortgage will be held for 8 more years. Thus if no refinancing takes place, the existing loan will be 13 years old (out of its 30-year life) when it is repaid. If refinancing takes place, the new loan will be 8 years old (out of its 25-year life) when it is repaid. Note that at that future point in time, both mortgages will have the same remaining term (17 years).

This becomes an important consideration since the outstanding balances of the two loans will not be equal at that time. Other things constant, the lower the contract rate, the faster a loan will amortize.[20] In this case the refinanced loan will have a lower balance at that time than the existing loan. This is viewed as a savings to the borrower and would be considered a cash inflow. After the additional 8 years, the outstanding balance on the existing mortgage if refinancing did not take place would be $85,934. With refinancing, the balance on the new loan would be $84,618. Note that the prepayment penalty on the existing loan has expired. This produces a savings at that time of $1,316. The net present value equation now would be

$$\text{NPV} = \$142.49 \ (\text{PVAIF}_{7.5/12,96}) + \$1,316 \ (\text{PVIF}_{7.5/12,96}) - \$3,979$$
$$= \$10,263 + \$724 - \$3,979$$
$$= \$10,987 - \$3,979$$
$$= \$7,008$$

The net present value is positive and the borrower would refinance.

Taking Out Equity. Suppose the borrower wants to take some equity out of the property. Maybe the borrower needs $30,000 for remodeling. If the borrower wants no up-front expenses, this means borrowing $134,866 ($99,471 + $5,395 + $30,000). The payment at 7.50 percent for 25 years is $996.65. Thus the borrower's new payment is $119.08 more than the current payment of $877.57. However, the borrower receives $30,000 cash at the time of refinancing. The NPV is:

$$\text{NPV} = -\$119.08 \ (\text{PVAIF}_{7.5/12,300}) + \$30,000$$
$$= -\$16,114 + \$30,000$$
$$= \$13,886$$

Summary

Table 6-11 summarizes the advantages and disadvantages of various AMI loans. Default risk is considered from the standpoint of both the provision for negative amortization and for increases in the payment-to-income ratio. The GPM and the PLAM have the greatest risk of default through negative amortization, while the ARM and FLIP loans join these two in terms of the likelihood that the payment-to-income ratio can increase. The standard, fixed-rate loan and the SAM are the only loans for which the payment cannot increase. In terms of interest rate risk, the ARM is superior to all other loans. Although both the GPM and the PLAM have provisions for negative amortization, the PLAM compensates for changes in the rate of inflation. Thus, the risk is less with the PLAM than with the GPM, which has a rather long duration.

Loans that do not allow the borrower to deduct all of the interest charges when they occur (GPM, PLAM) are inferior to those that do. ARMs have a moderate level of complexity because of the various cap, margin, and index choices. The GPM is the only AMI for which the payment schedule is predetermined at origination and is, therefore, not complex. When interest rates are high, the GPM, PLAM, and SAM lower the initial payments and solve the tilt problem. The FLIP constructs a graduated-payment schedule through an arrangement that raises the total finance charges to the borrower.

TABLE 6-11

Characteristics of Various Mortgages

	SFR	ARM	GPM	PLAM	SAM	FLIP
Default risk from neg. amortization	Moderate	Moderate	Large	Large	Little	Moderate
Default risk from payment/ income ratio	Moderate	Large	Large	Large	Little	Large
Interest and rate risk	Moderate	None	Substantial	Little	Little	Little
Tax savings	Standard	Standard	Poor	Poor	Standard	Standard
Level of complexity	Low	Moderate	Low	High	Moderate	Moderate
Affordability at higher interest rates	Poor	Moderate	Good	Excellent	Excellent	Moderate

Source: © 2014 OnCourse Learning

Those loans that rank highest in overall characteristics are the FRM and the ARM. This would explain their dominance in the mortgage market. This is true whether a borrower is seeking funds to purchase a real property or to refinance a property currently owned. Refinancing can be viewed essentially as a present value analysis. If the present value of the future payment savings exceeds the cost of the refinancing, it may make economic sense to refinance the loan.

Key Terms

11th District Cost of Funds Index	Life-of-loan rate cap
Adjustable-rate mortgage (ARM)	London Interbank Offered Rate (LIBOR)
Adjustment rate cap	Margin
Convertible	Negative amortization
Constant Maturity Treasury (CMT) Indexes	Periodic Adjustment Rate Cap
(Cost of Funds Index, COFI)	Pledged-account mortgage
Dual Index Mortgage (DIM)	Price level adjusted mortgage (PLAM)
Flexible loan insurance program (FLIP)	Rate cap
Frequency of rate change	Refinancing
Fully indexed rate	Reverse Mortgage
Graduated-payment mortgage (GPM)	Shared appreciation mortgage (SAM)
Historical replication	Simulation model
Index	Teaser rate
Initial-period discount	Tilt effect
Interest rate caps	

Review Questions

6-1.   Name two AMIs that solve the maturity mismatch problem of thrifts and explain how they do so.

6-2.   Identify seven common terms that characterize an ARM.

6-3.   What is meant by "pricing" ARM terms?

6-4.   How would a lender change the margin on an ARM (increase or decrease) in response to (a) imposing a 1 percent rate cap on a previously uncapped ARM, (b) granting an initial period discount, and (c) removing a life-of-loan cap? Explain each of your answers.

6-5.   What factors affect the share of newly originated mortgages that are ARMs?

6-6.   What are the major shortcomings of the graduated-payment mortgage?

6-7.   Explain how the price level adjusted mortgage compensates the lender for both the real rate of return and the rate of inflation.

6-8.   What are the major shortcomings of the price level adjusted mortgage?

6-9.   How is the amount of the share of property appreciation given to the lender for a SAM loan determined?

6-10.   From the borrower's perspective, what is the major drawback of the pledged account mortgage, or FLIP?

6-11. Why are GPMs and PLAMs poor AMIs from the standpoint of income tax regulations?

Problems

6-1. Given the following data, determine the first monthly payment for the following types of mortgages listed in a, b, c, and d.

Market rate	5%
Real rate	2%
Mortgage amount	$100,000
Maturity	30 years

a. Standard, fixed-rate mortgage
b. Price level adjusted mortgage
c. ARM, special first year rate 8 percent

6-2. Determine the first payment in the second year of the 1-year adjustable ARMs shown in the following table (mortgage amount at origination, $100,000; maturity, 30 years):

ARM	CONTRACT RATE	TEASER RATE	RATE CAP	MARGIN	YEAR 1 INDEX	YEAR 2 INDEX
A	6%	4%	1%	100	3%	4%
B	6	4	2	200	3	5
C	7	4	2	300	3	6

6-3. Suppose you are considering an ARM with the following characteristics:

Mortgage amount	$100,000
Index	1-year Treasury bill yield
Margin	2.50
Maximum annual adjustment	2%
Lifetime interest cap	6%
Discount points	2.00
Loan maturity	30 years

a. If the Treasury Bill yield is currently 3 percent, what is the monthly payment for the first year? (Assume the loan is fully indexed at the outset.)
b. If the index moves to 4.5 percent at the end of the first year, what is the monthly payment for the second year?
c. If the loan is paid off at the end of the second year, what is the effective cost (yield)?

6-4. Consider a PLAM with the following features:

Mortgage amount	$90,000
Mortgage term	30 years
Current real rate	3%
Inflation for the next 3 years respectively	2%, 3%, 5%
Mortgage payments adjusted annually	

a. What are the monthly payments for each of the first 3 years?

b. What is the effective cost if the loan is repaid at the end of the third year?

c. What is the effective cost if the loan is repaid at the end of the third year and the lender charges 2 discount points up front?

6-5.   Compare the following mortgages and determine which has the lower cost:

	FRM	ARM
Mortgage amount	$100,000	$100,000
Term	30 years	30 years
Discount points	2.00	3.25
Initial contract interest rate	5%	3%
Margin	. . .	2.75
Caps	. . .	2% annual, 6% lifetime
Index values	. . .	
EOY1	4%	
EOY2	5.5%	
Prepayment	End of year 3	End of year 3

6-6.   Determine the share of appreciation the lender should receive on the following SAM loan:

Loan-to-value ratio	90%
Market rate	12%
Rate on loan	10%
Lender's tax bracket	30%

6-7.   A widow wishes to take out a reverse annuity mortgage on her house. What annual payment can she get if she decides on a $100,000 debt at the end of 10 years, the current rate is 9 percent, and she wants to take a $10,000 advance?

6-8.   Five years ago a borrower incurred a mortgage for $80,000 at 10 percent for 30 years, monthly payments. Currently the market rate is 8 percent on 25-year mortgages. The existing mortgage has a prepayment penalty of 5 percent of the outstanding balance at prepayment for the first 10 years of the mortgage and the lender will charge 4 percent financing cost on a new loan. The borrower's opportunity investment rate is 8 percent. The borrower is considering refinancing the payoff of the loan (remaining balance + prepayment penalty).

a. If the borrower plans to hold either mortgage (the existing mortgage or the new mortgage) for the next 25 years, should he or she refinance?

b. If the borrower plans to hold the mortgage financing for 8 more years, should he or she refinance under the conditions in part a?

c. Assume everything in part a except that, instead of refinancing the outstanding balance, the borrower borrows $100,000. Should he or she refinance?

d. Suppose the financing costs of the new loan will be included in the loan amount and the new loan amortization will be 30 years. Should he or she refinance?

Notes

1. In today's mortgage market, lenders commonly offer the 15-year, fixed-rate mortgage as an alternative to the standard 30-year, fixed-rate loan. The shorter term loan, by nature, will repay faster, which can be an advantage to the mortgage lender in periods of slow prepayment (such as when interest rates are rising). The borrower would have to weigh the advantages of the shorter-term loan (such as faster equity buildup) against the disadvantages (such as a higher monthly payment). For an analysis of choosing between 15- and 30-year mortgages, see Richard A. Phillips, Eric Rosenblatt, and James H. Vanderhoff. The effect of relative pricing on the fixed-rate mortgage term decision. *Journal of Real Estate Research* 7 (Spring 1992), 187–194.

2. For an example of the research on teaser rates on ARMs, see Joel F. Houston, J. Sa-Aadu, and James D. Shilling. Teaser rates in conventional adjustable-rate mortgage (ARM) markets. *Journal of Real Estate Finance and Economics* 4 (March1991), 19–32. See also R. Green and J. Shilling. Do teaser rates on adjustable-rate mortgages make owner-occupied housing more affordable? *Journal of Housing Economics* 3 (December 1994), 263–282.

3. J. Sa-Aadu and J.D. Shilling. Tests of borrower perceptions in the adjustable-rate mortgage market: Do borrowers view ARM contracts as distinct? *Journal of Urban Economics* 36 (1994), 8–22.

4. B. Elledge, S. Fletcher, and G. Norris. Fumbles, oversights, and omissions: Bank ARM calculations. *Real Estate Review* 25 (Fall 1995), 48–54.

5. A paper by Scott, Houston, and Do shows that actually a hybrid PLAM that permits inflation-risk sharing and also accommodates a wide range of amortization-graduation schemes for loan repayment may be the optimal mortgage. See William H. Scott, Jr., Arthur L. Houston, Jr., and A. Quang Do. Inflation risk, payment tilt, and the design of partially indexed affordable mortgages. *Journal of the American Real Estate and Urban Economics Association* 21 (Spring 1993), 1–26.

6. J. Huston McCulloch. Risk characteristics and underwriting standards for price level adjusted mortgages versus other mortgage instruments. *Housing Finance Review* 5(Fall 1986), 65–97.

7. Joyce Manchester. Evidence of possible default under three mortgage contracts. *Housing Finance Review* 4 (January 1985), 517–536.

8. James Pesando and Stuart Turnbull. The timepath of homeowner's equity under different mortgage instruments: A simulation study. *House Finance Review* 4 (January 1985), 483–504.

9. Ann Dougherty, Robert Van Order, and Kevin Villani. Pricing shared appreciation mortgages. *Housing Finance Review* 1 (October 1982), 361–375.

10. Christopher J. Mayer and Katerina Simons. Reverse mortgages and the liquidity of housing wealth. *Journal of the American Real Estate and Urban Economics Association* 22 (Summer 1994), 235–255.

11. Peter VanderHart. An empirical analysis of the housing decisions of older homeowners. *Journal of the American Real Estate and Urban Economics Association* 22 (Summer 1994), 205–233.

12. Thomas P. Boehm and Michael C. Ehrhardt. Reverse mortgages and interest rate risk. *Journal of the American Real Estate and Urban Economics Association* 22 (Summer1994), 387–408.

13. Linda Klein and C.F. Sirmans. Reverse mortgages and prepayment risk. *Journal of the American Real Estate and Urban Economics Association* 22 (Summer 1994), 409–431.

14. Thomas J. Miceli and C.F. Sirmans. Reverse mortgages and borrower maintenance risk. *Journal of the American Real Estate and Urban Economics Association* 22 (Summer 1994), 433–450.

15. Revenue Ruling 77–135.

16. Revenue Ruling 51–83.

17. Revenue Ruling 70–647.

18. Amy Dickinson and Andrea J. Heuson. Explaining refinancing decisions using microdata. *Journal of the American Real Estate and Urban Economics Association* 21 (Fall 1993), 293–311.

19. T.L. Tyler Yang and Brian Maris. Mortgage refinancing with asymmetric information. *Journal of the American Real Estate and Urban Economics Association* 21 (Winter1993), 491–510.

20. This means that given two loans with everything equal except the contract rates, the loan with the lower contract rate will amortize faster and will have a lower outstanding balance at any point in time between inception and maturity. Only at the beginning and the end (when the balance is zero) will the balances on the loans be equal.

Web Sites

http://www.federalreserve.gov
Board of Governors of the Federal Reserve System. Provides various interest rate data

http://www.coldwellbanker.com
Provides tips on buying and financing a home. Online mortgage calculations are also available

http://www.countrywide.com
Provides online applications for mortgages, loan information and services, and information for real estate professionals

http://www.aarp.org/revmort/
Provides information on reverse mortgages

http://www.reversemortgage.org
Provides information on reverse mortgages

http://www.mtgprofessor.com
Provides answers to questions typically asked about mortgages

http://www.dinkytown.net
ARM calculator

http://www.hud.gov/buying/rvrsmort.cfm
Reverse mortgages for seniors

APPENDIX 6-A

Computing Initial Payment on a GPM Loan

To compute the first payment on a GPM loan, consider that the present value of the loan equals:

$$\text{Year 1}\left[\text{PMT}_1 \sum_{t=1}^{12} \frac{1}{\left(1+\dfrac{i}{12}\right)^t}\right]$$

$$\text{Year 2}\left[\text{PMT}_1(1+g)^1 \sum_{t=1}^{12} \frac{1}{\left(1+\dfrac{i}{12}\right)^t} \cdot \frac{1}{\left(1+\dfrac{i}{12}\right)^{12}}\right]$$

$$\text{Year 3} + \left[\text{PMT}_1(1+g)^1 \sum_{t=1}^{12} \frac{1}{\left(1+\dfrac{i}{12}\right)^t} \cdot \frac{1}{\left(1+\dfrac{i}{12}\right)^{24}}\right]$$

$$\vdots \qquad \vdots$$

$$\text{Year 6} - 30 + \left[\text{PMT}_1(1+g)^5 \sum_{t=1}^{300} \frac{1}{\left(1+\dfrac{i}{12}\right)^t} \cdot \frac{1}{\left(1+\dfrac{i}{12}\right)^{60}}\right]$$

where i is the contract rate, PMT_1 is the monthly payment for the first year, and g is the growth rate of payment. The solution to the equation involves finding the present value of annuities. Each year's series of payments is an annuity for 12 months. They each have a present value as of the first of the year in which they occur. In turn, each of these values has a present value. It works as follows:

- The PVIFA_1 for the first year payments is equivalent to their present value. The PVIFA_2 for the second year payments is equivalent to their present value as of the beginning of the second year. PV_2 is the present value, as of the loan origination, of PVIFA_2, and so forth. As an example, assume a loan for $100,000 at 12 percent with a 7.5 percent graduation in payments through the first 6 years. The following table computes the present value factors:

YEAR	PAYMENT	GRADUATED PAYMENT FACTOR	PVIFA	PVIA	FACTORS
1	PMT_1	1	11.255[a]	1	11.255
2	$\text{PMT}_1 (1.075)$	1.0	11.255	0.8874[b]	10.737
3	$\text{PMT}_1(1.075)^2$	1.1556	11.255	0.7876[b]	10.243
4	$\text{PMT}_1(1.075)^3$	1.2423	11.255	0.6989	9.772
5	$\text{PMT}_1(1.075)^4$	1.3355	11.255	0.6203	9.323
6–30	$\text{PMT}_1(1.075)^5$	1.4356	94.946[c]	0.5504	75.031
TOTAL					126.361

[a]*Present value interest factor of an annuity for 12 periods at 1 percent.*
[b]*Present value of future sum discounted at 12 percent.*
[c]*Present value interest factor of an annuity for 300 periods at 1 percent.*

$PMT_1 \times 126.36 = \$100,000.$ Therefore, $PMT_1 = \$100,000/126.36 = \$791.39.$

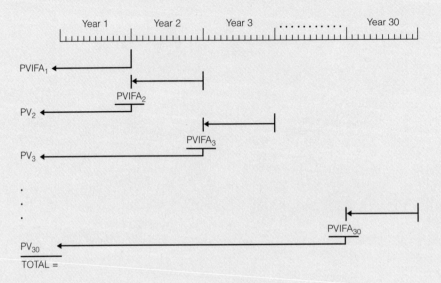

FEDERAL REGULATION OF FINANCIAL INSTITUTIONS RELATED TO THE MORTGAGE MARKET

LEARNING OBJECTIVES

After reading this chapter, you should understand how the federal government regulates mortgage lenders. You will know the regulatory responsibilities of the various government agencies involved in this regulation. The agencies enforce regulations established by law or within the authorization of the agencies themselves. You will understand which agencies are responsible for which institutions, activities, and markets. You will understand the basis for their authority in regulating the mortgage market. You should understand that there are many regulations pertaining to financial institutions and markets that are not related to mortgage lending. These aspects of regulation will not be covered in this chapter. Finally, you should understand the concept of systematic risk within the financial market.

INTRODUCTION

The federal government has vast regulatory oversight of the financial markets. The U.S. Congress has, over a long period of time, passed laws that establish regulatory agencies that have oversight over financial markets. Occasionally, the U.S. Congress will change the regulatory structure by adding or removing regulatory agencies and laws and restructuring the regulatory environment. Although the regulatory environment encompasses the entire financial market, this chapter focuses on those agencies and laws that have an impact on mortgage lending.

There are four components of financial regulation. One is safety and soundness. The safety and soundness of financial institutions has as its secondary goal a more stable and less risky economy. A second component is deposit insurance. An example would be the establishment of the **Federal Deposit Insurance Corporation (FDIC)** to insure the deposits at commercial banks (and now, savings and loan associations and mutual savings banks). The main purpose of deposit insurance is to prevent depositors from taking out their funds en masse or as in a "run on the bank." A widespread "run on the bank" could lead to economic recession or "panic" as money is removed from the economic system in large amounts. A third component is assurance of adequate capital for financial institutions. Capital, or equity, is basically, the net worth of a financial institution. Net worth, of course, is the value of the institution's assets less its liabilities. Adequate capital will help ensure that a particular or even a large number of institutions will not "fail." Lack of adequate capital will expose a financial institution to failure if, for example, its assets are risky (and therefore subject to a decline in market value) or its liabilities are extremely short term (and subject to higher interest payments to depositors when the liabilities mature). The fourth component is a more recent one and is related to systematic risk. Briefly **systematic risk** refers to those risks that will affect all financial institutions simultaneously. The risk is widespread in the economy and exposes all financial institutions, not just single institutions, to risk. A good example of systematic risk is the real estate "bubble" that "burst" in 2006–2007 and caused widespread financial problems to numerous financial institutions. Nonsystematic risk, on the other hand, affects only a single financial institution. An example would be the risk posed by incompetent management of the institution.

QUICK OVERVIEW OF SYSTEMATIC RISK

Systematic risk within the financial market exists when a large portion of the firms in the market face financial failure simultaneously. They face simultaneous financial risk because they are all affected by the same national economic conditions or are so interrelated, financially, with one another, that the failure of one or a few large firms will precipitate the failure of other firms. An example of an economic condition that is "systematic" is the widespread decline in housing values that, in turn, led to a significant decline in the value of mortgage-backed securities (MBSs) and derivatives in the secondary mortgage market.

Within the financial market, the debt obligations of one financial institution may represent the assets of another institution. This means that if the first institution fails and is unable to meet its debt obligations, the assets of the second institution are compromised and may suffer a decline in value. In turn, the second institution may be unable to meet its debt obligations that are the assets of a third institution. The process of a "domino" collapse can, therefore, pose risk to the entire financial system. Below we present a more in depth review of "systematic" financial risk.

WHAT DO FINANCIAL REGULATORS DO?

At present financial regulators related to the mortgage market perform the following tasks.

Regulate Types of Financial Institutions. If a financial firm chooses to become a depository institution (commercial bank, savings and loan association, credit union), then depending on other factors, they will be regulated by agencies concerned with that type of financial institution. The **Federal Reserve System** (also known as *the Fed*) and the FDIC generally regulate commercial banks with a federal charter. State chartered banks may or may not be regulated by the Fed but will fall under the regulation of the FDIC. **Government sponsored enterprises (GSEs)**, such as Freddie Mac and Fannie Mae, are regulated by the Federal Housing Finance Authority (FHFA).[1]

Regulate Types of Risk. Whether it is systematic or nonsystematic, regulators are concerned with the risk that financial institutions may fail. Even the failure of one or a few large financial institutions can cause a domino effect in which other institutions fail and thus the cascade of failures become systematic. The **Financial Stability Oversight Council (FSOC)** has the duty of preventing, as much as possible, systematic risk.

REGULATING THE INSTITUTIONS

The regulation of institutions engaged in mortgage lending has been somewhat simplified by the Wall Street Reform and Consumer Protection Act of 2009 otherwise known as the **Dodd-Frank Act**. This act eliminated some regulatory agencies that affected mortgage lending. Table 7-1 shows the current regulatory environment *only* for institutions involved in mortgage lending.

Much of this structure will be discussed later in this chapter and in future chapters.

REGULATING RISK

The Dodd-Frank Act designated the FSOC as the agency to assess the systematic risks of financial institutions. The Fed will, under the Act, serve as the regulator and the FDIC will have resolution authority for institutions designated as risky by the FSOC. Regulating systematic risk boils down to requiring adequate capital.

TABLE 7-1

Federal Financial Regulators Related to Mortgages (2012)

REGULATORY AGENCY	INSTITUTIONS REGULATED	REGUALTORY POWERS	OTHER AUTHORITY
Federal Reserve System	Bank holding companies and subsidiaries, savings and loan holding companies and subsidiaries, state banks that are members of the FRS, any firm designated as systematically significant by the FSOC	Lender of last resort (discount window), can shut down risky institutions with consent of 2/3 of FSOC	
Office of the Comptroller of the Currency	National banks and federally chartered thrifts		
Federal Deposit Insurance Corporation (FDIC)	Federally insured depository institutions and state banks and state chartered thrifts that are nonmembers of the FED	After determining threat of failure the FDIC may use insurance funds to assist institutions at risk and/or guarantee payment of deposits	
National Credit Union Administration (NCUA)	Federally chartered or insured credit unions	Liquidity lender to credit unions experiencing a liquidity problem	Operates the National Credit Union Share Insurance Fund (NCUSIF) similar to the FDIC
Federal Housing Finance Agency (FHFA)	Fannie Mae, Freddie Mac, Federal Home Loan Banks	Since 2008 acts as a conservator of Fannie Mae and Freddie Mac	
Bureau of Consumer Financial Protection	Nonbank mortgage-related firms (and other institutions not related to mortgages)		Writes rules authorized by the federal consumer financial protection laws.

Source: © 2014 OnCourse Learning

TABLE 7-2
Capital Standards for Federally Regulated Depository Institutions

AGENCY	CAPITAL STANDARDS
OCC	Minimum risk-based capital ratio of 8%. Asset values are risk-weighted. Highly rated institutions (Tier I) that have highly diversified assets and no undue interest rate risk exposure and are well managed may have a minimum ratio of 3%. For other institutions the minimum ratio may be 4%
FDIC	Same as the OCC
Federal Reserve System	Member banks must meet an 8% minimum capital ratio and 4% for Tier I capital
NCUA	Minimum ratio is 7% of risk-weighted assets

Source: © 2014 OnCourse Learning

Adequate capital (equity) will allow a financial institution to weather financial problems. Systematic risk can occur when one or a few large financial institutions are unable to meet the financial obligations of their debt. Consider that their debt is the asset of another financial institution and the "cascade" of financial failure becomes evident. Thus, if a sufficient number of firms have adequate capital the "cascade" of risk will not lead to widespread financial systematic risk.

The financial risk of a particular financial institution will be related, to a great extent, to the riskiness of its assets. Thus, sound capital adequacy guidelines would require institutions with more risky assets to have greater levels of capital (equity).

The Basel Accords. The **Basel Accords** is an international framework for adequate capital guidelines. The guidelines are promulgated under the guidance of the Bank for International Settlements. The guidelines link the risk of assets to the capital requirements. The guidelines are generally not mandated for U.S. institutions at this time. However, federal regulators use a version of the Basel Accords for the institutions they regulate but are generally mandated by provisions of the Dodd-Frank Act.

Included in the Dodd-Frank Act are provisions for stricter guidelines for "systematically significant firms", that is firms for which their financial failure is likely to affect the financial health of other firms. The Act requires capital standards on a "consolidated" basis for financial holding companies. It also requires the federal banking regulators to make the capital standards countercyclical, increasing in times of economic expansion and vise versa.

Table 7-2 shows the capital standards for federally related depository institutions. It should be noted that this table represents a summary only of the minimum capital requirements. A more detailed description can generally be found at the regulators' Web pages. In addition, the regulators conduct internal assessments of the regulated institutions under what is known as the **CAMELS system**. The **Federal Financial Institutions Examinations Council (FFIEC)** coordinates the CAMELS rating system. CAMELS in an acronym for *C*apital adequacy, *A*sset quality, *M*anagement, *E*arnings, *L*iquidity, and *S*ensitivity to market risk.

BANKING REGULATORS

Commercial banks have two different types of charters: federal (national banks) and state. Virtually all of these two types of banks are federally insured by the FDIC and would, therefore, fall under FDIC supervision. The primary regulator for federal banks is the **Office of the Comptroller of the Currency (OCC)**. The primary regulator for the state chartered banks is the Fed. The **National Credit Union Administration (NCUA)** that administers a deposit insurance program separate from that of the FDIC regulates credit unions. All of these regulators are concerned with the quality of the loans made by the regulated institutions, including, of course, both commercial and residential mortgage loans. There are several risks that are of concern. Default risk is the risk that the borrower will fail to meet interest and/or principal payments on the mortgages. Interest rate risk is also important because to one degree or another financial institutions will make mortgage loans with a long maturity and will accept deposits from customers with a short maturity. This maturity mismatch can cause problems if interest rates rise because the financial institutions will be required to pay higher rates as their short-term liabilities mature and roll over. Meanwhile, they will not be receiving higher interest rates on their long-term mortgage loans (their assets) because of their lengthy maturity. It is the maturity mismatch that contributed to widespread failure of savings and loans in the 1980s and early 1990s. Financial regulators will encourage the institutions to borrow longer-term (issue longer-term certificates of deposits, for example) and lend shorter-term (adjustable rate mortgages that adjust for the interest rate every year, for example). The maturity mismatch problem was discussed at length in Chapter 5. In short, financial regulators will consider expected default rates, prepayment rates, interest-rate exposure, and other risks when examining loans made by the regulated institutions. If the regulators find that a particular institution is exposed to excessive risk, they can order the institution to sell off risky loans and take other steps to correct a risky balance sheet. Since both commercial and residential mortgages involve default, interest rate, and prepayment risks the oversight of commercial bank lending practices has a great effect on the nation's mortgage market.

A CLOSER LOOK AT THE REGULATORS OF MORTGAGE LENDERS

Office of the Comptroller of the Currency

Established in 1863 as a part of the Department of the Treasury this regulator supervises federally chartered commercial banks. It was originally charged with replacing bank notes (issued by each bank) with a uniform national currency. The OCC enforces safety and soundness of nationally chartered banks. Failure to respond to OCC's concerns could result in a suspension of a bank's national charter. The OCC is also the primary regulator for federally chartered **thrift institutions**.[2]

In 2010 the OCC supervised 1,487 national banks (22 percent of all commercial banks) with assets of $8.5 trillion (71 percent of all commercial bank assets). Prior to 2011, thrifts were regulated by the Office of Thrift Supervision (OTS). OTS, established in 1989 as a result of the widespread failure of savings and loans, was eliminated and its duties were merged with the OCC in 2011. The OCC has a primary interest in the national mortgage market and issues a quarterly report, the OCC Mortgage Metrics report that provides standardized measure of mortgage loan performance serviced by national banks and thrifts. The OCC also issues the annual Survey of Credit Underwriting Practices. This report analyses the inherent credit risk of bank and thrift portfolios

The Code of Federal Regulations (CFR). Figure 7-1 can be used to ascertain the real estate–related regulations applicable to the OCC and other regulators. The code indicates that the OCC sets real estate lending and appraisal practices for national banks and federally chartered savings and loans. An interesting portion of the code indicates that banks regulated by the OCC can make real estate loans uninhibited by most state laws and regulations regarding: credit laws, loan-to-value ratios, due-on-sale clauses, escrow accounts, credit reports, and so forth.

FIGURE 7-1	Regulatory Structure Summary

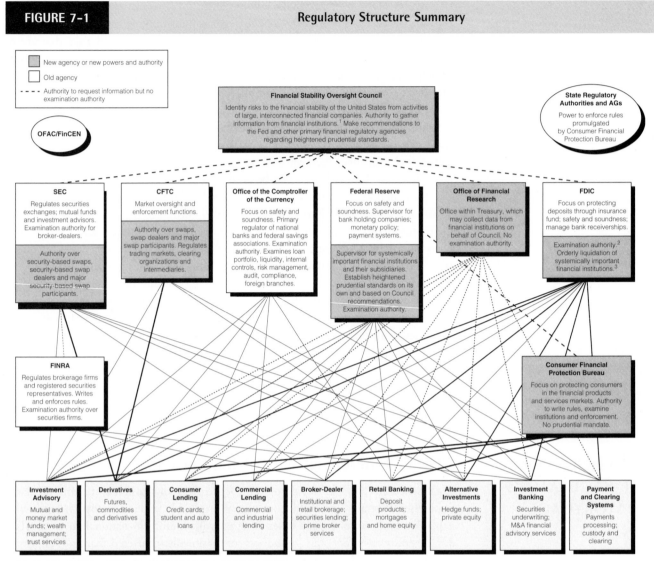

Note: Black lines from SEC and CFTC represent enhanced authority over existing relationships

Source: http://articles.businessinsider.com/2012-04-05/wall_street/31291695_1_systemically-dodd-regulations

Federal Deposit Insurance Corporation (FDIC)

Created in 1933 this regulator provides deposit insurance to lending institutions. As of June 2012, the FDIC insured 6,222 commercial banks and 1,024 thrifts. It manages the insurance fund, supervises financial institutions, and manages (in receivership) failed institutions. As a receiver of failed institutions, it liquidates the assets and/or arranges for mergers with financially sound institutions. Deposits are insured up to $250,000 (as of 2008, and indexed thereafter for inflation).[3] The FDIC is the primary regulator for state-chartered banks that are not members of the Fed and all state-chartered thrifts. The FDIC can also identify financial institutions that pose systematic risk (too big to fail) and impose more stringent capital requirements and require the institution to draw up plans for an orderly liquidation. In October 2008, the FDIC announced it would temporarily insure unsecured debt of banks, thrifts, and certain holding companies as well as business accounts regardless of dollar amounts. The Dodd-Frank Act made this expansion of insurance permanent.

The Federal Reserve System (Fed)

The Board of Governors of the Federal Reserve System (1913) are charged with providing stability to the banking sector through their management of bank reserves.[4] In addition, the Fed has authority to regulate the safety and soundness of member banks. The Fed is the primary regulator of bank and nonbank financial institutions that are deemed systemically significant by the FSOC. For such "too big to fail" firms, the Fed may require enhanced capital levels.

National Credit Union Administration (NCUA)

The NCUA was established by the Federal Credit Union Act of 1934. Since 1970 the NCUA regulates federal credit unions and the state credit unions that elect federal deposit insurance. As of June 2012, there were 6,961 member institutions representing 93,147,804 members. Similar to the FDIC, it administers the National Credit Union Share Insurance Fund to insure the deposits at member institutions. The NCUA has the authority to enact administrative orders regarding persons employed by credit unions. The three most common administrative orders are

1. order to cease and desist, which may include an order to make restitution;
2. order of prohibition, which prohibits a person from ever working for a federally insured financial institution; and
3. order assessing civil monetary penalties.

Credit unions have significant amounts of residential mortgages in their portfolios.

Federal Housing Finance Agency (FHFA)

The Housing and Economic Recovery Act of 2008 replaced the Office of Federal Housing Enterprise Oversight (OFHEO) and the Federal Housing Finance Board (FHFB). The OFHEO had been the primary oversight agency for Fannie Mae and Freddie Mac. During the housing "boom" of the 1990s and early 2000s (and for many years previously), these two GSEs issued vast amounts of debt and, with the proceeds, purchased a large amount of residential mortgages (and some mortgage derivative securities).[5] At the end of 2010, their combined debt and obligations exceed $6.7 trillion. The housing collapse that began in 2006 lead to record numbers of foreclosures and subsequent losses on mortgage investments by the two GSEs. The financial and "accounting" problems of the GSEs that accompanied the housing collapse are discussed in detail in Chapter 10.

As a result, the FHFA was given enhanced safety and soundness oversight over the GSEs. The FHFA can set capital standards and order the GSEs to cease activities considered financially unsound and divest themselves of risky assets. The FHFA can also replace management of the GSEs if they deem to exist unsound management practices.

Bureau of Consumer Financial Protection (BCFP)

The Dodd-Frank Act created the **Bureau of Consumer Financial Protection (BCFP)**. This agency is designed to create protection for consumer loans including residential mortgages. It is an independent agency within the Fed. It oversees consumer-related financial transactions including deposits, mortgages, credit cards, debt collection, real estate settlement procedures, and financial data processing. This agency is charged with enforcing consumer protection laws. Regulatory authority is different for institutions with less than and greater than $10 billion in assets.

Certain exempt entities are those that provide consumer debt incidental to the sale of a nonfinancial good or service such as automobiles, insurance, real estate (brokers), and depository institutions with less than $10 billion in assets. The BCFP also is a rule-making body under the Federal Credit Reporting Act (1970) as amended under the Consumer Credit Protection Act in June 1968. Many of its rules pertain to credit reporting agencies (for example, Fair Isaac Corporation, FICO). Since the BCFP, at this time, is in its initial rule-making stages, readers are encouraged to visit the BCFP Web site for ongoing rule-making changes.

Financial Stability Oversight Council (FSOC)

The FSOC is chaired by the Secretary of the Treasury. Other members consist of the heads of the Federal Reserve System, FDIC, OCC, NCUA, Securities and Exchange Commission, Commodities Futures Trading Corporation, FHFA, BCFP, and one member with insurance expertise. The FSOC is charged with identifying and ameliorating systematic risk (too big to fail). The FSOC coordinates information sharing among all of the financial regulators and identifies areas where lapses in regulation could expose the financial industry to systematic risk. The FSOC can, upon review of possible shortcomings in regulation, propose additional regulations to the U.S. Congress. That is, it cannot by itself enact additional regulations; it can only suggest such changes to Congress. The FSOC can approve decisions by the Federal Reserve to close firms that pose a significant systematic risk.

The FSOC operates under the Office of Financial Stability (OFS, established in October 2008) within the Office of the Treasury. The OFS was established by the Emergency Economic Stability Act of 2008 that also established the Troubled Asset Relief Program (TARP). The activities under the TARP program ceased in 2010, but the OFS continues to promote initiatives to aid homeowners facing foreclosure.

Federal Financial Institutions Examinations Council (FFIEC)

The FFIEC was established in 1979 pursuant to title X of the Financial Institutions Regulatory and Interest Rate Control Act to coordinate federal regulation of lending institutions. Because there are several regulators of commercial banks, savings and loan associations, and credit unions, the FFIEC is charged with making regulations uniform and harmonious. The FFIEC was also charged with coordinating regulation among the states; it established the State Liaison Committee composed of representatives of state supervisory agencies. The chair of this committee is a representative of the council. The council was given additional statutory responsibilities under the Housing and Community Development Act of 1980. Under these responsibilities, the council collects data required under the Home Mortgage Disclosure Act (HMDA) and makes them available to the public. FFIEC examiners evaluate lending institutions for risk, safety, and soundness.

Regulation of Mortgage and Derivative Securities

The "securitization" of the mortgage market has led to a significant role for the secondary mortgage market. Firms involved with the securitization of mortgages basically issue debt and, with the proceeds of the debt, purchase mortgages from depository institutions. The debt is backed up by the mortgages, and hence the term *securitization of mortgage debt*. The debt issued by the secondary market firms is generally referred to as MBSs. In addition, mortgage derivative securities (you will learn more about them in Chapter 11) such as interest-only and principal-only securities, inverse floaters, collateralized debt obligations (CDOs), and others are created in the secondary mortgage market. All of these mortgage-backed and derivative securities are traded daily in the secondary mortgage market. The task of clearing trades of MBSs and derivatives is performed by the Fixed Income Clearing Corporation (FICC) under the direction of the Chicago Mercantile Exchange Clearing House (CMECH). Within the FICC is the Mortgage-Backed Securities Division (MBSD). The MBSD provides automated trading, trade confirmation, risk management, and pool notification to the market. The U.S. Securities and Exchange Commission regulates the MBSD, as a unit of the CMECH.

REGULATION OF MORTGAGE LOAN ORIGINATORS: AN ANSWER TO A CLASSIC AGENCY PROBLEM

The housing crisis that began in 2006–2007 was due, in part, to "risky" or subprime residential loans that, in retrospect, should not have been made. The collapse of housing prices exposed many of these loans to default and foreclosure. Many "subprime" loans were originated for the purpose of resale to the secondary mortgage market. The relationship between mortgage originators and the secondary mortgage market was characterized by classic agency problems.[6] Mortgage originators, either at depository institutions, or as mortgage brokers receive compensation for originating loans that they sell off to the secondary mortgage market. As such, they have an incentive to originate as many loans as feasible, sometimes without regard to the safety of the loans. By paying a guarantee fee to secondary mortgage market entities such as Fannie Mae and Freddie Mac, some mortgage originators were able to sell off risky loans while reaping origination fees and yield spread premiums.

It was the agency problem and the loan origination activities of some **mortgage loan originators (MLOs)**[7] that provided the incentive for the Secure and Fair Enforcement for Mortgage Licensing Act of 2008 (S.A.F.E. Act). The S.A.F.E. Act established federal registration requirements for individuals who act as residential MLOs and is employed by a financial institution that is regulated by a federal regulator (agency-regulated institutions).[8] Under the S.A.F.E. Act, the regulating agencies developed rules that required all MLOs to register with the National Mortgage and Licensing System and Registry.[9] Upon registering an MLO is assigned a unique identifier, which consumers may use to access information about a particular MLO including name and any alias, employment history as well as disciplinary and criminal history. The identifier is also required to be placed on all loan documents submitted for loan purchase by Fannie Mae and Freddie Mac. The act was intended to provide nationwide uniform licensing standards for MLOs. The Dodd-Frank Act allowed for the transfer of regulations under the S.A.F.E. Act to the Consumer Finance Protection Board. Figure 7-1 presents a summary of the regulatory structure discussed in this chapter.

A Closer Look at Systematic Risk

The recent changes in the regulation and legislation related to financial institutions involved in mortgage lending have focused, in part, on what we have referred to as "systematic risk." In short, systematic risk refers to risk that affects a large portion of the financial system at the same time. In the late 2000s, there was widespread failure of large financial institutions including Bear Stearns, IndyMac Federal Bank, the **Federal National Mortgage Association (Fannie Mae)**, the **Federal Home Loan Mortgage Corporation (Freddie Mac)**, Lehman Brothers, American International Group (AIG), and Citigroup. It should be noted that these financial institutions were involved in the mortgage market but not as traditional depository institutions. By traditional **depository institutions**, we mean commercial banks, savings and loan associations, mutual savings banks, and credit unions. The failed institutions noted above were, primarily, "**investment bankers**," institutions that traded in mortgages and mortgage derivative securities among themselves. The failures of one or a few of these firms would cause failures of others. To see this, consider a financial institution that purchases mortgages from depository institutions or mortgage brokers (originators of the mortgages to homeowners). They will purchase the mortgages with money raised by issuing bonds called residential mortgage-backed securities (RMBSs). The bond buyers are promised interest and principal payments from proceeds of the interest and principal payments on the mortgages by the homeowners. But the process does not stop there. The bond buyers will often purchase the bonds with money raised by issuing their own debt, generally called **collateralized debt obligations(CDOs)**. These CDOs will have various "tranches" or classes that promise payments in a structured order. That is, the lower rated tranches will absorb all losses from defaults first, and if exhausted (worthless), the next tranche up will begin to absorb default losses, and so forth. The lower tranches often consisted of subprime loans.[10] The **rating agencies** (Standard & Poor's, Moody's, Finch) would give higher ratings to the tranches that would absorb losses later and lower ratings to the tranches absorbing losses sooner. But, it does not stop here. CDO buyers would raise the required funds from issuing additional CDOs called CDO-squared. Sometimes, they would create the CDOs squared from the lower tranches of the CDOs. Thus, the CDO-squared would, in reality, consist of tranches that would all absorb default losses first.

In addition, investors who were aware that many of the CDOs and CDO-squared consisted of subprime loans would "bet" against them. They would do so by purchasing insurance from a large financial institution (such as AIG) that would pay off if there was a decline in the value of the mortgage derivative.[11]

The large increase in the volume of subprime loans (from 9 percent of new mortgage originations in 2001 to 40 percent in 2006) meant that an increasing number were finding their way into the secondary mortgage market and the mortgage derivative securities. The large increase in subprime loans resulted in large-scale agency problems. Originators of the subprime mortgages had an incentive to sell them off to the secondary mortgage market, passing on the risk to investors in RMBSs. As long as house prices were increasing, even the RMBSs backed by subprime loans would be viewed as relatively riskless. This is because if a homeowner was, for some reason, unable to meet his or her payment obligations the worst-case scenario would involve a foreclosure where the proceeds would exceed the mortgage debt obligation.

Now, how does systematic risk arise? When house prices began a free fall in 2007, it became evident that many of the mortgage-backed bonds and derivatives were in danger of a decline in value or becoming worthless. Now, consider that the debt obligation of one large financial institution is the asset of another. And the asset of that financial institution backs up its debt that is an asset of a third institution. Failure of the debt obligation on one institution endangers the assets of another and so forth in a cascading effect. This process of cascading failure can be slowed or halted altogether if financial institutions have sufficient equity capital. The losses on their assets are absorbed by a reduction in the value of their equity capital (stockholders) and not in the value of another firm's assets. However, in an effort of increase their return on capital many financial institutions became highly leveraged.

That is, their debt-to-equity ratios were very high. Prior to the financial collapse many investment bankers had debt-to-equity ratios of 25 to 1.[12] Furthermore, when failing, the financial institutions found it difficult to raise additional capital because stockholders are reluctant to invest in failing firms.

Summary

The financial crisis precipitated by the crisis in the (subprime) mortgage market beginning in 2007 led to a fundamental restructuring of the regulation of financial institutions. The crisis can be briefly explained as follows. First, the agency problem in the market encouraged lenders (and mortgage brokers) to originate and sell off subprime mortgages to the secondary mortgage market. Next, financial institutions packaged the subprime loans into RMBSs, CDOs, and other derivative securities. Third, the major rating agencies rated many of these securities at levels not warranted by the riskiness of the subprime loans. Major financial institutions invested in the MBSs. In addition, some investors "bet" against the MBSs by insuring them against a decline in value. They did so by buying credit default swaps (CDSs) from such insurance firms such as AIG. Furthermore, the debt obligations were the assets of other financial institutions, creating substantial systematic risk. The "house of cards" so to speak, was set up by the view that house prices would not decline so that even subprime mortgages would be safe investments.

Once house prices began to collapse in 2007, the "house of cards" began to collapse leading to the widespread failure of financial institutions and the bail out by the federal government of institutions viewed as "to big to fail."

In response to the financial crisis, the federal government passed legislation, primarily the Dodd-Frank Act, aimed at preventing a reoccurrence of a widespread financial meltdown. The regulations included those aimed at making sure financial institutions had adequate capital (equity) to prevent a systematic meltdown. Agencies were established with the goal of regulating the market (including the rating agencies and mortgage originators).

It should be noted that throughout history, financial crises were followed by financial regulations. This was so after the stock market crash of the 1930s and the savings and loan crisis of the 1980s and 1990s. It would be expected that in the future there may be more financial crises and that, accordingly, the regulatory landscape may change again.

Key Terms

Basel Accords

Bureau of Consumer Financial Protection (BCFP)

CAMELS system

Collateralized Debt Obligation (CDO)

Depository Institutions

Dodd–Frank Act

Federal Deposit Insurance Corporation (FDIC)

Federal Financial Institutions Examinations Council (FFIEC)

Federal Home Loan Mortgage Corporation (Freddie Mac)

Federal National Mortgage Association (Fannie Mae)

Federal Reserve System

Financial Stability Oversight Council (FSOC)

Government Sponsored Enterprises (GSEs)

Office of the Comptroller of the Currency (OCC)

Investment banker

Rating agencies

Mortgage Loan Originator (MLO)

Systematic risk

National Credit Union Administration (NCUA)

Thrift institutions

Review Questions

7-1.   What are the four components of financial regulation?

7-2.   In regards to financial risk what is "systematic risk"?

7-3.   What are the major regulators of financial institutions involved in mortgage lending?

7-4.   What is the primary function of the federal Stability Oversight Council (FSOC)?

7-5.   How does adequate capital (equity) of financial institutions affect systematic risk?

7-6.   What is the "CAMELS" rating system?

7-7.   Regarding depository institutions, what is interest rate risk?

7-8.   What is the role of the Federal Housing Finance Agency (FHFA) in regards to the Government Sponsored Agencies (GSEs, such as Fannie Mae, Freddie Mac, and Federal Home Loan Banks)?

7-9.   What is the primary role of the Bureau of Consumer Finance Protection (BCFP)?

7-10.   What are the major provisions of the Secure and Safe Enforcement of Mortgage Licensing Act (S.A.F.E.)?

7-11.   How did the rating agencies (Standard & Poor's, Moody's, etc.) play a role in the collapse of the subprime mortgage market?

7-12.   What are CDOs and CDO-squared?

Notes

1. Fannie Mae (Federal National Mortgage Association) and Freddie Mac (Federal Home Loan Mortgage Corporation) are former federal government mortgage agencies that were privatized. They are referred to as Government Sponsored Enterprises (GSEs). Although they are private corporations, they enjoy their status as "quasi" government agencies. The perception that the federal government would not allow them to fail has allowed them to raise funds through bond issues at low (subsidized) interest rates. As such, the federal government retains oversight of the GSEs.

2. "Thrift institutions" is a collective name for savings and loan associations, mutual savings banks, and credit unions.

3. Temporary by Section 135 of the Emergency Economic Stabilization Act of 2008 made permanent by the Dodd-Frank Act.

4. Banks lend money in the form of demand deposits (checking accounts) that comprise the bulk of the nation's money supply. They must keep reserves with the Federal Reserve System as a percent of their demand deposits. Thus, by controlling the reserve ratio and the amount of reserves, the Federal Reserve System can affect the amount of money in the economy.

5. Another, smaller, GSE is the Federal Home Loan Banks. They are also included in the regulations of the FHFA. By far the largest of the GSEs are Fannie Mae and Freddie Mac.

6. The agency problems led some mortgage originators to make loans that were not in the best interest of the borrower or the purchaser of the mortgage. It should be noted that, while many mortgage originators did not make risky and subprime loans for their own financial benefit, the agency problems were sufficient to induce some originators to engage in originating loans that were risky and not in the best interest of the secondary mortgage market.

7. A mortgage loan originator (MLO) is defined as any individual who both takes residential loan applications and "offers or negotiates" residential mortgage loan terms.

8. That is, the Federal Reserve System, Office of the Comptroller of the Currency, the Federal Deposit Insurance Corporation, and the National Credit Union Administration.

9. Registration was required between January 31, 2011, and July 29, 2011. National registration was required to prevent MLOs from "jumping" borders if they were banned or disciplined in one state or local jurisdiction.

10. Mortgage loans are typically classified as prime or nonprime, depending on the risk that a borrower will default on the loan. Nonprime loans are further distinguished between "subprime" and "alternative-A" (Alt-A), again depending on credit risk. Generally, borrowers qualify for prime mortgages if their credit scores are 660 or higher and the loan-to-value ratio is below 80 percent. Borrowers with lower credit scores or other financial deficiencies, such as a previous record of delinquency, foreclosure or bankruptcy, or higher loan-to-value ratios, are more likely to qualify only for a nonprime loan

11. For an informative and enjoyable book on this topic readers are urged to read *The Big Short; Inside the Doomsday Machine* by Michael Lewis, W.W. Norton & Company.

12. For every dollar in equity they issued $25 in debt. Commercial banks, subject to minimum capital requirements by their regulators had debt-to-equity ratios of 12 to 1.

Web Sites

http://www.occ.treas.gov/

Thrift financial reports and annual reports of the OCC. Of special interest are the quarterly OCC Mortgage Metrics reports and the Survey of Credit Underwriting Practices.

http://www.fdic.gov/

The Uniform Bank Performance Reports (UBPR) allows access to the financial condition of any insured commercial bank or thrift. Also available are statistics and historical trends of insured institutions. This cite also has data on Regional Economic Conditions (RECON) at the state and county level including real estate activity.

http://www.federalreserve.gov/

Economic and research data of all types including flow of funds data that includes debt and equity financing of real estate properties. Also available are academic and professional publications including consumer guides to mortgages and refinancing mortgages.

http://www.ncua.gov/

Financial performance reports, enforcement actions, other data related to membership.

http://www.fhfa.gov/

Monthly and quarterly housing price index: national, regional, state, and city. U.S. Housing Market Conditions: housing production, markets, affordability, foreclosures, and trends on a national and regional and historical basis.

http://www.consumerfinance.gov/

Data under Regulation C (home mortgage disclosure regulation). Asset exemptions for reporting institutions.

http://www.treasury.gov/initiatives/fsoc/Pages/default.aspx

Data under the Home Affordable Mortgage Program (HAMP) by MSA (annual reports, final rules).

http://www.ffiec.gov/

Annual reports, access to Central Data Repository Public Data Distribution. This site provides financial and structural information on FDIC-insured institutions. Access is also available for Uniform Bank Performance Reports. Most data can be downloaded in Excel format.

FEDERAL HOUSING POLICIES: PART I

LEARNING OBJECTIVES

The subject of Chapters 8 and 9 is federal housing policies. Federal laws greatly influence the practices of individuals and institutions involved in financing residential property. After reading this chapter, you should understand how federal legislation has affected the mortgage and housing markets in terms of affordability, efficiency, and competition. You should understand how legislation has been passed to increase affordability of housing through subsidies to lenders and borrowers. You also should understand how the federal government has sought to foster efficiency in the housing and mortgage market, and you should know the various laws that have been enacted to promote competition in the real estate services industry. Chapter 9 deals with issues of equity and discrimination in housing.

INTRODUCTION

The U.S. Congress has determined that housing issues are a concern of the federal government. Through a series of acts, it has set as a priority the availability of adequate and affordable housing for all citizens regardless of race, gender, national origin, or religious affiliation. Federal legislation addresses four housing market issues: affordability, efficiency and stability, competition, and equity. In this chapter, we cover the first three. The important concepts of equity and discrimination are dealt with in Chapter 9.

HOUSING AFFORDABILITY

Federal programs designed to make housing more affordable can be categorized into three areas: economic support of financial institutions that supply mortgage funds; guarantee of mortgage insurance, direct grants, and subsidies; and income tax provisions.

Economic Support of Financial Institutions

The federal government has provided economic support to financial institutions that supply mortgage funds. This financial support has allowed the institutions to deliver mortgage funds at a lower cost than they otherwise could. Economic support has come from two sources: (1) loans at below market rates to savings institutions and commercial banks and (2) subsidized insurance of deposits. Both programs have reduced the cost of funds, both borrowed funds and deposits, for financial institutions. The following discussion focuses on subsidies to savings institutions.

Federal Home Loan Bank Act (1932). This act established the Federal Home Loan Bank Board and 12 district banks. The board was terminated in 1989. Its role was to act in a supervisory capacity. The role of the banks is to provide liquidity to member associations, such as thrifts, in periods when deposit growth slows or declines. The liquidity is needed because member associations hold assets in the form of long-term mortgages—loans definitely not payable on demand. Also, prior to the development of a secondary mortgage market, it was difficult for thrifts to meet liquidity needs created by an outflow of deposits by selling off mortgages.

The Federal Home Loan Banks (FHLBs) obtain a significant amount of the funds that they lend to thrifts from the sale of FHLB bonds in the capital market. Member associations are required to purchase stock in the FHLBs. This initial capital serves as a solid equity base to support the bond issues. Although the bonds are not guaranteed by the U.S. government, the banks operate under a federal charter and government supervision. Also, when a district bank advances a loan to a member association, it requires collateral, such as mortgages held in the portfolio of the association. Such a loan is called a *secured advance*. The bonds that district banks sell in the capital market must be backed in equal amount by these secured advances plus government securities or cash. These factors combine to make the FHLB bonds virtually risk free. The low interest paid by the banks allows them to advance loans to their member associations at a reduced rate.

The borrowing and lending activity of the district banks is portrayed in Table 8-1. The data show how the net deposit gain of savings and loan associations slowed when market interest rates rose. Note the slowdown in 1966, 1969, 1974, and, particularly, 1981. We do not include data subsequent to the Garn–St. Germain Act of 1982 because bank advances to thrifts rose significantly as a result of this act. Net FHLB advances followed deposit flows, rising when deposits slowed and falling (through repayments) when deposit flows increased. Also, the changes in the amount of FHLB bonds outstanding followed closely the advances by the banks to member thrifts.

Figure 8-1 shows what occurs to FHLB bonds and advances to thrifts when interest rates cause deposit inflows to slow. As interest rates fall, the reverse process occurs.

National Housing Act (1934). This act, in addition to creating the Federal Housing Administration, established the Federal Savings and Loan Insurance Corporation (FSLIC), which was abolished in 1989 and merged with the Federal Deposit Insurance Corporation (FDIC). The purpose of this agency was to insure consumer deposits against loss. It assessed institutions a "flat" rate of one-twelfth of 1 percent of total deposits as a premium. Deposit insurance allows thrifts to take on excess risk. Without it, depositors would recognize the risk of a thrift's investments and withdraw their funds, effectively closing down the thrift. The rate

TABLE 8-1

Interest Rates, S&L Deposits, FHLBB Advances, and FHLBB Bond Activity: 1965–1981 (in millions)

	10-YEAR TREASURY BOND YIELD	NET DEPOSIT GAIN[a]	NET FHLB ADVANCE[b]	CHANGE IN CONSOLIDATED BONDS AND DISCOUNT NOTES OUTSTANDING
1965	4.28	8,409	672.3	852.0
1966	4.92	3,589	937.8	1,638.0
1967	5.07	10,574	(2,549.0)	(2,799.0)
1968	5.65	7,381	873.4	641.0
1969	6.67	3,954	4,030.0	3,721.0
1970	7.35	10,809	1,325.6	1,767.1
1971	6.16	27,465	(2,678.4)	(3,349.1)
1972	6.21	32,113	42.5	(169.0)
1973	6.84	19,984	7,168.6	7,778.3
1974	7.56	15,705	6,657.3	4,995.9
1975	7.99	42,118	(3,959.8)	(3,062.3)
1976	7.61	49,991	(1,982.6)	(1,762.9)
1977	7.42	50,453	4,310.9	1,389.0
1978	8.41	44,350	12,497.2	9,100.4
1979	9.44	38,968	9,168.0	5,262.2
1980	11.46	41,211	7,124.7	6,896.8
1981	13.91	13,481	16,231.4	16,862.5

[a]*Deposit inflows less withdrawals for all FHLB member associations.*

[b]*New advances to associations less payments.*

Source: © 2014 OnCourse Learning

FIGURE 8-1 **Flow of Funds Through FHLBs When Interest Rates Rise**

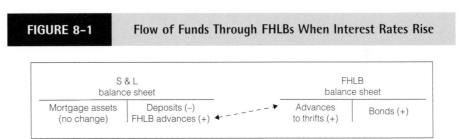

Source: © 2014 OnCourse Learning

---

was flat in the sense that it was based on the amount of an institution's deposits rather than on risk factors. There are several sources of institutional risk:

1. *Interest volatility risk.* Changes in market interest rates cause the market value of assets to *fall relative to liabilities* (because of maturity mismatch).
2. *Credit risk.* Borrowers may default on their obligations.
3. *Liquidity risk.* An unpredictable surge in deposit net withdrawals may occur.
4. *Internal fraud risk.* Misappropriation of funds by management is one example.
5. *Miscellaneous risk.* Risk from foreign exchange, risk of losses from subsidiaries, and risk from unforeseen regulatory actions are included in this category.

Of the sources of risk identified in the preceding list, the first two have been critical for most thrifts. Risk-averting institutions are likely to seek out investments that reduce their maturity mismatch and default exposure. On the other hand, risk- (and return-) seeking institutions are likely to acquire long-term or speculative investments. Equity participations (see Chapter 19) in commercial real estate developments are an excellent example of the latter.

A low, flat-rate insurance premium structure has two faults. First, it misprizes risk and, therefore, encourages thrifts to assume more risk than they could without the insurance. Second, it is distributionally unfair, forcing conservatively managed institutions to subsidize those with risky investments. If regulators are quick to close a thrift as its capital level diminishes and before it has negative net worth, then the risk will be borne by the stockholders—not by the depositors or the government. However, since many thrifts have been undercapitalized to begin with and since bureaucratic regulators are slow to recognize problem thrifts, the deposit insurance ends up as a subsidy to the stockholders of risk-seeking thrifts.

Furthermore, the value of deposit insurance to an institution will vary directly with (1) interest rate volatility, (2) the institution's asset—liability maturity mismatch, and (3) the institution's capital-to-asset ratio. In 1983, McCulloch estimated that FSLIC deposit insurance was worth 2.1 percent of its liabilities per year for an institution with a capital-to-asset ratio of 0.01 and an asset–liability maturity mismatch of only 1 year.[1]

In a competitive market, the value of the government-provided insurance subsidy will be shifted forward to borrowers and backward to depositors. Low insurance premiums explain why, in some years, the yield on money market accounts exceeded that of short-term Treasuries and why the majority of mortgage loans have always been of the fixed-rate type.

Mortgage Insurance, Direct Grants, and Subsidies

The National Housing Act, which established the **Federal Housing Administration (FHA)**, provides for the bulk of benefits in this category. Insurance, direct grants, and subsidy programs are carried out under the direction of the Department of Housing and Urban Development (HUD), within which the FHA is located.

Mortgage Insurance

The FHA provides default insurance on a variety of mortgage types for a cost that many believe is less than that justified by the risk. The various government-sponsored insurance programs are detailed in Chapter 14 and are only briefly mentioned here. The largest FHA insurance program is the One to Four Family Home Mortgage Insurance Program (Section 203 of the National Housing Act). Other FHA insurance programs target loans for high-risk residential properties and include insuring loans for home improvement in declining neighborhoods (Section 223[e]), for home improvement in urban renewal areas (Section 220), and for construction of cooperative housing (Section 213). FHA insurance is also available for types of mortgages such as graduated payment mortgages (GPMs, Section 245a), home equity conversion mortgages (HECMs, section 255), and adjustable rate mortgages (ARMs, section 251).

Still other FHA insurance programs target loans for high-credit-risk borrowers and include insuring loans for special credit risks (those with a less-than-exemplary credit history [Section 237]), for multifamily properties whose tenants are from moderate-income families (Sections 221 [d] [3] and 221 [d] [4]), and for rental housing for the elderly (Section 231). Finally, there are programs that target socially desirable properties such as nursing homes, intermediate-care facilities, board-and-care homes (Section 232), hospitals (Section 242), and group medical practice facilities (Title XI).

Without these insurance programs, it is doubtful that lenders would make many of these high-risk loans, even those for single-family houses. FHA premiums historically have appeared to be less than what would be necessary to compensate for the default risk of residential loans. From 2007 through 2011, the average loan-to-value ratio on home purchases was 95 to 96 percent. Because housing prices rose substantially during the 1960s, 1970s, and early 1980s, there were relatively few defaults on FHA-insured, single-family loans during this period. The premiums charged by the FHA did not appear to be low, relative to the risk at that time. This situation changed in the mid-1980s through the early 1990s. Housing price appreciation slowed nationally, and prices declined in locally depressed areas such as the oil-patch states of Texas and Louisiana. Rising numbers of defaults led to large losses for the FHA (see Chapter 14). Since the FHA is backed by the full faith of the U.S. government, lenders are willing to make loans backed by this agency, despite the losses that result from failure to underwrite loans and correctly price insurance. In contrast, when a private mortgage insurer misprizes insurance and suffers large losses, lenders will transfer their business to other insurers. The ability of a private mortgage insurer to pay claims is very important to a lender.[2] Several private mortgage insurers went bankrupt during the late 1980s and early 1990s. In short, the backing of the government has allowed the FHA to subsidize home buyers by charging them a premium that is less than what private insurers would be able to charge, especially for high loan-to-value ratio loans.

It is uncertain how long the government may use the backing of the Treasury to subsidize the insurance premium on FHA loans. There has been a movement to make the FHA actuarially sound. In fact, the Cranston–Gonzalez National Affordability Housing Act of 1990 provided for a restructuring of the premium for FHA insurance to accomplish this purpose. The annual charge (premium) has been replaced by a combination of both an up-front and an annual charge. In addition, the Cranston–Gonzalez act requires that the FHA become actuarially sound in terms of having adequate capital to meet foreseeable future losses. It established minimum capital ratios that have to be met.

The FHA also has a loss mitigation program aimed at avoiding losses on loans due to delinquency and foreclosure. This program encourages lenders to avoid losses on delinquent loans through forbearance, modification, and partial claims (a loan from the FHA to borrowers sufficient to reinstate delinquent loans). This program requires lenders (that is, it is not optional) to inform borrowers of their loss mitigation options. Failure to follow the loss mitigation requirements can result in a termination of the lender from the FHA program.

One must realize that opposing a move to actuarial soundness will be political pressures to make housing affordable, especially for first-time home buyers. If the FHA premium reflects the full risk of high loan-to-value ratio loans, it will obviously reduce housing affordability for those home buyers with little equity to invest in housing.

The subprime mortgage crisis of 2007–2011 also affected FHA loans. The crisis was precipitated by a sharp decline in housing prices. Houses financed with FHA loans were not immune to the decline in housing values. During this period, the percent of FHA loans that were high loan-to-value ratios (96 to 98 percent) increased. The percentage of these loans was approximately 40 percent in 2007. By 2010 the proportion increased to approximately 68 percent. For all loans ever originated with FHA insurance, the serious delinquency rate (SDR, 90+ days delinquency, borrower bankruptcies, and foreclosures) averaged approximately 9 percent. During 2007 and 2008, this rate averaged about 20 percent. The FHA capital reserve account was $19.9 billion in March 2009. By December 2011, the capital reserve had been reduced to $6.3 billion. Loan losses from the mortgage crisis contributed to this decline in capital.

Direct Grants

In addition to its mortgage insurance program, HUD administers many **direct grant** programs. Begun in 1974 the **Community Development Block Grants** program provides funds to cities and urban counties on a formula basis to entitled communities to carry out a wide range of community development projects. Some of the activities that can be carried out with community development funds include the acquisition of real property; the rehabilitation of residential and non-residential properties; and the provision of public facilities, such as water and sewerage treatment plants, street maintenance, and neighborhood centers. All projects must benefit low- and moderate-income persons. HUD determines the amount of each grant by using a formula comprised of several measures of community need. The formula includes such measures as poverty, housing overcrowding, and the age of the housing stock.

Community Development Block Grants for States and Small Cities is a similar program for states and smaller cities. No less than 70 percent of the grant money can be used for projects that benefit low- and moderate-income persons. The grant period is specified by the state but not to exceed 3 years. Some activities include rehabilitation of residential and commercial properties, providing public facility improvements (water, sewers, streets, etc.) and homeowner assistance. The HUD secretary's Discretionary Fund provides community block grants to those communities not eligible for the first two types of grant. These grants are available for the insular areas such as Guam, the Virgin Islands, and American Samoa. Grants in this category are also available for Indian tribes, Alaskan Native villages, and work-study programs. The fiscal year (FY) 2011 appropriation for this program was $3.336 billion.

Rental Rehabilitation Grants are available to cities and states to encourage rehabilitation of rental properties. Rental Rehab funds (generally up to $15,000 per unit) may cover up to half the total eligible rehabilitation costs of a project. After rehabilitation, at least 70 percent of the occupants must be low-income families (less than 80 percent of the median income for the area). Some funds also must be used to aid large families. Rents subsequent to rehabilitation cannot be limited by rent control. The FY 2004 appropriation for this program was $4.5 billion.

Under the **Urban Homesteading Program**, federally owned properties (primarily foreclosed FHA, Veterans Administration [VA], or FMHA-insured properties) are transferred to local governments that have a homestead program approved by HUD. They, in turn, transfer the properties to low-income families (family income does not exceed 80 percent of the median family income in the area) for a nominal sum. The homesteaders must occupy the property for at least 5 years and bring the property up to code standards. After these requirements have been met, the homesteaders receive fee-simple title to the property.

The **Emergency Shelter Grants Program** provides grants to states and cities to rehabilitate and convert buildings for shelter for the homeless. The program was established by Section IV of the Stewart B. McKinney Homeless Assistance Act of 1987. Participating local jurisdictions must submit a comprehensive homeless assistance plan (CHAP) outlining the need for assistance, the inventory of facilities available to serve the homeless, and a strategy to meet the long-term needs of the homeless. The act authorized $125 million for FY 1991, $138 million for FY 1992, and $156.8 million for 1995. In FY 2004, the allocation was $153 million. Funds can be used to pay for maintenance costs, utilities, insurance, and furnishings, but no salaries for staff to operate a shelter may be paid out of grant funds.

The **Self–Help Homeownership Opportunity Program (SHOP)** provides funds for eligible nonprofit organizations to establish an infrastructure whereby low-income persons and families can gain homeownership through sweat equity. Funds are used for eligible expenses, but potential homeowners must agree to contribute significant amounts of work toward the construction of the housing units. This program requires community participation by volunteers who have expertise in renovations. FY 2003 funding was $25 million.

The **Brownfields Economic Development Initiative (BEDI)** was begun to aid communities in redevelopment of abandoned and underused industrial and commercial properties that may be contaminated with hazardous materials. The goal of this program is to return abandoned and contaminated properties to productive economic use. The 2007 outlay was $22 million. After 2008 this program was not retained as a separate program.

The **Housing Opportunities for Persons with AIDS (HOPWA)** program was established in 1992 to address the specific needs of persons with AIDS. The program provides grants to state and local communities and nonprofit organizations for projects that benefit low-income persons who have been medically diagnosed with AIDS. The grants can be used to acquire, construct, and rehabilitate housing units. The AIDS Housing Opportunity Act requires that 90 percent of the available funds be allocated based on the number of AIDS cases and highest incidence of AIDS. The 2004 appropriation was $294.75 million for the benefit of 73,700 households.

Subsidies

HUD also has several **subsidy** programs, whereby the department pays a portion of housing costs for low-income families. The most well known of the subsidy programs is the Lower Income Rental Assistance, or Section 8, Program. Under this program, HUD makes up the difference between what low- and very low-income households can afford and the approved rent for an adequate housing unit. Eligible tenants must pay the highest of either 30 percent of adjusted income, 10 percent of gross income, or a portion of welfare assistance designated to meet housing costs. The subsidized housing must meet certain safety and sanitation standards. The rent cannot exceed the fair market rent for the local area. Funding under this program is no longer available for new construction or for substantially rehabilitated dwellings.

A related program is the Section 8 Existing Housing Voucher Program. It gives assisted families a greater choice of selection by allowing them to rent units with rents above the fair market rent. Monthly housing assistance payments are based on the difference between a payment standard for the area (not the actual rent) and 30 percent of the family's monthly income. Preference is given to those families currently occupying substandard housing or who are involuntarily displaced or are paying more than half their income for rent.

The Section 8 Moderate Rehabilitation Program is a subsidy program that encourages the rehabilitation of dilapidated dwellings. A local Public Housing Agency (PHA) administers the program by selecting landlords to participate on a competitive basis. Landlords agree to rehabilitate properties to meet certain safety and sanitation standards. The PHA sets the rents, based on the costs of maintaining and managing the property. HUD makes the subsidies available for 15 years. Eligible tenants must pay the highest of 30 percent of adjusted income, 10 percent of gross income, or a portion of welfare assistance designated for housing. Preference is given to very-low-income families currently occupying substandard housing or who are involuntarily displaced or paying more than half their income in rent.

Very-low-income families are those whose income is less than 50 percent of the median family income. Low-income families include those whose income is less than 80 percent of the median family income. Family size adjustments allow for higher limits (and lower for smaller families, the base being four members). For example, an eight-family member household can qualify with 132 percent of the median family income.

Home and Hope Programs

The Cranston-Gonzalez National Affordability Housing Act of 1990 had as its primary purpose an increase in the supply of affordable housing for low-income and very-low-income families. It also was designed to improve housing opportunities for disadvantaged minorities (including Native Americans), increase the supply of supportive housing for persons with special needs (such as those with disabilities), and retain dwellings produced for low-income families with federal assistance (such as low-income housing) so as to prevent their conversion into standard housing. The two main parts of the program are Title II, the HOME Investment Partnership Act, and Title IV, the Homeownership and Opportunity for People Everywhere (HOPE) Program.

The HOME program is structured around a loan arrangement whereby the federal government sets up a local home Investment Trust Fund that can be drawn from to increase the supply of low-income housing. Local jurisdictions can use the funds to construct or rehabilitate existing low-income housing. Income from the housing is intended to be returned to the trust for further investment. This portion of the act emphasizes the need to rehabilitate existing structures, rather than produce new dwellings. The act authorized $1 billion for FY 1991 and approximately $2 billion for FY 1992 for this purpose. These funds may not be used to defray administrative expenses. Also, HUD can place limits on the per-unit cost of the dwellings, according to the cost of construction in the area. Local jurisdictions are required to match the federal funds at no less than 25 percent for rental assistance programs, 33 percent for rehabilitation of existing structures, and 50 percent for new construction. In general, HUD allocates funds by formula among eligible state and local governments. The FY 2011 appropriation was $1.607 billion subject to some small set-asides for Indian tribes, insular areas, management information systems, and housing counseling.

The HOPE program is structured as a grant. Grants can be used by local jurisdictions to rehabilitate public housing (and relocate tenants during the rehabilitation) and to acquire public housing for the purpose of transferring ownership to eligible families. Grants also can be used to aid in the formation of rental management corporations for public housing. The goal here is to privatize public housing so as to reduce future deterioration of these properties. The act allocated $68 million in FY 1991 and $380 million in FY 1992 for these purposes. Local jurisdictions are required to match a minimum of 25 percent of the federal grant under the HOPE program. Although still on the books, there have been no additional funding requests under this program since 1995. Up-to-date information for these and all HUD subsidy programs can be obtained by visiting the HUD Web site referenced at the end of this chapter.

Social Programs of the Government Sponsored Enterprises

Later, in Chapter 10, you will learn about the government-sponsored enterprises (GSEs) Fannie Mae and Freddie Mac. These two agencies are actually private corporations but with original federal government charters. Because they were originally created by the federal government to participate in the secondary mortgage market and because they enjoy the reputation of being supported by the federal government, they have had certain social responsibilities imposed on them by Congress. As a result, both agencies have active programs designed to bring affordable housing to underserved segments of the population. As an example, Fannie Mae has several social programs. The Mortgage Consumer Rights Agenda is a program designed to reduce regulatory barriers to lending, encourage responsible lending practices, and combat predatory lending. By 2004 Fannie Mae had committed over $80 million for local antipredatory initiatives. The National Minority Homeownership Agenda is a program designed as a challenge to the mortgage finance industry to create 5 million new minority homeownerships by the year 2010. In 2002 it served approximately 977,000 minority families through this program. The e-Homeownership Initiative is a program designed to lower the cost of mortgage credit through the expanded use of the Internet. The Affordable Rental Housing Leadership Initiative is a program intended to increase investment in low-income multifamily housing. As a result of the subprime crisis that began in 2006, Federal National Mortgage Association (FNMA) initiated Fannie Mae's HomeStay program in 2007. The program allowed many subprime borrowers to refinance into safer loans. It also provided over $10 million in grants to support foreclosure prevention counseling. In 2008 Fannie Mae initiated the Keys to Recovery program. This initiative allowed refinancing for many "underwater" borrowers up to 120 percent of the properties current value (important because of the nationwide decline in property values), allowed borrowers in hard-hit communities to remain in their property on a rent-to-own basis, and allocated $10 billion to State Housing Finance Agencies (HFAs) for first-time home buyers. Fannie Mae also initiated the MyCommunityMortgage program. This program provides low-income borrowers with special features on conventional loans such as 100 percent financing, low mortgage insurance premiums, and a 40-year amortization period.

Finally, the two GSEs are able to purchase loans with a lower rate of interest than would otherwise be the case because they are able to issue bonds with low rates of interest. They can issue the bonds with low rates because they enjoy the perception that they are federal agencies. In 2003 the Congressional Budget Office (CBO) estimated that the implied federal subsidy resulted in a gain of more than $15 billion per year to the two agencies. (In 2000 the CBO estimate was $10.6 billion.)

The GSEs have other special federal benefits including

- GSEs have lower capital requirements than other financial institutions (increasing their leverage).
- Federal support allows the GSEs to issue callable long-term debt.
- GSE debt securities are eligible for open market transactions by the Federal Reserve System.
- GSE debt securities are eligible for investment, without limit, by federally insured banks and thrifts.
- GSE securities held by banks and thrifts require only a 20 percent risk weighting under the Basel Accord.
- The U.S. Treasury is authorized to purchase up to $2.25 billion of their debt securities.
- GSEs are exempt from state and local taxes.
- GSEs are exempt from filing with the Securities and Exchange Commission (SEC); thus, they do not have to disclose financial data on a timely basis).
- GSEs have exclusive charters, which limit competition.

Income Tax Provisions

For simplicity, the annual cost for an owner-occupant of housing under the current tax law can be stated as

$$C = [(1 - t)(i + p) + m + d - f]H \qquad \text{(Equation 8-1)}$$

where C is a dollar cost, H the value of the house, t the owner's personal tax rate, i the interest rate on the mortgage (the amount of the mortgage is assumed to be identical in amount to H), p the property tax rate, m maintenance and miscellaneous costs as a percent of H, d the rate of

$$C = [(1 - 0.3)(0.12 + 0.02) + 0.01 - 0.06] \times \$100,0$$
$$= (0.098 + 0.01 - 0.06) \times \$100,000 = \$4,800$$

depreciation, and f is the rate of annual inflation in housing values. Housing inflation reduces the cost of housing and is subtracted from the cost of housing. Assume, for an individual in the 30 percent tax bracket, a house with a value of $100,000, a mortgage rate of 12 percent, property taxes of 2 percent, miscellaneous expenses and depreciation of 1 percent, and housing inflation of 6 percent. The annual cost of housing for this person is $4,800. This simple equation can be used to estimate the approximate changes in the total housing cost that result from changes in the components. The components of the equation reflect current tax treatment by the federal government. Both interest charges on mortgages (for primary residences) and property taxes (if itemized) can be deducted for the purpose of determining taxes. Prior to 1997 gains were not taxed as long as the homeowner purchased a new house within 2 years with a higher value than the basis of the old property. Now, the Tax Relief Act of 1997 allows a $250,000 capital gain tax exclusion for single taxpayers and a $500,000 exclusion for married taxpayers as long as they have resided in the house for 2 of the 5 years prior to sale. This provision effectively eliminates capital gains taxation on housing for the vast majority of U.S. citizens. (If the purchase of the new residence is less than the sales price of the old residence, there will be some tax due. The amount that is sheltered is equal to the difference between the cost of the new residence and the basis of the old residence.) The full amount of housing appreciation f is deducted from the cost.

Many have argued that the current tax treatment favors the production of owner-occupied housing. If interest costs and property taxes were not deductible and owners had to pay tax on the appreciation in house values, the annual housing cost in our example would be expressed as

$$C = [i + p + m + d - f(1 - t)]H$$
$$C = [0.12 + 0.02 + 0.01 - 0.06(0.7)] \times \$100,000 \qquad \text{(Equation 8-2)}$$
$$C = 0.108 \times \$100,000 = \$10,800$$

or more than double the tax-subsidized cost.

A complete model of owner-occupied housing is much more complex than the simple equation presented here. A complete model would have to take into account such factors as the tax treatment of rental property (with a deduction for depreciation, for example), the impact of inflation on the cost of rental housing relative to owner-occupied housing, the interaction of inflation and nominal interest rates, and the distribution of households among income classes.

Nonetheless, many have concluded what the simple equation here shows—that current tax laws significantly reduce the cost of owner-occupied housing and encourage its production. Follain and Dunsky examined the demand for the amount of mortgage debt demanded by U.S. homeowners as a function of the tax rate at which mortgage interest payments can be deducted. They concluded that the elasticity of the demand for mortgage debt with respect to a decrease in the rate at which interest is deductible was 21.5 in 1983 and 23.5 in 1989.[3] Harvy Rosen estimates the increase in the home ownership is 2.5 to 5.4 percent (depending on family income) as a result of the tax advantage.[4]

EFFICIENCY AND STABILITY

Legislation designed to foster stability and efficiency in the mortgage and housing market has focused on two areas: (1) creating liquid and efficient markets for loans and (2) deregulating the market.

Efficient Markets

Capital is used more efficiently and channeled into productive uses when the market for capital is large and liquid. More lenders are willing to invest in debt instruments if they know there is a large, liquid market within which these instruments can be resold. This eliminates marketability risk, which otherwise requires a rate premium. For many years, this was not the case for residential mortgages. Many loans were originated and held in the portfolios of lenders until they either prepaid or matured. Consequently, rates on mortgages were relatively high and reflected the default, interest rate, and marketability risks of the lenders' portfolios. Stated differently, the mortgage market was not well integrated into the overall capital market, the latter being large, liquid, and efficient. When not integrated, shifts in the supply and demand for mortgages would cause a divergence between the mortgage rate and capital market rates. The integration of the mortgage market into the larger capital market required the introduction of securitization.

Securitization refers to the process whereby individual, liquid mortgage loans are packaged into securities that are large, riskless (default), and sold on organized exchanges. The process of securitization, by expanding the market for a particular type of debt instrument, lowers the yield required by lenders. Although many private financial institutions undertake to securitize mortgages today, the initial task of securitization took place through the activities of the federal government. The structure of the secondary mortgage market is outlined in detail in Chapter 10, so we present only a summary of the legislation here.

The National Mortgage Association of Washington (1938), shortly renamed the FNMA, was authorized to create a secondary market for FHA loans. (Another purpose was to gain greater acceptance of this new loan insurance by standing ready to buy and sell them.) Most of its activities involved buying the loans and holding them in its own portfolio. It raised borrowed money in the capital market to finance its purchases. Later, it was allowed to purchase VA loans, and in 1970 the FNMA was given authorization to purchase conventional loans.

The **Housing and Urban Development Act** (1968) privatized the FNMA (partially to remove its financial activities from the federal budget), while allowing the association to retain a $2.25 billion line of credit with the U.S. Treasury. The act also established the Government National Mortgage Association (GNMA). This agency, housed within HUD, does not buy mortgages. Rather, it guarantees the payment of principal and interest on the securities that are created and backed by mortgages.

The Emergency Home Finance Act (1970) grew out of the success of FNMA and GNMA in creating a liquid market for government-underwritten loans. The industry pressed for more government support of the conventional loan market, and this act created a new secondary mortgage market agency, the Federal Home

Loan Mortgage Corporation, with an objective to create a secondary market for conventional loans. The act also allowed FNMA to purchase conventional loans. The FHLMC issued the first conventional mortgage pass-through security (see Chapter 10) in 1971—the mortgage participation certificate.

Deregulation

During the 1960s and 1970s, regulation of mortgage lenders interfered with an efficient flow of capital through the mortgage market. The two most noticeable areas of inefficient regulation were federal Regulation Q limits on institutional deposits and state-imposed ceilings on the rate lenders could charge on mortgages. The Regulation Q limits caused funds to flow out of depository institutions and, therefore, out of the mortgage and housing market. The usury ceilings in various states caused mortgage money to dry up in those states when interest rates rose to cyclical peaks. Well-intentioned laws designed to keep the cost of mortgage funds low for the consumer resulted in unavailable loans, as funds flowed to unrestricted, nonhousing capital markets.

In the early 1980s, the Depository Institutions Deregulation and Monetary Control Act (1980) deregulated financial institutions in an attempt to solve these problems. The act eliminated limits both on deposit rates and on mortgage loan rates. It established the Depository Institutions Deregulation Committee to gradually phase out the Regulation Q limits over a few years. In the early 1980s, this committee, composed of the heads of the regulatory agencies, eliminated deposit-rate ceilings on first one and then another type of deposit until the rates on all deposits were set by market forces and competition. The act also overrode all state usury ceilings for federally related loans. (Actually, in the year before, the Housing and Community Development Amendments exempted all FHA-insured loans from state and local usury limits.)

The combination of the development of the secondary mortgage market and deregulation has led to a greater integration of the mortgage market into the capital market. In the early 1980s, less than 5 percent of newly issued, fixed-rate conventional mortgages were securitized. By the late 1980s, more than half were securitized by the government agencies.

Hendershott and Van Order conclude that this rise in the securitization of mortgages has led to a substantial increase in the degree of integration.[5] They analyzed the relationship between the rate on GNMA bonds and that on conventional loans from the 1970s through the 1980s. Hendershott and Van Order viewed the GNMA rate as a capital market rate because GNMA bonds sell in a large and liquid market and are guaranteed against default by the U.S. government. They found that, during the early 1970s, the fraction of the change in the GNMA yield that was reflected in the conventional rate within 2 weeks was only one-sixth. By the early 1980s, the fraction rose to nearly one-half, and by the late 1980s, it had risen to nearly 100 percent. Hendershott and Van Order conclude that, while conventional rates may have been too high or too low relative to GNMA rates in the past, they are currently in line.

COMPETITION IN THE REAL ESTATE FINANCE MARKET

Congress has passed several acts designed to make the real estate finance market more competitive. Economic models have demonstrated the benefits of competition in terms of the efficient allocation of resources. Competitive models assume that market participants have full knowledge of all relevant prices and alternatives. Knowledge of the prices of factors of production and of goods and services is an essential (but not sufficient) condition for a market to be competitive. Accordingly, legislation affecting the competitiveness of the mortgage market has been aimed at making more information available to consumers.

Interstate Land Sales Full Disclosure Act

The **Interstate Land Sales Full Disclosure Act (ILSFDA,** 1968) makes it unlawful to offer certain types of land for sale in interstate commerce without disclosing particular information, both to HUD and to prospective purchasers. Motivation for the act came out of hearings by the U.S. Senate Special Committee on Aging, during which testimony was given about land schemes aimed at the elderly. Through manipulative practices (such as land parties) and pressure sales tactics, the elderly often were enticed into purchasing nearly worthless land in swamps, deserts, or remote areas. The ILSFDA is administered by the Office of Interstate Land Sales Registration (OILSR) within HUD. The act applies to all subdivisions within the same promotional scheme (that is, they need not be physically contiguous) that are divided or in the future will be divided into 50 or more lots. A lot is defined as a piece, division, unit, or undivided interest in land. It can include leases, condominiums, and time-sharing arrangements. Subdivisions where the minimum lot is five acres or more are exempt from the provisions of the act. Another exemption is the sale or lease of a subdivision where the purchaser or spouse personally inspects the property, the so-called on-site exemption. Also exempt is the sale or lease of lots where a residential or commercial building exists or is required to be built by the buyer within 2 years of purchase. These exemptions reflect the purpose of the law to restrict the promotion and sale of raw, remote, and nearly worthless land to buyers who have little or no knowledge of the property.

Under this law developers must do two things. First, they have to register a statement of record with the OILSR. The statement of record must list, among other things, the developers involved and the characteristics of the land. Second, the developers must provide to each prospective buyer or lessee a property report. The property report is similar to the statement of record and is designed to provide basic information about the subdivision. The report also advises the prospective buyers that they should seek professional advice, such as from an attorney, before purchasing any lot. A willful violation of the act can result in a penalty of 5 years imprisonment and/or a $10,000 fine. A suit for damages can also be brought by the purchaser of the land in either state or federal court.

Consumer Credit Protection Act

Title I of the Consumer Credit Protection Act (Truth-in-Lending Law, 1968), containing the **Truth-in-Lending** and Fair Credit Billing acts, requires lenders to provide full information about any loan they grant to a customer. The act gives the board of governors of the Federal Reserve System the authority to set standards and regulate this portion of the act. The regulatory requirements established by the board are referred to as **Regulation Z**, and they became effective July 1, 1969. They apply to both consumer loans (installment and revolving credit) and to residential mortgages. Loans exempt from Regulation Z include commercial and agricultural loans, loans from a securities dealer to a customer to purchase securities (margin account), student loans, and loans over $25,000 not secured by real property. Residential loans covered by the act include those used to purchase a one- to four-family dwelling, including condominiums, mobile homes, and trailers. Loans for transactions involving dwellings with more than four units are considered commercial and are not covered by the regulations. Also, an owner-seller of a single-family residence who extends credit to a purchaser is not required to conform with the regulations. The regulations do apply to second mortgages. The regulations are not intended to set maximum or minimum loan terms but rather to ensure the consumer is made fully aware of the essential terms of any loan. The motive is to provide consumers with sufficient and early information so that they may shop and compare charges among various loans.

Disclosure must be made in writing and in a form the borrower may keep. Disclosures must be made prior to the consummation of the loan or within 3 business days after the lender receives an application for the loan. This 3-day period coincides with the same period of time that a lender has to provide good faith estimates of settlement costs under the **Real Estate Settlement Procedures Act (RESPA)** (discussed later in this chapter). If the lender does not know the precise credit terms, the lender must make the disclosures based on the best information reasonably available and must indicate which items are estimates.

The two most important loan features that must be revealed to the consumer are the total finance charges and the **annual percentage rate (APR)** of interest. These two items must be made more "conspicuous" than any other items of disclosure.

Total Finance Charges

Finance charges are the total of all charges over the life of the loan and include interest charges, origination fees (points), discount points, appraisal and credit report fees, premiums for creditor life and accident insurance (should the borrower die, the mortgage balance will be paid), and mortgage insurance premiums. Not included in finance charges are any fees that would be associated with the sale of the property, even if no mortgage were involved. These typically include application fees, charges for delinquent payments or default, sales taxes, transfer taxes, recording fees, attorney fees, title examination fees, deed preparation fees, and the like. In some cases, the lender may charge the seller of the property "points" for extending a mortgage to the buyer. Such charges are not considered finance charges under Regulation Z, even if the seller of the property raises its price to recoup the cost of the points. The same is true for any other seller-paid fees, such as mortgage insurance premiums.

In addition to the amount of the total finance charges, the lender must disclose the number, amount, and due date of each payment. Disclosure also is required for any prepayment penalties, delinquency and penalty charges, and prepaid finance charges. Prepaid finance charges represent an interest charge for the first partial month payment until regular payments begin.

Annual Percentage Rate

Recall from Chapter 4 that the annual percentage rate (APR) is the effective yield on a loan. The APR on a loan is similar to the yield-to-maturity concept. It will be greater than the contract rate of interest when there are up-front finance charges, such as origination and discount points. To recall how the APR is calculated, first consider a simple mortgage with no finance charges other than the contract rate of interest. The contract rate establishes the payment. When additional finance charges are considered, the monthly payment remains the same and the lender may quote the same contract rate, 10 percent. Origination and discount points will have the effect of reducing the amount of the effective loan amount below the face value. The right side of the equation is the monthly payment annuity. If the left side (loan amount) is reduced, then the equation will no longer be in balance. Balance is restored by raising the discount rate. The discount rate that restores the balance is the APR. It is found just as the internal rate-of-return is calculated in traditional capital budgeting problems or commercial real estate investment analysis. As in those

FIGURE 8-2	APR as a Function of Holding Period

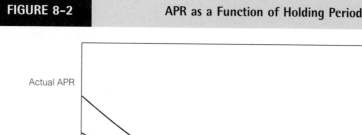

Source: © 2014 OnCourse Learning

cases, lenders have no set formulas that will conveniently yield the APR. Computer programs are available to search for the correct APR.

The regulations require that the APR reported to the borrower be within 0.125 percent of the true APR (0.25 percent for ARMs). Thus, if a fixed-rate mortgage had an APR of 10.57 percent and the lender reported it as 10.5 percent, he or she would be within the allowed tolerance. A lender may be absolved from any error that is made if the calculation was made through the use of a calculation tool (for example, a computer program) used in good faith. To be absolved, the lender must have taken reasonable steps to verify the accuracy of the calculation tool.

As shown in Chapter 4, the lender calculates the APR of a 30-year loan on the basis of a holding period of the same length. If the borrower repays the loan prior to its maturity, the actual cost increases. The discount and origination points are "spread out" over a fewer number of years. For loans prepaid early in their life, the actual cost can be substantially greater than the contract rate. The actual cost is inversely related to the holding period of the loan. Regulation Z does not require that these other costs be disclosed, only the one based on a 30-year holding period.

Depending on the borrower's expected holding period for a loan, the APR revealed by the lender can lead to an incorrect choice of loans. To see this, consider two loans, A and B, with different contract rates and up-front points. The actual APRs for each loan as a function of the holding period are shown in Figure 8-2.

Mortgage A has the lower "Reg. Z" APR (based on the term of the loan, N). If the borrower plans to hold the loan less than T^* years, mortgage A will have the higher actual APR. Most borrowers are likely not sophisticated enough to make these subtle distinctions. Yet, there is no current requirement that a loan's APR based on different holding periods be disclosed. Furthermore, there is evidence that home buyers have reasonable knowledge about their expected tenure in a house. Linneman and Voith analyzed data from the Michigan Panel Study on Income Dynamics.[6] They found that many people, including new homeowners, who indicated that they expected to move in the near future did, in fact, do so. They argue that since many moves are anticipated by home buyers, APR schedules based on different tenure periods would provide useful information.

Regulation Z and Alternative Mortgage Instruments

Special rules apply to some of the alternative mortgage instruments discussed in the previous chapter, including graduated-payment mortgages, adjustable-rate mortgages (ARMs), shared appreciation mort gages, buydown mortgages, and home equity loans. Examples are included in Appendix 8-A.

Graduated-Payment Mortgages. Consider a graduated-payment mortgage with a 5-year graduation period and a 7.5 percent yearly increase in payments. The loan amount is $44,900 and carries a 14.75 percent rate of interest. Finance charges include two discount points ($898) and an initial mortgage insurance premium of $225. The following equation can be used to compute the APR:

$$\$43,777 = \frac{446.6}{(1 + r/12)^1} + \cdots + \frac{479.67}{(1 + r/12)^{13}} + \cdots + \frac{515.11}{(1 + r/12)^{25}}$$
$$+ \frac{553.13}{(1 + r/12)^{37}} + \frac{593.91}{(1 + r/12)^{49}} + \cdots + \frac{673.68}{(1 + r/12)^{360}}$$

The resulting APR is 15.37 percent. The lender must advise the borrower that any negative amortization is a finance charge and not part of the amount financed. A sample disclosure appears in Appendix 8-A.

Adjustable-Rate Mortgages. The major problem with estimating the APR on ARMs is that the future payments are not known with certainty. They will go up or down with movements in the index. Disclosure of finance charges is generally based on the initial terms of the loan. Lenders cannot assume that interest rates will change in either direction.

Many ARMs carry a reduced interest rate for the initial period. In such cases, the APR is computed as a time-weighted average of the rates over the life of the loan. For example, consider an ARM with a 2 percent margin, originated when the index is 10 percent. The contract rate, if fully indexed, would be 12 percent. The lender may agree to a first-year rate of 9 percent. In this case, the APR, assuming no other finance charges, would be 11.90 percent, based on the first year at 9 percent and the remaining years at 12 percent. If the loan were for $100,000, the lender would have to disclose that there would be 12 payments of $804.62, and 348 payments of $1,025.31. The lender also must disclose general information about its ARM loans, including the margin; the index used and where information on the index is published (such as the *Wall Street Journal*); the frequency with which the rate can change; any caps on the interest rate change, either periodically or over the life of the loan; any cap on the payment change; and any provision for negative amortization. The lender also is required to provide the borrower with an example showing how payments on its ARM loan would have changed over a recent period of time. Historical indexes are used for this purpose. An example of these disclosures also appears in Appendix 8-A.

Shared Appreciation Mortgages. With this type of loan, the lender receives a share of the appreciation in the value of the property in return for a reduction in the initial rate of interest. Since the amount of the appreciation is unknown when the loan is originated, all disclosures must be based on the original, fixed interest rate.

Buydown Mortgages. In certain transactions, the seller or another third party may agree to pay an amount to the lender to reduce the borrower's payments or to reduce the interest rate for a portion of the loan's term. If the lower rate is reflected in the terms of the contract, then the disclosures must take the buydown into account. As with ARMs, the APR must be a composite rate that takes into account the lower initial rate and the higher subsequent rate. Payment disclosures also must reflect the two levels. If the lower rate is not reflected in the contract (as might be the case where a side contract is made between the party providing the buydown and the borrower), then the disclosure provided by the lender cannot reflect the buydown. The effect of all borrower buydowns must be included in the disclosure.

Home Equity Loans (HELs). These loans are usually open-ended; the borrower can "take down" amounts as needed up to a level determined by the value of the equity in the property. There is no amortization schedule, but the loan will generally stipulate minimum monthly payments. The rate on HELs is almost always variable and tied to some money market index, such as short-term Treasury yields. HELs can be best described as open-ended, nonamortizing, ARMs.

Disclosure regulations require that the lender inform the borrower that the lender will acquire a security interest in the home. The lender also must inform the borrower that certain conditions may allow the lender to terminate the loan (require full payment of the balance), deny any further extensions of credit, or reduce the credit limit. One such condition would be the failure to meet repayment terms as determined by agreement between the lender and borrower. Payment terms also must be disclosed, including the periodic rate, how the rate is determined, and a statement that paying only the interest charge will not reduce the principal of the loan. The lender also must provide an example of how payments would behave based on a $10,000 extension of credit and the most recent 15-year history of the index value. The example must reflect all significant loan terms, such as negative amortization, rate carryover, rate discounts, and rate and payment limitations that would have been affected by the index movement during that period.

The board of governors of the Federal Reserve System made several additional minor changes in disclosure requirements as a result of the Home Equity Loan Consumer Protection Act of 1988 (HELCPA). Lenders are no longer required to provide HEL disclosures to a borrower as a result of the latter's inquiry into credit other than an HEL. Also, fees charged to a borrower who voluntarily closes out an HEL account prior to its scheduled maturity need not be disclosed. Since hazard insurance is already carried on the property securing most HELs, the lender need not disclose the amount of insurance premiums but only that property insurance is required.

Other Regulation Z Requirements

Under Regulation Z, the borrower has the right to rescind the credit transaction within a short period after it has been consummated. This right allows the cancellation of any agreement that the borrower may have been pressured into accepting. The borrower may cancel the transaction within 3 business days or the receipt of the notice of rescission, whichever occurs later. If a complete and accurate disclosure of the finance charges as required by the regulation has not been made, then the 3-day rescission period is extended until such disclosures are made. The borrower may not waive the **right of rescission** unless a financial emergency arises, and then he or she may do so only in writing. There can be no preprinted forms for this purpose. The right of rescission does not apply to first mortgages on residential properties where the borrower is not a natural person (if the borrower is a corporation, for example) or if the loan is for a business purpose. Also, the borrower does not have a right to rescind a mortgage transaction for other than a principal dwelling. A borrower cannot rescind a loan made to purchase a second, or a vacation, home. An example of a rescission form is included in Appendix 8-A.

Regulation Z also prescribes certain practices for advertising in the print media (newspaper, billboards, fliers, window displays, and the like). If the advertisement contains any information about a single financing term, such as the down payment, installment payments, number of payments, or length of the loan, then it must also disclose all the other terms, including the cash price; down payment; number, amount, and due dates of payments; and the APR of interest. Furthermore, such information cannot be relegated to the "fine print" section of the advertisement.

Finally, Regulation Z provides for both civil remedies and criminal penalties. The civil remedy is an amount equal to twice the finance charge involved (but not less than $100 or more than $1,000), plus attorneys' fees and court costs. Additional damages suffered by the borrower also can be recovered. If, for example, the borrower obtains a loan with an advertised APR of 10 percent and it turns out that the lender miscalculated and the actual APR is 11 percent, the borrower may claim damages. Specifically, the borrower might have been able to obtain another loan with a true APR of 10 percent. The borrower can seek reimbursement for the difference in the finance charges. Criminal penalties for noncompliance (a misdemeanor) include 1 year in jail or a $5,000 fine, or both. Lenders can avoid the civil and criminal penalties if the violation was the result of a miscalculation, but the borrower may still seek damages.

Regulation Z and the Dodd Frank Act

As seen in Chapter 7, the mortgage crisis of 2007–2011 led to a significant overhaul of the financial institution regulatory framework. The Dodd-Frank Act was the centerpiece of this change in the regulatory landscape. The mandates of the Dodd-Frank Act are still being implemented today. Many rules and regulations under the Act may not be settled for several years. In the meantime, a brief synopsis of Dodd-Frank and Regulation Z is as follows.

Oversight of Regulation Z was transferred from the Federal Reserve System to the Consumer Financial Protection Bureau (CFPB). The program retains its title, Regulation Z. In addition to ensuring that adequate information be provided to mortgage consumers, the CFPB was given authority to amend the Regulation Z requirements to address problems leading to the recent mortgage crisis. Additional requirements include:

1. Lenders will be required to confirm the ability-to-pay status of borrowers. The assessment of the ability-to-pay will include confirmation of income and assets, employment status, the monthly payment on mortgage and mortgage-related obligations, current debt obligations, and credit history. Most, if not all, of these requirements were already in place for various mortgage insurance applications (VA, FHA, PMI). They will now be applied to all loans regardless of insurance status.

2. Lenders will be able to originate what is referred to as "qualified" mortgage that provides special protection from liability. Such qualified mortgages must avoid many of the provisions that led to the housing and mortgage crisis. They cannot contain provisions for negative amortization, interest-only payments, balloon payments, or terms exceeding 30 years. Also, points, origination and other fees may not exceed 3 percent of the loan balance, income and assets of the borrower are verified, and the scheduled principal and interest payments must fully amortize the loan over the loan's period.

3. There may also be a limit on the loan's provision for prepayment penalties. Prepayment penalties discourage borrowers from refinancing their mortgage when interest rates decline. For this reason, lenders have typically lowered the

loan's interest rate if there was an agreement for a prepayment penalty. The provision to eliminate the prepayment penalty may, therefore, result in an increase in loan rates overall.

The final rules and regulations are, as of now, not established. The reader is encouraged to visit the CFPB Web site, law & regulation page, for more information.

Home Ownership and Equity Protection Act

The Home Ownership and Equity Protection Act (HOEPA, 1995) is an amendment to the Truth-in-Lending Act (TILA) intended to stop abusive or predatory lending practices to borrowers who already own a home and wish to borrow against their equity. For home equity loans, the lender must give the borrower certain disclosures in writing at least 3 business days prior to closing. The information includes a notice that the borrower could lose his home and any equity in the home if the obligations under the loan are not met. The disclosure also includes the annual percentage rate, the amount of the payments, and, if applicable, certain variable-rate information. The law also bans from the high-rate, high-fee loans such terms as balloon payments due in less than 5 years, an interest rate that increases in the event of a default, and most prepayment penalties. Lenders are also prohibited from engaging in a pattern or practice of lending based on home equity without regard to the borrower's ability to make the loan payments. Lenders may also not make direct payments to home improvement contractors. Borrowers also have 3 business days to rescind any loan contract.

On July 14, 2008, the Federal Reserve made amendments to Regulation Z (which administers the HOEPA) that became effective October 1, 2009. The revisions increased the regulation of subprime mortgage and tightened the requirement that lenders verify the income and assets of the borrower. Also, for a defined category of high-priced mortgages the revisions impose more restrictions on lenders including limiting prepayment penalties, requiring escrows for property taxes and hazard insurance, and considering the ability of borrowers to meet payments. As long as a loan is a closed-end loan (one whose balance may not increase during the term of the loan) and is on a principal residence, the loan may be a higher-priced loan. A higher-priced loan is defined as one that has an APR that is 3 percentage points (or more) than comparable maturity Treasuries on a first-lien loan and 5 percentage points on a second-lien loan. For higher-priced loans, there are four protections. First, lenders will not be allowed to engage in a "pattern and practice" of making higher-priced loans without regard to the borrower's ability to repay the loan other than from the property itself. Second, in making loans lenders may rely only on income and assets that are verifiable. The revisions list the documents, such as W-2s, bank statements, and so on, that the lenders should rely on. Third, prepayments penalties are restricted for the higher-priced loans. The prepayment penalty must expire at least 60 days before an interest rate adjustment is due (as with an ARM). Fourth, lenders may not grant a loan secured by a first lien without establishing an escrow account for property taxes and hazard insurance.

The Dodd-Frank Act transferred regulation of HOEPA loans to the CFPB. Recently the CPFB announced new rules and regulations related to HOEPA loans. The new rule proposal reduces the interest rate caps, limits the fees and points to five, stringently restricts balloon payments, requires homeowner counseling when HOEPA is triggered, and limits prepayment penalties. It also expands HOEPA to include purchase money mortgages, refinances, closed-end home equity loans, and open-end credit plans making a HOEPA apply to most mortgage scenarios other than reverse mortgages.

State Antipredatory Lending Laws

Since the early 2000s, the various states have passed antipredatory lending laws. The laws defined abusive practices most of which include

- Loan flipping—repeatedly refinancing loans and charging high fees each time.
- Excessive fees, exceeding those justified on economic grounds. Such fees include points, prepayment penalties, single premium insurance (to cover the balance of the loan in the event of death of the borrower), and balloon payments.
- Asset-based lending (based on the borrower's assets rather than the ability to make loan payments).
- Outright abuse and fraud.

Appendix 8-B at the end of the chapter is a summary of the state antipredatory lending laws.

Real Estate Settlement Procedures Act

This legislation was passed in 1974 in response to complaints by consumer groups concerning the costs of completing a residential property transaction. Not only were the costs of settlement becoming expensive, but many consumers expressed a frustration over understanding and controlling the various cost elements. The heart of this legislation mandates that reasonable estimates of all **settlement charges** be made known prior to settlement. Just a listing of the possible settlement charges provides an idea of the confusion faced by the typical borrower. Such charges might include an appraisal fee, a credit report fee, inspection fee (termites, for example), mortgage insurance premium, notary fees, title insurance, title search fee, document preparation fee, prepaid interest, attorneys' fees, recording fee, real estate transfer fee (sometimes called document stamps), sales commissions, and service charges.

Another concern among consumer groups was the manner in which the settlement process lent itself to the practice of kickbacks. Lenders in search of business might be tempted to give kickbacks to real estate salespersons in exchange for directing home buyers to them. Title companies might, in turn, give kickbacks to the lender for directing business to them, and so forth. Since the average home buyer is unaware initially of all of the players in the settlement procedure, it is a ripe area for consumer abuse. Consumer groups felt that some of the settlement services were well overpriced, either in terms of the value to the borrower or the cost of supplying the service. RESPA was designed to make markets more competitive by requiring the dissemination of information to consumers and prohibiting certain practices, particularly kickbacks.

Disclosure Requirements

Three disclosure requirements are mandated by RESPA. First, at the time of the application, the borrower must be given a copy of a booklet that completely details RESPA and the information that must be disclosed. The booklet comes from HUD and provides an explanation of the settlement process and indicates the standard practices and procedures. The booklet also indicates the remedies that are available to the loan applicant in the event the settlement fails to conform to RESPA requirements.

The second disclosure requirement is a "good faith estimate" of the settlement charges that are likely to be assessed against the borrower at settlement. If a range of values is provided for a particular service, then the range must be based on actual experience. The lender also must disclose any special relationship that exists between the lender and another service provider. For example, if the lender uses only one attorney to review the settlement, then the lender must disclose any business relationship that may exist between them. Exhibit 13-5 on the closing disclosure (CD) shows a typical good faith estimate. The lender must also provide the borrower with a servicing disclosure statement. This statement must indicate (1) whether the servicing of the loan may be assigned, sold, or transferred to another party at any time during the life of the loan; (2) the percentage of loans made by the lender in the last 3 calendar years for which servicing has been assigned, sold, or transferred; and (3) the estimated percentage of all loans made by the lender for which servicing may be transferred during the 12-month period after the closing.

The **Uniform Settlement Statement** is the third disclosure required by RESPA. It is made on a form provided by HUD. It contains a list of all the charges to be made against the borrower and a complete accounting of all disbursements to be made at settlement. The borrower has the right to review this statement prior to the date of settlement. The Uniform Settlement Statement must be accurate and must contain no estimates of values. Lenders must retain a copy for at least 2 years and cannot assess a charge for completing the form.

RESPA covers all first mortgages that are secured by one- to four-family residences and made by a federally regulated or insured lender. It does not cover mortgaged property in excess of 25 acres, home-improvement loans, loans to finance the purchase of land where no proceeds are used to construct a dwelling, construction loans to developers, or the execution of land sales contracts.

Regulation of Abusive Practices

Regulation of practices under RESPA deals with potentially **abusive practices**, such as kickbacks, required use of certain title services, and unduly large escrow accounts. RESPA requires that the payment of money or something of value be for actual services rendered (that is, not a kickback). If payment exceeds the value of services provided, then it is assumed that a kickback has been provided.

Abusive practices are monitored closely, especially in cases where one of the parties can "control" the direction of business to certain service providers. Real estate salespersons often can direct the home buyer to a certain lender. That lender, in turn, can often direct the borrower to a particular attorney, appraiser, or title company. Payments from lenders to REALTORS® are suspect, as are payments from attorneys, appraisers, and title companies to lenders.

"Kickbacks" need not involve actual payments but can come in the form of price concessions. In 2000 several private mortgage insurance (PMI) companies were sued for "kickbacks" on pool insurance. Pool insurance is insurance on a large pool of mortgages. If a lender sells a large pool of mortgages to Fannie Mae or Freddie Mac, then the latter will charge the lenders a much smaller guarantee fee if the lender has purchased pool insurance. The suit alleged that the PMIs were charging a very low premium fee on the pool insurance to gain more "regular" business of the lenders. If this were so, then the PMIs would be able to charge a higher fee on individual mortgages, for example. It should be noted that late in 2000 the cases were dismissed under a summary judgment. The case is mentioned only to show how real estate settlement providers must be careful to avoid relationships that may suggest improprieties such as kickbacks.

A particularly sticky problem arises when a mortgage broker originates a loan at a slightly higher interest rate than the going rate (say, 8.5 instead of 8 percent). In addition to receiving the normal origination fees and discount points, the broker may be able to sell the mortgage at a slight premium to another lender. This premium is termed a yield spread premium (YSP). In some recent cases, however, it has been charged that the premium paid by the lender is additional compensation to the mortgage broker beyond the normal discount points and origination fees and, therefore, prohibited by RESPA. In light of several recent court cases regarding YSPs, HUD has issued an opinion the YSPs are not a violation of RESPA rules as long as the amount provided to the mortgage broker reasonably reflects the value of services provided by the broker including expenses, the market value of the use of facilities (office), and consulting services.

RESPA also prohibits a mandatory requirement that the borrower obtain title insurance from a certain title company and limits the amount of funds that can be required in an escrow account. Generally, no more than one-twelfth of the annual taxes and hazard insurance can be included in the monthly payment. Lenders may require an additional amount be placed in escrow to cover any unexpected increases in taxes or insurance. This contingency is limited to one-sixth the current estimate of a reasonable annual charge.

Remedies Under RESPA

Unlike the Land Sales Full Disclosure Act and Regulation Z, RESPA does not provide for either an equitable remedy or a right of rescission. Nothing in the act affects the validity or enforceability of any sale, contract for the sale of real estate, or any loan agreement. Also, unlike the other two acts, the borrower can contract away his rights under RESPA. The act does, however, provide for damages for violations of the abusive practices defined above. In such cases, the damaged party can recover attorneys' fees and treble damages. There is also a criminal penalty for abusive practices. Finally, if the laws within a given state provide greater protection than RESPA, those laws will supersede RESPA.

As with Regulation Z, Dodd-Frank mandates that oversight of the RESPA regulations be transferred to the CFPB. Recently the CFPB has issued proposed rules that have not, at this time become effective. One of the more important rules that is expected will be that the Regulation Z and RESPA forms be combined into one, easier to read, and consistent disclosure form for borrowers.

RESPA'S Effect on Settlement Services

To assess the need and usefulness of RESPA, we next analyze the market for **settlement services**. Consider the market for settlement services in the absence of any RESPA regulation. The first thing that the reader should understand about most settlement services is the basis of their value. The purpose of many settlement services is to protect the collateral of the lender. Although paid for by the borrower or the seller of the property, the demand for these services is created by the lender. The borrower, more often than not, will be unaware of either the value of the services or the major suppliers in the local market. Examples of such settlement services are mortgage insurance, title search and insurance, and escrow services. Mortgage insurance protects the lender in the dual event that the borrower defaults and the value of the collateral (residence) is less than the loan balance at the time of default. A title search assures the lender that there are no prior liens on the property that would jeopardize the lender's security. Title insurance hedges the lender against the possibility that the title search was done incorrectly or that fraud or forgery (not detectable by a title search) has occurred within the chain of prior transactions. Escrow accounts ensure that the property taxes and hazard insurance fees are current. The value of settlement services, then, derives from their risk-reduction properties.

The second thing that the reader should be aware of is the inelasticity of demand for settlement services. The demand for settlement services is not responsive to their price for several reasons. One, in aggregate, settlement costs represent a small proportion of either the total transaction or the borrower's total consumption expenditures. Also, they occur infrequently. Consumers are less likely to shop around for services that are purchased so infrequently or represent such a small portion of the overall transaction. Even though the services are demanded by the lender, they are paid for by the borrower.

Third, the suppliers of settlement services (mortgage insurers, title insurers, and so forth) have no incentive to advertise directly to the borrowing public. The borrowing public purchases the services only infrequently, and the public is not the primary beneficiary of services; lenders are. Advertising expenditures for PMI companies range from only 2 to 5 percent of total operating costs, for example. These factors combine to create a system where the cost of services will exceed their value, and referral fees or kickbacks become a common method of soliciting business.

The above discussion indicates the potential for overpricing of settlement services and the accumulation of excess profits by service providers. Evidence of overpricing and excess profits is difficult to obtain, however, because so little is known about the cost curves of providers, either individually or as an industry. Also, although the demand for settlement services as a package is inelastic, the demand curve faced by each individual service provider may be elastic. That is, although the individual borrower has no incentive to shop around for settlement services, lenders may. They have more time, know the market better, and are knowledgeable about the quality of services provided by suppliers.

There also exists the possibility that, whereas individual services may be overpriced, the combined package of settlement services and loan charges may be competitively priced so that no excess returns are earned by any single service provider. This may be so even in the absence of regulations, such as those contained in RESPA. Although this sounds like a contradiction, Villani and Simonson make such a point.[7] They argue that RESPA may have reduced the prices of individual services while at the same time allowing the price of the entire settlement package to increase.

To understand their argument, consider a situation, again in the absence of RESPA, in which some service providers are competitive, for example, lenders. There are many lenders, entry into the market (especially for mortgage bankers) is not difficult, and borrowers easily can compare and shop around for the best loan terms. Now assume that other service providers are not in a perfectly competitive market. For example, title companies: There may be only a half-dozen or so represented in most regions of the country, they face an inelastic demand curve, and entry into the market may be regulated by state laws. As a result, they charge rates above those that would be charged had their services been priced competitively. Since each firm charges a rate above its marginal cost, it will seek to expand its sales and capture a larger portion of the market. There is no incentive to advertise to the general public, so solicitation of business will take place through revenue sharing (kickbacks) with lenders who refer business to the title companies.

The referral fees (kickbacks) become part of the income of lenders and part of the expenses of title companies. Since the lenders are offering a product in a competitive market, they will price their product in a manner that reflects their expenses and revenues (including the referral fees from title insurers). Since each lender perceives that he or she will receive a referral fee from a title insurer for each loan generated, he or she has an incentive to compete with other lenders to generate loans. The ultimate beneficiary is the borrower, who may face lower interest rates or discount points and origination fees. Since lenders know the title insurance market and can shop for title companies, they will extract larger and larger referral fees, until the title company's excess profits are eliminated. The pressure of competition at the point of loan origination forces the lender to pass these referral fee revenues along to the borrower in the form of reduced loan charges. The result of this whole process is a fee structure in which the price paid for title insurance is above the value of the service, the total package of settlement fees and loan charges is competitively priced, and no single service provider makes excess profits.

Curiously, under such a scenario, introducing RESPA-type legislation could actually increase the total cost of settlement. Besides requiring additional paperwork and legal fees, RESPA prohibits referral fees. But, referral fees may make the total settlement process competitive, at least in this hypothetical example. Without referral fees, title companies may keep more of the excess profits generated by their relatively less competitive market position. On the other hand, RESPA-required disclosure may make consumers more aware of the cost of settlement charges, such as title insurance, and more likely to shop for services. This would make that sector of the market more competitive. The causal evidence suggests that the profitability of title companies has declined since RESPA. Pre- and post-RESPA financial data for the title insurance industry are provided in Table 8-2. The table shows that operation revenues have had a somewhat steady increase across pre- and post-RESPA. Likewise, operation expenses have increased steadily. Claims losses have increased over the entire period; however, the increase has been especially dramatic from 1982 to 1992. The operation expense ratio and the combined ratio have increased generally with some dramatic swings in value. One should interpret the data carefully. For one thing, housing sales slowed considerably in the 1980s as interest rates rose to record highs.

The title industry is one of high fixed costs and low variable costs (see Chapter 14). Unlike other insurance companies, title insurance companies are unable to reduce expenses when revenues drop. Even with the recovery in real estate in the mid-1980s, title industry profitability did not return to its pre-RESPA levels. On balance, there is no evidence that profits in this industry were abnormally high, relative to other industries, either before or after the act. Plotkin reports that the rate-of-return on invested capital from the underwriting activities of all title insurance companies averaged 4.8 percent from 1970 through 1974.[8] This compares to a rate-of-return on capital of 10.2 percent for a broad spectrum of U.S. industries, as computed by the SEC and the Federal Trade Commission.

RESPA'S Effect on Real Estate Sales

After RESPA was passed, technological developments and a changing market structure created conflicts of interest within the mortgage origination sector of the market. Advances in computer technology gave birth to **computer loan origination systems (CLOs)**. CLOs allowed borrowers to view, and in some cases apply for, loans from an extensive list provided by lenders. The ability of borrowers to select loans by computer led some large institutional lenders to align themselves with real estate sales firms to capture the borrower at the point of first contact. Traditional mortgage lenders, particularly mortgage bankers, saw the new alignments between the large institutional investors and the real estate sales firms as a threat to their market share. They claimed that such arrangements had the potential of violating Title 8 of RESPA.

TABLE 8-2
Financial Performance of Title Companies; Pre- and Post-RESPA

YEAR	SINGLE-FAMILY HOME SALES (THOUSANDS)	TOTAL OPERATING REVENUE OF TITLE COMPANIES	TOTAL OPERATING EXPENSES OF TITLE IND.	LOSS (CLAIMS) (IN DOLLARS)	OPERATION EXPENSE RATIO	COMBINED RATIO
1968	2507	367.7	306.0	4.9	83.2	87.2
1969	2071	383.7	321.0	4.8	83.7	81.3
1970	2097	375.0	337.1	4.9	89.9	93.5
1971	2674	525.2	421.5	6.2	80.2	83.5
1972	2970	644.4	514.1	7.0	79.8	83.4
1973	2968	720.6	604.0	10.2	83.8	88.5
1974	2791	674.9	617.3	14.4	91.5	98.0
1975	3025	684.9	618.6	20.3	90.3	99.0
1976	3710	899.7	773.9	17.9	86.0	92.3
1977	4469	1,181.8	996.4	18.8	84.3	89.6
1978	4803	1,509.2	1,338.7	20.5	88.7	93.7
1979	4536	1,548.6	1,411.6	24.4	91.2	96.2
1980	3518	1,403.9	1,380.6	30.0	98.3	104.9
1981	2854	1,496.5	1,504.2	35.3	100.5	108.6
1982	2403	1,445.8	1,464.3	33.4	101.3	109.7
1983	3320	2,181.9	1,954.0	31.4	89.6	95.9
1984	3467	2,612.8	2,383.7	44.2	91.2	99.1
1985	3820	2,956.9	2,699.7	48.9	91.3	99.0
1986	4225	3,770.0	3,279.6	331.7	87.0	95.8
1987	4108	4,218.3	3,834.4	324.8	90.9	98.6
1988	4180	4,055.8	3,777.4	389.4	93.1	102.7
1989	3974	4,107.1	3,871.8	390.2	94.3	103.8
1990	3754	4,092.9	3,890.4	410.2	95.1	105.1
1991	3695	4,231.3	4,025.3	424.4	95.1	105.2
1992	4089	5,231.9	4,725.3	387.7	90.3	97.7
1993	4453	5,936.9	5,336.6	343.1	89.7	95.5
1994	4587	5,860.2	5,453.5	315.3	93.1	98.5
1995	4553	4,842.7	4,590.0	282.3	90.0	95.8
1996	4954	5,552.7	5,205.9	270.9	93.6	98.5
1997	5686	6,180.5	5,788.9	286.8	93.7	94.1
1998	5856	8,276.8	7,676.2	294.0	92.7	96.6
1999	6085	8,496.0	7,900.0	324.7	92.9	97.1
2000	5990	7,869.2	7,448.8	394.8	94.7	100.0
				Average 1968—1974	84.6	88.8
				Average 1975—2000	92.3	99.0

Source: Title Insurance Industry Statistics, *Washington, DC: American Land Title Association, 2002.*

CLOs, introduced in the early 1980s, are of two types. One type is a loan information network that allows all lenders the opportunity to display their loans and rates to potential borrowers. Borrowers view the alternative loans and then make separate contact with the lender. The loan listings are updated periodically, either by the lenders or the staff employed by the CLO system. The listings usually are displayed on a computer terminal in a participating REALTOR'S® office. Another type of CLO is the integrated origination and processing system. These networks contain loan applications that are filled out on a computer screen and transmitted to a centralized processing and underwriting station for approval. The real estate salesperson takes the application information from the borrower at the point of sale. This type of CLO system also may allow the salesperson to track the loan through its processing stages. This type of CLO generally will have some sort of a prequalification program to make an initial indication of the likelihood that the loan will be approved.

CLOs are either private networks or open networks. Private networks only offer the loans chosen by the sponsor of the network, and only affiliated originators may use the system. Open networks allow any lender who pays a participation fee to list loans on the system and receive processed loans. Private networks have been the object of criticism by those who think they may lead to violations of RESPA.

One example of a controversial private network is Citicorp's Mortgage Power Program. This program began in 1981 on a limited, regional basis and, by 1990, accounted for approximately 5 percent of the national first-mortgage market. The program lined up participating REALTORS® and offered loans at attractive terms to home buyers. In effect, Citicorp used the program to reach the home buyer at the first point of contact, the real estate salesperson.

By marketing its loans in this manner, Citicorp avoided large marketing costs, including those hard (bricks-and-mortar) costs required to open offices throughout the country. Because of these lower marketing costs, Citicorp was able to offer loans with fewer or no origination points or other fees. The participating real estate sales firms were able to charge a fee for their service and still remain competitive.

Critics of the Citicorp program claimed the relationship was a form of disguised referral fees. Instead of charging points for the loans and sending a portion to the referring real estate sales firm, Citicorp simply reduced its origination fees and allowed the real estate firm to substitute its own charges.

Participants claimed that the charges made by the real estate sales firms were compensation for financial advice and loan consultation—charges allowed under RESPA. Citicorp, in fact, sought the opinion of HUD before implementing their program on a nationwide basis. In 1986 the general counsel of HUD issued an opinion that Mortgage Power did not violate RESPA.

Citicorp's position was buttressed by two court cases, *United States v. Graham Mortgage Corp.* and *Eisenberg v. Comfed Mortgage.*[9] In these cases, the courts basically said it was not clear that HUD had intended that the definition of settlement charges include the origination of a loan. One can understand, however, why traditional lenders would be threatened by a mortgage origination system that attracts the consumer at the point of sale and give sales firms the incentive to divert loan business to large institutional investors.

In 1992 HUD issued a rule that allowed companies to pay employees for referrals to affiliated firms as long as customers were informed about the affiliation. In response to pressure from lenders (the Mortgage Bankers Association filed a lawsuit), the Clinton administration requested HUD to revise the rules. The revision, issued in 1994 and proposed as a final rule in 1996, revoked the 1992 rule allowing referrals. It did, however, create several exemptions. The 1996 rule allowed, for example, a managerial employee to be compensated if a certain percentage of his or her clients do business with affiliated firms. He or she cannot be paid on a per-referral basis. Also, a nonmanagerial employee who does not provide settlement services (stockbroker, for example) can be paid for referrals. Finally, a financial services representative who markets services for several companies can be paid on a commission basis but cannot perform settlement services. This 1996 rule also eliminates exemptions for CLOs where the borrower pays the fee but allows all CLO fees (by borrowers, lenders, or others) if the fee reasonably relates to the value of services provided. The revisions incorporated in the 1996 rule brought more complaints from settlement provide and HUD delayed implementation until July 1997. Finally, the 1996 revisions included a policy statement that defined acceptable services of a CLO. The statement indicated that a CLO may

- provide information concerning products or services.
- prequalify a prospective buyer.
- provide consumers with an opportunity to select ancillary services.
- provide prospective borrowers with information regarding the rates and terms of loan products.
- collect and transmit information on properties for evaluation by lenders.
- provide loan origination, processing, and underwriting services.
- make final funding decisions.

Real estate sales firms appear anxious to participate in CLO networks. Some large firms that currently participate include Coldwell Banker Residential Group, Better Homes and Gardens Real Estate Service, and Realty World Corporation. The following chart shows the advantages and disadvantages of CLO systems as perceived by advocates and opponents:

ADVANTAGES	DISADVANTAGES
Less costly form of loan origination for lenders	Danger of steering business and paying referral fees (kickbacks)
Access to more geographically dispersed markets	Less professional loan counseling and less quality control
Incentives for aggressive rate competition	Loss of lender identity
Side-by-side loan comparisons for borrowers	Closing off of a sizable portion of the
Reducing processing and approval time	market to traditional lenders

Internet Lending

The referral of borrowers to certain lenders has taken a twist with the advent of Internet lending. Many real estate sales firms have created a presence on the Internet where potential home buyers can access information on available properties anywhere in the United States. Now, some of these firms have made agreements with mortgage lenders to be exclusive providers of loans to their customers. In April 2000, for example, mortgage-select.com signed an agreement with Realty.com making the former the exclusive provider of origination and pre-approval services to the latter's network of "Site Select" Web sites for its real estate agents. Under the terms of the agreement, home buyers who visit the Web site of Realty.com would be able to immediately access mortgage-select.com to evaluate the financial arrangements of their home purchase.

The increasing presence of lenders in CLOs and recently on the Internet has given them a powerful position in the home purchase-settlement process. With the increase in their presence has come a movement to allow lenders to make themselves a one-stop center. In July 2002 HUD proposed some rule changes that would, according to the department, reduce the cost of settlement to the consumer by allowing lenders to package all of the closing costs themselves, the so-called one-package rule. Under this rule, a lender could offer a guaranteed price for all settlement services. Essentially, the lender would contract with other settlement service providers, such as title companies, obtain quotes on the services, and offer the entire package to the borrower.

HUD believes lenders would compete with one another to offer the lowest "one-package" deal to their consumers. This means that lenders would, in turn, negotiate the lowest prices from other settlement service providers. Lenders would have to provide borrowers with an enhanced good faith estimate of costs or a guaranteed mortgage package (GMP) in place of the standard good faith estimate. HUD estimated that the one-package deal could save the average borrower as much as $1,000 on settlement costs.

As of mid-2004, this proposed rule has continued to be debated by industry participants. Nonlenders, such as title insurance companies, feel threatened by the central role that lenders would have and have proposed "two-package" deals whereby nonlenders would be able to offer their own "package."

The proposed rule ran into significant trouble when, in 2004 despite President Bush's backing, the Mortgage Bankers Association pulled their support of the rule change. Some lenders contend that they do not need the proposed one-package rule formerly instituted by HUD to offer such a service. They point out that they would be able to contract with other service providers for services at an agreed on price as long as there were no kickbacks or charge for a service not actually provided and as long as the costs are itemized on the HUD-1 settlement sheet. They also cite support from several court cases in 2003 and 2004 that allowed lenders to charge a "profit" on such services. The court decisions said that lenders could contract for a service from another settlement service provider at an agreed on charge and then add a "profit margin" and charge the borrower more for the service. The court decisions have allowed the surcharge by lenders as long as there are no kickbacks involved. In summary, the trend in settlement services appears to be that "one-stop" shopping will be the future of settlement services as long as kickbacks are not involved.

As of the fall of 2012, the CFPB was formulating new rules to combine the forms from Regulation Z (TILA) and RESPA. The first new proposed form (the Loan Estimate) is designed to provide disclosures that will help consumers understand the costs (and risks) of the loan that they are applying for. It would replace the Good Faith Estimate (HUD) and the Truth-in-Lending disclosures (Federal Reserve System). The second form (the CD) is designed to help consumers understand all of the costs associated with the loan closing. It would replace the HUD-1 and the TILA disclosures. The disclosure will have to be provided at least 3 business days prior to the loan closing. The new forms will reconcile any differences between the old TILA and RESPA forms as well as adding several other mandated disclosures. Excluded from the new mandates are home equity and reverse mortgage loans.

Since this is an ongoing process, readers are encouraged to learn more by accessing the document 201207 cfpb on the enclosed CD.

Homeowners Protection Act

The **Homeowners Protection Act** (HPA, 1998) requires lenders to inform the borrower, up front and annually, that he or she has the right to request a cancellation of mortgage insurance if the amount of equity in the residence reaches a certain level. It also mandates an automatic cancellation of mortgage insurance when the equity reaches certain amounts. For this purpose, equity is defined as the original purchase price less the loan balance. Under this law, the lender must disclose to the borrower at closing the type of mortgage insurance (lender paid or borrower paid) that is in force under the loan terms. For fixed-rate mortgages, the lender must provide to the borrower the following three items:

1. A description of the borrower's right to request cancellation of mortgage insurance once the equity in the residence reaches 20 percent (loan-to-value ratio of 80 percent). (Also, the lender must indicate that the mortgage insurance will be automatically canceled when the equity reaches 22 percent.)

2. An amortization schedule indicating the date at which the borrower may request cancellation and the date the lender will automatically cancel the mortgage insurance.

3. Information as to whether the loan is considered high risk by Fannie Mae or Freddie Mac. If the loan is considered high risk, then the mortgage insurance can be canceled no later than the loan's half-way point.

For ARMs the required three disclosures are the following:

1. A notice that the borrower may request cancellation when the equity reaches 20 percent and that the lender will notify the borrower when that date is reached.

2. Information that the insurance will be automatically canceled when equity reaches 22 percent.

3. Information as to whether the high-risk exception applies.

When the lender pays the premium on the mortgage insurance, the borrower is almost always charged a slightly higher interest rate to cover the premium expense. In this case, the HPA law requires the lender to inform the borrower of this fact. The lender must also provide the borrower with information that compares the benefits of lender-paid versus borrower-paid mortgage insurance.

Under the law, the mortgage insurance must be canceled if the mortgage's loan-to-value ratio is less than 80 percent, the borrower has not been more than 30 days late on a payment in the last 12 months or more than 60 days late in the last 2 years, and the property value has not declined subsequent to purchase. Insurance must be automatically canceled when the loan-to-value ratio reaches 78 percent and the borrower is not delinquent on the current payment and the loan is not considered high risk.

Practical Effect of the HPA

You will notice that equity is defined as the original purchase price of the residence less the current loan balance. Thus, the only buildup of equity under this law is through loan amortization. There is no buildup of equity through appreciation in the market value of the residence. This restriction can have a dramatic effect on the point at which mortgage termination becomes effective. For a 95 percent loan-to-value mortgage at 8 percent interest, the 80 percent loan-to-value point is reached in approximately 13 years. At higher interest rates, the cancellation point is even longer. Yet, the National Association of REALTORS° has data that indicate that the average homeowner moves approximately every 7 years (and presumably pays off the old loan). Also, according to data from the Mortgage Insurance Association of America (MICA), the average loan that is insured with private mortgage insurance is paid off in approximately 4 years. MICA estimates that less than

4 percent of the loans insured by PMI would be eligible for termination under the HPA law.

More loans would be eligible for cancellation, of course, if the equity in the property is defined as the current value of the residence less the current balance on the loan. Since 1968 the median price of residential properties in the United States has risen, on average, 6.5 percent annually. A $100,000 property purchase in 1980 would be worth $210,837 in the year 2000 if it increased only 3.8 percent annually, the appreciation rate applicable for that time period. Employing the conservative 3.8 percent appreciation rate that has occurred since 1980 (and the scheduled amortization of the loan), one can calculate the increase in property prices and, there fore, the increase in equity that occurs. Under such a scenario the 78 percent loan-to-value ratio occurs in the fifth year of the loan.

As the law is currently written, it is unlikely that large numbers of homeowners will be eligible for protection. Few borrowers will hold their loan long enough to acquire the required equity through loan amortization only.

Summary

The influence of the federal government in housing issues is pervasive. Legislation is concerned with making housing more affordable, with making borrowers more knowledgeable, and with making the market for housing and mortgages more efficient. The greatest success of the government has occurred in the area of pioneering the secondary mortgage market. The secondary mortgage market has made home financing less expensive by creating a liquid market for mortgages. The government also has made housing more affordable by subsidizing the cost of funds for mortgage lenders, subsidizing costs for mortgage default insurance, and providing direct grants and subsidies for low-income families for the purchase or rental of housing. Rules and regulations designed to make more information available promote competition. Legislation in this area is focused on the cost of credit and the costs associated with residential real estate transactions.

Key Terms

Abusive practicesAnnual percentage rate (APR)

Brownfields Economic Development Initiative (BEDI)

Community Development Block Grants

Computer loan origination systems (CLOs)

Direct grant

Emergency Shelter Grants Program

Federal Housing Administration (FHA)

Finance charges

Homeowners Protection Act

Housing and Urban Development Act

Housing Opportunities for Persons with AIDS (HOPWA)

Interstate Land Sales Full Disclosure Act (ILSFDA)

Real Estate Settlement Procedures Act (RESPA)

Regulation Z (Truth-in-Lending)

Rental Rehabilitation grants

Right of rescission

Securitization

Self-Help Homeownership Opportunity Program (SHOP)

Settlement charges

Settlement services

Uniform Settlement Statement

Subsidy

Urban Homesteading Program

Truth-in-Lending

Review Questions

8-1. What are the four housing market issues addressed by federal legislation?

8-2. Describe the federal programs that provide financial support to depository institutions.

8-3. Indicate the main role of the Federal Home Loan Banks and how they finance their operations.

8-4. a. Indicate the source of risk for thrifts.
       b. How did deposit insurance fail to account for such risks?

8-5. How have federal guarantees allowed the FHA to subsidize mortgage insurance?

8-6. Describe at least three HUD grant programs for low-income family housing.

8-7. a. What is the motivation behind the Interstate Land Sales Full Disclosure Act?
       b. What types of properties are covered by the act?

8-8. What are the two main disclosures required by Regulation Z?

8-9. Explain why adding discount points raises the APR on a mortgage.

8-10. What is the effect of prepayment on the actual APR? Explain.

8-11. What are the remedies under Regulation Z for the failure of a lender to adequately disclose financing charges?

8-12. What was the motivation for the Real Estate Settlement Procedures Act?

8-13. What are considered abusive practices under RESPA?

8-14. Discuss the market for settlement services and the arguments for and against the need for regulation.

8-15. Discuss the major provisions of the Homeowners Protection Act.

8-16. List several special benefits received by the GSEs (FNMA and FHLMC).

8-17. What types of predatory lending practices are prohibited under most state laws?

Problems

8-1. Determine the annual percentage rate per Regulation Z for the following mortgages:

MORTGAGE	COUPON RATE (%)	MORTGAGE AMOUNT ($)	DISCOUNT POINTS	MATURITY (YEARS)	APR
A	11	100,000	500	30	___
B	10	100,000	2,500	30	___
C	8	100,000	3,000	15	___

8-2. For Problem 8-1, which mortgage would you choose if you anticipated selling your residence at the end of (a) 1 year, (b) 5 years, (c) 15 years?

8-3. Determine the APR of the following 30-year mortgage for the indicated holding periods (amount, $100,000; coupon, 10 percent; cost of discount points, $4,000).

MORTGAGE	HOLDING PERIOD (YEARS)	APR
A	5	——
B	10	——
C	25	——

8-4. What is the APR for the following ARM loan?

Amount, not applicable; fully indexed rate: 9 percent first year (only); teaser rate: 7 percent; no discount points.

Notes

1. J. Huston McCulloch. Interest-rate sensitive deposit insurance premia: Adaptive conditional heteroscedastic estimates. Unpublished manuscript. The Ohio State University, 1983.

2. Standard and Poor's provides ratings for private mortgage insurers, just as it does for corporate bonds. Mortgage lenders consider the ratings to be an important barometer of an insurer's claims-paying ability.

3. James R. Follain and Robert M. Dunsky. The demand for mortgage debt and the income tax. *Journal of Housing Research* 8(2) (1997), 155–199.

4. Harvey S. Rosen, Housing decisions and the U.S. income tax. *Journal of Public Economics* 11 (Feb. 1979), 1–23.

5. Patric Hendershott and Robert Van Order. Integration of mortgage and capital markets, Working Paper No. 89–4. Tempe, AZ: Center for Financial Systems Research, Arizona State University, 1989.

6. Peter Linneman and Richard Voith. Would mortgage borrowers benefit from the provision of APR schedule? *Housing Finance Review* 4 (January 1985), 569–576.

7. Kevin Villani and John Simonson. Real estate settlement pricing: A theoretical framework. *AREUEA Journal* 10 (Fall 1982), 249–275.

8. Irving Plotkin. *On the Theory and Practice of Rate Review and Profit Measurement in Title Insurance.* Cambridge, MA: Arthur D. Little, 1978.

9. 564 F. Supp. 1239 (E. D. Mich. 1983), rev'd 740 F. 2nd 414 (6th Cir. 1984), reh'g den.

Web Sites

http://www.hud.gov/funds/index.cfm
Information on HUD programs for subsidized housing

http://www.allregs.com
Home lending regulations and compliance for FNMA and GNMA programs

http://www.stopmortgagefraud.com
A site by the Mortgage Bankers Association of America to aid in fighting predatory lending

http://archives.hud.gov/pubs
A complete listing and description of all HUD programs as of 2006

APPENDIX 8-A

ARM Examples

VARIABLE-RATE
MORTGAGE
SAMPLE

This disclosure describes the features of the adjustable-rate mortgage (ARM) program you are considering. Information on other ARM programs is available on request.

How Your Interest Rate and Payment Are Determined

- Your interest rate will be based on an index rate plus a margin.
- Your payment will be based on the interest rate, loan balance, and loan term.
  —The interest rate will be based on the weekly average yield on U.S. Treasury securities adjusted to a constant maturity of 1 year (your index), plus our margin. Ask us for our current interest rate and margin.
  —Information about the index rate is published weekly in the *Wall Street Journal.*
- Your interest rate will equal the index rate plus our margin unless your interest rate "caps" limit the amount of change in the interest rate.

How Your Interest Rate Can Change

- Your interest rate can change yearly.
- Your interest rate cannot increase or decrease more than 2 percentage points per year.
- Your interest rate cannot increase or decrease more than 5 percentage points over the term of the loan.

How Your Monthly Payment Can Change

- Your monthly payment can change yearly based on changes in the interest rate.
- For example, on a $10,000, 30-year loan with an initial interest rate of 9.71 percent (the rate shown in the interest rate column below for the year 1987), the maximum amount that the interest rate can rise under this program is 5 percentage points, to 14.71 percent, and the monthly payment can rise from a first-year payment of $85.62 to a maximum of $123.31 in the fourth year.
- You will be notified in writing 25 days before the annual payment adjustment may be made. This notice will contain information about your interest rates, payment amount, and loan balance.

Example

The example below shows how your payments would have changed under this ARM program based on actual changes in the index from 1977 to 1987. This does not necessarily indicate how your index will change in the future. The example is based on the following assumptions:

Amount	$10,000	Caps	2 percentage points annual interest rate
Term	30 years		5 percentage points lifetime interest rate
Payment adjustment	1 year	Index	Weekly average yield on U.S.

Interest adjustment   1 year   Treasury securities adjusted to a
Margin   3 percentage points   constant maturity of 1 year

YEAR (AS OF 1ST WEEK ENDING IN JULY)	INDEX (%)	MARGIN[a] (PERCENTAGE POINTS)	INTEREST RATE (%)	MONTHLY PAYMENT ($)	REMAINING BALANCE ($)
1977	5.72	3	8.72	78.46	9,927.64
1978	8.34	3	10.72[b]	92.89	9,874.67
1979	9.44	3	12.44	105.67	9,832.70
1980	8.51	3	11.51	98.79	9,776.04
1981	14.94	3	13.51	113.51	9,731.98
1982	14.41	3	13.72[c]	115.07	9,683.39
1983	9.78	3	12.78	108.25	9,618.21
1984	12.17	3	13.72[c]	114.96	9,554.39
1985	7.66	3	11.72[b]	101.08	9,456.03
1986	6.36	3	9.72[b]	88.13	9,311.25
1987	6.71	3	9.71	88.07	9,151.55

[a]*This is a margin we have used recently; your margin may be different.*

[b]*This interest rate reflects a 2 percentage point annual interest rate cap.*

[c]*This interest rate reflects a 5 percentage point lifetime interest rate cap.*

To see what your payments would have been during that period, divide your mortgage amount by $10,000; then multiply the monthly payment by that amount. (For example, in 1987 the monthly payment for a mortgage amount of $60,000 taken out in 1977 would be: $60,000/$10,000 = 6; 6 × $88.07 = $528.42.)

RESCISSION MODEL FORM (GENERAL)

Notice of Right to Cancel

YOUR RIGHT TO CANCEL

You are entering into a transaction that will result in a [mortgage/lien/security interest] [on/in] your home. You have a legal right under federal law to cancel this transaction, without cost, within 3 business days from whichever of the following events occurs last:

1. the date of the transaction, which is _____; or
2. the date you received your Truth-in-Lending disclosures; or
3. the date you received this notice of your right to cancel.

If you cancel the transaction, the [mortgage/lien/security interest] is also canceled. Within 20 calendar days after we receive your notice, we must take the steps necessary to reflect the fact that the [mortgage/lien/security interest] [on/in] your home has been canceled, and we must return to you any money or property you have given to us or to anyone else in connection with this transaction. You may keep any money or property we have given you until we have done the things mentioned above, but you must then offer to return the money or property. If it is impractical or unfair for you to return the property, you must offer its reasonable value. You may offer to return the property at your home or at the location of the property. Money must be returned to the address below. If we do not take possession of the money or property within 20 calendar days of your offer, you may keep it without further obligation.

How to Cancel

If you decide to cancel this transaction, you may do so by notifying us in writing at (creditor's name and business address).

You may use any written statement that is signed and dated by you and states your intention to cancel, or you may use this notice by dating and signing below. Keep one copy of this notice because it contains important information about your rights.

If you cancel by mail or telegram, you must send the notice no later than midnight of

(date)

(or midnight of the third business day following the latest of the three events listed above). If you send or deliver your written notice to cancel some other way, it must be delivered to the above address no later than that time.

I Wish to Cancel

_____

Consumer's Signature   Date

Convenient Savings and Loan   Account number: 4862-88

Michael Jones
500 Walnut Court, Little Creek USA

ANNUAL PERCENTAGE RATE	FINANCE CHARGE	Amount Financed	Total of Payments
The cost of your credit as a yearly rate.	The dollar amount the credit will cost you.	The amount of credit provided to you or on your behalf.	The amount you will have paid after you have made all payments as scheduled.
15.37%	$177,970.44	$43,777	$221,548.44

Your payment schedule will be:

Number of Payments	Amount of Payments	When Payments Are Due
12	$446.62	Monthly beginning 6/1/81
12	$479.67	" " 6/1/82
12	$515.11	" " 6/1/83
12	$553.13	" " 6/1/84
12	$593.91	" " 6/1/85
300	varying from $637.68 to $627.37	" " 6/1/86

Security: You are giving a security interest in the property being purchased.

Late Charge: If a payment is late, you will be charged 5% of the payment.

Prepayment: If you pay off early, you
☒ may   ☐ will not   have to pay a penalty.
☒ may   ☐ will not   be entitled to a refund of part of the finance charge.

Assumption: Someone buying your home cannot assume the remainder of the mortgage on the original terms.

See your contract documents for any additional information about nonpayment, default, any required repayment in full before the scheduled date, and prepayment refunds and penalties

_____
e means an estimate

APPENDIX 8-B   State Antipredatory Lending Laws

STATE	STATUTORY CITATION	FLIPPING BANNED	NEGATIVE AMORTIZATION BANNED	PREPAYMENT PENALTIES BANNED	FINANCING CREDIT INSURANCE BANNED	CONSUMER CREDIT COUNSELING PROVISION	HIGH DEBT-TO-INCOME RATIO PROVISION (ABILITY TO REPAY LOAN)
Arkansas	Ark. Stat. Ann. §23–53–101 *et seq.*	X	X		X	Third party required	Give due regard
California	Cal. Financial Code §4970 *et seq.* and §4973 *et seq.*	X	X			Disclosure	Presumption at 55%
Colorado	Colo. Rev. Stat. §5–3.5–101 *et seq.* and §38–40–105	X	X			Notification	Give due regard
Connecticut	Conn. Gen. Stat. §36a–746 *et seq.* and §36a–521		X			Notification	Presumption at 50%
D.C.	D.C. Code Ann. §26–1114. and §26–1151.01 *et seq.*		X	X			Give due regard
Florida	Fla. Stat. §494.0078 *et seq.*	X	X			Notification	Give due regard
Georgia	Ga. Code §7–6A–1 *et seq.*	X	X		X	Third party required	Presumption at 50%
Illinois	Ill. Rev. Stat. ch. 815, 137/1 *et seq.* and ch. 765, 77/70	X	X		X	Notification	Presumption at 50%
Indiana	Ind. Code 4–6–12 and 24–9–1 *et seq.*		X		X	Third party required	Give due regard
Kentucky	Ky. Rev. Stat. §294.010 *et*	X	X		X	Notification	Presumption at 50%

STATE	STATUTORY CITATION	FLIPPING BANNED	NEGATIVE AMORTIZATION BANNED	PREPAYMENT PENALTIES BANNED	FINANCING CREDIT INSURANCE BANNED	CONSUMER CREDIT COUNSELING PROVISION	HIGH DEBT-TO-INCOME RATIO PROVISION (ABILITY TO REPAY LOAN)
	seq. and §360.100						
Louisiana	La. Rev. Stat. Ann. 6:1096(G) and 9:3572.6(C)						
Maine	Me. Rev. Stat. Ann. tit. 9–A, §2–509, tit. 9–B, §429; tit. 9–A, §8–103, §8–206–A, tit. 9–A, §10–102 and tit. 33, §506, 2007 Chapter 273, 2008 Chapter 471	X	X	X	X	Third party required	Give due regard
Maryland	Md. Commercial Law Code §12–127, 12–311, 12–409.1 and 12–1029	X	X		X	Third party required	Presumption at 45%
Massachusetts	Mass. Gen. Laws Ann. ch. 183C, 1 et seq.		X	X		Third party required	Presumption at 50%
Michigan	Mich. Comp. Laws §445.1631 et seq.		X		X	Notification	
Minnesota	2007 Chapter 18 Minn. Stat. §58.137	X				Notification	Requires verification
Missouri	Mo. Rev. Stat. 375.937						

(Continued)

STATE	STATUTORY CITATION	FLIPPING BANNED	NEGATIVE AMORTIZATION BANNED	PREPAYMENT PENALTIES BANNED	FINANCING CREDIT INSURANCE BANNED	CONSUMER CREDIT COUNSELING PROVISION	HIGH DEBT-TO-INCOME RATIO PROVISION (ABILITY TO REPAY LOAN)
Montana	Mont. Code Ann. §32–5–306						
Nebraska	Neb. Rev. Stat. §45–702, 45–704 and 45–705				X		
Nevada	Nev. Rev. Stat. §598D.010 *et seq.*			X	X		Give due regard
New Jersey	N.J. Rev. Stat. 46:10B-22 *et seq.*		X		X	Third party required	
New Mexico	N.M. Stat. Ann. §58–21 A–1 *et seq.*	X	X	X	X	Third party required	Give due regard
New York	N.Y. Banking Law 6–l	X	X		X	Notification	Give due regard
North Carolina	N.C. Gen. Stat. §24–1.1 E, §24–1.1 F, §24–10.2 and §53–243.01 *et seq.*	X	X			Third party required	Presumption at 50%
Ohio	Ohio Rev. Code Ann. §1322.062, §1322.07, §1322.08, §1345.01 *et seq.* and	X	X		X		Give due regard/ Presumption at 50%

STATE	STATUTORY CITATION	FLIPPING BANNED	NEGATIVE AMORTIZATION BANNED	PREPAYMENT PENALTIES BANNED	FINANCING CREDIT INSURANCE BANNED	CONSUMER CREDIT COUNSELING PROVISION	HIGH DEBT-TO-INCOME RATIO PROVISION (ABILITY TO REPAY LOAN)
	§1349.25 *et seq.*						Give due regard
Oklahoma	Okla. Stat. tit. 14A, §3–204 and tit. 59, §2081 *et seq.*	X					
Pennsylvania	Pa. Cons. Stat. 63, §456.101 *et seq.*					Notification	Presumption at 50%
Rhode Island	R.I. Gen. Laws §34–23–5R.I. Gen. Laws §34–25.2–1 *et seq.*	X	X		X	Third party required	Presumption at 50%
South Carolina	S.C. Code Ann. §37–23–10 *et seq.*	X	X		X	Third party required	Presumption at 50%
Tennessee	Tenn. Code Ann. §45–20–101 *et seq.*	X	X				Presumption at 50%
Texas	Tex. Finance Code §343.001 *et seq.* and Tex. Gov. Code §2306.001 *et seq.*		X	X			Give due regard
Utah	Utah Code Ann. §61–2d–101 *et seq.*		X		X	Notification	
Virginia	Va. Code §6.1–422.1 and §6.1–422	X					

(Continued)

STATE	STATUTORY CITATION	FLIPPING BANNED	NEGATIVE AMORTIZATION BANNED	PREPAYMENT PENALTIES BANNED	FINANCING CREDIT INSURANCE BANNED	CONSUMER CREDIT COUNSELING PROVISION	HIGH DEBT-TO-INCOME RATIO PROVISION (ABILITY TO REPAY LOAN)
Washington	Wash. Rev. Code §31.04 et seq.						
West Virginia	W.Va. Code §31–17–1 *et seq.*			X			
Wisconsin	Wis. Stat. Ann. §428.202 *et seq.*	X	X		X	Notification	Give due regard

Definitions of provisions:

Flipping: refinancing an existing mortgage loan with no benefit to the consumer; also referred to as churning.

Negative amortization: payment terms under which the outstanding principal balance will increase at any time over the course of the loan because the regular periodic payments do not cover the full amount of interest due or terms under which the aggregate amount of the regular periodic payments would not fully amortize the outstanding principal balance.

FEDERAL HOUSING POLICIES: PART II

LEARNING OBJECTIVES

After reading this chapter, you should be aware of how federal laws protect the home buyer from discrimination in sales and financing. You should know the major provisions of the Fair Housing Act (and amendments), the Home Mortgage Disclosure Act, the Community Reinvestment Act, and the Equal Credit Opportunity Act. You also should know the theories of discrimination, and what types of discrimination may or may not have occurred in the housing market.

INTRODUCTION

Legislation intended to make the housing market equitable has been aimed at what has been perceived as discriminatory practices in the sale, financing, and rental of houses. Since discrimination on the basis of race, creed, gender, or national origin is decidedly un-American and against the public interest, the federal government has taken an active role in outlawing practices considered to be discriminatory.

EQUITY IN HOUSING

Two principal acts address housing discrimination: the 1968 **Fair Housing Act** addresses discrimination in the sale of houses and the 1974 Equal Credit Opportunity Act (as amended in 1976) deals with discrimination in the financing of houses. Other legislation includes the 1975 **Home Mortgage Disclosure Act** and the 1978 **Community Reinvestment Act.** A complete list of legislation affecting housing and lending is provided in Appendix 9-A.

Fair Housing Act

The Fair Housing Act (1968) was passed as Title VIII of the Civil Rights Act of 1968. It prohibits discrimination in the sale or rental of residential dwellings (or vacant land intended to be used as such) on the basis of race, color, religion, or national origin. Gender was added as a protected class by the Housing and Community Development Act of 1974. Families (those with children under 18) and the handicapped are protected under the Fair Housing Amendment Act of 1988. Under the act, as amended, it is unlawful to:

- Refuse to sell or rent, or refuse to negotiate to sell or rent, or to otherwise make unavailable a residential dwelling to those in the protected groups.
- Modify the terms or conditions of a sale or rental on the basis of group membership.
- Advertise that the sale or rental is available to only certain groups.
- Represent to any member of a protected group that a residential dwelling is unavailable for sale or rent when in fact it is.
- Attempt to induce a sale of dwelling units by representing that individuals of any classification are moving into the neighborhood.
- Modify the terms of a mortgage based on the classification of the borrower in a protected group.
- Deny access to a multiple listing service to any individual in a protected group.
- Deny or make different terms or conditions for home loans by commercial lenders.

The first condition specifically includes brokers in addition to the owner of the property. Condition 5 makes it illegal to engage in what is commonly referred to as blockbusting. In its most unethical form, **blockbusting** has been used by the unscrupulous to drive prices down so that properties can be purchased cheaply. The "blockbuster" will typically make a statement that certain minority groups are moving into the neighborhood and that property owners should sell quickly at a reduced price to avoid further depreciation. Blockbusters may even pay, or otherwise encourage, a member of a minority group to purchase or show an interest in purchasing neighborhood properties. All this is illegal under the act.

The act does exempt some property owners from its provisions (although no exemptions are made for racial discrimination). An owner-occupant who does not employ a broker or use discriminatory advertising to sell or rent the property is exempt. There are restrictions on who constitutes an owner-occupant, however. For example, the exemption does not apply to anyone owning more than three houses. Also, religious organizations can give preference for their members as long as they do not discriminate on the basis of color, race, gender, national origin, handicap, or families with children. Private clubs also may restrict occupancy of dwellings to their members as long as the facilities are not operated commercially for a profit. For rentals of an apartment or a house with a shared common area or a dormitory at an education institution, a preference for gender may be used in an advertisement.

Title VIII also calls for the development and implementation of affirmative, fair-marketing plans in which participants in the Department of Housing and Urban Development (HUD) housing plans must employ an affirmative program to attract buyers and tenants from all minority and majority groups. HUD also has instituted, under Title VIII, voluntary affirmative marketing agreements (VAMAs) with the nation's major housing industry groups, including the National Association of REALTORS®. The agreements commit the participants to activities designed to make the industry aware of its responsibilities under the law.

The act provides for two legal remedies, which can be pursued simultaneously or in sequence. First, a complaint can be filed with HUD, which will either refer the case to a state agency, if the laws of the state grant essentially the same rights and remedies, or, if not, HUD will investigate the complaint itself. Unable to issue any cease-and-desist orders, HUD will seek an informal reconciliation of the matter. Its investigation will be conducted at no expense to the complainant, and any evidence it uncovers can be used under the second remedy—a civil suit in federal district court.

A civil suit must be filed within 2 years of the discriminatory act unless the complaint is first filed with HUD. The federal court can order the discriminatory behavior stopped and fine the offender up to $1,000. In rare cases of a widespread pattern of abuse by an offender (cases of general public importance), the attorney general of the United States may file a civil suit. In fiscal year 1988, HUD received 4,658 complaints; conciliation was attempted in 1,539 and was successful in 1,122.

Evidence of discrimination is often difficult to accumulate. Government investigators may, therefore, use a system of "checking" or "testing." They may send a black and an equally qualified white buyer into a predominantly white neighborhood to see if the seller of the property or the broker treats the two identically. If the seller or broker tells the black "buyer" that a contract on the house was just signed that day, but tells the white "buyer" (arriving later) that the property is still for sale, the "checkers" would have gathered sufficient evidence to be used in court. There are public and private entities at the local level that support antidiscrimination practices. The Fair Housing Initiatives Program (FHIP) of HUD was established by the Housing and Community Development Act of 1992 to provide funding to these entities. The activities involve programs to prevent or eliminate discrimination in housing and include programs of enforcement, voluntary compliance, and education and outreach.

At present there are no protections under the FHA for sexual orientation or gender identification (LBGT). However, in 2012 HUD's Office of Fair Housing and Equal Opportunity issued regulations to prohibit LBTG discrimination in federally assisted housing programs. In addition approximately 15 states have enacted laws addressed to discrimination in housing related to sexual orientation, gender identity, or both.

Equal Credit Opportunity Act

This act extended the civil rights momentum of the 1960s to credit markets. Though not strictly limited to consumer credit, it concentrates on this area of the capital market. The **Equal Credit Opportunity Act (ECOA)** (1974) grew out of a series of hearings held in 1972 on discrimination against women in the credit market. Witnesses testifying at the hearings of the National Commission on Consumer Finance (NCCF) in May indicated that (especially) married women faced difficulties in obtaining credit. Later in that year the NCCF report was cited by the Senate Committee on Banking, Housing, and Urban Affairs as justification for federal legislation. The Senate developed a version of a bill that became law in October 1974. This version prohibited discrimination in credit markets based on gender and marital status. Subsequently, the House of Representatives Committee on Banking, Currency, and Housing pushed for an expansion to include discrimination on the basis of age, race, national origin, religion, and color. The Senate amended this bill by adding yet two more protected classes, those receiving income from welfare and those who had, in good faith, exercised their rights under the ECOA. The revised bill became law in March 1976. The act requires lenders to notify applicants of a decision within 30 days of the application for credit and to provide written reasons for any denial of credit. The act specifically prohibits lenders from requesting certain information from applicants including:

- whether or not the applicant has children.
- whether or not there exist child care problems.
- whether or not there may be interruption of income due to future childbirth.
- whether or not the applicant receives alimony, child support, or separate maintenance.
- whether or not the applicant is widowed, divorced, or single.
- whether or not the applicant has a listed telephone number.

One difficulty in interpreting and enforcing this legislation has been differentiating between those acts (such as denial of credit) that are discriminatory and those that represent legitimate efforts of lenders to screen applicants for credit. The act assigns that task to the Federal Reserve Board. In Regulation B, the Board states that it is illegal to discriminate by treating one candidate for credit "less favorably" than another. Accurately defining and interpreting discriminatory behavior is more difficult than making this statement, however.

There are at least three ways in which discriminatory lending behavior can be defined or identified. One is the **effects method.** Under this method, discrimination is said to exist if members of minority groups are underrepresented in the class of credit recipients. That is, they represent a smaller proportion of those receiving credit than they do in the general population. Under the **intent approach,** discrimination is held to have existed if a lender intends to treat minority groups less favorably. Finally, the **practices approach** to discrimination holds that discriminatory behavior exists when a lender fails to adhere to a set of guidelines governing the do's and don'ts of the lending procedure. As an example, board guidelines prohibit the use of "Mr." and "Mrs." on credit application forms and require that a married woman's credit history be considered independently of that of her spouse. Failure to adhere to these "practices" may result in a finding of discriminatory behavior. Lenders are careful to avoid any prohibited practices in taking and evaluating credit applications.

Legitimate credit screening may result in fewer credit approvals for members of minority groups than their proportion in the general population. If, for example, income is a legitimate screening device and blacks have, on average, less income than whites, then the result will be that blacks are underrepresented in the creditworthy group. This is so, even though race is not a screening factor. This makes the effects approach to discrimination difficult to interpret and enforce. In addition, strict compliance with an effects approach would result in more credit granted to unworthy candidates (based on income) and less to worthy candidates. This would raise the total cost of credit (through a greater number of defaults) to all groups.

It is also difficult to determine a lender's intent. Lenders are not likely to admit discriminatory intent. For these reasons, the federal government has focused on the practices approach to regulate discrimination and enforce the ECOA, although Regulation B does mention the effects test in a footnote to Section 202.6(a).

The need for legislation to prevent discrimination in the credit market can be addressed both theoretically and empirically. Theoretically, some markets may be more open to discrimination than others. Whether that is true of the credit market can be partially answered through empirical studies. We look at both approaches.

THE ECONOMIC THEORY OF DISCRIMINATION

There are two models of discrimination in credit markets. They derive from work done primarily in the economics of labor-market discrimination. One theory states that individuals or firms have a "taste" or **preference for discrimination.** This simply means that firms or individuals may derive psychological, but not monetary, satisfaction from discrimination. The other theory states that firms or individuals gain economically from discrimination because there are costs associated with gathering sufficient information to make unbiased decisions.

"Taste" for Discrimination

One of the first economists to explore the implications of this form of discrimination was Becker.[1] According to this model, an individual or firm has a taste for discrimination if he acts as though he is willing to pay (perhaps in the form of reduced profits) to be associated with some types of people and not others. It is important to note the economic costs associated with discrimination. If, for example, a man and a woman are equally qualified and skilled in all respects for a position, yet the firm hires the man at a higher salary, then it is incurring an additional labor expense for no additional return.

Becker argued that in a perfectly competitive market, firms with a taste for discrimination would, in the long run, be driven out by lower cost firms without such a preference. That is, the firm with the lowest cost (least discrimination) could undersell all other firms. Although perfect competition in the product market may limit the amount of discrimination, it also may be limited (in long-run equilibrium) in the case where the market is dominated by a monopolist with a taste for discrimination. In this latter case, the owner(s) of the firm would not be maximizing the value (stock) of the company. He could obtain a higher income by selling the firm to new owners who would not discriminate. The new owners would be willing to pay a higher price for the firm because they could manage it more efficiently—that is, without costly discrimination.

One area where discrimination might survive the rigors of the marketplace would be publicly regulated companies. They have a monopoly or near monopoly in the market for their products. Their profit margin is often regulated. Since excess profits may be regulated away by a mandated price reduction, managers may prefer to take their returns in a nonpecuniary form such as discrimination. This consideration opens up the possibility of discrimination in credit markets when and where financial institutions are heavily regulated. During the 1960s and 1970s, there was a climate of regulation and discouragement of competition. The 1980s brought on deregulation and a spirit of competition. Discrimination in credit markets would have been more likely to survive in the earlier period. Yet, several studies found strong inter-institutional competition during the earlier period.[2]

It should be noted that discrimination can persist in a competitive market under some circumstances. Ferguson and Peters[3] point out that Becker had previously indicated that the ability of nondiscriminating competitors to compete away discrimination depended on their production functions. Specifically, if production costs rise sharply with output then one or a few nondiscriminating firms would be unable to capture the industry's entire output. Ferguson and Peters argue that portfolio costs in a lender's "production function" cause it to be nonlinear, which in turn leads to rationing where discrimination can take place.

Economics of Information

A second theory of discrimination derives from a branch of economic theory termed the **economics of information.** Traditional models of perfect competition assumed that all market participants have complete knowledge of product prices and factor productivity (labor, for example). More recent economic models recognize that information is not a free good. Time and money must be used to acquire information. Often the expense of obtaining information may be greater than the benefits. In such a case, discrimination may occur. Here, let us offer a simple working definition of discrimination. Consider discrimination to be "the act of attributing to an individual a characteristic that is known to be true of the group to which he belongs." Without knowledge about the individual, he is tagged with a group characteristic.

A good example relates to automobile insurance. Young males are charged higher rates because as a group they have more frequent and serious accidents than females. Yet, one particular male may have less risk of having an accident than most women. The cost to insurance companies of discovering this information would be prohibitive relative to any benefits. As a result, insurance companies charge all young males higher rates than females. Information about certain driver characteristics that may bear on the severity and frequency of accidents may not be costly to obtain. If married drivers or good students tend to have fewer accidents, then insurance companies might offer discounts to males in these classes because it is not costly to obtain this information.

A similar scenario occurs in credit markets. Prior to ECOA, lenders would compute a "credit score" based on the economic characteristics and group membership of the applicant. Lenders may have operated in the belief that the marital status of an applicant, for example, provided additional useful information concerning the likelihood of default. That is, given two applicants with an identical economic situation, a married applicant may be less likely to default than an unmarried applicant. Being married would increase the probability of obtaining credit. Information on marital status is also inexpensive to obtain.

Now that ECOA is law, lenders cannot obtain or use such information to make a loan decision. The impact of ECOA on the allocation of credit depends on whether such group membership affects the likelihood of default. If group membership (such as marital status) does not actually affect the probability of default, then the ECOA restrictions would have no effect on credit screening. It would prevent lenders from considering information that was useless anyway. However, if group membership does affect the probability of default, then prohibiting the use of this information will have an effect. It will raise the probability of acceptance of a random applicant from a "risky" group and lower the probability of acceptance of a candidate from a less risky group. This would result in an increase in the proportion of defaulted loans and in the total cost of lending.

Lenders would be expected to attempt to reduce costs by taking other nonprohibited actions. The lender might use a subset of information collected without cost to indirectly screen those who could apply for credit in the first place. If the lender decided to accept an application, then he or she would seek out additional (costly) information on the applicant. The indirect screening could take the form of refusing applications from certain neighborhoods. An overt refusal to take applications from within a certain area would open the lender to criticism. Indirect screening might take place in more subtle forms, such as failing to open up lending offices in the designated neighborhood. This would be detrimental to a whole class of borrowers that the ECOA was designed to protect. There was some indication that lenders, in fact, responded in this manner to the ECOA. Concerned about this type of lender behavior, the Congress passed the Fair Lending Practices Regulations and the Community Reinvestment Act in 1978, both of which are discussed later in this chapter.

EMPIRICAL EVIDENCE OF DISCRIMINATION

There are several interesting empirical issues raised by the previous discussion. One question involves the extent to which membership in any particular demographic group provides information about credit risk. Another concern is the extent to which lenders discriminated against certain groups prior to the enactment of ECOA. Finally, there is the question of whether or not the ECOA has resulted in a reduction in undue discrimination and greater credit opportunities for those in groups protected by the act.

Group Membership and Credit Risk

Tests designed to determine if membership in a particular group affects payment performance are difficult to perform. Data are available on the default experience of actual borrowers and their group membership. But borrowers cannot default until they are given credit. Therefore, any selection bias by lenders automatically would bias the results of a study of default behavior. Some studies have attempted to overcome this "acceptance bias" through statistical techniques. Group characteristics of interest include gender, age, marital status, and race.

Chandler and Ewert analyzed 2,000 credit card applicants and account holders at a large bank from 1971 through 1974.[4] They found that, after correcting for economic variables, females had a better payment record than males. Boyes, Hoffman, and Low analyzed the payment history of a large number of credit card holders.[5] They discovered that older borrowers, other things being equal, had better credit histories. Avery analyzed approximately 9,900 new accounts opened between 1968 and 1970 at a consumer finance company.[6] He also found that older borrowers had better creditworthiness. Insofar as marital status is concerned, Avery also found this to be important. Married debtors were better credit risks. However, Boyes, Hoffman, and Low found no relationship between marital status and credit risk. Both of these later studies found race to be a significant factor. After controlling for other variables, it appeared that blacks defaulted more often than whites. It must be pointed out, however, that these studies were based on the experience of only two creditors and only for those borrowers accepted for credit. Any selection bias whatsoever tends to bias the results.

Existence of Discrimination

Evidence of lender discrimination on the basis of a group characteristic may show up in a difference in the default rate between members of that group and general debtors. If lenders unwarrantedly discriminated against members of a particular group, they would require of them higher standards of creditworthiness or higher interest rates on loans. There is no evidence that lenders charged differential loan rates based on membership in a particular group. If discrimination did occur, it would be through the application of tougher qualifying standards. This would, in turn, lead to a lower default rate among members of the group(s) discriminated against. For this reason some research into this issue has focused on default rates among various groups. Peterson and Peterson[7] and Peterson[8] looked at the default rates on consumer loans given to 37,000 customers at 30 banks from 1965 through 1971. The data identified the gender of the borrower and the type (purpose) of consumer loan. For most types of loans, the authors found no difference in default rates between male and female borrowers. However, females did default at a disproportionately higher rate for used car loans and at a disproportionately lower rate for home improvement loans. This suggests that there may have been some discrimination in favor of females for car loans and against them for home improvement loans. The authors also found no evidence that females were charged higher interest rates on any type of loan. Marshall analyzed the applications of a large number of borrowers at two finance companies.[9] He found no discrimination on the basis of gender. He did find that older applicants were more likely to be rejected than would be predicted on the basis of their credit scores. In another study Shay and Sexton constructed two scoring models to predict acceptance or rejection for credit.[10] In one model they entered variables for gender, marital status, and age. They found no additional predictive ability for the model that included the group variables. Their results also failed to find evidence of lender discrimination. Altman et al. used much the same methodology and found some evidence of discrimination on the basis of these three group characteristics.[11]

Evidence concerning racial discrimination in credit markets also is mixed but leans toward the view that it was not pervasive either prior or subsequent to ECOA. Responses to surveys that solicit consumer perceptions of discrimination also indicate that loan decisions based on group characteristics are not pervasive. Survey evidence reveals that most consumers did not believe that they had been subject to discriminatory treatment in the credit market.

Effects of ECOA

Economic theory predicts that discrimination by firms is costly in (long-run) competitive markets. Available evidence suggests that the practice of discrimination in the credit market was not pervasive prior to ECOA. If this is the case, it appears that the legislation should have little or no impact on either the total amount of credit available or on its distribution among potential borrowers. Post-ECOA studies of the credit market suggest that the legislation has not made more credit available to protected classes than would otherwise be the case. In fact, the opposite may have occurred. By preventing lenders from considering group membership, credit available to some protected classes may have been reduced. This is particularly so for females. Chandler and Ewert built several statistical models to predict acceptability for credit.[12] In some they included a variable for gender; in others they did not. The latter would be equivalent to compliance with ECOA. The model that included the variable for gender led to a higher acceptance for female applicants than the model that complied with ECOA. The results suggest that credit risk is affected by gender, and that females, other things being equal, represent less of a risk. If lenders are not able to identify the gender of the applicant, females may lose this advantage. Shinkel found that exclusion of all variables covered by ECOA led to an increase in defaults of up to 2.6 percent, with a reduction in lender profits of 2 percent to 16 percent.[13]

Effects of FHA

Has the Fair Housing Act resulted in a greater access to housing for minorities? According to Bostic and Martin[14] the answer is yes if one factor is in fair housing policy enforcement. They looked at black homeownership rates by census tract from the U.S. Census for 1970, 1980, 1990, and 2000. They compared these data to legal actions initiated (at county level) under Title VIII of the Fair Housing Act. Many legal actions initiated did not result in actual litigation since many cases were settled. In the 1990s HUD managed approximately 3,445 cases annually on a national level. The authors created variables that reflected the intensity of legal actions initiated such as the number of enforcement activities relative to the population in a county containing the census tract in question. Overall, they found a positive and statistically significant relationship between fair housing policy enforcement and black homeownership growth. They also found that black homeowners gained access to higher-income neighborhoods during the 1970 to 2000 timeframe. The authors note that much of their result reflected affluent black homeowners moving out of poverty-stricken central cities to more affluent suburbs. They also point out that their research in no way indicates that fair housing laws have solved all problems associated with black homeownership in America.

In summary, four general statements can be made. First, economic theory suggests that discrimination is costly to the individual or the firm with a taste for discrimination. In a competitive market, low-cost producers (nondiscriminators) will attain a competitive edge. Credit markets, especially subsequent to deregulation, are characterized by large numbers of firms and competition. Second, the empirical evidence suggests that lenders engage in little discrimination. Third, as a result, it is doubtful that ECOA has had any significant impact on making credit available to qualified individuals who would otherwise be cut out of the market because of race, marital status, age, or religion. Fourth, the ECOA does say something about principles of fair-lending practices and, as such, is a valuable statement. Fifth, fair housing laws appear to more important than equal credit laws.

Home Mortgage Disclosure Act and Community Reinvestment Act

These two acts are closely related to ECOA and reflect the concern of the federal government that all citizens have access to credit markets, regardless of the neighborhood in which they wish to live. The first act discourages lending institutions from avoiding certain neighborhoods, and the second encourages them to evaluate and actively lend in their defined community. The **Home Mortgage Disclosure Act (HMDA)** (1975) requires a depository institution with assets exceeding $32 million ($10 million prior to September 1996 and $28 million prior to December 1999) to compile a report on the distribution of its loans, by number and dollar amount, within and outside of any Standard Metropolitan Statistical Area (SMSA) where it has a main or branch office. Nondepository institutions are exempt from the report if they have assets less than $10 million or originate less than 100 home purchase loans annually. The report must indicate the distribution of loans by census tract, and the lender must make it available for public inspection. The 2000 census data were used for all loans made after January 1, 2003. State-chartered institutions are exempt from the disclosure requirements if they are subject to state laws that are substantially similar to HMDA requirements. HMDA disclosure statements are available on the Web site of the Federal Financial Institutions Examination Council (FFIEC).

Some major changes in the HMDA were included in the 1989 Financial Institutions Reform, Recovery, and Enforcement Act (FIRREA). The changes expanded coverage to include mortgage lenders not affiliated with depository institutions and to include data on home improvement loans. In addition, the changes required institutions to report the race, sex, and income of mortgage and home improvement loan applicants and borrowers. Depository institutions with less than $30 million in assets are exempt from these additional provisions, however. In 1991 the Federal Reserve Board issued revised rules that required reporting of data on home improvement loan refinancing and on rejected loan applications submitted through brokers or correspondents. The revisions also made it clear that civil money penalties could be imposed for violations of the act. At one time the Federal Reserve Board restricted the meaning of those "in the mortgage business" to lenders whose mortgage business was 10 percent or more of their total loan origination business. Because many lenders also issued large amounts of non-mortgage loans (credit cards for example) in 2002 the Board amended the HMDA scope of regulation to lenders who made more than $25 million in mortgage loans annually. Such lenders are now considered to be in "the business of mortgage lending."

A recent study by Munnell, Browne, McEneaney, and Tootell using the HMDA data shows that the denial rate for whites who apply for mortgages is 6 percentage points lower than the denial rate for comparable minority applicants. The study concludes that this is due to discrimination since the study controls for applicant characteristics considered by lenders in approving loans.[15] A subsequent editorial in *Forbes* magazine by Brimelow and Spencer[16] challenges this claim of discrimination, citing the Federal Reserve's own finding that the average mortgage default rate for minority neighborhoods is the same as the rate for white neighborhoods. Their rationale is that discriminating lenders would be granting loans to riskier whites while denying them to relatively more qualified minorities. However, a revisiting by Carr and Megbolugbe reinforces the Munnell et al. study by showing that a close examination of the data reveals an even stronger statistical case for discrimination than was originally reported.[17]

As of 2008 mortgage lenders must collect and report the following data for each loan: Date application received, type of application (Federal Housing Administration [FHA], Veterans Administration [VA], etc.), the purpose of the loan (purchase, home improvement, refinancing), whether the application resulted in an origination or denial, property type (one-to-four family, multifamily, manufactured, whether the property would be owner-occupied, amount of the loan requested, action taken (approval, denial, and the date), ethnicity, race, and gender of the borrower, gross annual income of the borrower, for higher price loans the rate spread above the yield on a comparable Treasury security that exceeds 3 percentage points for first lien loans and 5 percentage points for junior lien loans, whether the loan was subject to (Home Ownership and Equity Protection Act) HOEPA (see previous chapter), and lien status (first, junior or not home-secured).

As of November 1978, the **Community Reinvestment Act (CRA)** (1978) requires all federally regulated financial institutions (primarily commercial banks, savings and loan associations, and mutual savings banks) to publicize their lending activities within their community. Under the act an institution must

1. Define its "community" by preparing a map, indicating the area from which it accepts deposits and to which it makes loans.

2. List and make available to the public and regulators the types of credit services available.

3. Post a notice in its place of business indicating that its lending practices are being evaluated by their federal regulator and that the public can appear and make comments at any hearing for the purpose of authorizing any expansion.

4. Make a periodic report (community support statement) to its regulator concerning its efforts to serve the credit needs of its community.

Based on the community support statement, federal regulators can make written evaluations of an institution's record of meeting the credit needs of the community and can deny a request for expansion to any institution that fails to comply with these provisions.[18]

By amendments made by FIRREA, each evaluation will have a public and confidential section. Under the public portion, the regulatory agency will rate the institution's record of meeting the community's credit needs as either outstanding, satisfactory, in need of improvement, or in substantial noncompliance. The confidential portion is designed to protect the identity of complainants. In 1991 the Federal Housing Finance Board ruled that the Federal Home Loan Bank (FHLB) System could deny access to long-term FHLB advances (loans) by member thrifts that have poor evaluations. If an institution has an outstanding or satisfactory evaluation of its statement, it will be deemed to be in compliance. If it receives a lower evaluation, it must indicate how it expects to cure the deficiencies in an action plan. Access to long-term FHLB advances will be restricted if an institution has a community support action plan disapproved or fails to substantially meet the goals of the action plan within 1 year.

The reason for these acts is that Congress was concerned that discriminatory lending practices could take place other than at the point of loan application. Specifically, citizen groups had long charged that lenders discriminated by refusing to make any loans (or a reduced amount of loans) in certain neighborhoods populated by a greater proportion of individuals in protected groups, especially racial minorities. They claimed that lenders would draw a red line on a map indicating the neighborhoods within which they would not make mortgage loans. The term **redlining** became synonymous with this discriminatory practice.

Those who defended the practice claimed that lenders were simply identifying neighborhoods where the risk of mortgage lending was greater than normal. Default risk is greatest where property values are likely to decline subsequent to originating loans. Borrowers will exercise their put option when the value of the property falls below the amount of the loan. The risk is greater if the borrower lacks sufficient assets that the lender can pursue in satisfaction of any deficiency. The combination of falling property prices and low levels of wealth are typical of neighborhoods that are in transition from predominantly white to a mixture of white and racial minorities. It is likely that property values stabilize when the transition is complete and a neighborhood is populated predominantly by a racial minority. If lenders are not averse to default risk, then the redlining practice would appear to be racially motivated. Critics of redlining claim that the practice not only discriminates against that segment of the population that needs access to credit the most, but that it also contributes to the decline of neighborhoods. They argue that the inaccessibility of mortgage funds lowers the demand for properties and causes their values to fall. Owners, in turn, have little incentive to maintain their properties. In addition, they are denied access to home improvement loans. The result is a deterioration of the properties within the redlined area. Whether redlining causes deterioration in neighborhoods or deterioration causes redlining is a difficult cause-and-effect relationship to disentangle. Proponents on each side of the issue have their own points of view.

A related issue is the practice of **FHAing** a neighborhood. Critics of redlining argue that lenders would originate only (or predominantly) FHA mortgages within a redlined area. If there is a greater risk of default within certain areas, then this would be a reasonable response by a lender. As we will see in Chapter 14, the FHA fully insures the lender against all elements of loss. For conventional loans the lender would either be self-insured, if he or she held the loan in his or her own portfolio, or would require private mortgage insurance (PMI), which is a coinsurance relationship, however. This means that, under the PMI contract, the lender absorbs a portion of the loss (much like the deductible on your automobile insurance).

Critics of FHAing argue that this practice also contributes to neighborhood decay. They claim that because all elements of loss are covered and the FHA often acts slowly in resolving their claims, many properties in default are left to deteriorate and become the target of vandalism. Whatever the arguments on each side of the issue, Congress sought a prohibition against the practice of redlining. They saw it as a civil rights issue and not a risk management issue and passed these two acts.

EMPIRICAL EVIDENCE ON REDLINING

Redlining can occur in several forms. Lenders may make fewer total loans, fewer home improvement loans, or fewer conventional loans in certain neighborhoods. The motive for redlining can either be risk aversion or discrimination. If redlining occurs because of risk aversion, lenders would be expected to make fewer (conventional) loans in neighborhoods that are undergoing a transition from predominantly one race to another. If redlining occurs because of discrimination, lenders would be expected to make fewer loans in any neighborhood with a significant minority population, whether changing or stable. Empirical research is concerned with all of these issues. Hutchinson, Ostas, and Reed studied the lending behavior of four large savings and loan associations in Toledo, Ohio, in 1975.[19] They looked at total loans, home improvement loans, and the proportion of loans that were conventional in each of Toledo's 123 census tracts. Explanatory variables were taken from the 1970 census and included the percentage of the population that was black, the change in the percentage that was black (from 1960 to 1970), the average age of structures, unemployment rate, median income, the percentage of the population over 55, the average duration of residency, and several other factors. They concluded that the racial composition of a census tract had no effect on the total loans originated within that area. Racial composition did affect the proportion of loans with conventional financing and the number of home improvement loans, both being reduced in tracts with more blacks. Hutchinson, Ostas, and Reed discovered that the proportion of conventional loans was minimized when the percentage of a tract's black population reached approximately 45 percent. Tracts with a homogeneous racial composition (either predominantly white or predominantly black) had higher proportions of conventional loans. The authors concluded that lenders perceive transitional neighborhoods as risky and prefer to originate government-insured loans in those areas.

One could argue that the experience of a sample of four lenders is not representative of the market, that even if those lenders redlined certain neighborhoods (in terms of FHAing or home improvement loans), those neighborhoods may have had access to other lenders and suffered no lack of borrowing opportunities. Ahlbrandt looked at all mortgage loans made in each of the census tracts in Pittsburgh in 1973 and 1974.[20] Explanatory variables included median family income, percentage of units vacant, percentage of units that were owner-occupied, percentage of the population that was black, the change in the percentage black from 1960 to 1970, and the crime rate. Ahlbrandt found that income and neighborhood risk factors (such as crime) were the most important determinants of the number of loans made within a census tract.

The number of loans made was positively related to the change in the percentage of black families. This result could be due to the fact that transitional neighborhoods will have more property sales and thus a higher demand for new mortgages. An important finding was that lenders attach more importance to income and neighborhood risk factors in areas with high black populations. Stated differently, a black in such a neighborhood may be required to have more income to qualify for a loan than otherwise would be the case. This conclusion is valid,

Ahlbrandt points out, only if one can infer a correspondence between census tract characteristics and mortgage applicant characteristics.

More evidence of discrimination surfaced in a report by the Federal Reserve. Based on 1990 Home Mortgage Disclosure Act data, the report was released in late 1991. The data were derived from reports from 9,300 lenders covering 6.4 million loan applicants. The Federal Reserve noted the denial rate on loans of families with similar incomes but of different races. Overall, 14.4 percent of all whites applying for conventional loans were denied credit. In contrast, 21.4 percent of Hispanics and 33.9 percent of blacks were denied credit. Interestingly, Asians appeared to be the most favored; only 12.9 percent were denied a loan. In the lowest income group, the rejection rate was 23.1 percent for whites, 17.2 percent for Asians, 31.1 percent for Hispanics, and 40.1 percent for blacks. The pattern remained the same for high-income groups: Rejection rates were 8.5 percent for whites, 11.2 percent for Asians, 15.8 percent for Hispanics, and 21.4 percent for blacks.

The pattern also was much the same for government-backed loans (FHA and VA). Here the rejection rates were 12.1 percent for whites, 12.8 percent for Asians, 18.4 percent for Hispanics, and 36.9 percent for blacks. Similar differences in rejection rates were noticed for home improvement loans.

Interestingly and reflecting previous studies, the report found that the racial mix of the neighborhood was important. The rate of denial to minority families increased as the proportion of minorities in the neighborhood increased. For conventional loans the denial rate was 12 percent for areas with less than 10 percent minority residents, and 24 percent in areas that were 80 percent or more minority. For government-backed loans the pattern was similar.

The Federal Reserve indicated that the results should be interpreted with caution. The HMDA data reveal little about the financial characteristics of the applicants other than their income level. The level of assets, previous credit history, and other factors were not available when the report was prepared. Nonetheless, unless credit histories and asset levels vary systematically with race, the results indicate a possible trend of discrimination. A 1999 study by the Urban Institute, *Mortgage Lending Discrimination: A Review of Existing Evidence*, thoroughly examined many of the issues raised in regards to the methodology used in the Boston Fed study. It concluded that:

- The large difference in loan denial rates by race could not be explained by such factors as data errors, omitted variables, or interaction between factors that influence loan approval.

- The Boston Fed study proves neither the existence of differential treatment discrimination in loan approval nor the absence of disparate impact discrimination.

- The study presents strong evidence of differential denial rates that establish a presumption of discrimination and effectively shifts the burden of proof to the lenders.

Recent years have seen a renewed interest in racial discrimination in mortgage lending. It is felt that, in some cases, minorities may be held to a higher standard of loan qualification than nonminorities. If this is the case, then logically, default rates for minorities should be less than the default for nonminorities. Berkovec, Canner, Gabriel, and Hannon tested this theory by examining a sample of FHA loans over the period 1987–1989.[21] They found the exact opposite result. Their results indicated a higher likelihood of default by minority households. They found that the proportion of minorities in a census tract is not strongly correlated with default.

Calem, in a 1996 study, took a different tack.[22] He examined whether minority loan applicants were denied credit more frequently than nonminority applicants because of information externalities (such as the number of house sales in the area). For predominantly nonminority neighborhoods he found the number of sales in the area for the previous year had a positive effect on the loan approval rate. For minority neighborhoods, however, he found, even in the case of few previous sales, the approval rate exceeded approval rates in nonminority areas.

Fair Housing Amendments Act of 1988

This act, signed in September 1988, became effective in March 1989. It prohibits discrimination in renting on the basis of age, number, and gender of children in the family. It also adds persons with disabilities to the set of protected groups under the Fair Housing Act of 1968. Its passage was partially the result of complaints by families with children that they had been denied access to rental dwellings or charged higher rental rates. Apparently, the charges were based on practice. A 1980 HUD survey showed that 50 percent of rental units nationwide limited access to families according to the number, age, or gender of their children.[23] Twenty-five percent excluded families with any children. Landlords defended the practice by stating that rental units that accepted families with children incurred higher operating costs.

Familial status under the act includes a parent or other adult having custody of one or more children under the age of 18. It also covers any person who is pregnant or in the process of securing custody of a child under 18. Dwellings covered by the act include apartment complexes, single-family units, condominiums, mobile home parks, and cooperative apartments. The exemptions under the 1968 act remain in effect, however. In addition, housing units for older adults are exempt from the act, provided 80 percent of the dwellings are intended to be occupied by at least one person over the age of 55, if all occupants are over 62 years of age (including spouses), or if such units are operated under a state or federal program designed to assist the elderly. Originally the units had to further satisfy a facilities and services test (unless it was not practical to do so) that demonstrated they were specifically designed to meet the physical and social needs of older persons. However, the **Housing for Older Persons Act** (HOPA, 1995) eliminated the requirement that the housing had to meet the "significant facilities and services" designed for the elderly. A HUD rule (April 2, 1999) in the Federal register implements the HOPA and details those provisions of the Fair Housing Act that pertain to senior housing. Relief under the act has been strengthened. It is now the responsibility of the U.S. government to represent the interests of the individual in cases alleging violations. Also, individuals are allowed to pursue civil action on their own and may be awarded punitive damages by the court.

Goebel and Rosenberg looked at the effect on operating expenses of renting to families with children.[24] Prior to the enactment of the federal legislation, 16 states had enacted some sort of antidiscrimination law based on familial status. Apartment owners in these states would not be able to exclude families with children. Goebel and Rosenberg analyzed the financial statements of a large number of apartment complexes in both states that allowed discrimination and those that did not. In addition to the law in each state, they used demographic and economic variables and the physical characteristics of each apartment complex to explain the level of rents and operating expenses.

They found that rents were higher in states with antidiscrimination laws—that is, in states where families with children could not be excluded. They found no difference in operating expenses, however. The additional rent could not be justified on the basis that admitting families with children raised operating costs. They concluded that antidiscrimination laws in this instance may have hurt those they were intended to protect. One shortcoming of their research was that although they had identified apartment complexes by the laws of the state in which they were located, they did not identify apartment complexes strictly by whether or not they rented to families with children. That is, in those states where discrimination was allowed, some complexes would have discriminated and some would not have. Each type was not identified.

In regard to individuals with disabilities, the law defines such a person as one having:

- A physical or mental impairment that substantially limits one or more major life activities.
- A record of having such an impairment.
- Being regarded as having such an impairment.

Individuals who do not have, or are limited by, impairment but are regarded as having an impairment by another person are also protected. The act extends protection to persons who live with or intend to live with an individual who has a handicap. Congress has extended the original definition of handicapped to include those with acquired immunodeficiency syndrome (AIDS) or human immunodeficiency virus (HIV) infection. With regard to accommodations, housing providers must make reasonable modifications of the structure to allow a person with a handicap to use the dwelling. They must also make **reasonable accommodations** in rules, policies, practices, or services if they are necessary for a person with a disability to use the facility. Common areas must be accessible and hallways and doors must be built so as to allow wheelchairs to travel unobstructed. Buildings that have an elevator, four or more units, and are ready for occupancy after March 13, 1991, must conform to these provisions. In May 2004 HUD released new guidelines strengthening its view on "reasonable accommodations" for the disabled. Among other things the new guidelines prohibit an apartment owner from banning the use of scooters and carts in common areas. The guidelines stress the need for property owners to make reasonable accommodations for disabled persons. Reasonable accommodations are those that are not expected to place an undue (financial) burden on the property owner. State antidiscrimination laws that are more stringent will supersede this federal law.

Violence against Women Act VAWA (2005)

The VAWA was originally passed in 1994 and reauthorized in 2000 and 2005. The latest reauthorization adds to the FHA a prohibition against the eviction of women who are victims of domestic violence, dating violence, and stalking. The act applies only to public housing and Section 8 housing. It does not cover private housing and other federally subsidized housing. It prohibits evictions based on real or perceived domestic violence, dating violence, or stalking. Examples of prohibited cause of eviction include:

- Assault by a family member.
- Assault by a significant other not living in the household.
- Damage to apartment during an incident of domestic violence.
- Noise from a domestic violence incident.

Summary

One of the major areas of concern for federal policies toward housing has been discrimination, especially racially based discrimination. Laws have been enacted to discourage discriminatory practices in the sale and financing of houses. The Fair Housing Act of 1968, the Housing and Community Development Act of 1974, and the Fair Housing Amendment Act of 1988 together prohibit discrimination in the sale of properties on the basis of race, color, national origin, gender, familial status, and nature of handicap. The ECOA of 1974 (and amendments in 1976) makes it illegal to discriminate in lending on the basis of age, race, color, national origin, and gender. The Home Mortgage Disclosure Act of 1975 and the Community Reinvestment Act of 1978 prevent lenders from discriminating against minorities by redlining certain areas. All of the acts list practices that are illegal and require brokers and lenders to adhere to a set of guidelines to avoid discrimination.

Economic theory suggests that in a competitive market pure discrimination is costly and should not be pervasive. The empirical evidence suggests that there has been some limited discrimination in the lending area. Discrimination in the sales area, especially on the basis of race, is more likely. Whether or not the legislation outlined in this chapter has had a profound effect in changing the practices of brokers and lenders, the laws may make a difference on the margin and also offer a positive statement concerning the type of behavior that is appropriate for public policy.

Key Terms

Blockbusting

Community Reinvestment Act (CRA)

Economics of information

Effects method

Equal Credit Opportunity Act (ECOA)

Fair Housing Act

FHAing

Home Mortgage Disclosure Act (HMDA)

Housing for Older Persons Act

Intent approach

Practices approach

Preference for discrimination

Reasonable accommodations

Redlining

Review Questions

9-1.   List and discuss the major federal legislation designed to promote equity in the housing market.

9-2.   If I own a house and advertise a room for rent, under the Fair Housing Act may I refuse to rent to an individual based on his religion? Race? Explain.

9-3.   What is the motivation behind the Equal Credit Opportunity Act?

9-4.   Indicate three ways in which discriminatory lending practices can be defined. How does Regulation B attempt to define such practices?

9-5.   What are the two economic theories of discrimination?

9-6.   Do empirical studies support the need for discriminatory lending practices? Explain.

9-7.   Has ECOA reduced the amount of discriminatory lending practices?

9-8.   What is the motivation behind the Home Mortgage Disclosure Act and the Community Reinvestment Act?

9-9.   a. What is redlining?
       b. What is FHAing?

9-10. Discuss the requirement of "reasonable accommodations" under the Fair Housing Act Amendments of 1988.

9-11. Discuss the implications of the Violence Against Women Act for women who rent public or Section 8 housing.

Notes

1. G.S. Becker. *The Economics of Discrimination*, 2nd ed. Chicago: University of Chicago Press, 1971.

2. See, for example, R.P. Shay. Factors affecting price, volume, and credit risk in the consumer finance industry. *Journal of Finance* (May 1970), 503–515; W.L. Sartoris. The effects of regulation, population characteristics, and competition on the market for personal cash loans. *Journal of Financial and Quantitative Analysis* (September 1972), 1931–1956; and G.E. Boczar. Competition between banks and finance companies: A cross section study of personal loan debtors. *Journal of Finance* (March 1978), 245–258.

3. M. Ferguson and S. Peters. Is lending discrimination always costly? *Journal of Real Estate Finance and Economics* 21(1) (July 2000), 23–44.

4. G.G. Chandler and D.C. Ewert. Discrimination on the basis of sex under the Equal Credit Opportunity Act, Working Paper No. 8. West Lafayette, IN: Credit Research Center, Purdue University, 1976.

5. W.J. Boyes, D. Hoffman, and S. Low. Lender reactions to information restrictions: The case of banks and the ECOA. *Journal of Money, Credit, and Banking* (May 1986), 211–219.

6. R.B. Avery. Discrimination in consumer credit markets. *Research Papers in Banking and Financing Economics*. Washington, DC: Board of Governors of the Federal Reserve System, 1982.

7. R.L. Peterson and C.M. Peterson. Testing for sex discrimination in commercial bank consumer lending, Working Paper No. 10. West Layfayette, IN: Credit Research Center, Purdue University, 1978.

8. R.L. Peterson. An investigation of sex discrimination in commercial banks' direct consumer lending. *Bell Journal of Economics* 12 (Autumn 1981), 547–561.

9. J. Marshall. Discrimination in consumer credit. In A. Heggestad and J.J. Mingo, eds., *The Costs and Benefits of Public Regulation of Consumer Financial Services*. Cambridge, MA: ABT Associates, 1979.

10. R.P. Shay and D.E. Sexton. Anti-discrimination laws in consumer credit markets: Their impact on creditors approval applications. In A. Heggestad and J.J. Mingo, eds., *The Costs and Benefits of Public Regulation of Consumer Credit Financial Services*. Cambridge, MA: ABT Associates, 1979.

11. E.I. Altman et al. *Application of Classification Techniques in Business, Banking, and Finance*. Greenwich, CT: JAI Press, 1981.

12. G.G. Chandler and D.C. Ewert. Discrimination on the basis of sex under the Equal Credit Opportunity Act, Working Paper No. 8. West Lafayette, IN: Credit Research Center, Purdue University, 1976.

13. B.A. Shinkel. The effects of equal credit opportunity legislation in consumer finance lending. *Journal of Business Research* (March 1980), 113–134.

14. R.W. Bostic and R.W. Martin. Have anti-discrimination housing laws worked? Evidence from trends in black homeownership. *Journal of Real Estate Finance and Economics*. 31(1) (2005), 5–26.

15. Munnell, L. Browne, J. McEneaney, and G. Tootell. Mortgage lending in Boston: Interpreting the HMDA data, Working Paper 92–7. Federal Reserve Bank of Boston, 1992.

16. P. Brimelow and L. Spencer. The hidden clue. *Forbes* (January 4, 1993), 48.

17. J.H. Carr and I.F. Megbolugbe. The Federal Reserve Bank of Boston study on mortgage lending revisited. *Journal of Housing Research* 4(2) (1993), 277–313.

18. In 1991 the Federal Reserve Board voted against the merger between First Interstate BancSystem of Montana and Commerce BancShares of Wyoming after a group of Northern Cheyenne Indians challenged the lending record of First Interstate Bank of Colstrip, Montana, with regard to loans (or lack of loans) made on the Cheyenne reservation. In the same year, consumer groups challenged the merger between First Interstate Bank and Security Pacific, based on the former's high rejection rate of black and Hispanic loan applicants.

19. P. Hutchinson, J. Ostas, and D. Reed. A survey and comparison of redlining influences in urban mortgage lending markets. *AREUEA Journal* (Winter 1977), 463–472.

20. R. Ahlbrandt. Exploratory research on the redlining phenomenon. *AREUEA Journal* (Winter 1977), 473–481.

21. J. Berkovec, G. Canner, S. Gabriel, and T. Hannon. Race, redlining, and residential mortgage loan performance. *Journal of Real Estate Finance and Economics* 9 (1994), 263–294.

22. P. Calem. Mortgage credit availability in low- and moderate-income minority neighborhoods: Are information externalities critical? *Journal of Real Estate Finance and Economics* 13 (1966), 71–89.

23. R.W. Marans. Measuring restrictive rental practices affecting families with children. Washington, DC: Office of Policy Planning and Research, Department of Housing and Urban Development, 1980.

24. P. Goebel and S. Rosenberg. Economic analysis of the impact of antidiscrimination legislation based on familial status, Working Paper. Texas Tech University, February 1990.

Web Sites

http://www.bazelon.org
　Coalition to Preserve the Fair Housing Act

http://www.govtrack.us/congress
　Tracks congressional legislation (introduced, voted by senate, house, passage, signed by president, etc.)

http://www.nami.org
　Information from the National Alliance for the Mentally Ill. Do a quick search for housing.

http://www.hud.gov/offices/fheo/index.cfm
　Office of Fair Housing and Equal Opportunity

http://www.justice.gov/crt/about/hce/caselist.php
> Cases of the housing and civil enforcement section of the U.S. Department of Justice

http://www.hud.gov/offices/fheo/library/huddojstatement.pdf
> Guide for reasonable accommodations under the Fair Housing Act

http://www.mrsc.org/subjects/planning/housing/housing.aspx
> Municipal Research and Services Center of Washington. Provides information on federal laws and regulations regarding housing.

APPENDIX 9-A

Summary of Major Federal Legislation Affecting Real Estate

1932—Reconstruction Finance Act. This act created the Reconstruction Finance Corporation for the purpose of giving liquidity to commercial banks during the Depression.

1932—Federal Home Loan Bank Act. Established the Federal Home Loan Bank System composed of the Federal Home Loan Bank Board and 12 regional banks. One purpose of the banks was to provide liquidity to thrifts.

1932—Home Owners' Loan Act. This act established the Home Owners' Loan Corporation to purchase and refinance defaulted home loans.

1934—National Housing Act. Established the Federal Housing Administration and the Federal Savings and Loan Insurance Corporation. The former insured long-term, fixed-rate loans, and the latter insured the deposits of thrifts against default.

1938—National Mortgage Association of Washington. Established to provide secondary market support for the newly created FHA loans. It was later changed to the Federal National Mortgage Association.

1944—Serviceman's Readjustment Act. Established a mortgage insurance program to be housed within the Veterans Administration.

1949—Housing Act. Proclaimed that the national housing goal was to provide "a decent home and suitable living environment for every American family." It also consolidated the lending programs of the Farmers Home Administration and authorized urban renewal projects.

1959—Housing Act of 1959. Authorized long-term, direct loans through HUD to private, nonprofit sponsors to construct rental and cooperative housing facilities for the elderly and handicapped.

1961—Consolidated Farmers Home Administration Act. Extended the authority of this agency to make residential loans to nonfarmers in rural areas.

1965—Housing and Urban Development Act. Consolidated many housing agencies into the Department of Housing and Urban Development (HUD).

1966—Interest Rate Readjustment Act. Authorized the setting of maximum rates on deposits at thrifts and created the 0.25 percent differential between the maximum rate for thrifts and that for commercial banks.

1968—Fair Housing Act (Title VIII of Civil Rights Act). Prohibited discrimination in real estate sales and mortgage lending on the basis of race, color, national origin, or religion.

1968—Interstate Land Sales Full Disclosure Act. Required the complete disclosure of all relevant facts concerning the interstate sale of certain types of undeveloped land.

1968—Consumer Credit Protection Act. The first title of the act, known as Truth-in-Lending, authorized the Federal Reserve Board to formulate regulations concerning the advance disclosure of certain financial information about consumer loans. The regulations were known as Regulation Z. Title VI of the act is known as the Fair Credit Reporting Act, which established disclosure requirements regarding the information that can be used to grant or deny a loan.

1968—Housing and Urban Development Act. This act privatized the Federal National Mortgage Association (FNMA) and continued its authorization to provide secondary market support for mortgage lending. It also created a new agency, the Government National Mortgage Association (GNMA).

1969—National Environmental Policy Act. This act requires the preparation of an environmental impact statement for real estate developments.

1970—Emergency Home Finance Act. Created a new secondary mortgage market agency, the Federal Home Loan Mortgage Corporation, to support the secondary market in conventional loans originated by thrifts. It also gave FNMA authority to purchase conventional loans in addition to FHA/VA loans.

1974—Flood Disaster Protection Act. Effective in the following year mortgage loans could not be made for the purpose of purchasing dwellings in a flood area unless borrowers obtained flood insurance.

1974—Real Estate Settlement Procedures Act (RESPA) (amended in 1976). This act and the amendments require that mortgage lenders provide borrowers with an advance disclosure of all loan settlement costs and charges. The act also prohibits kickbacks to any person for referring business.

1974—Equal Credit Opportunity Act (ECOA) (amended in 1976). The act prohibits discrimination in lending on the basis of gender, age, marital status, race, religion, or the fact that the applicant receives public assistance (welfare). If rejected, the applicant must be notified within 30 days of the reasons for the rejection.

1975—Home Mortgage Disclosure Act. This act requires the disclosure of an institution's mortgage loans by census tract or zip code. The intention of the act is to prohibit redlining.

1976—ECOA amendments. "Added to the 1974 act the following protected classes; race, color, religion, national origin, age, receipt of pubic assistance, and good faith exercise of rights under the Consumer Credit Protection Act."

1976—RESPA amendments. Requires lenders to provide a good faith estimate of settlement costs and a HUD booklet. Also, a Uniform Settlement Statement (HUD-1) must be provided to the borrower before or at the loan settlement.

1977—Housing Financial Discrimination Act. Requires that all lenders provide a "Fair Lending Notice" to loan applicants with information indicating it is illegal to discriminate in lending based on (a) trends and characteristics of the neighborhood surrounding the housing accommodation to be acquired, and (b) race color religion sex, marital status, national origin, and composition of the neighborhood.

1978—Fair Lending Practices Regulations. These FHLB regulations require member thrifts to develop written underwriting standards, keep a loan registry, not deny loans on the basis of the age of the dwelling, and direct advertising to all segments of the community.

1978—Community Reinvestment Act. This act requires federally insured thrifts to adopt a community reinvestment statement. The statement must define the community in which the institution makes loans, maintain a file for public inspection, and post a notice of the CRA requirements.

1979—Housing and Community Development Amendments. This legislation exempts FHA-insured mortgages from then-current state usury laws that established interest rate ceilings.

1980—Depository Institutions Deregulation and Monetary Control Act. Through this act commercial bank and thrift deposit rate ceilings were gradually eliminated (by the Depository Institutions Deregulation Committee, DIDC). The act also overrode all state usury laws for all types of loans. It also simplified the truth-in lending standards and eased lending restrictions for banks and thrifts.

1980—Omnibus Reconciliation Act. Placed limitations on the volume of tax-exempt mortgage revenue bonds that states and municipalities were allowed to issue.

1982—Garn–St. Germain Act. Preempted state due-on-sale restrictions; allowed thrifts to make consumer, commercial, and agricultural loans; and provided FSLIC and FDIC assistance to institutions with deficient net worth.

1984—Deficit Reduction Act. Extended the tax exemption for qualified mortgage subsidy bonds issued by states and local governments.

1984—Secondary Mortgage Market Enhancement Act (SMMEA). Overrode state laws that (a) limited investments in mortgage securities by state-regulated investors such as life insurance companies and pension funds and (b) required tough registration requirements (blue-sky laws) for mortgage securities. The legislation allowed states to take back this authority by legislative vote within 7 years. By October 1991, the deadline for this option, about half the states had done so.

1986—Tax Reform Act (TRA). Reduced the corporate tax rate from 46 percent to 34 percent and reduced the bad debt deduction from 40 percent to 8 percent. It also provided for 3-year carrybacks and 15-year carryforwards for the net operating loss (NOL) of savings and loan associations.

1987—Competitive Equity Banking Act. Established to make thrifts competitive with commercial banks, it gave them the flexibility to form different types of holding companies and authorized a $10.8 billion FSLIC recapitalization.

1987—Stewart B. McKinney Homeless Assistance Act. Provided grants through HUD for assisting the homeless. Participating jurisdictions must provide a Comprehensive Homeless Assistance Plan (CHAP) to receive funds that may be used to support the operations of shelters for the homeless.

1988—Home Equity Loan Consumer Protection Act. This act loosened the reporting requirements for home equity loans under Regulation Z.

1989—Financial Institutions Reform, Recovery, and Enforcement Act. This act restructured the regulation of the thrift industry. It replaced the FSLIC with the Resolution Trust Corporation and placed it under the control of the FDIC, changed the FHLBB to the Office of Thrift Supervision and placed it under the U.S. Treasury, established risk-based capital requirements for thrifts, prohibited acquisition of certain investments by thrifts, and required that appraisals on mortgaged properties be done by "certified" appraisers.

1990—Cranston–Gonzalez National Affordable Housing Act. This act contains several programs to increase housing affordability for low-income families. Title II, the HOME Investment Partnerships Act, made available about $3 billion to participating local jurisdictions to construct and preserve housing for low-income families. Title IV, the Homeownership and Opportunity for People Everywhere (HOPE) program made $448 million in grants available for rehabilitations of public housing. Other provisions created incentives for owners of low income housing not to remove units from this market.

1992—RESPA Amendment (see 1974). The coverage of RESPA is extended to include subordinate financing.

1992—HMDA Amendment (see 1975). Mortgage companies and other nondepository institutions are required to comply with HMDA.

1993—Tax Act. Increased the marginal tax rate on personal income to 39.6 percent but kept the long-term capital gains tax rate at 28 percent. Losses and credits from certain real estate activities are no longer disallowed by the passive loss rules starting in 1994. This relief is designed especially for real estate brokers, salespeople, and other real estate professionals. It increased the write-off period for nonresidential real estate from 31.5 years to 39 years for properties placed in service after May 12, 1993. By relaxing some debt-financed real property exceptions, the tax act made it easier, in limited ways, for pension funds and other exempt organizations to invest in real estate. It also made low-income rental housing tax credits for investors permanent. Among other changes, units occupied by full-time students qualify for these credits, starting in 1993.

1994—Community Development Bank Bill. This new legislation was designed to aid the expansion of the secondary market for commercial and multifamily real estate mortgage loans. The bill helps reduce securitization transaction costs, expand investor markets, and facilitate banks' entry into the secondary market by extending to all highly rated commercial and multifamily real estate securities the same benefits enjoyed by similar residential securities under SMMA (see 1984).

1995—Home Ownership and Equity Protection Act (HOEPA). Amends the Truth in Lending Act (TILA) and provides special protections for borrowers in certain non-purchase, high-cost loans secured by their homes.

1995—Housing for Older Persons Act. This act states that it is legal for communities to market themselves as age-restricted provided that they maintain that 80 percent of the occupied units are occupied by at least one person who is 55 years of age or older. It also exempted from personal liability individuals who relied in good faith on an application for an exemption related to older persons.

1997—Taxpayer Relief Act. First $500,000 of gain ($250,000 for single persons) on the sale of residence is exempted from taxes if taxpayer resided in house 2 of the 5 years prior to sale. Capital gains rate on commercial properties reintroduced effective May 7, 1997.

1998—The Homeowners Protection Act of 1998 (HPA). Requires lenders to inform borrowers (up front and annually) about their right to request cancellation of their mortgage insurance and to automatically cancel the mortgage insurance for those who do not request it when the equity in the residence reaches certain levels.

1999—REIT Modernization Act of 1999 (RMA). This act allows REITs to own 100 percent of a taxable subsidiary (TRS). Taxable subsidiaries are those that provide otherwise taxable services. The TRS cannot exceed 20 percent of the value of the REIT's assets. This act is intended to make it easier for REITs to manage real estate properties where some of the services are nonrental in nature.

2000—E-Sign Act. Promotes the growth of online commerce including real estate transactions.

2002—Small Business Liability Relief and Brownfields Revitalization Act. This act promotes the redevelopment of brownfields (contaminated properties) through federal funding and liability relief.

2003—American Dream Downpayment Act. Provides an average of $5,000 in grants to low-income families in 2003 and 2004 to help with downpayments and closing costs of their first home.

2003—REIT Improvement Act of 2003. Purpose is to clarify and correct some issues associated with the Reit Modernization Act of 1999. For one thing it eliminates barriers to foreign investment in U.S. REITs and allows the Internal Revenue Service (IRS) to impose monetary penalties for reasonable violations of the REIT tests rather than imposing a loss in REIT status.

2005—Violence Against Women Act Reauthorization (originally passed in 1994 and reauthorized in 2000). Protects women in public housing and Section 8 vouchers (only) from discriminatory evection based on domestic violence, sexual assault, and stalking.

2008—Housing and Economic Recovery Act (HERA, passed in 2008, effective July 30, 2009). This act applies to all purchases and refinances for both primary and secondary houses including home equity loans. The intention of the law is to bring more transparency to the lending process by restricting unreasonable fees and requiring disclosures including an appraisal on the property. It established the Federal Finance Housing Agency and the federal Housing Finance Oversight Board.

2008—Secure and Fair Enforcement for Mortgage Licensing Act of 2008 (SAFE Act). Requires states to establish a registration and licensing system for mortgage loan originators (MLOs). See Chapter 7 for more detail.

2009—American Recovery and Reinvestment Act of 2009. This act was part of the 2009 stimulus plan for the economy. It provided a tax credit of up to $8,000 for first-time home buyers (depending upon the price of the house and the buyer's income).

2010—Dodd-Frank Wall Street Reform and Consumer Protection Act of 2010. This Act made the most significant changes in the financial regulatory landscape since the Great Depression of the 1930s. It affects all federal financial regulatory agencies. See Chapter 7 for more information.

THE SECONDARY MORTGAGE MARKET

LEARNING OBJECTIVES

The purpose of this chapter is to introduce you to the workings of the secondary mortgage market. After reading this chapter, you should know why the secondary mortgage market exists, how this market developed, how the market works, why it is important for a more efficient allocation of funds in the real estate market, what the major secondary mortgage market agencies are, and what portion the market commands in real estate lending. You should also understand how agency problems and the sub-prime mortgage crisis of 2007 to 2010 affected the major secondary mortgage market entities. You will see that the crisis led to the failure of several private firms engaged in the secondary mortgage market as well as a bailout of the government sponsored enterprises (Fannie Mae and Freddie Mac).

Issues such as factors that influence the size and timing of cash flows and the valuation of mortgage-backed securities and derivative securities are also discussed in the next chapter.

INTRODUCTION

We begin this chapter by answering two important questions: (1) What is a secondary mortgage market? (2) Why does it exist? The answers to these questions will give you a sound understanding of the nature of the secondary mortgage market.

NATURE OF THE SECONDARY MARKET

What Is a Secondary Mortgage Market?

A secondary mortgage market is one in which existing mortgages are bought and sold. This is in contrast to the primary market, where mortgages are originated. Mortgages are originated by the initial lenders, such as thrifts or mortgage bankers. Some thrifts and all mortgage bankers then sell these loans in the secondary market. By definition, the owner of a mortgage that was purchased in the secondary market did not originate the loan. Agencies and firms that purchase mortgages in the secondary market most often raise the funds required for the purchase by issuing bonds or other types of debt

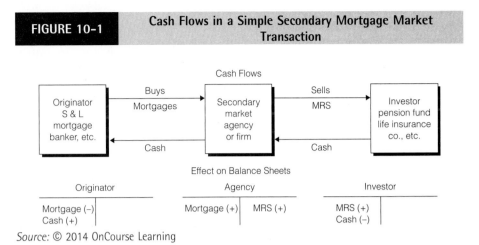

FIGURE 10-1 · **Cash Flows in a Simple Secondary Mortgage Market Transaction**

Source: © 2014 OnCourse Learning

instruments. They will pledge the mortgages (now their assets) as collateral for the debt they issue. The debt issue is termed a **mortgage-backed security (MBS)** because it is backed up, or **collateralized**, by mortgages. Mortgage-backed securities are also bought and sold and are considered part of the secondary mortgage market.

A very simple example of how funds might flow in this market is shown in Figure 10-1. The ultimate source of the funds is the investors who purchase the bonds (mortgage-backed securities) from the secondary mortgage market agency or firm. The agency or firm then uses the funds to purchase mortgages from, for example, a thrift. The thrift uses the funds to originate mortgages. Although the transactions occur in the reverse order and take some time, it may be useful to think of the entire process as occurring instantaneously as described. The important thing is that investors supply the funds and homeowners use them to purchase residences. As a result, the amount of funds flowing into mortgages is not restricted by the amount that thrifts and banks can raise through deposits alone.

Note that the simple process described here has created a series of assets and liabilities even though there is only one source (investors) and only one use (homeowners) of funds. The homeowner's asset (residence) is partially offset by a liability (mortgage). The mortgage is an asset to the secondary market entity and is offset by a liability (MBS). The MBS is, in turn, an asset for the investor. There is no limit to the number of assets and liabilities that can be created in the secondary mortgage market. The investor, for example, might fund the purchase of the mortgage-backed securities by issuing its own form of debt and using the mortgage-backed securities as collateral. In this case, there would be two mortgage-backed securities ultimately backed by the mortgages. We will see an example of just such a secondary mortgage market transaction in the following.

Why Does the Secondary Mortgage Market Exist?

We all have a picture in our mind of Jimmy Stewart, as the beleaguered savings and loan association president in *It's a Wonderful Life,* fending off a mob of depositors anxious to get their money. Either because of rumors of fiscal mismanagement of the institution or just a need for liquidity in times of unemployment, a "run" on the bank was just the sort of dramatic occurrence movie audiences could relate to. In *It's a Wonderful Life,* Jimmy Stewart tried to persuade the anxious depositors that their funds were safe but tied up in the form of residential loans to their neighbors. Such ugly scenes were not far from reality in times when financial institutions faced severe liquidity constraints that resulted from an inability to quickly sell some of their assets in a liquid, efficient market.

Other than stocks and bonds held by commercial banks, much of the assets of lending institutions, particularly thrifts, were illiquid mortgage loans. Up until as recently as the late 1960s, it was very difficult for many thrifts to sell their mortgage assets. There were two reasons for this.

First, their mortgage assets were not homogeneous. The portfolio of a thrift would consist of many different loans with different interest rates, dates of maturity, and loan-to-value ratios. Selling $25 million or $50 million of loans with such different characteristics could be very difficult. Second, potential buyers were concerned with the default risk, particularly of conventional loans. Investors nationwide had little or no ability to judge the soundness of loans that were underwritten by a localized thrift.

As a result of the inability to buy and sell mortgages, there was often a persistent mismatch of the supply and demand for capital. The mismatch took two forms. First, there was a regional mismatch. This occurred when there was a greater supply of capital (deposits) in one region and a greater demand (for mortgages) in another. A more stable region with moderate housing growth will have an excess supply of savings, and a rapidly growing area with significant additions to the housing stock will have a deficiency of capital. A secondary market for mortgages alleviated this mismatch by allowing thrifts in capital-surplus areas to take their excess deposits and purchase mortgages from thrifts in capital-deficit areas. Second, there was an institutional mismatch in the sense that traditional mortgage lenders may have had insufficient funds to meet the mortgage demand, and other nonmortgage intermediaries may have had a need to invest funds in long-term assets. This occurred, for example, when individuals began to place more of their savings with pension funds and less with thrifts and banks. The latter have fewer funds with which to originate mortgages, whereas the former have a need to invest in long-term assets. The secondary mortgage market offered a solution to this mismatch by facilitating the sale of mortgages from the thrifts and banks to pension funds.

The secondary mortgage market, then, developed because it solved these two mismatch problems. Additionally, the growth of this market in the 1970s and 1980s was stimulated by other developments. During this time, life insurance companies gradually reduced their presence in the mortgage market. There was a need for their correspondent mortgage bankers to find new sources of funds to purchase the loans they originated. Also, pension funds grew in size and needed investments of a long-term nature. We noted in earlier chapters that thrifts were particularly vulnerable to the interest rate risk that resulted from their maturity mismatch and an increase in the volatility of interest rates. Pension funds and long-term investors would be able to handle this risk better. At the same time, some secondary market firms began to purchase mortgages, either because of their risk preference or their ability to issue mortgage-backed securities that matched the maturity of the mortgages they purchased. By the 1980s numerous thrifts attempting to avoid interest rate risk sold so many of the loans they originated that they essentially became mortgage bankers. Investors in mortgage-backed securities did not wish to take on default risk, however. So another impetus to the development of a secondary mortgage market was the federal government's willingness to support it through guarantees of timely and full payment.

Finally, the federal government encouraged the development of the secondary mortgage market by overriding state laws that hindered its development. Many states had laws that limited investment in mortgage-backed securities by state-regulated investors, such as life insurance companies and pension funds, and had tough securities registration requirements (blue-sky laws). In 1984 Congress passed the Secondary Mortgage Market Enhancement Act (SMMEA) to overcome these obstacles. The act removed state-imposed limits on the types and quantities of mortgage-backed securities that investors could purchase. At the same time, it exempted mortgage securities from state securities registration requirements. (The charters of Freddie Mac and Fannie Mae exempt them from the registration laws as well.)

At the time the act was passed, Congress gave the states the option of taking back the authority for setting limits on investments by state-regulated investors if the state legislatures voted to override SMMEA within 7 years. By October 1991, the deadline for the override, 21 states had voted to override the preemption from state investment laws and another 5 opted to override the preemptions on the blue-sky laws. The remaining states, about one-half, are bound by the provisions of SMMEA.

MORTGAGE-BACKED SECURITIES

Characteristics of Mortgage-Backed Securities

The key to a successful secondary market for mortgages is the creation of mortgage-backed securities (MBSs) that are acceptable to investors. Acceptable securities have the three following characteristics:

1. MBSs will have some form of **credit enhancement.** This means that the MBS will have less default risk than the underlying mortgages that serve as collateral. The safety of MBSs can be enhanced by any of several methods. The methods are outlined in a comparison of MBSs in Table 10-1. Just as with corporate bonds, many MBSs are rated by Standard and Poor's and Moody's for their safety. Many investors, such as pension funds, are prohibited by state law from investing in securities that have less than an investment-grade rating. As a result, a strong rating will broaden the market for the MBS and make it more liquid. This increases the need for credit enhancement.

2. MBSs need to avoid **double taxation.** A secondary market entity that issues MBSs and uses the funds to purchase mortgages will have interest revenue, which it passes through to the investors in the MBSs. MBS issuers must make sure that their revenues and the cash flows to the investors are not both taxed. Otherwise, the double taxation will offset any benefits of the arrangement.

3. MBSs need to tailor their cash flows so as to appeal to investors. Many investors do not desire to invest in securities whose cash flows exactly replicate that of a mortgage. If the cash flows from the mortgages can be rearranged in amount and timing and then distributed to the MBS investors, the market for them will be larger and more liquid.

TABLE 10-1
Mortgage-Backed Securities

	TYPICAL CREDIT ENHANCEMENT	EXTENT TO WHICH CASH FLOWS REARRANGED
Pass-through	FHA/VA loans in pool Agency guarantee	None
Mortgage-backed bonds	Agency equity Pool insurance	Moderate
Mortgage pay-through bonds	Agency equity Pool insurance	Moderate
Collateralized mortgage obligation	Agency equity Pool insurance Letter of credit	Substantial
Debt of agency	FHA/VA loans in pool	Moderate

Source: © 2014 OnCourse Learning

Types of Mortgage-Backed Securities

There are four principal types of mortgage-backed securities:

1. Mortgage pass-through securities
2. Mortgage-backed bonds
3. Mortgage pay-through bonds
4. Collateralized mortgage obligations

MORTGAGE PASS-THROUGH SECURITIES

Pass-through securities were the first popular MBSs. The early successful pass-throughs were promoted by the Government National Mortgage Association (GNMA), a federal agency within the department of Housing and Urban Development (HUD), in the mid-to-late 1960s. With a pass-through, the investor is said to have an undivided interest in the pool of mortgages. The investor has an "ownership" position in the mortgages. What this means is that he or she will receive the mortgage payments (principal and interest) and any prepayments just as if he or she were the lender.

Here is a simplified example of how a pass-through works. A thrift (or other originator) groups or packages together, say, 100 fixed-rate loans of $100,000 each, all with the same maturity and contract rate of interest—assume 30 years at 10 percent. It will next issue $10 million in bonds to obtain the cash to finance the mortgages. The bonds may have a minimum denomination of $25,000. Four hundred such bonds will be backed by the pool of mortgages. The bonds promise a 9.5 percent yield. Note that the mortgage originator earns 10 percent on the mortgages and pays 9.5 percent to investors in the bonds. The difference, 0.5 percent, will be shared by the originator who services the loan and the agency that provides for credit enhancement. In the case of GNMA bonds, that agency guarantees the timely payment of interest and principal and collects a small fee. Additional enhancement is gained by the provision that the mortgages be held in the hands of a trustee. Investors are satisfied with the 9.5 percent yield because of the credit enhancement and the high yield relative to other "safe" investments.

Assume that an investor buys two bonds ($50,000). At the end of the first month, the mortgagors will remit their payments. If all do so, then the total payments on the $10 million in mortgages will be $87,756.27, of which $83,333.33 will be interest and the remainder, $4,422.94, will be principal. The investors will receive this principal (proratedly) and interest at 9.5 percent, or $83,589.61 ($4,422.94 + 0.095/12 × $10,000,000). The investor holding two bonds will receive 0.5 percent (2/400) of this amount, or $417.95, of which $22.11 will be principal reduction. The principal balance of his two bonds at the end of the first month will be $49,977.89. The investor will receive the same amount the following month, assuming that no mortgagor in the pool decides to prepay his or her entire loan. If during a given month one or more mortgagors repay their loans, because of a move to a new residence, for instance, the entire amount of the prepayment will be divided proratedly to the investors in the pass-through bonds. In that month the investors' checks will be unexpectedly large and the principal balance of the bond will be reduced more quickly than normal. Essentially, bond investors have a small section of a larger portfolio of loans and receive cash flows that replicate those of a mortgage originator that retains loans in its portfolio.

Investors are attracted to pass-throughs because of their relatively high-yield, liquidity, and risk-free qualities. However, many investors do not like the uncertainty of the timing of the cash flows, due to unpredictable prepayments of mortgages.

Also, mortgages prepay more quickly when interest rates drop, so that the prepayments must be reinvested at lower market rates. Investors in pass-throughs face the same callability risk as mortgage lenders. For these reasons, other MBSs have been developed to avoid the uncertainty surrounding the timing of the cash flows.

Some pass-throughs are rated by the rating agencies (Standard and Poor's and Moody's). Those agencies review the credit risk of the collateral as affected by the types of property, their location, and loan-to-value ratios. They will also rate the capability of the issuer to make cash advances to cover the principal and interest on delinquent and defaulted properties.

Some lenders have pools of mortgages that carry neither Federal Housing Administration/Veterans Administration (FHA/VA) nor **private mortgage insurance (PMI).** These pools are difficult to securitize into pass-throughs because of their default risk. Often the lenders do not wish to purchase pool insurance but prefer to self-insure the loans. **Pool insurance** is PMI on the entire pool, not the individual mortgages. Usually only a small percentage—for example, 10 percent—of the pool is insured. A pass-through structure that allows for the loans' securitization is the **senior/subordinated pass-through.** In this arrangement, the lender creates two securities from a pool of mortgages, one having the priority of receiving payments from the pool. From a $100 million pool of mortgages, the lender may create a senior pass-through with a principal balance of $94 million. Since the $94 million pool is secured by $100 million in mortgages, it can be described as overcollateralized.

The lender typically will sell the senior security and retain the rights to the cash flows on the subordinated security—the remaining $6 million, in this example. This overcollateralization enhances the safety of the senior security and gives it investment-grade quality, because cash flows from $100 million in mortgages are available to meet the payments on only $94 million in pass-throughs. A moderate number of delinquencies and defaults from the pool can occur before the payments on the senior pass-throughs are threatened. Instead of insurance or government guarantees, the overcollateralization provides the credit enhancement.

If properly constructed, the senior securities will receive an investment-grade rating from the rating agencies. The agencies will assign an appropriate level of subordination, considering the level of credit risk inherent in the pool. The credit risk is determined by considering the likely amount and timing of defaults, the time required to resolve defaults, and the likely recovery from foreclosures. If an investment grade is assigned, the securities will trade at prices that yield 20 to 40 basis points less than whole-loan pass-throughs (those without overcollateralization). If a significant number of defaults occur early in the life of the pool, then some payments on the senior security may be missed. This risk is reduced, however, by increased levels of overcollateralization.

To see how this type of pass-through works, consider a popular arrangement called the interest shifting mechanism. Under this type of senior/subordinated structure, payments from the mortgage pool are made to both the senior pass-through holders and the holder of the subordinated interest (the lender usually retains the subordinated interest, but on occasion may sell it).

However, a disproportionate share of the payments from the pool (including prepayments) is shifted to the senior pass-through holders. This has the effect of lowering the principal balance on the senior security more rapidly than that on the subordinated interest, increasing the level of subordination and safety of the senior security. In addition, the securities can contain a provision that, if losses through delinquency and default are large enough to endanger the promised payments to the senior security, then all future cash flows can be reassigned to that security until a specified level of subordination is achieved.

Since the senior securities are priced higher than whole-loan pass-throughs (they trade at lower yields), the pickup in value accrues to the lender who retained the subordinated security. In simple terms, the lender may be able to sell the $94 million in pass-throughs for $95 million. Since the lender retains the $6 million in subordinated loans, the total value of the pool to the lender is $101 million. Value has been created by the subordination process. The lender incurs the risk of loss, however, if the default rate on the pool becomes excessive. All defaults are charged to the subordinated position. The lender will benefit from the arrangement as long as losses from defaults are less than the $1 million "profit" picked up from the sale of the senior position. A yield comparison of nonsubordinated pass-throughs with subordinated securities is made in Chapter 11.

MORTGAGE-BACKED BONDS

Mortgage-backed bonds (MBBs) are mortgage-backed securities that promise payments similar to corporate bonds. That is, they promise semiannual payments of interest only until maturity, with the face value due at maturity. The mortgages are owned by the issuer of the bonds; investors have no ownership interest in the mortgages. These bonds are issued primarily by private financial firms. They are usually, but not always, backed by conventional residential and commercial mortgages. The maturity on the bonds will be less than that on the mortgages, and the yield will be slightly below that on the mortgages. Credit enhancement is accomplished through overcollateralization. This means that the face value of the pool of mortgages will be greater than that of the bonds. The issuer makes up the difference with the equity contribution. Figure 10-2 shows an example where an issuer sells $100 million in MBBs, adds an additional $25 million, and purchases $125 million in conventional mortgages. The issuer will attempt to estimate the cash flows coming in from the pool of mortgages, but there will be some uncertainty due to prepayments. Also, the maturity of the MBBs will be less than that of the mortgages, but likely longer than the average life of a mortgage. For example, the maturity on the MBBs may be 15 years and that on the mortgages 30. However, because of prepayments, the average life of the mortgages may be, say, 12 years. A small percentage of mortgages will last the full 30 years, of course. Finally, there is some danger that some of the mortgages may default, and if they are without FHA/VA or PMI, the MBB issuer will sustain a loss on such loans.

Hopefully, if all goes well, the issuer will take the monthly interest and principal payments from the pool of mortgages and invest them in a fund that earns interest. Then, semiannually, the issuer will remit interest payments to

FIGURE 10-2	Cash Flows for a Mortgage-Backed Bond

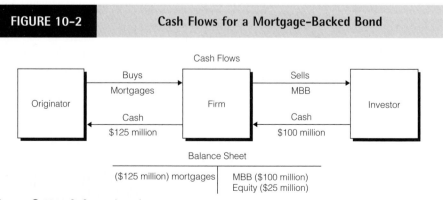

Source: © 2014 OnCourse Learning

the bondholders from this fund. Any prepayments of mortgages are added to the fund. The fund should continue to grow since interest, principal, and prepayments from the pool of mortgages will be larger than the interest payments on the bonds. At the maturity date, the fund should be large enough to pay the face value of the bonds. Any residual left over will be returned to the issuer as a return on the $25 million equity investment. An example of the cash flows and the pricing of MBBs is provided in the Chapter 11.

Uncertainty surrounding the achievement of the scenario just mentioned is the reason for the overcollateralization. If insufficient funds are available to pay off the principal on the bonds, then some of the mortgages will have to be sold. This would be true if there were fewer prepayments of mortgages than expected, if there were a large number of defaults, or if the interest rate earned on the reserve fund dropped to a low level. The mortgages are usually placed in the hands of a trustee who will mark-to-market any changes in the value of the mortgages and make sure that the agreed-on overcollateralization is maintained (125 percent, in this example). **Mark-to-market** refers to valuing the mortgages on a frequent basis as a result of the changes in interest rates. A rise in rates, for example, will cause the market value of mortgages to fall, thus endangering the value of the collateral. If the overcollateralization falls below the agreed-on limit, the trustee will require that the issuer purchase additional mortgages from its own sources and add them to the pool.

Rating agencies such as Standard and Poor's and Moody's rate the MBBs. They consider a number of factors:

- *The quality of the mortgages in the pool.* Mortgage quality will be affected by insurance backing (FHA/VA or PMI), loan-to-value ratios, status as residential or commercial, first or second mortgages, and so forth.
- *The interest rate spread between that on the mortgages and that on the MBBs.* The greater the spread, the higher the safety.
- *The likely rate of prepayments of the mortgages.* Low-interest mortgages are less likely to prepay if interest rates have risen, for example.
- *The geographic diversification of the mortgages in the pool.*
- *The amount of overcollateralization.*

All of these considerations affect the rating and, therefore, the amount of overcollateralization chosen by the issuer. The extra $25 million in mortgages is a buffer against the uncertainty of the rate of prepayment and the risk of default. Some issuers will enhance the credit rating of the MBBs further by providing for pool insurance or a letter of credit from a large commercial bank.

MORTGAGE PAY-THROUGH BONDS

Mortgage pay-through bonds (MPTBs) are mortgage-backed securities that are a cross between pass-throughs and MBBs. As with MBBs the issuer retains ownership of the pool of mortgages and issues the MPTB as a debt obligation. The issuer also will over collateralize the debt obligation. Just as with a pass-through, the cash flows to the investor are based on the coupon rate of interest, while principal from amortization and prepayments is passed through as received from the pool of mortgages. Thus, the investor in these bonds faces the same callability risk as those in pass-throughs. Paythroughs are also rated by the agencies, based on the same factors associated with MBBs. Because the scheduled amortization of the mortgages and prepayments is passed through to reduce the principal of the bonds, the extent of overcollateralization is less than with MBBs.

COLLATERALIZED MORTGAGE OBLIGATIONS

Collateralized mortgage obligations (CMOs) go the farthest in rearranging the uncertain cash flows from a pool of mortgages into those desired by investors. The restructuring of the cash flows is the most complicated of all mortgage-backed securities. The object of CMOs is to rearrange the mortgage cash flows into several different bond-like securities with different maturities. The different bond classes are called **tranches.** A typical CMO will have three or four tranches. Because the cash flows from the mortgage pool are uncertain, there will be a tranche into which all residual cash flows accrue. This residual tranche often will be "owned" by the issuer of the CMO. Thus, the issuer will have to have an equity interest in the CMO. The cash flows that accrue to residual are a return-on-equity. A detail of the cash flows of a CMO is outlined in the next chapter, but the basic structure is presented in Table 10-2.

In this example, an issuer sells $100 million in CMOs, adds $6 million of its own equity funds, and purchases $106 million of 10 percent mortgages. The CMO is overcollateralized by $6 million, or 6 percent, of the issue. The CMO has three bond-like tranches and a residual class. The Tranche A bonds earn the lowest rate, 9.25 percent. The other tranches earn somewhat more because of their longer maturity, which results from the order in which cash flows received from the mortgages are distributed to the various tranches. Tranche A bondholders are paid off first. In addition to interest, Tranche A bondholders receive (1) any scheduled amortization of the mortgages, (2) any prepayments of the mortgages, and (3) deferred interest earned by the Tranche Z bondholders but transferred to the Tranche A bondholders. The principal amount of the Tranche A bonds is reduced by these three items. If a large number of prepayments occur, the maturity of the Tranche A bonds will be shortened. For this reason, the maturity of these bonds is stated as a range of 5 to 9 years. Tranche B bondholders receive interest payments only, but no repayment or prepayment of principal until the Tranche A bondholders are completely paid. After the Tranche A holders are paid, the Tranche B holders receive all repayments and prepayments of principal, as well as interest deferred and transferred from Tranche Z. This pattern is followed for the remaining tranches. In any year, payments not given to any of the tranches create a residual that accrues to the equity interest of the issuer. This description of the cash flows omits a discussion of loan losses due to defaults and foreclosures of the underlying mortgages. Any loan losses will, of course, reduce the amount available to be disbursed to the bond (CMO) holders. Some CMOs are structured to provide that all of the losses due to defaults and foreclosures will be assigned to the last tranche, protecting the senior tranches. In the event the principal from the last tranche is exhausted by loan losses then additional loan

TABLE 10-2

Structure of a Collateralized Mortgage Obligation

ASSETS	LIABILITIES	MATURITY (YEARS)	COUPON (PERCENT)	AMOUNT
Mortgages $106,000,000	Tranche A	5–9	9.25	$ 30,000,000
Yield 10%	Tranche B	9–14	9.50	30,000,000
	Tranche C	12–17	10.00	25,000,000
	Tranche Z	28–30	10.50	15,000,000
	Equity			6,000,000
TOTAL $106,000,000				106,000,000

Source: © 2014 OnCourse Learning

losses will be assigned to the next highest tranche. A simplified example of the cash flows where loan losses are considered is provided in the next chapter.

A careful inspection of the detailed cash flows of this CMO in the following chapter may clear up any uncertainties as to the flow pattern of funds from the mortgage pool to the various tranches of the CMO. Some CMOs are backed not by a pool of mortgages but by an MBS issued by another agency. Thus, a private firm might purchase pass-throughs issued by GNMA and rearrange the cash flows to meet the needs of investors. In this situation, the market experiences a "layering" of mortgage-backed securities.

A special form of CMO is a stripped MBS. Generally, two classes are established. One class of investors has the right to receive all interest payments from a pool of mortgages, while the other has the right to receive all the principal payments—both scheduled amortization and prepayments. The interest-only (IO) and principal-only (PO) securities have some peculiar payment patterns, especially when interest rates are volatile. Some investors purchase them to hedge against the effect of interest rate changes on their other assets. These are also discussed in Chapter 11.

Swaps

A **swap** is a secondary mortgage market transaction that occurs when a lender sells mortgages to an agency that in turn issues an MBS, such as a pass-through, back to the lender. Early in the development of the secondary market came the realization that, for various reasons, the investor in the MBS might very well be the lender that desired to sell the portfolio of mortgages. In such a case, the agency would "swap" the mortgages for the MBS. Why would a lender such as a thrift prefer to hold an MBS backed by its own pool of mortgages rather than the pool itself? The cash flows associated with the underlying pool of mortgages are not altered, yet resources are expended in converting the pool to an MBS. Efficient market theory would predict a loss in value due to these expended resources.

One reason for a swap lies in the liquidity advantage of an MBS over individual loans. Thrifts can use them as collateral to borrow funds (this was especially true when Regulation Q set limits on the rate they could offer on deposits but not on borrowed funds). They also can sell them more quickly if there is a need for cash, such as to meet the demands of net withdrawals of deposits. Even if it sells the MBS, the lender will likely retain the servicing and receive a servicing fee. The lender will receive a rate on the MBS from 0.25 percent to 0.5 percent less than that on the pools of mortgages it originally owned. The spread is the agency's fee for underwriting and guaranteeing the mortgages in the pools and the timely payment of interest and principal. Also, the MBSs are considered an investment in real estate for those regulatory rules that require a certain percentage of assets of thrifts to be held in such investments.

Some secondary mortgage market agencies and firms specialize in one or two types of MBSs, while others issue a variety. These agencies and firms are discussed later in this chapter.

RESIs

Although most mortgage-backed securities provide some sort of credit enhancement, there are exceptions. For example, in 2004 Bank of America issued some structured MBSs that passed all of the credit risk through to the bondholders. The securities, called **real estate synthetic investment securities (RESI)**, are rated by agencies such as Moody's or Standard and Poor's. The bonds are structured so that losses from default are passed to the lowest rated classes first. Ratings ranged from a low of B-3 to a high of A-2 by Moody's Investor Service. The securities were backed by, primarily, jumbo loans. Because the default risk is passed through to the bondholders, the return on the RESIs is quite high. In 2004, when rates on home loans were approximately 6 percent, investors in lower-graded RESIs were getting approximately 15 percent.

Commercial Mortgage-Backed Securities

The counterpart to the securitization of residential mortgages is the **commercial mortgage-backed security (CMBS)**. CMBSs got their start with the savings and loan crisis of the late 1980s when the Resolution Trust Corporation (RTC) took over many failed S&Ls and needed to dispose of the commercial loans on their books. The RTC packaged many of the loans into pools and sold CMBSs backed by the pools. RTC issuance of CMBSs peaked in 1992 when they represented 63 percent of all CMBS issues in that year. The basic CMBS issue created by the RTC included two tranches, one a senior and the other a subordinated tranche. The **senior tranche** received all principal payments including prepayments as well as any cash flows from foreclosures. The **subordinated tranche** bore all losses from defaults. The RTC completed its mission and disbanded in 1995. The private market then filled the CMBS void left by the RTC's departure.

The process of securitization is essentially the same as for a CMO except that commercial mortgages back the bonds that are issued. Commercial mortgages, of course, include mortgages on commercial properties such as hotels, office buildings, warehouses, hospitals, shopping centers, and so forth. A secondary mortgage market entity will issue bonds to be used to acquire the commercial mortgages. The CMBSs can be backed up in several ways. First, they may be backed up by a pool of many different mortgages on many different properties. Second, the CMBS can be backed up by a single loan on a very large property (such as Rockefeller Center in New York City). Third, the CMBS may be backed up by a single loan made on many properties.

The process begins when a pool of mortgages is warehoused until a sufficient volume is reached. Information on the loans and the properties that back them are then sent to a rating agency such as Standard and Poor's, Moody's, or Fitch ICBA. The rating agencies will review the commercial loans and the properties that back them and then issue a credit rating based on the likelihood of default. After a preliminary assessment of the assets underlying the commercial mortgage the rating agency will conduct site visits to the property and analyze the strength of the underlying regional economy in which the property is located. The rating agency will next review the legal documents associated with the loan. Factors that are favorable to a good rating include a well-diversified loan portfolio in terms of property type and geographical area, borrowers who have no history of default, loans with high loan-to-value ratios, and good debt coverage ratios. In a 1997 study Harding and Sirmans[1] found that the most important factors in determining the required rate of return on a given tranche of a CMBS were (1) the quality of the loan (loan-to-value ratio and debt service coverage ratio), (2) the property type (multifamily properties were viewed as more safe than hotel and office properties), and (3) the existence of cross-collateralization (loan collateralized by more than one property). A study by Fitch ICBA[2] in 1997 also found the default rate on CMBSs to be low when the properties involved were multifamily (3.9 percent) but high when the property was a hotel (4.2 percent). This study also found that variable-rate loans were more likely to default (5.4 percent) than fixed-rate loans (3.5 percent).

Once rated, the loans are then contributed to a **Real Estate Mortgage Investment Conduit (REMIC)**. Just as with a CMO, often the CMBSs backed by the pool of loans in the REMIC will be structured into different tranches with different maturity dates. Also, just as with a CMO, the early tranches will receive interest and principal and prepayments prior to the later tranches. Additionally, the CMBS may be structured so that any losses from the commercial mortgage pool, say, because of a default, are allocated entirely to the later tranches. Thus the later tranches are paid later and suffer any default losses disproportionately to the earlier tranches. For this reason the rating agencies will rate the later tranches lower and the required rate-of-return will be higher. It is not unusual to see an early tranche rated AAA and a later tranche in the same CMBS to be rated BBB–, for example. In the late 1990s Standard and Poor's reported that the 15-year cumulative default rate on its database involving 6,700 obligors was 1.06 percent for AAA-rated loans and 4.21 percent on its BBB-rated loans. The default rate was 42.72 percent on CCC-rated loans.

The initial success of the CMBSs came from the fact that many investors desired to receive the high yields resulting from lending on commercial properties but also wanted the diversification benefits of having their investment in a CMBS backed by many loans in a single pool. The rating of the CMBSs by the rating agencies was an essential ingredient in the process of developing the market for CMBSs. One drawback, however, was the heterogeneous nature of the loans in the pool. A pool of residential loans is often more homogeneous in terms of interest rate, maturity, and loan-to-value ratio. Commercial mortgages, on the other hand, share few terms in common with each other. So it was essential for the rating agencies to rate the CMBSs and each of their tranches so as to provide the market with a guide to pricing.

In 1995 the amount of CMBS's outstanding was $29.1 billion. A decade later the 2005 outstanding amount had reached $540.8 billion. At the end of the second quarter of 2012 the outstanding amount was $669.6 billion. It is clear CMBSs have become a major source of capital for the commercial real estate market. We will explore this market in more detail in Chapter 17, Sources of Funds for Commercial Real Estate Properties.

Credit Tenant Lease Security

A **credit tenant lease (CTL) security** is a special form of mortgage security. A mortgage debt security called a CTL is issued and is backed by real estate. In the case of a CTL, the purchaser has an extra layer of protection. With a CTL the borrower, say, the developer of the property, issues the CTLs and then collateralizes them with the property and the rent to be received from the tenants of the property. The tenants will be directed to make lease payments to a trustee who, in turn, makes interest payments to the holders of the CTLs. As with CMOs the CTLs can have various tranches. If the tenants fail to make their lease payments (say, the tenants go bankrupt), the owner of the CTL has recourse to the property as collateral. Because of the manner in which the CTLs are collatealrized, their default risk is a function of both the financial position of the tenants (who make lease payments) and the value of the property. When a credit agency such as Moody's rates a CTL, it will look at the financial position of the tenant. It will also consider the "loan-to-dark" value of the property. The loan-to-dark ratio is the ratio of the loan amount to the value of the property if vacant, or dark. The value of a property is less when vacant than when it has tenants because to lease a property the owner of the property must incur expenses such as renovation, tenant improvements, and leasing commissions. The rating agency will also look at the term of the lease versus the maturity date on the CTL. It is desirable, from the standpoint of the CTL holder, for the term of the leases backing it up to be longer than the maturity date on the CTL. In 1992 slightly less than $1 billion in CTLs was issued. By 1999 the issuance had risen to well over $3 billion.

Credit, Counterparty Risks, and Credit Default Swaps

Consider an owner of a debt security such as an MBS. The MBS could have been issued by Fannie Mae, Freddie Mac, or a private issuer such as a large investment banker. The MBS would, of course, be backed by a pool of mortgages purchased by the MBS issuer. **Credit risk** refers to the risk that the MBS issuer may default on the obligation. The issuer may not be able to pay interest or principal on the MBS because of a deterioration in the value of the mortgage portfolio. The MBS will lose value and, in worst case scenario, may be worthless.

Counterparty risk refers to the risk that either party to a contract may default. Such a situation may exist in what is referred to as a **credit default swap (CDS)**. The owner of the MBS may wish to "insure" against a loss in its value should the MBS issuer default. The particular MBS is referred to as a **reference entity**. The owner will buy a CDS. A CDS is an over-the-counter instrument which means that it is not traded on an organized exchange such as stock exchange. It is a private deal between two parties involving, generally, more than $5 million. Major financial institutions such as Citibank or Credit Suisse have credit default swap desks that trade in these instruments. The owner of the MBS will contact the CDS desk and propose to buy a CDS. The owner of the MBS will agree to make a series of annual payments for a period of time generally running from 2 to 10 years (with 5 years being the most popular term of a CDS). The annual payments are called the **price** or the **spread** of the CDS. In return the seller of the CDS will agree to make a payment back to the MBS owner in the event that there is a default, or other **credit event**, and consequently a loss in value of the MBS. Other credit events (other than a default) include bankruptcy, debt restructuring, obligation acceleration (obligations of the issuer become due prior to their originally scheduled maturity date), or rating change (by, say Standard and Poor's or Moody's). The price or the spread is stated in terms of a percentage of the nominal value of the MBS. For example, if the spread is 150 basis points (1.5 percent), the owner of the MBS will agree to pay an annual fee to the CDS seller equal to $150,000 on $10 million worth of MBSs. So counterparty risk is present with a CDS if the buyer of the CDS fails to make the annual spread payments or the seller of the CDS fails to make a reimbursement in the event of a credit event.

When a credit event results in a loss of value to the MBS, settlement is made by the seller of the CDS in one of two ways. With a **physical settlement** the owner of the MBS tenders the instrument to the seller in exchange for a cash payment equal to the par or face value of the MBS. With a **cash settlement** the seller of the CDS pays the owner an amount equal to the difference between the par or face value and the new (lower) market value of the MBS.

Subsequent to the CDS transaction the probability of a credit event may change and the MBS owner may profit accordingly. If, for example, the probability of a credit event for the MBS increases the spread, in the CDS market, will increase to, say, 250 basis points. The MBS owner may then *sell* (not buy as in the original CDS transaction) another CDS. The payments it receives on this subsequent transaction will exceed the payments it makes on the original transaction, making a tidy profit.

History of CDSs

CDSs were invented in 1997 by JPMorgan Chase as a regulatory loophole that allowed financial institutions to shift the risk of default without having the shift count against regulatory capital requirements. Federal regulation (as with the Securities and Exchange Commission) became illegal with the Commodity Futures

Modernization Act of 2000 (which also created the so-called Enron loophole). Prohibitions on the types of transactions such as CDSs were in force since the Shad-Johnson Accord of 1982. The Modernization Act was a companion bill to an 11,000-page omnibus spending bill rushed through Congress before the 2000 Christmas holiday and signed by President Clinton on December 21, 2000. The Modernization Act was never debated and no hearings were held on its provisions.

Without any regulation the market for CDSs exploded in volume. Soon parties were buying CDS protection on bonds that they didn't even own. This would be the same as having hundreds of parties buy fire insurance on your house. Buyers of CDSs were not so much protecting themselves against default losses as betting on whether or not there would be a default. Before the 2000 Act the market value of CDSs was estimated at $900 billion. By the end of 2007 the CDS market had a notational value of $45 *trillion*. The **Depository Trust Clearing Corporation** (DTCC), which runs a warehouse for CDS trade confirmations itself held 29.2 trillion as of December 26, 2008. By buyer protection (owners of the MBS) there were $85 billion in CDSs for residential mortgage-backed securities and $11 billion in commercial CMBSs.

It should be noted that many of the CDSs are "stacked." For example, the seller of a CDS on a reference entity may, in turn, buy a CDS on the same entity (perhaps to take advantage of an arbitrage opportunity because of a small difference in the spread). If the notional amount on each CDS is $10 million, then there will be $20 million recorded as CDSs. Yet there is only one level of risk, on the original $10 million. If the reference entity defaults and its bonds are only worth $5 million, the buyer of the CDS will pay $5 million but will receive $5 million as a seller of the second CDS.

In 2008 two events related to CDSs occurred. One event was the federal government bailout of insurance giant AIG. AIG had purchased a large volume of CDSs, many on MBSs. The subprime mortgage meltdown caused many of the MBSs to decline in value and endangered the solvency of AIG. Second, in late 2008 the federal government took over Freddie Mac and Fannie Mae. This takeover was actually considered to be a credit event that would trigger payments on their CDSs. Fortunately the government takeover actually assured the face value of the Fannie Mae and Freddie Mac MBSs so that there would appear to be little loss to be paid by the buyers of their CDSs.

Tax and Accounting Issues of Mortgage-Backed Securities

Secondary mortgage market agencies and firms that issue MBSs backed by pools of loans have always had to wrestle with the issue of double taxation. Essentially, cash flows from the mortgages to the agency or firm and then to the investors. If the cash flows are taxable when received by the agency, and then again by the investors, the tax burden would be so great as to eliminate the advantages of securitization of mortgages. Avoidance of the double taxation was accomplished in the early years by the creation of a **grantor trust** to own the mortgages. The grantor trust worked especially well for pass-through securities. If the provisions of a qualified grantor trust are met, then the trust is not taxed, only the investor in the pass-through. To qualify, a grantor trust must (1) have a limited life, (2) be self liquidating (no assets remain after investors are paid off), and (3) require no active management of the assets after they are placed in trust. One can see why a pass-through easily fits these requirements.

When CMOs were developed to meet the cash flow demands of investors, tax and accounting problems developed. Many CMO issuers transferred (sold) the underlying loans to a trust to gain the favorable tax treatment and also to remove the loans from their balance sheet (as was the case with pass-throughs). Many thrifts, and certainly mortgage bankers, did not want to carry the loans as assets and MBSs as liabilities on their balance sheets (however, some originators did want to treat CMOs as a financing). Transfer to a trust appeared to solve both problems. The IRS and the accounting profession complicated this arrangement, however. In March 1985, the **Financial Accounting Standards Board (FASB)** ruled that an issuer must treat a CMO as a financing (debt), even when the loans are transferred to a trust, if the issuer holds more than a "nominal" residual interest in the collateral. But requirements by the rating agencies for overcollateralization create residual interests that are not nominal. In addition, the size of the residual may increase if prepayments are slower than expected or if reinvestment income exceeds expectations. Some CMO issuers responded by creating a second trust to own the residuals (an owner's trust). Investors could purchase certificates of beneficial interest.

But this did not solve the tax problem. The IRS ruled that CMOs using the trust arrangement were similar to a corporation retaining control and having an equity interest (the residual). The trust arrangement also required active management, because the cash flows not currently distributed to security holders had to be reinvested for later delivery. A few originators who did not mind avoiding the trust arrangement carried the mortgages as assets and the CMOs as debt. For them, the problems were not as severe. However, the residual interest meant that they could not borrow against the full amount of the debt.

Because of these problems, secondary mortgage market participants urged Congress to consider remedial legislation. It came as part of the Tax Reform Act of 1986. The legislation established REMIC as an entity that could issue CMOs and not be subject to double taxation. A partnership, trust, or other corporation may elect REMIC status and maintain separate records relative to the mortgage pool and management of the funds related to the pool. For tax purposes, income is recorded as received from the pool of mortgages and deductions are allowed for interest paid (on the CMO tranches) to investors and for other pool-related expenses. The net income then can be passed-through to the owner of the residual (usually the CMO issuer) as income or loss.

An agency, trust, or firm retains this favorable tax status as long as it does not engage in any prohibited transactions, including (1) receiving income from any asset that is not a "qualified mortgage," (2) receiving fees or compensation for services (other than servicing income from the mortgage portfolio), or (3) buying or selling mortgages out of the pool (except as the pool is liquidated if all proceeds are disbursed within 90 days).

If desired, the user of a REMIC can avoid reporting the mortgages as assets and the CMOs as liabilities; the REMIC is a stand-alone activity. The issuer will report a gain or loss on the "sale" of the mortgages into the REMIC trust, however. If the issuer wants to avoid a loss on the "sale," it will simply report the residual interest owned in the REMIC as an asset. Figure 10-3 shows how REMIC transactions work.

Now that we have considered several types of mortgage-backed securities, let's review the agencies and firms that are active in the market. Several entities currently issue mortgage-backed securities or have in the past:

- Federal National Mortgage Association (FNMA, Fannie Mae)
- Government National Mortgage Association (GNMA, Ginnie Mae)
- Federal Home Loan Mortgage Corporation (FHLMC, Freddie Mac)
- Federal Home Loan Banks (FHLB)
- Federal credit agencies
- State and local credit agencies
- Private firms

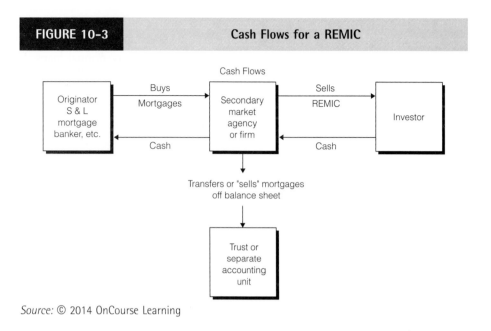

Source: © 2014 OnCourse Learning

SECONDARY MORTGAGE MARKET AGENCIES AND FIRMS

Federal National Mortgage Association

Congress established the **Federal National Mortgage Association (FNMA)** in 1938 as a subsidiary of the Reconstruction Finance Corporation (RFC). The main purpose was to form secondary market support for FHA and, later, VA loans. Up until the 1980s, the FHA and VA set a limit on the rate interest lenders could charge on these loans so as to keep housing affordable. As interest rates rose, lenders were reluctant to originate FHA and VA loans because of the large amount of points they would have to charge. Additionally, the value of existing loans declined with rising rates. Fannie Mae's purpose was to stand ready to purchase these loans at face value from originators, so as to replenish their funds for new originations. Even though their value was less than face, Fannie Mae hoped to sell them back at face or at a gain when interest rates dropped. In a sense, it was Fannie Mae's purpose to ride the interest rate cycle and take on interest rate risk. Fannie Mae obtained the funds to purchase mortgages by issuing long-term bonds. However, it faced substantial interest rate risk and in the early days relied on the Treasury to cover losses.

In 1950 the agency was transferred to the Housing and Home Finance Agency (an agency that was created in 1942 and later made part of HUD). Its life there was short-lived; it was rechartered and became a separate agency in 1954. The recharter assigned three tasks to Fannie Mae: (1) continued enhancement of the secondary mortgage market for FHA and VA loans, (2) liquidation of properties and mortgages acquired by default, and (3) management of a subsidized loan program. The recharter also contained a provision that transformed Fannie Mae into an essentially private entity. For this purpose, the 1954 re-chartering authorized the issuance of nonvoting preferred and common stock. This would both provide for the restructuring of Fannie Mae as a corporation and provide additional funds with which it could purchase mortgages.

Fannie Mae supports the secondary mortgage market by issuing mortgage-backed securities and purchasing mortgages. Credit enhancement comes from the ability of Fannie Mae to borrow from the U.S. Treasury, and its equity results from the sale of common and preferred stock. Originally, Fannie Mae was authorized to purchase FHA and VA loans, but in 1970 Congress, in an act that established the Federal Home Loan Mortgage Corporation (see following), allowed the agency to purchase conventional loans. Fannie Mae holds most of these loans in its own portfolio but occasionally sells some of its inventory to control its interest rate risk exposure. In the 1970s Fannie Mae issued mostly short-term debt, so it faced the same sort of maturity mismatch and interest rate risk problem that thrifts did. It was, essentially, a large thrift. In 1981 its portfolio of $61.4 billion dollars in long-term mortgages was financed partially by $21.2 billion dollars in short-term debt. The amount of liquidating assets within 1 year was $3.6 billion, which produced a 1-year maturity gap of $17.6 billion. This gap represented 29 percent of the agency's assets.

Then, during the mid-1980s FNMA reduced its interest rate risk by issuing pass-throughs and CMOs and by purchasing adjustable-rate mortgages. By the end of 1988, the liquidating assets and maturing liabilities within 1 year were equal ($36 billion each), so that the 1-year maturity gap was zero. Since that time, the agency has had a more balanced portfolio of assets and liabilities. Table 10-3 shows information about FNMA during the decade of the 2010s. The information is very telling regarding the rise and fall of the housing market. As background you should know that up until 2006 the housing market in the United States was very robust. Residential prices were increasing rapidly during this time. Then, in late 2006 the housing bubble "burst" and residential prices fell dramatically, in some area losing 50 percent of their 2006 value. During the period of rapidly rising prices the risk of default was seen by most as nonexistent. As long as property prices were rising and it was perceived would continue to rise the risk of default and foreclosures was seen as very unlikely. After the market crashed in late 2006 delinquencies, defaults, and foreclosures became widespread. Eventually, this affected the financial performance of FNMA and resulted in its rescue and takeover by the federal government.

Let's take a closer look at the data in Table 10-3. On the first line note that from 2000 to 2003 there was a significant increase in the number of mortgages purchased by FNMA and significant purchase thereafter. The third line indicates that, beginning in 2002 FNMA began to acquire subprime mortgages at an increasing rate. FNMA did so at the request of the federal government in order to expand home ownership to previously marginal borrowers. Recall, as long as residential prices were perceived to increase the sub-prime mortgages were not seen as risky in terms of default and foreclosure. In 2004 alone FNMA purchased nearly $67 billion in subprime mortgages. From 2002 to 2007 FNMA purchased $170 billion in subprime mortgages. Line six shows the guarantee fee income for FNMA. When a mortgage originator sell a mortgage to FNMA the latter requires that the former agree to re-purchase the mortgage at its face value (balance) if, for some reason there is a default. However, the originator can transfer the default risk, along with the mortgage by paying FNMA a guarantee fee. In essence, FNMA is accepting the default risk in return for a fee. Now, if house prices are expected to continue to increase then the risk of default is low and the guarantee fee income is appealing to FNMA. Notice how the guarantee fee income was increasing during the period when FNMA was purchasing more subprime loans shortly before the housing collapse (2006). This may be an indication that mortgage originators perceived the guarantee fee to be worth paying so as to avoid having to re-purchase loans that may be likely to default.

Next, line four indicates how FNMA raised funds to purchase the mortgages. It shows that FNMA issued $211 billion in mortgage-backed securities (MBS) in 2000. In 2003, the year that FNMA purchased a large amount of mortgages it issued $1.22 Trillion in MBSs. Because FNMA was paying less interest on the MBSs than it received on its mortgage assets its net interest income (interest

TABLE 10-3
Federal National Mortgage Association—Selected Market Activity and Financial Data

YEAR	2000	2001	2002	2003	2004	2005	2006	2007	2008	2009	2010	2011
Addition to Assets												
Purchases (Mortgages)	237446	$586,804	$820,964	$1,353,389	$604,505	$558,489	$545,025	$704,668	$617,235	$720,165	$625,129	$582,475
Purchases (Mortgage Related Securities)	129716	$209,124	$268,574	$408,606	$176,385	$62,232	$102,666	$69,236	$77,523	$161,562	$44,495	$20,760
Subprime Mortgage Purchases			$4,963	$25,769	$66,827	$24,469	$35,606	$15,628	$637	$0	$0	$0
Funding												
MBS Issuances	211662	$528,422	$743,630	$1,220,066	$552,482	$510,138	$481,704	$629,607	$542,813	$807,853	$629,746	$598,672
Earnings												
Net Interest Income	5674	$8,090	$18,426	$19,477	$18,081	$11,505	$6,752	$4,581	$8,782	$14,510	$16,409	$19,281
Guarantee Fee Income	1351	$1,482	$2,516	$3,432	$3,784	$4,006	$4,250	$5,071	$7,621	$7,211	$202	$227
Credit Related Expense	94	$78	$273	$353	$363	$428	$783	$5,012	$29,809	$73,536	$26,614	$27,498
Net Income	4448	$5,894	$3,914	$8,081	$4,967	$6,347	$4,059	−$2,050	−$58,707	−$71,969	−$14,014	−$16,855
Return on Equity	25.60%	39.80%	15.20%	27.60%	16.60%	19.50%	11.30%	−8.30%	NM	NM	NM	NM
Balance Sheet												
Total Assets	675224	$799,948	$904,739	$1,022,275	$1,020,934	$834,168	$843,936	$882,547	$912,404	$869,141	NM	NM
Total Debt	642682	$763,467	$841,293	$961,280	$953,111	$764,010	$767,046	$796,299	$870,393	$774,544	NM	NM
MBS Outstanding	706722	$863,445	$1,040,439	$1,300,520	$1,480,047.0	$1,598,918	$1,777,550	$2,118,909	$2,289,459	$2,432,789	$2,399,577	$2,433,708
Mortgage Quality												
Single Family Serious Delinquency	0.45%	0.55%	0.57%	0.60%	0.63%	0.79%	0.65%	0.98%	2.42%	5.38%	4.48%	3.91%
Credit Loss as Percent of Guaranteed Book	0.01%	0.01%	0.01%	0.01%	0.01%	0.01%	0.02%	0.05%	0.23%	0.45%	0.77%	0.61%
U.S. Treasury Purchase of FNMA Preferred Stock									$16,200	$60,000	$15,000	$25,800

NM = Not Meaningful
Single Family Homes are Seriously Delinquent when the Borrower has Missed Three or More Consecutive Payments and the Loan has not Brought Current
Credit Losses are Chargeoffs, Net of Recoveries and Foreclosed Property Expense.
On September 7, 2008 the Federal Government Placed FNMA into Conservatorship. The Federal Housing Finance Agency is the Conservator
Source: Federal Housing Finance Agency

income less interest expense) rose steadily. Net interest income reached its peak in the 3-year period 2002–2004. Its return on equity was 27.6 percent in 2003, a great time to be a stockholder in FNMA.

Next, look at the percentage of single-family residences (for which FNMA held a mortgage) that were in serous delinquency (loans 90 days with no payment or brought current). The rate was inconsequential in 2000 at less than one-half of 1 percent. By 2005–2006 danger signs were on the horizon as the delinquency rate rose to about three-quarters of 1 percent. Then in 2008 the delinquency rate accelerated to 2.42 percent. This increase was due to the combination of FNMA's large portfolio of subprime loans and the collapse of housing prices in 2007. The delinquency rate continued to be very high through 2011, the latest year of available data.

By 2008, 2 years after the peak in housing prices, it was evident that FNMA was in severe financial difficulty. Net income was nearly $70 billion negative that year. As a result, the federal government, which had an implicit guarantee of the MBSs, did several important things. First, it gave FNMA an infusion of funds when the United States Treasury purchased some of FNMAs preferred stock (that was essentially worthless on the stock market). Beginning in 2008 the Treasury purchased $16.2 billion in stock. By the end of 2011 it had purchased about $117 billion in preferred stock from FNMA. Second, the Federal Reserve System purchased stock as well. Third, by authorization under the Housing and Economic Recovery Act of 2008 (HERA) FNMA was placed under conservatorship by the Federal Housing and Finance Agency. In essence this gave complete control over the operations (including naming directors) of FNMA.

By 2012 it appeared that FNMA was on its road to recovery, so-to-speak. It reported a first quarter profit of $2.7 billion and did not require further government support. It returned $2.8 billion to the U.S. Treasury. By the end of the first quarter FNMA had returned a total of $22.57 billion in dividends. In addition, by agreement with the U.S. Treasury, FNMA has agreed to reduce its portfolio size in an orderly fashion. By an agreement in 2009, FNMA will reduce its portfolio size 10 percent annually with a goal of reaching $250 billion by 2022. However, a further agreement increased the annual reduction to 15 percent of its portfolio annually, reaching the $250 billion goal by 2018. FNMA's portfolio was $789 billion at the end of 2010 and $708 billion at the end of 2011. In addition, the U.S. Treasury replaced the requirement that it receive an annual 10 percent dividend with a return of all profits until the Treasury's position is eliminated. Finally, the FHFA has pursued a strategy of requiring mortgage originators to buy back loans that did not meet underwriting and eligibility requirements. For example, in the first quarter of 2010 lenders were required to re-purchase $3.1 billion in loans. As of 2012 the future of FNMA was uncertain. In all likelihood it will be smaller, more diligent in loan underwriting and perhaps, returned to the stockholders as a publicly traded corporation.

Government National Mortgage Association

In 1968 Congress passed the Housing and Urban Development Act. Among other things the act established the **Government National Mortgage Association (GNMA)** and placed it in the newly formed Department of Housing and Urban Development. Ginnie Mae relieved FNMA of two of its functions: the management and liquidation of previously originated (FHA) mortgages and the loan subsidization program. Under the latter program, termed the special assistance function (SAF), Ginnie Mae subsidized the cost of housing for low-income families. A typical arrangement, called a **Tandem Plan**, authorized Ginnie Mae to make low-interest loans to qualified families. It then would sell the loans at a discount to Fannie Mae. The discount allowed FNMA to earn a market yield. Ginnie Mae absorbed the loss—the difference between the amount of the loan originated and the discounted price received from FNMA. It was Ginnie Mae's only primary market activity. These two functions were never a large part of Ginnie Mae's operations, however. Rather, the agency was given an important third function—support of the secondary mortgage market.

Ginnie Mae's secondary mortgage market operations have been somewhat focused. The agency supports the FHA and VA (and, to a small extent, the Farmers Home Administration) loan market by guaranteeing pass-through securities. Credit enhancement on the pass-throughs comes from two sources. First, the underlying loans are guaranteed against default by the FHA and the VA. Second, Ginnie Mae guarantees the timely payment of interest and principal. So, even if there is a default on some of the loans in the pool, pass-through investors will not have to wait until a claim is made to the FHA or the VA to obtain payment. The originator of the mortgages is required to make monthly payments to the investors in the pass-throughs and then seek reimbursement from the FHA, VA, or the Rural Housing Service (RHS). If the originator cannot make the payment, Ginnie Mae will.[3]

It is important to note that Ginnie Mae itself neither purchases mortgages nor issues securities. A balance sheet of Ginnie Mae would show that for its pass-through activity it holds no mortgages nor issues any debt. The agency's activities can be understood by considering its early operations in support of the FHA and VA loan market. Later modifications in operations have been minor. Figure 10-4 shows a typical early Ginnie Mae arrangement. It is useful to view the process in stages.

FIGURE 10-4	Creation of a GNMA Pass-Through Security

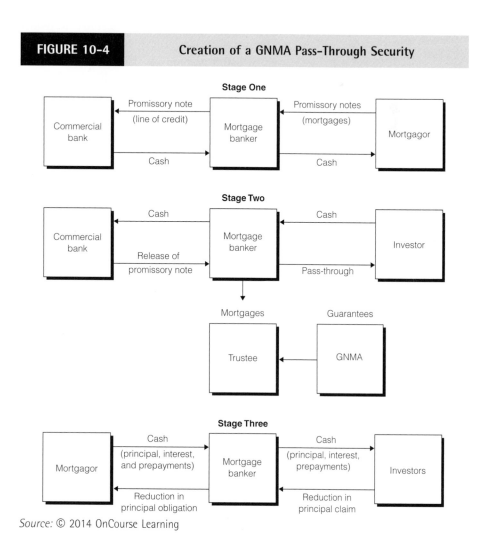

Source: © 2014 OnCourse Learning

In Stage One a mortgage originator, say, a mortgage banker, obtains a line of credit from a commercial bank with which to make mortgage loans. As the loans are made, the line of credit is taken down, and the loans are pledged as collateral for take-down. This is termed **warehousing**. In this fashion, the originator accumulates a pool of, say, $100 million in total value mortgages. All mortgages must have the same maturity (within a year) and the same rate of interest (within one percentage point), be guaranteed by the FHA, VA, or RHS (Rural Housing Service), and be within 24 months of origination (except for the multifamily mature loan program). Next, the originator will request that the pool be qualified for a pass-through security to be issued. Ginnie Mae will qualify the pool if it meets the restrictions mentioned and some other minor conditions. The originator must pay a nonrefundable fee ($500 on the first $1.5 million and $200 for each additional million in the pool) with its request for qualification.

In Stage Two the originator issues the pass-through securities. They will be sold through securities dealers and investment banking firms. They were sold, usually on a forward basis, through an organization called the Ginnie Mae Dealers Association that was merged into the Public Securities Association (PSA) in 1982. Buyers include banks, thrifts, pension funds, life insurance companies, and individual investors. The originator pays off the line of credit with the funds obtained from the sale of the securities. The mortgages then are transferred to a trustee. The trustee makes sure that the pass-through investors are paid off whenever there is a prepayment of the mortgage.

In Stage Three principal and interest payments are made to the investor. The principal of the investor's security is reduced by the amount of the scheduled amortization and any prepayments. The pass-through will bear a rate of interest that is 0.5 percent less than that on the mortgages. If the rate on the mortgages is 10 percent, then the rate on the pass-through will be 9.5 percent. The difference is split between the originator (44 basis points) for servicing the loans and Ginnie Mae (6 basis points) for its guarantee of timely payments. Ginnie Mae uses these funds to make payments (on defaulted loans) to the pass-through investors in the event the originator cannot.

In 1983 Ginnie Mae loosened the provision that all mortgages in a pool had to have the same interest rate. Under the Ginnie Mae II program, loans can be mixed as long as the difference in rates among the mortgages is no greater than 1 percent. The program also allows seasoned or existing mortgages to be included in the pool.

Table 10-4 shows the recent activity of the GNMA. At the end of September 2011 the total assets was $18.851 billion. Over the years past earnings from their guarantee fees have been deposited directly with the U.S. Treasury ($7.213 billion) or invested in U.S. Treasury securities ($2.216 billion). Liabilities totaled only $3.089 billion. The difference between assets and liabilities is called investment in the U.S. government. This account is similar to "stockholders equity" because GNMA is a government agency. Their total revenues, $1.064 billion, in fiscal year ending September, 2011 came from their investment in U.S. Treasury securities ($208,100,000) and guarantee fees ($856,500,000). At the end of fiscal year 2011 there were $1.221 trillion in GNMA bonds outstanding. More information on GNMA securities can be found on the GNMA Web site, www.ginniemae.gov.

Federal Home Loan Mortgage Corporation

In 1970 mortgage-backed securities backed by pools of FHA- and VA-insured loans were well established. A large percentage of mortgage loans were conventional, however. Sixty-five percent of all one- to four-family mortgages that were originated in that year were conventional. Furthermore, thrifts dominated the conventional loan

TABLE 10-4

Ginnie Mae Financial Highlights, Fiscal Years 2009 to 2011

SEPTEMBER 30	2011	2010	2009
(Dollars in thousands)			
Balance Sheets Highlights and Liquidity Analysis			
Funds with U.S. Treasury	$7,210,300	$6,650,500	$5,253,800
U.S. Government Securities	$2,126,800	$3,551,200	$9,235,800
Other Assets	$9,514,000	$6,861,600	$1,184,800
Total Assets	$18,851,100	$17,063,300	$15,674,400
Total Liabilities	$3,089,300	$2,485,500	$1,638,100
Investment of U.S. Government	$15,761,800	$14,577,800	$14,036,300
Total RPB Outstanding[1]	$1,221,685,233	$1,046,179,139	$826,016,583
LLR[2] and Investment of U.S. Government	$16,157,600	$15,582,700	$14,596,200
Investment of U.S. Goverment as a Percentage of Average Total Assets	87.77%	89.06%	91.85%
LLR and Investment of U.S. Government as a Percentage of RPB	1.32%	1.49%	1.77%
Capital Adequacy Ratio[3]	1.30%	1.47%	1.73%
Highlights From Statements of Revenues and Expenses & Profitability Ratios Year Ended September 30			
MBS Program Income	$856,500	$742,900	$547,800
Interest Income	$208,100	$269,000	$109,500
Total Revenues	$1,064,600	$1,011,900	$657,300
MBS Program Expenses	$72,800	$72,700	$55,400
Administrative Expenses	$11,000	$10,300	$8,600
Fixed Asset Amortization	$9,900	$9,500	$5,100
Total Expenses	$93,700	$92,500	$69,100
Recapture of Provision (Provision for Losses)	$394,600	$(730,000)	$(78,600)
Total Gains (Losses)[4]	$(181,500)	$352,100	$—
Excess of Revenues Over Expenses	$1,184,000	$541,500	$509,600
Total Expense as a Percentage of Average RPB	0.0083%	0.0099%	0.0099%
Recapture (Provision) for Loss as a Percentage of Average RPB	0.0348%	(0.0780%)	(0.0112%)

[1]*Remaining Principal Balance (RPB) of Ginnie Mae MBS; this does not include $8.8M of GNMA Guaranteed Bonds*
[2]*Loan Loss Reserve (LLR)*
[3]*LLR and Investment of U.S. Government divided by the sum of Total Assets and Remaining Principal Balance*
[4]*Total Losses from credit impairment of mortgage loans held for investment, net and loss on MSR o!set by the gain on sale of securities*
Source: www.ginniemae.gov

market. Seventy percent of loans originated by thrifts were conventional. Mortgage bankers, on the other hand, dominated the FHA and VA market. Ninety-four percent of their loans were this type. Thus, up to 1970 government support of the secondary mortgage market aided the FHA and VA sector and mortgage bankers. There was a perceived need for government support for conventional lenders and thrifts that were experiencing interest rate risk.

In 1970 Congress passed the Emergency Home Finance Act. Title III of this act chartered the **Federal Home Loan Mortgage Corporation (FHLMC)**, or Freddie Mac. It authorized the corporation to purchase conventional and FHA and VA loans. It also authorized the purchase of conventional loans by Fannie Mae. To date, Freddie Mac has specialized in conventional mortgages and Fannie Mae in FHA and VA mortgages. The corporation's initial capital came from the sale of $100 million in nonvoting common stock that was sold to the 12 district **Federal Home Loan Banks**. It also issued 15 million shares of preferred stock at the end of

1984 to the Federal Home Loan Banks, which in turn issued them to their members (thrifts). This issuance was part of the effort to help troubled thrifts survive in the mid-1980s. Freddie Mac stock is traded on the New York Stock Exchange.

Freddie Mac obtains its funds by issuing a wide variety of debt and mortgage-backed securities discussed in the following sections.

Discount Notes and Debentures

Freddie Mac issues debentures in minimum denominations of $10,000 and increments of $5,000. It also issues discount notes (maturity of 1 year or less) with a minimum denomination of $25,000 and increments of $1.

Mortgage Participation Certificates

The Freddie Mac **participation certificate (PC)** is the corporation's pass-through security. First sold in 1971, pools now consist of conventional fixed-rate, 30-year mortgages, 15-year mortgages, adjustable-rate mortgages, and multifamily mortgages. The corporation guarantees the timely payment of interest and principal. Freddie Mac assumes the mortgage credit risk on the underlying mortgages (the risk that the borrower will default on the loan) by guaranteeing the payment of interest and principal to the holders of its PCs.

Collateralized Mortgage Obligations

First issued in 1983, Freddie Mac CMOs are available in several classes with varying stated maturities. Semiannual principal payments are allocated to each class of the CMO in the order of the stated maturity. No principal is paid to an investor in a class until earlier maturity classes are retired. Holders of each class of CMOs receive semiannual interest payments on the unpaid principal balance of their bonds at the coupon rate for the class. Interest on the accrual class is paid out only on the full payment of all other classes of bonds. Although they are the general obligation of Freddie Mac, each CMO is backed by its own pool of mortgages that is owned by, and held in, its own portfolio.

Guaranteed Mortgage Certificates

Issued early on, **guaranteed mortgage certificates (GMCs)** have not been sold directly by Freddie Mac since 1979. They represent an undivided interest in a pool of mortgages owned by Freddie Mac. The certificates pay a guaranteed minimum principal annually and interest semiannually.

Table 10-5 shows much of the same information for the FNMC as does Table 10-3 for FNMA. Much of the discussion mirrors that for FNMA since the housing crisis affected each equally and the federal government took over the operations of FHLMC at the same time as it did FNMA. As with FNMA the purchases of mortgages and mortgage-related securities rose steadily and peaked in 2007. It funded the purchases by issuing mortgage-backed securities. Likewise its earnings were substantial prior to the mortgage crisis and then became significantly negative after 2007. The quality of the mortgage portfolio declined prior to the mortgage collapse. The single-family serious delinquency rate was approximately one-half of 1 percent prior to 2007 but reached 3.89 percent in 2009. As with FNMA the U.S. Treasury purchased large sums of FHLMC stock from 2008 through 2011.

Federal Home Loan Banks

The Federal Home Loan Bank System is made up of 12 regional banks that are owned by member banks (and other institutions) that are the actual stockholders. Currently, membership in the FHLBs is open to all depository institutions as well as certain other financial institutions. As of 2008 there were 5,858 commercial

TABLE 10-5

Federal Home Loan Mortgage Corporation—Selected Market Activity and Financial Data

YEAR	2000	2001	2002	2003	2004	2005	2006	2007	2008	2009	2010	2011
Addition to Assets												
Purchases (Mortgages)	$174,043	$393,634	$543,848	$716,775	$367,524	$292,845	$364,301	$487,711	$381,557	$491,921	$401,750	$341,118
Purchases (Mortgage Related Securities)	$91,896	$248,466	$299,674	$385,078	$223,299	$325,575	$241,205	$231,039	$297,614	$238,835	$51,828	$120,001
Subprime Mortgage Purchases												
Funding												
MBS Issuances	$166,901	$389,591	$547,312	$713,787	$365,108	$397,867	$360,023	$470,976	$357,861	$475,412	$393,037	$317,261
Earnings												
Net Interest Income	$3,758	$7,448	$9,525	$9,498	$9,137	$4,627	$3,412	$3,099	$6,796	$17,073	$16,856	$18,397
Guarantee Fee Income	$1,243	$1,381	$1,527	$1,653	$1,382	$2,076	$2,393	$2,635	$3,370	$3,033	$143	$170
Credit Related Expense	$75	$39	$126	$2	$140	$347	$356	$3,060	$17,529	$29,837	$17,891	$11,287
Net Income	$3,666	$3,158	$10,090	$4,816	$2,937	$2,113	$2,327	–$3,094	–$50,119	–$21,553	–$14,025	–$5,266
Return on Equity	39.00%	20.20%	47.20%	17.70%	9.40%	8.10%	9.80%	–21.00%	NM	NM	NM	NM
Balance Sheet												
Total Assets	$459,297	$641,100	$752,249	$803,449	$795,284	$798,609	$804,910	$794,368	$850,963	$841,784	NM	NM
Total Debt	$426,899	$578,368	$665,696	$739,613	$731,697	$740,024	$744,341	$738,557	$843,021	$780,604	NM	NM
MBS Outstanding	$576,101	$653,084	$729,809	$752,164	$852,270	$974,200	$1,122,761	$1,381,863	$1,402,714	$1,495,267	$1,467,985	$1,422,081
Mortgage Quality												
Single Family Serious Delinquency	0.49%	0.62%	0.77%	0.86%	0.73%	0.53%	0.42%	0.65%	1.83%	3.98%	3.84%	3.58%
Credit Loss as Percent of Guaranteed Book	0.01%	0.01%	0.01%	0.01%	0.01%	0.01%	0.01%	0.03%	0.20%	0.41%	0.72%	0.68%
U.S. Treasury Purchase of FHLMC Preferred Stock									$45,600	$6,100	$13,000	$7,617

NM = Not Meaningful

Single Family Homes are Seriously Delinquent when the Borrower has Missed Three or More Consecutive Payments and the Loan has not Brought Current

Credit Losses are Chargeoffs, Net of Recoveries and Foreclosed Property Expense.

On September 7, 2008 the Federal Government Placed FHLMC into Conservatorship. The Federal Housing Finance Agency is the Conservator

Source: Federal Housing Finance Agency

banks, 1,183 thrifts, and 1,113 credit unions, and insurance companies as members. In 1997 the Federal Home Loan Bank of Chicago began purchasing pools of (conforming) mortgages from the member institutions. The program is called the **Mortgage Partnership Finance Program (MPFP).** Today, nine of the banks offer this program through the Chicago bank. Three other FHLBs offer their own mortgage purchase programs. The major difference in the FHLB programs and those of Fannie Mae and Freddie Mac relate to the assumption of credit risk. Credit risk is the risk of default by the mortgagor (homeowner). When Fannie Mae and Freddie Mac purchase mortgages they assume this risk but charge for it by assessing a fee to the seller (mortgage originator). Under the MPF the credit risk is retained (most of it anyway) by the seller. The FHLB will, in turn, pay a fee (up to 10 basis points on the outstanding balance) to the seller for assuming this risk. As with Fannie Mae and Freddie Mac the FHLBs retain the market risk (the risk that the value of the mortgages will change when interest rates change). The members of the FHLB set up a First Loss Account equal to 1 percent of the outstanding balance of the mortgage pool that is sold to the FHLBs. In addition, the mortgage must have PMI if the loan-to-value ratio is greater than 80 percent. Thus, if there is a default the loss is covered first by the homeowner's equity, next by PMI, and third by the First Loss Account. In the event that the First Loss Account is exhausted, the seller (members) provide an additional layer of protection. They establish a loss amount such that the probability of losses in excess of said amount is less than that faced by investors in Moody's AA-rated bonds. For these layers of protection the FHLBs are willing to pay the previously mentioned 10 basis points as a fee.

The main advantage of selling loans to the FHLBs as opposed to Fannie Mae and Freddie Mac is the fee income the sellers receive for managing the credit risk. If a seller has a record of originating loans with a very low, if not zero, default rate, it will pay for that seller to receive a risk management fee from the FHLB rather than pay the same to Fannie Mae and Freddie Mac.

In 2002 the FHLBs acquired $45.7 billion in conforming mortgages from their members. The MPF program purchased $27.9 billion and the Mortgage Purchase Program purchased $17.8 billion. By the beginning of 2008 the FHLBs had funded $166.2 billion in loans through these programs. However, in early 2008 the Chicago bank announced it was suspending the MPF program effective in July, 2008. The bank cited risk factors (likely associated with large loan losses associated with the housing market collapse in 2006 and 2007). The bank did indicate it would aid its members by pursuing alternative, off balance sheet, secondary mortgage market outlets.

Federal Credit Agencies

There are several **federal credit agencies** that, in part, support the primary and secondary mortgage market.

Farm Credit System. In 1987 Congress passed the Agricultural Credit Act. The purpose was to consolidate and coordinate the activities of three agriculturally related systems: the Federal Land Banks, the Federal Intermediate Credit Banks, and the Banks for Cooperatives. The first two were merged into a system of 37 farm credit banks and the latter renamed the Federal Credit Banks. The farm credit system is divided into 12 farm credit districts. The farm credit banks make direct loans for agricultural purposes, including the purchase of rural homes. The banks obtain their funds by issuing securities through the Credit

Banks Funding Corporation located in New York. The securities are called Farm Credit Systemwide Obligations and consist of both discount notes and long-term bonds. In March 2008 the system had $197.4 billion in assets, of which $165 billion was in loans.

Federal Agricultural Mortgage Corporation (FAMC; Farmer Mac). A third creation of the Agricultural Credit Act, this corporation was intended to act similarly to GNMA and FNMA, but for farm mortgages. This institution, housed in the Farm Credit System, examines pools of farm mortgages, places a guarantee on the timely payment of principal and interest, and permits underwriters to sell pass-throughs in the secondary market. Unlike the full guarantee of timely payments granted by GNMA, FAMC guarantees the timely payment of 90 percent of the principal and interest payments. Credit enhancement (funds to allow the guarantee of payments) comes from three sources: (1) a $1.5 billion line of credit from the U.S. Treasury; (2) $20 million in equity raised by selling stock to banks, insurance companies, and farm system institutions; and (3) the fees the agency charges for the guarantee. FAMC charges 50 basis points plus an annual fee of 0.5 percent of the outstanding pool balance.

Farmer Mac was originally capitalized by a $20 million subscription sale of common stock, which was sold primarily to financial institutions that deal with agricultural loans. To qualify as an agricultural loan, a loan must be secured by land or improvements used for the production of at least one agricultural commodity. This includes rural housing loans that finance single-family residential dwellings in rural areas with populations not greater than 2,500 and with a maximum purchase price of $100,000.

Although established in 1987, the implementation of Farmer Mac's underwriting program was delayed to 1992. In that year Farmer Mac issued its first guaranty certificates worth $233 million. These securities were collateralized by agricultural loans originated by Travelers Insurance Company. At the end of 2007 the corporation had $4.574 billion in short- and long-term obligations outstanding.

Rural Housing Service (RHS). The RHS (formerly the Farmers Home Administration), housed in the Department of Agriculture, extends loans to rural areas for farms, houses, and community facilities. Until 1975 the agency raised some funds through the sale of Certificates of Beneficial Ownership (CBOs). Current sources of funds include a line of credit with the U.S. Treasury and the sale of its loans to the private sector or to trusts, which in turn create pass-through securities. The direct loans made by RHS are restricted to areas with a population of less than 10,000 and to low- and moderate-income families. Maximum income limits (adjusted family income) are set and vary by section of the country and size of the family. The loans made by the agency are typically below-market-rate loans. They are sold at a discount, with the agency bearing the loss. The term for a direct loan is typically 33 years; however, loans for up to 38 years may be made for applicants whose annual income does not exceed 60 percent of the median income for the area. Each county has a different maximum loan amount that may not exceed the market value of the property. The payment for principal, interest, property taxes, and insurance (PITI) cannot exceed 29 percent for very-low-income families or 33 percent for low-income families and the family must personally occupy the dwelling. Section 504 loans are for repair of existing properties. It is for families with very-low income (less than 50 percent of the median income in the area) that cannot obtain repair loans elsewhere. The loan cannot exceed $20,000 and the interest payment is 1 percent annually.

Financing Corporation (FICO). The Financing Corporation was chartered by the Federal Home Loan Bank Board under the Competitive Equality Banking Act of 1987. It was formed to help solve the deepening crisis of widespread insolvency among thrifts. The purpose of FICO was to recapitalize the FSLIC, which was in danger of insolvency itself as a result of the costly resolutions of many failed thrifts. FICO was authorized to issue $3 billion in nonvoting capital stock and up to $10.825 billion (no more than $3.75 billion in any 1 year) in debt securities. The proceeds are to be transferred to the FSLIC for use in resolving problems with failed thrifts. The bonds are not guaranteed by either the U.S. government or the FSLIC. Since 1989 the annual level of debt for this agency has been $8.17 billion.

Federal Financing Bank (FFB). This bank was established by the Federal Financing Bank Act of 1973 to consolidate and reduce the government's cost of financing a variety of federal agencies and other borrowers whose obligations are guaranteed by the federal government. The bank issues debt to obtain funds with which to purchase the obligations of two dozen or so federal agencies. Most of the mortgage- and housing-related agency obligations are excluded. Examples of agencies whose obligations are purchased include the Tennessee Valley Authority (TVA), Rural Electric Administration (REA), National Aeronautics and Space Administration (NASA), Small Business Administration (SBA), postal service, and many others. Two housing-related obligations that the bank can purchase are those issued by HUD to support Section 108 guaranteed loans and low-rent public housing. In 2007 the bank had $31.969 billion in debt outstanding and $34.673 billion on its loan portfolio. In its loan portfolio it held $791 million in HUD low-rent public housing loans and $5 million in HUD Community Development Block Grant loans.

State and Local Credit Agencies

We saw in Chapter 7 how the various state Housing Finance Agencies (HFAs) issue mortgage revenue bonds that carry a low rate of interest because of their tax exemption. Another activity of the HFAs is their outreach to the secondary mortgage market. HFAs fund FHA-insured and VA-guaranteed loans that are packaged into securities guaranteed by GNMA. They also participate in affordable housing initiatives offered by Freddie Mac and Fannie Mae. In 1989, HFAs originated approximately $9 billion in CMOs through the secondary mortgage market.

Private Firms

Numerous private firms have entered the secondary mortgage market. Once the government agencies demonstrated the need for the market and Congress passed enabling legislation, many private firms saw a profit in securitizing mortgages. The private companies do everything that the government-related agencies do. They purchase mortgages for securitization and exercise swaps. Credit enhancement comes from pool insurance or overcollateralization or both. The mortgage-backed securities that they issue are rated by rating agencies such as Moody's and Standard and Poor's. Many of the private firms specialize in loans that the government agencies either cannot or do not wish to securitize, such as nonconforming and jumbo loans. Some large thrifts or other financial institutions create subsidiaries to carry on the specialized function of mortgage securitization.

Currently, several large financial institutions, such as Bank of America, Deutsche Mortgage Securities, Merrill Lynch Mortgage Investors, Morgan Stanley, Wells Fargo, and Washington Mutual are active in issuing CMO pass-throughs. Additionally, there are dozens of small financial institutions active in the market.

Developing a Secondary Mortgage Market: A Year-by-Year Summary

There have been more changes in the mortgage market since 1980 than in any other comparable period. We review some of the events during this period on a year-by-year basis. These events paint a picture of a revolution in mortgage financing. There appears to be no limit to the imagination of market participants in creating financial instruments designed to provide funds to the ultimate user, the mortgage borrower.

1981   Freddie Mac introduces Guarantor, the first swap program for conventional, fixed-rate mortgages. Disintermediation is a problem for thrifts, and they can use the Freddie Mac PCs as collateral for borrowing funds outside of Regulation Q limits. They also can sell the PCs to raise funds to meet deposit withdrawals without reporting a loss on their income statement. A sale of the original loans that were swapped would have generated losses, because they were predominantly low-rate loans.

1982   Conventional mortgage rate peaks at 16.5 percent. GNMA securitizes more than $12 billion in one-to four-family mortgages. Freddie Mac more than doubles its holdings of one-to four-family mortgages, from $19.5 billion in 1981 to $42.6 billion in 1982.

1983   In June, Freddie Mac issues the first CMO for $1 billion. The issue sells out in 1 week. By December, there are 12 issues of CMOs for nearly $4.7 billion. Life insurance companies and pension funds are the major investors in the long-term tranches of the CMOs. Private firms such as First Boston and Salomon Brothers purchase Ginnie Mae pass-throughs and convert the cash flows to CMOs. American Southwest Financial forms a consortium of 35 builders to securitize mortgages on the properties they sell.

1984   The Home Mortgage Acceptance Corporation (HOMAC) is started. This firm will aid the home building industry by securitizing FHA- and VA-insured mortgages made by builders on their properties. In February they sell $18 million in CMOs. Freddie Mac begins buying 1-, 3-, and 5-year ARMs for the first time. Later in the year, they move to standardize ARMs by setting restrictions on the terms of ARMs that they will purchase. Lenders begin to adopt this standardization, since many desire the ability to sell their loans in the secondary market. Cumulative CMOs reach $3 billion. Citicorp Homeowners Mortgage Acceptance Corporation introduces the first CMO backed by mortgages without a federal (FHA or VA) guarantee. The Secondary Mortgage Market Enhancement Act is passed. It provides secondary mortgage market issuers an exemption from state security registration laws and legal investment restrictions. To qualify under the act, the mortgage securities must be rated in one of the two top categories by at least one rating agency. This act effectively placed Freddie Mac and Fannie Mae obligations on a par with U.S. Treasury securities. The act also authorized these two agencies to purchase second mortgages and increase their activity in the securitization of multifamily mortgages.

1985   Freddie Mac issues PCs in book-entry form through the Federal Reserve Bank of New York book entry system. Rapid expansion of the secondary mortgage market requires that action. Trading volume of mortgage-backed securities jumps from $131 billion in1981 to nearly $1 trillion in 1984. Later in the year, Fannie Mae also converts to the book-entry system. The first CMO backed by commercial mortgages is issued by Penn Mutual Life Insurance Company. It is a $204.8 million AAA-rated issue. Fannie Mae issues its first MBS denominated in yen. In further "layering" of the secondary market, EPIC Acceptance Corporation issues a $100 million CMO backed by Freddie Mac PCs. It is over collateralized by 30 percent. HOMAC expands its activities to include conventional mortgages (including jumbo loans).

1986   The Tax Reform Act (TRA) is passed. The act authorizes the issuance of Real Estate Mortgage Investment Conduits (REMICs). They offer alternative tax treatment for multiclass pass-through securities. REMICs avoid the double-taxation problem for actively managed pass-throughs, yet allow the issue to be treated as a sale of assets for accounting purposes. The act also places limits on the total amount of mortgage revenue bonds that can be offered by state housing agencies. It eliminates the installment sales treatment of builder bonds, effectively closing down HOMAC. Secondary mortgage market activity heats up: Freddie Mac increases the maximum loan amount on single-family properties to $133,250. Freddie Mac sells a record $2.6 billion in PCs in February and closes a single $3 billion swap deal in June. It begins selling multifamily PCs on a weekly basis. Ginnie Mae issues a record $135 million in ARM securities and reaches the $300 billion milestone for total securities guaranteed. Fannie Mae purchases a record $6.6 billion in mortgages in the second quarter. Fearing interest rate risk, it sells off $10 billion in fixed-rate loans.

1987   Freddie Mac raises the maximum loan limit on single-family residences to $153,100. It also swaps $1 billion in PCs for fixed-rate mortgages with Amerifirst Mortgage Company. Fannie Mae issues its first REMIC, backed by $500 million of FHA and VA loans. It is a stripped security divided into two classes. One class receives 99 percent of the principal payments and 62 percent of the interest payments (resulting in a 5 percent coupon rate). The other class receives 1 percent of the principal and 38 percent of the interest (resulting in a 3.05 percent coupon rate). The agency also announces it will purchase 7- and 10-year balloon mortgages to create a market for this type of loan. Ginnie Mae announces an increase in its guarantee fee from 6 to 10 basis points, and then later rescinds the increase after heavy criticism from lenders. Private firms become more active and innovative. Mechanics and Farmers Saving Bank issues the first publicly offered security backed by biweekly mortgages. First Boston Corporation issues the first CMO with a securitized residual class. This means that the class shares some of the scheduled principal payments, making it more liquid and easy to understand. The first REMIC backed by commercial mortgages is a $200 million issue by Security Pacific Merchants Bank.

1988   To avoid problems with excessive teaser-rate discounts, Freddie Mac requires that borrowers qualify for the loan at the maximum rate for the second year (or it will not purchase the loan). The agency also announces a $1 billion multiclass PC to be is sued through a REMIC, the largest ever. Fannie Mae issues the first REMIC backed by ARMs; Glendale Federal Savings and Loan of California is the originator of the $200 billion in loans in the pool. The agency also issues its first "megapool," allowing investors to combine existing mortgage-backed securities into larger instruments. HUD announces that it will consider having the FHA insure price level adjusted mortgages. Federal Home Loan Bank Board Chairman Danny Wall raises his estimate of the cost of resolving insolvent thrifts from $22 billion to $30 billion.

1989   Federal Home Loan Bank Board announces a new rule to take over troubled thrifts before they become insolvent. It also announces plans to sue large accounting firms that failed to detect financial problems in thrifts that they audited. The Government Accounting Office suggests that the thrift industry should be overhauled, starting with a split of the Federal Home Loan Bank Board and the FSLIC. The Chicago Board of Trade announces a new cash-settled, mortgage-backed futures and a futures/options contract. They are listed monthly, based on the current GNMA coupon, and traded 4 months in the future. Freddie Mac announces a stripped Giant PC program. The interest-only and principal-only strips will be formed by using several fixed-rate PCs. The agency also issues the 100th series of multiclass mortgage PCs. The Financial Institutions Reform, Recovery, and Enforcement Act is passed.

1990   Jack Kemp, secretary of HUD, launches a nationwide search for certified public accountants to put his agency in fiscal order. President Bush says the $164 billion financing enacted to solve the thrift problem may not be enough. The Office of Thrift Supervision issues Bulletin 38, which places seven types of CMO/REMIC products in the 100 percent risk class for the purpose of determining thrift capital requirements. Freddie Mac issues its first MBS backed by ARMs pegged to the London Interbank Offer Rate (LIBOR). It also announces five REMICs, backed by gold PCs.

1991   U.S. House of Representatives approves $78 billion in funding to keep the Resolution Trust Corporation (RTC) running so it can solve the thrift problem. The RTC swaps $70 million in loans with the Federal Home Loan Mortgage Corporation. The loans came from the failed Imperial Federal Savings and Loan Association. It also sells $833 million in mortgage-backed securities, the largest single MBS sale ever. Congress considers passing legislation that would require government-sponsored enterprises (GSEs), such as Fannie Mae and Freddie Mac, to be adequately capitalized and supervised. Provisions of any legislation would require GSEs to obtain Triple-A ratings on their MBSs by the rating agencies. By midyear, 84 percent of all FHA/VA mortgages and 32 percent of conventional mortgages have become securitized.

1992   Congress passes the Housing and Community Development Act, an extensive housing law that consists primarily of modifications to existing programs. It includes the Federal Housing Enterprises Financial Safety and Soundness Act, which rewrites the congressional charters for Fannie Mae and Freddie Mac to establish safe goals for financing affordable housing and housing in central cities and other underserved areas. The revised charters also set standards to protect against any future savings and loan-type failures.

1993   Mortgage debt held by all mortgage pools and trusts reaches $1.5 trillion; 36 percent of all mortgage debt outstanding in the nation.

1994   At the end of March, 87 percent of all FHA/VA and 42 percent of conventional mortgages have been securitized.

1995   The fiscal 1995 HUD appropriations act revises the mortgage limits under the Federal Housing Administration Section 203(b) home mortgage program such that the maximum limit is 75 percent of the current Federal Home Loan Mortgage Corporation limit.

1996   Freddie Mac announces the purchase of $1.075 billion in mortgage revenue bonds from housing finance agencies.

1997   The FHA and VA approve Freddie Mac's Loan Prospector, an automated loan processing program that allows lenders to use the Internet to approve FHA and VA loans almost instantaneously. The Federal Home Loan

1998   Bank of Chicago becomes the latest GSE by purchasing loans from its members under the Mortgage Partnership Finance Program.

1998   Freddie Mac issues the largest REMIC ever, which is in excess of $5 billion. The issue is made up entirely of Gold PCs. Freddie Mac announces a new product, Alt 97SM, which allows cash-strapped homeowners to acquire a residence with as little as 3 percent down payment.

1999   Freddie Mac announces the first 10-year Reference Note Program, a $4 billion transaction. In August, Freddie Mac announces that over 1.8 million loan submissions have been processed through Loan Prospector®.

2000   Freddie Mac issues a $5 billion tranche of Euro Reference notes for the European investment market. Ginnie Mae's outstanding balance of securities passes the $600 billion level for the first time. It backed $105.5 billion in securities in FY 2000. Fannie Mae announces record earnings for the year, $4.45 billion, up 15 percent from 1999.

2004   The Office of Federal Housing Enterprise Oversight requires Fannie Mae to resolve several severe accounting problems that led to the resignation of top management.

2008   Congress passes the Housing and Economic Recovery Act to increase regulatory oversight of the GSEs in light of recent accounting irregularities at Fannie Mae. In September Fannie Mae and Freddie Mac were taken over by the federal government with the Federal Housing Finance Agency operating as their conservator.

THE SECURITIZATION OF AMERICA'S MORTGAGES

Table 10-6 shows the amount of residential (1–4 family and multi-family) mortgages outstanding by type and by holder (owner as an asset). By mid-2012 there was approximately $10 trillion dollars in single-family mortgages and $850 billion in multi-family mortgages outstanding. The amounts held by commercial banks, savings institutions (savings and loans, mutual savings banks, and credit unions) are not securitized. These loans are originated by the institutions and held in their portfolio as assets. To focus on securitization, review the figures for federal and

TABLE 10-6

Residential Mortgage Debt Outstanding—Including Securitized Debt Million of Dollars)

	2010	2011	2012Q2
All Holders			
Type of Property			
1-4 Family	$10,422,777	$10,167,078	$10,028,032
Multi-Family	$842,773	$847,660	$849,652
Type of Holder			
Commercial Banks			
1-4 Family	$2,202,728	$2,147,003	$2,163,551
Mult-Family	$197,149	$189,188	$197,031
Savings Institutions			
1-4 Family	$430,480	$407,032	$345,623
Mult-Family	$61,248	$62,095	$50,773
Life Insurance Compaies			
1-4 Family	$6,163	$6,351	$6,712
Mult-Family	$47,246	$49,378	$50,574

**TABLE 10-6
(Continued)**

	2010	2011	2012Q2
Federal and Related Agencies			
Ginnie Mae			
1-4 Family	$5,277	$7,328	$7,755
Mult-Family	$0	$0	$0
Fannie Mae			
1-4 Family	$2,819,447	$2,790,029	$2,791,133
Mult-Family	$170,550	$176,898	$180,809
Freddie Mac			
1-4 Family	$1,799,256	$1,733,215	$1,675,687
Mult-Family	$85,883	$82,311	$79,597
FHLB			
1-4 Family	$61,019	$53,292	$51,643
Mult-Family	$25	$21	$21
FDIC			
1-4 Family	$2,686	$812	$1,095
Mult-Family	$181	$86	$37
FHA			
1-4 Family	$803	$1,207	$1,361
Mult-Family	$3,273	$3,174	$3,141
Mortgage Pools or Trusts			
Ginnie Mae			
1-4 Family	$1,037,538	$1,186,432	$1,247,890
Mult-Family	$52,223	$60,486	$65,167
Fannie Mae			
1-4 Family	$27,015	$26,514	$24,700
Mult-Family	$1,857	$1,702	$1,598
Freddie Mac			
1-4 Family	$4,243	$3,838	$3,641
Mult-Family	$12,838	$24,178	$32,310
Private Mortgage Conduits			
1-4 Family	$1,290,562	$1,097,948	$1,007,157
Mult-Family	$98,724	$91,059	$83,347
Individual and Others			
1-4 Family	$700,855	$671,321	$664,116
Mult-Family	$100,666	$96,265	$94,499
Other			
1-4 Family	$34,705	$34,756	$35,968
Mult-Family	$10,910	$10,819	$10,748
Securitized Mortgages			
1-4 Family	$7,745,212	$7,569,917	$7,473,722
Mult-Family	$522,766	$532,920	$537,348
Percent Securitized			
1-4 Family	74.31%	74.46%	74.53%
Mult-Family	62.03%	62.87%	63.24%

Source: Federal Reserve Sysytem

related agencies and mortgage pools and trusts. Most, but not all, of the mortgages in these categories are considered securitized (in essence, originated but not held in the portfolio of the originator). Non-securitized loans in this category would consist of loans held by Ginnie Mae, the FDIC and the FHA. They are essentially loans foreclosed on and held by these agencies until they can be sold. The total of the securitized single-family loans held by the federal agencies and pools (except as just noted) was approximately $7.5 trillion in mid-2012. The amount of multi-family loans was $537.3 billion. The data indicate that 74.53 per cent of all single-family loans and 63.24 percent of all multi-family loans were securitized in mid-2012. Because of the mortgage crisis that began in 2007 the total amount of mortgage debt outstanding has actually decreased somewhat from 2010 to 2012.

REGULATION OF GOVERNMENT-SPONSORED ENTERPRISES

Government-sponsored enterprise (GSE) is a term used to describe FNMA and FHLMC. These agencies are not official departments or branches of the U.S. government. Yet, they were originated through federal legislation and in the eyes of the investing public appear to enjoy the backing of the federal government. In fact, although the federal government does not guarantee the obligations of these two GSEs, Congress has expressed the feeling that in the event of default, they may be required to expend federal dollars to pay off investors who may have purchased their obligations. Notice that these two agencies operate similarly to, but not exactly as, thrifts. They issue debt to purchase long-term mortgages. Some of the debt is short term. Thus, the agencies face interest rate risk. In addition, any uninsured mortgages held by the agencies would pose a threat of default risk. The GSEs face several areas of risk. First there is management and operating risk if the management of the GSEs fails to operate them efficiently. There is also the risk of asset devaluation if defaults on their mortgage portfolios increase above normal or acceptable levels. In recognition of these risks, in 1992 Congress passed the Federal Housing Enterprise Financial Safety and Soundness Act. Although there was no indication, at the time, that default rates on the GSE's mortgage portfolios would pose a problem, the act, nevertheless, addressed this possibility in terms of its capital (equity) guidelines for Fannie Mae and Freddie Mac. To establish and monitor the capital guidelines the Act created the Office of Federal Housing Enterprise and Oversight (OFHEO) within the Department of Housing and Urban Development. The act set two levels of capital guidelines, minimum and critical. In addition, it authorized the director of OFHEO to establish a third, and more rigorous, risk-based guideline. Under this guideline the director could simulate a 10-year "stress" period (high default rates) that includes large movements in interest rates and house prices. The capital sufficient to meet the default risk during this stress period established this guideline.

Although the OFHEO director established the risk-based guideline, the act set the minimum and critical guidelines. The minimum capital was set equal to 2.5 percent of the aggregate on-balance sheet assets plus 0.45 percent of the unpaid principal balance of mortgage-backed securities plus 0.45 percent of the off-balance-sheet obligations of the enterprise. The critical capital level was established at 1.25, 0.25, and 0.25 percent of the same items. An enterprise was deemed adequately capitalized if its capital exceeded the rigorous risk-based capital guideline. It was deemed undercapitalized if its capital was less than the risk-based guideline but greater than the minimum. It was considered significantly undercapitalized if its capital was less than the minimum but above the critical guideline.

Finally, an enterprise was considered critically undercapitalized if its capital was less than the critical guideline. In the latter case it would have to submit a capital restoration plan and could be placed into conservatorship. In addition, the director of OFHEO could limit the growth and activities of the enterprise. The OFHEO had the authority to propose changes in the risk-based capital requirements and to require that the GSEs adhere to generally accepted accounting principles (GAAP). OFHEO found that in the late 1990s, for example, Fannie Mae violated GAAP in its reporting of various components of net income. In 2004 OFHEO concluded that Fannie Mae had engaged in pervasive and willful violations of GAAP to (1) smooth the year-to-year reporting of net income to show stable and growing income (to disguise its riskiness), and (2) meet income goals that would allow senior management to earn compensation based on earnings per share. There were two areas of accounting irregularities in particular: one related to amortization of premiums and discounts and one related to derivatives and hedging activities. Without going into detail in regard to GAAP and accounting rules, here is a simple example of Fannie Mae's accounting irregularities. If Fannie Mae held a mortgage that had a coupon rate slightly higher than the market rate, Fannie Mae booked it as a premium loan. Fannie Mae was required to amortize this premium (for example, show a reduction in the value of the premium as an expense, thus reducing net income) as a function of market conditions. In 1998 there was a drop in interest rates, which resulted in an unexpectedly large amount of refinancing (prepayments) of the mortgages they held. GAAP required that Fannie Mae report approximately $400 million in that year as premium amortization expenses. Instead it reported only $200 million in 1998 and deferring the remaining $200 million to 1999. Had Fannie Mae reported the entire $400 million in 1998 it would have reduced its earnings per share and senior management would have lost their eligibility for bonuses. The EPS that would have met the requirement for management bonuses would not have been met had more than $200 million be expensed. OFHEO concluded that 1998 was not an isolated event but rather one that kicked off an effort to smooth income recognition by (1) not recognizing expenses below certain thresholds and (2) deferring income and expenses (sometimes for several years), which exceeded certain thresholds. By 2004 OFEHO entered into an agreement with the Board of Directors of Fannie Mae to (1) implement correct accounting standards, (2) move to a capital surplus equal to 30 percent of its required minimum capital, (3) recalculate its earnings for all quarterly periods beginning in 1998, (4) review its top management compensation structure, (5) appoint an independent chief risk officer, and (6) agree to not allow its mortgage portfolio assets to exceed a specified amount. The initial cap was set at $727.75 billion but since has been changed by developments that led to an eventual takeover of the GSEs as discussed in the later sections of this chapter.

Effect of the Housing Market Crash on the GSEs

The accounting problems discussed earlier were only a small part of the problem facing the GSEs. After many years of rising house prices, the market began to collapse, nationally, in mid-2006. The GSEs, (as well as other private secondary mortgage market entities) held large volumes of sub-prime mortgages in their portfolios. They also held large volumes of adjustable-rate mortgages that had re-set provisions to higher interest rates after an initial period of time. As long as house prices continued to rise, the default rate on the subprime loans would remain low. In Chapter 12 we explain that sufficient equity in a house will prevent or discourage a homeowner from defaulting on a loan even if he or she becomes unable to make the payment. That is, if a homeowner becomes unable to make the payment on a loan because of a loss of income or because of a payment increase as a result of a re-set of the interest rate on an ARM he or she will not default if there is positive equity to be captured through a sale of the property. However, the drop in housing values beginning in 2006 and continuing through 2008 along with the ARM re-sets created an environment where defaults on their mortgage portfolio became much more likely. The sub-prime mortgages presented one problem, the ARM re-sets another. To understand the ARM re-set problem you must consider the agency problem between mortgage bankers and the secondary mortgage market. Mortgage bankers have no funds of their own but originate mortgages to be sold in the secondary market. Furthermore, in addition to origination fees, mortgage bankers can earn significant fees in the form of yield spread premiums (YSPs). The YSP is an amount the mortgage banker receives over and above the amount of the loan. If, for example, a mortgage banker can convince a borrower to take out a mortgage with a market rate (say, 6 percent) that re-sets after 2 years to a higher rate (say, 10 percent), he or she will be able to sell that loan in the secondary market for a substantial premium (a $200,000 loan may be sold for $220,000) based on the yield spread (10 percent versus 6 percent). The mortgage banker has an incentive to place borrowers in these ARM re-set loans. But this increases the risk of default, especially if house prices fall, because the borrower may be less able to make the loan payments after they re-set.

By 2008 the decline in housing values had dire financial consequences for the GSEs. As indicated earlier, the value in their stock fell precipitously as it became evident that the value of their mortgage portfolios was falling below the value of their debt obligations. Also, in the face of the rapid decline in stock values it became known that the CEOs of both GSEs were receiving very large compensation packages along with valuable "golden parachute" retirement provisions.

The accounting problems, the housing market decline, rising default rates, ARM re-sets, and general decline in the mortgage portfolios of the GSEs led the Congress to pass the Housing and Economic Recovery Act of 2008.

The Housing and Economic Recovery Act of 2008

This act was signed into law by President Bush on July 30, 2008. It was intended to place more restrictive regulations on the GSEs. This act eliminated the OFEHO and replaced it with **Federal Housing Finance Agency (FHFA)**. The Act had three parts: one addressing housing finance reform, a second addressing foreclosure prevention, and a third addressing tax-related provisions.

HOUSING FINANCE REFORM

This section of the Act brought in the Federal Home Loan Banks as GSEs. It also extended regulation beyond the GSEs to include directors, officers, employees, controlling stockholders, agents, consultants, and other persons who participate in the management or conduct of the GSEs. The FHFA took over the duties of the former OFHEO but also had expanded regulatory powers. The director of FHFA is prohibited from having any financial interest in a regulated GSE. The director of FHFA can also limit the compensation of the GSEs' CEOs including golden parachute payments. The FHFA is empowered to require regulated agencies to submit regular reports, including financial statements on as fair value basis. Penalties for failure to provide the report or to provide reports with misleading information may result in a fine of as much as $1 million per day.

The Act vests the director of FHFA with broader powers to establish or change risk-based capital standards. It can raise the standards to the extent needed to ensure that the GSEs operate in a financially safe and sound manner. It also applied the risk-based capital standards to the FHLBs. Also, regulated entities that fail to be adequately capitalized are prohibited from making capital distributions (dividends) that would place the entity in a lower capital classification and must submit a capital restoration plan to FHFA.

Also included in this Act was the Secure and Fair Enforcement for Mortgage Licensing Act of 2008 (SAFE Mortgage Licensing Act). This Act promotes the establishment by the states of a National Mortgage Licensing System and Registry. The objectives of this Act include a nationally uniform license application and reporting requirements of loan originators, a licensing database, providing consumers with accessible information on the employment history and enforcement actions against loan originators, providing comprehensive training and examination requirements related to subprime mortgage lending, and facilitating the collection and disbursement of consumer complaints on behalf of state regulators.

FORECLOSURE PREVENTION

There are several key provisions here. The Act limits the ability of lenders to foreclose on properties owned by members of the armed services for 9 months following the period of military service and limits the rate of interest over such period to 6 percent. It raises the upper limit on the value of houses financed by FHA loans beginning in 2009. It revises the minimum cash down payment on FHA loans (and disallows the seller of the property from funding this down payment). It also increases the upper limit on the initial (up-front) mortgage insurance premium on FHA loans.

TAX-RELATED PROVISIONS

There are two main provisions. The Act provides a refundable tax credit for first-time home buyers equal to the lesser of 10 percent of the purchase price or $7,500 for the tax year of the purchase. However, this credit must be re-paid by the taxpayer over 15 years with equal installments at no interest. The credit is phased out for high-income taxpayers, however. Second the Act increases the standard deduction for the taxable year to the lesser of (1) its allowable deduction for state and local property taxes or (2) $1,000 (joint return).

The Subprime Mortgage Crisis Forces the Federal Government to Takeover Fannie Mae and Freddie Mac

By mid-2008 the large losses on low-quality mortgages had taken their toll on these two GSEs. Furthermore, the Housing and Economic Recovery Act of 2008 had failed to prevent the financial bleeding of the GSEs. They were losing money primarily because of their loan write-offs (for which they had accepted guarantee fees) and their book net worth was negative. The market value of Fannie Mae was $7.6 billion in August 2008 down from $38.9 billion at the end of 2007. Freddie Mac's market value of equity fell from $22 billion to $3.3 billion over the same period. In the second quarter of 2008 alone Fannie Mae had net income of negative $2.603 billion.

Many financial economists had always thought that had the two GSEs ever been in a position to default on their bonds that the federal government would come to the rescue of the bond investors, many of which were banks and large financial institutions. The believed so because of the "federal" in the names of the GSEs. And so it was.

On September 7, 2008 (while the financial markets were closed) the Federal government announced its takeover of Fannie Mae and Freddie Mac. The FHFA placed them under conservatorship. Under the takeover the U.S. Treasury received $1 billion of senior preferred stock with warrants representing an ownership stake of 79.9 percent of the two GSEs. The Treasury initially received 10 percent interest on this stock but in 2011 an agreement was made whereby the GSE's would return all their profits to the Treasury so as to pay down their indebtedness. The government also pledged to support the bonds (including subordinated debt) of the two agencies. Thus, Fannie Mae and Freddie Mac debt essentially become obligations of the federal government. The government also required the agencies to reduce their holdings of mortgages. Neither portfolio could exceed $850 billion in mortgages as of December 31, 2009. Furthermore initially the portfolios were to be reduced by 10 percent each year until they reach $250 billion. Now, that reduction has been accelerated to 15 percent annually. Finally, the U.S. Treasury agreed to purchase $5 billion per month of their bonds, for a period of time.

The failure of the two mortgage giants occurred in part because of agency problems. First, mortgage brokers originated loans for which they would not hold in their own portfolio but would sell off to the secondary mortgage market. Their incentive was to originate as many loans as possible earning commissions and yield premium spreads while shifting the risk to the secondary market. They responded to this incentive by originating many subprime (and fraudulent) loans. Also, since lenders were required to "take back" any problem mortgage for which they did not pay a guarantee fee to the GSEs, they paid these fees. The guarantee fee income, in turn, boosted the bottom line of the GSEs and its stock price. Senior management at the GSEs had stock options. In 2007, CEO Richard Syron received $14.3 million in stock options as part of $19.8 million in total compensation.

Also, as part of the takeover the government promised financial support to the Federal Home Loan Banks that had, themselves, purchased mortgages from their member (savings and loans) institutions.

Summary

The secondary mortgage market is one in which existing mortgages are bought and sold. Purchased mortgages are "repackaged" and their cash flows converted into various types of mortgage-backed securities, such as MBBs and CMOs. These mortgage-backed securities also are bought and sold in the secondary mortgage market. The secondary market exists to facilitate the flow of funds from areas or institutions with a surplus of capital to areas or institutions with a deficit. The flow is facilitated by the creation of liquid, default-free, mortgage-backed securities. The secondary market also allows originators of mortgages to shift interest rate risk to investors, who are in a better position to handle the risks. Players that facilitate transactions in the secondary market include government agencies, such as the Government National Mortgage Association, the Federal Home Loan Banks, and the Federal National Mortgage Association, as well as private firms, such as First Boston or Salomon Brothers. These agencies and firms specialize in rearranging the cash flows from pools of mortgages into debt instruments that appeal to investors.

The federal government has actively supported the secondary mortgage market by its guarantee of some bonds (GNMA), its line of credit from the U.S. Treasury (FNMA), and legislation that facilitates the formation of conduits (REMICs) that have favorable tax rules. The secondary mortgage market has been so successful in meeting the needs of its participants that, by 2012, 74 percent of all single-family residential mortgage debt had been securitized.

Because two agencies, FNMA and FHLMC, were established by federal legislation and enjoy the perception of federal backing, legislation was passed aimed at regulating these government-sponsored enterprises in terms of capital requirements reflecting their credit, interest rate, and management risks. Even with these regulations in place the mortgage crisis of 2007 to 2012 led to large losses for the GSE's. This eventually had to be taken over by the federal government in September 2008 and placed into conservatorship with the federal Housing Finance Agency. They also received significant financial support from the United States Treasury and Federal Reserve System.

Key Terms

Cash settlement

Collateralized

Collateralized mortgage obligations (CMOs)

Commercial mortgage-backed security (CMBS)

Counterparty risk

Credit default swap (CDS)

Credit enhancement

Credit event

Credit risk

Credit tenant lease (CTL) security

Depository Trust Clearing Corporation

Double taxation

Federal Agricultural Mortgage Corporation (FAMC)

Federal credit agencies

Federal Financing Bank (FFB)

Federal Home Loan Banks (FHLB)

Federal Home Loan Mortgage Corporation (FHLMC)

Federal Housing Finance Agency (FHFA)

Federal National Mortgage Association (FNMA)

Financial Accounting Standards Board (FASB)

Government National Mortgage Association (GNMA)

Government-sponsored enterprise (GSE)

Grantor trust

Guaranteed mortgage certificates (GMCs)

Mark-to-market

Mortgage pay-through bonds (MPTBs)

Mortgage-backed bonds (MBBs)

Mortgage-backed security (MBS)

Mortgage Partnership Finance Program

Participation certificate (PC)

Pass-through securities

Physical settlement

Pool insurance

Private mortgage insurance (PMI)

Real Estate Mortgage Investment Conduit (REMIC)

Real estate synthetic investment securities (RESI)

Reference entity

Secondary mortgage market

Senior tranche

Senior/Subordinated pass-through

Spread (price)

Subordinated tranche

Swap

Tandem Plan

Tranches

Warehousing

Review Questions

10-1. What are the benefits of a well-organized secondary mortgage market? List at least three.

10-2. What are two forms of a supply-and-demand mismatch solved by the secondary mortgage market?

10-3. What are mortgage-backed securities?

10-4.   What are desirable characteristics of mortgage-backed securities?

10-5.   List and give a brief description of the types of mortgage-backed securities.

10-6.   What are the advantages of a collateralized mortgage obligation over a straight pass-through security?

10-7.   Explain what credit enhancement is, and list a few ways in which it is accomplished in the secondary mortgage in debt.

10-8.   What is a stripped mortgage-backed security?

10-9.   Define a swap and indicate why some lenders use them.

10-10.   Explain what a REMIC is and why Congress passed legislation to provide for it.

10-11.   List and briefly describe several secondary mortgage market agencies.

10-12.   Compare and contrast the three federally sponsored agencies. Include in your comparison the types of mortgages they purchase and the types of securities they issue.

10-13.   Describe current regulation of government-sponsored agencies.

10-14.   List the characteristics of mortgage-backed securities that make them acceptable to investors.

10-15.   Compare and contrast a commercial mortgage-backed security with a collateralized mortgage obligation.

10-16.   Describe the major characteristics of a credit tenant lease security.

10-17.   What is the major advantage for depository institutions when selling their loans to the FHLBs under the Mortgage Partnership Finance Program as opposed to Fannie Mae or Freddie Mac?

10-18.   What is the difference between credit risk and market risk insofar as residential mortgages are concerned?

10-19.   Give two examples of an agency problem that led to the financial problems at Fannie Mae and Freddie Mac.

10-20.   Describe how a credit default swap works.

10-21.   Briefly explain how the mortgage crisis beginning in 2007 led to the financial problems with the GSE's.

10-22.   Briefly explain the steps that the federal government took to support the GSE's failing financial position as a result of the mortgage crisis.

Notes

1. John P. Harding and C.F. Sirmans. Commercial mortgage-backed securities: Anintroduction for professional investors. *Real Estate Finance* 14(1) (Spring 1997), 43–51.

2. Fitch IBCA. Trends in commercial mortgage default rates and loss severity—1997 update. (July 20, 1998).

3. In the early years of operation, GNMA had two programs: a straight pass-through, which provided for the payment of interest and principal only if paid by the mortgagors, and a partially modified pass-through, which provided for interest payment (but not principal) whether or not collected. Recent GNMA programs are all fully modified pass-throughs that pay interest and principal whether or notcollected.

Web Sites

http://www.ginniemae.gov
Information on GNMA programs and securities

http://www.freddiemac.com
Information on the Federal Home Loan Mortgage Corporation including articles from its journal, *Secondary Mortgage Markets*

http://www.rurdev.usda.gov/rhs/
Information on Rural Housing Service programs

http://www.fhfb.gov
Site of the Federal Housing Finance Board

http://www.dtcc.com
Data on CDSs from the Depository Trust Clearing Corporation

MORTGAGE DERIVATIVE SECURITIES AND STRUCTURED FINANCE

LEARNING OBJECTIVES

The topic of this chapter is the valuation of mortgage securities. After you have read this chapter, you should understand how the cash stream from a pool of mortgages flows through to investors in various types of mortgage securities. You should understand how the cash flows of mortgage securities differ from one another in terms of their amount and timing. You also should know how changes in interest rates affect the value of mortgage securities. You will also see how prepayment and default assumptions affect the cash flows of mortgage securities. You will see why the values of mortgage securities behave differently from one another in response to changes in interest rates. You will discover how some mortgage securities can be used to hedge against interest rate risk inherent in more traditional debt securities.

INTRODUCTION

In this chapter, we analyze the cash flows and valuation of several types of mortgage securities: pass-throughs, mortgage-backed bonds, collateralized mortgage obligations (CMOs) (including the interest-only and principal-only strips), and servicing rights. These securities are called mortgage-related and mortgage-derivative securities. A **mortgage-derivative security** is any security for which the cash flows derived from mortgages are rearranged in terms of amount and timing. They include all of the securities discussed so far except for pass-throughs. In valuation, particular attention is paid to how changes in the market rate of interest affect the cash flows and value of these securities.

It is well known how changes in the rate of interest affect the value of traditional debt securities. For these securities, future expected cash flows are fixed in terms of amount and payment dates. For fixed-rate obligations such as Treasury bonds or (noncallable) corporate debt, an increase in the market rate of interest will lower their values. The amount and timing of the future cash flows are unchanged, although the discount rate is raised. The reverse is true for a decrease in the market rate. Furthermore, the longer the duration (similar to maturity) of the obligation, the greater will be the change in value as a result of a change in market rates. However, mortgage securities are very dissimilar to these traditional types of debt.

The most striking difference is that for mortgage securities, both the timing and the amount of future expected cash flows are dependent on changes in the rate of interest. Not only does a change in the market rate of interest affect the rate used to discount the cash flows of a mortgage security, the change also affects the time pattern of the cash flows. Since the amount and timing of the cash flows are contingent on interest rates, they are referred to as **interest rate contingent securities**. All of this makes the valuation of mortgage-derivative securities somewhat of an intricate exercise. As a foundation, we begin with a review of the valuation of traditional debt securities and then move to mortgage-related securities (MRSs).

VALUATION OF TRADITIONAL DEBT SECURITIES

By a traditional debt security, we mean an obligation for which the issuer has promised a fixed payment on certain dates. A noncallable corporate security, for example, pays a semiannual interest payment that is fixed in its dollar amount and a return of the face principal amount at maturity. The size and timing of the payments are not contingent on future levels of interest rates. The value of the security depends on the discount rate employed to find the present value of the cash flows. Initially, if the coupon rate of interest equals the market discount rate for the security, it sells at face (par) value. This is usually the case when the bond is originally issued, because the corporation will attempt to set the coupon payment equal to the current market rate. As market rates change over the life of the bond, so will its value—in the typical inverse relationship. As an illustration, consider the value of the bond described in Table 11-1. The bond is a noncallable corporate bond with a remaining life of 19 years. It carries a 10 percent coupon and was issued and sold at par a year earlier.

TABLE 11-1

Valuation of Traditional Debt Security

Bond description:

Annual coupon rate 10%; face value, $1,000; semiannual coupon, $50; number of periods to maturity, 38 (19 years); duration, 9.9 years

CURRENT MARKET RATE (%)	VALUE ($)
6	1,449.85
7	1,312.62
8	1,193.68
9	1,090.25
10	1,000.00
11	920.97
12	851.54
13	790.31
14	736.13
15	688.01

Valuation Formula: $PV = \dfrac{\$50}{1 + r/2} + \dfrac{\$50}{(1 + r/2)^2} + \cdots + \dfrac{\$1050}{(1 + r/2)^{38}}$

or

$$PV = PV/FAr_{\%,\,38} \times \$50 + PV/Fr_{\%,\,38} \times \$1000$$

Three concepts are important: valuation, yield-to-maturity (YTM), and the sensitivity of the value to changes in interest rates.

Valuation. Note that the bond in the example promises to pay $100 annually—$50 every 6 months. This promised payment is fixed. Its value can be found by discounting the expected cash flows by the current discount rate. Two elements comprise the remaining cash flows—the 38 semiannual payments of $50 and the face value of $1,000, to be paid at the end of the nineteenth year. Again, higher discount rates create lower values and vice versa. As an illustration, if the market rate of interest is 12 percent, then the value is found by

$$\$851.54 = \frac{50}{(1.06)^1} + \frac{50}{(1.06)^2} + \cdots + \frac{50}{(1.06)^{38}} + \frac{1000}{(1.06)^{38}}$$

Yield-to-Maturity. The function of the discount or premium on a bond is to cause its yield to equal the current discount rate. When the market rate of interest is 12 percent, investors require the expected yield on the bond in our example to also be 12 percent. For a bond selling at a discount, the higher yield is obtained in two parts—coupon payments and capital gain. The latter is the difference between the amount paid for the bond and its face value at maturity ($1,000 − 851.54). An approximation of the YTM can be found by utilizing the following formula:

$$\text{YTM} = \frac{C + [FV - p_0]/N}{(p_0 + FV)/2} \qquad \text{(Equation 11-1)}$$

where C is the annual cash coupon, N is the number of years to maturity, P_0 is the purchase price, and FV is the face value at maturity. The formula puts the yield on an annual basis and has two components—the cash coupon and the amount of appreciation in the value of the security. This latter component is represented by the total capital gain (FV − P_0) divided by the number of years to maturity. Together, these two components of annual return are divided by the average investment in the security. You should note that this is an approximation only. It is used here to show how the yield is affected by the discount from the face value. For our example,

$$\text{YTM} = \frac{\$100 + [(\$1000 - \$851.54)/19]}{(\$851.54 + \$1000)/2} = \frac{107.81}{925.11} = 11.65\%$$

which is close to the precise yield of 12 percent.

Sensitivity of Prices to Changes in Interest Rates: Duration. Note that although the bond's current maturity is 19 years, its duration is 9.9 years. It is the bond's duration that determines the change in its value as a result of changes in the rate of interest. This can be seen by reviewing the formula that relates the percentage change in the price of a debt security to its duration:

$$\triangle P/P = -D(\triangle r/(1 + r)) \qquad \text{(Equation 11-2)}$$

As an exercise, note the change in the price of the corporate bond in Table 11-1 when the market interest rate changes from 10 to 9 percent. The percentage change in the price of the security is given by

$$0.0925 = -9.9(-0.01/1.1)$$

If the duration of a security is unknown, one can avoid the tedious calculations necessary to determine it by using Equation 11-2. If one accepts the fact that securities trading in liquid markets are priced efficiently, then simply rewrite the equation as

$$D = -\triangle P/P \times (1 + r)/\triangle r \qquad \text{(Equation 11-3)}$$

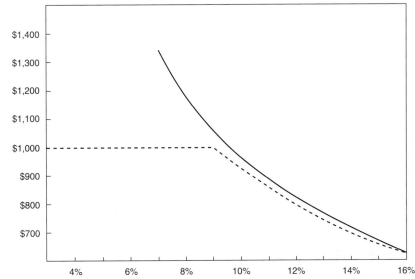

| FIGURE 11-1 | Value of Traditional Debt Security Coupon, 10%; Maturity, 19 Years |

Source: © 2014 OnCourse Learning

and solve for its duration. This is a quick and easy way in which to approximate the duration of a security. In the above example, note that

$$9.9 = 0.090 \times (1.1/0.01)$$

Later, we will use this estimation method to determine the duration of MRSs.

The value profile of the corporate bond in Table 11-1 is shown in Figure 11-1. It relates the value of the bond as a function of the market (discount) rate of interest. It is downward sloping throughout and has a convex shape. One characteristic of securities is their convexity, which refers to the extent to which the value profile in Figure 11-1 is more or less convex. The value of the security increases as the discount rate approaches zero. This is because the bond is noncallable; the issuer must make the remaining coupon payments as promised even if the market rate falls. A callable bond would not increase in value below a certain low interest rate. Its value profile would appear as the dashed line in Figure 11-1. When the market rate of interest falls sufficiently below the coupon rate, the company will call it and pay an amount equal or close to its face value. It will raise the funds necessary to call the bond by issuing new bonds at the lower market rate.

The principles of valuation, YTM, and the sensitivity of prices to changes in interest rates can be very different for MRSs, which we consider next.

MORTGAGE-RELATED SECURITIES

The cash flows and valuation of MRSs differ from traditional debt securities of the type examined above. This is because the amount and timing of the cash flows depend on changes in the level of interest rates. To see this, consider a pool of several hundred mortgages. In any one period (month), the cash flows from that pool will consist of three elements: (1) scheduled amortization of principal, (2) interest on the remaining principal, and (3) prepayments of a portion of the pool.

The first two elements are the standard principal and interest payments. For a standard fixed-rate, fixed-payment mortgage, the payment is constant, with a declining portion represented by interest and an accelerating portion as principal. The third element is any prepayment of one or more mortgages prior to the maturity. Most loans are prepaid prior to maturity. The average life of standard mortgages is from 9 to 15 years.

For a pool of mortgages (with no defaults), the following is true. First, the total amount of principal (both scheduled and prepayments) that will be paid from the pool will not depend on changes in the interest rate. Changes in the interest rate may cause the principal payments to be delayed or accelerated, but the total amount paid will equal the initial principal in the pool. In other words, there is no question as to the amount to be received in the future, only to its timing.

Second, the interest payments in any 1 month will depend on the amount of principal outstanding at the beginning of that month. Thus, if the principal payments are delayed, more total interest payments will be coming from the pool. Conversely, if principal payments are accelerated by early prepayments, the total amount of interest payments will be reduced. For interest payments, uncertainty surrounds both the amount and the timing of the payments.

Third, changes in the market rate of interest will affect the timing of prepayments. If interest rates remain unchanged, a "normal" rate of prepayment results from homeowners selling their properties due to lifestyle changes. (Also, a default and foreclosure will result in a prepayment.) A change of occupation, a divorce, a decision by the homeowner to consume more or less housing than at present may lead to a prepayment of the existing loan. Beyond this normal rate, changes in interest rates will have an impact on prepayment rates. If interest rates rise, then more loans will have a coupon rate that is lower than the market rate. Prepayments of these low-rate loans will slow. Some homeowners will defer taking on a new job or a move to a new residence because they would face a higher house payment for the same amount of housing. Conversely, if rates fall, prepayments will accelerate. Even if the homeowner does not anticipate selling the residence, he or she will have an incentive to refinance his or her loan at a lower rate. By exercising the call option, his or her loan is prepaid. Thus, changes in the rate of interest will affect the amount and timing of the cash flows from a pool of mortgages and, in turn, the cash flows to the MRSs. We begin by reviewing the cash flows of a pass-through security.

Pass-Throughs

As with all MRSs, the timing and amount of cash flows from a pool of mortgages backing a pass-through are crucial for valuation. The expected rate at which mortgages from a pool will prepay is critical to the valuation exercise. There are several models of expected prepayments that have been or are currently used to value pass-through securities.

Twelve-Year Prepaid Life

During the 1970s, the standard approach to valuing pass-throughs was to assume that the mortgages in the pool would all prepay at the end of 12 years, the so-called average life of mortgages. The 12-year average life was based on Federal Housing Administration (FHA) data. It was soon discovered that this assumption led to misleading results. All pass-throughs do not prepay at the same rate. Changes in interest rates will cause some to prepay faster than others. Pools of mortgages with coupon rates above the market rate will prepay faster than those with coupons at the market rate. Pools with low-coupon mortgages will prepay more slowly. This method has been abandoned in favor of more sophisticated models.

Constant Prepayment Rate

One commonly used method is to assume that mortgages in a pool prepay at a constant rate. A pool's **constant prepayment rate (CPR)** for a given period is the percentage of the mortgage principal in the pool at the beginning that prepays during the period. The beginning balance is computed net of scheduled amortization. For example, consider a pool with a monthly CPR of 1 percent (12 percent annually). If, at the beginning of the month, the principal in the pool is $1 million and the scheduled amortization is $10,000, then the expected prepayment is $9,900 ($1,000,000 − $10,000 × 0.01).

The effective annual CPR for this example is 11.36 percent. Total prepayments for the year will be $113,600 (11.36% × $1,000,000), not 12 × $9.900 = $118,800. The reason it is less than 12 percent is that the 1 percent prepayment rate is applied each month to a declining principal balance (sort of compounding in reverse). The assumed CPR for a given pool will depend on the coupon rate of the pool in relation to market rates.

FHA Experience

The FHA periodically publishes a schedule of the survivorship of FHA loans for each of the 30 years of their maturity. The schedule is based on the prepayment behavior of all FHA loans insured since 1957. An example is presented in Table 11-2. Note that 87.289 percent of all FHA loans originated since 1957 survived 5 years, and 82.38 percent survived 6 years. This tells us that 4.91 percent (87.289 − 82.38) of all FHA mortgages outstanding at the beginning of their sixth year were prepaid in that year.

The prepayment rates can be used to estimate those on a pool of mortgages. Different models of prepayments may assume faster or slower attrition than the FHA experience. A rate-200 percent FHA indicates that a pool is expected to prepay twice as fast as the overall FHA experience, while a rate-50 percent FHA indicates a prepayment rate that is one-half that of the FHA experience.

The advantage of using the FHA experience is that it allows for a variation in the assumed prepayment rate by year. This reflects the fact that the probability of prepayment varies by year. The probability of prepayment is low in the initial years of a mortgage, rises and reaches a peak between 5 and 8 years, and falls thereafter. The disadvantage is that these rates are based on the behavior of all

TABLE 11-2
FHA Mortality Table; Original Term, 30 Years

YEAR	PERCENT EXISTING AT BEGINNING OF YEAR	PREPAID DURING YEAR	YEAR	PERCENT EXISTING AT BEGINNING OF YEAR	PREPAID DURING YEAR
1	1.00	0.00837	16	0.44062	0.03028
2	0.99163	0.03100	17	0.41034	0.03037
3	0.96063	0.04171	18	0.37997	0.03057
4	0.91892	0.04603	19	0.34940	0.03074
5	0.87289	0.04909	20	0.31866	0.03105
6	0.82380	0.04956	21	0.28761	0.02953
7	0.77424	0.04668	22	0.25808	0.02793
8	0.72756	0.04399	23	0.23015	0.02625
9	0.68357	0.04093	24	0.20390	0.02450
10	0.64264	0.03784	25	0.17940	0.02271
11	0.60480	0.03595	26	0.15669	0.02089
12	0.56885	0.03399	27	0.13580	0.01907
13	0.53486	0.03241	28	0.11673	0.01725
14	0.50245	0.03127	29	0.09948	0.02181
15	0.47118	0.03056	30	0.07767	0.07767

Source: © 2014 OnCourse Learning

FHA loans. If the FHA experiences were broken down by periods, radically different prepayment rates might be observed. Loans originated in a year of high interest rates (such as 1981) and followed by a drop in interest rates would prepay much faster in the early years. The reverse would be true for loans originated in a year of low rates (such as 1974) and followed by an increase.

Public Securities Association Model

The current industry standard is the **Public Securities Association (PSA) prepayment rate** model. It combines the information contained in the FHA experience tables with the simplicity of the CPR model. The PSA benchmark assumes that the annual CPR on a monthly basis is 0.2 percent in the first month and increases by 0.2 percent each month thereafter until month 30, at which time the CPR is 6 percent. The annual CPR remains at that level for the remaining 330 months. Multiples of the PSA benchmark are interpreted in terms of this base model. A 200 percent PSA assumes that the loans prepay at 0.4 percent in the first month, 0.8 percent the second month, and so forth, until they level off at 12 percent in month 30. Figure 11-2 shows the base PSA and two multiples.

Future cash flows are estimated by taking the scheduled principal and interest payments and adding the assumed PSA prepayment rate. Once the cash flows are so estimated, the value of the pass-through can be determined by use of the standard discounted cash flow model.

Econometric Prepayment Models

Many Wall Street firms as well as the secondary mortgage market agencies have developed **econometric prepayment models** to predict prepayments of pools of mortgages for each month remaining for the pool. A number of variables that affect prepayments are included in the model: the age of the mortgages, the season of the year, current and projected interest rates relative to the coupon on the mortgages, geographical location of the properties that back the mortgages, and

FIGURE 11–2	PSA and Multiples of PSA

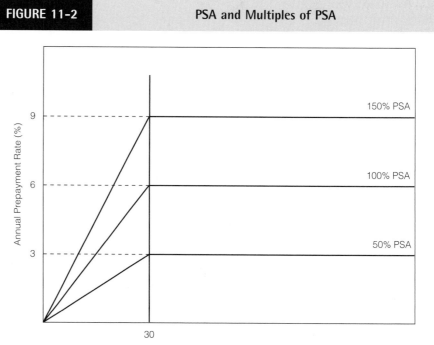

Source: © 2014 OnCourse Learning

borrower characteristics such as age, income, and wealth. Such a model was developed by Merrill Lynch's Mortgage-Backed Securities Research Department and based on the prepayment rates on a portfolio of conventional loans held by Freddie Mac. The model explained 85 percent of the historical variation in prepayment rates. The level of interest rates is important, of course, because these determine the probability that mortgagors will exercise the prepayment option. Location also can be important because mortgages turn over more frequently in some parts of the country than in others. Also, seasonal patterns in home sales will translate into seasonal patterns of prepayment rates. Borrower characteristics may indicate the propensity to relocate.

Econometric models can be used to forecast the prepayment rate for each month in the future. The accuracy of any such models becomes diminished for more distant months. Also, the predicted prepayment rates may appear very unlike the PSA-model rates. But once the prepayment rates are determined, then the cash flows can be estimated and a value placed on the pool via standard discounted cash flow analysis. The results can be expressed in terms of a PSA prepayment rate by finding the particular PSA-type rate that yields the same value for the security.

Refinancing Models

Telerate Advanced Factor Service. In May 1991 Telerate Mortgage Market Services introduced a market database for the purpose of predicting prepayment activity. Their Advanced Factor Service (AFS) estimates prepayments based on data gathered from title search companies. When homeowners decide to prepay their existing mortgage, a title search is performed as part of the refinancing process. Thus, title search activity will precede the actual refinancing by one to several months. This information can be used, essentially, as an early warning of near future refinancing's (prepayments).

Mortgage Bankers Association Weekly Mortgage Application Survey. A similar data set is the weekly report issued by the Mortgage Bankers Association. The data are compiled from a survey of approximately 20 large national mortgage bankers. Data relating to the purpose of the loan are collected and of interest is the purchase or refinance decision. Changes in application volume are related to a baseline index date of March 16, 1990. Here, again, the data provide an early warning of near future refinancings.

Changes in Interest Rates and Prepayment Behavior

Many studies have demonstrated that one of the most important variables that affect the prepayment behavior of a mortgage pool is the relationship between current market rates and pool rates. Common sense would tell us that if the current rate is above the contract rate, borrowers will have little incentive to prepay. Moreover, regardless of the size of the positive differential, prepayments will occur at a uniformly slower pace, dictated by noneconomic factors such as job relocation, divorce, and so forth. When market rates fall below the contract rate, prepayments should accelerate until a sufficiently large negative differential is reached, at which point they should level off. Some have suggested that this behavior leads to the relationship characterized in Figure 11-3. Tests confirm that this is, in fact, the case. Navratil looked at the prepayment behavior of several hundred Government National Mortgage Association (GNMA) pools.[1] He found that the interest rate differential between the current market rate and that on a pool was the single most important determinant of prepayments and, furthermore, that the data fit the curve in Figure 11-3 very well.

FIGURE 11–3	Interest Rate Differential and Prepayment Rates

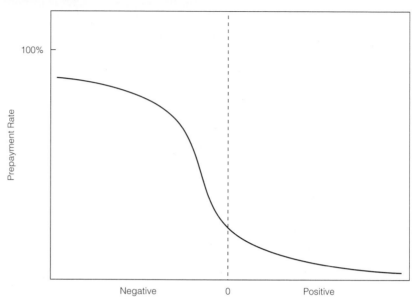

Source: © 2014 OnCourse Learning

As an example, for the average 12 percent pool in Navratil's study, the expected prepayment rate was 1.5 percent with no interest differential. It rose to 8.4 percent when the market rate fell 200 basis points below the pool, and to 30.9 percent for a 400-basis point differential. When the market rate was above the contract rate, little change was seen in the prepayment rate. It fell to 1 percent for a 200-basis point differential. He also found that the elasticity of the change in the prepayment rate with respect to the interest rate differential was greatest for the 200- to 300-basis point negative differential. The duration of the mortgage pool was similarly affected. With no differential, the duration on the average 12 percent pool was 6.4 years. It fell dramatically to only 2.5 years for a 400-basis point negative differential but remained between 5 and 6 years for all positive differentials.

Green and Shoven analyzed the probability of a given mortgage prepaying as a function of changes in interest rates.[2] They looked at the prepayment behavior of nearly 4,000 mortgages held by California savings and loans from 1975 through 1982. As market rates rose, the value (to the lender) of low-rate loans and the probability of their prepayment fell. Their average time to payoff was extended. They analyzed both loans with a due-on-sale feature and those without one. They found that a 10 percent reduction in value reduced the probability of prepayment by 35 percent for loans with a due-on-sale clause and by 63 percent for those that were assumable. The average time to payoff for a 10 percent mortgage was 5.83 years, if the market rate was also 10 percent. It rose to 7.331 years if the market rate increased to 12 percent and the loan had a due-on-sale clause, and to 10.337 years if the mortgage was assumable. Milonas and Lacey found that both the interest rate differential and the shape of the term structure affected prepayment rates.[3] They found that the interest rate differential was the key to predicting prepayments, but they also discovered that expected future rates were important. Even if the current rate was above the contract rate (the prepayment option was out-of-the-money), they found there was a greater likelihood of increased prepayments if rates were expected to rise further. Instead of maximizing the value of the prepayment option, homeowners were maximizing their utility from relocating. They also found that prepayment behavior operated with a lag. As interest rates fell, prepayments rose—but with at least a 3-month lag.

Next, we explore how the prepayment rate affects the cash flows, values, and yields on pass-through securities. Later, we analyze their effect on other MRSs.

Effect of Prepayments on the Cash Flows of Pass-Throughs

The assumed rate of prepayments will have a significant impact on the timing of the cash flows from a pool of mortgages. In turn, it will affect the value of those cash flows. Consider the examples presented in Tables 11-3 and 11-4.

The pool of mortgages at issue consists of $106 million in fixed-rate, 30-year amortizing loans that carry a 10.25 percent coupon rate. It might be useful to consider the pool as one big mortgage for the total amount of the pool. In Table 11-3, we assume that the prepayment rate is 0 percent PSA. This means that there are no prepayments at all. The table can be used as a comparison for models that assume a positive PSA prepayment rate. The annual payment necessary to amortize a $106 million fixed-rate mortgage is $11,479,564. As with this type of loan, the payment consists of interest and principal. The former portion falls and the latter rises through time.

If one were to discount the cash flows presented in Table 11-3 at the mortgage coupon rate (10.25 percent), the present value of all the payments would be, of course, $106 million. The present value of the interest portion would be $89,277,157, or 84 percent of the total present value of the cash flows. Since there are no prepayments at all, the total interest payments and their present value are larger than any model that includes positive prepayments.

The cash flows from this pool, assuming a 100 percent PSA, are shown in Table 11-4. In year 1, scheduled principal and interest payments are the same as in the case of no prepayments. At the end of the first year, it is assumed that approximately 1.3 percent of the remaining balance prepays. The beginning

TABLE 11-3

Cash Flows from Pool of Mortgages

YEAR	BALANCE END OF YEAR ($)	PRINCIPAL ($)	INTEREST ($)	PREPAYMENTS	TOTAL ($)
\multicolumn{6}{l}{Initial balance, $106,000,000; PSA 0%; coupon, 10.25%}					
0	106,000,000	—	—	—	—
1	105,385,436	614,564	10,865,000	0	11,479,564
2	104,707,878	677,557	10,802,007	0	11,479,564
3	103,960,871	747,007	10,732,558	0	11,479,564
4	103,137,296	823,575	10,655,989	0	11,479,564
5	102,229,304	907,992	10,571,573	0	11,479,564
.	.	.	.	.	.
.	.	.	.	.	.
.	.	.	.	.	.
.	.	.	.	.	.
29	10,412,303	9,444,266	2,035,298	0	11,479,564
30	0	10,412,303	1,067,261	0	11,479,564
Total		106,000,000	238,386,935	0	344,386,935
PV at 10.25%		16,722,843	89,277,157	0	106,000,000

Source: © 2014 OnCourse Learning

TABLE 11-4

Cash Flows from Pool of Mortgages

Initial balance $106,000,000; PSA, 100%; coupon, 10.25%

YEAR	BALANCE END OF YEAR ($)	PRINCIPAL ($)	INTEREST ($)	PREPAYMENTS ($)	TOTAL ($)
0	106,000,000	—	—	—	—
1	104,015,425	614,564	10,865,000	1,370,011[a]	12,849,575
2	99,523,055	668,749	10,661,581	3,823,620	15,153,950
3	93,135,241	710,017	10,201,113	5,677,797	16,588,928
4	86,860,047	737,815	9,546,362	5,537,378	15,821,555
5	80,935,662	764,691	8,903,155	5,159,695	14,827,541
.	.	.	.	.	.
.	.	.	.	.	.
.	.	.	.	.	.
.	.	.	.	.	.
29	1,870,495	1,804,751	388,935	119,245	2,312,931
30	0	1,870,493	191,725	0	2,062,218
Total		34,958,128	138,017,824	71,041,872	244,017,824
PV at 10.25%		8,399,418	66,083,742	31,516,840	106,000,000

[a](106,000,000 − 614,564) × 0.013

Source: © 2014 OnCourse Learning

balance in year 2 is less than that in the case of no prepayments. As a result, the interest payments in year 2 will also be less. Total scheduled amortization and prepayments are $106 million ($34,958,128 + $71,041,872), but the timing of their receipt is accelerated. The present value of the cash flows remains $106 million but is now distributed differently between principal and interest. The present value of interest payments is only $66,083,742, or 62 percent of the total, mainly because the total amount of the interest payments is reduced. The present value of the principal payments is increased, not because that total is any different, but because principal payments are accelerated in timing. The earlier a cash flow is received, the greater will be its present value. Further increases in the PSA rate will lead to additional reductions in the present value of the interest payments relative to that of the principal payments. The relationship between the present values of the two components as a function of the PSA rate is shown in Figure 11-4.

Recall that the PSA model assumes that the prepayment rate on a pool of mortgages will rise through month 30 and then level off. This produces a "spike" in the third year of the cash flows. Cash flows under the PSA model will rise for 3 years and then decline. Larger PSA rates produce more pronounced "spikes" in the third year. The profiles of the cash flows of a pool of mortgages under various PSA assumptions are shown in Figure 11-5.

Discount and Premium Pass-Throughs

The effect of the assumed prepayment rate is crucial to the valuation of pass-throughs that sell at a discount or premium. Debt obligations sell at a discount when the market rate is above the coupon rate, and at a premium when the rates are reversed. For pass-throughs, prepayments complicate their valuation. To see

FIGURE 11-4	Proportion of Total Present Value of Cash Flow of Principal and Interest

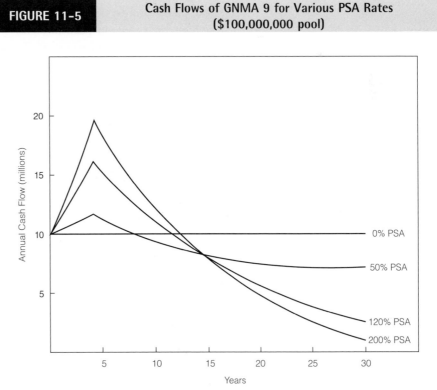

Source: © 2014 OnCourse Learning

FIGURE 11-5	Cash Flows of GNMA 9 for Various PSA Rates ($100,000,000 pool)

Source: © 2014 OnCourse Learning

this, consider first traditional debt securities that sell at a discount. The appreciation in value from purchase to maturity is part (or all) of the yield. A debt obligation maturing in 2 years with a $1,000 face value (and no coupon payments) will be priced at $826.44 to yield 10 percent. Over the 2-year period, the $173.56

appreciation represents the yield to the investor. But what would happen to the yield if, for some reason, the debt issuer were to prepay the face value 1 year after purchase? The 1-year gain of $173.56 on the investment would represent a yield of 21 percent. Conversely, a delay of the repayment of the principal would lower the yield. For discounted debt securities, accelerated prepayments increase the realized yield and delayed prepayments lower the yield. Investors that price pass-through securities on an expected rate of prepayment will realize yields that are different from expected if prepayments accelerate or slow. The reverse is true, of course, for premium pass-throughs. Here, the coupon on the mortgages is above the market yield, and investors benefit if the prepayments are delayed and suffer if they are accelerated.

Price and Yield Behavior of Pass-Throughs

We can now analyze how the price and YTM of pass-through securities behave in response to changes in interest rates. Their behavior is different from standard debt instruments because of their prepayment (call option) feature.

Pass-Through Prices. At any time, pass-throughs of several different coupons are trading in the market. A pass-through will have a coupon reflecting the level of mortgage rates when it was issued. Since interest rates are cyclical at any given time, available pass-throughs will reflect a range of coupons. Figure 11-6 shows the prices on October 1, 2004, of seasoned GNMA and Federal National Mortgage Association (FNMA) pass-throughs. On that date, the market rate on new mortgages was approximately 6 percent.

Note that the price curves became flat above the 6 percent coupon level. This is called **price compression** and reflects the market perception of prepayment behavior for high coupon pass-throughs. The value of the high coupon is offset by the higher expected prepayments. Recall that accelerated prepayments reduce the yield on premium pass-throughs. The higher prepayments are expected on

| FIGURE 11-6 | Prices of GNMA and FNMA Pass-Through; October 2004 |

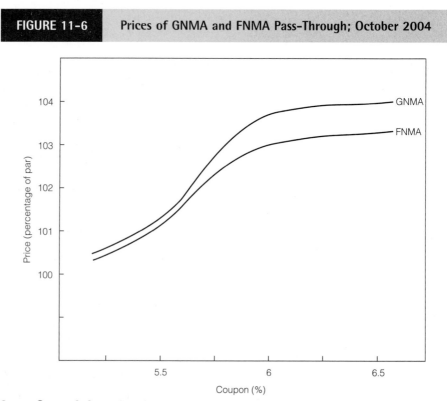

Source: © 2014 OnCourse Learning

these pass-throughs because of the opportunity of mortgagors to call the loan and refinance it. Another way of viewing the price of premium pass-throughs is to realize that investors require a higher yield (lower price) to compensate for the fact that they are purchasing a callable debt instrument. Furthermore, the call option is "in the money" for premium pass-throughs. For rates below 6 percent, the prices reflect the differences in coupons. This is so because there are no expectations of accelerated prepayments for the discounted pass-throughs.

Changes in the market rate of interest will have two impacts on the value of pass-throughs. Both the discount rate and the assumed rate of prepayments will change. Figure 11-7 shows the projected price paths for a discounted and a premium GNMA pass-through (5 and 7 percent coupons, respectively, when the market rate is 6 percent). The shapes of the curves are different from one another and reflect the difference in the prepayment rates. The price of the GNMA 5 changes for either a decrease or increase in the market (discount) rate. It currently sells at a discount. If rates increase, prepayments are expected to slow. In this case, the discount rate rises and the prepayments slow. Both factors cause a decrease in price. If a moderate decline in rates occurs, the price of the GNMA 5 will rise. The discount rate is lower and prepayments are expected to accelerate as rates drop. For large reductions in the interest rates, the value will continue to increase, but at a slower rate, because the large amount of the refinancing would have already occurred.

The shape of the price path of the GNMA 7 is somewhat different. It lies everywhere above that of the GNMA 5 because of the larger coupon. It is a premium security and its price will fall with an increase in rates for the same reasons as the GNMA 5. For a moderate decline in rates, the value will not change much, however. The increase in the value caused by the lower discount rate is offset by a reduction in value caused by the acceleration of prepayments. Recall that accelerated prepayments reduce the yield on a premium pass-through. Investors will require compensation in the form of a lower price. For a large reduction in the level of rates, the effect of the lower discount rate will dominate the prepayment

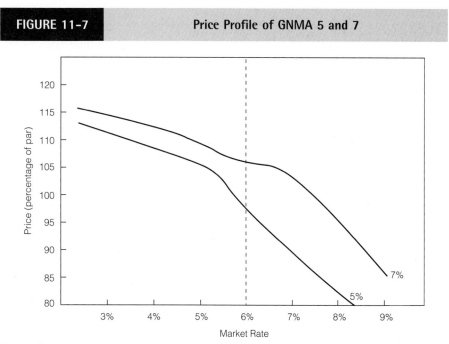

FIGURE 11-7	Price Profile of GNMA 5 and 7

Source: © 2014 OnCourse Learning

| FIGURE 11-8 | Projected Yield-to-Maturity, GNMA 5 and 7 |

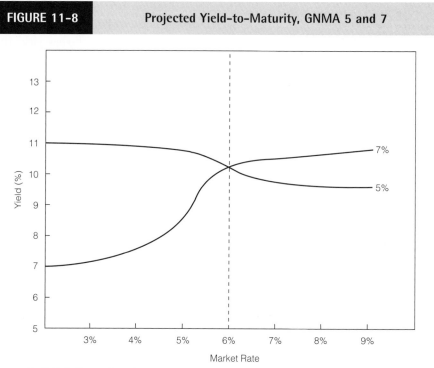

Source: © 2014 OnCourse Learning

behavior as, again, much of the prepayment activity would have occurred during a moderate decline in rates.

Pass-Through Yields. Figure 11-8 illustrates the effect of changes in the market rate of interest on the yield-to-maturities of the GNMA 5 and 7. First, consider an increase in rates. Prepayments for both pass-throughs will slow. A slower prepayment rate will reduce the yield on the discounted pass-through, because the principal is received later in the security's life. The slower prepayment rate raises the yield on the premium, however. The higher coupon rate is earned on a loan balance that does not contract as rapidly as ordinary. As interest rates fall, prepayment rates accelerate. This causes the yield on the GNMA 5 to rise and that on the GNMA 7 to drop. The prepayment rate on the GNMA 7 will be faster than that of the GNMA 5 because the interest rate differential will be larger, making refinancing more profitable for the mortgagor. Because the yields of the two pass-throughs react differently to both increases and decreases in market rates, a good hedging strategy would be to purchase a balanced portfolio of both.

We saw above that, under some circumstances, a change in market rates may not cause a large change in the price of a pass-through. This was true, for example, for the premium GNMA 7 for moderate declines in interest rates. In that example, an increase in value due to the decline in the discount rate was offset by an acceleration in the prepayment rate. In effect, the duration of the security was shortened, thereby moderating the effect of the change in rates on price.

Effective Duration of Pass-Throughs. The duration of pass-throughs is impossible to measure by calculating the amount and timing of future cash flows because they are affected by uncertain prepayments. Nonetheless, it is possible to determine the **effective** or **implied duration** by observing the price behavior of various pass-throughs in response to changes in interest rates. The example in Table 11-5 will clarify this. The market prices of a GNMA 7 are given for the base rate, 6 percent, and a change of the rate by 25 basis points in both directions. The price

TABLE 11–5

Calculation of Effective Duration of GNMA 7

	INTEREST RATE (%)		
	5.75	6.00	6.25
Projected prepayment rate	230	200	180
Price at 200 PSA	105.25	104.25	103.16
Price at projected prepayment rate	104.80	104.25	103.46

Source: © 2014 OnCourse Learning

at the base rate ($104.25) is necessary to produce an expected yield of 6 percent. If market rates rise by 25 basis points, the price of the pass-through will fall. The price will increase with a fall in rates. However, the expected prepayment rate also rises and falls with changes in the market interest rate. The change in the assumed prepayment rate has the effect of moderating the price changes as a result of changes in market rates.

The example shows two prices of the pass-through for a fall in market rates and two prices for an increase. In each case, one price is that required to produce the new yield, assuming the prepayment rate remains constant and does not change with the market rate. The other price is that necessary to produce the new yield, assuming the prepayment rate does change when the market rate changes, which is much more likely. Take, for example, an increase in the market rate by 25 basis points. This will produce a fall in the value of the security. If one assumes that the prepayment rate is not affected by the rise in the market rate, then the new price will be $103.16. But if it is assumed that the prepayment rate will slow, then the market price will fall but will still be higher, $103.46. The increase in value ($103.46 − $103.16) is the result of the slowing of the prepayment rate on a premium pass-through. Of course, the reverse argument can be used to demonstrate that when market rates fall, the increase in value will be moderated by the acceleration in prepayments.

The effective or implied duration of the security under each set of assumptions can be calculated with Equation 11-3. If this is done, it can be shown that the changes in the prepayment rates reduce the effective duration of pass-through securities. In other words, the change in the prices of pass-throughs as a result of changes in interest rates is not as dramatic as with conventional debt securities with the same duration. As an illustration, the duration calculated using the unadjusted price data is

$$D = \frac{104.25 - 103.16}{104.25} \times \frac{1.0625}{0.0025}$$

$$= \frac{1.09}{104.25} \times 425 = 4.44 \, \text{years}$$

Using the adjusted price data the duration is

$$D = \frac{104.25 - 103.46}{104.25} \times \frac{1.0625}{0.0025}$$

$$= 0.007578 \times 425 = 3.221 \, \text{years}$$

The uncertainty surrounding the prepayment rates on pools of mortgages complicates their valuation. The complication has led to the creation of other MRSs that are more easily priced by investors. Nonetheless, pass-throughs remain popular and provide returns from 100 to 200 basis points above those on other default-free securities such as U.S. Treasury obligations. As long as they exist, prepayment assumptions will play an intricate part of the pricing in the marketplace.

The following three examples illustrate the importance of prepayment assumptions for one discounted and two premium pass-throughs.

EXAMPLE 1

In the late 1970s and early 1980s market interest rates were at high levels. Ginnie Mae pass-throughs originated a few years earlier were selling at substantial discounts. An investor's realized yield would depend, in part, on the prepayment rate. Realized yields would be greater than expected if prepayment rates were faster than expected. As a result, a great deal of attention was devoted to the identification of pools that were likely to have prepayment rates that were faster than the average. Some members of the Ginnie Mae Dealers Association claimed a specialization in identifying the "fast-pay" Ginnie Maes and promised superior returns to their clients who purchased them.[4] They were called "speed freaks" in the financial press. Their identification of the pools that would prepay at a fast rate was based primarily on the pools' prepayment histories to date, a rather naive model. Simply put, pools that had prepaid faster than the average were expected to continue that behavior. Interest in identifying the so-called fast-pay pools declined with the introduction of more sophisticated econometric models to estimate future prepayment rates. It was also soon realized that, historically, fast-pay pools had a tendency to slow their rate of prepayment. Needless to say, this led to undesirable investment results.

EXAMPLE 2

The second example concerns premium GNMAs. In March 1989, when mortgage rates were in the neighborhood of 10 percent, the FHA sent out several thousands of letters to homeowners who still had insured mortgages with a 15 percent coupon or higher. The FHA was concerned about the risk posed by the homeowners' possible inability to meet the payments on these high-rate mortgages. They offered a **Streamline Refinance Plan (SRP)**, whereby homeowners could refinance their existing loans with lower rate, FHA-insured loans with virtually no refinance costs. The moderate refinance costs could furthermore be included in the amount of the new loan. Basically, the homeowner could refinance the existing loan with no out-of-pocket funds and still reduce the monthly payment. The result, of course, would be a dramatic one-shot increase in the amount of prepayments of GNMA 15s and above. The marketplace realized this, and over the next several weeks the price of GNMA 15s fell, relative to other GNMAs, by about 200 basis points. Holders of GNMA 15s lost about $22 million in the value of their securities as a result of the unexpected acceleration in prepayments.[5]

EXAMPLE 3

Our third example continues with the SRP program. In mid-1990 the Office of the Inspector General of Housing and Urban Development (HUD) announced that it was investigating certain scams associated with the SRP program. Apparently, several lenders were profiting from the program by offering to refinance high-rate loans, but only at a half-point or so below the contract rate and not at the market rate. These lenders would place newspaper ads that read "Lower Your FHA Mortgage with No Out-of-Pocket Costs and No Paper Work." With the market rate at about 10 percent, the lenders involved in the scam would offer the no-cost refinancing plan to those with, say, 13 percent loans. By offering the refinance at 12 percent, they could sell the new loans into Ginnie Mae pools that would sell for about 102 to 104 percent of par. The lenders would absorb the refinancing costs, which were less than the premium earned on the pool. Then a few months later, they would offer the same borrower an opportunity to refinance down again, but still at an above-market rate. The lender would insure a profit on the second and any subsequent refinancings that were above market. Losses were suffered by the pass-through security holders, who purchased their pass-throughs at a premium, only to have them prepaid shortly thereafter. On the first refinancing, the involved lenders would tell borrowers that only one refinancing rate was available at the time, but would give them a "Free Refinance Certificate" or a "Preferred Borrower Certificate" for the next refinancing.

Senior/Subordinated Pass-Throughs

In the previous chapter, we discussed the structure of a senior/subordinated pass-through. With this arrangement, a pool of mortgages is securitized into a senior pass-through with a principal balance somewhat less than the principal of the pool. The senior security has enhanced rights to the cash flows from the entire pool. The subordinated security, usually retained by the lender who sells the senior pass-through, bears all of the default risk. Since there is little or no default risk with the senior security, it will command a premium. The lender captures this premium as a reward for enhancing the credit of the senior by absorbing the entire default risk in the subordinated position. If the premium exceeds the present value of future default risks of the pool, the lender benefits. If, however, there is a severe incidence of default in the pool, the lender may receive a very low or negative return on the subordinated position.

Figure 11-9 is an approximation that compares the yields on a whole mortgage pool with those on the subordinated position as a function of various foreclosure rates. For low foreclosure rates, the lender's return on the subordinated position is greater than that on the pool as a whole. This is so because the lender receives a premium on the sale of the senior position. This premium is considered a cash flow to the subordinated position. As long as the foreclosure rates in years 2 to 4 are less than 2 percent, the yield on the subordinated position will exceed that on the whole pool. Lenders who may be in a better position to judge the default risk of a portfolio of loans that they originate can obtain better yields by creating the senior/subordinated securities. This is, in effect, a form of leveraging. Superior expected yields are created on the subordinated position. The trade-off is the increased risk of the subordinated position. With sufficient foreclosures, the yield

FIGURE 11-9 | **Yield Comparison of Whole Mortgage Pool and Subordinated Security; Senior Security Sold to Yield 40 Basis Point Difference, GNMA 10**

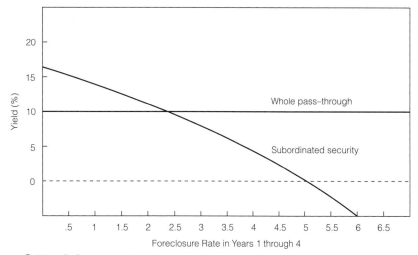

Source: © 2014 OnCourse Learning

on the subordinated position becomes less than that on the whole pool and can even become negative.

We next look at pricing considerations of mortgage-backed bonds.

Mortgage-Backed Bonds

The cash flows of mortgage-backed bonds are designed to appear as traditional noncallable debt. They promise periodic coupon payments and a return of the face value at maturity. They are priced the same as traditional debt securities. The discount rate may reflect risk if the issue is not sufficiently overcollateralized, however. In addition, there is the issue of valuing the residual interest. Let's consider the simple example in Table 11-6. There, we see that $100 million in mortgage-backed bonds is collateralized by $110 million in conventional, fixed-rate, 30-year mortgages, each having a 10.5 percent coupon. The mortgage-backed bonds promise a 9.5 percent coupon payable semiannually for 20 years with repayment of face value at maturity. The cash flows are analyzed on an annual basis for simplicity. At first, we make the assumption that there are no prepayments, but that there is a default rate of 0.5 percent annually for 10 years, applied to the beginning pool balance less scheduled amortization. Cash inflows from the pool not delivered as interest to bond investors are placed in a sinking fund for the repayment of principal at maturity. The fund earns 8 percent. No payments are made to the residual (equity) position until after the bonds mature.

Two important observations can be made. First, the fund balance in year 20 in this example is $105,760,237, sufficient to make the maturity payment ($100 million). Second, the residual payments in the last column have a net present value of $224,138 when discounted at the rate of the pool, 10.5 percent. Taken together, this means that the securitization was successful. The overcollateralization was sufficient to make the promised payments to the bondholders, and the residual payments provided a return-on-equity to the agency issuing the bonds.

The firm issuing the bonds would like to keep the amount of equity (overcollateralization) as small as possible to maximize the return on investment. The bond buyers, on the other hand would like to see the amount of equity as large as possible to guarantee payment of interest and principal. As noted previously, one of the things that the rating agencies will examine closely in the rating process is the amount of overcollateralization. The rating agencies will determine the adequacy of the overcollateralization by considering the impact of several key variables on the balance in the sinking fund at maturity (year 20, in this example). Variables that affect the sinking fund balance include the prepayment rate on mortgages in the pool, the reinvestment rate on the sinking fund, the initial overcollateralization, and the default rate.

The effect of changes in these variables on the sinking fund balance at maturity is shown in Table 11-7. Each variable is changed in isolation from the others to show the effect on the fund balance. There are several interesting relationships. First, a small increase in the initial amount of overcollateralization has a magnified impact on the terminal fund balance. An increase in initial equity of $2.5 million (from $110 million) raises the sinking fund balance in year 20 by $12,284,070. This is due to the reinvestment of a larger volume of cash flowing into the sinking fund. Second, even a slight increase in the default rate has a dramatic impact on the sinking fund balance. An increase to 0.007 percent for the first 10 years is sufficient to drop the fund balance below that necessary to redeem the bonds. Not only is the value of the defaulted mortgages lost, but so are the principal and interest payments and reinvested funds. Third, an increase in the yield on the sinking

TABLE 11-6
Cash Flows of Mortgage–Backed Bonds

YEAR	POOL BALANCE ($)	PRINCIPAL AND INTEREST ($)	PREPAYMENT	DEFAULT ($)	CASH INFLOW ($)	PAYMENT TO BOND HOLDERS ($)	FUND ($)	RESIDUAL PAYMENT ($)
1	110,000,000	12,158,133	0	546,959[a]	12,158,133	9,500,000	2,658,133[b]	0
2	108,844,908	12,097,342	0	540,881	12,097,342	9,500,000	5,468,126[c]	0
3	107,635,399	12,036,856	0	534,501	12,036,856	9,500,000	8,442,432	0
4	106,365,759	11,976,671	0	527,787	11,976,671	9,500,000	11,594,497	0
5	105,029,705	11,916,788	0	520,705	11,916,671	9,500,000	14,938,845	0
6	103,620,331	11,857,204	0	513,216	11,857,204	9,500,000	18,491,157	0
.	.	.	.	.	.	.	.	.
19	76,898,349	11,563,723	0	0	11,563,723	9,500,000	96,015,290	0
20	73,408,952	11,563,723	0	0	11,563,723	109,500,000	5,760,237	5,760,237
21	69,553,168	11,563,723	0	0	11,563,723	0	0	11,563,723
.	.							
30	10,464,908	11,563,723		0	11,563,723			11,563,723

Mortgage $110,000,000
Coupon 10.5%
Bonds $100,000,000
Coupon 9.5%
Maturity 20 years
Equity $10,000,000
%PSA 0
Default rate
First 10 years 0.005
NPV equity 224,138[d]
Fund balance
Year 20, $105,760,237

[a] 0.005 × ($110,000,000 − $608,133)
[b] $12,158,133 − $9,500,000
[c] $2,658,133 × 1.08 + ($12,097,342 − $9,500,000)
[d] $10,224,138 − $10,000,000

Source: © 2014 OnCourse Learning

TABLE 11–7

Year 20 Fund Balance for MBB

INITIAL MORTGAGE POOL ($)	FUND BALANCE ($)	DEFAULT RATE	FUND BALANCE ($)	YIELD ON FUND	FUND BALANCE ($)	PSA PREPAYMENT RATE FUND (YEAR 1)	BALANCE ($)
110,000,000	105,760,237	0.005	105,760,237	0.08	105,760,237	0	105,760,237
112,500,000	118,044,303	0.006	102,651,606	0.08125	107,295,582	0.05	126,269,237
115,000,000	130,328,368	0.007	99,565,138	0.0825	108,855,597	0.075	122,217,256
117,500,000	142,612,434	0.008	96,500,677	0.08375	110,440,682	0.10	117,341,525
120,000,000	154,896,000	0.009	93,458,067	0.085	112,051,241	0.125	113,015,338
125,000,000	179,464,632	0.01	90,437,154	0.08675	113,687,688	0.15	109,482,052

Source: © 2014 OnCourse Learning

fund has a positive effect on the fund balance, but not as dramatically as one might think. Finally, the fund balance will rise with increases in the PSA prepayment rate, reach a maximum, and then fall. For small levels of the prepayment rate, more cash flows are available to be placed in the sinking fund prior to year 20. That is, some payments from the mortgage pool that would have been paid subsequent to the maturity date of the bonds are paid prior to that date. This increases the balance of the fund at maturity. But if the prepayment rate is too great in the early years of the pool's life, a reverse effect will occur. The prepayments are made into a pool that is earning a rate of return generally less than that on either the mortgages or the bonds. Thus, excessive prepayment rates adversely affect the sinking fund balance at maturity, because principal is taken from a mortgage pool earning 10.5 percent and placed in a fund earning 8 percent.

Some factors may interact in their effect on the sinking fund balance. If market interest rates fall, prepayments will accelerate. Furthermore, the excess payments are placed in a sinking fund for which the reinvestment rate also has fallen. In this example, if the interest rate earned on the fund balance drops to 7.5 percent and the prepayment rate rises to 10 percent in the first year, the fund balance in year 20 will be only $94,202,239.

These considerations point out the need for sufficient overcollateralization. Rating agencies will consider some worst-case scenarios when determining the minimum acceptable level for overcollateralization. If their overcollateralization is insufficient, the bonds will receive a low rating and not be available for investment by a wide class of regulated investors. To obtain a high rating, the issuer will have to provide more collateralization or provide other forms of credit enhancement, such as pool insurance or insurance on the individual loans. The rating on the bonds (and the current level of market rates) will determine the discount rate for valuing the mortgage-backed bonds. If the rating is adequate and the discount rate equals the coupon rate, the bonds will sell at par when issued. A subsequent change in market rates or a change in their rating will affect the discount rate and the value of the bonds in the same manner as in Table 11-1.

Collateralized Mortgage Obligations

The cash flows from a pool of mortgages to the various tranches and residual class of a CMO can be complicated. We continue with the example discussed in the previous chapter. For convenience, the structure of the CMO is repeated in Table 11-8. Before you analyze the cash flows, notice some relevant characteristics of this CMO. First, the coupon yield on the mortgages is 10.25 percent. This is greater than the coupon yield on the first two tranches, which make up the majority

TABLE 11-8
Structure of CMO Example

Pool balance, $106,000,000; coupon rate, 10.25%; maturity; 30 years			
CMO TRANCHES	**COUPON**	**MATURITY (YEARS)**	**AMOUNT ($)**
Tranche A	9.25	5–9	30,000,000
Tranche B	9.50	9–14	30,000,000
Tranche C	10.00	12–17	25,000,000
Tranche Z	10.50	26–30	15,000,000

Source: © 2014 OnCourse Learning

(60 percent) of the total CMO issue. Additionally, the CMO is over collateralized by $6 million. Thus, assuming no default risk, the cash flows from the mortgage pool will be sufficient to meet the payments on the CMO. Recall that any prepayments from the mortgage pool are passed along to the bondholders; there is no sinking fund that will have the potential of earning less than the coupon rate on the bonds. In other words, the CMO issuer faces no interest rate or reinvestment risk. The longest maturity tranche does have a higher yield than the shorter maturity tranches and the yield on the mortgage pool. But it has a small outstanding principal. With this in mind, let's look at the cash flows from the mortgage pool to the security holders and the residual class. One possible scenario is presented in Tables 11-9 through 11-12.

Column 6 of Table 11-9 shows the total cash flows from the pool for each year of its 30-year life. The total cash flows are the total of the scheduled principal and interest and the prepayments. Prepayments are based on the 100 percent PSA model, which implies a first-year rate of approximately 1.3 percent of the pool balance after scheduled amortization.[6] The last column in this table shows the remaining principal owed to the security holders. The amount for the first year is the original principal less scheduled amortization and prepayment from the pool ($100,000,000 − $614,564 − $1,370,011). All principal reductions from the pool are passed through to security holders.

Next, Table 11-10 shows the payments to the first two classes of securities. Bondholders for Tranche A receive all principal payments from the pool plus the deferred interest from the Tranche Z bondholders. Skipping down to Table 11-11, you will notice that in the first year the accrued interest for this class is $1,575,000. This amount is added to the principal prepayments ($1,370,011) and scheduled amortization ($614,564) from the pool, and the total ($3,559,575) is paid to the Tranche A bondholders as a reduction in their principal. These bondholders also receive their 9.25 percent coupon payments of $2,775,000, for a total of $6,334,575. The Tranche B and C bondholders only receive coupon payments ($2,850,000 and $2,500,000, respectively). Total cash flows to all bondholders equal $11,684,575. Because $12,849,575 is available from the pool, the difference ($1,165,000) goes to the residual (equity) holders.

This process continues year by year until year 5. In that year, the total cash available from the pool ($14,827,541) is more than sufficient to pay off the remaining principal and accrued interest for the Tranche A bonds. The excess principal payment from the pool in this year is next applied to the principal of Tranche B. Coupon payments for Tranche C bonds are made and deferral of the interest on the Tranche Z continues. By now, the total owed to Tranche Z bondholders is $24,711,701. The Tranche B bondholders are paid off by year 9, and Tranche C bondholders by year 12. After year 12, the accrued interest is paid each year along with principal reductions from the pool. Because the pool's balance is still sizable in relation to that of Tranche Z ($47.5 million versus $41.5 million),

TABLE 11-9

Cash Flows from Mortgage Pool

Initial balance, $106,000,000; coupon rate, 10.25%; maturity, 30 years; PSA, 100%

YEAR	(1) POOL BALANCE END OF YEAR ($)	2 = (3) + (4) SCHEDULED PRINCIPAL AND END OF YEAR ($)	(3) AMORTI-ZATION ($)	(4) INTEREST ($)	(5) PREPAY-MENTS ($)	6 = (2) + (5) TOTAL AVAILABLE FOR DISTRIBUTION ($)	(7) AMOUNT OWED TO SECURITY HOLDERS ($)
0	106,000,000						100,000,000
1	104,015,425	11,479,564	614,564	10,865,000	1,370,011[a]	12,849,575[b]	98,015,425[c]
2	99,523,055	11,330,330	668,749	10,661,581	3,823,620	15,153,950	93,523,055[d]
3	93,135,241	10,911,131	710,017	10,201,113	5,677,797	16,588,928	87,135,241
4	86,860,048	10,284,177	737,815	9,546,362	5,537,378	15,821,555	80,860,048
5	80,935,662	9,667,846	764,691	8,903,155	5,159,695	14,827,541	74,935,662
6	75,340,138	9,088,452	792,547	8,295,905	4,802,977	13,891,429	69,340,138
7	70,052,814	8,543,781	821,417	7,722,364	4,465,907	13,009,688	64,052,814
8	65,054,231	8,031,753	851,339	7,180,413	4,147,244	12,178,997	59,054,231
9	60,326,059	7,550,410	882,351	6,668,059	3,845,821	11,396,230	54,326,059
10	55,851,031	7,097,914	914,492	6,183,421	3,560,535	10,658,449	49,851,031
11	51,612,876	6,672,536	947,805	5,724,731	3,290,350	9,962,886	45,612,876
12	47,596,257	6,272,651	982,331	5,290,320	3,034,289	9,306,939	41,596,257
13	43,786,714	5,896,731	1,018,114	4,878,616	2,791,428	8,688,159	37,786,714
14	40,170,614	5,543,340	1,055,201	4,488,138	2,560,900	8,104,239	34,170,614
15	36,735,091	5,211,127	1,093,639	4,117,488	2,341,883	7,553,010	30,735,091
16	33,468,009	4,898,824	1,133,477	3,765,347	2,133,605	7,032,429	27,468,009
17	30,357,908	4,605,238	1,174,767	3,430,471	1,935,334	6,540,572	24,357,908
18	27,393,967	4,329,246	1,217,560	3,111,686	1,746,381	6,075,627	21,393,967
19	24,565,960	4,069,794	1,261,913	2,807,882	1,566,094	5,635,888	18,565,960
20	21,864,223	3,825,891	1,307,880	2,518,011	1,393,857	5,219,748	15,864,223
21	19,279,614	3,596,606	1,355,523	2,241,083	1,229,086	4,825,692	13,279,614
22	16,803,481	3,381,061	1,404,901	1,976,160	1,071,232	4,452,293	10,803,481
23	14,427,634	3,178,434	1,456,077	1,722,357	919,770	4,098,204	8,427,634
24	12,144,309	2,987,951	1,509,118	1,478,833	774,207	3,762,157	6,144,309
25	9,946,146	2,808,883	1,564,091	1,244,792	634,072	3,442,955	3,946,146
26	7,826,158	2,640,546	1,621,066	1,019,480	498,922	3,139,468	1,826,158
27	5,777,708	2,482,298	1,680,117	802,181	368,332	2,850,631	0
28	3,794,488	2,333,534	1,741,319	592,215	241,901	2,575,435	0
29	1,870,493	2,193,686	1,804,751	388,935	119,245	2,312,931	0
30	0	2,062,218	1,870,493	191,725	0	2,062,218	0

[a]($106,000,000 − $614,564) × 0.013

[b]$11,479,564 + $1,370,011

[c]$100,000,000 − $614,564 − $1,370,011

[d]$98,015,425 − $668,749 − $3,823,620

Source: © 2014 OnCourse Learning

some payments will be left over for the residual tranche. After Tranche Z is paid off in year 26, all remaining pool payments accrue to the residual class. The final table, Table 11-12, shows the cash flows accruing to the residual class beginning with the $6 million investment. The internal rate of return and the net present value of the cash flows also are given.

Because CMOs are structured differently than pass-throughs, prepayment behavior affects their pricing and yield behavior in a different fashion. The price

TABLE 11-10
Payments to Tranche A and B Bondholders

	TRANCHE A				TRANCHE B			
YEAR	(1) PRINCIPAL OUTSTANDING ($)	(2) REDUCTION IN PRINCIPAL FROM POOL AND TRANCHE Z ($)	(3) COUPON ($)	(4) TOTAL = (2) + (3) ($)	(5) PRINCIPAL OUTSTANDING ($)	(6) REDUCTION IN PRINCIPAL FROM POOL AND TRANCHE Z ($)	(7) COUPON ($)	(8) TOTAL ($)
0	30,000,000				30,000,000	0		
1	26,440,425[a]	3,559,575[b]	2,775,000[c]	6,334,575	30,000,000	0	2,850,000	2,850,000
2	20,207,680	6,232,744	2,445,739	8,678,483	30,000,000	0	2,850,000	2,850,000
3	11,896,751	8,310,929	1,869,210	10,180,139	30,000,000	0	2,850,000	2,850,000
4	3,496,517	8,400,234	1,100,450	9,500,684	30,000,000	0	2,850,000	2,850,000
5	0	3,496,517	323,428	3,819,945	25,223,961	4,776,039[d]	2,850,000	7,626,039
6					17,033,708	8,190,252	2,396,276	10,586,529
7					8,879,209	8,154,499	1,618,202	9,772,702
8					712,397	8,166,812	843,525	9,010,337
9						712,397	67,678	780,075

[a] $30,000,000 − $3,559,575

[b] $614,564 + $1,370,011 (Table 11-9) + $1,575,000 (Column 6, Table 11-11)

[c] $30,000,000 × .0925

[d] $764,691 + $5,159,695 (Table 11-9) + $2,348,171 (Column 6, Table 11-11) − $3,496,517 (payoff of Tranche A)

Source: © 2014 OnCourse Learning

TABLE 11-11

Payment to Tranche C and Z Bondholders

	TRANCHE C				TRANCHE Z					
YEAR	(1) PRINCIPAL OUTSTANDING ($)	(2) REDUCTION IN PRINCIPAL FROM POOL AND TRANCHE Z ($)	(3) COUPON ($)	(4) TOTAL ($)	(5) PRINCIPAL OUTSTANDING ($)	(6) ACCRUED INTEREST ($)	(7) ACCUMULATED ACCRUED INTEREST ($)	PREPAYMENT ($)	INTEREST ($)	TOTAL ($)
0	25,000,000				15,000,000					
1	25,000,000	0	2,500,000	2,500,000	16,575,000	1,575,000	1,575,000	0	0	0
2	25,000,000	0	2,500,000	2,500,000	18,315,375	1,740,375	3,315,375	0	0	0
3	25,000,000	0	2,500,000	2,500,000	20,238,489	1,923,114	5,238,489	0	0	0
4	25,000,000	0	2,500,000	2,500,000	22,363,531	2,125,041	7,363,531	0	0	0
5	25,000,000	0	2,500,000	2,500,000	24,711,701	2,348,171	9,711,701	0	0	0
6	25,000,000	0	2,500,000	2,500,000	27,306,430	2,594,729	12,306,430	0	0	0
7	25,000,000	0	2,500,000	2,500,000	30,173,605	2,867,175	15,173,605	0	0	0
8	25,000,000	0	2,500,000	2,500,000	33,341,834	3,168,229	18,341,834	0	0	0
9	17,483,333	7,516,667	2,500,000	10,016,667	36,842,726	3,500,893	21,842,726	0	0	0
10	9,139,819	8,343,514	1,748,333	10,091,847	40,711,213	3,868,486	25,711,213	0	0	0
11	626,986	8,512,833	913,982	9,426,814	44,985,890	4,274,677	29,985,890	0	0	0
12	0	626,986	62,699	689,685	41,596,257	4,723,518	26,596,257	3,389,633	4,723,518	8,113,152
13					37,786,714	4,367,607	22,786,714	3,809,542	4,367,607	8,177,149
14					34,170,614	3,967,605	19,170,614	3,616,101	3,967,605	7,583,706
15					30,735,091	3,587,914	15,735,091	3,435,522	3,587,914	7,023,437
16					27,468,009	3,227,185	12,468,009	3,267,082	3,227,185	6,494,267
17					24,357,908	2,884,141	9,357,908	3,110,101	2,884,141	5,994,242
18					21,393,967	2,557,580	6,393,967	2,963,941	2,557,580	5,521,522
19					18,565,960	2,246,367	3,565,960	2,828,007	2,246,367	5,074,373
20					15,864,223	1,949,426	864,223	2,701,737	1,949,426	4,651,163
21					13,279,614	1,665,743	(1,720,386)	2,584,609	1,665,743	4,250,353
22					10,803,481	1,394,359	(4,196,519)	2,476,132	1,394,359	3,870,492
23					8,427,634	1,134,366	(6,572,366)	2,375,847	1,134,366	3,510,213
24					6,144,309	884,902	(8,855,691)	2,283,325	884,902	3,168,226
25					3,946,146	645,152	(11,053,854)	2,198,163	645,152	2,843,316
26					1,826,158	414,345	(13,173,842)	2,119,988	414,345	2,534,334
27					0	191,747	(15,000,000)	1,826,158	191,747	2,017,904

Residential Real Estate Finance

TABLE 11–12
Residual Cash Flows to Equity

IRR, 13.89%; net present value at 13%, $325,940	
YEAR	CASH FLOW ($)
0	(6,000,000)
1	1,165,000[a]
2	1,125,467
3	1,058,788
4	970,871
5	881,556
6	804,900
7	736,987
8	668,660
9	599,488
10	566,602
11	536,072
12	504,103
13	511,009
14	520,533
15	529,573
16	538,162
17	546,330
18	554,105
19	561,515
20	568,585
21	575,339
22	581,801
23	587,991
24	593,931
25	599,639
26	605,135
27	832,727
28	2,575,435
29	2,312,931
30	2,062,218

[a] *12,849,575 (Column 6, Table 11-9) − 6,334,575 (Column 4, Table 11-10) − 2,850,000 (Column 8, Table 11-10) − 2,500,000 (Column 4, Table 11-11)*

Source: © 2014 OnCourse Learning

and yields on the shorter term classes will not vary in response to prepayments as much as with pass-throughs. It is this characteristic that makes CMOs appealing to some investors. The importance of the prepayment behavior on the effect of yields on the various tranches is greater for bonds sold at a discount or premium. Recall that for a discounted security, an acceleration in prepayments increases the yield and a delay reduces the yield. The opposite is true for securities sold at a premium.

Assume that the market initially employs a discount rate different from the coupon rate on the securities and prices them under a 100 percent PSA model. In this case, the market assumes that the cash flows displayed in Tables 11-10 and 11-11 will occur. Table 11-13 shows the effect of changes in the prepayment rate on yields. For example, assume that investors initially employ a 10.25 discount rate to value the cash flows of Tranche A under the 100 percent PSA model. Since the coupon rate is 9.25 percent, the issue will sell at a discount. The present value for the cash flows of Tranche A shown in Table 11-13 is $29,257,585. Given this price for the security at issue, the actual yield will depend on the

TABLE 11–13

Prepayment Rates and Yield Behavior; CMO Tranches and Residual Class

INITIAL DISCOUNT RATE AND PRICE		PSA RATE					
		0%	50%	100%	150%	200%	500%
Tranche A:							
Coupon, 9.25%;	0.1025						
Principal, $30,000,000	$29,257,585	0.0987	0.1009	0.1025	0.1038	0.1049	0.1092
	0.0825						
	$30,772,244	0.0863	0.0841	0.0825	0.0812	0.0801	0.0798
Tranche B:							
Coupon, 9.50%;	0.105						
Principal, $30,000,000	$28,611,057	0.1019	0.1034	0.105	0.1064	0.1077	0.1132
	0.085						
	$31,482,680	0.0881	0.085	0.0835	0.0823	0.0823	0.0768
Tranche C:							
Coupon, 10.00%;	0.11						
Principal, $25,000,000	$24,159,905	0.1081	0.1092	0.11	0.1110	0.1121	0.1179
	0.09						
	$26,610,312	0.092	0.091	0.09	0.0889	0.0878	0.0821
Tranche Z:							
Coupon, 10.50%;	0.115						
Principal, $15,000,000	$16,928,790	0.1069	0.1117	0.115	0.1166	0.1184	0.1291
	0.095						
	$17,373,272	0.0919	0.0944	0.095	0.0934	0.0916	0.081
Residual class							
investment, $6,000,000		0.158	0.142	0.1389	0.1348	0.1322	0.1302

Source: © 2014 OnCourse Learning

realized prepayment behavior of the pool. The yield will be as low as 9.87 percent for 0 percent PSA prepayments and as high as 10.92 for 500 percent PSA prepayment rates.

If the Tranche A cash flows are initially discounted at 8.25 percent, the issue will command a premium ($30,772,244). Slower realized prepayment rates will increase the actual yield, and accelerated prepayment rates will lower the yield. The changes in the yield for the discounted and premium cases are comparable for this tranche. The example for the Tranche A securities is repeated for the other tranches. Several things should be noted. First, for the shorter tranches, there is little change in the yield as prepayment behavior changes. The change in the yield for the longer maturity Tranche Z is more pronounced, however. This is expected, since changes in prepayments will have a greater effect on the actual maturity (duration) of this class. Second, since the price paid for the residual is the amount of the equity investment ($6 million), we report only the internal rate of return (yield-to maturity) for this class as prepayment behavior is modified. The effect of prepayments is greatest for the residual. Figure 11-10 depicts the relationship between yields and prepayment behavior for a hypothetical CMO (other than the example used here). Here, you can see how prepayment behavior affects the yields on the various tranches of a CMO.

We also can demonstrate the effect on the price of the various tranches in the simple case where each tranche has the same coupon rate and it is below the market rate (so that the securities sell at a discount when initially issued). Figure 11-11 shows that the value of each later maturity tranche is progressively lower, as would

| FIGURE 11-10 | Yield-to-Maturity for CMO Tranches (discounted) |

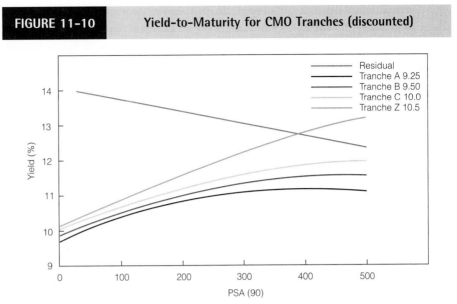

Source: © 2014 OnCourse Learning

| FIGURE 11-11 | Effect of Prepayment Assumptions on Value of Discounted CMO Tranches |

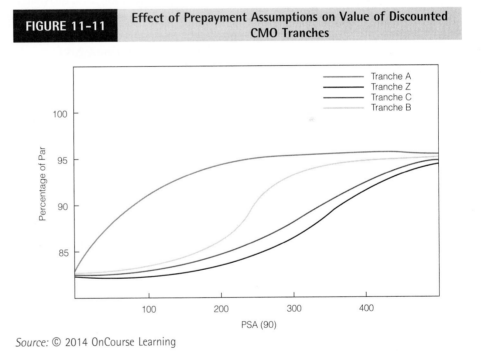

Source: © 2014 OnCourse Learning

be expected. Also, all values increase with expectations of accelerated prepayments. For zero prepayments, the values converge. They also draw near in value for very fast prepayments because their values become close to the remaining balance.

Cash Flows with Default Losses

It should be obvious that the cash flows from the mortgage pool and, therefore, the cash flows to various tranches of the CMO can be affected by defaults on the mortgages. Many CMO tranches are structured so that the default losses are first allocated to the last (most risky) tranche. If and when the principal on the last tranche is exhausted, additional default losses are assigned to the next highest tranche and so forth. When a mortgage goes into default and foreclosure, there will likely be a loss on that mortgage. The loss will likely be a portion of the mortgage balance because the property can almost always be sold at some positive amount. In this section, we define a **default loss** percent as the loss after the sale of the property. Thus, if the mortgagor defaults on a $200,000 property and the recovery from foreclosure is, say $100,000 then the default loss would be 50% on that mortgage.

Tables 11-14 through 11-17 show the cash flows from a hypothetical CMO with defaults. Note that there are five tranches with progressively higher interest rates that reflect the loss allocations from defaults. In this example, the default rate has been set at a modest one-half of 1 percent for the life of the pool. Default losses are expressed as a percentage of the pool balance and are assigned at the end of the year. Notice that the balance of tranche Z is not exhausted until year 25 of the pool (Table 11-16). Note from Table 11-17 that the return to the equity position is 9.87%. It is assumed in this example that no default losses are assigned to the equity position, but each CMO arrangement can be different.

Tables 11-18 to 11-21 show the cash flows from a CMO where the assumed default losses are increased (1 percent in years 1 to 3, 4 percent in years 4 to 8, and 2 percent for the remaining 22 years). Note that tranches Z and D are both exhausted. Also, note that the return on the equity position is 10.59 percent. The return to the equity position is somewhat higher because obligations to the two last tranches have been exhausted from the default losses. This is a hypothetical example, and you should be aware that there are as many different arrangements with default losses as there are CMOs.

Next note that with even a moderate amount of default losses, the Z tranche is in danger of being exhausted. Later in this chapter, we discuss collateralized debt obligations (CDOs). A CDO is essentially another CMO that is created not through the purchase of mortgages, but, rather, through the purchase of tranches. If a CDO is created through the purchase of only Z tranches from a CMO then *all* of the tranches of the CDO will be vulnerable to even modest default losses. Finally, some entities created CDOs from the tranches of another CDO and are called CDOs-squared. Needless to say, with any default losses at all the value of the CDOs-squared may be eliminated.

Interest-Only and Principal-Only Strips

One interesting way in which the cash flows from a mortgage pool have been rearranged has been to *strip* off the rights to receive the principal payments and the

TABLE 11-14
CMOs with Default Rates

TRANCHES	AMOUNT ($)	RATE (%)
A	25,000,000	7.00
B	25,000,000	7.50
C	20,000,000	8.00
D	20,000,000	10.00
Z	10,000,000	12.00
Equity	6,000,000	
fund rate		5.00
Pool rate		10.00
Default rate		
Years 1–3		0.50
Years 4–8		0.50
Years 9–30		0.50

Source: © 2014 OnCourse Learning

TABLE 11-15

Cash Flows from Pool with Default Rates

YEAR	BEG. BAL ($)	P&I ($)	INTEREST ($)	PRINCIPAL ($)	BAL ($)	DEFAULT ($)	CUM. DEFAULT ($)	END BAL ($)
1	106,000,000	11,244,400	10,600,000	644,400	105,355,600	526,778	526,778	104,828,822
2	104,828,822	11,188,178	10,482,882	705,296	104,123,526	520,617	1,047,396	103,602,908
3	103,602,908	11,132,237	10,360,291	771,947	102,830,961	514,154	1,561,550	102,316,806
4	102,316,806	11,076,576	10,231,681	844,896	101,471,911	507,359	2,068,910	100,964,551
5	100,964,551	11,021,193	10,096,455	924,738	100,039,813	500,199	2,569,109	99,539,614
6	99,539,614	10,966,087	9,953,961	1,012,126	98,527,488	492,637	3,061,746	98,034,851
7	98,034,851	10,911,257	9,803,485	1,107,772	96,927,079	484,635	3,546,382	96,442,443
8	96,442,443	10,856,701	9,644,244	1,212,456	95,229,987	476,149	4,022,532	94,753,837
9	94,753,837	10,802,417	9,475,384	1,327,033	93,426,804	467,134	4,489,666	92,959,670
10	92,959,670	10,748,405	9,295,967	1,452,438	91,507,231	457,536	4,947,202	91,049,695
11	91,049,695	10,694,663	9,104,970	1,589,694	89,460,002	447,300	5,394,502	89,012,702
12	89,012,702	10,641,190	8,901,270	1,739,920	87,272,782	436,363	5,830,866	86,836,418
13	86,836,418	10,587,984	8,683,642	1,904,342	84,932,076	424,660	6,255,526	84,507,416
14	84,507,416	10,535,044	8,450,742	2,084,302	82,423,114	412,115	6,667,642	82,010,998
15	82,010,998	10,482,369	8,201,100	2,281,269	79,729,729	398,648	7,066,291	79,331,081
16	79,331,081	10,429,957	7,933,108	2,496,849	76,834,232	384,171	7,450,462	76,450,061
17	76,450,061	10,377,807	7,645,006	2,732,801	73,717,260	368,586	7,819,048	73,348,674
18	73,348,674	10,325,918	7,334,867	2,991,051	70,357,623	351,788	8,170,836	70,005,835
19	70,005,835	10,274,288	7,000,583	3,273,705	66,732,130	333,660	8,504,497	66,398,469
20	66,398,469	10,222,917	6,639,847	3,583,070	62,815,399	314,077	8,818,574	62,501,322
21	62,501,322	10,171,802	6,250,132	3,921,670	58,579,652	292,898	9,111,472	58,286,754
22	58,286,754	10,120,943	5,828,675	4,292,268	53,994,486	269,972	9,381,444	53,724,513
23	53,724,513	10,070,339	5,372,451	4,697,887	49,026,626	245,133	9,626,578	48,781,493
24	48,781,493	10,019,987	4,878,149	5,141,838	43,639,655	218,198	9,844,776	43,421,457
25	43,421,457	9,969,887	4,342,146	5,627,741	37,793,716	188,968	10,033,744	37,604,747
26	37,604,747	9,920,038	3,760,475	6,159,563	31,445,184	157,225	10,190,970	31,287,958
27	31,287,958	9,870,437	3,128,796	6,741,642	24,546,317	122,731	10,313,702	24,423,585
28	24,423,585	9,821,085	2,442,359	7,378,727	17,044,859	85,224	10,398,926	16,959,634
29	16,959,634	9,771,980	1,695,963	8,076,016	8,883,618	44,418	10,443,344	8,839,200
30	8,839,200	9,723,120	883,920	8,839,200	0	0	10,443,344	0
TOTALS		313,979,207	218,422,552	95,556,656		10,443,344		

Source: © 2014 OnCourse Learning

interest payments from the mortgages. An investor who purchases the **principal-only (PO) strip** will have the right to receive all the principal payments whenever they are received. The same is true for the **interest-only (IO) strip**. The total amount of the principal payments will equal the initial pool balance. Because prepayments are unpredictable, the exact timing of the PO payments will not be known. If prepayments accelerate, more of the principal will be returned sooner rather than later. The total amount of interest payments will not be known. Interest payments are made each period on the basis of the principal outstanding in that period. Here, accelerated prepayments reduce the principal outstanding and, therefore, the interest payments for all remaining periods. Thus, accelerated payments may be advantageous for the PO investor and disadvantageous for the IO investor.

The role of market interest rates in the value of the POs and IOs is interesting. Changes in interest rates will have two impacts on each of these strips. First, a move in interest rates changes the discount rate used to value all securities. Second, a move in rates alters the prepayment behavior of mortgage pools and,

TABLE 11–16
Cash Flows to Tranches with Default Rates

TRANCHE A END BAL (%)	TRANCHE A INTEREST (%)	TRANCHE B END BAL (%)	TRANCHE B INTEREST (%)	TRANCHE C END BAL (%)	TRANCHE C INTEREST (%)	TRANCHE D END BAL (%)	TRANCHE D INTEREST (%)	TRANCHE Z END BAL (%)	TRANCHE Z INTEREST (%)	TOTAL (%)
25,000,000	1,750,000	25,000,000	1,875,000	20,000,000	1,600,000	20,000,000	2,000,000	9,473,222	1,136,787	8,361,787
25,000,000	1,750,000	25,000,000	1,875,000	20,000,000	1,600,000	20,000,000	2,000,000	8,952,604	1,074,313	8,299,313
25,000,000	1,750,000	25,000,000	1,875,000	20,000,000	1,600,000	20,000,000	2,000,000	8,438,450	1,012,614	8,237,614
25,000,000	1,750,000	25,000,000	1,875,000	20,000,000	1,600,000	20,000,000	2,000,000	7,931,090	951,731	8,176,731
25,000,000	1,750,000	25,000,000	1,875,000	20,000,000	1,600,000	20,000,000	2,000,000	7,430,891	891,707	8,116,707
25,000,000	1,750,000	25,000,000	1,875,000	20,000,000	1,600,000	20,000,000	2,000,000	6,938,254	832,590	8,057,590
25,000,000	1,750,000	25,000,000	1,875,000	20,000,000	1,600,000	20,000,000	2,000,000	6,453,618	774,434	7,999,434
25,000,000	1,750,000	25,000,000	1,875,000	20,000,000	1,600,000	20,000,000	2,000,000	5,977,468	717,296	7,942,296
25,000,000	1,750,000	25,000,000	1,875,000	20,000,000	1,600,000	20,000,000	2,000,000	5,510,334	661,240	7,886,240
25,000,000	1,750,000	25,000,000	1,875,000	20,000,000	1,600,000	20,000,000	2,000,000	5,052,798	606,336	7,831,336
25,000,000	1,750,000	25,000,000	1,875,000	20,000,000	1,600,000	20,000,000	2,000,000	4,605,498	552,660	7,777,660
25,000,000	1,750,000	25,000,000	1,875,000	20,000,000	1,600,000	20,000,000	2,000,000	4,169,134	500,296	7,725,296
25,000,000	1,750,000	25,000,000	1,875,000	20,000,000	1,600,000	20,000,000	2,000,000	3,744,474	449,337	7,674,337
25,000,000	1,750,000	25,000,000	1,875,000	20,000,000	1,600,000	20,000,000	2,000,000	3,332,358	399,883	7,624,883
25,000,000	1,750,000	25,000,000	1,875,000	20,000,000	1,600,000	20,000,000	2,000,000	2,933,709	352,045	7,577,045
25,000,000	1,750,000	25,000,000	1,875,000	20,000,000	1,600,000	20,000,000	2,000,000	2,549,538	305,945	7,530,945
25,000,000	1,750,000	25,000,000	1,875,000	20,000,000	1,600,000	20,000,000	2,000,000	2,180,952	261,714	7,486,714
25,000,000	1,750,000	25,000,000	1,875,000	20,000,000	1,600,000	20,000,000	2,000,000	1,829,164	219,500	7,444,500
25,000,000	1,750,000	25,000,000	1,875,000	20,000,000	1,600,000	20,000,000	2,000,000	1,495,503	179,460	7,404,460
25,000,000	1,750,000	25,000,000	1,875,000	20,000,000	1,600,000	20,000,000	2,000,000	1,181,426	141,771	7,366,771
25,000,000	1,750,000	25,000,000	1,875,000	20,000,000	1,600,000	20,000,000	2,000,000	888,528	106,623	7,331,623
25,000,000	1,750,000	25,000,000	1,875,000	20,000,000	1,600,000	20,000,000	2,000,000	618,556	74,227	7,299,227
25,000,000	1,750,000	25,000,000	1,875,000	20,000,000	1,600,000	20,000,000	2,000,000	373,422	44,811	7,269,811
25,000,000	1,750,000	25,000,000	1,875,000	20,000,000	1,600,000	20,000,000	2,000,000	155,224	18,627	7,243,627
25,000,000	1,750,000	25,000,000	1,875,000	20,000,000	1,600,000	19,966,256	1,996,626	0	0	7,221,626
25,000,000	1,750,000	25,000,000	1,875,000	20,000,000	1,600,000	19,809,030	1,980,903	0	0	7,205,903
25,000,000	1,750,000	25,000,000	1,875,000	20,000,000	1,600,000	19,686,298	1,968,630	0	0	7,193,630
25,000,000	1,750,000	25,000,000	1,875,000	20,000,000	1,600,000	19,601,074	1,960,107	0	0	7,185,107
25,000,000	1,750,000	25,000,000	1,875,000	20,000,000	1,600,000	19,556,656	1,955,666	0	0	7,180,666
25,000,000	1,750,000	25,000,000	1,875,000	20,000,000	1,600,000	19,556,656	1,955,666	0	0	7,180,666

TABLE 11-17
Cash Flows to Residual with Default Rates

NET CASH	FUND	TRANCHES	
FLOW (%)	BALANCE (%)	TOTAL (%)	RESIDUAL (%)
2,882,614	2,882,614	99,473,222	
2,888,866	5,915,610	98,952,604	
2,894,623	9,106,014	98,438,450	
2,899,845	12,461,160	97,931,090	
2,904,486	15,988,705	97,430,891	
2,908,497	19,696,637	96,938,254	
2,911,823	23,593,292	96,453,618	
2,914,404	27,687,361	95,977,468	
2,916,177	31,987,906	95,510,334	
2,917,069	36,504,370	95,052,798	
2,917,003	41,246,592	94,605,498	
2,915,894	46,224,815	94,169,134	
2,913,647	51,449,703	93,744,474	
2,910,161	56,932,349	93,332,358	
2,905,324	62,684,290	92,933,709	
2,899,012	68,717,517	92,549,538	
2,891,093	75,044,485	92,180,952	
2,881,418	81,678,128	91,829,164	
2,869,828	88,631,862	91,495,503	
2,856,146	95,919,601	91,181,426	
2,840,179	103,555,760	90,888,528	
2,821,717	111,555,265	90,618,556	
2,800,528	119,933,556	90,373,422	
2,776,360	128,706,594	90,155,224	
2,748,261	137,890,185	89,966,256	
2,714,135	147,498,829	89,809,030	
2,676,808	157,550,578	89,686,298	
2,635,978	168,064,085	89,601,074	
2,591,314	179,058,603	89,556,656	
2,542,454	190,553,988	89,556,656	100,997,332
		IRR =	9.87%

Source: © 2014 OnCourse Learning

TABLE 11-18
CMO'S with Default Rates

TRANCHES	AMOUNT ($)	RATE (%)
A	25,000,000	7.00
B	25,000,000	7.50
C	20,000,000	8.00
D	20,000,000	10.00
Z	10,000,000	12.00
Equity	6,000,000	
fund rate		5.00
	Pool rate	10.00
	Default rate	
	Years 1–3	1.00
	Years 4–8	4.00
	Years 9–30	2.00

Source: © 2014 OnCourse Learning

TABLE 11-19

Cash Flows from Pool with Default Rates

YEAR	BEG. BAL ($)	P&I ($)	INTEREST ($)	PRINCIPAL ($)	BAL ($)	DEFAULT ($)	CUM. DEFAULT ($)	END BAL ($)
1	106,000,000	11,244,400	10,600,000	644,400	105,355,600	1,053,556	1,053,556	104,302,044
2	104,302,044	11,131,956	10,430,204	701,752	103,600,292	1,036,002	2,089,559	102,564,289
3	102,564,289	11,020,637	10,256,429	764,208	101,800,081	1,018,000	3,107,560	100,782,080
4	100,782,080	10,910,430	10,078,208	832,222	99,949,858	3,997,994	7,105,554	95,951,863
5	95,951,863	10,474,013	9,595,186	878,827	95,073,037	3,802,921	10,908,476	91,270,115
6	91,270,115	10,055,053	9,127,012	928,041	90,342,074	3,613,682	14,522,158	86,728,391
7	86,728,391	9,652,851	8,672,839	980,011	85,748,380	3,429,935	17,952,094	82,318,444
8	82,318,444	9,266,737	8,231,844	1,034,892	81,283,552	3,251,342	21,203,436	78,032,210
9	78,032,210	8,896,067	7,803,221	1,092,846	76,939,364	1,538,787	22,742,223	75,400,577
10	75,400,577	8,718,146	7,540,058	1,178,088	74,222,489	1,484,449	24,226,673	72,738,039
11	72,738,039	8,543,783	7,273,804	1,269,979	71,468,060	1,429,361	25,656,034	70,038,699
12	70,038,699	8,372,907	7,003,870	1,369,037	68,669,662	1,373,393	27,029,427	67,296,269
13	67,296,269	8,205,449	6,729,627	1,475,822	65,820,447	1,316,408	28,345,836	64,504,038
14	64,504,038	8,041,340	6,450,404	1,590,936	62,913,101	1,258,262	29,604,098	61,654,839
15	61,654,839	7,880,513	6,165,484	1,715,029	59,939,810	1,198,796	30,802,894	58,741,014
16	58,741,014	7,722,903	5,874,101	1,848,802	56,892,212	1,137,844	31,940,739	55,754,368
17	55,754,368	7,568,445	5,575,437	1,993,008	53,761,360	1,075,227	33,015,966	52,686,133
18	52,686,133	7,417,076	5,268,613	2,148,463	50,537,670	1,010,753	34,026,719	49,526,917
19	49,526,917	7,268,734	4,952,692	2,316,043	47,210,874	944,217	34,970,937	46,266,656
20	46,266,656	7,123,360	4,626,666	2,496,694	43,769,962	875,399	35,846,336	42,894,563
21	42,894,563	6,980,893	4,289,456	2,691,436	40,203,127	804,062	36,650,399	39,399,064
22	39,399,064	6,841,275	3,939,906	2,901,368	36,497,696	729,953	37,380,352	35,767,742
23	35,767,742	6,704,449	3,576,774	3,127,675	32,640,067	652,801	38,033,154	31,987,266
24	31,987,266	6,570,360	3,198,727	3,371,634	28,615,632	572,312	38,605,466	28,043,319
25	28,043,319	6,438,953	2,804,332	3,634,621	24,408,698	488,173	39,093,640	23,920,524
26	23,920,524	6,310,174	2,392,052	3,918,122	20,002,403	400,048	39,493,688	19,602,354
27	19,602,354	6,183,971	1,960,235	4,223,735	15,378,619	307,572	39,801,261	15,071,047
28	15,071,047	6,060,291	1,507,105	4,553,186	10,517,861	210,357	40,011,618	10,307,503
29	10,307,503	5,939,085	1,030,750	4,908,335	5,399,168	107,983	40,119,601	5,291,185
30	5,291,185	5,820,304	529,119	5,291,185	0	0	40,119,601	0
TOTALS		243,364,554	177,484,155	65,880,399		40,119,601		

Source: © 2014 OnCourse Learning

therefore, the amount and timing of the cash flows of the POs and IOs. Thus, for the strips, we have

PO: interest rate ↑	discount rate ↑	value ↓
interest rate ↑	prepayments ↓	value ↓
net effect		value ↓
IO: interest rate ↑	discount rate ↑	value ↓
interest rate ↑	prepayments ↓	value ↑
net effect		value ↑

To understand how changes in interest rates affect the cash flows and values of the strips, first refer back to Figure 11-3, which shows the prepayment rates on a mortgage pool as a function of the market rate of interest. The figure shows that prepayments change little as rates rise but accelerate sharply as they fall until they reach a sufficiently low market rate, at which point they level off again. We reproduce this curve in Figure 11-12 for two GNMAs, one with an 8 percent coupon

TABLE 11-20
Cash Flows to Tranches with Default Rates

TRANCHE A		TRANCHE B		TRANCHE C		TRANCHE D		TRANCHE Z		TOTAL ($)
END BAL ($)	INTEREST ($)	END BAL ($)	INTEREST ($)	END BAL ($)	INTEREST ($)	END BAL ($)	INTEREST ($)	END BAL ($)	INTEREST ($)	
25,000,000	1,750,000	25,000,000	1,875,000	20,000,000	1,600,000	20,000,000	2,000,000	8,946,444	1,073,573	8,298,573
25,000,000	1,750,000	25,000,000	1,875,000	20,000,000	1,600,000	20,000,000	2,000,000	7,910,441	949,253	8,174,253
25,000,000	1,750,000	25,000,000	1,875,000	20,000,000	1,600,000	20,000,000	2,000,000	6,892,440	827,093	8,052,093
25,000,000	1,750,000	25,000,000	1,875,000	20,000,000	1,600,000	20,000,000	2,000,000	2,894,446	347,334	7,572,334
25,000,000	1,750,000	25,000,000	1,875,000	20,000,000	1,600,000	19,091,524	1,909,152	0	0	7,134,152
25,000,000	1,750,000	25,000,000	1,875,000	20,000,000	1,600,000	15,477,842	1,547,784	0	0	6,772,784
25,000,000	1,750,000	25,000,000	1,875,000	20,000,000	1,600,000	12,047,906	1,204,791	0	0	6,429,791
25,000,000	1,750,000	25,000,000	1,875,000	20,000,000	1,600,000	8,796,564	879,656	0	0	6,104,656
25,000,000	1,750,000	25,000,000	1,875,000	20,000,000	1,600,000	7,257,777	725,778	0	0	5,950,778
25,000,000	1,750,000	25,000,000	1,875,000	20,000,000	1,600,000	5,773,327	577,333	0	0	5,802,333
25,000,000	1,750,000	25,000,000	1,875,000	20,000,000	1,600,000	4,343,966	434,397	0	0	5,659,397
25,000,000	1,750,000	25,000,000	1,875,000	20,000,000	1,600,000	2,970,573	297,057	0	0	5,522,057
25,000,000	1,750,000	25,000,000	1,875,000	20,000,000	1,600,000	1,654,164	165,416	0	0	5,390,416
25,000,000	1,750,000	25,000,000	1,875,000	20,000,000	1,600,000	395,902	39,590	0	0	5,264,590
25,000,000	1,750,000	25,000,000	1,875,000	19,197,106	1,535,768	0	0	0	0	5,160,768
25,000,000	1,750,000	25,000,000	1,875,000	18,059,261	1,444,741	0	0	0	0	5,069,741
25,000,000	1,750,000	25,000,000	1,875,000	16,984,034	1,358,723	0	0	0	0	4,983,723
25,000,000	1,750,000	25,000,000	1,875,000	15,973,281	1,277,862	0	0	0	0	4,902,862
25,000,000	1,750,000	25,000,000	1,875,000	15,029,063	1,202,325	0	0	0	0	4,827,325
25,000,000	1,750,000	25,000,000	1,875,000	14,153,664	1,132,293	0	0	0	0	4,757,293
25,000,000	1,750,000	25,000,000	1,875,000	13,349,601	1,067,968	0	0	0	0	4,692,968
25,000,000	1,750,000	25,000,000	1,875,000	12,619,648	1,009,572	0	0	0	0	4,634,572
25,000,000	1,750,000	25,000,000	1,875,000	11,966,846	957,348	0	0	0	0	4,582,348
25,000,000	1,750,000	25,000,000	1,875,000	11,394,534	911,563	0	0	0	0	4,536,563
25,000,000	1,750,000	25,000,000	1,875,000	10,906,360	872,509	0	0	0	0	4,497,509
25,000,000	1,750,000	25,000,000	1,875,000	10,506,312	840,505	0	0	0	0	4,465,505
25,000,000	1,750,000	25,000,000	1,875,000	10,198,739	815,899	0	0	0	0	4,440,899
25,000,000	1,750,000	25,000,000	1,875,000	9,988,382	799,071	0	0	0	0	4,424,071
25,000,000	1,750,000	25,000,000	1,875,000	9,880,399	790,432	0	0	0	0	4,415,432
25,000,000	1,750,000	25,000,000	1,875,000	9,880,399	790,432	0	0	0	0	4,415,432

Source: © 2014 OnCourse Learning

TABLE 11-21

Cash Flows to Residual with Default rates

NET CASH FLOW ($)	FUND BALANCE ($)	TRANCHES TOTAL ($)	RESIDUAL ($)
2,945,827	2,945,827	98,946,444	
2,957,703	6,050,822	97,910,441	
2,968,544	9,321,907	96,892,440	
3,338,097	13,126,099	92,894,446	
3,339,861	17,122,265	89,091,524	
3,282,268	21,260,646	85,477,842	
3,223,060	25,546,739	82,047,906	
3,162,080	29,986,156	78,796,564	
2,945,289	34,430,753	77,257,777	
2,915,813	39,068,103	75,773,327	
2,884,386	43,905,895	74,343,966	
2,850,850	48,952,039	72,970,573	
2,815,033	54,214,674	71,654,164	
2,776,750	59,702,157	70,395,902	
2,719,745	65,407,010	69,197,106	
2,653,162	71,330,523	68,059,261	
2,584,722	77,481,771	66,984,034	
2,514,214	83,870,073	65,973,281	
2,441,409	90,504,986	65,029,063	
2,366,067	97,396,302	64,153,664	
2,287,924	104,554,042	63,349,601	
2,206,703	111,988,447	62,619,648	
2,122,102	119,709,971	61,966,846	
2,033,798	127,729,267	61,394,534	
1,941,444	136,057,174	60,906,360	
1,844,669	144,704,702	60,506,312	
1,743,071	153,683,008	60,198,739	
1,636,221	163,003,379	59,988,382	
1,523,653	172,677,202	59,880,399	
1,404,872	182,715,934	59,880,399	122,835,535
		IRR =	10.59%

Source: © 2014 OnCourse Learning

and one with a 12 percent coupon, and assume that the current market rate is 9 percent. Note the inflection points (the point at which the curves become flat) in the two curves. Those points occur approximately where the market rate would equal the coupon rate for each pool. At the base market rate of 9 percent, the prepayment rate on the 12 percent pool is significantly greater than that on the 8 percent pool, as would be expected. If rates rise, there is little change in the prepayment rate on the 8 percent pool because the prepayment option, which is already "out of the money" for this pool, becomes even more so. Also, as rates rise, the call option on the 12 percent pool, which is "in the money," becomes less valuable and eventually becomes "out of the money." Thus, prepayments for this pool drop dramatically as the market rate rises. The important thing to note is that the inflection point in each curve occurs where the market rate would equal the coupon rate. With this in mind, we can turn to a valuation of the IOs and POs.

Figure 11-13 shows the value of a GNMA 8 and its component IO and PO for various market interest rates. When the market rate equals the coupon rate, the pass-through is valued at or near par. The actual value will depend on investors'

| FIGURE 11-12 | Annual Prepayment Assumptions as a Percentage of Outstanding Balance, GNMA 8 and 12 |

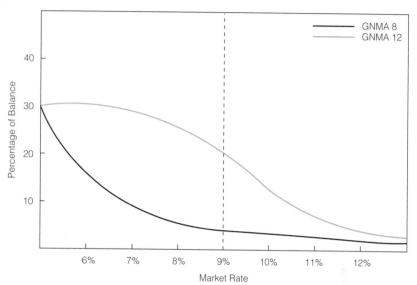

Source: © 2014 OnCourse Learning

| FIGURE 11-13 | Value of GNMA 8, IO, and PO; Various Market Rates |

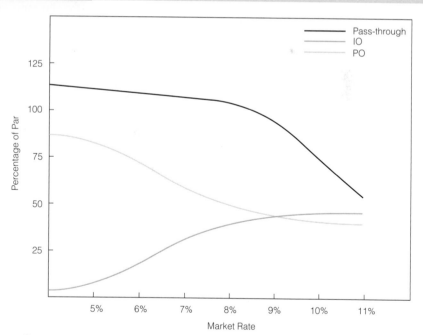

Source: © 2014 OnCourse Learning

expectation of future interest rates and the expected volatility of interest rates. If investors expect high volatility in interest rates, this will increase the value of the call option, raise the required yield, and result in a lower price. Here, we assume the rates are not expected to change and that there is low volatility.

The value of the pass-through is the sum of the component IO and PO. The shape of the value profiles can be explained as follows. If interest rates rise above the coupon rate, prepayments will slow. The effect of the increased rate and the slowing of the prepayments will combine to reduce the value of the PO. The increase in the market rate raises the discount rate used to value the PO cash flows. At the same time, the slowing of the prepayments will push the PO cash flows (unaltered in total amount) further back in time. The same is not true of the IO. Although there is an increase in the discount rate, the total amount of interest payments to be received is augmented. These two effects tend to cancel each other, and there is little change in the value of the IO for rising market rates. The sum of the components, the value of the pass-through, declines as the effect on the value of the PO outweighs that on the IO. When market rates decline, there is little change in the value of the pass-through.

For a sufficiently large drop in rates, prepayment of much of the pool becomes likely, so that it is valued at or near par. The values of the two strips nearly mirror each other. The decline in the market rate makes prepayments accelerate and substantially reduces the total cash flows expected on the IO. The cash flows on the PO are again unaltered but now accelerated. The combined effect of a reduction in the discount rate and the expectation that more of the cash flows will be received sooner rather than later raises the value of the PO. For very low rates, the prepayment rate is so high that the value of the PO approaches that of the pass-through and the value of the IO approaches zero.

The shapes of the value profiles for the IO and PO will not be the same for all pass-throughs. Figure 11-14 shows the profiles for a GNMA 12, a premium GNMA. For an increase in the market rate, the value of the IO increases dramatically, as the in-the-money call option approaches the out-of-the-money range (12 percent). The rise in the value of the IO is matched by a decline in the value of the PO, again for the same reason—the fall in the value of the call option. Since the base market rate is 3 percentage points below the coupon, prepayment behavior is not expected to change dramatically for further reduction in the market rate. This, in turn, leads to little change in either strip or the pass-through itself.

| FIGURE 11-14 | Value of GNMA 12, IO, and PO; Various Market Rates |

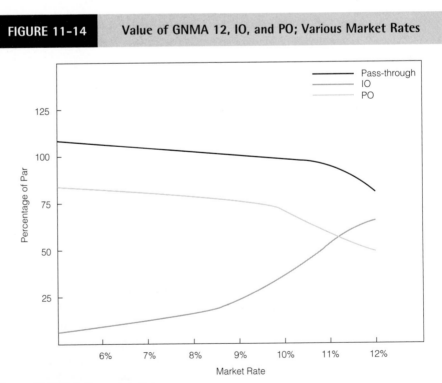

Source: © 2014 OnCourse Learning

As opposed to traditional debt securities, the value of the IO strip moves in the same direction as market interest rates. This means that an IO strip has **negative duration**. This does not mean that the weighted average life of the cash flows is negative. That does not appear to be sensible. What it means is that the value of the IO strip will not decline with a rise in rates, as a traditional debt security will. This makes the IO strip a useful security to hedge interest rate risk. For a lender or other institutional investor with traditional debt securities, the addition of IO strips will hedge the return on the portfolio. If rates rise, a decline in the market value of the traditional debt securities will be partially offset by a rise in the value of the IO strip. The curves in Figures 11-13 and 11-14 indicate that the value of the IO strip is most sensitive to changes in the market rate when this rate is between 100 and 300 basis points below the coupon on the pool. Thus, investors who desire to obtain the hedging benefits of the IO strip should purchase strips of pass-throughs 100 to 300 points above the market rate.

Floaters and Inverse Floaters

Some investors in mortgage-backed securities (MBSs) may have a need for bonds with a rate of interest that moves with the market rate. Financial institutions, for example, have short-term liabilities (savings deposits) with interest rates that move with the market. They thus have a need to invest in assets with rates that match those on their liabilities. **Floaters** are classes of a CMO that have a rate that moves with the market. They operate just like an adjustable-rate mortgage (ARM) would. A floater can be created out of a particular tranche of a CMO while the remaining tranches have the more typical bond-like payments described previously. The interest payment on the floater is usually pegged to a short-term interest rate such as the monthly London Interbank Offered Rate. This rate, called the LIBOR, is a short-term rate that European banks charge one another for short-term borrowing. It is similar to the federal Funds Rate in the United States. The rate on a floater will be set at a certain number of basis points over the LIBOR rate (similar to a margin on an ARM).

One of the problems with creating a floater from a CMO tranche lies in the possibility that market rates may rise significantly above the rate on the underlying mortgage pool. If the pool of mortgages is receiving an 8 percent coupon and the rate on the floater rises above this rate there will be a loss on this tranche. To solve this problem, an inverse floater is created out of the same tranche. An **inverse floater** is a bond for which the interest rate moves in the opposite direction to market rates. The rate on the inverse floater will move opposite to the rate on the floater. The formula for determining the rate on the inverse floater will be set so as to ensure that the total interest payment from the tranche will be constant regardless of the movement of interest rates.

As an example, assume that a $100,000,000 tranche supported by 8 percent coupon mortgages is structured to create floaters and inverse floaters with a total interest payment of 7.5 percent. Next, assume that the floater portion of the tranche is backed by 75 percent of the tranche or $75,000,000 and the inverse floater is supported by the remainder. The rate on the floater is set at the 1-month LIBOR plus 0.5 percent. If the 1-month LIBOR is initially 3.75 percent, then the rate on the floater will be 4.25 percent. The rate on the inverse floater, I, will be set at

$$I = C - 3 \times \text{LIBOR}$$

In this formula, C is a cap on rate for the inverse floater, the highest rate possible assuming that the LIBOR goes to zero. If, for example, the cap is set at 28.5 percent, then the initial rate on the inverse floater, I, will be

$$I = 28.5\% - 3 \times 375\% = 17.25\%$$

The "value" of 3 in the formula reflects the fact that the floater portion of the tranche is three times as large as the inverse floater portion. In this case, the weighted-average coupon (WAC) rate of the entire tranche is

$$
\begin{aligned}
&= 0.75 \times F + 0.25 \times I \\
&= 0.75 \times (L + 0.5) + 0.25(C - 3 \times L) \\
&= 0.75 \times L + 0.375 + 0.25 \times C - 0.75 \times L \\
&= 0.375 + 0.25 \times C
\end{aligned}
$$

If the WAC is set at 7.5 percent then

$$7.5 = 0.375 + 0.25 \times C$$

and

$$7.125 = 0.25 \times C$$

Thus, C is set at $7.125/0.25 = 28.5$ percent.

Although beyond the scope of this text, you should realize that many other securities can be created from a pool of mortgages. As an example floater/inverse IO floaters have been created from IO strips. The combinations of interest contingent securities (derivatives) that can be created are, quite literally, infinite.

Servicing Rights

Next, we turn to the valuation of another derivative of mortgages, **servicing rights**. When lenders sell off loans that they originate, they often retain the servicing rights to those loans. Sometimes they may sell the servicing rights as a separate package. In either case, the proper valuation of the servicing rights is important. Servicing a pool of loans includes some or all of the following: collecting monthly payments, maintaining escrow accounts for property taxes and hazard insurance, forwarding proper payments to purchasers of the loans, sending notices of delinquency and default, initiating foreclosure procedures on defaulted loans, and making claims to the mortgage insurer for losses on defaulted loans. The revenues associated with servicing loans include the servicing fee, float on the escrow accounts, and float between the receipt of the monthly payment and the payment of proceeds to the purchaser of the loans. Costs associated with servicing a pool include administrative costs and overhead. The cash flows available from servicing will equal the revenue less the costs.

The servicing fee is generally between 0.25 and 0.5 percent of the mortgage balance, usually three-eighths of a percent. The costs will vary with the balance of the mortgages but will include a fixed component, such as administrative and overhead costs. The value of the servicing rights is the present value of the net income from servicing. Those cash flows will behave similarly to an IO strip. This is because the major portion consists of the servicing fee, which is expressed as a percentage of the outstanding balance of the pool, just as interest payments are.

To make the analysis more concrete, we provide an example of the servicing cash flows from a pool of mortgages in Table 11-22. For simplicity, we assume no revenues are associated with float on the escrow account or on the timing of payments from the pool to the investors. Servicing costs in the first year equal $30 per year plus 0.0002 percent of the ending pool balance. They grow at 4 percent

TABLE 11-22

Valuation of Servicing Rights

Discount rate, 12%; pool balance, $100,000; coupon rate, 10%; initial P&I, 10,608

YEAR	BEGINNING BALANCE ($)	PAYMENT ($)	ENDING BALANCE ($)	PREPAYMENT ($)	SERVICING INCOME ($)	SERVICING COST ($)	NET ($)
1	100,000	10,608	99,392	1,292	375.00	52.00	323.00
2	98,100	10,470	97,440	3,605	367.87	53.67	314.21
3	93,835	10,083	93,136	5,352	351.88	54.86	297.02
4	87,784	9,503	87,059	5,217	329.19	55.63	273.56
5	81,842	8,934	81,092	4,860	306.19	56.41	250.49
6	76,232	8,398	75,457	4,522	285.87	57.25	228.62
7	70,935	7,895	70,133	4,203	266.01	58.15	207.86
8	65,930	7,422	65,102	3,902	247.24	59.10	188.14
9	61,200	6,977	60,343	3,616	229.50	60.12	169.38
10	56,727	6,559	55,840	3,347	212.72	61.20	151.52
11	52,494	6,166	51,577	3,091	196.85	62.35	134.51
12	48,486	5,796	47,538	2,849	181.82	63.56	118.27
13	44,689	5,449	43,709	2,620	167.59	64.83	102.75
.	.	.	.	.	.	.	.
.	.	.	.	.	.	.	.
.	.	.	.	.	.	.	.
25	11,305	2,596	9,839	590	42.39	86.00	(43.61)
26	9,250	2,440	7,735	464	34.69	88.30	(53.62)
27	7,271	2,294	5,704	342	27.27	90.69	(63.43)
28	5,363	2,156	3,742	224	20.11	93.18	(73.07)
29	3,518	2,027	1,843	110	13.19	95.75	(82.56)
30	1,732	1,906	(0)	(0)	6.50	98.43	(91.93)

PV at 12% $1,588

Source: © 2014 OnCourse Learning

annually thereafter. For the 100 percent PSA model, the value of the servicing rights is $1,588 per $100,000 in mortgages.

The value of the servicing rights under the 200 percent model is only $1,235, or 78 percent of the value under the 0 percent model.

Changes in interest rates will affect the value of the servicing rights in much the same way as they affect an IO strip. A fall in rates will cause the discount rate to fall, but the rate of prepayments to accelerate. Prepayments eliminate all future revenue associated with the terminated loan, although fixed expenses for the pool may continue. The combined effect will reduce the value of the servicing rights significantly.

Often, mortgage originators will retain excess servicing rights. Excess servicing consists of servicing fees greater than the "normal" compensations for the services provided. This generally occurs when the mortgages are sold with a promised rate somewhat less than the coupon on the mortgage. For example, a mortgage originator may sell a pool of 9.5 percent mortgages with a promised 9 percent rate to the investor or secondary mortgage market agency. The originator retains the 50 basis points (if there is no guarantee fee) for servicing. This is greater than the normal 25 or so basis points. Sometimes the spread may be 100 or more basis points. The greater the spread, the larger the excess servicing retained by the originator.

There are several reasons why originators may retain excess servicing fees. First, MBSs usually have coupons in one-half-point intervals; one-quarter-point interval securities trade at relatively unattractive prices. In the above example, the mortgage-backed security has a 9 rather than a 9.25 rate. Second, premium securities may sell at relatively unattractive prices because of investors' apprehension about paying a premium for a security that may repay at par at any time. If mortgages are originated at 10 percent and rates decline to 9.25 percent, the originator may prefer to sell a 9 percent security below par rather than a 9.5 percent security above par. The lower rate results in higher excess servicing fees. Third, originators often mix loans with different coupons in the same pool. As a result, some loans in the pool may have excess servicing, even when the pool on average has no excess servicing.

Financial Accounting Standards Board (FASB) Statement Number 65 ("Accounting for Certain Mortgage Banking Activities," September 1982) requires that excess servicing, after adjustment for expected prepayments, be capitalized at the time of the mortgage sale. The resulting asset is designated "excess servicing rights" and is generally amortizable over the expected life of the servicing contract. Although originators followed these guidelines for accounting purposes, many used a different tax treatment. To see why, consider the notion that the lower the promised coupon on the mortgages sold, the lower the price obtained by the seller (originator). Thus, by retaining excess servicing, the loans were sold at a discount or a loss over their basis at origination. By retaining excess servicing, originators could show a loss on their mortgage sales for tax purposes. For example, a $100 million pool of mortgages may be sold for only $95 million, producing a $5 million loss.

In 1991 the Internal Revenue Service (IRS) put a stop to this practice with Revenue Ruling 91–46. The ruling required that the fair market value of the excess servicing be allocated between the servicing rights and the mortgage pool. In the above example, if the value of excess servicing is determined to be $5 million, then the basis of the pool is considered to be $95 million. Since that is also the sales price in the example, there would be no loss for tax purposes. IRS Procedure 91–50 also indicates the acceptable amount of normal servicing for one- to four-family residential mortgages. Those normal servicing fees are 25 basis points for conventional, fixed-rate loans; 44 basis points for FHA and Veterans Administration (VA) loans; 44 basis points for loans with an original balance of less than $50,000, and 37.5 basis points for other loans, including adjustable rate loans.

Buyers of servicing rights would like to amortize their investment as quickly as possible for tax purposes. Amortization is writing off the investment on the books similar to depreciation on real property. The IRS had, for years, required a constant amortization on the entire pool of mortgages at a constant rate regardless of how the pool actually paid down (as a result of prepayments). Buyers of pools requested the ability to write off mortgages as they actually prepaid. In early 2000, the IRS compromised and allowed mortgage servicers to break a pool of mortgages down and reassemble them for amortization purposes. The subgroups will be based on their expected amortization. So, mortgages that may be expected to prepay early can be placed in a subgroup and then that subgroup may be amortized more quickly than other subgroups.

Accounting and Valuation Issues: Mark-to-Market

So far in this chapter we have not discussed the issue of the effect of mortgage defaults on value of MBSs, CMOs, and other mortgage derivatives. First, one must realize that it is possible to construct several layers of mortgage-derivative securities

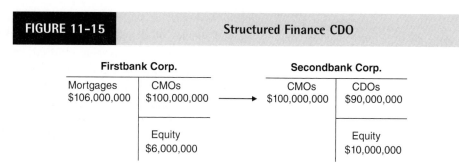

FIGURE 11-15 **Structured Finance CDO**

Firstbank Corp.			Secondbank Corp.	
Mortgages $106,000,000	CMOs $100,000,000 →		CMOs $100,000,000	CDOs $90,000,000
	Equity $6,000,000			Equity $10,000,000

Source: © 2014 OnCourse Learning

from a single mortgage pool. To understand this concept, refer to Figure 11-15. The left-side panel shows the original creation of $100,000,000 in CMOs from a pool of mortgages by the Firstbank Corp. These are the CMOs illustrated in Tables 11-8 through 11-12. The process of creating mortgage derivatives can stop with the left-side panel. However, there is no need to do so. Instead of multiple investors purchasing the CMOs from Firstbank, it is possible that the entire CMO issue could be purchased by the Secondbank Corp. The Secondbank Corp., in turn, obtains the funds to purchase Firstbank's CMOs from issuing its own debt obligations, in this case more generally known as **collateralized debt obligations** or CDOs.

In fact the CDOs in this example are sometimes referred to as **structured finance CDOs**. It is even possible that the CDOs of the Secondbank Corp. could be sold to the Thirdbank Corp. that obtained its funds from issuing its own CDOs called **CDO-squared**.

Returning to the Secondbank Corp., the investors who purchase the CDOs may require that Secondbank Corp. maintain certain levels of equity, say, in this case, one-ninth of the outstanding principal balance of the CDOs. That is, if the amount of equity falls below one-ninth of the outstanding principal value of the CDOs the Secondbank Corp. will be required to raise more capital (sell stock) to bring the equity value in line with the one-ninth requirement.

So, what happens if there is deterioration in the underlying collateral, the mortgages held by Firstbank Corp.? If, for example, a large portion of the mortgages experience default, the cash flows to the CMOs and therefore the value of the CMOs, will be reduced.

Mark-to-Market Requirements

Accounting rules and government regulation (Securities and Exchange Commission [SEC]) both may require what is called **mark-to-market** accounting. FASB statement No. 157 "Fair Value Measurements" became effective for fiscal years beginning after November 15, 2007. In brief, FAS 157 requires corporations to adjust the book value of their assets to the lower of their original cost or their current market value. If, for example, the value of the CMOs held as assets by Secondbank Corp. fall to $80 million (because of defaults in the mortgages held by Firstbank Corp.), the $20 million loss will be expensed by Secondbank Corp. and reflected in a reduction of its equity (now at negative $10 million). Investors in the CDOs may now require Secondbank Corp. to issue more stock (equity) to bring the equity level back up to $10 million (a **margin call**). If any financial institution in the chain of mortgage derivatives is unable to raise capital a "chain reaction" of financial institution failures may result.

Adding to the problem is the ability of financial institutions such as Secondbank Corp. to adequately value their CMOs. There may not be a large active market for their CMOs so that market prices are simply unavailable. FAS 157 allows Secondbank Corp. to estimate the market value of their CMOs on "other" information such as the value of similar mortgage derivatives or models that pre-dict the impact of defaults on mortgage derivatives. But these methods are, at best, estimates of market value. Indeed, Secondbank Corp. may feel that the CMOs are more valuable than estimates based on similar securities or on models.

An example of a margin call is the requirement of Guggenheim Structured Real Estate Advisors, LLC to seek addition equity capital in late 2008. The com-pany sought $300 million to meet the margin call and reduce debt. One of its equity investors, the Oregon Investment Council (the council invests Oregon's public employees retirement fund) authorized an additional $100 million invest-ment in equity in Guggenheim in October 2008.

In 2007 and 2008, the mark-to-market requirements contributed to the finan-cial crisis created by the subprime meltdown. As a result, Congress passed the **Emergency Economic Stabilization Act of 2008**. The act was passed into law on October 3, 2008. Section 132 of the act gave the SEC the authority to suspend mark-to-market accounting rules if it determines such a suspension is in the public interest and will protect investors.

Data on Mortgage Pools

The market value of MBSs depends to a certain extent on individual characteristics of the mortgages in the pools that back them. Pool characteristics can affect the rate of delinquency, default, and prepayment. For this reason, MBS investors demand as much information as possible about pool characteristics. As an example, when GNMA pools were first formed and pass-throughs issued, the pools often were formed from mortgages from a defined geographic area. Thus, knowing which mortgage banker may have issued the pool gave investors knowledge about the geographic area in which the loans were originated. This information was valu-able because mortgages from some areas, such as Southern California, had higher prepayment rates than those from other areas. Some geographic areas also may be more vulnerable to high default rates. By the early 1980s, many lenders had expanded into the national market and GNMA mortgage pools were formed from mortgages originated over wide geographic (national) areas. As a result, such pool information was no longer valuable for these pass-throughs.

However, other pool characteristics, including those for nonstandard loans, remain available and are important to investors. As an example, a mortgage pool may consist of a variety of ARMs with many different terms. One pool may have a complexity of terms, including periodic rate cap, lifetime cap, index, margin, adjustment frequency, and convertibility. Secondary market agencies such as Fred-die Mac will issue pool information on the amount of the principal balance having these various features. Other pools may consist of relocation mortgages. Relocation mortgages are mortgages given to key employees of firms as part of a relocation package. They may have different prepayment behavior than standard mortgages. Still other pools may be buydown mortgages. The ability of the borrower to meet the regular payments after the buydown period likewise may cause the prepayment behavior to vary from that of standard mortgages.

If a pool of mortgages consists of standard fixed-rate, fixed-payment mortgages with a variety of coupons and ages, there is valuable investor information that is pertinent. Since 1983 Freddie Mac has made available information on the original WAC and weighted-average remaining maturity (WARM) of each pool, so inves-tors could judge the likely prepayment rate and age of the loans in those pools. Beginning in 1987, the WAC and WARM of each pool were updated annually and quartiles reported. Quartiles are the sequential interest rate and age ranges into which one-quarter of the loans in a pool fall. Since 1991, WACs and WARMs and quartiles have been updated monthly. Also since 1991, data are available monthly on a pool's weighted-average loan age (WALA), weighted-average original loan term (WAOLT), updated longest maturity date (ULMD), and average original loan size (AOLS). All of this pool information can be used, along with current market rates, to judge the future prepayment behavior of the pool. As an example, investors may have different prepayment projections if the loans in a pool average $50,000 as opposed to $200,000.

Each of the secondary market agencies has automated telephone services through which investors can obtain detailed information on pools. Ginnie Mae has a service through Chemical Bank, Freddie Mac has Freddie Answers, and Fannie Mae has PoolTalk. Often, the investors can download information on many pools into their personal computers. They then can analyze the pool information to make pricing decisions. Also, data on pools are available from private firms that specialize in such services. Examples include the Bond Buyer; Capital Market Decisions, Inc.; Financial Publishing Co.; Interactive Data Corporation; and Telerate Systems, Inc. Given the increase in the volume of data available on pools, the market for MBSs is very efficient compared to markets for other assets.

VALUE CREATION IN MORTGAGE-RELATED SECURITIES

In each case of the creation of MRSs, the cash flows from a pool of mortgages are delivered, often rearranged in terms of amount and timing, to investors in the securities. No additional cash flows are added to the pool. Cash flows available to investors come from the pool only. In fact, some cash flows are absorbed by the owners of the additional resources used to create the MRSs. Such parties as underwriters, investment bankers, trustees that hold the mortgages, security brokers, and their staffs absorb cash flows from mortgage pools. The question that presents itself is this: How can value be created through a system that does not add additional productive resources, but rather absorbs cash flows from the existing portfolio? The three most common answers follow.

1. Securitization makes the mortgage market larger and more liquid. By eliminating liquidity risk, value is created.

2. Mortgage securitization often rearranges the cash flows of a pool into less and more risky components. Different investors may have a need and therefore value differently the partition of the cash flows. As an example, investors seeking a hedge against interest rate risk may value the IO strip for this reason. Certainly, the different risk preference of investors gives rise to **value creation** by rearranging the cash flows in this manner.

3. Value can be created for one party by the existence of asymmetric information. In the case of the senior/subordinated pass-through, the lender may have superior information concerning the credit risk of the pool. Since outsiders do not have this information, they will attach greater value to the senior security than would be the case if they had full information. The lender with the information captures the increased value by selling the senior at a premium and retaining the subordinated interest, which, the lender knows, does not have significant default risk.

The fact that such a great percentage of mortgages has been securitized in the secondary mortgage market indicates that the process creates value over and above the value of the resources required to accomplish the securitization.

Summary

The valuation of MRSs, including the behavior of their YTM and duration, is different from that of traditional debt securities. The cash flows depend, to various degrees, on the payment behavior of pools of mortgages. The cash flows from a pool of mortgages consist of the scheduled amortization, interest on the remaining balance, and any prepayments of loans. As such, the cash flows associated with MRSs are interest contingent. This means that changes in the market interest rate have two effects on the value of the MRS. First, the discount rate changes. As with traditional debt securities, the change in the market rate will have an effect on the value of the MRS in the opposite direction. Second, the timing and/or amount of the cash flows will change. This effect can either reinforce or counteract that of the discount rate. If the change in the market rate causes the total payments to increase or to occur sooner, the value of the MRS will increase, and vice versa.

Pass-through securities represent an ownership interest in a pool of mortgages. The cash flows of pass-throughs behave precisely as those of the mortgages in the pool. Prepayment behavior will have an impact on the yield of discounted and premium pass-throughs. If the principal on a discounted pass-through is received sooner than expected, the YTM will be greater than anticipated. Thus, a drop in interest rates will increase the YTM on discounted pass-throughs as prepayments accelerate. The opposite is true for premium pass-throughs.

Several types of MRSs rearrange the cash flows from a pool of mortgages into various components, some of which are more and some of which are less interest contingent. The extent of the repackaging can either reduce or enhance the interest-contingent character of their payments. Some tranches of a CMO, for example, are constructed so that interest only is received and the maturity of the obligation occurs within a narrow range of years, regardless of the prepayment behavior of the mortgage pool. They go the furthest in creating MRSs that mimic the cash flow payments of traditional debt securities. The creation of the tranches also produces a residual component, which may be more interest contingent than the pool as a whole.

A CMO of particular interest is the interest-only and principal-only division of the cash flows. The holder of the IO receives only the interest payments from the pool of mortgages, while the PO holder receives only principal payments (both scheduled and prepayment). When market interest rates change, the values of these securities behave very differently from each other. When market rates rise, the value of the PO drops considerably as the discount rate increases and the fixed amount of principal payments are extended in time through the slowing of prepayments. When rates fall, the value of the PO drops considerably for the same reasons. When interest rates rise, the value of the IO actually may increase. Because prepayments from the pool are slowed, the increase in the total amount of cash received on the IO enhances its value. The IO is one security used by investors to hedge their portfolio of traditional debt securities against changes in value through the interest rate cycle.

The value of servicing rights behaves similarly to the IO. The servicer of a pool of loans receives compensation defined as a percent of the outstanding balance—thus the similarity to an IO. When prepayments accelerate, the total payments for the servicing decrease. The value of servicing rights on the marketplace will depend on expectations of charges in interest rates and the effect on the prepayment behavior of the mortgage pool.

The interest-contingent nature of the cash flows of MRSs makes the estimation of future prepayments essential to proper valuation. Several models have been used, including the history of FHA loans, a Constant Prepayment Rate CPR, and the repayment model of the PSA. In addition, econometric models have been used to estimate future prepayment behavior. These models identify the functional relationship between various variables (such as interest rates and the yield curve) and the prepayment behavior of a pool of mortgages. Finally, value is created through mortgage securitization if the resulting securities trade in a more liquid market or meet the risk preferences of different types of investors. Value also is created for one party when there is asymmetric information concerning the risk of a mortgage pool.

Key Terms

CDO-squared	Margin call
Collateralized debt obligations	Mark-to-market
Constant prepayment rate (CPR)	Mortgage-derivative security
Default loss	Negative duration
Econometric prepayment models	Price compression
Effective (implied) duration	Principal-only (PO) strip
Emergency Economic Stabilization Act of 2008	Public Securities Association (PSA) prepayment rate
Floaters	Servicing rights
Interest rate contingent securities	Streamline Refinance Plan (SRP)
Interest-only (IO) strip	Structured finance CDOs
Inverse floater	Value creation

Review Questions

11-1. a. What is meant by interest (rate) contingent securities?
  b. Give three examples of a claim on cash flows that is interest rate contingent. Explain.

11-2. Why are pass-through securities considered "callable" bonds?

11-3. List and explain three methods of predicting prepayments on a pool of mortgages.

11-4. Given a GNMA 10 pool of mortgages, would you expect prepayments to accelerate greatly if the market rate of interest fell from 15 to 14 percent? From 10 to 8 percent? Explain any difference in your answer.

11-5. Explain what "overcollateralized" means and why overcollateralization exists. Give an example.

11-6. a. What is meant by the "effective" or "implied" duration of a mortgage pool?
  b. How does it differ from the duration of a traditional noncallable corporate bond?
  c. How can it be measured?

11-7. What are senior/subordinated pass-throughs? How do they provide for credit enhancement?

11-8. Compare and contrast the characteristics of mortgage-backed bonds with those of collateralized mortgage obligations.

11-9. a. Explain what interest-only and principal-only strips are.

b. Explain why the value of an interest-only strip goes up when market rates of interest go up.

c. Explain why interest-only strips are excellent investment vehicles to hedge against interest rate risk. In this regard, define negative duration.

11-10.   a. What are servicing rights?

b. Explain why the value of servicing rights declines as prepayments are expected to accelerate.

11-11.   Explain how the securitization of mortgages can create value.

11-12.   Explain what floaters and inverse floaters are.

11-13.   Explain how mark-to-market rules can cause financial problems to companies that issue CDOs.

11-14.   Explain how default losses can be allocated to tranches in a CMO.

11-15.   Explain how default losses on a CMO tranche can be magnified for a CDO.

Problems

All Files MBB

11-1.   Given the following information about a pool of fixed-rate mortgages, perform the calculations indicated.

Amount	$110 million
Coupon rate	11%
% PSA	100%

Year 1, 1.3%; year 2, 3.7%; year 3, 5.75%; year 4, 6%

For the first 4 years, show (a) the end-of-year pool balance; (b) scheduled principal and interest payments; and (c) total cash flows.

All Files MBB

11-2.   Perform the calculations in Problem 11-1 assuming a PSA of 50 percent.

11-3.   a. Calculate the effective duration from the following yield and price data on an FNMA 11.

	MARKET RATE	
	10%	10.25%
Price	105.125	104.25

b. Would the duration calculated be greater or less if the price change did not reflect a change in the assumed PSA prepayment rate? Explain.

All Files MBB

11-4.   Given the following information on a mortgage-backed bond, perform the calculations indicated.

POOL DATA	
Amount	$120 million
Coupon rate	11%
Maturity	30 years
% PSA	0%
Default rate	0.5% first 5 years

BOND DATA	
Amount	$110 million
Coupon rate	10%
Maturity	20 years
Yield on fund	7%

For the first 4 years, show the
a. end-of-year pool balance.
b. default losses.
c. cash inflow from pool.
d. payment to bondholders.
e. end-of-year fund balance.

All Files MBB

11-5. a. Perform the calculations in Problem 11-4 assuming no default rate at all.
     b. When the default rate drops from 0.005 to 0, who benefits—the bondholders or the equity holders? Explain.

All Files CMO

11-6. Given the following information, perform the calculations indicated.

POOL DATA	
Amount	$106 million
Coupon rate	10.5%
Maturity	30 years
PSA	100%

Year 1, 1.3%; year 2, 3.7%; year 3, 5.75%; year 4, 6%

TRANCHE DATA	COUPON RATE (%)	AMOUNT ($)
Tranche A	9.50	30,000,000
Tranche B	9.75	30,000,000
Tranche C	10.25	25,000,000
Tranche Z	10.50	15,000,000
Equity		6,000,000
Total		106,000,000

a. For the first 4 years, show the
    1. end-of-year pool balance.
    2. total funds available for distribution.
    3. end-of-year amount owed to security holders.
b. For the first 4 years, show the principal outstanding and cash distributions to holders of the A, B, and C tranches.
c. For the first 4 years, show the principal outstanding for Tranche Z.
d. For the first 4 years, show the cash flows to the residual (equity) interest.

11-7. Assume that the rate on a floater is set at LIBOR 12.5 percent, that the floater portion of a class is 80 percent, and that the weighted-average coupon of the floater plus inverse floater should be 8 percent. Determine the cap on the formula for the inverse floater that will accomplish this.

Notes

1. Frank Navratil. The estimation of mortgage prepayment rates. *Journal of Financial Research* 8 (Summer 1985), 107–117.

2. Jerry Green and John Shoven. The effects of interest rates on mortgage prepayments. *Journal of Money, Credit, and Banking* 18 (February 1986), 41–59.

3. Nikolaos Milonas and Nelson Lacey. An examination of GNMA prepayments. Office of Policy and Economic Research, Federal Home Loan Bank Board (May 1988).

4. This association was subsequently merged into the Public Securities Association.

5. See Terrence M. Clauretie, Mel Jameson, and Ronald Rogers. A note on refinancing costs, prepayment assumptions, and the value of mortgage-backed securities. *Journal of Real Estate Finance and Economics* 3 (September 1990), 295–330.

6. Years 2, 3, and 4 will have prepayment rates of 3.7, 5.75, and 6 percent, respectively.

Web Site

http://www.ginniemae.gov
    Site for GNMA

APPENDIX 11-A

A Primer on Mortgage Derivatives and Structured Finance

MEANINGS OF RATINGS ON SECURITIES

Most investors don't have the time or expertise to determine how risky any given investment is. So they depend on the ratings agencies to tell them how risky or safe a particular investment is.

Many investing organizations have a simple rule: They will not invest in anything but AAA rated securities. The CFO of a company will say, "We manufacture widgets, and we're experts at that. We're not experts at evaluating investment risks. So we invest ONLY in the safest securities, the AAA-rates securities. Period."

So if you're an investment broker and you want sell securities that aren't AAA-rated, then you've got a problem, because a lot of investors won't touch them at any price. The simplest solution is to find a way to turn lower-rated securities into AAA-rated securities, and that's where the structured finance magic comes in, as you will see.

There are three major ratings agencies—Standard & Poor's, Moody's Investors Service and Fitch Ratings. The ratings they provide indicate the probability of default within the next year.

The following table gives the S&P ratings, along with the probability of default for each:

RATING	DEFAULT PROB.	RATING	DEFAULT PROB.	RATING	DEFAULT PROB.
AAA	.094%	BBB+	.603%	CCC+	27.280%
AA+	.094%	BBB	.978%	CCC	29.945%
AA	.1255%	BBB−	1.482%	CCC−	31.827%
AA−	.137%	BB+	3.750%	CC	37.738%
A+	.174%	BB	5.000%		
A	.304%	BB−	7.500%		
A−	.343%	B	9.1112%		
		B	9.432%		
		B−	12.745%		

And so, for example, if you purchase a BB bond that will pay you $1000 at maturity in a year, then there's a 5% chance that you won't receive that $1000, and a 95% chance that you will.

Computing Present Value of a Future Payment

If you're going to receive $1000 a year from now, how much is that $1000 worth today?

That depends on the market interest rate. For simplicity, we'll assume throughout this article that the market interest rate is 6%.

So, if I deposit $50 in a bank that pays 6% interest per year, then at the end of a year I'll have $50*(1 + 6%) = $50*(1.06) = $53.

Now, turn the computation upside down. If I'm going to receive $1000 a year from now, then the "present value" of that $1000 is $1000/(1+6%) = $1000/(1.06) = $943.40.

That's a "present value" computation for future payment.

Computing Expected Value of an Uncertain Payment

Suppose that the year is up, and I now have a bond that's going to pay me $1000 today, but it's not certain—but there is a 5% probability of default. What's the value of that bond?

There's a 95% probability that I'll receive $1000 today, and a 5% probability that I'll receive nothing. The "expected value" is: ($1000*95% + $0*5%) = $950.

I know that this seems strange; after all, how can $950 be the "expected value," when you won't receive $950 under any circumstances: you'll receive either $0 or $1000, but never $950.

The answer is that "expected value" is a mathematical term from the Theory of Probability. Imagine that you have an infinite number of these bonds, all being paid today. As you redeem one bond after another, some paying $0 and some paying $1000, what's the AVERAGE amount that will be paid per bond? The average is $950, the expected value.

COMBINING PRESENT VALUE AND EXPECTED VALUE

Now let's assume that I have an IOU that will pay $1000 in a year, with a 5% probability of defaulting. If I wanted to sell that IOU to someone else, what's a fair price for the IOU today?

Here we have a payment in the future, and a payment that's uncertain. So we have to combine present value and expected value computations.

Well, there's a 5% probability of default, and a 95% probability that $1000 will be paid, then the IOU is worth its expected value a year from now, which is $1000*95% = $950 a year from now.

The present value of that $950 is $950/1.06 = $896.22.

So, if I want to sell the IOU to someone, a fair price would be the present value of the expected value, or $896.22. If I wanted to make a commission, then I'd sell it for, say, $925, and earn essentially a commission of ($925 − $896.22) = $28.78.

HOW TO CREATE A CDO

If you want to understand how to create a collateralized debt obligation (CD0), then this example tells you how to do it. In actual practice, where there are many different ratings levels (tranches), the computations are a lot more complex, but the basics are contained in this simple example.

You have to know a little bit about computing probabilities to understand this example, but if you work it through to the end, we think you'll understand what happened:

- Suppose that two people each owe me $1000. That is, I have two IOU certificates, X and Y, from two different people, each of which will pay me $1000 a year from today.

- However, because both of these people are unemployed, there may be a default on one or both of X and Y. I estimate that there's a 5% chance of default on each of X and Y, and in case of default I get nothing.

- Note from the table above that X and Y each have an S&P rating of BB (5% probability of default).

- What's the "real value" of X and Y today? It depends on the current market interest rate, so let's assume the current market interest rate is 6%, as we have before. Now we have to compute the expected value of the present value, as follows: The "present value" of $1000 to be paid a year from now is $1000/(1 + 6%) = $1000/1.06 = $943.40. However, there's only a 95% chance of being paid, so the EXPECTED value today of the present value is $1000/1.06*(95%) = $896.23. That's the expected value of the present value, and it's fair to call that the "real value" of each of X and Y today, and that would be a fair price to sell either X or Y for.

- I'd like to get some money right away, so I offer to sell you X for $896.23. You say, "That's a fair price, but it's a BB rated security, and I only buy securities rated A or above. The 5% default rate is too high for me, even though the price is fair."

- OK, so I have a problem. I'd like to sell X and Y, but many people won't buy such risky investments, even at a fair price that takes the risk into account.

- So, I combine X and Y into a single pot called a CDO (collateralized debt obligation). I create two new investment certificates, P and Q, that will pay out according to the following rules:

  - If EITHER X or Y pays out (does not default), then the owner of P will get $1000. P is the "high-rated tranche."
  - If BOTH X and Y pay out, then the owner of Q will get $1000. Q is the "low-rated tranche."

  So now, P and Q are certificates that, like X and Y, each may pay $1000 a year from now, but because of the rules they have different probabilities of payout, and therefore different real values today.

- What's the probability that P will pay out $1000? The probability of payout from each of X and Y is 95%, and we assume that those are INDEPENDENT probabilities. (Remember that assumption, because we'll come back to it later.) So the probability that EITHER X or Y will pay out is 1−(1−95)*(1−.95) = 1−0.0025 = .9975 = 99.75%. So the probability that P will default is 0.25%, which gives it an A rating (which requires a default probability of 0.343% or lower). The magic has started: I've taken two BB rated securities, and created from them an A rated security. So P is A rated, so it meets your criteria for investing, and you'll now be willing to buy P for a fair price.

- I wanted to keep this example simple, so the rating comes out to A. If I manipulated the numbers a little differently, I could easily have gotten the rating to come out to AAA, which is what the financial engineers do in actual practice.

- What's the probability that Q will pay out $1000? That equals the probability that BOTH X and Y will pay out. That probability is 0.95*0.95 = 0.9025 = 90.25%. So the probability of default is 9.75%, and so Q is a CCC+ rated security. So the magic has a downside, as well. I started with two BB rated securities (X and Y), and ended up with two securities (P and Q) with different ratings, A and CCC+, respectively. There are some investors who are willing to purchase CCC+ securities, provided that they pay a fair price. Let's now compute what that fair price is.

- What are the fair values for P and Q? Using the same kind of computation as above for computing the fair values for X and Y (the expected value of the present value), I get the following: Fair value for P = $1000/1.06*(99.75%) = $941.04. Fair value for Q = $1000/1.06* (90.25%) = $851.42.

- Assuming that there are no defaults, what are the interest rates earned by purchasers of P and Q at those prices? Interest rate for P = 1.06/99.75% − 1 = .062 = 6.2% Interest rate for Q = 1.06/90.25% − 1 = .174 = 17.4%

- Those are damn high interest rates. So here's what I do. I tell you, "I'm going to sell you this A-rated security P for $943.40. At the end of a year, you'll receive $1000, which means you'll get 6% interest. That's a great deal!" Huh? What happened? First, I "forgot" to mention to you that the security P might default. In fact, I'll tell you that these things "are so safe that they NEVER default. You can count on it!!" If you don't understand structured finance then you won't even ask the right question. Second, I keep the difference as a commission. The fair price is $941.04, and I sell it to you for $943.40. So I keep the difference, or $2.36. You have no idea I've done this, because all you've seen is the price $943.40. Now, $2.36 might not seem like much, but in actual practice we'll be dealing with CDO security pools valued at a hundred million dollars in a single deal. That makes the commission $236,000—on a single deal! If I'm a good salesman and I put together a hundred of these deals a year, then I'll make tens of millions of dollars in commissions.

If security P doesn't default, then you'll earn your 6% interest, and you should be happy. If you've bought millions of P's, then you'll probably have defaults in 0.25 % of them. The nominal value of each of those P's is $943.40, which is what you paid for it. But when they start defaulting, then a lot of them will have to be "written down," based on the real volume of defaults.

- For example, if you have $10 million (nominal value) of these things in your portfolio, then you may have to write them down to $9.8 million, and take a $200,000 charge.

That's bad enough, but now suppose that all the X's and Y's that were securitized into P and Q were "liar-loan" mortgages, approved for homeowners with no income, no assets, no job, and no chance of making the payments. Then the defaults will rise much higher, and you'll have to write down a lot more. Typical write-down amounts during the mortgage melt-down for major investment bankers have been in the neighborhood of 20-40 cents on the dollar. So if you have $10 million (nominal value) of these things in your portfolio, then you'll have to write them down to $2-4 million.

- What went wrong? Remember, a few paragraphs back, we said that the probability of payout from each of X and Y is 95%, and we assume that those are INDEPENDENT probabilities. Well, if X and Y are both related to subprime mortgages, then these probabilities are no longer independent, and so the computations come out wrong.

- What about security Q in the above example? It's rated CCC+ and pays 17.4% interest, so there are several things I can do with it:

  I can easily sell it as a "junk bond" for the "fair price" of $851.42, because it pays 17.4% interest.

  I can use the same trick as with the high-rated security. Instead of giving you 17.4% interest, I'll raise the price so that you get only 10% interest, and I'll keep the difference as a commission. Since you have no idea I've done this, you'll think that I'm really giving you a deal with this huge 10% interest.

  I can pool a whole bunch of similar CCC+ securities and repeat all the steps in the example above, creating a new CDO from the junk securities in the last CDO. The result is called a "CDO-squared," because it's a CDO that backed by other CDOs.

  I can insure the low-rated securing with a bond insuring agency, in order to bring its rating up to AAA. And so, we started out with X and Y, which would have given us a little money a year from now. We used a variety of "structured finance" tricks, I lie a little, I forget to mention some things, and so I get a lot more money, and I get it today rather than a year from now.

  All the steps in the above example are used in the creation of "real life" CDOs. The only difference is that "real life" CDOs are much more complicated because:

- Instead of just X and Y, there are hundreds of millions of dollars worth of securities used as input.

- Furthermore, the input securities are themselves at different ratings levels, and so the arithmetic of combining these becomes a lot more complicated.

- Also, the output is not just two tranches, a "high-rated" tranche P and a "low-rated" tranche Q, but a dozen or so different tranches, with different ratings (AAA, AA+, AA, AA−, A+, A, A−, BBB+, etc.)

- When there are multiple tranches, a "cascade rule" is put into effect, similar to how payments are made to P and Q in the above example: All the income is pooled, and the high-rated tranches are paid off first. Next, the middle-level tranches are paid off and, if there's enough income, the lower-rated tranches are paid. This "cascade rule" is very important, and we'll illustrate it later.

But whatever the complexity of the "real world" CDO, it's based on exactly the same principles as illustrated by the above example, using the same kinds of computations for "present value" and "expected value."

THE MAKING OF A MORTGAGE CDO

Making a CDO – Step 1

The individual mortgages are not the X's and Y's in the example above—those come in the next step. These are the individual mortgages that are sliced and diced to get the X's and Y's.

Several thousand loans go into a single pool, labeled "RMBS trust" (residential mortgage backed security). In order to provide "diversity," different kinds of loans from all over the country are combined into this pool.

That way, the investors are protected, since risk is spread around. These assumptions made sense in earlier decades, but in the last decade they were not applicable because the mortgage melt-down caused defaults to be dependent on the systematic risk of the economy.

Making a CDO - Step 2

The RMBS Trust is "securitized"—sliced and diced into individual securities called "Residential Mortgage Back Securities," or RMBS. These securities are the X's and Y's that will form the CDO.

In our example above, the X's and Y's had equal risk, both B-rated. In real world examples, the original mortgage loans that went into the RMBS Trust had various levels of risk, so when they're sliced and diced into RMBS securities, those securities have multiple levels of risk as well, and so have different ratings. These different levels are called "tranches." The AAA-rated securities are low-risk tranches, and the low-rated securities are high-risk tranches. The levels of risk are created by the process of assigning default losses to the lower tranches first and higher tranches later.

Just as the X's and Y's could be sold as is, the RMBS bonds could be sold as is. Fair prices and interest rates could be computed for each rating level, and bonds at each level could be sold.

Therefore, a "cascade rule" is set up. All the income for all the bonds goes into a pool, and the highest-rated bonds get paid off first. As more money comes in, the lower-rated bonds get paid off as well. If enough money comes in, then everyone gets paid. However, with default losses some tranches (lower) suffer greater losses than the remaining tranches.

Making a CDO - Step 3

The low-rated bonds in the RMBS pool can't easily be sold because they're too risky, so the trick is to get them an AAA rating.

The low-rated bonds are moved over into a new pool called a collateralized debt obligation (CDO). That is, they represent the assets of a new pool financed by the creation of additional debt obligations or CDOs.

Making a CDO - Step 4

Although all these bonds were low-risk, they can still be sorted by risk within the low risk category. Then a "cascade rule" is put into effect for the CDO, just as it was for the RMBS, so that income is first paid to the highest rated bonds, and additional income is paid to the lower-rated bonds.

This CDO itself contains lower-rated securities, and those can be passed off to a new CDO, creating a "CDO-squared." There's no limit to the ingenuity that financial engineers can display.

Making a CDO - Step 5

Income to the CDO goes to the high-rated bonds first, and liabilities are assigned to low-rated bonds first. That way, the high-rated bonds are more likely to be paid, while the low-rated bonds are more likely to default.

Making a CDO – Step 6

When the CDO was created, most of the securities were AAA-rated.

When the mortgage meltdown began in 2007, ratings agencies were forced to reexamine their ratings of CDO securities, and hundreds of billions of dollars worth have already had their ratings lowered several notches, making many of them almost worthless.

Source: This appendix is adapted from a discussion by John J. Xenakis, Generational Dynamics and is published with his permission. A more complete explanation with diagrams and graphics is available at: http://www.generationaldynamics.com/cgi-bin/D.PL?d=ww2010.i.cdo080123

CONTROLLING DEFAULT RISK THROUGH BORROWER QUALIFICATION, LOAN UNDERWRITING, AND CONTRACTUAL RELATIONSHIPS

CHAPTER
12

LEARNING OBJECTIVES

This chapter discusses controlling default risk through borrower qualification, loan underwriting, and contractual relationships in the note and mortgage or deed-of-trust. After reading this chapter, you should be familiar with the important borrower and property characteristics that are the focus of borrower qualification. You also should understand the legal relationship between the lender and the borrower and how contractual provisions give each party rights and obligations. You should see how many of the contractual relationships protect the lender from default risk. In short, you should understand how the lender controls for default risk from the qualification of the borrower through the structuring of the legal contracts supporting the loan.

INTRODUCTION

One of the major risks faced by mortgage lenders is **default risk**, the risk that the borrower will fail to make timely payments or repay the loan principal amount. The risk is greater when property values fall, because the likelihood increases that the value of a particular property will fall below the balance of the loan. Lenders use several precautionary measures to mitigate default risk, including closely scrutinizing the financial position of the borrower, accurately estimating the value of the property that serves as collateral, and employing legal instruments (deeds-of-trust and mortgages) with provisions that protect the interest of the lender. Although the lender garners as much information as possible and uses legal instruments to guard against default risk, the legal system affords some rights to borrowers as well. These rights, along with such unforeseen events as localized recessions that dampen property values, ensure that some default risk will remain for the mortgage lender. In Chapter 14, we will discuss the business of default risk insurance.

BORROWER QUALIFICATION AND LOAN UNDERWRITING

Borrower qualification and loan underwriting refer to the process of determining and controlling default risk. In general, mortgage credit analysis includes (1) determining the maximum loan amount, (2) estimating settlement requirements and costs, (3) analyzing credit history, (4) calculating effective income, (5) estimating monthly housing expense, and (6) assessing ability to repay mortgages and other liabilities in a timely fashion. When a borrower defaults on a loan, the lender must take legal action (foreclosure) to obtain payment of the loan. The lender will liquidate the property and make a claim to the insurer (discussed in Chapter 14). Alternatively, the lender can make a claim and deliver a deed to the property to the insurer. The process can be time-consuming and expensive, because the lender must pay legal fees, property taxes, maintenance expenses, hazard insurance, repairs, and so forth. Proper borrower qualification can minimize this risk. Some reasons for rejection are (1) borrower cannot support the payments, (2) borrower has a bad credit history (especially pertaining to mortgage repayment), and (3) borrower is currently delinquent.

One technique used by lenders is credit scoring. The best known company providing credit scores is Fair, Isaac, and Company (FICO). FICO uses credit, income, outstanding debt and debt utilization over the years, access to credit, and other indicators to determine how likely the borrower is to repay the debt. A numerical score is developed ranging from 300 to 900. The cutoff score for Fannie Mae and Freddie Mac is 620. Scores less than this are considered subprime. The weights used in deriving the FICO score are payment history (35 percent), amount of debt (30 percent), the length of time the borrower has used credit (15 percent), the borrower's very recent credit history (10 percent), and the borrower's credit mix (10 percent). Historically, credit scores have not been released to borrowers. The major argument is that borrowers must be observed going about their business as usual. For example, the borrower may close out a rarely used credit card if this improves the credit score. There is some push for disclosure. Congress is considering the Fair Credit Full Disclosure Act.

Theories of Default

There are two theories of default risk: the **ability-to-pay theory** and the **equity theory**. Borrower qualification addresses both theories.

Ability-to-Pay Theory

The ability-to-pay theory states that default and default risk occur when the borrower cannot make the monthly payments on the loan. Loss of employment, disputes that emerge from a divorce proceeding, and an unexpected addition to the family are some reasons why borrowers may fail to make their loan payments. After several payments are missed, the foreclosure procedure will begin. Borrower qualification involves an analysis of borrower characteristics, such as the number of dependents and the amount and stability of family earnings. Research conducted to explain or predict default and delinquency under this theory has focused on such borrower characteristics as family size and source of income.

Equity Theory (The Put Option)

The equity theory of default focuses on the amount of equity in the property. This theory states that no borrower with substantial positive equity would default, even if unable to make the monthly payment. The borrower instead would sell the property in the market and pay off the loan, capturing the equity. On the other hand, if there is negative equity (the value of the property is less than the amount of the loan), default may occur even if the borrower is able to make the monthly payment.

The equity theory of default is also termed the *put option theory* of default. When the loan is made, the borrower acquires a put option. Simply stated, whenever the value of the house is less than the value of the loan, it is optimal for the borrower to give (put to) the lender the house rather than repay the loan. The borrower benefits if he puts a $100,000 house to the lender in satisfaction of a $150,000 mortgage debt. Some borrowers in this situation may decide not to default because they may personally value the property or feel an obligation to pay the debt.

Although the lender may be able to seek a court judgment for the loss (called a deficiency judgment), this may, in practice, be difficult. The cost of pursuing the judgment in court and the ability of defaulters to declare personal bankruptcy can mitigate the power of the deficiency judgment. Also, some states prohibit deficiency judgments by statute.

At the time the loan is originated, the lender will ensure that the appraised value of the house is greater than the amount of the loan. Notwithstanding, the put option may have value if, subsequently, the value of the property falls below the amount of the mortgage loan. When this occurs, the put option is "in the money." The put option will have greater value where the loan-to-value ratio is high and the variance in property price changes is great.

Studies of Delinquency and Default

Studies of delinquency and default have included variables that are expected to be related to both the equity theory and the ability-to-pay theory. A survey of the mortgage default literature by Quercia and Stegman shows that, consistently, home equity or the related measure, loan-to-value ratio, is the main characteristic influencing the default decision.[1] Other factors found to be important are transactions costs and the difficulty of estimating the value of the default option. In an early study of defaults, von Furstenberg analyzed the default rates on Federal Housing Administration (FHA) loans grouped by the policy year (the year the loans were originated and insured).[2] He considered the original maturity of the loans, the original loan-to-value ratio, and whether or not the loan was for a new or existing property. He found that shorter maturity loans (20-year versus 30-year loans) and loans on new houses were much less likely to default. Holding these two variables constant, he discovered that the original loan-to-value ratio was the single most important factor governing defaults over the life of the loans. In a similar study of VA loans, von Furstenberg considered not only the original loan-to-value ratio but also the age (time from origination to default) of defaulted loans.[3] He found that defaults peak between 3 and 5 years subsequent to origination, and the loan-to-value ratio is the predominant determining factor in explaining defaults. In another study of the loan portfolio of a large Pittsburgh savings and loan association, von Furstenberg and Green found that delinquencies behaved similarly to defaults; they were related primarily to the loan-to-value ratio, the age of the mortgage, and the type of property (new or existing).[4]

Variables related to the ability-to-pay theory, such as family size and source of income, also have been used to explain default. In an early study, Morton analyzed borrower characteristics in terms of their importance in causing delinquency or foreclosure.[5] He analyzed the loan performance of 24 Connecticut lenders and found that the number of dependents and the employment status of the borrower were very important in explaining defaults. Employment as a salesman was by far the most significant job classification related to defaults.

On a macro level, unemployment may be expected to affect defaults. In a study of mortgages insured nationally by the Mortgage Guaranty Insurance Corporation, Campbell and Dietrich found that the regional rate of unemployment contributed to an explanation of delinquency and default rates.[6]

Finally, in a test of the ability-to-pay and equity theories of default, Jackson and Kaserman concluded that the evidence supports the latter theory.[7] Using a large number of FHA loans that were originated in or close to the year 1969, they found the loan-to-value ratio a better predictor of default than the payment-to-income ratio of the borrower.

The reader should note, however, that there is no inherent conflict between the two theories of default. Negative equity is likely a necessary but not sufficient condition for default. A home owner with negative equity in his or her residence may prefer to make the monthly payments. He or she may do so out of a sense of obligation, a fear of a bad credit rating, or because the house has more value to him or her than it would in the market.

Once default occurs, the natural progression is for the lender to initiate foreclosure proceedings. However, as Ambrose and Capone point out in a 1996 study, foreclosure can be the most costly post-default outcome.[8] As a result, lenders may attempt to recover the debt without going through the foreclosure process by offering the borrower some alternatives such as deed in lieu of foreclosure (voluntary title transfer), allowing the borrower to sell the property even at a loss, or arranging a work-out agreement to lower payments. Ambrose and Capone do a simulation in which the results show that lenders can find profitable opportunities in extending foreclosure alternatives.

Lenders, however, face a "moral hazard" problem by offering alternatives to foreclosure. The willingness of lenders to negotiate a less costly solution to default may act as a signal to other borrowers that their cost of default has decreased and this, in itself, may lead to more defaults. In this regard, Clauretie and Jameson conclude that loan renegotiation does not occur frequently enough to warrant its consideration in mortgage pricing models.[9]

However, Ambrose and Buttimer indicate that there can be a potential payoff for lenders from foreclosure alternatives.[10] Using an option-based model of default they argue that forebearance, pursuit of antideficiency judgments, and, especially, pointing out the value of future credit reputation to the borrower may be valuable alternatives to foreclosure.

Characteristics of the Property

Lenders require that an appraisal of the property be performed as part of the qualification procedure. The appraisal will usually be done by an independent, third-party appraiser. For all Federal Housing Administration (FHA), Veterans Administration (VA), and conventional loans regulated by a federal financial institution, the appraisal process and form are standardized, and federal law requires the appraiser to be state licensed or certified. A Freddie Mac/Fannie Mae uniform report is shown in Exhibit 13-1 (on the Web site). The appraiser will note on the form the physical characteristics of the property, such as the square footage, number of bedrooms, and structure (frame, masonry, concrete). The appraiser also will indicate the property's location, such as urban, rural, or floodplain. Next, the appraiser will determine the recent selling price of at least three nearby and comparable properties in forming an opinion of value. Finally, the value of the residence as a rental property will be considered. Even though the intended use is for owner occupancy, its value as reflected by the economic market rent it could command is considered an appraisal method.

Conforming conventional loans have guidelines set by the major secondary market agencies that purchase them. Other conventional loans have no set guidelines. Loans in excess of 95 percent loan-to-value ratio are not common, and most lenders require private mortgage insurance on all loans with loan-to-value ratios in excess of 80 percent.

Characteristics of the Borrower

Though different in detail, procedures for borrower qualification for conforming conventional, FHA, and VA loans are similar. They involve a determination of the ability of the borrower to make mortgage payments out of the family income. The qualification procedures consider the type and stability of income, supplemental sources of income, nonmortgage debt obligations, and living expenses.

Borrower qualification for conforming conventional, FHA, and VA loans all compare maximum ratios of housing-related expenses to either gross or after-tax income. Table 12-1 compares these definitions and ratios. Ratios for nonconforming

TABLE 12-1

Comparison of Borrower Qualification Guidelines

	CONFORMING CONVENTIONAL	FHA	VA	
			RESIDUAL METHOD	INCOME RATIOS
(1) Monthly income	Verifiable gross income	Verifiable gross income	Net effective income (gross less federal taxes)	Gross income
(2) Monthly housing interest expense	Principal, interest, taxes, insurance (PITI)	Principal, interest, taxes, insurance, association fees (TMP)	Principal, interest, taxes, insurance, utilities, maintenance	Principal, taxes, insurance, association fees
(3) Other monthly expense	State and local taxes, car payment, installment loans, child support, other debt obligations	Installment debt, loan payments, child support, state and local taxes, credit card payments, other debt obligations	State and local taxes, Social Security, taxes, installment debt, retirement contributions, life insurance premiums, loan payments	Installment debt, loan payments, child support, state and local taxes, other debt obligations
(4) Minimum residual			Food, clothing, transportation, medical care, personal items; by region and family size, homeowner association dues	
Maximum ratio 2/1	Generally 28% Should not exceed 33% [80% L/V]	29%		
Maximum ratio (2+3)/1	Generally 36% should not exceed 41% [80% L/V]	41%		41%
Minimum excess residual ratio [(1)−(2)−(3)−(4)]/(4)			20%	

conventional loans will vary by lender but will approximate those in the table. Borrower qualification is based on several criteria that include credit scoring, income, assets, total indebtedness, and other factors. The first factor, credit scoring, is a statistical method that lenders use to quickly and objectively assess the credit risk of a loan applicant. It is also useful in setting prices for prime and subprime loans. A **subprime loan** is one made to a borrower who does not have a top grade credit record. Because subprime loans command higher interest rates, careful use of the loans can enhance profitability.

Typically, current market rates on conforming loans are easily accessible. They are quoted widely in newspapers, on the Internet, and so on. Because subprime loans are based on risk-based pricing, rates are not quoted publicly. Instead they are negotiated based on the riskiness of the borrower.

Risk-based borrowing matches the borrower to a series of risk profiles and rates the likelihood that the loan will be repaid. Scores range from 350 indicating high risk to 950 indicating low risk. The most widely used credit score is FICO, which was developed by Fair, Isaac and Company. Credit scores are based strictly on the information in the borrower's credit profile and do not consider factors such as income and demographic factors such as race, gender, or marital status. Credit history would contain information regarding the borrower's current debt level, past delinquencies, types of credit, length of credit history, and the number of recent credit checks. The weight given these factors in calculating the credit score are typically: 35 percent for payment history, 30 percent for the current level of indebtedness, 15 percent for types of credit, 15 percent for length of credit history, and 5 percent for number of inquiries. The most important factor is simply paying bills on time. Even a small balance should not be allowed to become delinquent.

Access to the Internet increases the ease of rate shopping by borrowers. Procedural changes in credit scoring are designed to minimize the negative impact of rate shopping. For example, if the borrower is shopping for a mortgage, consumer-initiated inquiries within the last 365 days from mortgage-related entities are ignored for the first 30 days. Afterwards, multiple inquiries within the next 14 days are counted as one although each inquiry still appears on the credit report.

Because profiling differs across lenders, no fixed set of criteria exists. However, borrowers are generally placed into a set of A, A–, B, C, D, or F categories. The A borrower has a low default rate and can obtain a higher loan-to-value ratio loan. An A– borrower is slightly riskier—perhaps due to late payments. The B borrower may be self-employed and have trouble documenting income. The underwriter looks for reasonable explanations for delinquencies. A C borrower has only fair credit and high debt ratios. The underwriter looks for ability and willingness to repay the debt. A D borrower has poor credit and high debt ratios. These loans have a good chance of going into foreclosure. The underwriter must ensure that the collateral is sufficient to guarantee payment. An F borrower is currently in bankruptcy or foreclosure. These ratings are discussed in greater detail later in this chapter.

Legislation such as the Fair and Accurate Credit Transaction Act of 2003 is designed to ensure fair treatment in applying for credit. First, this law allows every borrower to obtain a free copy of his or her credit report each year. Second, the law attempts to reduce identity theft by requiring merchants to delete all but the last five digits of a credit card on store receipts. Third, the law creates a national system of fraud detection that requires only one telephone call by the victim. Fourth, the law encourages lenders and credit agencies to take preemptive action by identifying patterns of theft.

Current technology advances and sophisticated information-gathering systems have made it possible for lenders to increase their subprime lending. As a result, over the decade ending in 2007, a wave of new loans with low interest rates and low or no down payments entered the market. These loans allowed borrowers who would ordinarily not qualify for financing (such as low-income borrowers) to achieve the dream of home ownership. This behavior was encouraged based on the benefits of home ownership such as wealth building, neighborhood and family stabilization, and crime reduction. However, many of these loans were written under terms that borrowers could not support in the long run.

Mortgages and the Internet

A number of Web sites offer mortgages directly to consumers. A borrower can now negotiate a loan over the Internet. The expanded use of the Internet for mortgage lending is happening for a couple of reasons. First, it eliminates the need to travel to the mortgage lender's office. This may eliminate having to travel long distances or through congested areas. Second, borrowers with less-than-perfect credit records can avoid meeting face to face with the loan officer. Even people with perfect credit may prefer the anonymity of applying over the Internet.

A mortgage negotiated over the Internet may have a lower origination fee but other fees are likely to be about the same as a regular mortgage. But the anonymity of the Internet works both ways. The borrower does not have a real person with whom to discuss financial needs, and anonymity provides shady operators a cover behind which they can take advantage of unwary borrowers.

HUD/FHA Guidelines

The Department of Housing and Urban Development (HUD) requires that FHA-approved lenders use a percentage calculation to help determine an applicant's eligibility for a loan. Lenders follow a mortgage credit analysis worksheet in which two **payment-to-income ratios** are utilized: (1) the ratio of the monthly **total mortgage payment (TMP)** to **gross monthly effective income** (referred to as the "front end" ratio) and (2) the sum of TMP and other monthly expenses to monthly effective income (referred to as the "back end" ratio). Effective income is the borrower's and co-borrower's regular plus supplemental gross income. Payment-to-income ratios that exceed 31 and 43 percent (includes principal and interest, escrow deposits for taxes, hazard insurance, mortgage insurance premium, homeowners' dues, etc., and all recurring monthly revolving and installment debt such as car loans, personal loans, student loans, credit cards, etc.) generally will lead to a denial of the loan application. These ratios also hold for newly constructed homes that are identified as being "energy-efficient homes." In fact, the FHA has an "energy-efficient mortgage" in which the borrower can buy or refinance and incorporate in the cost of energy-efficient improvements.

Definition of Housing Expenses

Whereas borrower qualification for conventional loans may focus on only the principal, interest, taxes, and insurance (PITI), the FHA adds to PITI the monthly mortgage insurance premium (MIP) and any homeowner association or condominium fees.

The total fixed payment is determined by adding to the TMP any installment debt, child support, and other debt payments (such as on an automobile loan). Any installment payment that is scheduled to be paid off within 6 months can be excluded from this definition. The idea is to estimate the total monthly obligation for which the borrower will be committed over an extended period of time. This total should not exceed 43 percent of gross monthly effective income.

Definition of Income

Gross monthly effective income is determined by HUD as the gross income from all sources that can be expected to continue for the first 5 years of the mortgage. The dual qualifying ratios computed with respect to gross income can be exceeded if there are significant compensating factors such as the following:

- The borrower has a conservative attitude toward the use of credit and has accumulated liquid assets (other than by gift).
- The borrower has at least a 10-percent investment in the property.
- The borrower's housing expenses are increased only slightly as a result of the purchase.
- The borrower has other compensation not reflected in the effective income figure.
- A considerable amount of the borrower's effective income is from nontaxable sources.

Self-employed borrowers can pose some difficult problems for estimating effective income. A borrower is considered self-employed if he or she has a 25 percent or greater ownership in a business. For such borrowers, the lender must verify at least 2 years of income. An average income figure must be used for the purpose of qualification. Furthermore, the self-employed borrower must have been self-employed for a minimum of 2 years. A person who has been self-employed between 1 and 2 years must have at least 2 years' previous employment to qualify. No person self-employed for less than a year can qualify for an FHA-insured loan.

HUD/FHA employs an accept/reject decision based on the following four factors of credit rating:

1. Credit characteristics.
2. Stability of effective income.
3. Adequacy of effective income.
4. Adequacy of wealth or assets.

A rejection in any category will lead to a denial of the loan.

VA Borrower Qualification

The VA mortgage loan program is designed to help veterans finance the purchase of homes with favorable loan terms and at competitive interest rates. VA mortgages are available from private lenders to buy owner-occupied homes, town houses, condominiums, and mobile homes; to repair or improve a home; and to refinance. Basic characteristics of VA loans are no down payment, limits on closing costs paid by the buyer, and no prepayment penalty. Typical requirements are (1) eligibility with loan entitlement, (2) the home must be owner-occupied, (3) the borrower must meet income requirements, and (4) the borrower must have good credit. The VA makes direct loans only to Native Americans on trust land or in some cases of veteran disability. Otherwise, loans are made by local lenders and are guaranteed by the VA.

The VA offers loans with a maximum term of 30 years and 32 days and can be a fixed-rate loan, a graduated-payment loan, an adjustable-rate mortgage, or a growing equity mortgage. The growing equity mortgage allows for gradual annual increases in payments with all extra applied to the mortgage principal. Increases may be fixed (3 percent per year, for example) or tied to some index. No down payment is required if the value of the property exceeds the purchase price or cost. A down payment is required on the graduated-payment mortgage because of negative amortization. The interest rate is negotiated and only reasonable closing costs can be charged. These might include a VA appraisal, credit report, survey, title insurance, recording fees, an origination fee, and discount points.

Wartime veterans are eligible for a VA loan if they have served 90 days of active duty during a "hot war." This would include (1) World War II (1940–1947), (2) the Korean conflict (1950–1955), (3) the Vietnam War (1964–1975), and (4) the Persian Gulf War (1990–present). Peacetime service requires a minimum of 181 days of continuous active duty. For reservists and national guardsmen, 6 years of service is required for eligibility. Others that may qualify for a VA loan include certain U.S. citizens who served in the armed forces of an allied country in World War II or their unremarried surviving spouses, and the spouse of any veteran listed as missing in action or a prisoner of war for 90 days or more.

The VA employs a two-step method using ratios similar to those employed in FHA qualification. The ratios are displayed in Table 12-1. The residual method has been used for many years; the income ratio method was added in October 1986.

Residual Method

The **residual method** is similar to that used by the FHA, except that an additional category of obligations is added to the analysis—monthly living costs such as food, clothing, and transportation. The VA begins with the same definition of housing expenses as the FHA—PITI—and then adds utilities and maintenance costs. Additional monthly payments are added as well. Here, the VA includes state and local taxes, retirement contributions, Social Security taxes, and life insurance premiums. Finally, the VA adds cost-of-living expenses to this total. Estimates of these costs, called minimum residual income, are made by region and family size.

The total of all these costs is then subtracted from net effective income (gross income less federal income taxes) to arrive at excess residual income. Under VA guidelines, this excess residual income should be at least 20 percent of the minimum required residual if the borrower fails the income ratio method described next.

Income Ratio Method

The **income ratio method**, similar to the FHA's method, is used in conjunction with the residual method. The income concept is gross income as opposed to net effective income. Here, PITI is used as a definition of housing expenses, and other monthly expenses include loan repayments, installment obligations, and child support. The sum of the housing plus other expenses should not exceed 41 percent of gross income. If the expenses exceed this ratio, then the residual method can be employed. Also, the previous credit history of the applicant as indicated by his or her wealth, borrowing decisions, and credit history is considered by the VA. The VA will look at the work history and stability of earnings of the borrower. The number and ages of dependents is also a factor, as is the size of the down payment on the property.

Conforming Conventional Loan Qualification

Unlike government-insured loans, there are no nationally uniform guidelines for conventional loan underwriting. The Federal National Mortgage Association (FNMA) and the Federal Home Loan Mortgage Corporation (FHLMC) purchase conventional loans from lender/originators. These agencies have established qualification guidelines to which the loan application must conform. Because nonconforming loans would not be purchased by these large secondary market agencies, most conventional loans are originated under their guidelines. If these guidelines are not met, the loan will not be available for purchase by the agencies and is therefore unlikely to be offered by lenders that do not hold their originations in their own portfolio. Due to the efficiencies of the secondary mortgage market, conforming loans often carry interest rates 10 to 50 basis points lower than nonconforming loans. Exhibit 12-8 (on the CD) shows an FNMA/FHLMC residential loan application form used for borrower qualification.

For 95 percent loan-to-value loans, FNMA requires that the mortgage payment not exceed 25 percent of gross income and that the total of the payment and other obligations not exceed 33 percent of gross income. The limits are 28 percent and 36 percent, respectively, for less than 95 percent loan-to-value loans.

Table 12-2 indicates that the federal agencies have other guidelines that pertain to loans other than the standard fixed-rate type. As an example, FNMA will not purchase adjustable-rate mortgages (ARMs) with negative amortization. The FHLMC will, but require a 10 percent down payment. The same is true for graduated-payment ARMs.

Also, Freddie Mac and Fannie Mae determine a loan limit subject to an annual survey of home purchase prices conducted by the Federal Housing Finance Board (FHFB). As of 2007, the limit is $417,000 for a one-unit property in most of the United States. Higher limits apply in Alaska and Hawaii and properties larger than one unit. By law, since 1981 the Fannie Mae and Freddie Mac loan purchase limit is adjusted annually on the basis of the October-to-October percent change in the average home price reported in the FHFB's monthly survey of terms on conventional home mortgages.

Borrower Qualification Comparison

Table 12-3 shows the relevant values and ratios for the Smith family example. The family meets all of the ratio tests with the exception of a high loan-to-value conventional loan and a low residual income ratio. If the family were to fail the VA test using the income ratio method, the VA would look next to the residual income. Here, the family appears to have difficulty, since the residual income is less than the 20 percent guideline.

Computing the various ratios involved in borrower qualification can be time-consuming. Fortunately, software programs are available that make the computations easy. As additional information is made known, the user can simply input the new data into the program to automatically calculate the new ratios. Spreadsheet programs are also ideal for this type of analysis.

Recently lenders have been assigning letter grades to loans based on the credit history of the applicant. Lenders commonly refer to loans as A, B, and C loans. Under the A rating, the borrower can have no more than 38 percent of income allocated to pay debt, has no late mortgage payments in the last 2 years, no bankruptcy in 10 years, and no more than one 30-day late installment payment or 60-day late credit card payment. For a B loan, no more than 50 percent of the borrower's income may be allocated to debt service, no more than three 30-day late

TABLE 12-2
Federal Agency Guidelines for Purchased Conventional Mortgages

	INSURANCE LOANS ALLOWED?	MINIMUM DOWN PAYMENT	MINIMUM DOWN PAYMENT FOR REGULAR ARMS	MINIMUM DOWN PAYMENT FOR REG. AM.ARMS	GRADUATED PAYMENT ARM	BUILDER BUYDOWNS	REFINANCED LOANS	PMI MORTGAGE INSURANCE REQUIRED	TITLE INVESTOR REQUIRED
FANNIE MAE	Yes, maximum 80% loan-to-value ratio	10% (with tougher income standards if less)	10%	Not acceptable	Not acceptable	Fixed rate, less than 10% down limited to 3%; 10% down limited to 6%. ARM, no contributions	10%	Yes, if loan-to-value ratio more than 80%	Yes
FREDDIE MAC	Yes	5%	5%	10% Max 125% neg. amortization	10% down 5%, 7.5% adjustment for first 5 years	Value of buydown less than 10% of loan amount; annual increase in payment 7.5% or less	10%	Yes, if loan-to-value ratio more than 80%	Yes

Source: © 2014 OnCourse Learning

TABLE 12-3
Borrower Qualification Ratios for Smith Family

	CONFORMING CONVENTIONAL	FHA	VA	
			RESIDUAL METHOD	INCOME RATIOS METHOD
(1) Income	$3,600	$3,600	$3,200	$3,600
(2) Housing expense	800	800	950	800
(3) Other monthly expenses	600	600	850	600
(4) Minimum residual			1,193	
Ratio one (2/1)	22.22%	22.22%		
Ratio two (2+3)/1	38.99%	38.89%		38.89%
Minimum expense [(1)−(2)−(3)−(4)]/4			17.35%	

Source: © 2014 OnCourse Learning

mortgage payments in the last year (no 60-day late payments at all), and no more than four 30-day late installment loan payments or two 30-day late credit card payments. Also, the borrower must have no declared bankruptcy in the last 2 *to* 4 years. A C loan limits debt payments to 55 percent of income, and allows no more than four 30-day late installment loan payments or four 60-day late credit card payments. The borrower must not have declared bankruptcy in the last 2 years.

CONTRACTUAL RELATIONSHIPS IN RESIDENTIAL LOANS

This section describes the generic characteristics of legal instruments that deal with residential finance. The actual characteristics vary from state to state and from region to region. Many provisions are subject to negotiation between the borrower and the lender, although this seldom occurs. Some of the provisions of the legal instruments discussed here maybe modified or obviated by state law. In addition, there may be conflicts between provisions allowed or prohibited by the various states and those required by the federal government through such regulatory agencies as the Office of Thrift Supervision.

Often, state legislatures pass laws (or state courts make decisions) that protect the borrower in a financial transaction. As an example, many state laws disallow prepayment penalties on mortgages, thus preserving the value of the borrower's prepayment option. Remember, then, that many of the provisions discussed further in this chapter may not be valid in some states or for some mortgages originated by federally regulated thrifts or purchased by federal secondary mortgage agencies.

Promissory Notes

In a residential finance arrangement, the borrower promises to repay the lender by signing a **promissory note**. The promissory note contains the important provisions of the loan. The mortgage or trust deed collateralizes the property for the lender in the event of borrower default. The mortgage or trust deed also has important provisions. Default generally is defined as any failure on the part of the borrower to meet the terms of the promissory note. That can include failure to make interest and principal payments, property tax payments, hazard insurance payments, and so forth. The promissory note can be sold by the lender to another investor.

When this is done, the mortgage or trust deed also is transferred. A sale or assignment of the latter without the sale of the note is meaningless. The security for the debt has no value apart from the debt itself.

Types of Promissory Notes

A promissory note can be either a recourse note or a nonrecourse note. A **recourse note** is one in which the lender has the right to pursue other assets of the borrower in the event that, through a default and foreclosure, the liquidation value of the residence is insufficient to satisfy the debt. In this situation, there is a deficiency and the lender can obtain a court-ordered judgment for the amount of the deficiency. A **nonrecourse note** limits the lender's remedy to the value of the residence that serves as collateral. This is done through the exculpatory clause, which literally means "to hold blameless." Although the terms of a note may determine its status, state legislation may prohibit certain loans from being recourse notes. Seller carryback loans and home improvement loans often are required to be nonrecourse. A seller carryback exists when the owner-seller of the residence agrees to grant a loan to the buyer instead of receiving cash. A handful of states (six as of 2009) require that first mortgages be nonrecourse through antideficiency judgment legislation. In these states, the lender is unable to pursue a judgment for the deficiency. His or her recourse is only to the residence securing the loan. Some states allow deficiency judgments on first mortgages so that the lender can proceed against the borrower's remaining assets. Of course, if the borrower has few remaining assets, his or her ability to declare personal bankruptcy may discourage the lender from incurring the legal expenses required to pursue a deficiency judgment. Deficiency judgments are discussed in detail in Chapter 14.

Provisions of Promissory Notes

Amount, Consideration, and Payer. Since a note has value, the lender must give consideration to make it enforceable. Usually that consideration is the amount of the loan (cash). It also can be personal property, or in the case of seller carrybacks, real estate. The amount to be repaid must be contained in the note as well as the person or entity to be repaid. If the words "or order" appear after the identification of the lender as payee, the lender can sell the note or designate another to collect the payments. Because of the large secondary mortgage market, virtually all notes have this provision.

Interest and Payment. The note will indicate the annual rate of interest and the date from which interest begins to accrue. For adjustable-rate mortgages, the note will indicate the date that the interest rate may change (anniversary date), the basis on which the new rate will be calculated (index), and any limitations (caps) on the interest change or the payment change. In the case where payments (but not the interest rate) are capped, the note also will explain the provisions for negative amortization. For the standard fixed-rate, amortizing loan, the amount of the installment payment (principal and interest) and due dates will be noted. Some notes may provide that the loan be amortized over a period longer than the final payment date. In this case, some unamortized principal will remain on the final due date. The entire principal will come due and is referred to as a "balloon payment." Legislation in some states requires written notice by the note holder within a certain time frame (say, 6 months) that the balloon payment is coming due.

Interest can be charged using an accrual or an add-on method. The former is by far the most common method and exists when the installment payment covers both interest and principal reduction. Interest is charged only on the unpaid balance. The latter exists mainly in debt not related to real estate. Here, interest is computed for the entire amount of the loan and added on at the beginning.

Assignment Provision. Many notes provide that in the case of default, the borrower assigns the right to receive rents or other income from the property to the lender. This prevents the borrower from obtaining benefits from ownership while not paying the interest payments to the lender.

Lock-In Clause and Prepayments. Mortgage notes contain a phrase similar to "and the borrower promises to pay the installment amounts or more…." The "or more" portion of the clause allows the borrower to prepay any portion or all of the debt at any time prior to the term of the loan. Borrowers are more likely to prepay their loan when interest rates fall below the note rate. They refinance the existing note with a new note to take advantage of lower market rates. Since this prepayment (call) option has value, lenders may prefer to "lock in" the borrower by excluding this portion of the installment payment clause. Competition between lenders, state legislation, case law, and the regulations of federal agencies that insure loans (FHA, VA) have virtually eliminated the **lock-in clause**. As a result, the bulk of residential mortgages gives the borrower the right to prepay at any time.

An alternative to the lock-in provision is a lender-imposed prepayment penalty fee. If the fee is large enough, the borrower will not prepay the loan when interest rates fall below the note rate. Here again, competitive forces, state legislation, and federal regulations have severely limited the use of prepayment penalties. Where they do exist, they are likely to be limited by legislation. The penalty may be limited in amount (say, the next 6 months' interest) or in time (within only the first 3 years of the loan). Prepayment penalties are not allowed in the case where the loan is accelerated because of a transfer of the property and the lender's exercise of the due-on-sale provision. Prepayment penalties are common on commercial real estate loans.

The general disuse of the lock-in clause or prepayment penalties on residential mortgages means that the majority of borrowers are free to exercise prepayments when it is advantageous to do so.

Default, Late Performance, and Acceleration. The note often will stipulate that if the borrower is late in paying the installment amount, a fee can be charged for the late performance. It also will indicate the number of days that the payment can be late before the loan is considered to be in default. In the event of default, the note will stipulate that the borrower is required to pay attorneys' and other legal fees necessary to cure the default. These fees are added to the amount of the indebtedness that is secured by the residence. The acceleration clause indicates that in the event of default, the lender can require that the entire amount of the debt become due. There will be statutory limitations on the exercise of this lender option, however. The equitable right of redemption, available in all states, allows the borrower to cure the default up to several days before a trustee's sale of the property by bringing the debt (including any legal and other foreclosure fees) current. Additionally, most states require that a sale date be set at least 3 months subsequent to the notice of default (NOD). In the unusual event that the note is unsecured, the acceleration clause may be immediately enforceable.

Escrow (Impound) Accounts. Since the residence is security for the note, lenders often require that payments for hazard insurance and property taxes be made as part of the regular installment payment and placed in an account for disbursement to the proper parties. The lender needs to ensure that the hazard insurance is paid, because a loss of value due to a fire, for example, would reduce or eliminate the security for the note. Property tax payments also must be made, because any lien placed on the property for failure to pay taxes is superior to the lien of the lender. In some states, lenders can require an escrow account on some types of loans. Such accounts generally will be present on loans of greater than 90 percent loan-to-value ratio and on loans guaranteed by a government agency (FHA, VA). Lenders may not charge a fee for handling the account, and the borrower has the right to an end-of-year accounting and to have any excess accumulated funds returned.

Lenders can require a cushion of one-sixth of the total amounts paid out of the account (approximately 2 months' worth). RESPA does not require escrows to be present. This is up to the lender. Also, HUD does not require interest to be paid on accounts. Some states do but many do not.

Guarantor. Often an individual other than the borrower may guarantee the payment of the note. This individual is called a **guarantor**. Lenders will require a personal guarantee when the borrower is a corporation or a limited partnership. This alleviates an agency problem. A major stockholder of a corporation could borrow money in the corporation's name and then waste the assets of the corporation (transfer them to another corporation, for example). Additionally, the note may be secured by the corporation's property and not the stock of the corporation. In an unusual twist, the guarantor may end up with a greater liability than the borrower in states where antideficiency judgment legislation exists. Such legislation may not apply to guarantors. Thus, the borrower, even if a corporation, would be protected by the antideficiency legislation, but the guarantor would not. The lender would pursue the guarantor for any deficiency.

Due-on-Sale Clause. We learned in earlier chapters that assumable loans contain a valuable option. If market rates rise above the rate on the loan, it will have greater value if assumed than if prepaid when the property is sold. The value of the assumability option is capitalized to a certain extent into the value of the property. We also learned that the right to assumability was so valuable as to be the subject of expensive litigation. Since the Garn–St. Germain Act, virtually all due-on-sale clauses are enforceable. Recall that the regulatory authorities convinced Congress that enforcement was required to mitigate the interest rate risk faced by depository institutions and protect their solvency. Also under the act, a sale means any conveyance of any interest, including a lease, further encumbrance, or some types of transfers.

Rather than sell a property financed with a due-on-sale note, the owner may attempt to take advantage of the low rate on the note by leasing the property.

A long-term lease would have a present value close to that of the property, yet the owner would make payments based on the note's low rate. Under the Garn–St. Germain Act, any leasehold interest greater than 3 years in length could represent a transfer of interest for the purpose of enforcing the due-on-sale clause. A lease with an option to purchase the property would also trigger the due-on-sale provision, even if less than 3 years.

Also, the creation of a junior lien on the property may trigger the due-on-sale clause for properties that contain more than one residential unit or are not owner-occupied (transfer of the right of occupancy). In addition, a foreclosure on the junior trust deed can activate the due-on-sale clause for all residential properties.

Residential properties often are transferred from one party to another on death, divorce, or simply through a voluntary transfer (parents to children). In such situations, the transfer of the property will not activate the due-on-sale clause, unless the new owner does not occupy the residence or the property is not a single-family residence.

A transfer of the property to a trust likewise will not trigger the due-on-sale clause if the owner remains the beneficiary and there is no change in occupancy. The Office of Thrift Supervision (OTS) regulations generally will not require an enforcement of the clause as a result of transfers involving single-family residences to be owner-occupied. Also, a lender that accepts payments on the original note from the new owners of the property may have waived his right to enforce the due-on-sale clause. OTS regulations are not intended to override state laws with regard to waivers.

Then there is involuntary conversion. If a fire completely destroys a residence, the lender has the right to require that the proceeds from insurance be applied to paying off the note rather than to rebuilding the property. The lender is more likely to require the repayment if market interest rates are substantially higher than that on the note. The borrower would be forced to rebuild the residence via a high-rate loan. In some states, however, the courts have sided with the property owner and required the lender to extend the terms of the original note. They cite the long-term expectations of each party to the contract and indicate that, as long as there is no threat to the security for the note, the borrower should be able to use insurance proceeds to rebuild the house.

Lenders may allow a loan to be assumed even if there is a due-on-sale clause. In such cases, the lender is allowed to, and may, charge an assumption fee. However, the fee cannot consist of "points" ordinarily associated with new loans. Case law in some states has made it clear that large assumption fees imposed by lenders during high-interest-rate periods constitute an unreasonable constraint on alienation (the right to convey property to another). In order not to be unreasonable, the fee should reflect the expenses incurred by the lender in transferring the note to the new owner (credit evaluation, for example).

Sale, Transfer, or Assignment of the Note

The sale of notes and transfer of mortgages and trust deeds are two independent events. There are several means by which the sale (transfer) of the note can occur. One is by absolute assignment. Here, the seller retains no property rights or liabilities. The buyer of the note will not have recourse to the seller in the event of a default. To ensure no future liability, the seller may endorse the back of the note with the words "endorsed without recourse."

A second type of transfer is by endorsement. This leaves the seller personally liable to the buyer. In the case of future default on the note, the buyer can seek compensation from the seller for any loss incurred.

Finally, a transfer by guarantee occurs when a third party, not a party to the transaction, guarantees to the buyer that the note will be paid in full. The guarantee is really a separate transaction between the note buyer and the guarantor.

Deed-of-Trust or Trust Deeds

The **deed-of-trust** or trust deed is an instrument that serves as security for a note. A third party to the lender-borrower relationship is added to hold the deed in trust. The trustee is usually a bank, attorney, title company, or other individual. There is generally no prohibition of the lender also serving as trustee, but this is unusual. The trust deed usually will say something to the effect that "the borrower grants and conveys to the trustee in trust, the following real property...." In reality, the borrower retains the right to use the property as he or she sees fit—to possess, encumber, or sell it. Should the borrower default, the trustee, having a deed, is in a position to quickly liquidate the property. A typical trust deed will identify the parties and have several provisions.

Parties to the Trust Deed

There are three parties to the trust deed: the borrower (trustor, who is also usually the owner of the property), the lender (beneficiary), and the trustee. The trustor can own and encumber a part interest in real estate (for example, of two individuals owning real estate, one can encumber his or her part interest). The beneficiary is the individual entitled to repayment of the note. Thus, if the note is sold, the buyer becomes the beneficiary under the new arrangement. Most of the provisions of a note are designed to protect the interest of the lender/beneficiary. Under most provisions, he or she can require that taxes and insurance be paid (placed in escrow), that the property be maintained, and, most important, he or she can liquidate the property if the borrower fails to make his or her payments. The borrower/trustor has the right to use the property within any limitations established by the covenants and restrictions. He or she can also sell or lease the property. Many of the borrower's rights are given by state law rather than the trust deed. State law may require that interest be paid on the tax and insurance escrow account, or that the borrower has a right to an accounting of all amounts paid and owing if he or she has received a notice of default. Some state laws are potentially valuable to the borrower. They may give the borrower the right to redeem the property even after foreclosure (for a specified period of time). We will discuss state laws in more detail in Chapter 14. The only duties of the trustee are to act fairly without bias and to return the property title to the borrower when he or she receives documentation that the note has been paid.

Provisions of a Trust Deed

The provisions of the trust deed outline the rights and obligations of the lender/beneficiary and the borrower/trustor. In addition, the trust deed also may include many of the same provisions of the promissory note, such as those related to payments, escrow accounts, the due-on-sale clause, actions in the event of default, and so forth.

Assignment of Rents. In the event of a default, this provision allows the lender to collect any rents from the property and apply them to the debt. In the unlikely event that the rents are substantial, they may be sufficient to cure the default. This provision prevents "equity skimming" by the borrower. Equity skimming occurs when an original or subsequent borrower (by assuming the loan) invests little equity in the property. He or she then collects rents from the property but makes no repairs or debt payments. The amount pocketed easily can exceed the initial equity after a few months. The borrower then defaults on the loan. If the lender has the right to intervene and collect the rents, this behavior is discouraged.

Waste. The borrower agrees to keep the property in good condition so as not to lose value. In this way, the value of the collateral is not impaired.

Nonwaiver. The lender's failure to exercise a right given in the trust deed is not to be construed to prohibit the exercise of the right in the future.

Security Protection. The borrower must reimburse the lender for the costs of protecting the property from adversary interests in the event that the borrower fails to do so.

Successors and Assigns. Any person or entity who receives an interest in the property must adhere to the same provisions as the borrower.

Substitution of Trustee. This provision allows the lender to replace the trustee, assuming the proper papers are filed with the county recorder.

Reconveyance. On payment of the indebtedness, this provision directs the lender to give the note and trust deed to the trustee, who in turn delivers the title to the borrower.

Release Clause. This provision is typical for large residential real estate developments, where the land is used as collateral for a development loan. It allows the borrower to have some portion of the collateral (land) released from the provisions of the note and trust deed in return for a partial payment of the debt. This allows the borrower/developer to sell off parcels of the development without having to pay the entire debt. Usually, the lender will make sure that the value of the remaining collateral still exceeds the amount of the remaining debt.

Owner-Occupancy. By this provision, the owner promises to occupy the property. This prevents borrowers from purchasing the property as an investment. As we will see in Chapter 14, "investment properties" have a higher incidence of default than do owner-occupied properties. This also prevents equity skimming.

Award from Eminent Domain. Should the property be expropriated by a governmental authority, the lender can claim the proceeds from the action to satisfy the debt. Otherwise, if the borrower received the proceeds, he or she could default on the debt and the lender would have no collateral.

Covenants and Restrictions. These appear in the trust deed and can limit the use of the property by the borrowers in many ways. They may be as substantial as a prohibition of the use of the property as a business, or as minor as a limitation on the number of pets.

Summary

In this chapter we saw how lenders manage default risk from the borrower qualification stage to the provisions in the mortgage and/or trust deed. At the borrower qualification stage, lenders are concerned that the value of the property that serves as collateral is greater than the amount of the loan. They also are concerned with the ability of the borrower to make the monthly payments. A great deal of stress is placed on the amount and stability of applicants' income, the size of the mortgage payments, and other nonmortgage debt obligations. Both government (FHA, VA) and private mortgage insurers have an interest in managing default risk. Many borrower qualification standards are set by them. Government agencies, such as the Federal National Mortgage Association and the Federal Home Loan Mortgage Corporation, purchase conventional mortgages and also are concerned with default risk. They establish their own qualification standards for conforming loans.

Most of the provisions in the mortgage and/or deed-of-trust protect the lender in case of default. The lender can step in and collect any rents or proceeds from insurance claims or eminent domain awards. The lender also can foreclose on and sell the property to recover the amount of the indebtedness. The lender can require the owner to maintain the property in good condition. Although the deed-of-trust may give the borrower some rights, most are given by state law. They include the right to cure a deficiency and reinstate the loan by making required payments. In some states, the right extends for a period beyond the foreclosure and liquidation of the property.

Key Terms

Ability-to-pay theory of default

Deed-of-trust

Default risk

Equity theory of default

Gross monthly effective income

Guarantor

Income ratio method

Lock-in clause

Nonrecourse note

Payment-to-income ratios

Promissory note

Recourse note

Residual method

Subprime loan

Total mortgage payment (TMP)

Review Questions

12-1. a. State and explain the two theories of default.
b. Which theory makes more "intuitive" sense?

12-2. a. What is a deficiency judgment?
b. How useful are deficiency judgments in mitigating losses through borrower default?

12-3. Explain default as a put option held by the borrower.

12-4. Define borrower qualification.

12-5. Contrast borrower qualification under VA and FHA procedures. Describe the residual and income ratio methods.

12-6. List four contractual relationships in a mortgage that are designed to protect the interest of the lender.

12-7.   Indicate how state laws can require provisions in mortgages to protect the borrower.

12-8.   What is the difference between a recourse and a nonrecourse promissory note?

12-9.   List at least seven important provisions of promissory notes.

12-10.   a. What is a trust deed?
b. Who are the parties to a trust deed?
c. What are the duties of the trustee?

12-11.   List and explain at least five provisions of a typical trust deed.

Problem

12-1.   Assume the following monthly data for the Jones family:

JONES FAMILY	LOAN AMOUNT, $85,000
Gross income	$3,400
Federal taxes	425
PITI	795
Utilities and maintenance	160
Other debt payments	625
Social Security, retirement, life Insurance, state, and local taxes	235
Minimum residual	1,200

a. Compute the relevant qualifying ratios for (1) an FHA loan and (2) a VA loan.

b. Under which ratios, if any, would the Jones family qualify for a loan?

Notes

1. R.G. Quercia and M.A. Stegman. Residential mortgage default: A review of the literature. *Journal of Housing Research* 3(2) (1992), 341–379.

2. G. von Furstenberg. Default risk on FHA insured home mortgages as a function of the terms of financing: A quantitative analysis. *Journal of Finance* 24 (1969), 459–477.

3. G. von Furstenberg. The investment quality of home mortgages. *Journal of Risk and Insurance* 37 (1970), 437–445.

4. G. von Furstenberg and J.R. Green. Estimation of delinquency risk for home mortgage portfolios. *AREUEA Journal* 2 (Summer 1974), 5–19.

5. T.G. Morton. A discriminant function analysis of residential mortgage delinquency and foreclosure. *AREUEA Journal* 3 (Fall 1975), 73–90.

6. T. Campbell and J. Kimble Dietrich. The determinants of default on insured conventional residential mortgage loans. *Journal of Finance* 38 (1983), 1581–1596.

7. J.R. Jackson and D.L. Kaserman. Default risk on home mortgage loans: A test of competing hypotheses. *Journal of Risk and Insurance* 47 (1980), 678–690.

8. B. Ambrose and C. Capone. Cost-benefit analysis of single-family foreclosure alternatives. *Journal of Real Estate Finance and Economics* 13 (1996), 105–120.

9. T. Clauretie and M. Jameson. Residential loan renegotiation: Theory and evidence. *Journal of Real Estate Research* 10 (1995), 153–161.
10. B. Ambrose and R. Buttimer. Embedded options in the mortgage contract. *Journal of Real Estate Finance and Economics* 21(2) (September 2000), 95–111.

Web Sites

http://www.bostonfinancial.com
Information on risk mitigation for lenders, investors, and REITs

http://www.housebuyingtips.com
Provides a comprehensive guide for buying a home

http://www.reinfo.com
Provides information for buyers and sellers of homes plus a nationwide referral network for finding real estate agents

http://www.hsh.com/calc-amort.html
Income qualification, housing affordability calculator

http://www.nahb.com
Information on building or buying a new home

http://www.mortgageunderwriters.com
Mortgage underwriting guidelines

http://www.fdic.gov/bank/analytical/working/wp2003_06/index.html
Bank loan underwriting practices

http://www.frbsf.org/publications/economics/papers/2007/wp07-33bk.pdf
Subprime mortgage delinquency rates

LOAN ORIGINATION, PROCESSING, AND CLOSING

LEARNING OBJECTIVES

After reading this chapter, you should have an understanding of the steps involved in processing a loan application and closing a mortgage. You should know the data that must be collected and analyzed, the forms used throughout the process, and the regulations that must be observed. You also should understand the operation of mortgage bankers. (Please note that all exhibits referred to in this chapter can be accessed on the publishers Web site.

INTRODUCTION

In most cases, processing a residential loan transaction is a detailed step-by-step procedure. For government-insured loans, there is little variation, either in the process or in the documents used. The general process is the same for all types of residential loans, but for convenience our description will rely heavily on FHA loan transactions. The forms and procedures employed in loan processing do change periodically. As a result, should you ever be engaged in this type of activity, you will need to refer to the latest guidelines and practices.

LOAN PROCESSING

Loan processing involves several steps, including property appraisal, analysis of application (borrower information collection and verification), submission for credit approval, and closing the loan. At each step of the way, forms are used to organize the process and to keep track of loans that are in the "pipeline." The mortgage loan process is a complex transaction and borrowers should not hesitate to seek advice from knowledgeable sources. At the start of the process the borrower, through consultation with a loan officer, will complete a Uniform Residential Loan Application (Form 1003/URLA). The application has various sections that deal with different aspects of the loan including type of mortgage and loan terms, property information, borrower information, employment information, income relative to housing expenses, and net worth. In addition, the borrower's credit report is typically used to assess the borrower's credit status.

Early in the loan process, the loan documentation type must be established. Depending on market conditions and regulatory constraints, several "doc types" may be considered. First is the "full doc" where the information provided by the borrower is verified from various sources. A second type is "stated income, verified assets" where the borrower's income is "stated" by the borrower in good faith (may be popular with tip-based and bonus-based income) and assets are verified. A third type is "stated income, stated asset" where the borrower's income and assets are "stated" by the borrower in good faith and are not verified by the lender. The income and assets must be legitimate funds and not obtained through illegal means such as money laundering or theft. A fourth type of loan is the "no doc" loan where no information is provided relative to the borrower's income and assets and the loan is based primarily on the borrower's credit and repayment history.

Property Appraisal

Property appraisal is one of the first steps in the loan process. The **appraisal** is generally made after the application for a loan. However, a developer who contemplates building and selling houses with Federal Housing Administration/Veterans Administration (FHA/VA) financing will request an appraisal in conjunction with a master certificate of reasonable value (MCRV). The MCRV process allows for an appraisal of the property prior to the loan application and will establish both maximum values of the properties and maximum loan amounts if financed with FHA/VA loans.

The three stages in the appraisal process are ordering the appraisal, monitoring the appraisal, and evaluating (reviewing) the appraisal.

Ordering the Appraisal. The procedures for ordering conventional appraisals vary from lender to lender and from investor to investor. Most lenders are free to choose their own appraiser. Since January 1995, a **uniform residential appraisal report** has been used for nearly all loans, including those intended for sale to Fannie Mae or Freddie Mac and those insured by the FHA or VA. They are available only to direct endorsement lenders (see Exhibit 13-1 on the Web site). Separate forms are used for condominiums (Exhibit 13-2) and for small (generally, up to four families) residential income properties (Exhibit 13-3). Since 1994, lenders have been able to choose the appraiser in FHA/VA loan applications, whereas previously these agencies assigned appraisers to the property. The loan officer generally provides to the appraiser a request for determination of reasonable value (provides the appraiser information on the subject property) and the contract or preliminary title report (provides legal documentation regarding the property).

The regulatory environment of appraisers is shown in Figure 13-1. The Financial Institutions Reform, Recovery, and Enforcement Act of 1989 (FIRREA) mandated that state-certified or licensed appraisers must be used in appraisals involving federally related mortgage transactions after July 1, 1991.[1]

Under the act, each federal regulatory agency (Federal Reserve Board, FDIC, Office of the Comptroller of the Currency, Office of Thrift Supervision [formerly the Federal Home Loan Bank Board FHLBB], and the National Credit Union Administration) establishes appraisal guidelines for the appraising of federally related transactions. Virtually all mortgages are federally related, because they are insured by the FHA, guaranteed by the VA, originated by federally insured institutions, or originated for sale to federal secondary mortgage market agencies. FIRREA mandates that, at a minimum, all appraisal work must conform to the Uniform Standards of Professional Appraisal Practices (USPAP) as established by the Appraisal Standards Board of the Appraisal Foundation.[2]

| FIGURE 13-1 | Appraisal Regulation |

State Government
and Private Organizations

Federal Government
Organizations

State Certification Boards

Certify and license
appraisers

Appraisal Foundation

Composed of Appraisal
Institute plus other
appraisal organizations

**Federal
Regulatory Agencies:
FED, FDIC, OTS, NCOA**

1. Requires appraisals
   in conformity
   with GAAS

2. Determines which
   federally related
   mortgage transactions
   are to be appraised
   by certified and which
   by licensed appraisers

**Federal
Financial Institutions
Examination Council**

Supervises

**Appraisal
Qualifications
Board**

Administers
Uniform State
Certification
Examination

**Appraisal
Standards
Board**

Establishes
Generally Accepted
Appraisal Standards
(GAAS)

**Appraisal
subcommittee**

Appraisers

Monitors activities of

Source: © 2014 OnCourse Learning

The regulatory agencies can establish additional standards for the institutions they regulate. The act distinguishes between certified and licensed appraisers, the former of which must meet a stricter set of requirements. It delegated the certification and licensing to individual states. The state certification agencies must establish certification requirements in conformity with criteria established by the Appraiser Qualification Board of the Appraisal Foundation. The Appraiser Qualification Board assists the stat by administering the Uniform State Certification Examination.

To see that the state certification agencies are doing their job in screening appraisers for certification and licensing, the act further establishes a government regulatory authority, the Appraisal Subcommittee of the Federal Financial Institutions Examination Council. This council oversees the various federal regulatory agencies.

Using a noncertified or nonlicensed appraiser in connection with a federally related mortgage transaction can result in a fine of $25,000 for the first violation and $50,000 for subsequent violations.

Monitoring the Appraisal. At this stage, the loan processor makes sure that the appraisal is performed within the time specified by the Department of Housing and Urban Development (HUD) (if an FHA loan) or by a private investor or secondary market agency. The processor makes certain that the appraiser gains access to the property and is paid on receipt of the report.

Evaluating the Appraisal. For government-insured loans, the lender will not receive a copy of the appraisal itself, only a conditional commitment (HUD-FHA) or certificate of reasonable value. If the appraised value appears to be low, the lender may request a reconsideration. To do so, the lender must provide detailed data on at least three comparable properties. The same appraiser makes the second appraisal, and if the lender is still dissatisfied, HUD will assign a staff appraiser to handle a second reconsideration.

For VA-guaranteed loans, the value established is an "as-is" value and requires that the veteran acknowledge the condition of the property prior to closing. HUD-FHA appraisals, on the other hand, may require that repairs be made if the health and safety of the occupants are endangered by a defect. In some cases, the lender can request that HUD-FHA waive repairs if he or she feels that the defects do not materially affect the value of the property. If repairs are not waived, the seller must be informed so that the necessary repairs can be made.

The lender will receive a complete appraisal report for conventional loans. An **underwriter** or **review appraiser** will review the report for acceptability. The review may include visits to the property and a check on the transaction prices of any comparables used by the original appraiser. If the review is done only in the office of the review appraiser, it is called a **desk review**. The review appraiser will consider several important elements of the appraisal, including the physical characteristics of the subject property, the neighborhood, present and alternative land uses, predominant occupancy (owner-occupied versus rental units), price range of single-family properties, and range in age of properties. The appraisal report must indicate if the property is located in a HUD-identified flood hazard area. Flood zones are rated A if it is likely that the property will be invaded by water, B if there is only a minimal chance of water invasion, and C if there is virtually no chance of flooding. Flood insurance is required for properties located in an A zone but is optional for B and C properties.

Note that under the *di minimus* rule, it is not required for lenders to have an appraisal performed if the loan is for less than $200,000 and the lender will retain the loan in its portfolio. However, since most lenders would like to reserve the option to sell the loan they will generally require an appraisal.

The valuation section of the appraisal will indicate how the appraiser arrived at the opinion of value. Generally accepted appraisal standards require that the appraiser consider three approaches to the determination of value: cost, market, and income.

The **cost approach** is based on the premise that the buyer will not pay more for a property than for a comparable property with the same utility. Thus, the value of the property cannot be greater than the cost of replacing it. These are the steps in the cost approach:

1. Estimate the value of the land as vacant.
2. Estimate the cost of replacing the improvement.
3. Estimate depreciation for the improvement. This may be of three types:
    a. Physical deterioration (deferred maintenance, peeling paint, sagging shutters, etc.)
    b. Functional obsolescence (bad floor plan, no air conditioning in south Florida, etc.)
    c. Economic obsolescence (changing neighborhood characteristics, busy street, etc.)
4. Subtract 3 from 2.
5. Add 1 plus 4 to arrive at total value.

In estimating depreciation, physical and functional obsolescence are generally internal to the property and may be **curable**. A problem is considered curable if the cost to remedy is not greater than the value added by making the repair. Economic obsolescence is external to the property and is generally **incurable**. Economic depreciation is caused by factors that are beyond the control of the individual homeowner. The amount of street traffic is an example. We should point out, however, that all external factors are not detrimental. A property that adjoins a golf course would have its value affected favorably.

The general limitation of the cost approach is that cost is not necessarily equal to value. For example, if you built an expensive home in an industrial district you would likely soon discover the difference between cost and value.

The **market approach** is based on the premise that transaction prices of similar properties (comparables) in the neighborhood are good indicators of value. The appraiser will generally utilize at least three comparables. The appraiser will make adjustments to the comparables for differences in physical characteristics of the properties relative to the subject property. For example, the appraiser may deduct $1,300 from the value of the comparable because it had a fireplace and the subject property does not. Typically, several adjustments are made. Besides physical characteristics, the review appraiser will also examine factors such as location, time on the market, and financing.

The **income approach** says that the value of the property is a function of the income that accrues to it. Thus, this approach arrives at a value by capitalizing the potential rent on the property using either an income multiplier or overall capitalization rate. For example, if a property produces $1,000 per month in gross rent and the appropriate gross rent multiplier (value divided by gross monthly rent) is 100, then the estimated value for the property is $100,000. The gross rent multiplier can be derived by dividing the transaction prices of recently sold comparable properties by the rent paid on those properties.

Alternatively, the appraiser may use the overall capitalization rate to determine value. The overall capitalization rate is the reciprocal calculation of income multiplier and is defined as net operating income (NOI as defined in Chapter 15) divided by the value of the property. Again, comparable properties are generally used to determine the overall capitalization rate. Thus, if a property has NOI of $10,000 per year and the applicable capitalization rate is 10 percent, the indicated value of the property is $100,000.

The review appraiser will next determine the loan-to-value ratio. A loan guaranteed by the VA may not exceed the value of the property, and the FHA sets limits on the loan-to-value ratio. These limits vary from program to program but are generally above 90 percent. Conventional lenders will establish a maximum loan-to-value ratio for loans without private mortgage insurance. Generally, loans above 80 percent loan-to-value ratio will require insurance. The cost of the insurance will vary with the loan-to-value ratio. Loan-to-value ratios are computed by using the appraisal value or the contract price, whichever is less.

The estimates of value produced by the three approaches will likely not be equal. Thus, in the **reconciliation phase** of the appraisal, the appraiser will consider each estimated value and arrive at a final estimate. Given the complexities of the process mentioned earlier, one understands that appraisal is a "subjective art" rather than an "exact science" as the appraiser considers the reliability of each estimate based on such factors as quality and quantity of data.

Analysis of Application

This stage of loan processing involves a complete analysis of the financial position of the borrower and the disclosure of information required by the Real Estate Settlement Procedures Act (RESPA), Regulation Z, and the Equal Credit Opportunity Act (ECOA). RESPA requires that lenders provide, in advance, general information about the settlement costs (Exhibit 13-4) and, within 3 days after receiving the application, a statement of the estimated costs of settlement and monthly payments (Exhibit 13-5). Also within this 3-day period, the lender must provide the borrower with a good-faith estimate (Exhibit 13-6) of the cost of the loan over its term, and it must include an estimate of the annual percentage rate (APR). The actual APR and total finance changes must be provided at or prior to settlement.

The FHA and VA use a joint application form for mortgages they insure (Exhibit 13-7). Fannie Mae and Freddie Mac have their preferred form for loans they buy (Exhibit 13-8). Some lenders prefer to take all loan applications on their own form and then transfer the data to the relevant application form. Some applications may be taken by an outside agent, such as a REALTOR® or builder. HUD requires that FHA loans entail a face-to-face meeting between lender and borrower at some time during the application stage.

Some of the more important items collected on the application form include the type of loan applied for, terms of the loan, purpose of the loan (construction loan, construction-to-permanent loan, existing property), names in which the title will be held, down payment and settlement charges, and borrower information. Important borrower information includes gross monthly income, other income, monthly housing expense, previous employment data, assets, liabilities, net worth, previous credit references, and a schedule of other real estate owned.

The loan processor is responsible for ensuring that RESPA requirements have been met regarding proper disclosure and documentation. The loan processor then verifies (to the extent agreed on) all the information in the application. In this phase of the loan process, the lender is concerned with two items: (1) the borrower's ability to make the down payment and monthly payments on the loan and (2) the accuracy of the financial data provided on the loan application. To address the first concern, the lender examines the borrower's liquid assets, the amount and stability of the borrower's income relative to housing expenses, and the past credit history of the borrower. On the second point, the lender must verify the accuracy of the financial data from independent, third-party sources. Financial data are verified as soon as possible, so that figures will not become outdated (verifications more than 90 days old are generally not acceptable for FHA loans).

The FHA, VA, and Fannie Mae use a common form for the verification of deposit (Exhibit 13-9). The FHA and VA use one form for the verification of employment (Exhibit 13-10), while Fannie Mae uses a separate form (Exhibit 13-11). The verification forms must be signed by the applicant and sent directly to the depository institution and employer for their signatures. Often the lender will have to verify the existence and worth of other assets, such as stocks, bonds, retirement funds, equity in other real estate, and the cash surrender value of life insurance policies. Lenders have their own forms for these verifications. The lender also will require at least a 2-year history of income from all sources. The history is required to judge the amount and stability of income.

Finally, the lender will verify the credit standing of the applicant. The lender will request a credit report from a credit reporting agency (bureau). The credit report will indicate any failure of the applicant to make timely payments to other creditors. Some creditors of the applicant may not report information to the credit bureau. In this case, the lender has to obtain a direct verification from them. The lender also will determine if there are any outstanding liens or judgments against the applicant in the public record.

Most verifications (credit reports) will be returned within 2 to 7 (employment) days. The lender must monitor the process to see that all verifications are received in a timely manner.

Submission for Insurance

When the verification of borrower information has been made and there are no major problems, the loan will be submitted for insurance. The FHA and VA have a common form for the submission (Exhibit 13-12). Most of the items on the form are self-explanatory, but a few comments are in order. If FHA credit approval is applied for, the lender will have to indicate which of the many FHA insurance programs is applicable. Each approved lender is assigned a 10-digit ID number that must be included in the application. Information on the borrower's race or national origin is sought for monitoring purposes. However, if the borrower prefers not to provide this information, it will not be included in the application for insurance.

Information on housing expenses, such as interest, hazard insurance, property taxes, utilities, and maintenance, must be included in the application. Information on the borrower's income assets and liabilities also is included.

The lender's certification portion of the application includes important information for the FHA or VA. By signing this portion, the lender certifies that all provisions and regulations of the FHA have been complied with. The lender also agrees to be responsible for any acts of its agents, such as the appraiser.

The borrower's certification portion of the application also contains important information for both the borrower and the insuring agency. The FHA is particularly interested in knowing if the borrower has ever defaulted on a previous residential loan, has other FHA-guaranteed loans, or intends to rent the property covered by the insurance. All of these factors affect the credit risk of the borrower. The FHA/VA also informs the borrower that, in the event the contract price exceeds the appraised value of the property, it is the borrower's responsibility to make up the difference through a cash down payment. The borrower also certifies that all information provided in the application is true and complete to the best of his or her knowledge.

Next, for FHA- and VA-insured loans, the lender prepares a loan analysis worksheet (Exhibit 13-13). If the worksheet is prepared properly, it will be given "priority" in processing by the local HUD office. The worksheet includes information on the borrower's (and co-borrower's) gross and net income; monthly payments for principal, interest, taxes, and insurance; other housing expenses; and other nonhousing monthly obligations. One purpose of the worksheet is to organize sufficient information to compute the ratios of net effective income to total housing expenses and total fixed payments. Another purpose is to determine if the borrower has sufficient liquid assets to meet the settlement requirements.

For FHA approval, the lender will submit a package consisting of the following documents:

1. Mortgage Credit Analysis Worksheet (Exhibit 13-13).
2. Application for commitment of insurance (Exhibit 13-12).
3. Copy of the sales contract.
4. All verifications of deposits (Exhibit 13-9).
5. All verifications of employment (Exhibit 13-10).
6. Credit reports.
7. Verifications of indebtedness.
8. Other supporting documents, such as sales contract on former residence, schedule of payments on a GPM, any buydown escrow agreement, and evidence of security for secondary financing.

Many lenders participate in the FHA's **direct endorsement program**. Under this program, the lender essentially performs the underwriting process. To become a direct endorser, a lender has to submit 15 or so test cases that the FHA will check. If there are no substantial differences between the underwriting process or decisions of the lender and the FHA for the test cases, approval will be granted for direct endorsement of subsequent loans. A lender that is a direct endorser is essentially an agent of the FHA. By being a direct endorser, the lender can save several days in the total processing time.

If the application for insurance is accepted, the FHA will issue a mortgage insurance certificate. The certificate will indicate the maximum mortgage amount (which may include the financing of the mortgage insurance premium), the interest rate on the loan, and the monthly payment. The commitment will have an expiration date beyond which the loan cannot be closed. If the commitment is conditional on modifications of the loan arrangement, the expiration date is 6 months after issue for existing properties and 1 year for new properties. For firm commitments, the expiration date is the expiration date of the conditional commitment, or 90 days from the date of the firm commitment, whichever is later.

The borrower should be aware that mortgage insurance is in addition to homeowners insurance. Homeowners insurance, designed to protect the lender from hazards such as natural disasters or accidents, is required on every loan. Mortgage insurance, when it is required, is paid along with homeowners insurance. These premiums may be paid outright by the borrower to the proper insurer or they may be paid through escrow. The borrower may be required to establish an escrow account with the mortgage lender into which payments are made on a monthly basis. These funds accumulate to pay the required premiums as they come due. Lenders may be willing to forego escrow for borrowers with high credit ratings by trading off a higher contract rate.

Loan Closing

Throughout this chapter loan documentation review and approval by underwriters have been discussed. This role of the underwriter is essential in ensuring that the documents meet the regulations set forth by governing agencies. The underwriter approves or denies the loan based on the loan program requirements and the borrower's ability to repay the loan.

Loan closing is composed of two distinct, but related, transactions. In one transaction, title to the property passes from the seller to the buyer. In the other, the buyer signs a promissory note. The closing involves preparing and assembling the legal documents necessary in the jurisdiction to carry out the closing transaction. In some areas of the country, the closing agent will prepare all of the documents. In other areas, the lender will prepare the documents and forward them to a closing agent to complete the process. In still other locations, the lender prepares the documents, carries out the closing, and records the documents. Regardless of the system used, there are certain documents that must be included in the closing transaction and recorded in the local courthouse. The note represents the borrower's promise to repay the loan. It states the terms of the loan, including the loan amount, interest rate, payments, due date, and so forth.

For some jurisdictions, the mortgage or deed-of-trust is standard. The Federal National Mortgage Association (FNMA) and Federal Home Loan Mortgage Corporation (FHLMC) use a joint form; the FHA and VA have similar but different forms. The mortgage or deed-of-trust will include much of the same basic information as the note and, in addition, will provide a legal description of the property.

The deed conveys title to the property from the seller to the buyer. The sellers identified in the deed as the grantors must be the owners-of-record, and the buyers indicated as the grantees must be the borrowers identified in the mortgage or deed-of-trust. The property identified on the deed also must be the same as that on the mortgage.

The settlement statement is a record of what went on at the closing. The record is kept on form HUD-1, a standardized settlement statement designed to comply with RESPA, which requires that the form be used for all "federally related" loans. There may be more than one copy of the HUD-1 form. The form given to the seller may or may not show the costs paid by the buyer, and vice versa.

The commitment should be part of the closing file. If an FHA commitment is involved, the borrower must sign certain certifications (Exhibit 13-14).

Truth-in-lending disclosure must be given to the borrower and must include the major financial terms of the loan (see Chapter 8).

Disbursement. Disbursement is part of the closing process and can be handled in a couple of ways. The lender may give the closing agent several checks payable to the ultimate recipients (title company, mortgage insurer, real estate agent, and so forth). Alternatively, the lender can give the closing agent one check for the full amount of the loan and payable to the agent. The agent then issues its own checks to the ultimate recipients.

Recording. The deed and the mortgage are recorded, so as to give notice to the public that the buyer is the new owner of the property and the mortgagee has a lien on the property. Recording is not necessary to enforce any claims made with regard to the transfer of the property or the indebtedness. It can, however, protect the owner against others that may claim also to have a valid deed or to protect the lender against those that may claim to have a senior lien against the property.

Mortgage Insurance Payments. We will limit our discussion of mortgage insurance to FHA insurance. The lender will instruct the closing agent to make a check payable to the secretary of Housing and Urban Development for the full amount of the mortgage insurance premium (MIP). The amount must agree with that indicated on the HUD-1 settlement form. Late charges and interest are assessed by HUD if the check is delayed. The check will accompany a Mortgagee's One-Time MIP Transmittal Form (Exhibit 13-15). In return, HUD will send the lender a Statement of Account, which summarizes the transaction. The lender then will file a submission for insurance, certifying that all FHA requirements have been met. The submission will include the statement of account, a mortgage insurance certificate, a copy of the note and mortgage, the original FHA firm commitment, the settlement statement, the federal truth-in-lending disclosure statement, a builder's warranty (if new construction), a mortgagee certification of repairs, and a mortgagee review certification.

The mortgagee's review certification is a signed document whereby the lender certifies that (1) the borrower has made at least the minimum cash investment, (2) the borrower has not paid any prohibited fees or charges, (3) all of the conditions imposed by the firm commitment have been met, (4) all repairs required by the firm commitment have been made, and (5) the terms of the mortgage conform to HUD requirements and the terms of the firm commitment.

MORTGAGE BANKING

Mortgage banking is the origination, servicing, and sale of mortgage loans by a firm or individual. Mortgage bankers specialize in the details of loan origination discussed in this chapter. Mortgage bankers are not depository institutions nor do mortgage bankers hold the loans they originate; they are not "portfolio" lenders. They are simply originators that process, close, and sell the loans they make. They often retain servicing rights, however. Loan servicing consists of several duties. It involves collecting monthly payments from the borrower, making sure escrow payments (impounds) are made for insurance and taxes, handling delinquencies and defaults, forwarding payments to the investor, and even inspecting properties on occasion. Mortgage bankers collect a fee for servicing the loans they originate.

The position of mortgage bankers relative to other mortgage originators increased steadily through the 1990s but began to decline in the 200s such that, by the end of 2008, market share had dropped below 20 percent.

Mortgage Brokers

Mortgage brokers act as an alternative to mortgage bankers. Mortgage brokers are licensed companies that offer mortgages from a variety of lenders. Mortgage brokers have the advantage of having access to a number of loan underwriters; thus, they can provide borrowers with their best loan options. Some mortgage brokers eventually evolve into broker-bankers, meaning the broker may be approved to be a banker for a larger lending institution once the broker has established good faith practices.

Sources of Funds

Mortgage bankers have two principal sources of funds. One is commercial paper. Commercial paper is a short-term (180 to 270 days) obligation that carries a rate about equal to the prime rate. Large mortgage bankers issue commercial paper. A second source of funds for mortgage bankers is short-term loans from commercial banks; these are called **warehousing loans**. A mortgage banker will ask for a line of credit for, say, $2 million. The mortgage banker will agree to a compensating balance, usually 20 percent of the maximum line of credit. Because mortgage loans are made from this line of credit, the mortgage banker will pledge those loans as collateral for the line of credit. That is, when the mortgage banker originates a mortgage for $100,000, he or she will simultaneously "take down" $100,000 of the $2 million line of credit and pledge the mortgage note for collateral. After the mortgage banker has originated $2 million in mortgages, he or she will sell them to an investor. The proceeds of the sale will pay off the line of credit at the commercial bank. Often, the mortgage banker will have received a commitment from an investor (FHLMC, for example) to purchase the loans for a set price. The warehousing cycle is complete and can be repeated. Each time, the mortgage banker usually retains the servicing of the loans. Mortgage brokers may also be allowed by loan underwriters to have a warehouse line of credit.

Revenues

Revenues for mortgage bankers come from four main sources. Mortgage bankers charge origination fees, usually 1 percent of the amount of the mortgage. They also charge a servicing fee, from 0.25 percent to 0.5 percent of the outstanding balance annually. Mortgage bankers also make some income on the difference between the rate earned on the mortgage and the rate paid for the line of credit at the commercial bank while the mortgages are being held and prepared for sale. This revenue is called the **warehousing rate difference**. Mortgage bankers also may earn revenue from a **marketing rate difference**. This is the difference between the amount originated and the amount received from the sale. Origination and servicing fees represent the largest portion of mortgage bankers' revenues.

Some mortgage bankers take advantage of economies of scale by purchasing the servicing rights of other originators. Because of fixed costs, as a mortgage banker grows in size, the average cost per serviced loan declines. Mortgage bankers who may be limited in the amount of mortgages they can originate can grow by purchasing the service rights to mortgages from other originators. Servicing rights are a sort of mortgage-derivative security in their own right, and their value depends on a host of assumptions regarding future interest rates and prepayments. Most rights sell for between 1.5 percent and 2.25 percent of the amount to be serviced. The valuation of servicing rights was discussed in Chapter 11.

Mortgage bankers are not regulated by any government agency as are thrifts and commercial banks. They are partnerships or corporations and, as such, are governed somewhat by state laws that address these forms of business. Other than that, there is no active regulation of mortgage bankers. Their activities are subject, however, to periodic audits if they are approved as lenders by the FHA or as lender/servicers by FNMA.

Summary

The steps involved in loan origination, processing, and closing are designed to reassure the parties to the transaction that their interests are protected. The buyer will want a clear (unencumbered) title to the property. The lender will want security for the loan. He or she will want to be assured that the buyer will make the required payments and that the value of the collateral (property) will be preserved through an accurate appraisal and by payment of property taxes and hazard insurance.

The lender also will desire insurance against events that would cause a loss, such as would result from a borrower default (mortgage insurance) or a clouded title that would jeopardize the lender's interest (title insurance). The insurance agencies will take steps necessary to verify that sufficient information has been gathered to assess the risk of default and loss.

At each step throughout the process, verifications of relevant facts, data, or information by outside parties will be required. The entire process can be appreciated as one in which each party takes the necessary steps to protect against loss.

Mortgage bankers are specialists in the origination, processing, and closing of residential loans. They do not hold loans in their own portfolios. They obtain sources of funds for lending by borrowing short-term from commercial banks (warehousing). After selling the loans, the mortgage bankers will repay this loan. Mortgage bankers obtain revenue primarily from servicing the loans they originate. Other sources of revenue include their warehousing rate difference and marketing rate difference.

Key Terms

Appraisal

Cost approach

Curable

Desk review

Direct endorsement program

Income approach

Incurable

Loan processing

Market approach

Marketing rate difference

Mortgage banking

Reconciliation phase

Review appraiser

Truth-in-lending disclosure

Underwriter

Uniform residential appraisal report

Warehousing loans

Warehousing rate difference

Review Questions

13-1. List and explain the steps in loan processing.

13-2. What is the importance of an appraisal in loan processing?

13-3. List and briefly explain the three basic appraisal methods.

13-4. What information concerning a loan applicant must be verified, and how is it verified?

13-5. In the realm of FHA insurance, what is a direct endorsement?

13-6. What two transactions take place in the loan closing?

13-7. What is a settlement statement?

13-8. What documents must be recorded and why?

13-9. Define mortgage banking.

13-10. What are the sources of revenue of mortgage bankers?

13-11. What is meant by the term *warehousing* of loans?

Notes

1. Because many states were late in passing legislation and establishing the rules and procedures for licensing and certification, the Federal Appraisal Subcommittee of the Federal Financial Institutions Examination Council extended the deadline to January 1, 1992. Then, in late 1991, Congress included a provision in some banking legislation that extended the deadline again, until January 1, 1993.

2. The Appraisal Foundation is a private organization made up of representatives of several appraisal groups, the largest of which is the Appraisal Institute (resulting from a merger in 1991 of the former American Institute of Real Estate Appraisers and the Society of Real Estate Appraisers).

Web Sites

http://www.hsh.com
   Housing and mortgage information

www2.cob.ilstu.edu/jwtrefz/FIL360/MORIGINA.DOC
   Loan origination, processing, and closing

MORTGAGE DEFAULT INSURANCE, FORECLOSURE, AND TITLE INSURANCE

LEARNING OBJECTIVES

After reading this chapter, you should understand the operations of three different default insurance plans: Veterans Administration (VA), Federal Housing Administration (FHA), and private mortgage insurance (PMI). You should understand the basic differences between the three insurance plans and be able to distinguish between partial insurance, full insurance, and co-insurance. You should also understand how foreclosure laws differ across states and how those laws affect mortgage insurance claims under the different insurance plans. Finally, you should understand the purpose of title insurance and appreciate the economics of the title insurance industry.

INTRODUCTION

In this chapter, we review the characteristics of default insurance, foreclosure laws, and title insurance. We begin with a description and comparison of three default insurance plans: VA, FHA, and PMI. These plans are different in terms of eligibility requirements, costs (premiums), loan limits, underwriting procedures, and coverage. Next, we will look at the foreclosure laws in various states. We will discuss the differences between judicial and power-of-sale procedures, equitable and statutory rights of redemption, and recourse and nonrecourse (antideficiency judgment) provisions. We will analyze the impact of the various foreclosure laws on default risk and on insurance claims under the coverage of the different insurance plans. We then will discuss title insurance—its purpose, nature, and cost.

MORTGAGE DEFAULT INSURANCE

The U.S. Department of Housing and Urban Development (HUD) has a number of diverse programs to support and promote housing such as: (1) insured energy-efficient loans, (2) insured loans for rehabilitation of properties, (3) insured loans for disaster victims, and (4) insured reverse annuity loans. Included in the HUD umbrella is the FHA. Since the FHA is one of the major government-sponsored mortgage default insurance programs, we will concentrate our discussion in this area.

Mortgage default insurance can take several forms. All insure the lender against losses that result from foreclosure. **Partial coverage** covers losses up to a certain percentage of the original amount of the loan. If the coverage is 20 percent, then all claims up to $20,000 on a $100,000 loan would be covered. Under **full coverage** all lender losses are covered. With **co-insurance** all losses up to a certain portion of the loan are covered. Losses above this amount are shared between the lender and the insurer in the same ratio. Thus, if the coverage ratio is 20 percent and there is a $30,000 loss on a $100,000 loan, the lender will cover $22,000 of the loss ($20,000 + 20 percent of the remainder). Later, we will see that the type of insurance affects the extent to which lenders have an incentive to control losses. The fourth type of mortgage insurance is **self-insurance**. With this insurance, lenders absorb the default risk themselves.

With respect to mortgage insurance and lenders, a couple of points should be made. First, the cost of the insurance is typically borne by either the borrower (in the case of FHA and PMI) or the federal government (VA). Second, the borrower may have no choice in carrying mortgage insurance if it is a qualifying contingency. For example, the guarantee on a VA loan is provided at no cost except for a required funding fee paid by the borrower at origination. This funding fee is not optional for the borrower. On FHA loans and loans covered by PMI, an up-front fee and a yearly premium are both paid by the borrower. Since FHA insurance covers the entire loan amount, historically the premium had to be paid by the borrower for the entire life of the loan (this has changed and will be discussed later) and payment of the premium is not optional. The same is true in general for conventional mortgages that have loan-to-value ratios greater than 80 percent; PMI is usually required.

Government-Sponsored Insurance

The two government-sponsored insurance programs are administered by the VA and the FHA. The VA is a partial insurance program; it covers losses up to a certain proportion of the loan amount. The FHA is a full insurance program; it covers all losses.

VA Insurance

VA insurance was created by the Serviceman's Readjustment Act of 1944 with Section 501 of the GI Bill of Rights. The VA was elevated to cabinet rank in 1989. The VA provides a guarantee program to assist eligible veterans and their immediate families (generally the spouse) in acquiring a home with little or no down payment. The home must be the veteran's primary residence. A veteran on overseas active duty may purchase a home as a primary residence for his or her immediate family. The VA provides default protection to the lender depending on the amount of the veteran borrower's eligibility. The VA does not protect the borrower against losses in default.

To be eligible for a VA loan, veterans must have served a minimum time on active duty. The time runs from 90 days for "hot" wars to 6 years for the reserves and National Guard. In general, service during peacetime requires 181 days of continuous active duty for eligibility. A veteran not on active duty must hold a discharge other than dishonorable. Unmarried surviving spouses of individuals who died while in service or as the result of a service-connected disability are generally eligible for a VA loan.

A Certificate of Eligibility certifies the veteran's **entitlement**, which establishes the maximum loan amount. The maximum entitlement at the inception of the program in 1944 was $2,000. As house prices have increased over the years, Congress has likewise increased the entitlement limit. Today, the veteran's basic entitlement is $36,000. For loans in excess of $144,000, however, additional entitlement up to an amount equal to 25 percent of the Freddie Mac conforming loan limit for single-family homes may be available. This loan limit can change periodically. As of 2008, the conforming loan limit is $417,000 in all states except Alaska and Hawaii.

The VA will guarantee up to 50 percent of a home loan up to $50,000. For loans between $45,000 and $144,000, the maximum guaranty is 40 percent of the loan up to $36,000. For loans greater than $144,000, the maximum guaranty is 25 percent of the Freddie Mac conforming loan limit for single-family homes. Most VA loans are handled by Ginnie Mae, which requires a 25 percent guaranty. The veteran may generally borrow an amount up to the reasonable value of the property or purchase price, plus the funding fee.

The VA guaranty provides an incentive for private lenders to make loans to veterans at favorable terms. If the borrower defaults and the lender takes a loss in foreclosure, however, the borrower may be responsible for repaying to the VA any monies paid by the VA to the lender. For loans closed on or after January 1, 1990, the defaulting borrower owes the VA money only if there was fraud, misrepresentation, or bad faith on the part of the borrower. VA loans approved prior to March 1, 1988, are fully assumable, and those approved subsequently are assumable subject to credit qualification of the buyer. For the former loans, the veteran is liable for the default of the buyer unless the veteran obtains a release of liability. For the latter loans, the buyer must assume full liability to repay the loan, including the indemnity liability of the VA. In either case, the VA loan always must have an entitlement attached to it. Thus, when a property is sold to a nonveteran, the selling veteran's entitlement remains with the property. Entitlement can only be restored by replacing it with another entitlement or by repaying the mortgage. One should note that restoration of entitlement is different from release of liability. For example, a veteran may allow the mortgage to be assumed by a nonveteran who qualifies. In this case the nonveteran could assume liability for the loan giving the veteran a release of liability. However, the veteran's entitlement would continue to be encumbered by the loan. Veterans who previously have used their entitlement may have an unused portion that they can apply to the purchase of another residence, even though the initial loan has not been paid off.

The VA guarantee entails a funding fee, which varies with the amount of down payment. For a 0 to less than 5 percent down payment, the funding fee is 2.15 percent of the loan amount. With at least 5 percent but less than 10 percent down payment, the fee is 1.5 percent; for a 10 percent or greater down payment the fee is 1.25 percent. The fee is higher for reservists/national guardsmen and for mortgage refinancings. The fee is waived for veterans entitled to compensation for service-connected disabilities. The fee may be included in the loan amount, provided the total does not exceed the VA limit. Existing single-family and two- and four-unit dwellings are eligible for insurance as long as the veteran occupies the property after the closing. New units are not eligible unless the builder has received prior approval or provides the veteran with an approved 10-year warranty.

Two or more veterans can use their entitlements to buy property together. The guaranty is based on each veteran's interest in the property but may not exceed the lesser of 40 percent of the loan amount or $36,000 ($60,000 for certain loans over $144,000). Also, a husband and wife who are both eligible can purchase property jointly but the amount of the guaranty may not exceed the lesser of 40 percent of the loan amount or $36,000 ($60,000 for certain loans over $144,000).

The VA also will guarantee qualifying graduated-payment loans. Because of the negative amortization feature, the veteran will be required to make a down payment and the rate on the loan may be slightly higher than on a standard loan. Starting in 1992, the VA has an adjustable-rate mortgage program. These are 1-year adjustables using the U.S. Treasury Bill yield index with annual and life-of-loan interest rate caps of 1 percent and 5 percent and a margin of 2.00. The VA will guarantee loans for home purchase, repair or improvement, and refinancing. This includes manufactured housing. The VA also provides refinancing loans.

Since 1992, market interest rates and discount points can be charged on VA loans. Any discount points paid by the borrower cannot be added to the loan amount. Previously, interest rates were set by the VA director and no points except the funding fee could be paid by the borrower.

Although closing costs can vary by custom across areas, the VA regulates them to some extent. For example, no commission or brokerage fees may be charged for closing a VA loan. The veteran will expect to pay reasonable closing costs that can generally include a VA appraisal, credit report, survey, title evidence, recording fees, a 1 percent origination fee, and discount points. The closing costs and origination fee cannot be included in the loan except in refinancing.

In foreclosure proceedings the VA historically paid the principal and interest due on the loan and took title to the property. With escalating foreclosures in the late 1980s the VA changed its policy to require notification of pending foreclosure. It then gets an appraisal and decides what action is in the best interest of the VA: take title to the property or simply pay the guaranty to the lender. With the latter procedure, the VA does not bid on the property at foreclosure. This leaves the lender to dispose of the property and alters the risk structure of the loan between the VA and the lender.

FHA Insurance

The Federal Housing Administration (FHA) was created by the National Housing Act in 1934 to encourage improvement in housing standards and conditions. At that time approximately two million construction workers were unemployed and a record number of home mortgages were in default. Only about 40 percent of households were homeowners and most mortgage loans were limited to 50 percent of property value and were 3- to 5-year balloon loans.

The primary function for the FHA has always been to provide a system of mutual mortgage insurance. The FHA has been part of HUD since 1965 and is completely self-supporting from insurance premiums. The mortgage insurance programs are designed to provide protection to private lenders against losses caused by defaults by borrowers. Like the VA, the FHA does not protect the borrower against losses of any kind, nor does it lend government funds directly.

Historically the FHA took title to property in foreclosure. Now its procedure is to get an appraisal and then decide whether to take title or simply pay the insurance claim and not bid at the foreclosure sale. The FHA has more than 50 different programs providing loans for homes purchases, home improvement, nursing homes, mobile home parks, and multifamily projects, among others. Along with typical mortgage financing, the FHA will make construction-to-permanent loans that can assist builders by allowing borrowers to be approved prior to construction.

Also, the FHA will do reverse mortgages allowing borrowers to convert equity into a monthly income or a line of credit. This loan is called the Home Equity Conversion Mortgage. Borrower requirements for this type loan are (1) at least 62 years of age, (2) own property, (3) occupy as principal residence, and (4) participate in a consumer information session. For this type of loan there are no income or credit qualifications and no repayment as long as the home is occupied as the principal residence by the borrower. Closing costs may be financed and financing is available for one- to four-unit properties. The mortgage amount is based on the age of the youngest borrower, the current interest rate, and the lesser of the appraised value or FHA limit. The maximum loan amount is $200,160 for a single-family home. For this loan, the FHA charges a 2 percent up-front premium and one-half of 1 percent on the outstanding balance annually.

Coverage under FHA insurance is different from the VA guarantee. The FHA insures the full amount of the loan in the event of default and foreclosure. To control risk, the FHA places a limit on the amount of the loan it will insure and underwrites the loan taking into consideration the borrower's income, credit and work history, funds available for settlement, and monthly housing expense. FHA insurance is open to any qualified resident of the United States. Citizenship is not required but the property must be the borrower's principal residence and must be located in the United States.

The contract interest rate and amount of discount points are allowed to float with the market and are negotiable with the lender. Discount points can be paid by either the buyer or the seller. Prior to November 30, 1984, the FHA had set a maximum interest rate the lender could charge and prohibited the buyer from paying the points (except for a one-point origination fee). The purpose of these limits was to protect borrowers. The reality however, was that when the market rate exceeded the pegged FHA rate, lenders charged points on FHA loans to equalize the rates. Since the borrower could not pay the points, they were charged to the seller who often raised the price of the house. This policy created such distortions in the credit market that the FHA abandoned the practice in favor of the current policy.

Loan Limits. The upper limit on the loan amount was once uniform nationally. This caused a shortage of FHA insurance in areas where housing was particularly expensive, such as Hawaii, Alaska, and portions of California. Consequently loan limits are allowed to vary depending on the cost of housing for a given area. For nonhigh-cost areas (about 2,300 counties in the United States), the limit is 48 percent of the Freddie Mac conforming loan limit. Currently the loan limits for nonhigh-cost areas are $271,050 for a single-family home, $347,000 for a two-unit property, $419,425 for a three-unit property, and $521,250 for a four-unit property.

High-cost area limits are also subject to a ceiling based on a percentage of Freddie Mac loan limits. In many high-cost areas (about 130 counties in the United States) the limit is set at 95 percent of the median house price in the Standard Metropolitan Area or county. Limits for Alaska, Guam, Hawaii, and the Virgin Islands may be adjusted up to 150 percent of loan limits to a maximum of $1,094,625 for a single-family residence. The limits are higher for multifamily properties. The FHA will finance up to four-unit properties as long as one unit is owner occupied.

Loan Assumptions. Prior to December 1, 1986, all FHA loans were simple assumptions. This meant that the buyer did not have to qualify to assume the mortgage. There was no release of liability for the seller unless requested and if the purchaser agreed to assume such liability. This remains the status of those loans. For loans originated between December 1, 1986, and December 14, 1989, assumptions made within 1 year of origination required a creditworthiness review of the persons seeking to assume the mortgage. After the initial period, the loan becomes a simple assumption. If the property is sold and the mortgage assumed, the seller remains liable for 5 years after the sale. The period was extended to 2 years if the assuming parties did not intend to occupy the residence. (Loans made to, or assumed by, nonowner-occupants are called investor loans and were eliminated in 1989.) For loans originated subsequent to December 14, 1989, a creditworthiness review is required for the entire life of the loan of all borrowers seeking to assume the loan. Nonowner-occupants (investors) may not assume any of these loans. That is, the assumptor must be an owner-occupant. With an acceptable borrower assuming the loan, the lender cannot refuse the seller a release of liability.

Refinancing. FHA loans can be refinanced, and cash can be obtained on owner-occupied properties up to 85 percent of the acquisition cost (appraised value plus closing costs). A borrower can refinance out of an insured, graduated-payment loan, but not into one. In March 1989, FHA announced its Streamline Refinance Plan (SRP) for very-high-rate mortgages (15 percent and above). Under the plan, FHA offered refinancing with little paperwork and the refinancing costs included in the new loan.

Loan-to-Value Ratios. The FHA has several loan programs, the most popular being the Section 203b program. This program insures standard 30-year, fixed-rate mortgages on one- to four-family houses. If the FHA application is accompanied by a certificate of veteran status, a discharged veteran can finance the entire value except for a $200 minimum. Otherwise a minimal down payment is required. The FHA uses the following calculations to determine the loan amount: (1) for a house with a price of $50,000 or less, 98.75 percent of the appraised value or the sale price, whichever is less; and (2) for a house with a price greater than $50,000, 97.75 percent of the lesser of appraised value or sale price. In 1991 HUD announced regulations that limited the percent of closing costs that could be financed to 57 percent.

The Section 245a program is the FHA's graduated-payment mortgage (GPM) plan. The borrower can qualify with less monthly income, but the down payment requirement is larger than the standard 203b loan because of the negative amortization. Depending on the plan selected, the payments will increase annually for 5 or 10 years and for various growth rates. Appendix 14-A compares the payments on three popular plans and the percent of the acquisition price that can be financed under the FHA GPM Plan III. As an example, for interest rates around 10 percent, the borrower must have a down payment of approximately 9 percent of the acquisition price.

Mortgage Insurance Premium. Prior to 1984 the FHA charged an annual premium (paid monthly) over the life of the loan. The annual premium was 0.5 percent of the outstanding balance. This amount was divided by 12 and added to the monthly payment. If a loan was prepaid, the borrower simply ceased to make premium payments but did not receive a refund.

From 1984 to 1991, the annual premium was dropped and the FHA charged a one-time, up-front premium only (except for loans on condominiums, which continued to have a monthly premium charged). The one-time **mortgage insurance premium (MIP)** was either paid in cash at closing or financed into the mortgage. If financed into the mortgage, the premium was 3.8 percent of the loan amount for a 30-year maturity. If paid in cash at closing, the premium was 3.661 percent.

In 1990 a new law established a phased-in reduction of the rate to a permanent 2.25 percent. This portion of the premium was renamed the up-front MIP. The permanent rate became effective in 1994. The up-front premium could be financed and was the same whether it was paid in cash or financed into the mortgage. The new law also reinstated the annual premium so that currently the FHA borrower pays both an up-front premium and an annual premium.

The amount of the reinstated annual premium is 0.50 percent of the outstanding balance. For loans originated before January 1, 2001, the length of time the premium has to be paid depends on the amount of down payment. With a loan-to-value ratio of less than 90 percent, the annual premium is assessed for the first 11 years of the loan's life. With a loan-to-value ratio of 90 through 95 percent, the premium must be paid for the full 30 years. If a mortgage has a loan-to-value ratio greater than 95 percent, the premium charge jumps to 0.60 percent and must be paid for the full life of the loan.

Beginning in April 2012, the annual premium for any loan with a term greater than 15 years is 1.20 percent if the loan has a loan-to-value ratio less than 95 percent and 1.25 percent if the loan-to-value ratio is greater than 95 percent. For 15-year loans, the annual premium is 0.35 percent (0.60 percent) if the loan-to-value ratio is greater (less) than 90 percent.

Starting January 1, 2001, the up-front premium was reduced from 2.25 percent to 1.50 percent. As of April 2012 the up-front premium is 1.75 percent. HUD also announced that for the first time new borrowers could suspend the annual premium once the mortgage is paid down to 78 percent of the purchase price. The insurance coverage would continue.

Beginning in July 2008 the FHA implemented a flexible premium pricing schedule. Up to this point, the up-front and annual premiums were the same across all borrowers, regardless of borrowers' credit standing. To treat FHA borrowers more equitably, under the new rule FHA's up-front insurance premium ranges from 1.25 percent to 2.25 percent with the lower premiums preserved for the least risky borrowers with strong credit histories.

Since the up-front premium is a lump-sum payment that covers the life of the loan, it is subject to a partial refund when a loan is prepaid. The FHA calculates the refund using a scale based on the number of years the loan has been outstanding. There is no refund if the loan is assumed.

At the end of 2012, massive losses from defaults on loans written during the housing bubble increased the likelihood of a taxpayer subsidy for the mortgage insurer. As of September 2012, the FHA faced a deficit of over $16 billion on its $1.1 trillion insured portfolio of mortgages. A bailout from the U.S. Treasury would be a first for FHA in its 78-year history. Partial blame for its financial woes could be placed on inflated house price resulting from the practice (banned since 2009) of sellers making down payments for buyers/borrowers.

The Rural Housing Service

The Rural Housing Service (formerly the Farmers Home Administration) has a guaranteed housing loan program. The program is designed to provide mortgage financing for rural areas. The program provides financing for new home loans, for construction-to-permanent loans, and loans to purchase existing homes, including repairs/improvements. Typical advantages of this program are (1) 100 percent loan-to-value ratio, (2) no mortgage insurance, (3) closing costs and the guarantee fee can be financed in many cases, (4) conventional appraisals are used, (5) not limited to first-time home buyers, and (6) 29 percent and 41 percent payment-to-income ratios. The program does impose some restrictions such as no swimming pools are allowed and financing does not cover manufactured homes. There is also a limit on the maximum loan amount.

One example of a Rural Housing Service loan is its Section 502 loan, which is primarily designed to help low-income individuals or households purchase homes in rural areas. Funds can be used to build, repair, renovate or relocate a home, or to purchase and prepare sites, including providing water and sewage facilities. To be eligible, applicants must have an income of less than 115 percent of the median income for the area and must be without adequate housing.

Private Mortgage Insurance

Private mortgage insurance (PMI) is provided by private companies that insure the lender against losses caused by borrower default. PMI plays a vital role in mortgage lending by protecting the lender against losses if the borrower defaults on the loan and by enabling borrowers with less cash for a down payment to have greater access to homeownership.

The industry dates to the early 1900s when title companies would acquire and resell mortgages—sort of a small secondary market. To make the market work, the loans were sold with a guarantee of payment as well as a guarantee of title. By the time of the Great Depression, there were hundreds of mortgage guaranty firms. Many of the firms were undercapitalized. Years of rising real estate values insulated them from default risk. The Depression years created a tremendous number of defaults, and many mortgage insurance companies failed and were unable to honor their commitments.

The widespread failure of the mortgage insurance companies was one of the motivations for the creation of FHA insurance during the Depression. Then, after World War II, the FHA insurance program was joined by the VA program. Both government programs were aimed at low- to moderate-income home buyers and placed limits on the amount of the loan. Bureaucratic rules also led to delays in processing on occasion. Because of the limitations of government insurance, conventional loans occupied a significant part of the mortgage market.

Private mortgage insurance reemerged in the late 1950s in Wisconsin with the formation of the Mortgage Guaranty Insurance Corporation. Other firms followed, and by the 1970s, there were a dozen or so large and mostly well-capitalized firms offering mortgage insurance. The restructured industry was based on solid capital requirements. Although PMIs are regulated by individual state agencies, all states require that insurers hold large reserves for possible losses. In addition to reserves for normal losses, PMIs must maintain a reserve sufficient to weather a severe economic recession or catastrophic depression.

COVERAGE

In general, PMI covers the top portion of the loan where the down payment is less than 20 percent. The lower the down payment, the greater the amount of coverage required. Coverage under a typical PMI policy is as follows. Assume the lender desires coverage for the amount of the loan in excess of 75 percent of the value of the property. The minimum mortgage insurance **coverage ratio** that will accomplish this is:

$$Coverage\ ratio = \frac{Mortgage\ balance - (0.75 \times Value)}{Mortgage\ balance} \qquad \text{(Equation 14-1)}$$

In the case of a \$90,000 mortgage on a \$100,000 house, the coverage would be

Coverage Ratio = (\$90,000 − \$75,000)/\$90,000 = 16.67% or 17%, *rounded*.

A typical claim with 17 percent coverage might appear as follows:

Principal balance due	\$ 88,915
Accumulated interest	7,900
Attorneys' fees	2,400[a]
Property taxes	1,040
Hazard insurance	650
Maintenance expense	360
Other foreclosure costs	200
Subtotal	101,465
Less rent received	1,300
Total claim	\$100,165

[a]*In most policies, the attorneys' fees are limited to 3 percent of the principal balance, plus accumulated interest.*

If the insurer believes that the property could be sold for more than \$100,165 after additional holding and transaction costs, the insurer will pay the claim and take possession of the house. If house prices are depressed, which is likely to be the case when borrowers default, the insurer will elect to pay the amount of the insurance, \$17,028 (\$100,165 × 0.17). This means that the lender could sell the property for \$83,137 (\$100,165 − \$17,028) after transaction costs and not suffer a loss.

The co-insurance factor provides an incentive for lenders to try to mitigate losses as much as possible, since, after they reach the limit, they share the bulk of additional default losses. Each PMI company has what is called a master policy, which governs the terms and conditions of the individual insurance policies. These master policies contain additional provisions intended to control losses. The following are some typical provisions.

- The lender shall pursue whatever foreclosure process is the quickest, unless the procedure precludes the possibility of pursuing a deficiency judgment (see the following for state foreclosure laws).
- Voluntary conveyance of title, or a deed-in-lieu-of-foreclosure, is encouraged, so as to avoid the legal expense of a foreclosure. Also, in many states a foreclosure action entitles the borrower to a lengthy period during which the property can be redeemed, and during which the borrower may be entitled to occupy the property rent free.
- Attorneys' fees are limited to 3 percent of the total claim (this prevents lenders from running up legal expenses for any attorney "friends"). Additional attorneys' fees are allowed if they are required to pursue a deficiency judgment against the borrower.
- Since the insurance company may reserve a right of subrogation (if allowed by state law, the insurer can pursue the borrower under any rights the lender has but does not exercise), the lender is not to undertake any action that would diminish the company's legal ability to seek compensation (if it does, a claim can be denied).
- The lender must make any repairs on the property to bring it to a condition that existed at the time the policy was taken out. This prevents the lender from neglecting the property to the detriment of the insurer. If the

repairs are not made, a claim cannot be filed. Only normal maintenance expenses can be included in the claim; major repairs are disallowed. So if the lender has allowed the property to deteriorate, repairs must be made prior to a claim being filed, and the cost of repairs cannot be included in the claim.

Figure 14-1 shows the procedures for the filing and resolution of a claim to a mortgage insurer (MI). For example, a loan is considered in default after three or four monthly payments have been missed. At that time, the lender must file a notice of default with the insurance company. If the loan is not brought current by the borrower, then the lender will seek to take title to the property, either through foreclosure or voluntary conveyance. After title is obtained, the lender will either sell the property for more than the amount of debt (there is no loss), sell the property for less than the amount of debt and submit a claim to the MI, or not sell the property but submit a preliminary claim. In the latter case, the MI will have two options—to pay the lender the percentage of the liability

FIGURE 14-1	**Claims Cycle**

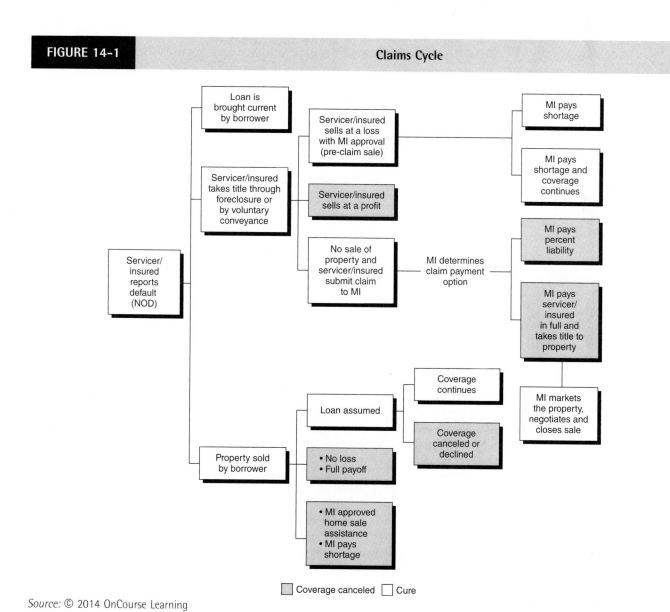

Source: © 2014 OnCourse Learning

established by the policy or to pay the claim in full and take title to and sell the property.

Fee Structure

The fee structure for PMI is somewhat different from that of government insurance. With PMI there is a relatively small up-front fee and an annual charge. If, after some years, the lender decides not to renew the policy, the annual fees cease. This fee structure has caused problems for the PMI industry. First, there is an adverse selection problem. What this means is that lenders have a tendency to cancel mortgage insurance on loans that, after the fact, turn out not to be risky. Local property prices may have risen significantly, for example. If loans continue to be risky, lenders continue to keep the policy in force by making payments (insurance companies cannot cancel insurance). Thus, after a period of time, insurance companies lose business on the good loans, but keep it on the more risky ones. Second, since the insurance can be canceled at any time, lenders may switch insurance companies if they feel that the claims-paying ability of a company is threatened by heavy losses or insolvency. Despite the heavy capitalization in the industry, several PMI companies failed in the mid- to late 1980s as a result of recessions in portions of the country and the tendency for lenders to switch policies away from financially weak insurance companies.

Comparison of Government and Private Mortgage Insurance Programs

Table 14-1 provides a summary of the similarities and differences between the FHA, VA, and PMI. The government programs have restrictions on the size of the loan that is insured, whereas PMIs do not. Although PMIs dominate the high-priced end of the mortgage insurance market, they still compete with FHA and VA insurance in the moderate price range. The VA has a modified co-insurance feature to the extent that all losses above the insured amount are absorbed by the lender. PMI companies engage in locational underwriting and can charge different premiums according to the risk of the loan, particularly the loan-to-value ratio. While the FHA insurance program charges annual premiums based on the loan-to-value ratio, the VA has a one-time, uniform, up-front fee. Both make insurance available irrespective of the location of the property.

TABLE 14-1

Mortgage Insurance Comparison

	FHA	VA	PMI
Limit on size of loan	Yes	Yes	No
Co-insurance feature	No	Modified	Yes
Uniform premium	Yes	N/A	No
Underwriting	No	No	Yes
Very low down payment loans	Yes	Yes	No
Fee structure	Partial up-front and annual	Up-front one-time	Partial up-front and annual
Available for new houses	Yes	Generally no	Yes

Source: © 2014 OnCourse Learning

As stated earlier, PMI firms charge an initial fee plus an annual charge. If the lender drops insurance, the PMI premium stops.

With both FHA insurance and PMI, the premium is canceled when the mortgage is paid in full. The Homeowners Protection Act of 1998 requires lenders to cancel the PMI coverage automatically when the loan-to-value ratio reaches 78 percent. Borrowers after July 29, 1999, can request that PMI be canceled once the loan-to-value ratio reaches 80 percent of the original property value. The Mortgage Insurance Companies of America estimates that about 1 million home buyers obtain PMI annually. The automatic cancellation does not apply to existing loans but existing homeowners have to be notified of their right to cancel.

The information that lenders must disclose to borrowers depends on the type of mortgage—fixed-rate or adjustable. For fixed-rate mortgages, the lender must provide to the borrower (1) a description of the borrower's right to cancel once the loan-to-value ratio reaches 80 percent (based on amortization or prepayments) and automatic cancellation at 78 percent loan-to-value ratio, (2) an amortization schedule showing the point at which the borrower can request cancellation and the date of automatic cancellation, and (3) information on whether this loan is a high-risk exception. In this case the insurance will be canceled no later than the loan's midway point. On a 30-year loan, this would be 15 years. For an adjustable-rate loan, the lender must provide to the borrower (1) a notice of right to cancel at the 80 percent loan-to-value ratio and that the lender will notify the borrower at this point, (2) a notice that the insurance will be automatically canceled at the 78 percent loan-to-value ratio, and (3) a notice of whether this loan is a high-risk exception.

Thus the law provides borrowers obtaining mortgages on or after July 29, 1999, two avenues for terminating mortgage insurance: requesting cancellation after 20 percent equity has been achieved and automatic cancellation at 22 percent equity. While automatic termination is based solely on the mortgage's initial amortization schedule, the law does require prepayments to be considered for borrower-initiated cancellation. The law does not require property value appreciation to be taken into account but it does not prohibit it either. Other requirements for cancellation other than the loan-to-value ratio are as follows: the borrower has not been more than 30 days late on a payment in the last 12 months or more than 60 days late in the past 24 months and the property value has not declined from its original value and there are no subordinate liens.

A new type of financing arrangement provides a way for borrowers to avoid paying PMI. This is the "piggyback" loan that stacks a small second mortgage on top of a primary mortgage. Because this arrangement is usually designed with an 80 percent first mortgage, 10 percent second mortgage, and a 10 percent down payment, they are often referred to as 80-10-10s. Other variations are also available. The primary mortgage is typically sold to Fannie Mae or Freddie Mac. The borrower not only has the advantage of not having to pay the insurance premium but the interest on the second mortgage is tax deductible and there is a faster buildup of equity. This type of financing can also be advantageous in purchasing higher-priced homes where the lender may restrict the loan-to-value ratio to 80 percent. However, with mortgage insurance premiums becoming tax-deductible starting in 2007, the borrower may find it more advantageous to pay the mortgage insurance than to get a piggyback loan.

The Housing/Mortgage Crisis and the Subprime Mortgage Market

The housing and mortgage crisis that started when the housing bubble burst in 2007 has been blamed on a number of factors. Because of these various factors, the borrowing power of the typical household in the United States increased substantially over the first half of the 2000s decade. These factors included low (and sometimes falling) interest rates, lenders willing to allow much higher debt-to-income ratios, interest-only mortgages, and low/no down payment loans. For example, in 2001 only one percent of new mortgages were interest-only. By 2005 this percentage had increased to almost 30 percent. Likewise, in 1989 the average down payment for a homebuyer was 20 percent and had declined to 12.24 percent by 2012.

The increase in borrowing power and the decline in lending standards resulted in increased demand for housing and rapidly increasing house prices. With this new-found wealth, households borrowed heavily against the equity in their homes. As a result, by the mid-2000s the average percentage of equity in homes had fallen below 50 percent for the first time since 1945.

The housing price bubble has been blamed on a number of factors. Some pointed to politicians and regulators as being blinded by the market ideology of "everyone a homeowner." Others blamed greedy speculators and others blamed regulators for keeping interest rates low. Still others pointed to the vast amount of money to be made and blamed mortgage lenders, real estate brokers, real estate appraisers, Wall Street investment firms, and ratings agencies. Whatever the case, by well into 2008 the mortgage delinquency rate had risen to 10 percent, housing inventories were up, and vacancies were at an all-time high. By the end of 2008, it was estimated that 16 percent of homeowners were "underwater" or owed more on their mortgage than the value of the house. Subprime mortgages and option adjustable-rate mortgages (ARMs) were even worse at 50 percent and 65 percent negative equity, respectively.

At its simplest, subprime lending is described as nonprime lending. This translates to high-cost lending due to risk and is generally associated with two characteristics: credit history of borrowers and down payment requirements. In the United States, a subprime mortgage is typically thought of as a loan that does not meet Fannie Mae or Freddie Mac requirements. Historically subprime mortgages have had lower loan-to-value ratios than prime loans, typically no more than 70 percent. Subprime lenders understood the risk of these loans and sought to protect themselves as much as possible against loss. With the housing boom in the mid-2000s, however, lenders relaxed subprime mortgages underwriting standards three ways: (1) writing subprime loans with very high loan-to-value ratios, (2) writing loans with very little or no documentation of the borrower's ability to pay, and (3) offering adjustable-rate loans with large built-in increases in monthly payment after 2 or 3 years.

Subprime loans generally have both higher upfront fees and ongoing costs relative to prime loans. A subprime loan has higher costs and is written at a higher interest rate than a prime loan due to the perceived risk of default. Although subprime loans were relatively rare before the mid-1990s, their use increased dramatically over the next decade, especially during the housing boom from 2002 through 2006, as an increasing number of households with less-than-stellar credit and limited wealth sought to become homeowners. Over the period 2004 to 2006, mortgage lenders made $1.5 trillion in high-interest loans. Most of these were subprime loans. For comparison, in 1994 the subprime market was one percent of the total mortgage market. By 2006, subprime mortgages made up 14 percent of total mortgages. The market expected interest re-sets on $362 billion of adjustable-rate subprime mortgages in 2008.

The subprime market was not reserved, however, for just weaker-credit borrowers. In 2005, 55 percent of subprime mortgages were originated by borrowers with credit scores high enough to qualify for prime loans. As of 2007 the value of subprime mortgages was estimated at $1.3 trillion with about 7.5 million subprime mortgages outstanding. The share of subprime mortgages to total originations was 5 percent in 1994 but had increased to 20 percent by 2006. Common features of subprime mortgages have been interest-only payments, pay option loans with adjustable rates, and hybrid mortgages with initial fixed rates that convert to adjustable rates after some initial period. For example, a popular hybrid has been the 2/28 loan, which offers a low fixed rate for the first 2 years then converts to a 1-year adjustable for the next 28 years.

Subprime lending became a controversial topic in the mid-2000s. Proponents argued that this segment of the mortgage market is essential for providing credit to borrowers who would otherwise have no access to credit and this served as a means for less creditworthy borrowers to become homeowners and create wealth. Opponents argued that some lenders have used the subprime mortgage market to target borrowers who could not fully understand the contract to which they were being obligated. Lenders were accused of writing contracts with exorbitant fees and with obscure terms and conditions.

Chomsisengphet and Pennington-Cross describe the evolution of subprime lending in the mortgage market.[1] They discuss that, although it can provide homeownership opportunities for an otherwise deprived set of borrowers, this type of lending can be risky for both borrower and lender. Their preliminary evidence shows that the probability of default is at least six times higher for subprime loans than prime loans. For example, although subprime ARMs represent only 6.8 percent of total mortgages they represented 43 percent of foreclosures started during the third quarter of 2007. They point out that subprime borrowers are also less likely to take advantage of lower rates by refinancing.

Chomsisengphet and Pennington-Cross show that the rate of securitization of subprime mortgages by the financial markets increased steadily starting in 1995. In 1995, 28.4 percent of subprime mortgages were securitized. By 2003, this percentage had risen to 58.7 percent. In 2006 $1.9 trillion of the $2.5 trillion in total mortgage originations that year were securitized. About 25 percent of these mortgage-backed securities were collateralized by subprime loans. Only about one-fourth of the subprime mortgages originated in 2006 were not securitized. As subprime woes increased in 2007, some of the major Wall Street firms were required to take substantial write downs on subprime mortgages and mortgage securities such as collateralized debt obligations.

STATE FORECLOSURE LAWS

The following discussion of state foreclosure laws will provide a background to assess the riskiness of the different mortgage insurance programs.

Foreclosure

Foreclosure is a legal process by which the property that serves as collateral on a loan is sold. Foreclosure takes place when the borrower defaults on the contractual obligations of the loan, usually by failing to make the required payments. Through the foreclosure process, the lender exercises his power to sell the property. In each state the process is governed by the terms of the loan contract and applicable state law. State laws differ in terms of the procedure that is permitted or mandated. State laws differ in three principal areas: procedures, redemption rights, and deficiency judgments.

Procedure

The two methods by which mortgaged property is sold in satisfaction of a defaulted obligation are foreclosure by judicial procedure and foreclosure by power-of-sale. In a limited number of states there is also a "strict foreclosure," which does not involve the sale of the property.

In a **judicial procedure foreclosure**, the lender must proceed through the courts to get a judgment against the borrower and a court order authorizing the sale of the property by an officer of the court. All states allow a judicial procedure, but in about half of the states, it is the only process permitted. All requirements for advertising the sale and giving notice to the appropriate parties are established by the statutes of each state. After the sale, a confirmation report is made to the court that ordered the sale. Then an officer of the court records and delivers the deed to the new owner and gives the proceeds of the sale, less court costs, to the lender(s) in order of their priority. Second and successive lien holders are paid after each prior lien holder has been paid in full. Any excess is given to the former owner (borrower). The priority of payment—court costs, lien holders in order, and the former owner—is mandated by the Uniform Land Transaction Act, to which most states adhere. If the proceeds of the sale are insufficient to pay court costs plus the amount due the lender(s), a deficiency results. As long as a state does not prohibit it, a deficiency judgment will be entered against the borrower for the amount of the deficiency. Because the foreclosure proceeds through the court, it generally results in a title that is solidly marketable. However, the procedure is often complicated, costly, and time-consuming. Just getting the case heard may take considerable time. In the meantime, the expenses associated with maintaining the property fall on the lender.

An alternative procedure allowed in many states is the **power-of-sale foreclosure**. The sale of the property can take place without a court order if the terms of the mortgage confer on the lender the right to sell the property in the event of a default. In such cases, there will most likely be a deed-of-trust held by a trustee. It is the duty of the trustee to make sure that the rights of both parties are protected and that there is no foreclosure sale without evidence of a default. The trustee is usually an attorney or bank. State laws protect the borrower by requiring that the sale be held at public auction and that ample notice of the sale be given. Proceeds of the sale go first to the cost of conducting the sale, including the reasonable costs of securing and holding the property, next to the amount of indebtedness, and, finally, any excess goes to the borrower.

If the proceeds from the sale are insufficient to cover the amount of the debt, the lender will have to initiate a court action to secure a deficiency judgment. Many states, however, require that a judicial procedure be used to obtain a deficiency judgment, denying it in the case of a power-of-sale foreclosure. The power-of-sale procedure is much quicker and less costly than the judicial procedure and is the preferred method in cases where it is permitted.

Equitable and Statutory Rights of Redemption

In all states a mortgagor who defaults on the loan may prevent the foreclosure sale by paying the full amount of the outstanding debt, including any back interest and expenses incurred by the lender. This is called the **equitable right of redemption.** The mortgagor can get a recordable release to clear the title. The equitable right of redemption is terminated by the foreclosure sale. The Uniform Land Transactions

Act limits the borrower's right to cure a default to once every 12 months. A defaulted borrower may sell his or her equitable right of redemption. The purchaser will then cure the loan and assume its liability.

A **statutory right of redemption** is the right of the borrower to regain the property lost in a foreclosure sale. The statutory right of redemption commences with the foreclosure sale or the termination of the equitable right of redemption. Not all states provide for statutory redemption. Two dozen or so states do. State statute determines the length of redemption, which varies between 1 and 18 months. The right is transferable. In a few states, the redemption period is available only if the foreclosure was by power-of-sale. The cost to redeem the property during this period is usually the amount paid at the sale plus interest and expenses (determined by the statute).

Some argue that the statutory right of redemption results in a weak title at foreclosure and discourages many from bidding at the sale of the property and thus increases the cost (loss) to the lender.

Deficiency Judgments

A **deficiency judgment** is a court-ordered judgment against the borrower for the difference between the value of the property (at foreclosure sale) and the amount of indebtedness (including delinquent interest and foreclosure costs).

Prompted by the large losses during the Great Depression, several states passed antideficiency legislation. Often, in a depressed real estate market, the only bidder at a sale of the property would be the lender. The lender would end up with the property and a judgment against the borrower. This appeared unfair to many. Antideficiency judgment legislation addressed this apparent inequity. Some states adopted modified antideficiency judgment legislation, whereby the amount of the deficiency was limited. In such cases, the amount was limited to the difference between the amount of the indebtedness and the fair market value of the property (not what the lender bid). The fair market value in such cases is determined by the court. Other states disallow a deficiency judgment if the lender bids at the sale of the property. Antideficiency legislation typically does not allow the borrower to waive this right in the mortgage contract.

Table 14-2 summarizes foreclosure procedures by state. Some additional subtle differences are not indicated in the table. For example, some states may apply somewhat different rules to residences located on certain size parcels of land.

Default Risk, Mortgage Insurance, and State Foreclosure Laws

Default risk on residential loans is often measured in terms of any negative equity in the property at the time of default. The presumed loss on a $100,000 loan when the property value is $90,000 is $10,000. The actual loss on a defaulted loan is much greater than the negative equity, however. When a lender forecloses on a property, significant costs arise. The cost of foreclosing and liquidating properties can be divided into three categories: transaction costs, property costs, and opportunity costs. Transaction costs include those involved with the foreclosure: attorneys' fees, trustee's fees, sheriff's cost of sale, broker's commission, title charges, and so forth. Property costs include those fees incurred by the lender to carry the property until liquidated: property taxes, hazard insurance, utilities, and repairs and maintenance. Opportunity costs include interest foregone on the investment value of the property.

TABLE 14-2

Comparison of Foreclosure Aspects by State

STATE	PREDOMINANT METHOD OF FORECLOSURE	MONTHS TO COMPLETE INITIAL ACTION	STATUTORY RIGHT OF REDEMPTION
ALABAMA	Power of sale	2	12 mo.
ALASKA	Power of sale	3	None (A)
ARIZONA	Power of sale	4	None (B)
ARKANSAS	Power of sale	5	None (C)
CALIFORNIA	Power of sale	5	None (A)
COLORADO	Power of sale	2	2.5 mo. (D)
CONNECTICUT	Strict foreclosure	6	None (E)
DELAWARE	Judicial	9	None
DIST. OF COLUMBIA	Power of sale	2	None
FLORIDA	Judicial	6	None
GEORGIA	Power of sale	1	None
HAWAII	Judicial (F)	6	None (F)
IDAHO	Judicial (G)	6	6 mo. (G)
ILLINOIS	Judicial	6	6 mo. (H,I)
INDIANA	Judicial	7	3 mo. (J,K)
IOWA	Judicial	6	6 mo. (L)
KANSAS	Judicial	4	12 mo. (M)
KENTUCKY	Judicial	9	None (N)
LOUISIANA	Judicial	4	None
MAINE	Entry & possession	1	12 mo.
MARYLAND	Power of sale	2	None
MASSACHUSETTS	Power of sale	9	None
MICHIGAN	Power of sale	4	6 mo. (O)
MINNESOTA	Power of sale	3	6 mo. (P)
MISSISSIPPI	Power of sale	1	None
MISSOURI	Power of sale	2	None (Q)
MONTANA	Power of sale (R)	1	None (R)
NEBRASKA	Judicial	7	None (J,S)
NEVADA	Power of sale	5	None (T)
NEW HAMPSHIRE	Power of sale	2	None
NEW JERSEY	Judicial	6	None (U)
NEW MEXICO	Judicial	6	1 mo. (V)
NEW YORK	Judicial	8	None
NORTH CAROLINA	Power of sale	1	None
NORTH DAKOTA	Judicial	3	6 mo. (L)
OHIO	Judicial	8	None
OKLAHOMA	Judicial	6	None (W)
OREGON	Power of sale	9	None (X)
PENNSYLVANIA	Judicial	6	None
RHODE ISLAND	Power of sale	1	None
SOUTH CAROLINA	Judicial	5	None (U)
SOUTH DAKOTA	Judicial	6	6 mo. (L,Y,Z)
TENNESSEE	Power of sale	1	None (C)
TEXAS	Power of sale	1	None
UTAH	Power of sale	5	3 mo. (J,A1)
VERMONT	Strict foreclosure	1	6 mo. (A2)
VIRGINIA	Power of sale	2	None
WASHINGTON	Power of sale	1 (A3)	None
WEST VIRGINIA	Power of sale	2	None
WISCONSIN	Power of sale (A1)	3	12 mo. (A1)
WYOMING	Power of sale (A1)	3	3 mo. (A1)

TABLE 14–2
(Continued)

Notes:	
(A)	Deed-of-trust. However, if there is a judicial foreclosure, there is a 12-month redemption period.
(B)	Judicial foreclosure under mortgage is also available. Time to complete would be 4 months followed by a 6-month redemption. However, if property was abandoned, the redemption can be reduced to 1 month if so stated in the decree.
(C)	Provided redemption rights have been expressly waived in the security instrument; if no waiver, redemption period is 12 months in Arkansas, 24 months in Tennessee.
(D)	Redemption period is 5 months on security instruments executed before July 1, 1965.
(E)	Redemption (law date) depends entirely on the equity in the property. If little or no equity exists, there is a 30-day law date prior to completion; otherwise, length is determined by the court.
(F)	Foreclosure by power of sale on entry and possession also available under deed-of-trust.
(G)	For properties of more than 20 acres, redemption is 12 months. Power-of-sale foreclosure also available under trust deed.
(H)	Statute permits both strict foreclosure (where value of property does not exceed 90% of debt) and foreclosure with consent of the mortgagor; in either case, the foreclosure sale is eliminated, the mortgagee waives deficiency judgment, and the decree vests title directly in the mortgagee subject to a 3-month redemption period.
(I)	Redemption is 6 months for sale if the judgment date is after January 1, 1982 (previously was 12 months from date of service).
(J)	The redemption period precedes sale in Indiana, Nebraska (court stays sale on mortgagor's request), Oklahoma (without court appraisement), Wisconsin (if judicial foreclosure is used), and Utah (if foreclosure is by power of sale). In Nebraska redemption can be only between day of sale and confirmation of sale.
(K)	On security instruments executed before July 1, 1975, redemption period is 6 months before sale; time to complete is then 10 months with a 12-month transfer time.
(L)	If security instruments specifically provide for 6-month redemption, period is 12 months. For Iowa, if the property was abandoned, redemption can be reduced to 2 months.
(M)	Provided no suit is instituted for deficiency, redemption period is reduced to 6 months in cases of abandoned property or on purchase money mortgages with less than a third down.
(N)	If foreclosure sale brings less than two-thirds of appraised value (court appraiser), there is a 12-month redemption period.
(O)	Redemption period is 12 months on security instruments dated prior to January 1, 1965. Redemption may be reduced if the property was abandoned.
(P)	If deed is executed after July 1, 1967, the redemption is 6 months provided the deficiency judgment was waived.
(Q)	Within 10 days after sale, mortgagor may give notice of intention to redeem, including security deposit for taxes, interest, etc.; the redemption period is then 12 months.
(R)	For estates of more than 15 acres, a mortgage is used and foreclosed judicially, 1 year redemption.
(S)	Foreclosure by power of sale is available under a deed of trust, effective 1965. Time of completion then would be 3 months; no redemption following sale.
(T)	Judicial foreclosure is available under a mortgage with a 12-month redemption following the sale.
(U)	Provided no suit is instituted for deficiency; otherwise, redemption is 6 months. In South Carolina, the redemption is 1 month if a deficiency judgment was obtained.
(V)	Provided mortgage specifically calls for shorter redemption period; otherwise, redemption period is 6 months.
(W)	Provided sale is with court appraisement; otherwise, there is a 6-month redemption period preceding the sale.
(X)	If security instrument was executed prior to May 26, 1959, judicial foreclosure is necessary with a 12-month redemption period following sale.
(Y)	Foreclosure by power of sale with service is also available for properties of less than 40 acres.
(Z)	Redemption period can be extended to 24 months upon filing of affidavit to mortgagor, including provision of accruing taxes, interest, etc.
(A1)	Judicial foreclosure is also available. If used, the 6-month redemption period precedes the sale. In Utah the 6-month redemption would follow the sale. In Wyoming a 3-month redemption follows the sale plus 30 days for successive lien holders.
(A2)	For mortgages executed after April 1, 1968, the redemption period is 6 months from date of judgment unless a shorter period is granted per the complaint. Redemption is 12 months for mortgages executed before April 1, 1968.
(A3)	Loan must be in default at least 120 days before day fixed for sale.

Source: Mortgage Bankers Association, a State Legislative Compilation.

The longer and more costly the foreclosure procedure, the greater these costs will be. An early study done for the Federal Home Loan Bank Board found that the loss on a defaulted loan as a percent of the loan balance was as little as 6.4 percent in states with quick and inexpensive foreclosure procedures and as great as 53 percent in states with lengthy and expensive procedures.[2] Clauretie found that the average loss suffered by the FHA on foreclosed loans in Illinois from 1972 through 1988 was $25,316.[3] Illinois law requires a judicial procedure and provides a statutory right of redemption. The average loss in the neighboring state of Michigan, for the same period, was $15,847. Michigan allows a power-of-sale foreclosure. Thus, it appears that the risk of default comes not only from a decline in property prices that might produce negative equity, but also from the cost of the foreclosure and property liquidation process. Some state laws facilitate the process, while others create an economic burden on the lender.

A process that helps contain costs would allow a power-of-sale foreclosure and provide for no statutory right of redemption. By shortening the process, the power-of-sale provision reduces the carrying costs, foregone interest, and opportunity costs. Bidding should be more rigorous at the liquidation sale if there is no statutory right of redemption. Laws that provide for deficiency judgments also should reduce default losses. Lenders can pursue a judgment to reduce losses.

Even if the borrower lacks funds to pay the full amount of the deficiency judgment, a threat of its use by the lender may suggest a settlement, which, to some extent, reduces the loss. In short, lenders can liquidate the property quickly, obtain a better price, and pursue the borrower for deficiencies in states with laws that are favorable to the lender.

Lender–Insurer Incentive Conflicts

Because most residential loans are insured by either government agencies or by private companies, the risk of loss from default and foreclosure becomes a concern of the insurers as well. Moreover, the form of the insurance contract, in combination with various state laws, may affect the risk exposure of the insurer.

This risk results from any incentive provided by the insurance contract for the lender to control foreclosure costs. Consider, for example, that the FHA provides full coverage for losses, while PMI is a co-insurance relationship. Since all losses are covered under FHA insurance, lenders would have no incentive to either pursue the most expeditious foreclosure process or a deficiency judgment. Under PMI, however, lenders share a portion of the loss in excess of the coverage ratio. They will have an incentive to foreclose quickly, if they have a choice of procedure (judicial versus power-of-sale) and will pursue a deficiency judgment. There is some evidence that this is exactly what occurs. Clauretie and Herzog analyzed the risk faced by mortgage insurers in terms of dollar losses from claims per dollar insured.[4] The average loss rate for PMIs from 1980 through 1987 was 1.2 percent. The loss rate varied by state, from a low of 0 in Hawaii (1980) to a high of 9.75 in Wyoming (1987).

Some of the variation was due to local economic conditions, but much was due to differences in state foreclosure laws. The authors found that the PMI loss rates were 12 percent and 25 percent higher in states that required a judicial procedure and mandated a statutory right of redemption, respectively. Losses were reduced by 29 percent in states that allowed a deficiency judgment. For FHA loans, the judicial procedure and statutory right of redemption increased the loss rate by 60 percent and 65 percent, respectively. FHA losses were not affected by the presence of a deficiency judgment. This would be expected since lenders have no incentive to pursue these judgments under FHA insurance.

TITLE INSURANCE

Real estate property is exchanged through a transfer of the title to the property. Title conveys legal rights to the use of the property from the seller to the buyer. The buyer desires to have a bundle of legal rights to the property that is as unencumbered as possible. Government may always restrict or deny certain property rights through its police powers. Examples include the ability to restrict the use of the property through zoning ordinances, the right to take the property for public purposes (eminent domain or expropriation), the need to require that all or portions of the property be used for public services (easements for utilities, for example), and the right to place taxes on property for revenue generation. Beyond these government powers, however, the buyer desires an unencumbered and "clear" title, free from restrictions by private parties.

Title insurance is obtained at the point at which property is transferred. It insures against the risk that clear title may not be transferred to the buyer. It does not insure against any loss that may result from government restriction of property rights, such as zoning legislation or eminent domain. Title insurance involves a **title search**, a process that reviews each transfer of title to the property throughout its history. The search reviews public records for occasions where clear title to property may not have been transferred. Most people think that clear title to property may be endangered by some ancient event in the history of the property. They envision the discovery of a document that shows there was a fraudulent transfer by an unscrupulous long-lost relative sometime in the 1800s, or that an ancient treaty with Native Americans was misinterpreted, or a land grant from an early Spanish king was never really made. They look on title insurance as protection against such claims. Although title insurance may cover such events, that is not the primary purpose of a title search or title insurance. Most failures of a transfer of clear title occur as a result of much more recent events.

Another common misconception that some people have is that title insurance is generally not necessary. They reason that if the seller of the property had a title search and received clear title when he or she purchased the property, then the title must still be unencumbered. Nothing could be further from the truth. Most encumbrances or obstacles to a transfer of clear title are recent and subsequent to the last transfer. The most obvious is a mortgage (deed-of-trust) that exists because the present owner financed the purchase of the real estate. But other encumbrances also may exist. There may be a second mortgage, taken out subsequent to the last transfer of the property. There may be a **lien** on the property as a result of the failure of the present owner to pay local property taxes. The Internal Revenue Service may have placed a lien on the property if the owner has not paid his federal income taxes. There could be a mechanic's lien on the property if the owner had repairs or additions made and did not pay the contractor. There may even be a lien for failure to pay water or sewerage bills. Furthermore, these liens can appear quite quickly on the property. A title search is designed to discover these encumbrances. They will be listed on a preliminary title search and must be removed (generally by paying them off) when title is transferred.

When property is transferred, a search of the title takes place and a title insurance policy is issued. There is a standard policy, called the **American Land Title Association (ALTA)** that is used nationally by the dozen or so national title insurance companies. That policy insures the lender and the new owner separately against certain losses.

Both parties are insured for losses if (1) title to the property is vested with the wrong party; (2) a lien or encumbrance remains after the transfer; (3) title is unmarketable; (4) the land physically abuts one or more streets, yet the owner fails to receive ordinary access rights; (5) the mortgage is unenforceable; (6) the lien of the mortgage is shown incorrectly as far as its order of priority; or (7) an assignment of the mortgage is invalid.

If a property is purchased without financing (all cash), the new owner does not have to purchase title insurance. He can assume the risk. If he does purchase insurance, it will involve an "owner's policy." In this case, only items (1) through (4) previously listed will be covered. The amount of the coverage can vary up to the value of the property. Owner's policies will not cover any losses that result from liens on the property known to exist prior to the sale. In other words, if a lien on the property is discovered by the title search and it is not removed on transfer of title, the title insurance will not insure against any loss that results from the lien. Liens discovered through the title search will be listed as "exceptions" on the insurance policy; that is, they are not covered. Although this does not appear to be fair to the property buyer, note that he or she will have recourse to the conveyer (title transfer company or attorney) if clear title is not transferred. So, if the conveyer makes a search of the title, discovers a lien, transfers title, and does not cause the lien to be removed, the new owner will have recourse to the conveyer but not the title insurance company.

The lender, on the other hand, will require the new owner to purchase a "lender's policy" that will cover the additional factors (5) through (7) mentioned earlier. Also, the lender's policy will cover losses that result from known liens or other encumbrances discovered in the search process. Because of the additional coverage, the lender's policy is somewhat more expensive than the owner's policy. The amount of the coverage is usually equal to the amount of the loan, which can be less than the value of the property. Finally, if a new owner purchases a property with all cash, he or she may wish to pay a larger premium to obtain a lender's policy. This is permissible.

Title insurance is different from other types of insurance (property and casualty insurance, for example) in several respects. First, title insurance covers losses caused by events that occur prior to the payment of the premium. Property and casualty, life, and health insurance all cover losses that occur subsequent to the payment of the premium. Second, and as a result, the title insurance company or its agent will make every effort to ensure that losses do not occur as a result of past events in the chain of title. The largest element of cost for title insurers is the expense incurred by searching public records for encumbrances and evidence of errors in the transfer of title prior to the current transaction. The company must hire individuals trained in searching the records. In many areas of the country, insurers maintain their own records, which replicate the public records. This is termed a **title plant**. The daily updating of the information in the title plant can be costly. The costs of maintaining a title plant and searching the records is the largest single expense for title insurers. In short, the administrative expenses associated with title insurance are substantially greater than those for other types of insurance.

In general, known risks are not covered by title insurance. Risk elimination as a result of a careful title search by the title company reduces the number of claims. Title insurance generally does not insure known defects and losses resulting from zoning and environmental regulations, eminent domain, and defects subsequent to the date of the policy. When problems arise, the title policy will usually contain a clause obligating the title company to defend the insured to the extent that the dispute involves a defect covered by the policy. Losses from claims are much less for title companies than other types of insurance. As a percent of revenues, claims may run 40 percent to 90 percent for property and casualty companies. During particularly bad years, claims losses may exceed 100 percent of premium revenues for certain of these companies. For title insurance companies, claim losses run between 4 percent and 7 percent of premium income. Thus, the bulk of the premium for property and casualty insurance covers the risk of loss from a claim, while that for title insurance covers the cost of maintaining the title plant and searching the records.

Finally, since a large proportion of the premium is used to pay administrative and operating expenses, less of the premium is available to employ for investment income. Net investment income averages about 11 percent of premiums earned for property and casualty companies and only 4 percent for title companies. The large fixed administrative costs associated with running a title plant makes title insurance companies vulnerable to the real estate cycle. Premium income is earned on real estate transactions, obviously, and when interest rates rise and there is a drop in, especially, commercial real estate activity, the premium income of title insurance companies drops substantially.

Summary

Lenders that desire to insure their loans against the risk of loss have a choice of government or private insurance programs. In either case, the loans must meet the qualifications of the insurers. The FHA and VA set loan-to-value and size limits on loans they insure. For this reason, many large loans are insured by private mortgage insurers. The VA provides partial coverage, while the FHA provides full coverage for all losses. PMI insurance covers up to an agreed-on proportion of the loan. If the loss exceeds this proportion, the lender and insurer share the additional loss. This is a co-insurance relationship.

If a default on a loan occurs, state laws regulate the foreclosure process. Some states require the process to be carried out in a judicial arena, while others permit a trustee to sell the property under a power-of-sale procedure. The latter is by far the least expensive of the two procedures. If the value of the property is insufficient to cover the amount of indebtedness, a deficiency results. Most states allow the lender to pursue a judgment on this deficiency, but a half-dozen or so prohibit deficiency judgments if a power-of-sale foreclosure procedure is implemented.

State laws regulating foreclosure can affect the total loss incurred on defaulted loans. Judicial procedures and statutory rights of redemption increase the cost of foreclosure (and the loss) as a result of a default. Antideficiency statutes also increase the loss by limiting the recourse of the lender. Historical data on claims made to mortgage insurers, both private and government, indicate that required judicial procedures and statutory rights of redemption increase the risk of loss on default.

Title insurance insures the lender (and borrower) against a loss due to a defect in the title. Borrowers' policies do not insure against liens or defects on the property known to exist before its sale. Lenders' policies insure against loss from any lien or defect that exists prior to the sale, known or unknown.

Key Terms

American Land Title Association (ALTA)	Coverage ratio
Co-insurance	Deficiency judgment

Entitlement

Equitable right of redemption

Foreclosure

Full coverage

Judicial procedure foreclosure

Lien

Mortgage default insurance

Mortgage insurance premium (MIP)

Partial coverage

Power-of-sale foreclosure

Private mortgage insurance (PMI)

Self-insurance

Statutory right of redemption

Title plant

Title search

Review Questions

14-1. Define and explain the different types of mortgage insurance coverage. Give an example of each.

14-2. Compare and contrast the FHA and VA insurance programs.

14-3. How does the FHA determine its premium on its standard (203b) program?

14-4. Compare private mortgage insurance programs to the government programs.

14-5. Compare and contrast the two predominant methods of foreclosure as determined by state law.

14-6. Differentiate between an equitable right of redemption and a statutory right of redemption.

14-7. Explain how state foreclosure laws can affect the loss on a loan and the claim made to the mortgage insurer.

14-8. Define title insurance and indicate what losses it is intended to cover.

14-9. Differentiate between an owner's (borrower's) and a lender's title policy in terms of coverage.

14-10. Compare and contrast title insurance with property and casualty insurance.

Problems

14-1. Given the following information, determine (a) the maximum mortgage amount for which the applicant will qualify; and (b) the percentage of the allowable closing costs that can be financed with FHA insurance.

VALUE OF PROPERTY

Sales price	$180,000
Appraised value	$178,000
Allowable closing costs	$2,400

14-2. What would be your answer to parts (a) and (b) in Problem 14-1 if the sales price and appraised value were both $46,000 and the allowable closing costs were $1,200?

14-3. Assume the following information on a residential loan default:

Value of house at foreclosure sale	$100,000
Balance of loan at time of last payment	$120,000
Original loan amount	$125,000
Delinquent interest payments	$4,000

Foreclosure costs

Attorneys' fees	$5,000
Court expense	$300
Real Estate Owned expenses	
Maintenance	$800
Hazard insurance	$400
Property taxes	$550
Repairs	$700

Determine the amount of the loss for which the lender will receive reimbursement if the loan was insured or guaranteed by (a) the FHA, (b) the VA, or (c) a typical PMI with a 15 percent coverage ratio. In each case indicate the proportion of the loss that would not be covered and, thus, must be borne by the lender.

14-4.　For Problem 14-3, what would the value of the house have to be, other things unchanged, for the lender to bear no portion of the loss under a private mortgage policy?

14-5.　Alternatively for Problem 14-3, if the value of the house remains at $100,000, what would the private mortgage insurance coverage ratio have to be in order for the lender to bear no portion of the loss?

Notes

1. S. Chomsisengphet and A. Pennington-Cross. The evolution of the subprime mortgage market. Federal Reserve Bank of St. Louis *Review* 88(1) (January/February 2006), 31–56.

2. Touche, Ross & Co. The costs of mortgage loan foreclosures: Case studies of six savings and loan associations. Washington, DC: Touche, Ross & Co., April 1975.

3. T. Clauretie. Foreclosed laws and FHA losses: Illinois and neighboring states, Office of Real Estate Research Paper No. 79. Champaign-Urbana: University of Illinois, May 1990.

4. T. Clauretie and T. Herzog. The effect of state foreclosure laws on loan losses: Evidence from the mortgage insurance industry. *Journal of Money, Credit, and Banking* 22(2) (May 1990), 221–233.

Web Sites

http://www.creditscoring.com
Information on status of credit scoring

http://www.fico.com/en/Pages/default.aspx
Information on credit scoring

http://www.fanniemae.com
Information about the Federal National Mortgage Association and the housing finance system

http://www.freddiemac.com
Information about the Federal Home Loan Mortgage Corporation

http://www.hsh.com
Information on conventional mortgages and other loans

http://www.hud.gov
>   Housing information (FHA included) and consumer alerts from the Department of Housing and Urban Development

http://www.mbaa.org
>   Mortgage Bankers Association

http://www.va.gov
>   Information on VA mortgages

http://moremortgagemeltdown.com/download/pdf/T2_Partners_presentation _on_the_mortgage_crisis.pdf
>   Overview of the Housing and Economic Crisis

http://real-estate-law.freeadvice.com/real-estate-law/mortgage_matters/ 1289/
>   Home Foreclosure Process

http://www2.cob.ilstu.edu/jwtrefz/FIL360/NDEFINSU.DOC
>   Mortgage default insurance, foreclosure, and title insurance

PART 3

Commercial Real Estate Finance

*I*n this section, we cover topics related to financing commercial real estate properties. Commercial real estate includes all nonresidential properties and multi-family residential properties. Commercial real estate is varied, including office facilities, warehouses, industrial complexes, shopping centers, hospitals, hotels, motels, and many other types of properties. In this section, we focus on attributes of financing that are unique to commercial real estate projects. We also cover issues related to taxation and different forms of ownership structure, such as partnerships, corporations, and real estate investment trusts.

VALUE, LEVERAGE, AND CAPITAL STRUCTURE

LEARNING OBJECTIVES

This chapter deals with issues of using debt to finance commercial or income-producing real estate properties. After reading this chapter, you should understand that the value of an equity investment in real estate is dependent on the level and risk of the after-tax equity cash flows. You also should understand how the use of debt can alter these cash flows. When the use of debt alters the amount or risk of the equity cash flows, the value of the equity position likewise will change. In this regard, there may be an optimal amount of debt to use. Too much or too little debt may not maximize the value of the equity. You should understand the concept of an optimal balance of debt and equity financing. There are arguments as to whether or not the use of an optimal amount of debt can change the value of a real estate equity investment. You also should understand how more practical institutional matters, such as the peculiarities of the tax laws and the risk of individual property types, affect the debt structure of real estate investments.

INTRODUCTION

Regarding commercial real estate properties, we are concerned with three fundamental principles in this chapter: value, financial leverage, and optimal capital structure. They are all interrelated. In this chapter, we will be concerned with the central issue of the value of using debt financing in real estate investments. Even without considering such institutional factors as tax laws and the legal aspects of debt contracts, one set of arguments suggests that financial leverage can affect the value of the equity position in a positive way. That is to say, leverage has value in and of itself. Within this set of arguments, the suggestion is also made that the use of too much debt can be risky and not desirable. Although the use of debt can be fruitful, there are also reasons why real estate cannot or should not be financed totally with debt. This suggests the use of an optimal amount of debt or an optimal capital structure. We will see that an optimal capital structure may be enforced by lenders who see it in their best interest to restrict the amount of debt. This, and other institutional factors, will affect the amount of debt financing.

On the other side of the issue is a proposition that the use of debt does not or cannot, per se, enhance the value of a real estate investment. This side of the argument implies that, ignoring institutional factors, there is no benefit from the use of debt and, therefore, no optimal capital structure.

Leverage by itself has no value, according to this argument. Whichever series of arguments appears to be most reasonable, we are left with explaining the widespread use of debt financing in real estate. So we conclude this chapter with possible explanations for the persistence of this form of real estate investment financing, as well as a discussion of some institutional factors that affect the amount of debt used to finance real estate investments. We first begin with some broad concepts.

VALUATION OF REAL ESTATE INVESTMENTS

General Principles

The valuation of real estate is conceptually no different from the valuation of other assets. The value of an income-producing asset, real estate included, is a function of the income that accrues to the asset. Income is generally measured as cash flow and is discounted using an appropriate interest rate.

This **discounted cash flow (DCF) model** is

$$\text{Value} = \sum_{i=0}^{n} \frac{\text{CF}_i}{(1+r)^i} \qquad \text{(Equation 15-1)}$$

For some assets, such as Treasury securities, valuation is simple because the cash flows are easily determined. For other investments, the determination of the cash flows and the proper discount rate may be more formidable and less certain.

Commercial real estate investment is one of the most difficult areas in which to apply the valuation model. For many real estate investments, both the expected cash flows and the proper discount rate are difficult to determine. Consider the following nonexhaustive list of commercial real estate investments: hotels, motels, urban office buildings, suburban office buildings, shopping malls, strip centers, warehouses, mini-warehouses, theme parks, restaurants, fast-food facilities, nursing and convalescence centers, hospitals, apartment complexes, casinos, and private schools.

Valuing the above types of real estate can be complicated since the cash flows can derive from two different sources: the nature of the real estate and the nature of non-real estate sources of value, such as the talent of the management team that directs the business enterprise. It is often difficult to separate the two sources of value, and failure to account for the business enterprise component may lead to mistakes in valuation. For example, the expected cash flows for an existing fast-food facility may be a function of two separate considerations. One consideration would be the value of the real estate: its location, state of repair, attractiveness of the facility, and so forth. The other would be the managerial talent of the present owners, the franchise name, and other non-real estate–related assets. The investor may buy the facility at the full value of the cash flows generated by the two sources and then cannot replicate the managerial talent or other non-real estate sources of cash flow. He may have paid too much because the cash flows subsequent to purchase may fall short of those expected. Although the value of the whole enterprise would be less than expected (and paid for), the value of the real estate itself may not have changed at all.

The identification of the cash flows from real estate may be less a problem for those facilities that are essentially rental in nature. Examples include office buildings, warehouses, and apartment complexes. But even in these cases, the property management function can be very important. An investor can purchase such a property, finance it with debt, fail to manage it properly, and be forced to default on the loan. Many improperly managed real estate investments have failed, but in other cases properties have been purchased, managerial talent applied, and fortunes made. What may appear to be a failure to value real estate properly may have been a failure to measure the non-real estate sources of cash flows. Bear in mind as we discuss the valuation of real estate that a portion of the cash flows may be derived from the non-real estate assets that occupy the realty.

The more uncertainty there is in the amount and timing of an asset's cash flows, the more difficult it is to value the asset precisely. However, the use of debt in real estate investment will have the effect of partitioning the cash flows from the investment into two parts: the return to the debt and the return to the equity. Of the two, the payments to the debt are generally more stable and predictable. In fact, if the debt is noncallable[1] and sufficiently collateralized by the real estate (the probability of default is minimal), the amount and timing of the payments will be nearly certain.

Financial Leverage

Financial leverage (henceforth referred to simply as leverage)[2] is the use of debt to finance a portion of a real estate investment. Although not all debt is structured alike, it is generally characterized by an obligation fixed in amount. Interest payments on the fixed obligation can be fixed or variable. When debt has a fixed amount and a fixed rate, the debt service or payments are stable and predictable. **Equity** is the difference between the value of the asset and the amount of debt and is therefore a residual. Equity holders have a claim on the cash flows of the asset after all obligations, including payments on the debt, have been met. For this reason, it is said that equity holders have a claim on the residual cash flows of the asset.

Leverage, the Return on Equity, and Value

The use of debt is common in real estate investing. Several arguments support the use of debt in financing real estate investments. Before we look at a complex real estate investment, it will help to present the arguments in favor of leverage by using the very simple example that follows.

Assume an asset "valued" at $100 produces an expected annual cash flow of $10 in perpetuity (forever). Although the expected cash flow is $10 each year, also assume there is a 50–50 chance that the cash flow will either be $8 or $12 (you should verify that, with these probabilities, the expected cash flow is $10). With this example in mind, let's look at leverage and value.

There are several general arguments that the use of debt enhances the value of the equity interest in real estate. One argument for the use of leverage claims that debt financing increases the **return on equity** and its **value**. The trick that accomplishes this task is the use of debt at a cost less than the expected return on the asset. Consider an investor whose total wealth is $100 in cash. If he or she purchases our simple asset with cash (he or she does not borrow), the expected return on the investment will be 10 percent ($10/$100). Now, if the investor can borrow up to 80 percent of the value of the asset at, for example, 8 percent, he or she can purchase the investment with only $20 of his or her own equity. From the $10 expected annual cash flow, he or she pays $6.40 ($80 × 0.08) in interest. The residual $3.60 represents an 18 percent ($3.60/$20) return on investment. If there are four other like assets available, the investor could purchase them with the remaining $80 in cash. Total expected cash flow after paying interest would be $18 (5 × $3.60), or 18 percent on his or her $100 investment. Had he or she purchased only one asset with all equity, the return would be only 10 percent. The advantage of leverage comes from the opportunity to borrow (use outside sources of funds) at a cost (rate) less than the return from the asset acquired with the borrowed funds.

Another way of looking at the effects of leverage in this simple example is to analyze the investor's wealth position. If he or she purchases one asset with all equity, his or her wealth position is $100. If he or she uses leverage and purchases five assets, his or her wealth position is the value of the five equity interests. The annual cash flows from those five equity interests total $18. The value of the equity cash flows depends on the investor's discount rate. Even using a 10 percent discount rate, the value of his or her wealth position is $180 ($18/0.10). It is clear that those with a limited access to equity would desire to use as much debt as possible. This allows those with limited equity to control as much in the way of real estate assets as possible and thereby increase their wealth.

There is a caveat here, however. Since the annual cash flow from the asset is uncertain and may vary from an expected value of $10, the **risk** to the equity position is magnified by the leverage. Recall that there is a 50–50 chance that the cash flows from the asset can be either $8 or $12. With a cash flow of $8, the residual is $1.60 after payment of the $6.40 in interest, and in the second case it is $5.60. The return on equity is either 8 percent or 28 percent. Below, we will consider an argument that the increase in risk eliminates the value enhancement. For example, if the augmentation in risk causes the investor's discount rate to increase to 18 percent, then the value of the equity position in the five assets would be $100 ($18/0.18), the same as the 100 percent equity investment in one asset. Nonetheless, the ability for an investor to acquire more real estate assets with a given amount of equity leads to a second consideration for the use of debt financing—portfolio effects.

Portfolio Considerations

Beyond these theoretical arguments, the case can be made that leverage allows for an increase in the diversification of a portfolio of assets. In the above example, the use of leverage has allowed the investor with limited equity funds to invest in five assets as opposed to one. In the context of real estate, diversification has potential benefits. It has been shown that the returns on different property types or on properties in different regions of the country are not perfectly correlated. As you will see in a later chapter, the lack of perfect correlation allows portfolio construction to reduce the risks associated with investment in one or a few properties. Thus, debt financing is particularly attractive to those desiring to construct a portfolio but with limited access to equity funds. As you will see next, debt also may have value in terms of risk allocation to investors with different risk preferences.

Division of the Cash Flows

Leverage divides the uncertain cash flows of the asset into two components: one of less risk and one of more risk than that of the asset in total. In the above example, as long as the annual cash flow from the asset does not drop below $6.40, the interest payment on the debt will be made. Ignoring default risk (which can be managed), the debt lender has the right to a $6.40 annual payment. The amount is known and will not vary. The equity investor has the right to the residual. But given the possible cash flows in the example above, the return on equity will be either 8 percent or 28 percent.

Value can be created through this division of the cash flows of the asset if the debt holder and the equity holder have different risk-return preferences. Simply put, more risk-averse "investors" will become debt lenders, and less risk-averse investors will become equity holders. The equity investors take on more risk for the increased return. But their risk preference is such that it is a desirable trade-off. The debt holders take on less risk for less return (8 percent on debt versus

| FIGURE 15-1 | Risk-Return Preferences |

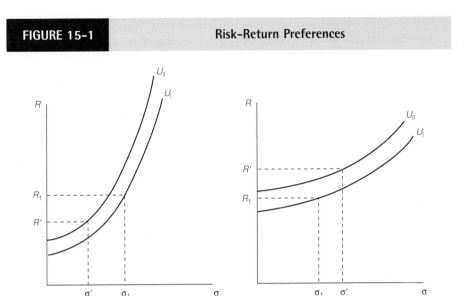

Source: © 2014 OnCourse Learning

10 percent on the asset). Their risk-return preference makes the trade-off for them desirable as well. The situation is graphically displayed in Figure 15-1.

The utility indifference curves for the more and less risk-averse investors are shown in the left and right panels, respectively. A utility curve shows the trade-off of risk and return for which an investor is indifferent. One can begin by assuming they are equal equity partners in a real estate investment. The cash flows of the investment have risk equal to $2 \times \sigma_1$, so each share the risk, σ_1. The total expected return is R_1, so they each share that as well. It may be possible to rearrange the risk and return of the cash flows and move each "partner" to a higher indifference curve. The strongly risk-averse investor has a steeply sloped utility curve. This means he or she is willing to give up substantial expected return for a reduction in risk. The mildly risk-averse investor has a gradually sloped utility curve, indicating it takes relatively little added return to take on additional risk. The risk-averse investor can agree to a debt position with little risk, σ', in exchange for a reduction in return to R' and still move to a higher indifference curve. This transfers more risk σ and return R to the less risk-averse equity investor, who also moves to a higher utility curve.

The actual ending positions will be determined by the relationship of the trade-off of risk and return. That relationship will depend on the nature of the risk and return of the cash flows of the investment. Offhand, one cannot determine any "formula" for the trade-off. However, given the slopes of the curves in Figure 15-1, it certainly appears reasonable that both investors can move to higher utility curves by rearranging the cash flows into debt and equity (residual). Since both types of security holders move to higher levels of utility, value is created by the division of the cash flows in the manner indicated.

Tax Deduction of Interest Payments

Now consider that interest payments are deductible as an expense for tax purposes. For each dollar in interest paid, net income is reduced by $1. This means that the government "rebates" a portion of the interest expense in the form of tax relief. If the tax rate of the holder of the real estate is 28 percent, then for every dollar in interest expense the after-tax cost is only 72 cents. This has the effect of lowering the after-tax cost of the investment and makes debt financing advantageous. Another way of visualizing the benefit of debt financing is to consider that a property generates only so many dollars of net operating income (NOI). If fewer dollars are given to the U.S. Treasury because of the tax laws, more can be divided between the debt and equity security holders, raising their values. An example of tax savings is illustrated in the next section.

Finally, the reader should note that the previous example illustrates what can be termed **positive leverage**. That is, the use of debt at a cost less than the return on the asset increases the return on equity. (Whether it also increases the required return, or discount rate on equity, has been mentioned and is another consideration.) Leverage also can be negative or neutral. **Negative leverage** occurs when the cost of debt is greater than the expected return on the asset. In this case, the return on the asset must be used to compensate the lender at a higher rate, reducing the expected return to the equity position. In our simple example, if the cost of debt is 12 percent, then the interest charge on an $80 loan would be $9.60, leaving only $0.40 for the equity holder, or a 2 percent rate of return.

As you might guess, **neutral leverage** occurs when the cost of debt equals the expected return on the asset.[3] In this case, the return on equity is not affected by the use of debt. In summary, leverage may create value if the return on assets exceeds the cost of debt, there is a portfolio effect, and interest is tax deductible.

DEBT AND RETURNS TO EQUITY: A REAL ESTATE EXAMPLE

To understand the effect of leverage on the value of a real estate investment, one must first understand the cash flow structure of a real estate project. The total cash flows are comprised of two components: (1) operating cash flows (rental revenues, etc.) and (2) cash flows from the resale of the property. Tables 15-1 and 15-2 show the calculation of the after-tax cash flows from operations and resale of the property. Although taxes are considered in the cash flows, in this chapter we are primarily concerned with structuring and evaluating the cash flows. A more detailed discussion of the tax treatment of real estate follows in Chapter 16. The cash flow structure is also expanded to reflect this in Chapter 16.

Table 15-1 shows that, beginning with gross rent (GR), one subtracts vacancy (VAC) and adds other income (OI) (sources such as paid parking, vending

TABLE 15-1

After-Tax Cash Flow from Operations

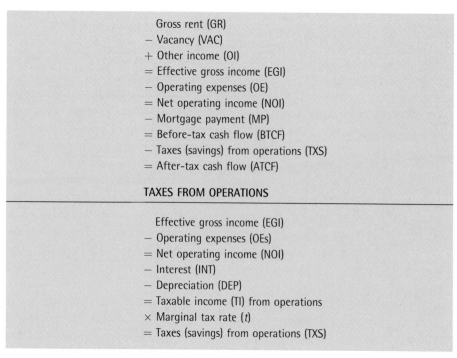

Gross rent (GR)
− Vacancy (VAC)
+ Other income (OI)
= Effective gross income (EGI)
− Operating expenses (OE)
= Net operating income (NOI)
− Mortgage payment (MP)
= Before-tax cash flow (BTCF)
− Taxes (savings) from operations (TXS)
= After-tax cash flow (ATCF)

TAXES FROM OPERATIONS

Effective gross income (EGI)
− Operating expenses (OEs)
= Net operating income (NOI)
− Interest (INT)
− Depreciation (DEP)
= Taxable income (TI) from operations
× Marginal tax rate (t)
= Taxes (savings) from operations (TXS)

Source: © 2014 OnCourse Learning

machines, and late fees on rents) to achieve effective gross income (EGI). Subtracting operating expenses (OEs) from EGI yields NOI. OEs may include management fees, property taxes, property insurance, pest control, cleaning services, utilities, and so on. To account for debt service, the mortgage payment (MP) is then subtracted from NOI to calculate the before-tax cash flow (BTCF) from operations. The remaining item to account for is the tax liability (or tax savings), which is calculated in the bottom portion of Table 15-1. This calculation is shown separately since taxes are based on taxable income and not cash flow.

As a general rule, a cash flow calculation will contain every item that is an actual cash inflow or outflow regardless of whether it is tax deductible. On the other hand, a taxable income calculation would contain all items that are tax deductible whether or not they are actual cash outflows. The upper part of Table 15-1 is consistent with the lower part down to NOI since OEs are tax deductible. From this point, however, only the tax-deductible portion (interest) of the MP is considered. Also, items that are tax deductible but not actual cash outlays (depreciation) are included.

Depreciation is a tax-deductible expense but not an actual cash outlay. Improvements on real property are considered physical structures that will deteriorate over time to a value of zero. Based on this, Congress has included in the tax laws a schedule by which real properties (along with other items) can be depreciated. The specifics of this schedule are discussed in Chapter 16. For now it is sufficient to say that the basis for depreciation is the sum of the value of the capital improvements and acquisition costs. Acquisition costs are costs related to acquiring the property, such as an appraisal or a survey. The current schedule is straight-line depreciation with midmonth convention. Residential income properties are depreciated 27.5 years straight-line while nonresidential income properties are depreciated over 39 years straight-line.

Once taxable income is known, the appropriate marginal tax rate is applied to calculate the tax liability or tax savings. Negative taxable income would produce an operating loss, which in turn would produce a tax savings. Thus, it may be possible to have a zero or negative BTCF but a positive after-tax cash flow.

Table 15-2 shows the after-tax cash flow from the resale of the property and the accompanying tax liability (savings) from the total gain. As seen, the sales price is derived net of selling expenses. Then the mortgage payoff is considered by subtracting the outstanding balance of the debt. Finally, the amount of tax (savings) is deducted (added) to produce the after-tax equity reversion.

The lower portion of Table 15-2 shows that the total tax due at resale is determined by the amount of total gain. The total gain has two components: the capital gain and the depreciation portion of the total gain. The total gain is the amount realized on sale minus the adjusted basis. Adjusted basis is the original purchase price plus any subsequent capital improvements plus acquisition costs minus accumulated depreciation. The depreciation portion of total gain is taxed at the applicable depreciation recovery tax rate (the current maximum is 25 percent), whereas the capital gain (assuming long-term) is taxed at the appropriate long-term capital gains tax rate (current maximum of 20 percent). Thus the total tax is the sum of the tax on the depreciation portion and the tax on the capital gain.

Once Tables 15-1 and 15-2 are in place, all the after-tax cash flows that accrue to the property are known except the initial outlay, that is, the initial equity investment. Mortgage lenders generally require the investor to make some equity investment in the project. This is reflected in the down payment. In addition, any acquisition costs and financing costs (costs related to acquiring the mortgage) are paid at the outset. These are typically paid from equity funds. Thus, the total equity outlay required at the outset will usually be the down payment plus acquisition costs

TABLE 15-2
After-Tax Equity Reversion

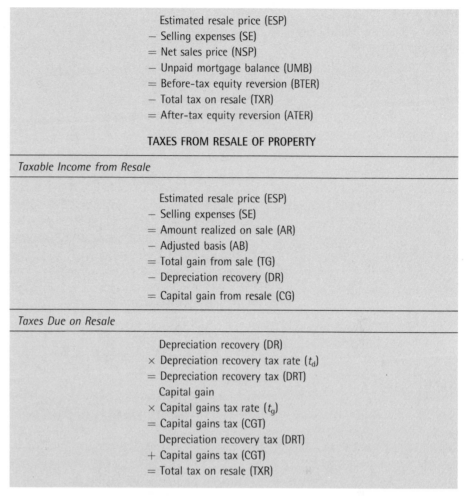

	Estimated resale price (ESP)
−	Selling expenses (SE)
=	Net sales price (NSP)
−	Unpaid mortgage balance (UMB)
=	Before-tax equity reversion (BTER)
−	Total tax on resale (TXR)
=	After-tax equity reversion (ATER)

TAXES FROM RESALE OF PROPERTY

Taxable Income from Resale

	Estimated resale price (ESP)
−	Selling expenses (SE)
=	Amount realized on sale (AR)
−	Adjusted basis (AB)
=	Total gain from sale (TG)
−	Depreciation recovery (DR)
=	Capital gain from resale (CG)

Taxes Due on Resale

	Depreciation recovery (DR)
×	Depreciation recovery tax rate (t_d)
=	Depreciation recovery tax (DRT)
	Capital gain
×	Capital gains tax rate (t_g)
=	Capital gains tax (CGT)
	Depreciation recovery tax (DRT)
+	Capital gains tax (CGT)
=	Total tax on resale (TXR)

Source: © 2014 OnCourse Learning

plus financing costs. In general, the initial equity investment would include any outlay paid by the equity investor. We are now ready to construct investor cash flows and to illustrate the effect of leverage.

Table 15-3 provides an example of multifamily investment property.

Basic Assumptions

Using the data in Table 15-3, the after-tax cash flows assuming no financial leverage are calculated in Table 15-4. We begin with this assumption so we can demonstrate the effects of leverage on the cash flows and value of the equity. GR in year 1 is $522,100, the VAC rate is 6 percent each year, and OI is 1 percent of GR. GR is expected to grow at 8 percent annually. The OE in the first year is 16 percent of the GR and grows at 7 percent annually thereafter. The property increases in value by 6 percent annually and is sold at the end of year 5.[4] The selling commission is 5 percent. Note that OEs can alternatively be stated as a percentage of EGI. The choice may be determined by local custom or by the client. Consistency with available benchmarks would be the objective.

Annual Operating Cash Flows

To begin, let's analyze the first year's cash flows in Table 15-4. In year 1 the GR is $522,100. Factoring in 6 percent VAC and 1 percent OI results in EGI of $495,995 for year 1. Deducting OEs (16 percent of the GR) results in a NOI of

TABLE 15-3

Property Data for Multifamily Investment Property

Project cost	
Land	$300,000
Building	$2,500,000
Total cost	$2,800,000
Equity investment	
Down payment	$2,800,000 less loan amount
Debt financing	
Initial Loan amount	Varies ($0 debt, Table 15-4; $1 million Table 15-6)
Interest rate	Varies (0% in Table 15-4; 9% in Table 15-6)
Loan term	30 years
Operating data	
Initial rent	$522,100
Growth in rent	8% per year
Vacancy rate	6% of gross rent each year
Other income	1% of gross rent each year
Operating expenses	16% of first year gross rent ($83,536)
Growth in operating expenses	7% per year
Growth in resale price	6%
Selling expenses	5% of resale price
Depreciation	Straight-line 27.5 years, midmonth convention, put into service at beginning of year
Holding period	5 years
Marginal tax rate	35%
Capital gains tax rate	15%
Depreciation recovery tax rate	25%

Source: © 2014 OnCourse Learning

$412,459. NOI is a net cash inflow—cash income less cash expenses. Since there is no MP, the NOI is also the BTCF. To derive the after-tax cash flow, we must compute the income tax liability. Expenses for tax purposes include depreciation and interest on debt. Depreciation is rounded to $87,000, assuming that the property was purchased on January 1 and sold on December 31, using the midmonth convention.[5] Since there is no debt, there are no interest expenses. The tax due is 35 percent of the taxable income ($325,459), or $113,911. For the first year, the after-tax cash flow is, therefore, $298,548. The after-tax cash flow can be computed similarly for each year.

For year 5, the after-tax cash flow is larger because revenues have grown faster than expenses.

Sale of Property

In this example, the property is sold at the end of the fifth year. The bottom portion of Table 15-4 shows the computation of the after-tax cash flow from the sale. By year 5, the value of the property has reflected the 6 percent annual growth in value and the property is sold for $3,747,032. The sales commission (5 percent) is $187,352, so that the net sales price is $3,559,680. The basis of the property has been reduced by accumulated depreciation and is $2,353,000. The resulting gain on the sale is $1,206,680. Of this amount, depreciation recovery (accumulated depreciation) is $447,000, which is taxed at 25 percent, producing a tax of $111,750. The remaining $759,680 is capital gain, which is taxed at 15 percent, yielding a tax of $113,952. Thus the total tax on resale is $225,702. The after-tax cash flow from the sale of the property is equal to the net sales price less the repayment of debt (none in this case) less the payment of taxes and is $3,333,978.

TABLE 15-4

Cash Flows from Operations (Initial Debt = $0)

YEAR	1	2	3	4	5
Before-Tax Cash Flows					
Gross rent (GR)	$522,100	$563,868	$608,977	$657,696	$710,311
− Vacancy (VAC)	31,326	33,832	36,539	39,462	42,619
+ Other income	5,221	5,639	6,090	6,577	7,103
= Effective gross income (EGI)	495,995	535,675	578,529	624,811	674,796
− Operating expenses (OEs)	83,536	89,384	95,640	102,335	109,499
= Net operating income (NOI)	412,459	446,291	482,888	522,476	565,297
− Mortgage payment (MP)	0	0	0	0	0
= Before-tax cash flow (BTCF)	412,459	446,291	482,888	522,476	565,297
Income Tax Liability (Savings)					
NOI	$412,459	$446,291	$482,888	$522,476	$565,297
− Depreciation (DEP)	87,000	91,000	91,000	91,000	87,000
− Interest (INT)	0	0	0	0	0
= Taxable income (TI)	325,459	355,291	391,888	431,476	478,297
× Marginal tax rate (t)	× 0.35	× 0.35	× 0.35	× 0.35	× 0.35
= Taxes (savings)	113,911	124,352	137,161	151,017	167,404
After-Tax Cash Flows					
Before-tax cash flow (BTCF)	$412,459	$446,291	$482,888	$522,476	$565,297
− Taxes (savings)	113,911	124,352	137,161	151,017	167,404
= After-tax cash flow (ATCF)	298,548	321,939	345,727	371,459	397,893

AFTER-TAX CASH FLOW FROM RESALE OF PROPERTY (Initial Debt = $0)

Before-Tax Equity Reversion					
Estimated sale price (ESP)				$3,747,032	
− Selling expenses (SE)				187,352	
= Net sales price (NSP)				3,559,680	
− Unpaid mortgage balance (UMB)				0	
= Before-tax equity reversion (BTER)				3,559,680	
Tax (Savings) on Resale					
Estimated sale price (ESP)				$3,747,032	
− Selling expenses (SE)				187,352	
= Amount realized on sale (AR)				3,559,680	
− Adjusted basis (AB)				2,353,000	
= Total gain (loss) on sale (TG)				1,206,680	
Depreciation recovery (DR)				447,000	
× t_d				× 0.25	
= Depreciation recapture tax (DRT)				111,750	
Capital gain (CG)				759,680	
× t_g				× 0.15	
= Capital gains tax (CGT)				113,952	
Depreciation recovery tax (DRT)				111,750	
+ Capital gains tax (CGT)				113,952	
= Total tax on resale (TXR)				225,702	
After-Tax Equity Reversion					
Before-tax equity reversion (BTER)				$3,559,680	
− Total tax on resale (TXR)				225,702	
= After-tax equity reversion (ATER)				3,333,978	

Source: © 2014 OnCourse Learning

Value of the Cash Flows

Table 15-5 summarizes the annual cash flows from this property. If the after-tax discount rate for equity is 12 percent, the value of the cash flows accruing to the owner is \$3,122,923. Using Equation 15-1, one calculates the net present value (NPV$_e$) of the equity position to be \$322,923. The **net present value (NPV)** is the present value of the cash inflows minus the present value of the cash outflows using the investor's risk-adjusted required rate of return as the discount rate. The NPV measures the increase or decrease in the investor's wealth by making this investment. This leads to the decision rule that independent projects with positive NPVs would be accepted and those with negative NPVs would be rejected. Zero NPVs would lead to indifference. If the investor faces capital rationing or is choosing between mutually exclusive investments, in general, that project or combination of projects with the highest NPV would be preferred. The equation for NPV is

$$NPV_e = \sum_{t=0}^{n} \frac{CF_t}{(1 + r_e)^t}$$ (Equation 15-2)

where CF$_t$ represents the equity cash flows in time t (both positive and negative), r_e is the discount rate for equity, and t is the number of time periods. For our example the NPV$_e$ would be

$$NPV_e = \$3,122,923 - \$2,800,000 = \$322,923$$

By setting the NPV equal to zero in Equation 15-2 and solving for r, one can derive the after-tax internal rate of return (IRR$_e$) for the equity. In this case, the after-tax IRR of 14.98 percent is slightly greater than the discount rate of 12 percent. The 14.98 percent is the "unlevered" (or overall) return on the project. If no debt is used, the return on equity is equal to the overall (unlevered) return on the project.

We know that the **internal rate of return (IRR)** is that rate at which the present value of the cash inflows equals the present value of the cash outflows, that is, the discount rate at which the NPV is zero. The IRR equation is written as

$$\sum_{t=0}^{n} \frac{CF_t}{(1 + IRR_e)} = 0$$ (Equation 15-3)

To make accept/reject decisions with IRR, the investor's risk-adjusted required rate of return is used as a benchmark. Independent projects with IRRs greater than the required return would be accepted, whereas those with IRRs less than the required return would be rejected. The investor is indifferent at the point where the two rates are equal. With our example, the project is acceptable since the NPV is positive and the IRR is greater than the required return.

Comparing NPV and IRR. In our example, we were making a simple accept/reject decision on an independent project (investing in this project has no effect on our

TABLE 15-5

Summary of After-Tax Equity Cash Flows; Multifamily Investment Property (Initial Debt = \$0)

YEAR	0	1	2	3	4	5
After-tax cash flows	(\$2,800,000)	\$298,548	\$321,939	\$345,727	\$371,459	\$397,893 +3,333,978
NPV at 12%	\$322,923					
After-tax IRR	14.98%					

Source: © 2014 OnCourse Learning

investing in other projects). In making a simple accept/reject decision on an independent project with conventional cash flows (an initial outlay followed by periods of cash inflows), the NPV and IRR techniques must agree on acceptance or rejection. Because of the nature of the calculations, there can be no conflicting recommendations. This assumes that an IRR can be calculated for the cash flows. In more complex decision making, however, the two techniques may present conflicting recommendations. For example, given two mutually exclusive projects, A and B, NPV may say choose project A, whereas IRR may say choose project B. This conflict is generally resolved in favor of NPV because it is a direct measure of the investor's change in wealth.

Another problem sometimes encountered with IRR is multiple rates of return; that is, it may be possible to calculate more than one IRR for a given set of cash flows. A general rule of thumb is that there is the possibility of having as many IRRs for a given set of cash flows as there are number of sign changes in the cash flows. For example, a set of cash flows with three sign changes may have three IRRs, two IRRs, or only one IRR. It is also possible to have a set of cash flows for which the IRR cannot be calculated.

Inherent in the discounting process used for deriving NPV and IRR is the assumption that the cash flows are reinvested at the rate of return used in the analysis. NPV assumes that cash flows are reinvested at the required rate of return. IRR assumes reinvestment at the IRR. Some would argue that NPV is more appropriate since it may be impossible to reinvest funds at the IRR, and it is more logical to assume that the investor will reinvest at least at the required rate of return.

Leverage and Value

We are now in a position to analyze the effect of debt on the value of the equity position. Tables 15-6 and 15-7 show the cash flows for the property, assuming that the owner can borrow $1 million at 9 percent for 30 years with annual payments. The first year's debt service payment, $97,336, will have to be paid from

TABLE 15-6

Operating Cash Flows; Years 1 through 5 (Initial Debt = $1,000,000)

YEAR	1	2	3	4	5
Before-Tax Cash Flows					
NOI	$412,459	$446,291	$482,888	$522,476	$565,297
− Mortgage payment	97,336	97,336	97,336	97,336	97,336
= Before-tax cash flow	315,123	348,955	385,552	425,129	467,961
After-Tax Cash Flows					
− Depreciation	$ 87,000	$ 91,000	$ 91,000	$ 91,000	$ 87,000
− Interest	90,000	89,340	88,620	87,836	86,980
= Taxable income	235,459	265,951	303,268	343,640	391,317
− Tax	82,411	93,083	106,144	120,274	136,961
= After-tax cash flow	232,712	255,872	279,408	304,855	331,000
AFTER-TAX CASH FLOW FROM SALE (YEAR 5)					
Resale price	$3,747,032				
− Selling expenses	187,352				
− Mortgage balance	956,094				
− Tax on resale	225,702				
= After-tax cash flow	2,377,884				

Source: © 2014 OnCourse Learning

TABLE 15-7

Summary of After-Tax Equity Cash Flows; Multifamily Investment Property (Initial Debt = $1,000,000)

YEAR	0	1	2	3	4	5
After-tax cash flows	($1,800,000)	$232,712	$255,872	$279,408	$304,855	$331,000 +2,377,884
NPV at 12%	$541,470					
After-tax IRR	19.48%					

the cash flows of the property. Table 15-7 shows that the value of the equity is $2,341,470, assuming that the owner applies the same 12 percent after-tax discount rate. He may not, but we will pursue this argument. Since the owner's contribution is $1,800,000, the NPV is $541,470 and the IRR is 19.48 percent. Because the NPV of the equity is greater, it appears that the use of leverage has created value.

One driving mechanism that has created the value in this example is the use of debt with an after-tax rate that is less than the after-tax rate of return on the all-equity property. The after-tax cost of debt is 5.85 percent (9% × [1 − 0.35]) and the after-tax IRR on the all-equity property is 14.98 percent. In essence, the investor is using outside funds with an after-tax cost of 5.85 percent to finance a property with an after-tax return of 14.98 percent. The "profit" on the portion financed by debt accrues to the investor.

Another factor creating value in this example is the reduction in taxes paid to the government. Whatever the cash flows generated by the intrinsic economic worth of the property, they will have greater value if a larger portion can be retained by the claimants (debt holders and equity holders) to those cash flows. In other words, if the use of debt causes the amount of taxes paid to fall, a greater amount of cash flows will be available to distribute to the lender (debt) and to the investor (equity). It stands to reason that they will reach an agreement (insofar as the interest rate on debt) that divides these tax-generated cash flows between them. In short, if the total available cash flows are greater, their value will be greater.

Optimal Capital Structure

Optimal capital structure refers to that proportion of debt and equity that maximizes the value of the property (or the value of both the debt and equity components). If value can be created, as indicated in the above fashion, then how much debt should be secured by the property? At first, one would be tempted to finance as much as possible, say, 99.9 percent. However, some practical considerations dictate against the use of so much debt. The risk of default increases with the use of debt. The cash flows available from the real estate investment are expected, not certain. If the cash flows of the property turn out to be substantially below expectations, both the value of the property and the ability of the owner to meet debt payments will fall. The property's value may fall below the amount of debt. If the debt is nonrecourse, the owner of the property will have a put option. He or she can put the (diminished) value of the property to the lender in satisfaction of the nominal amount of debt. To reduce the value of the put option, the lender will limit the amount of debt that the property can carry. Alternatively, the lender will require a higher interest charge for the greater use of debt. Since the greater use of debt increases the probability of default and the loss to the lender, it is reasonable to expect the lender to demand higher interest. If the interest charge becomes too great, the benefit of leverage will disappear. When the after-tax cost of debt exceeds the after-tax rate of return on the all-equity property, then reverse leverage will occur. In this case, more debt will cause the value of the equity to fall.

This analysis suggests that the use of debt creates value. Next, we review some counterarguments to this claim. However, keep in mind that the widespread use of debt to finance real estate properties implies that its use is valuable to owners and developers of real estate properties. It is likely some institutional factors also play a part in driving the use of debt to finance real estate.

Arguments against an Optimal Capital Structure

If we ignore the increase in the cash flows that occur because of deductibility of interest for tax purposes, there are some sound arguments to suggest that the use of debt financing cannot create value. The best way to proceed, then, is to assume that there are no taxes applicable to investment in real estate or the investor's tax bracket is zero. The first cogent argument that the use of debt cannot create value was first put forth by Modigliani and Miller in the context of corporate finance and stock values.[6] They argued that the use of debt by a corporation could not affect the value of the equity of the corporation. The basis of the argument was that the value of the corporation was determined by the amount and risk of the cash flows generated by the assets of the corporation and that dividing those cash flows into two components could not increase their value. More precisely, they argued that the division of the cash flows by the corporation could not create value because that division could occur outside the corporation through the use of "homemade" leverage. Investors will not value activities of the corporation that they can perform themselves. The authors proved their proposition through the use of an arbitrage argument. An arbitrage argument basically says that if riskless profits are available through the simultaneous buying and selling of securities (in their example, corporate stock), then such buying and selling will cause the prices of securities to change to eliminate the excess profits. We will illustrate this argument in the context of our real estate example.

Modigliani–Miller Proposition in a Real Estate Context. To understand this argument against value creation by the use of debt, assume the following:

1. Two (or two sets of) real estate properties are identical in all respects, including the physical characteristics and the expected amount and the risk of the annual cash flows.
2. One property (set) has no debt; it is an all-equity property. The other has $2 million in debt.
3. There are no taxes (interest is not tax-deductible).
4. Investors can borrow personally at the same rate as they can get for a mortgage on the property.
5. There are no transaction costs involved in buying and selling real estate properties.

Table 15-8 shows the expected cash flows for year 1 and the values of the properties obtained from discounting the cash flows to equity at 15 percent. In this version, the values are somewhat higher than those shown elsewhere because we have eliminated taxes. (We want to show the **Modigliani–Miller (MM) hypothesis** in a no-tax situation.) As expected, the value of the debt-financed property is higher than the all-equity property. The increase in value is due purely to the ability to borrow at a rate less than the return on the assets (equity).

The MM argument would proceed as follows. If the property values indicated in Table 15-8 existed, then the owner of Property B could engage in arbitrage.

TABLE 15-8
Cash Flow and Values

ALL EQUITY VS. DEBT FINANCE PROPERTIES YEAR 1 CASH FLOWS		
	PROPERTY A ALL EQUITY	PROPERTY B $2 MILLION DEBT (10.75%)
Gross revenue ($)	522,100	522,100
Net revenue ($)	495,995	495,995
Operating expenses ($)	83,536	83,536
NOI ($)	412,459	412,459
Interest ($)	0	215,000
After-tax cash flow ($)	412,459	197,459
Value of property ($)	3,363,197	3,648,130
Value of equity ($)	3,363,197	1,648,130
ARBITRAGE		
Sell B for ($)		3,648,130
Pay off mortgage ($)		2,000,000
Difference ($)		1,648,130
Borrow $2.0 million		2,000,000
		3,648,130
Buy A for ($)		3,363,197
Difference ($)		284,933

Source: © 2014 OnCourse Learning

He or she would sell the property for $3,648,130 and pay off the mortgage ($2,000,000). He or she would take the remaining $1,648,130 and borrow (personally) $2,000,000 at 10.75 percent. He or she now has $3,648,130, uses $3,363,197 to purchase Property A, and puts the remaining $284,933 "in the bank," so to speak. The first year, after-tax cash flow from Property A will appear as in Table 15-8—$412,459, from which he or she must make a $215,000 payment on the (personal) $2,000,000 loan, leaving $197,459.

This amount is the same as the cash flow from Property B. The investor thus has the same expected cash flow and the same risk, but now has an extra $284,933 "in the bank." He is clearly better off and therefore has an incentive to arbitrage in this fashion. But what does the arbitrage do to the property prices? If a sufficient amount of properties of the types described are available, and if there is pressure to sell property of Type B and buy property of Type A, their prices will change. Property A prices will rise, and Property B prices will fall. In fact, the process will continue until their prices are identical. At that point, one cannot say that the values of properties with debt financing are greater than all-equity properties.

It is important to note the heart of the MM argument. It says that as long as investors can borrow at the same rate offered by lenders on mortgaged properties, the creation of debt adds no value to the property. This is so because the debt can be created at the personal level (MM call this homemade leverage). Any value created by the use of debt can occur outside of the property level and, therefore, will not attach to the property. Also, if two properties, one with debt and the other with all equity financing, must sell for the same value, then the total value of the debt and equity for each property must be the same. But, we know that the use of debt financing at a rate less than the return on the property increases the expected return to the property. The implication, according to the MM model, is that the required rate of return on equity must rise with the use of debt. Referring back to Table 15-8, this means that the value of the equity would fall by the precise amount of the increase in debt. This would occur with a rise in the required return on equity. If, for example, the required return on equity rose to 29.53 percent when $2,000,000 in debt is used, then the value of the equity cash flows would be $832,944, and the total value of debt and equity would be $2,832,944, the same as the all-equity value.

What would cause the required return on equity to rise with the use of debt? The answer is an increase in the risk (variance) of the cash flows accruing to the equity holder. Recall from Chapter 3 and our simple example in this chapter that the variance in the cash flows to the equity holders increased with leverage. Although the expected return increases, so does the risk. Furthermore, for any given risk (of the cash flows from the property), as more debt is used, the variance in the cash flows to equity increases at accelerating rates. For sufficiently high levels of debt, the variance becomes so great that very high discount rates may be appropriate for valuing the equity position. The MM model argues that the equivalence of property prices implies that the discount rate must rise by precisely the amount necessary to equate the reduction in the value of the equity to the increase in the amount of debt.

Given the assumptions of the MM model, the conclusions are unarguable. But how do we reconcile this with the overwhelming use of debt to finance real estate properties? In the next section, we consider the effect of agency costs and the legal structure of debt financing for real estate.[7] Then we look at some other institutional and practical reasons for the use of debt financing.

Resolution of the Modigliani–Miller Proposition with the Use of Debt Financing for Real Estate Properties

We can reconcile the inescapable conclusions of the MM argument with the widespread use of debt financing in a couple of ways. One, of course, is the introduction of taxes. If the property is held in a nonpersonal form, as by a corporation, then the use of debt increases the amount of after-tax cash flows available to the owners. This was demonstrated earlier in the chapter.[8] The second important reason is agency costs.

Agency problems may be associated with the use of personal debt. In the case where the investor borrows personally and purchases a property with all equity, he or she has access to the same cash flows to pay the interest on the personal debt. The lender appears to be in no more of a risk position than if the loan were collateralized by the property, the cash flows being identical. However, if there is a default, our legal system provides first priority of loan payment to lenders who have a lien (mortgage) on the property. This means that there is added safety for the lender if the loan is secured by the property and not personally. Another way of looking at the situation is as follows. Suppose that the investor who borrows personally to purchase Property A in the above arbitrage example seeks another loan from another lender and pledges the property against that second loan. (He or she can add the $2 million loan to the amount in the bank if he or she desires.) In the event of default, the second lender will have priority in a claim to the property in satisfaction of the debt. The first lender will have to pursue the investor personally. However, the first lender is likely to anticipate the added risk this situation poses. The upshot is that the first lender will either require a much higher interest rate (eliminating the value of the debt financing) or insist on a first lien on the property. In the end, the value-creating debt financing is applied at the property level.

This situation does not run counter to the MM argument. What it does say is that if debt creates value, it is the legal system, whereby properties can serve as collateral for loans that creates a situation where the leverage occurs at the property level and not personally. Also, note that many investors do not use debt to acquire real estate investments. Some large institutional investors, such as life insurance companies and pension funds, purchase properties with all equity. The National Council of Real Estate Investment Fiduciaries (NCREIF) is an organization of more than 50 such institutional investors and real estate managers of equity properties. They own or manage more than 1,000 all-equity properties totaling more than $15 billion. Many such institutional investors do not have to pay taxes on income as received, however. This removes an incentive for them to use debt with its associated deductibility of interest payments.

Finally, let's consider some other institutional and practical considerations that affect the amount of debt used to finance real estate.

Some Practical Considerations in the Use of Debt to Finance Real Estate Properties

The above theoretical discussion on optimal capital structure can be used to explore the effect of some practical considerations on the use of debt in financing real estate properties. Several considerations will dictate the relative amounts of debt and equity that will be used by real estate investors. They include the form of ownership, access to equity capital markets, the risk of the property type, the cost of bankruptcy, special tax regulations, and the interest rate or cost of debt. Let's consider each in turn.

Form of Ownership. If real estate is owned by a corporate entity, the returns will be subject to double taxation. The value of the debt and equity of the real estate investment can be increased through the use of debt. Given the alternative legal structures under which real estate may be held (such as limited partnerships or nontaxable real estate investment trusts), it makes little sense to hold real estate in a corporate structure and incur the double taxation. If real estate is held in the corporate form, one would expect a liberal use of debt so as to reduce the taxable income of the corporation.

Access to Equity Capital Markets. The equity market for real estate is very limited. Although there is a limited market for interests in real estate investment trusts, there is no market for other forms of equity interests. Pension funds and life insurance companies own substantial amounts of equity real estate (though not in proportion to their total asset portfolios), but these equity interests are not traded on a market and are held for long-term investments by those institutions. Thus, most investors will have to make whatever equity resources they have go as far as possible in acquiring real estate investments. That is, relatively small, noninstitutional investors with limited equity will have to rely on debt financing to acquire real estate, since it is difficult to raise additional equity funds in any organized and liquid market. One would expect that small, noninstitutional investors would use a larger proportion of debt to acquire larger and more expensive properties.

Risk of the Property. Lenders that provide debt financing for the acquisition of real estate properties are risk averse. For this reason, they will require larger equity contributions for the purchase of real estate properties that they perceive to be risky. Certain property types are likely to be inherently more risky than others. Historically, the variance in the cash flows of urban office buildings has been greater than that for apartment complexes. In some regions of the country, the risk of a particular property type may be more or less than in other areas of the country. Knowledgeable local lenders will likely require higher equity contributions (lower debt ratios) to finance the purchase of real estate properties they perceive to be risky.

The Cost of Bankruptcy. This consideration is closely related to the risk of the property type. A note secured by the property can either be recourse or nonrecourse. A **nonrecourse note** means that the lender may look only to the property to satisfy the debt. From the lender's point of view, such a note is obviously more risky. A **recourse note**, on the other hand, is more risky for the investor. If the operating cash flows from the property fail to cover the debt service, the result may be default and foreclosure. If this should occur, then the investor may be personally liable for any deficiency between the amount of the debt obligation and the market value of the property. Taken together, this implies that lenders will prefer to advance greater amounts of debt only on less risky properties and only if the note is a recourse note. Investors will prefer nonrecourse notes on all properties but especially on risky properties. Other things being equal, one would expect to see investors maximize the use of debt when it is nonrecourse.

Special Tax Regulations. Here there are two issues to consider: the extent to which operating losses from the real estate investment can be used to offset OI and the tax rate. You will see in the next chapter that present tax laws severely limit the extent to which an investor can use an operating loss on a real estate property to offset other positive (taxable) income and thereby reduce tax liability. There are also limitations on the extent to which interest deductions can be used to reduce taxes. It was not always this way. These changes have reduced the value of the interest deduction and, therefore, the value of debt financing. If the depreciation deductions on a property are sufficient to minimize the NOI, this will further reduce the value of the interest deduction. Thus, one would expect to see less debt used to finance properties with large depreciation components. These are basically newer properties where the value of the improvements are large relative to the value of the (undepreciable) land. Of course, the lower the tax rate, the less the value of the interest deductions.

Interest Rate. One would expect that the lower the market rate of interest, the more debt would be utilized to purchase real estate properties. This is especially true if the factors that lower the market rate of interest have no effect on the cost of equity. In this case, debt becomes relatively cheaper than equity. Given the limited amount of equity available for real estate investment, this would imply that the market rate of interest is an important determinant of market values and activity. In fact, we know that over the cycle, lower interest rates bring about an increase in real estate transactions and real estate prices.

In summary, debt will represent a greater portion of the capital structure of real estate investments when (1) the corporate structure is used to acquire the investments, (2) the value of the investment is large (access to equity is limited), (3) the risk of the property as measured by the variance in the operating cash flows is small, (4) the cost of bankruptcy to the investor is low (the note is nonrecourse), (5) operating losses are available to offset OI and thereby reduce current taxes, (6) the depreciation component is small, (7) the tax rate is high, and (8) the market interest rate is low.[9]

Several of these factors may interact. If a property has a large depreciable base, but tax laws allow operating losses to offset other positive income, debt financing still will be valuable. If, however, there are restrictions on such a use of operating losses, there will be less of a need for the use of debt. The considerations discussed in this chapter have favored the use of debt to finance real estate investments. Historically, the tax laws have been favorable, access to equity markets limited, and the after-tax cost of debt low relative to equity. Regardless of the theoretical arguments on the existence of an optimal capital structure, more practical considerations such as limited equity markets, tax rules, property risk, and the legal enforcement of debt covenants have driven the use of debt in real estate finance.

REAL ESTATE INVESTING IN THE REAL WORLD

The cash flow examples presented in this chapter are designed to provide a good basis for making real estate investment decisions. The tables give a basis for structuring cash flows from different types of real estate investments. In reality, some projects may have additional factors that must be considered, as discussed next. In the process of purchasing property, the buyer may encounter various costs, referred to as **closing costs**. A buyer may incur costs such as an appraisal, mortgage origination fees, and document recording fees. These costs are typically paid by the buyer at the time the property is acquired. These costs, however, are not fully tax deductible in the year they are paid. To start, the buyer has to distinguish between **acquisition costs** and financing costs. Acquisition costs are costs related to acquiring the property. These are prorated relative to the value of the land versus the value of the improvement in relation to the total value of the project. The portion prorated to the improvement is included in depreciation and written off over the depreciable life of the asset. **Financing costs**, on the other hand, are costs related to acquiring the mortgage. These would include such costs as mortgage origination fees and discount points. Financing costs are written off on a straight-line basis over the life of the mortgage. Thus, for example, if a buyer incurred $15,000 in financing costs on a 30-year mortgage, the annual deduction would be $500. This amount would be reflected in both cash flow and taxable income. If the property is sold before financing costs are fully amortized, the remaining balance of financing costs can be deducted in the year of sale.

Another financing consideration is a mortgage **prepayment penalty**. Some mortgages assess the borrower a penalty if the mortgage is prepaid, that is, repaid before maturity. These penalties may be stated as a percentage of the outstanding balance at the time of prepayment or in some form of yield maintenance. A prepayment penalty can be treated as interest and is fully tax deductible in the year it is paid. The amount of the prepayment penalty would be included in both the cash flow and taxable income calculations.

A final factor that may have to be considered is a **replacement reserve**. In some investment projects, the owner may be required to maintain a reserve to replace items that are prone to wear out. This would include such things as heating and cooling systems, appliances, and carpet. If a reserve is required, it is likely to be included in OEs. However, a set-aside of funds is not a tax-deductible expense. If reserves have been deducted to derive NOI, they must be added back to taxable income. In discounted cash flow analyses, the amount of replacement reserves is not reflected in the cash flow from resale since it is assumed that the selling price has been reduced by the amount of the reserve.

Summary

The division of risky cash flows of a real estate investment can be beneficial if lenders and equity holders have different risk-return preferences. Lenders may be willing to accept a relatively low rate of return on debt as a trade-off for less risk. In turn, the equity holder is exposed to more risk, including that of losing the entire investment. The use of debt at a rate less than the expected return on an all-equity property will magnify the return (and the risk) to the equity position. For the less risk-averse equity investor, the trade-off is again beneficial. Some will argue that the arrangement creates value, and this explains the widespread use of debt to finance real estate properties.

Others would argue along the lines of the MM hypothesis that, in a world without taxes, the use of leverage cannot increase the value of real estate properties. The value of the property will be based only on the amount and risk of the cash flows it generates and not on how they are divided among different classes of claimants (debt and equity). An arbitrage example can be used to demonstrate this point. The arbitrage argument is based on the assumption that the property owner can use homemade leverage to produce the same cash flows as would result from debt financing on the property.

However, two major institutional factors drive the use of debt financing for the acquisition of real estate properties. First, our legal system allows lenders to receive priority of payment from the liquidation of a property in the event of default. This is one reason why debt may be applied at the property level and not the personal level. Second, in a world of taxation, the deductibility of interest payments for tax purposes may increase the total cash flows accruing to the claimants. This factor alone would provide an incentive for debt financing. If the total cash flows to the claimants are greater by virtue of debt financing, they can arrange financing terms that make them both better off at the expense of the U.S. Treasury. Institutional investors that have no need for the tax deduction are more inclined to purchase properties with all equity. Other factors also affect the optimal capital structures, including the risk of the property, the risk of bankruptcy, the availability of nonrecourse financing, the amount of the depreciation tax shield, the tax rate, and, of course, the level of market interest rates. In the next chapter, you will see how tax laws affect the financing of real estate properties.

Key Terms

Acquisition costs

Closing costs

Discounted cash flow (DCF) model

Equity

Financial leverage

Financing costs

Internal rate of return (IRR)

Modigliani–Miller (MM) hypothesis

Negative leverage

Net present value (NPV)

Neutral leverage

Nonrecourse note

Optimal capital structure

Positive leverage

Prepayment penalty

Recourse note

Replacement reserve

Return on equity

Risk

Value

Review Questions

15-1. Define the terms debt and equity. What are the major characteristics that distinguish debt and equity?

15-2. Define leverage.

15-3. Under what condition will the use of debt financing raise the return on equity?

15-4. How does the use of debt affect the cash flows of a real estate property in terms of a division of risk and return?

15-5. What is meant by optimal capital structure?

15-6. Why is 100 percent debt financing rare for real estate investments?

15-7. Present the arguments for and against the view that the use of debt can add value to the equity position in a real estate investment. Assume a no-tax situation.

15-8. Explain why the deductibility of interest payments for tax purposes has a positive effect on the use of debt.

15-9. How does our legal system influence the use of debt to finance real estate investments?

15-10. List several institutional factors that will affect the use of debt to finance real estate. Explain how each affects the use of debt.

Problems

15-1. Consider the following information on a real estate property with a value (cost) of $1 million:

ANNUAL CASH FLOW ($)	PROBABILITY
150,000	0.5
90,000	0.5

a. What is the expected return on this property?

b. If an investor can borrow 80 percent of the value of the property at 10 percent interest, what will be the expected return on equity?

c. Will the investor be in danger of insolvency by borrowing 80 percent of the value of the property (that is, will the annual cash flow be sufficient to meet debt obligation)?

d. Should the investor borrow to finance the acquisition of the property or purchase the property with 100 percent equity? Explain.

For Problems 15-2 through 15-5, assume the following basic data about a residential development.

Land cost	$300,000
Building cost[a]	$2,500,000
Total cost	$2,800,000
Holding period	5 years
Gross rent, year 1	$500,000
Vacancy rate	4%
Operating expense, year 1	15% of gross rent
Growth rates	
Gross rent	7%
Operating expense	7%
Resale price	7%
Resale expense rate	5%
Investor's tax bracket	35% on ordinary income
	25% on recapture of depreciation
	15% on excess gain over cost
Depreciation, residential	27.5 years
Property purchased	January 1
Financing:[b]	

DEBT (IN MILLION $)	COST OF DEBT	AFTER-TAX COST OF DEBT	DISCOUNT RATE ON EQUITY
0	N/A	N/A	0.15
1.4	0.09	0.0648	0.15
2.4	0.18	0.1296	0.15

[a]Depreciation year 1 = $87,121; years 2 through 5, $90,909.
[b]All debt amortized over 30 years.

All Files
Income
Property

15-2. a. Calculate the after-tax cash flows for the project, assuming no debt.
b. Calculate the present value of the equity position. (Note: not the net present value.)

All Files
Income
Property

15-3. a. Calculate the after-tax cash flows for the project, assuming $1.4 million in debt.
b. Calculate the present value of the equity position.

15-4. a. Calculate the after-tax cash flows for the project, assuming $2.4 million in debt.
b. Calculate the present value of the equity position.

All Files
Income
Property

15-5. Show the total value of the property (value of debt and equity) for each of the debt levels in the above three problems. What is the optimal capital structure?

Notes

1. Unlike owner-occupied residential financing, the use of prepayment penalties in commercial real estate financing is widespread.

2. This term should not be confused with operating leverage, which relates to the relationship between fixed costs and variable costs in business operations.

3. These relationships can be demonstrated algebraically. If the return on assets (ROA) is defined as net operating income (NOI) divided by assets (A), and the return on equity (ROE) is defined as NOI minus interest expense (rD, where r is the interest rate and D is debt) divided by equity, then

$$ROA = \frac{NOI}{A}$$

and

$$ROE = \frac{(NOI - rD)}{Equity}$$

Positive leverage implies that the return on equity is greater than the return on assets if the cost of debt r is less than ROA. That equation

$$\frac{(NOI - rD)}{(A - D)} > \frac{NOI}{A}$$

can be reduced to

$$r < \frac{NOI}{A}$$

4. One could argue that with revenue increasing by 8 percent and expenses increasing by 9 percent the property's value should increase by more than 6 percent. All other things being equal, this may be true. However, for purposes of illustration, here we assume that other market factors do not allow the property to grow at an amount in excess of 6 percent.

5. The current tax code requires that depreciation for multifamily housing be based on a straight-line write-off over 27.5 years. The property is assumed to be placed in service and also sold in the middle of the month. A full year's depreciation would be $2,500,000/27.5 = $90,909. Prorated over 11.5 months, the precise depreciation for the first year and the last year

would be $87,121. The remaining year's depreciation is rounded to $91,000 from $90,909.

6. Franco Modigliani and Merton Miller. The cost of capital, corporation finance, and the theory of investment. *American Economic Review* 48 (June 1958), 261–297.

7. Recall that agency costs refer to costs incurred by a principal to ensure that an agent operates in a manner that protects the interests of the principal. In the example that follows, the principal will be the lender, and the agent will be the investor-borrower. As you know, borrowers often have an incentive to act in their own interest and not that of the lender.

8. In a later paper, Modigliani and Miller recognize this tax issue and conclude that corporations should use as much debt as possible. Franco Modigliani and Merton Miller. Corporation income taxes and the cost of capital. *American Economic Review* 53 (June 1963), 433–443.

9. George Gau and Ko Wang looked at the debt (loan-to-value) ratios on 759 properties that were sold in Vancouver, Canada, between 1971 and 1985. They did not have sufficient data to test the effect of the tax environment, but they did find that many of the above considerations affected the debt ratio. Apartment complexes (considered to be low risk) had higher debt ratios than other property types. Older properties (with smaller depreciation bases) also had higher debt ratios, as did properties held by corporations. Higher-valued properties (where access to the equity market would be a concern) also had higher debt ratios. In short, they found that the theoretical and practical considerations discussed here played an important part in determining the capital structure of real estate investments. George Gau and Ko Wang. Capital structure decisions in real estate investment. *Journal of the American Real Estate and Urban Economics Association* 18 (Winter 1990), 501–521.

Web Sites

http://www.creonline.com
  Real estate investing articles

http://www.finance.yahoo.com/calculator/index
  Cash flow calculator

FEDERAL TAXATION AND REAL ESTATE FINANCE

CHAPTER

16

LEARNING OBJECTIVES

After reading this chapter, you should understand how the rules and regulations of federal income taxation affect both the value and financing decisions of real estate investments. You will understand how changes in the tax rules can alter the return on real estate investment. Despite the complexity of the tax regulations, you will understand the motivation behind them.

INTRODUCTION

Federal income tax rules and regulations affect both the value and return on real estate investments in different ways. An outline of the effect of current and recent tax rules on real estate investments and real estate finance is given in Figure 16-1, which also orders the discussion in this chapter. Figure 16-1 shows that federal tax rules affect real estate investments through two primary channels: how income is defined for tax purposes and, given the definition of income, how tax payments are determined.

The definition of income is affected by two considerations: allowance of items not involving cash outlays to be treated as expenses (namely, depreciation) and allowance of interest payments on debt to be treated as expenses. Limitations on these expenses, such as the rate at which real estate can be depreciated and the application of both original issue discount (OID) and investment interest rules to interest expenses, will affect the attractiveness of real estate investments.

As to the second major way in which tax rules affect real estate investments—determining the actual amount of taxes to be paid—several considerations should be kept in mind. First, there is the differential treatment of capital gains (especially long-term gains) versus ordinary income. A lower rate on the former will provide an incentive for taxpayers to hold long-term investments and to convert ordinary income to capital gains when possible. To the extent that real estate can be used as a vehicle to do this, a differential tax rate will favor real estate as an investment. Under the current tax rules, a gain from the sale of a depreciable asset will have two components: depreciation recovery and capital gain. Although

FIGURE 16-1	**Tax Regulations and Their Effects on the Value of Real Estate Investment**

After-tax cash flows are affected in two primary ways:

First

The definition of income for tax purposes differs from before-tax cash flows because:

1. Noncash expenses such as depreciation (which often creates "paper losses") are allowed

2. Interest payments on debt can be expensed, subject to
   a. original issue discount (OID) rules
   b. investment interest rules
   c. amortization of discount points

Second

Given income for tax purposes, the actual amount of taxes paid are affected by:

1. Differential tax rates on ordinary income and capital gains

2. Offset of losses against other sources of income; such losses are restricted by
   a. capital loss limitation rules
   b. defining narrow income classes and prohibiting cross-class offsets of losses
   c. establishing "at risk" rules

3. Providing for alternative minimum tax

4. Establishing favorable classes of real estate investment, such as
   a. low-income housing
   b. historical structures

Source: © 2014 OnCourse Learning

the tax rates on the two components can be different, both have maximum rates that are less than the maximum tax rate on ordinary income. The depreciation recovery portion of the total gain is the accumulated depreciation on the project and the remaining amount above depreciation recovery is treated as capital gain.

Second, allowing losses on real estate investments to offset income from other sources will reduce the investor's overall tax bill and increase the investment value of real estate. However, the extent to which losses from real estate may be used to offset income from other sources can be restricted by rules that (1) limit the amount of capital loss that can offset income from other sources, (2) allocate income into increasingly more narrow categories and prevent cross-category offsets, and (3) limit the amount of losses that can be recognized to the amount the taxpayer has "at risk" in the property.

Third, other rules can limit the total amount of tax advantages for a taxpayer. Currently called **alternative minimum taxes (AMTs)**, these rules may limit the use of some of the tax advantages present in real estate investments. Finally, the establishment of favored classes of real estate will encourage investment in real property. Special rules such as tax credits for developing low-income housing or rehabilitating historic buildings will encourage investment in those real estate projects.

Table 16-1 summarizes the effect of tax rules on the value of real estate as an investment and indicates the rules' current status (in boldface). You will note quickly that some of the current rules do not favor real estate investment as much as they have in past years. Prior to 1987 (the effective year of the **Tax Reform Act of 1986**), many of the tax rules would have favored real estate as an

TABLE 16-1

Tax Rules and Real Estate Investment

TAX RULE	TAX RULE FAVORS REAL ESTATE AS INVESTMENT	TAX RULE DOES NOT FAVOR REAL ESTATE AS INVESTMENT	IMPACT ON REAL ESTATE INVESTMENT
Depreciation			Substantial
A. Accelerated over short period	X		
B. Straight-line over extended period		X[a,b]	
Capital gains treatment			Substantial
A. Rate less than ordinary income	X		
B. Rate same as ordinary income		X	
Interest payments on debt			
A. Deductible as an expense	X		Substantial
B. Lender and borrower on different basis	X		Moderate
C. Lender and borrower on same basis		X	
D. Not imputed	X		Moderate
E. Imputed		X	
F. Investment interest limitation		X	Minor
Definition of income			
A. Broad categories	X		Substantial
B. Narrow categories		X	
Alternative minimum tax			Minor
A. Not enforced	X		
B. Enforced		X	
Favored types of investment			Moderate
A. Allowed	X		
B. Not allowed		X	

[a]*Boldface = Current tax rules.*

[b]*Real estate may still have an advantage over other assets that may not be depreciated.*

Source: © 2014 OnCourse Learning

investment. Now, real estate is placed on a more equal plane with other investments.

In general, four changes in the tax laws can affect real estate: (1) changes in marginal tax rates, (2) changes in methods of depreciation, (3) changes in the treatment of capital gains, and (4) changes in the ability to write off losses. The discussion in this chapter will help you understand how these factors affect investors' real estate investment decisions.

CLASSIFICATION OF REAL PROPERTY

For federal income tax purposes, real estate is classified into four categories depending on the purpose for which the property is used:

1. Property held as principal residence.
2. Property held for investment.
3. Property held for resale to others.
4. Property held for use in trade or business.

Our focus in this chapter is on income-producing real estate.

The tax treatment of **property held as principal residence** (commonly called owner-occupied) has some distinct differences from the other categories. Some of these differences are (1) individuals can deduct mortgage interest up to $1 million of acquisition indebtedness plus $100,000 of additional indebtedness for any purpose, (2) losses from the sale and most operating expenses are not tax deductible (only mortgage interest and property taxes are deductible), and (3) depreciation is not allowed. Effective for transactions after May 6, 1997, individuals who sell or exchange a principal residence that they owned and occupied for at least 2 of the 5 years preceding the sale or exchange can elect a $250,000 ($500,000 for joint filers) exclusion from income of gain from the sale or the exchange. This applies to only one sale or exchange every 2 years. A surviving spouse is eligible to file a joint return with the deceased spouse only for the year of the deceased spouse's death. This new exclusion replaces the rollover provision and the age 55 exclusion.

If a homeowner owns more than one home, the property most frequently used is considered the principal residence. If this is unclear the Internal Revenue Service (IRS) considers a set of facts and circumstances that would include factors such as the homeowner's place of employment, the principal abode for other family members, the address given on tax returns, driver's license, the homeowner's mailing address for bills, the location of the homeowner's banks, and the location of religious organizations, clubs, and so on with which the homeowner is affiliated.

Current rules on the treatment of principal residence allow the sale of vacant land that a homeowner owned and used as part of a principal residence to qualify for the exclusion if the sale of the house occurs within 2 years before or after the sale of the vacant land. The vacant land must be adjacent to the land containing the house. The two sales would be treated as one with the maximum exclusion of $250,000 ($500,000 for joint returns). For a home that has a mixed use of principal residence and business, a homeowner is not required to allocate the gain from the sale between business and residential use if the business use occurred within the same dwelling unit as the residential use. The homeowner would be taxed only on the depreciation recovery portion of the gain (that is, the homeowner's accumulated depreciation).

A homeowner who fails to qualify for the exclusion because of a change in employment, health, or unforeseen circumstances may be entitled to a reduced or partial exclusion. Failure to qualify would mean that the homeowner has failed to meet either the occupancy or the 2-year exclusion requirement. The partial exclusion is equal to a fraction of the full exclusion. To calculate the fraction, the numerator is the lesser of the time the homeowner owned or used the home during the 5-year period ending on the date of sale or, if shorter, the period of time between the date of the prior excluded gain and the date of the current sale. The denominator is 2 years (or the equivalent days or months).

Contrary to what you might think initially, most real estate investments do not fall into the category of **property held for investment**. This category applies when the real estate is held strictly for income or investment and the owner has no participation in the operations of the investment. This will generally include unimproved land and net leases. Recall that a net lease is one in which the tenant pays operating expenses (such as maintenance, property taxes, and insurance); thus, the property is held strictly for income and is not used in trade or business. Investments in this category are subject to limitations not placed on other classifications. First, the owner may face limitations on interest deductibility. Second, investments sold at a loss are subject to the limitations imposed by the capital loss provisions of the law.

Property held for resale to other is viewed as inventory and profits from its sale are taxed as ordinary income (as opposed to capital gains). Individuals who hold real estate as inventory in the ordinary course of business are treated as dealers and not investors. Examples are developers developing lots and home builders building houses for immediate resale. Real estate held in this fashion cannot be depreciated; however, losses on the sale of this inventory can be treated as operating losses and are tax deductible.

Property held for use in trade or business, referred to as a Section 1231 asset, is the most prevalent (and in general the most favorable) classification for income-producing real property. In fact, most income-producing real estate investments fall into this category. The key words establishing this category are *real estate owned and operated for the purpose of deriving rental income*. All operating expenses, mortgage interest, and depreciation are fully deductible from rental income. In addition, losses from the sale of the property are fully deductible.

TAX SHELTERS

A **tax shelter** is an investment structured so that tax rules and regulations are utilized to enhance its value. The value of the investment is increased because a significant portion of the investor's return is derived from tax savings on other income or tax-favored income on the investment itself. In other words, the total value of the asset would be the sum of its fundamental economic value and the tax shelter value. The tax laws are used to alter the amount and timing of the cash flows, as well as the discount rate used to value the cash flows. Real estate is one investment that has the potential to be used as a tax shelter. The organizational form of ownership of the real estate combined with tax laws causes the cash flows from the real estate investment to be larger, occur sooner, or both, than they otherwise would. Organizational forms for holding real estate investments include corporations (both subchapter S and C corporations), limited and general partnerships, real estate investment trusts (REITs), and sole ownership. Because tax rules are applied differently according to the organizational structure of the investment, both the rules and the structure combine to create a shelter.

In some cases, favorable tax rules will enhance the value of real estate investments that would have value in their absence. More importantly, tax rules may create value for real estate investments that otherwise would not have value or be economically feasible. It is this latter case that most aptly fits the definition of a tax shelter. Given sufficiently favorable rules, a real estate investment that otherwise would generate negative cash flows may provide the investor with positive cash flows. Although any investment that utilizes tax rules to enhance the value of its cash flows can be considered a tax shelter, the term is generally applied to situations where positive cash flows result strictly from the application of tax regulations.

Taxes, Cash Flows, and Discount Rates: Some Examples

First, let's distinguish between the **before-** and the **after-tax discount rate** used to value cash flows. Investors are concerned with the cash flow they receive after paying income taxes. If an investor in a 40 percent tax bracket owns a 5-year corporate (taxable) bond that pays $100 annually (a 10 percent coupon bond), his or her **after-tax cash flow** will be $60. If the (before-tax) market discount rate for this bond is 10 percent, we know it should be valued at par, $1,000. That is,

$$\$1000 = \frac{\$100}{(1.1)^1} + \frac{\$100}{(1.1)^2} + \cdots + \frac{\$1000}{(1.1)^5}$$

The investor employing a 10 percent discount rate values the asset at $1,000, even though it pays only $60 annually after taxes. That is, one way to value the asset is to apply a before-tax rate to the **before-tax cash flows**.

How would this same investor value an equally risky municipal bond of the same maturity that promised to pay $60 annually on which there would be no taxes? The

TABLE 16-2

Property Data for Multifamily Investment Property

Project cost:	
Land	$165,000
Building	$660,000
Acquisition costs	$ 14,000
Additional capital improvements	none
Total	$839,000
Financing data:	
Loan amount	$660,000
Interest rate (monthly pmt)[a]	10%
Term	20 years
Financing costs	4% of loan amount
Prepayment penalty	5% of outstanding balance
Equity investment	$205,400
Operating data:	
Gross rent year 1	$141,000
Vacancy rate	6% of gross rent
Other income	3% of gross rent
Operating expense	32% of gross rent
Growth rates:	
Gross rent	5% per year
Property value	5% per year
Other:	
Selling expenses at reversion	8% of selling price
Depreciation	residential straight-line
Marginal tax rate	35%
Depreciation Recovery Tax	25%
Capital gains tax rate	15%
Holding period	5 years
Required equity yield	10%

[a]*The monthly payment is converted to an annual debt service by multiplying the monthly payment by 12.*

Source: © 2014 OnCourse Learning

answer is that he or she would place the same value on the municipal as on the corporate bond. And this is the case. If the two equally risky assets promise the same cash flows after taxes, they should be valued identically. But this would require that the after-tax cash flows be valued not by a before-tax market discount rate but rather by the investor's after-tax discount rate. For each asset, the after-tax cash flow is the same, $60. If they have the same value, they should be valued with the same discount rate. In this case, the discount rate is the after-tax rate of $r(1 - T)$, where r is the before-tax market rate and T is the investor's tax rate. For each asset, we have

$$\$1000 = \frac{\$60}{(1.06)^1} + \frac{\$60}{(1.06)^2} + \cdots + \frac{\$1000}{(1.06)^5}$$

where $60 is the after-tax annual cash flow and 0.06 is the after-tax discount rate, $0.1 \times (1 - 0.4)$.

Let's look at a more complex example. Table 16-2 shows the operating data and assumptions for a multifamily investment under the current tax laws. Recall that the Tax Reform Act of 1986 (and the subsequent Tax Act of 1993) ushered in widespread changes in the tax law. These changes reduced the attractiveness of real estate as a tax shelter. Later, we will contrast cash flows under the current tax system to the cash flows under the more lenient tax rules of the early 1980s. This will allow us to demonstrate the effect of changes in the tax regulations on the value of real estate investments.

Table 16-3 shows the cash flows from operations for a 5-year holding period. To calculate the after-tax cash flows, it is necessary to determine the tax liability.

TABLE 16-3

After-Tax Cash Flow from Operations for 5-Year Holding Period

YEAR	1	2	3	4	5
Gross revenue	141,000	148,050	155,452	163,225	171,386
− Vacancy	−8,460	−8,883	−9,327	−9,794	−10,283
+ Other income	+ 4,230	+ 4,442	+ 4,664	+ 4,897	+ 5,142
Effective gross income	136,770	143,609	150,789	158,328	166,245
− Operating expenses	−45,120	−47,376	−49,745	−52,232	−54,844
Net operating income	91,650	96,233	101,044	106,096	111,401
− Mortgage payment	−76,430	−76,430	−76,430	−76,430	−106,065
Before-tax cash flow	15,220	19,803	24,614	25,336	5,336
− Taxes	−501	−2,149	−4,276	−6,532	+ 8,017
After-tax cash flow	14,719	17,654	20,338	18,804	13,353

TAXES FROM OPERATIONS

YEAR	1	2	3	4	5
Effective gross income	136,770	143,609	150,789	158,328	166,245
− Operating expenses	−45,120	−47,376	−49,745	−52,232	−54,844
Net operating income	91,650	96,233	101,044	106,096	106,0961
− Interest	−65,508	−64,365	−63,101	−61,706	−89,799
− Amortized financing cost	−1,320	−1,320	−1,320	−1,320	−1,320
− Depreciation	−23,390	−24,407	−24,407	−24,407	−23,390
Taxable income	1,432	6,141	12,216	18,663	-22,907
× t	× 0.35	× 0.35	× 0.35	× 0.35	× 0.35
Taxes	501	2,149	4,276	6,532	−8,017

AFTER-TAX EQUITY REVERSION

Estimated selling price	1,052,932
− Selling expense	−84,235
Net sales price	968,697
− Unpaid mortgage balance	−592,696
Before-tax equity reversion	376,001
− TXR	−49,455
After-tax equity reversion	326,546

TAXES FROM RESALE OF PROPERTY TAXABLE INCOME FROM RESALE

Estimated selling price	1,052,932
− Selling expense	−84,235
Amount realized	968,697
− Adjusted basis	−718,999
Gain from sale	249,698

TAXES FROM RESALE

Depreciation recovery	120,000
× t_d	× 0.25
Depreciation recovery tax	30,000
Capital gain	129,698
× t_g	× 0.15
Capital gain tax	19,455
Depreciation recovery tax	30,000
+ Capital gain tax	+ 19,455
TXB	49,455

(Continued)

TABLE 16-3
(Continued)

	SUMMARY OF AFTER–TAX CASH FLOWS					
YEAR	0	1	2	3	4	5
After–tax cash flow	−205,400	14,719	17,654	20,338	18,804	13,353
After–tax equity reserve						326,546
NPV @ 10%	$61,745					
IRP	16.72%					

Source: © 2014 OnCourse Learning

Several expansions are seen from the cash flow example presented in Chapter 15. First, with the debt financing, we now have financing costs. The total amount is $26,400 ($660,000 × 0.04) and, although paid at the outset, must be amortized over the life of the mortgage. This yields a deduction each year of $1,320. Note that in year 5 (the end of the holding period when the loan is repaid) the investor is allowed to take the unamortized balance ($21,120). We also have a prepayment penalty on the mortgage of 5 percent of the outstanding balance. The loan is repaid at the end of year 5, thus the investor incurs a penalty of $29,635 ($592,696 × 0.05). Since the penalty is an actual outlay, it is included in the mortgage payment for year 5. Since the penalty is treated as interest and is fully deductible in the year it is paid, it is included in the interest expense for year 5.

The depreciation deduction now includes the appropriate portion of acquisition costs. Remember that acquisition costs are costs related to acquiring the property. Acquisition costs are paid at the outset but are not fully deductible in the year they are paid. The portion of acquisition costs related to acquiring the improvement (versus the land) can be included in the depreciable basis and written off over the depreciable life of the mortgage. In our example, acquisition costs are $14,000 and the building portion of the total project cost is 80 percent. Thus $11,200 of the acquisition costs can be included in depreciation. This yields total depreciation of $671,200 ($660,000 + $11,200) and results in annual depreciation of $24,407. Remember that the first year and last year of the holding period must be adjusted for mid-month convention, thus the deduction in those years is $23,390 ($24,407/(11.5/12)). The specifics of calculating depreciation are discussed more fully later in this chapter.

With an initial equity investment of $205,400 (down payment plus financing costs plus acquisition costs), this project is acceptable at the required return of 10 percent. The NPV for equity is $57,718 and the IRR for equity is 16.33 percent.

By contrast, Table 16-4 shows a different picture for the same project under the tax treatment of the 1981 Tax Act. The generous depreciation allowances produce negative taxable income. These losses could be written off against income from other sources to produce tax savings and generate even larger after-tax cash flows. Even more interesting, the project now generates a higher rate of return and has a greater NPV. This shows that tax rules can affect the investment value of real property.

Because all the cash flows (including the initial equity investment for the project) are on an after-tax basis, the proper discount rate is the after-tax discount rate. Since neither acquisition costs nor financing costs are deductible at the outset and since the down payment is not tax deductible, these equity expenditures are after-tax costs.

TABLE 16-4

Comparison of Pre- and Post-1986 Tax Reform Act After-Tax Cash Flows

YEAR	POST-1986 TAX TREATMENT AFTER-TAX CASH FLOW	TAX TREATMENT PRE-1981 TAX ACT
0	−205,400	−205,400
1	14,719	43,081
2	17,654	38,089
3	20,338	36,506
4	18,804	34,979
5	13,353 + 326,546	28,587 + 262,805
NPV at 10%	$61,745	$97,493
IRR	16.72%	21.87%

Source: © 2014 OnCourse Learning

Two tax considerations drive the difference in pretax and posttax value in this example. First, the favorable depreciation allowance creates large and early tax rebates (think: time value of money). Second, the conversion of ordinary income to capital gains produces a favorable treatment. Each dollar of depreciation reduces ordinary income by $1 and reduces taxes by the investor's marginal tax rate in the year in which it occurs. It also reduces the book value of the property and, given the ultimate sale price, increases the capital gain in the year of sale. The capital gains tax rate is generally lower than the investor's marginal tax rate. Thus, the tax rules allow the investor to postpone paying taxes in the early years at the higher marginal tax rate in exchange for paying taxes at a lower rate when the property is sold—a good deal.

The example just discussed is a good illustration of how a property can be made more attractive through the application of favorable tax laws. There is some suggestion that the lenient tax laws of the early 1980s encouraged the development of real estate projects that were pure tax shelters.

REAL ESTATE TAX REGULATIONS

Figure 16-1 provides a useful outline to discuss tax regulations and their impact on real estate. The value of real estate can be affected by the interaction of several of the tax rules. We begin with a discussion of the manner in which tax regulations affect the definition of income.

Definition of Income

The definition of taxable income differs from the definition of before-tax cash flow for two reasons. One is the treatment of noncash expenses such as depreciation, and the other is the treatment of interest as an expense.

Noncash Expenses, Notably Depreciation

Since depreciation is a noncash expense, each dollar of depreciation results in a proportional tax savings equal to the marginal tax rate of the taxpayer. This is true whether the depreciation reduces reported profits, whereby tax dollars are saved, or whether it creates a loss that can be offset against other income, creating a tax "rebate." Three factors affect the value of the tax savings that result from depreciation—the amount of depreciation, the speed of write-off, and the marginal tax rate. The tax shelter provided by depreciation will be greater if the tax laws allow a greater amount of depreciation to be recorded early in the life of the investment and tax rates are high. The general formula for the present value (PV) of the **depreciation tax shield** is

$$PV = \sum_{t=1}^{n} \frac{D_t \times T}{(1 + r)^t} \qquad \text{(Equation 16-1)}$$

where D_t is the dollar amount of depreciation in period t, n is the number of periods over which depreciation occurs (not necessarily the period over which the investment is held), T is the marginal tax rate of the investor, and r is the discount interest rate.

During the last two decades, there have been several distinct periods marked by different tax treatments of depreciation. In the several years prior to 1981, real estate was depreciated over relatively long periods. This disadvantage was offset by the ability of investors to select one of a few accelerated methods of depreciation. A high top marginal tax bracket, 70 percent, added to the value of the depreciation tax shield during this time. From 1981 through 1986, the tax shield held its value. Although the top marginal tax bracket was reduced to 50 percent, the depreciation allowance was accelerated. After 1986, however, the value of the tax shield was reduced by lengthening the period of depreciation, eliminating accelerated methods, and reducing the top tax bracket to 28 percent. The Tax Act of 1993 raised marginal tax rates on ordinary income to a maximum of 39.6 percent and extended the term of depreciation for nonresidential property. Finally, in 1997 capital gains treatment was reintroduced. Let's review these six periods.

Pre-1981. Prior to the Economic Recovery Act of 1981, tax regulations placed commercial real estate into classes with rather long lives for the purpose of depreciation. Residential real estate (multifamily housing) was depreciated over 40 years. The rules allowed for several methods of accelerated depreciation, including the double-declining balance and sum-of-the-years' digits methods. It also allowed a taxpayer to shift from one method to another during the depreciation period if the switch resulted in a greater depreciation over the remaining period. The taxpayer also could choose a straight-line depreciation method. During this time, the top marginal tax bracket was 70 percent.

Depreciation in year t, (D_t) under the **straight-line method** is given by

$$D_t = \frac{C}{n} \qquad \text{(Equation 16-2)}$$

where C is the cost basis of the depreciable portion of the real estate and n is the term over which it is depreciated. Under the straight-line method, the property is considered to deteriorate at a constant rate over its depreciable life.

Under the **double-declining method**, the depreciation in the first year is double that under straight-line. For the second year, depreciation is double the amount that would be calculated if the remaining balance were depreciated under a straight-line method. This method provides for relatively large depreciation in the initial years and little in the later years.

Annual depreciation under the **sum-of-the-years' digits method** is given by a ratio for which the numerator n is the number of years remaining, the denominator (SYD) is the sum of the years in the depreciable life taken individually, and C is the cost basis of the depreciable portion of the real estate.

1981–1986. The most notable feature affecting real estate in the Tax Reform Act of 1981 was the establishment of a new method of depreciation, the **accelerated cost recovery system (ACRS)**. Real estate was placed in a category of 15 years. This increased to 18 years for 1984 and 1985 then to 19 years for 1986. The depreciation rates for the first 5 years were, respectively: 12, 10, 9, 8, and 7 percent (46 percent of total depreciation). The alternative straight-line depreciation for real estate in the 15-year class was 6.67 percent in each year (1/15). From 1981 to 1986, the top tax bracket was 50 percent. This system allowed for somewhat greater depreciation in the early years but also reduced the value of the depreciation shield by lowering the top tax rate (from 70 percent in previous years).

1986–1993. The Tax Reform Act of 1986 (TRA 1986) created the **modified accelerated cost recovery system (MACRS)**. This system eliminated accelerated depreciation and placed commercial real estate investments in two separate classes. Residential properties such as apartment houses were to be depreciated over 27.5 years, and nonresidential properties (office buildings, shopping centers, warehouses, and so on) over 31.5 years, both on a straight-line basis. This change eliminated accelerated depreciation and lengthened the depreciation period. At the same time, the top tax bracket was reduced to 28 percent.[1] These changes of lengthening the depreciation schedule, switching to straight-line depreciation, and lowering the marginal tax rates for personal income led to a significant reduction in the value of the depreciation tax shield.

The MACRS requires use of the **midmonth convention**, which assumes that the asset is placed into service in the middle of the month acquired. It also assumes that the asset is sold in the middle of the month. Thus, even if the asset is purchased on January 1, the maximum depreciation for the first year is 11.5 months. Likewise, if the asset is sold on December 31 of a later year, the maximum depreciation allowed for that year is 11.5 months.

1993–1997. The Tax Act of 1993 provided some further changes in the personal income tax structure: (1) the top marginal tax rate increased from 31 percent for 1992 to 39.6 percent for 1993; (2) the long-term capital gains tax remained at a maximum of 28 percent; (3) starting in 1994, losses and credits from certain real estate activities were no longer disallowed by the passive rules; and (4) the depreciation write-off for nonresidential real estate increases from 31.5 years to 39 years straight-line for properties put in service after May 12, 1993.

1997–2003. The Taxpayer Relief Act of 1997 increased the holding period for long-term capital gains to 18 months (for sales and exchanges after July 28, 1997). For sales with long-term gains after May 6, 1997, the maximum capital gains rate was 20 percent (10 percent in a 15 percent marginal bracket). Capital gain property acquired after December 31, 2000, and held for more than 5 years were taxed at the reduced rate of 18 percent. This provision did not benefit anyone until the year 2006. For individuals in the 15 percent bracket, the 10 percent rate for capital gains was reduced to 8 percent for assets meeting the 5-year holding period, regardless of the acquisition date. This reduction is only for capital gains after December 31, 2000. Effective May 6, 2003, the tax rate on long-term capital gains is 15 percent.

Post-2003. The Jobs and Growth Tax Relief Reconciliation Act of 2003 lowered the maximum marginal income tax rate for individuals to 35 percent. This produced six marginal tax rates for individuals ranging from 10 percent to 35 percent. The maximum tax rate on depreciation recapture for Section 1250 properties is 25 percent. Note that, under current tax rules, depreciation must be recaptured even though it is straight-line. In the past, only excess depreciation (the difference between accelerated and straight-line) had to be recaptured. The portion of the total gain remaining after depreciation is recaptured is treated as capital gain and is taxed at a rate up to 15 percent.

2013. In 2013 Congress allowed the Bush tax cuts from 2003 to expire. This resulted in the federal current income tax structure for individuals containing seven marginal tax rates: 10%, 15%, 25%, 28%, 33%, 35%, and 39.6%. The maximum tax rate on long-term capital gains also increased to 20 percent. Thus the applicable long-term capital gains tax rates are: 0% for the 10% and 15% marginal income tax brackets, 15% for the 25%, 28%, 33%, and 35% marginal income tax brackets, and 20% for the 39.6% marginal income tax rate.

Depreciation methods for the 1981–1986 and post-1986 tax periods are summarized in Table 16-5. The table shows the annual depreciation for a multifamily residential property with a depreciable base of $100,000. A good measure of the value of depreciation is the present value of the tax savings that results from the method. For each method, the table shows both the present value (using a discount rate of 10 percent) of the depreciation amount and the present value of the tax savings. The latter value is the former multiplied by the relevant top tax rate. For the ACRS, the present value of the

TABLE 16-5

Annual Depreciation: ACRS and Post-1986 Methods, Multifamily Residential Property

Depreciable Base, $100,000; Placed in Service, January 1

YEAR	1981–1986 ACCELERATED COST RECOVERY ($) SYSTEM (ACRS)[a]	POST-1986 TAX REFORM ACT OF 1986 ($) (TRA 1986)
1	12,000	3,485[b]
2	10,000	3,636
3	9,000	3,636
4	8,000	3,636
5	7,000	3,636
6	6,000	3,636
7	6,000	3,636
8	6,000	3,636
9	6,000	3,636
10	5,000	3,636
11	5,000	3,636
12	5,000	3,636
13	5,000	3,636
14	5,000	3,636
15	5,000	3,636
16	—	3,636
17	—	3,636
18	—	3,636
19	—	3,636
20	—	3,636
21	—	3,636
22	—	3,636
23	—	3,636
24	—	3,636
25	—	3,636
26	—	3,636
27	—	3,636
28	—	1,979
Present value at 10%	$56,790	$33,586
Present value × the marginal tax rate[c]	$28,395	$ 9,404

[a]*Fifteen-year depreciable term.*

[b]*Reflects the midmonth convention.*

[c]*Assumed to be 50 and 28 percent, respectively.*

Source: © 2014 OnCourse Learning

tax savings is $28,395 with a top tax rate of 50 percent. For the post-1986 period, the present value of the tax savings is $9,404 with a top tax rate of 28 percent.

This shows that the tax shelter component of the asset's value declined significantly as a result of the shift to straight-line, a lengthening of the depreciation period, and a reduction in marginal tax rates.[2] At first thought, one might be tempted to ask how a tax law (such as TRA 1986) that significantly lowers the tax rate can have an adverse effect on the value of real estate as an investment. After all, if the investor pays less taxes, should that not increase the value of any capital investment? The answer is yes. One recalls that the 1986 tax law not only lowered tax rates but also reduced the value of depreciation and eliminated the advantage of capital gains. High tax brackets favor real estate projects that produce paper losses, because a greater portion of the loss results in a tax savings on other income. Paper losses are enhanced by generous depreciation allowances. Low tax rates favor real estate investments that will show a profit, because fewer taxes are paid on such investments. To this extent, the change in the depreciation method accomplished one intended goal—to reduce investment in real estate projects that are not economically justifiable.

Taxes and Interest Payments

Income for tax purposes also is affected by the treatment of interest payments on debt that are generally considered an expense. Thus, for every dollar of interest paid, the tax due to the government is reduced by one dollar times the tax rate. We saw in the previous chapter how the equity yield is enhanced by the use of debt. This would encourage the use of debt financing. This is counterbalanced by default risk, which increases as the amount of debt increases.

In the past, real estate developers and investors have used this rule to reduce or avoid taxes in much the same fashion as the depreciation tax shield. The tax laws are designed to restrict abuses. Two examples are the original issue discount (OID) rules and the investment interest limitation rules.

Original Issue Discount Rules

By way of background, the term **original issue discount (OID)** refers to debt that is issued at a discount from the face value. Such debt may have no coupon or interest payments during its life but simply promises a face amount at maturity. Zero-coupon bonds issued by corporations are a good example. The present value (at 10 percent) of a $1,000 bond that pays no coupon interest and matures in 10 years is $385.54. The investor who purchases the bond receives a 10 percent return through appreciation in its value over the term of the bond. During this time, the investor receives no cash interest payments. Assuming interest rates do not change, the value of the bond will increase each year as it approaches maturity. At one time investors did not have to pay tax on the accretion in value, since they were receiving no interest payments. Later, the IRS ruled that investors had to pay tax on the annual accretion in value. Prior to 1984, the set of regulations covering these requirements were referred to as OID rules, and they were applied only to corporate debt securities. The Tax Reform Act of 1984 extended the OID rules to real estate lending such as mortgages. The rules are applied to the financing of real estate whenever the periodic interest payment is different from market rates. Several abusive practices led to the OID rules being applied to real estate.

One practice concerned the conversion of ordinary income to capital gains during times when there is a differential tax rate. A simple example will illustrate. A property owner may desire to sell a parcel valued at $1 million that originally was purchased for $800,000. The seller, in a high tax bracket, has no immediate need for cash, only future income. The seller is willing to finance the purchase price at 12 percent over 30 years. The annual payment would be $124,144, of which $120,000 would be interest in the first year. The seller must pay taxes on interest at the ordinary tax rate. What would happen if, instead, the seller raised his asking price to $1.4 million and charged 8 percent interest on a loan for $1.4 million over the same term? The annual payment would remain relatively the same at $124,358 of which interest in the first year would be $112,000. The seller would receive the same payment and be able to trade off less ordinary income in the future for more capital gains in the present (the capital gain increases to $600,000 from $200,000). Even on a time-unadjusted basis, the seller pays less total tax and has greater after-tax income.

Another abusive practice that led to the OID rules was the use of large amounts of nonrecourse debt to sell properties at inflated prices. Without getting too technical, **nonrecourse debt** is a loan for which the borrower is not personally liable. Generally, the lender can only look to the property as collateral and for payment of the debt. **Recourse debt** refers to debt for which the lender can look to the personal assets of the borrower in the event of default. In seller-financed transactions, the seller of the property becomes the lender, and the buyer becomes the borrower. As an example of abusive practices, assume that an owner of a property valued at $1 million sells it for $1.8 million and finances the major portion of the loan at a very low rate—for example, 4 percent. The payments on the loan may be no greater than a market interest loan for a smaller amount and a sale at the true value. But the higher transaction price allows the borrower to write off much larger amounts of depreciation. Taxpayers in high tax brackets can then use the loss to offset other income, a typical tax shelter. Meanwhile, the seller of the property reports the sale on an installment basis, avoiding immediate capital gains tax. If the value of the property rises sufficiently, the buyer will continue to make payments on the loan and eventually pay off the debt. If the property does not rise in value, the buyer may default on the loan, giving the property back to the original owner. The total tax savings to the buyer because of the depreciation may well exceed the down payment, so there is no loss on the default. The parties also benefit if the loan called for the accrual of interest. If the buyer was on an accrual and the seller on a cash basis, the former could take a deduction for the interest accrued but not paid, while the latter would not have to report interest income. As a result of these practices, the OID rules were enacted. At-risk limitations also were introduced as a result of the use of nonrecourse debt. (The at-risk limitation rule is discussed later in the chapter.) First applied to real estate under the Tax Reform Act of 1984, the OID rules remained intact under the more recent TRA of 1986. These rules require two things: that a market rate be imputed to seller financing if it carries a below-market rate and interest charge, and that income be reported annually. There are two tests to determine if the OID rules apply.

The **adequacy-of-interest test** says that if the stated interest rate is less than 110 percent of the applicable federal rate, an interest rate will be imputed at 120 percent of the applicable federal rate. The applicable federal rate is determined with reference to the rate on U.S. Treasury obligations with a maturity equal to that on the loan. Three categories have been established: loans of maturity less than 3 years, loans of maturity from 3 to 9 years, and loans of maturity after 9 years.

EXAMPLE

Assume that the applicable federal rate is 10 percent. The rate on a loan is 9 percent. Since the rate is less than 11 percent (110 percent of 10 percent), the imputed rate on the loan will be set at 12 percent (120 percent of 10 percent).

The **time-value-of-money test** is applied only in cases where the stated interest meets the adequacy-of-interest test, but payments are not paid at least annually or an interest rate must be imputed. In either case, the test requires that the effective interest rate on the loan be determined and the amount of interest treated as income to the lender and expense to the borrower. In short, the OID rules require that interest be imputed and reported as revenue (expense) annually.

There are some exceptions to the OID rules. They fall into two categories: those exempted under the 1984 act and those subsequently exempted under an amendment passed in October 1985. Exemptions under the original act include sales of farms by individuals for not more than $1 million, sales of personal residences under $250,000, and transactions between related parties under $500,000. For these transactions the **imputed interest rule** applies, but the rate is set at 10 percent for loans that carry a rate less than 9 percent. Also, the time-value-of-money rule is not applied. This means that a cash-basis seller need not report interest income until actually received, although the accrual-basis buyer can deduct the interest expense as incurred.

The amendments in 1985 liberalized the OID rules further. For transactions where the amount of the seller financing does not exceed $2.8 million, the interest rate for tax purposes will be the lower of 9 percent or 100 percent of the applicable federal rate. Also, the $2.8 million figure has been indexed for inflation since 1990. This reduces the minimum interest rate either 110 percent or 120 percent of the applicable federal rate requirement. For sales involving a sale-leaseback with any amount of seller financing, the OID rules apply. The OID rules also apply to any seller financing greater than $2.8 million. The amendments provide for the use of the cash-basis method of accounting for interest provided the financing is $2 million or less and both the lender and the borrower agree to elect the cash-basis method.

Investment Interest Payments

Another example of the use of tax laws to minimize after-tax income involved holding property for investment purposes. Again, at a time when there was a tax-rate differential on ordinary and capital gains income, it was possible to transfer ordinary income into capital gains using interest expense as the tax shield. Assume an investor purchases an asset that is not likely to produce an operating income, only capital gains. An example would be the purchase of raw land to be held for appreciation in value. The investor takes out a loan to purchase the property with only a small down payment. On an annual operating basis, the investor will show no income, only an interest expense. The resulting loss can be used to offset other income. Here, interest expense and not depreciation creates the tax shelter. Later, when the property is sold, the gain is taxed at a lower capital gain rate.

To curtail such arrangements, an **investment interest limitation** was placed on the deduction of interest payments by the Tax Reform Act of 1969. It was aimed at those instances where an investment was made in an asset that provided no annual operating income. Most such assets include stocks and bonds. Examples in real estate singled out by the 1969 act included raw land and net leased investments. With a **net leased investment**, the owner holds property for which all operating expenses, including property taxes, repairs, and other expenses, are paid by the tenant. The investment replicates the holding of an investment for which the investor makes no managerial decisions or incurs no operating expenses. TRA 1986 removed net leased investments from the limitation because such properties under the act were placed under passive loss limitations (discussed below). The purpose of the rule as it now stands is to limit the amount of an individual's annual interest deduction to the amount of the net investment income received. If insufficient net income is generated, interest expense may not be deductible on loans used to carry raw land investments.

E X A M P L E

An investor borrows $1 million at 10 percent to purchase land valued at $1.2 million in the hopes that it will appreciate in value. In the first year, he or she allows some development of minerals and receives royalties of $110,000. Investment expenses in the first year consist solely of property taxes of $35,000. The interest expense will be $100,000 (0.1 × $1,000,000). The investor may make the following deductions:

Royalty income ($)	110,000
Less property tax expense ($)	35,000
Equals net investment income ($)	75,000
Interest allowed ($)	75,000
Interest deferred ($)	25,000

Determination of Taxes

The above rules specify how income and expenses are defined for the purpose of determining taxable income. Given taxable income, other rules determine the amount of the tax liability. The tax liability will be determined by

1. Differential tax rates on ordinary income and capital gains.
2. Offsetting losses from one income source against other sources (passive loss limitations).
3. Applicability of AMTs.
4. Establishment of favored classes of investment.

Differential Tax Rates

Prior to TRA 1986 and subsequent to 1997, ordinary income and capital gains income were taxed at different rates. The lower rate on capital gains encouraged the conversion of ordinary income into capital gains whenever possible. The 1986 act retained the distinction between the two types of income but required capital gains to be treated as ordinary income up to a maximum rate of 28 percent. The maximum tax rate for individuals is 39.6 percent. Tax regulations continue to require that income be distinguished because differential rates seem to come and go, and capital losses (discussed below) continue to be restricted. However, the closer to equalization the rates, the less the incentive to design tax schemes and shelters that convert ordinary income into capital gains.

Limitation of Losses

Tax regulations limit the use of losses from one source to offset income from another source in three ways: capital loss limitation, passive loss limitation, and "at-risk" rules.

Capital Loss Limitation. The **capital loss limitation** rule allows the taxpayer to offset capital losses only against capital gains. This is so even if tax rates are the same for ordinary income and for capital gains. Capital losses in excess of capital gains can be used to offset other sources of income only up to $3,000 annually. The remainder must be carried forward and used in subsequent years to offset capital gains or another $3,000 in other income. This rule really does not prevent the use of real estate as a tax shelter. The value of real estate as a tax shelter derives mainly from operating losses that could, if allowed by the tax rules, be used to offset other sources of income. Present rules, such as the **passive loss limitation**, severely restrict such an offset, however.

Passive Loss Limitation. Real estate tax shelters existed because losses created through a depreciation write-off could be offset against other (non-real estate) income. The tax savings were a bonus to the positive cash flow of the investment. The government's answer to this "problem" was to create narrow categories of income. Losses in one class cannot be used to offset positive income in other classes. There are two general types of income, which we will refer to as business income and outside income. The latter generally includes salaries and wages from an occupation. TRA 1986 created the passive activities loss limitation (PALL) rule and established three classes within the category of business income: active, portfolio, and passive income. **Active income** consists primarily of earnings received from actively working in a business. Income from an active trade or business is further subdivided into income from real estate or business. **Portfolio income** is income received from investments, such as interest on bonds, dividends on stock, and capital gains from these investments. **Passive income**, the focus here, is income received primarily from real estate activities. Figure 16-2 summarizes the categories of income and indicates the extent to which loss can be offset by outside income.

A loss generated by an active trade or business can be used to offset outside income, just as under prior law. The taxpayer must participate "materially" in the active trade or business. To participate materially means to be involved on a regular, continuous, and substantial basis. Real estate is not generally considered to be an active business. Losses from real estate activities cannot be used to offset outside income (except for a $25,000 special exemption discussed below). In essence, no real estate business, regardless of the taxpayer's participation, can be considered an active trade or business. A real estate business is usually characterized by rental activity. Rental activity is activity that produces revenue for the use of tangible real property. One exception here is the lodging industry, which rents living space on a short-term basis. Thus, hotels and motels are one example of real estate in an active business class.

Portfolio losses (losses in this class occur almost exclusively through a capital loss—a loss on the sale of the capital asset) can be offset against portfolio gains and up to $3,000 in ordinary income annually. Dividends from a REIT or income from a real estate mortgage investment conduit (REMIC) are considered portfolio income. These instruments, although real estate related, are actually stocks and bonds. Income from REITs and REMICs cannot be used to offset **passive losses**.

Passive income consists of income not in the above classifications. It includes all nonactive real estate activity and all income from limited partnerships. Income from limited partnerships is passive income by definition. Thus, whether or not a limited partnership is engaged in a non-real estate trade or business or a real estate trade or business, the income is still classified as passive. Income received for personal services performed for a limited partnership is not passive income, however. If a limited partner receives a salary for preparing the accounts of the partnership, such income is considered outside income.

Given these classes, losses from one are not available to offset income from the others. The one exception is the active participant in a real estate investment. Up to $25,000 in losses from this class can be used to offset income from other classes (active non-real estate, portfolio, or outside income). The loss must be from actively participating in real estate. This means that the taxpayer must be actively involved in the real estate rental activity. To be actively involved is not the same as to be materially involved (the requirement for the non-real estate trade or business). Active involvement requires only that the taxpayer participate in a significant

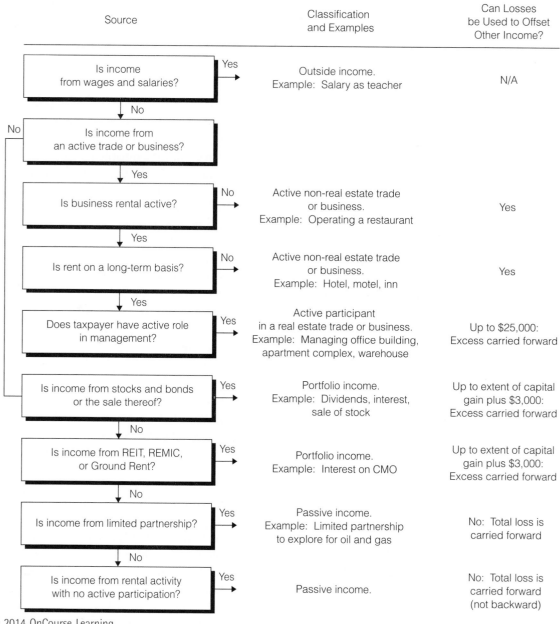

FIGURE 16-2   **Tax Reform Act of 1986 and Income Classification**

Source	Classification and Examples	Can Losses be Used to Offset Other Income?
Is income from wages and salaries? — **Yes**	Outside income. Example: Salary as teacher	N/A
Is income from an active trade or business?		
Is business rental active? — **No**	Active non-real estate trade or business. Example: Operating a restaurant	Yes
Is rent on a long-term basis? — **No**	Active non-real estate trade or business. Example: Hotel, motel, inn	Yes
Does taxpayer have active role in management? — **Yes**	Active participant in a real estate trade or business. Example: Managing office building, apartment complex, warehouse	Up to $25,000: Excess carried forward
Is income from stocks and bonds or the sale thereof? — **Yes**	Portfolio income. Example: Dividends, interest, sale of stock	Up to extent of capital gain plus $3,000: Excess carried forward
Is income from REIT, REMIC, or Ground Rent? — **Yes**	Portfolio income. Example: Interest on CMO	Up to extent of capital gain plus $3,000: Excess carried forward
Is income from limited partnership? — **Yes**	Passive income. Example: Limited partnership to explore for oil and gas	No: Total loss is carried forward
Is income from rental activity with no active participation? — **Yes**	Passive income.	No: Total loss is carried forward (not backward)

Source: © 2014 OnCourse Learning

sense, such as managing the property, making repairs, or arranging for repairs to be made. Taxpayers with an adjusted gross income (AGI) of less than $100,000 can use the entire $25,000 exemption. The exemption is reduced by 50 percent of the taxpayer's AGI above $100,000. It is eliminated for an AGI of $150,000 or above.

Use of Passive Losses. Unless the taxpayer is actively involved in a rental property, a gain or loss is categorized as passive income and losses. For each tax year, the taxpayer must net those losses and income. Each rental property is considered as a separate "activity." For each activity, positive net passive income is taxable and net passive losses must be carried forward to a future date. Passive losses cannot be carried back. The deferred (also called suspended) passive losses can be used to offset any positive passive income in future years, including any gain in the year the taxpayer disposes of the real estate activity. Any **suspended passive losses** that remain after the disposition of the entire activity can be used to offset outside income. Passive losses from an activity are suspended, but they are not lost.

The Tax Act of 1993 provides some easing of the passive loss rules for real estate brokers, salespersons, and other real estate professionals. The major benefit is that eligible taxpayers can deduct unlimited real estate activity losses from active income and portfolio income. Under the new law, individuals must meet these requirements: (1) More than half of all personal services they perform during the year must be for real property trades or business in which they materially participate and (2) they must perform more than 750 hours of service per year in those real estate activities. Thus, material participation requirements are met if the taxpayer is involved in real estate operations on a regular, continuous, and substantial basis. Real estate trades and businesses include real estate brokerage, management, rental, operation, leasing, development, construction, reconstruction, acquisition, or conversion.

Separate records should be kept for each passive activity of a taxpayer. The unused passive loss from an activity may be used to offset outside income in the year of disposition, even if there is positive passive income from other activities. An abandonment is considered a disposition of the property and will trigger the recognition of suspended losses. However, if the taxpayer transfers property to a related individual, the transfer will not be considered a disposition. Unused passive losses remain with the seller, who may use them to offset positive passive income until the property is fully disposed of. The government must have anticipated that a taxpayer would sell a property to a relative, use the suspended losses, and then repurchase the property.

Form of Organization. The passive loss limitation rules are modified, depending on the form of organization of the owner. Real estate property can be held by an individual, personal service corporation, limited partnership, a closely held C corporation, a regular C corporation, or an S corporation. A closely held C corporation (closed corporation) is one that is owned by a few stockholders or is a family business. It is not the same as an S corporation, which is also owned by a few stockholders but is taxed as a partnership. That is, it avoids the double taxation of a C corporation.

A closed corporation may use passive losses to offset active business income but not portfolio income. A regular C corporation can use passive losses to offset both active business income and portfolio income. Table 16-6 summarizes the use of passive losses to offset income according to the form of ownership.

TABLE 16-6
Passive Loss Limitations

	Can Passive Losses Offset	
FORM OF OWNERSHIP	ACTIVE BUSINESS INCOME?	PORTFOLIO INCOME?
Individual	No	No
Limited partnership	No	No
Personal service company	No	No
S corporation	No	No
Closely held C corporation	Yes	No
C corporation	Yes	Yes

Source: © 2014 OnCourse Learning

EXAMPLE

> A closely held C corporation has $200,000 in passive losses from an apartment complex (which it does not actively manage), $350,000 in positive income from a restaurant, and $50,000 in interest from bonds. The $200,000 can be used to reduce the income from the restaurant to $150,000 but cannot be used to reduce the portfolio income. Had the loss from the apartment complex been $400,000, it would reduce the income from the restaurant to zero and the remaining $50,000 loss would be carried forward.

The limitation of passive losses was clearly designed to curtail the use of real estate as a pure tax shelter. Under the new rules, passive activity is synonymous with real estate activity. These limitations, involving some rather complex rules, may have been overkill, however. TRA 1986, which defined the passive loss limitation, also extended the period of depreciation and lowered the top tax bracket. The treatment of depreciation alone probably would have been sufficient to eliminate most real estate tax shelters. A good example is the one used in the beginning of this chapter where the change in the depreciation rules destroyed the tax shelter character of the real estate investment. Certainly, the combination of the change in the treatment of depreciation and the limitation of passive losses has caused investors to concentrate on the true economic feasibility of real estate developments.

Capital Loss Limitation and Passive Loss Rule. Unused passive losses can be used to offset other sources of income on the disposition of the property. But what if there is a capital loss on the sale of the property? Is this loss a passive loss that can now be used to offset other income, or is a capital loss subject to the capital loss limitation? The answer is the latter. A capital loss is not exempt from the capital loss limitation rule simply because it is from a passive activity.

EXAMPLE

> Assume a taxpayer sells an apartment complex with a book value of $1 million for $950,000, incurring a $50,000 loss. The taxpayer also has $10,000 of suspended passive losses from previous years. The $10,000 can be used in full to offset other income. The $50,000 capital loss can be used only to offset capital gains plus $3,000 of ordinary income in the year of sale.

At-Risk Limitation

At-risk limitations were introduced by the Tax Reform Act of 1976 and were originally aimed at non-real estate shelters, such as oil and gas exploration ventures. Prior to the act, investors could purchase an "asset" at inflated prices with little of their own money and finance the remainder with nonrecourse debt. The heavy write-off of expenses would shelter other income from taxes. The cash flows from the tax shield were likely to be greater than the meager investment. If the venture failed, the investor would simply default on the nonrecourse debt. The 1976 act introduced the at-risk concept. Essentially, this rule limits cumulative losses on an investment to the amount that the investor actually has at risk.

The Tax Reform Act of 1986 applied the at-risk rules to real estate investments held by individuals, partnerships, and corporations, including closely held corporations. The crucial determination in applying the rule is the amount considered to be at risk. For a real estate investment, that amount is generally and initially the investor's cash contribution to the investment; the tax basis of any property that the investor contributes; amounts borrowed for use in the investment for which the investor is personally liable or has pledged other property; or amounts borrowed for use in the investment for which the investor is not personally liable but which are made by a qualified lender who is engaged in the business of making loans, such as a commercial bank, a savings and loan association, an insurance company, or a pension fund.

The qualified lender cannot be a promoter or a seller of the investment property. A lender becomes a promoter when a fee is received for a loan that is contingent on the amount of the investor's contribution. A qualified lender can have an equity participation in the investment property as long as the terms of the loan are common to those in the trade. If a lender who has an equity position in the investment makes a loan with an interest rate substantially below the market, with a term in excess of the life of the property, or with severe restrictions on the ability to foreclose, then the lender may be determined to be unqualified and the loan not considered an amount at risk.

Subsequent to the initial investment, the at-risk amount is increased by any additional contributions of the investor and reduced by any payments made to the investor. The at-risk test is applied before consideration of passive losses. If any loss is denied because of the at-risk test, that loss is not eligible to be a suspended passive loss and will therefore never be allowed to offset other income.

Alternative Minimum Tax Rules

Alternative minimum tax (AMT) rules were established in 1978 because some taxpayers with high incomes had so much of their income sheltered by tax preference items, a number of which relate to real estate. Essentially, the AMT rule establishes a minimal amount of income on which a tax is based and then sets a minimum tax rate. It does this by adding back some preference items to the adjusted income. It applies to both individuals and corporations. Currently we have two-tier rate structure that is 26 percent tax rate on income up to $175,000 and 28 percent tax rate on income above $175,000. Also, contributions of appreciated real, personal, and intangible property no longer create a tax preference item for the AMT. Tax preference items that must be added back are listed in Appendix 16-A.

The procedure for computing the AMT is as follows. The taxpayer begins with his or her regular taxable income and adds items known as **tax preference items**. He or she then makes deductions that are determined under the AMT rule and substitutes them for the regular deductions. The result is alternative minimum taxable income (AMTI). From AMTI an exemption of $45,000 ($33,750 for single taxpayers) was available in 2012 (the exemptions in 2011 were $74,450 for married filing jointly and $48,450 for single). Then, the appropriate AMT rate is applied. The taxpayer pays the higher of the regular tax or the AMT.

Favored Classes of Real Estate Investment

One tool by which the government encourages investment activity that has both social and economic value is the tax credit. A tax credit is different from a tax deduction. A deduction reduces taxable income and the value of the deduction is the amount of deduction times the marginal tax rate. A tax credit is a reduction in the taxes themselves and not taxable income. With a $1 tax credit, the taxpayer saves $1. Thus, tax credits can be a powerful motivating tool. Tax credits are available for the rehabilitation of historic structures and the development of low-income housing.

Rehabilitation of Historic Structures. The Revenue Act of 1978 established tax credits for the rehabilitation of historic structures. The credit was equal to 10 percent of the expenses required to rehabilitate qualified structures. TRA 1986 changed the credits and authorized a 10 percent credit for nonresidential structure built prior to 1936 and a 20 percent credit for any **certified historic structure (CHS)**, regardless of the year in which it was built. CHSs are structures that are on the National Register of Historic Places or are within registered historic districts. The rehabilitation must be certified by the secretary of the interior.

The tax credit can be used to offset taxes only on passive income, but it is treated as if it comes from a rental activity with active participation (management) by the taxpayer. Thus, the taxpayer is entitled to the $25,000 exemption for passive activities. A tax deduction of $25,000 will save $7,000 in taxes for a taxpayer in the 28 percent bracket. Therefore, the taxpayer may use up to $7,000 of the credit to offset outside income.

EXAMPLE

A taxpayer rehabilitates a non-CHS (nonresidential) structure built in 1924. It is eligible for the 10 percent credit. The taxpayer spends $120,000 to rehabilitate the structure, creating a $12,000 credit. He can use $7,000 of the credit to offset taxes on outside income. The remaining $5,000 may be used to offset taxes on passive income. If there is insufficient passive income, the unused tax credit is carried forward for use in future years. Finally, if the taxpayer uses the tax credit, the depreciable basis of the property must be reduced by the amount of the credit and depreciated with a straight-line method. This reduces the value of the credit somewhat.

Low-Income Housing Credits. Investors are eligible for tax credits on their investment in qualified low-income housing. There are two types of eligible property: new structures for which there are no other federal subsidies and properties for which there is some other form of federal subsidy (such as below-market interest loans or loans arranged through tax-exempt issues such as mortgage revenue bonds). In the first case, the credit will equal 9 percent of the "qualified basis" for each of the first 10 years. The qualified basis is that portion of the property used for low-income housing. For the second type, the credit is limited to 4 percent of the qualified basis over the first 10 years. If the project fails to meet the requirements for a credit in any 1 year, the previous tax credits can be recaptured. The credits are subject to the $25,000 exemption on passive losses. This means that the investor may use the credit to offset taxes up to $25,000 on nonpassive income annually. Again, for taxpayers in the 28 percent bracket, this results in a tax savings of $7,000. Any excess credit can be used to offset passive income or carried forward. The 1993 tax act makes the credit available for units occupied by full-time students and also eases various operating requirements for low-income housing.

EFFECT OF TAX REFORM ACT OF 1986 ON REAL ESTATE INVESTMENT

The Tax Reform Act of 1986 had a more dramatic impact on real estate than on any other investment activity. Rule changes were aimed specifically at reducing the value of real estate as a tax shelter. In this regard, there were three major changes: (1) a lengthening of the period of depreciation, (2) a limitation on the use of losses from real estate investment to offset other income, and (3) a lowering of the top tax rate. Real estate investment did retain some benefits, however. Interest on debt is deductible for tax purposes, and there are credits for investing in certain types of properties.

With the limitation of the pass-through of losses to partners, the advantage may have shifted to the corporate form of ownership. If the corporation has other sources of income, it can realize substantial tax savings. Furthermore, if these savings are reinvested in other assets (rather than declared as dividends), they will continue to generate cash flows free from taxation at the individual level. Nonetheless, the continued double taxation of corporation income will mean that some real estate will be developed through the partnership entity. Lentz and Fisher studied the impact of TRA 1986 on the form of ownership.[3] They concluded that although there were no conditions under which the corporate form of ownership would dominate prior to the act, that form of ownership may now be the value-maximizing organizational form. The corporate form of ownership, they claim, may be desirable for highly levered (interest tax deduction) depreciable property where a substantial amount of cash flows are retained by the corporation. The motivating factor is the ability of the corporation to utilize more of the losses to offset income. Also, cash flows are reinvested without being taxed. The authors also state that it is relatively more costly to set up a partnership and distribute the partnership interests than it is to establish the corporation. They suggest that real estate may be held less in the form of partnerships as a result of the 1986 act.

There is some evidence that this may be the case. In 1989 Nelson and Petska did a study of the number of real estate limited partnerships and their profit and losses for years before and after TRA 1986.[4] Using tax returns, they found that the number of limited partnerships in real estate fell as a result of the act. They also found that substantial losses were suspended and unavailable for tax relief. The number of limited partnerships with losses grew dramatically for several years prior to the 1986 tax act. In 1987 that number dropped dramatically.[5]

TAX-DEFERRED EXCHANGES OF REAL ESTATE PROPERTIES

There is one tax rule that does not affect the after-tax cash flows of operations from real estate or the ownership structure for holding real estate. Nonetheless, the rule has important implications for real estate investors. The rule is the Section 1031, or so-called **tax-deferred exchange rule**. A deferred exchange is defined as an exchange in which, pursuant to an agreement, the taxpayer transfers property held either for productive use in trade or business or for investment and subsequently receives property to be held either for productive use in trade or business or for investment.

Many real estate owners hold properties that, for various reasons, they would like to sell. Perhaps they do not envision the property as the type that would appreciate greatly in the future. Or perhaps there are too many management responsibilities with the property. The owner would like to remain a real estate investor, however. A sale (and purchase of another property) would accomplish the desired goal but may result in large tax payments if the basis in the property is low relative to the sales price. If a property worth $10 million (with a basis of zero dollars) is sold, the owner in a 30 percent tax bracket would have only $7 million after taxes to reinvest. One way around the problem is the use of the Section 1031 provisions. If the rules are followed, the investor may exchange one (or more) property for another. The new properties need only be "like-kind" properties. Virtually all real estate properties are considered like-kind. Owners may exchange farm land for apartment complexes, or office buildings for warehouses.

It is possible under Section 1031 to permanently defer the gain on investment real estate properties. As long as the investor keeps exchanging properties instead of selling, the equity buildup is not taxed. At the investor's death, the basis of the properties will automatically adjust to market value, eliminating all capital gains. Several basic requirements have to be met for the exchange to qualify as tax-deferred.

Basic Requirements

There are four requirements under Section 1031 rules. First, both the relinquished and the acquired property must be held for productive use in a trade or business or for investment. Thus, owner-occupied residences would not be eligible for a like-kind exchange. Second, both the property exchanged and the one received must be of like-kind. For real estate, this involves most any type as mentioned above. Third, the exchange must occur. The owner cannot sell one property for cash and immediately use the cash proceeds to purchase another property. There can be no intervening sale of the relinquished property, no matter how quickly the new acquired property is purchased. Finally, the basis in the acquired property will be equal to the basis in the relinquished property. The calculation of the basis must be adjusted if there is any non-real estate property (boot) involved. This is discussed shortly.

Three-Party Exchanges

You may wonder what transactions are available if an owner identifies a new property to be acquired, but the owner of the identified property does not wish to exchange it for the property in question. One way around this dilemma is the three-party exchange. Assume that the owner has a property A and desires to exchange it for property B. The owner of property B has no interest in owning property A, however. Under a three-party exchange, a third party interested in property A is found. Instead of buying A, the third party buys property B and then exchanges it for property A. All parties end up with the property they want: The third party gets A, the original owner gets B, and the owner of B gets cash.

Delayed Exchanges

What would happen if a third-party buyer for property A were available who wanted to own property A immediately, before the owner of A could identify another desirable property? In this case, there can be a delayed exchange. The owner of property A would transfer title (not sell) to the third party who, in turn, would agree to transfer a property identified by the owner of A at some time in the future. In such a case, the third-party buyer usually would deposit a sufficient sum of money in escrow to purchase the identified property at a later date. In this type of exchange, the owner of property A simply transfers title to the third party and says, "Some time in the future, I will identify other properties that you can purchase and deliver title to me."

Boot

Boot is a general term for property that is not like-kind. In a like-kind exchange, it is difficult to believe that real estate properties exchanged will have precisely identical values. If property A is worth $10 million, the owner may exchange it for another property worth $8 million and $2 million in cash. The cash is boot. In this case, the boot is a taxable portion of the exchange. If the investor is in the 30 percent tax bracket, then the tax due will be $600,000 ($0.3 \times \$2,000,000$). This is still better than a tax bill for $3 million if the property were sold outright. The basis of the acquired property will still be the basis of the relinquished property. In this example, it is zero.

Boot is not limited to cash. It can be any non-like-kind property, including the relief of a mortgage obligation. Assume in this example that there is a $1 million mortgage on the property to be relinquished. If the owner of the property to be exchanged (worth $8 million) exchanges that property and pays off the mortgage on the relinquished property plus $1 million, then the boot will consist of $1 million in cash and $1 million in mortgage relief.

Technical Requirements

Numerous technical requirements must be met if a like-kind exchange is to avoid taxation. Those who contemplate such an exchange are wise to seek the counsel of a tax specialist or a specialist in such exchanges. Most large urban areas have several such specialists who belong to a society or group of real estate exchangers. Here, we will mention a few of the most important technical requirements.

Time Limitation on Delayed (Deferred) Exchanges

The regulations contain three requirements that, if met, will satisfy a tax-deferred exchange. First, the replacement property must be identified by the owner of the relinquished property within an identification period. Second, the exchange must be completed within an exchange period. Third, the owner of the relinquished property must not be in constructive receipt of the proceeds from the transfer of the property.

The identification period begins on the date the relinquished property is transferred and ends 45 days thereafter. If more than one property is involved in the exchange, the period begins with the first transfer of a property. The exchange period begins on the date of the transfer of the relinquished property and ends 180 days later or on the due date of the tax return for the taxable year, whichever occurs first.

Multiple Property Tests

In a delayed transaction it may be difficult, if not impossible, to identify the property to be acquired within 45 days. The IRS rules permit the owner to identify several prospective properties within this time period, provided the three-property test, the 200 percent test, and the 95 percent test are met. The three-property test permits property owners to identify any three other properties to be exchanged without regard to their fair market values. The 200 percent test limits the identified properties to 200 percent of the fair market value of the properties relinquished. The 95 percent rule kicks in if the first two criteria are not met. Under this rule, the identification requirement is still met if at least 95 percent of the identified property is actually received by the termination of the 180-day exchange period.

Other Considerations

You should be aware of some other minor points concerning tax-deferred real estate exchanges. Incidental property may be involved in the exchange. This type of property is usually considered personal property (such as furniture and fixtures) but can be included in the real estate package as long as its value does not exceed 15 percent of the aggregate value of the replacement property. If the property to be acquired does not exist but is to be constructed, then the regulations require that as much detail as possible about the property be described within the identification period. Variations due to typical production changes are allowed. However, any additional construction after the property is received is not considered like-kind property, but rather will be considered boot. For the 200 percent test, the fair market value of the property to be produced is its value at the time it is to be received.

Recall that the owner of the property to be relinquished cannot receive any money from the transaction. Yet there is always the possibility that in a delayed transaction, the other party may not deliver title to the property as required under the exchange agreement. In this case, the property owner may require that the other party deposit a sum of money in an escrow account so as to guarantee delivery of the property to be acquired. Tax rules allow this arrangement as long as the property owner has not received any cash on delivery of the property to be relinquished.

Tax-deferred exchanges have obvious benefits for the property owner who desires to change the type of real estate investment without having to pay taxes and thereby reduce the size of the investment portfolio. Like so many other tax regulations, the rules involved in the tax-deferred exchange can be complicated. Property owners who anticipate an exchange are advised to seek professional help in structuring the transaction so as to comply with the applicable regulations.

EXAMPLE:
TAX DEFERRED
EXCHANGE

Suppose that Investor A owns a triplex that was bought 5 years ago and is currently worth $150,000. The property has an adjusted basis of $75,000 and Investor A owes $67,500 on the mortgage. He or she is seeking to buy a larger property and has found a quadruplex for sale by Investor B. This property is valued at $300,000 and is subject to a $217,500 mortgage. Table 16-7 shows the process of Investor A and Investor B doing a tax-deferred exchange.

In doing the exchange, the equities must balance. This may be done by giving cash (boot) or by refinancing one of the mortgages.

The recognized gain of $0 for Investor A shows that the $66,000 realized gain is completely deferred. The effect on the tax basis of the new property now owned by

TABLE 16-7

Tax-Deferred Exchange Calculations

	INVESTOR A	INVESTOR B
A. Equities must balance		
Market value of		
Property given	$150,000	$300,000
− Mortgage balance	67,500	217,500
= Equity given	82,500	82,500
+ Boot (unlike property)	0	0
= Total	82,500	82,500
B. Realized gain		
Market value of		
Property given	150,000	300,000
− Selling expenses	9,000	18,000
− Adjusted basis	75,000	270,000
= Realized gain	66,000	12,000
C. Recognized gain		
Net mortgage relief	0	150,000
− Boot given	0	0
− Selling expenses	9,000	18,000
+ Boot received	0	0
= Net boot received	0	132,000
Recognized Gain	0	12,000
(lesser or realized gain or net boot received)		
D. Tax basis of property received		
Adjusted basis	75,000	270,000
− Boot received	0	0
− old mortgage	67,500	217,500
+ Boot given	0	0
+ Selling expenses	9,000	18,000
+ Mortgage on new property	217,500	67,500
+ Recognized gain	0	12,000
= Tax basis of new property	234,000	150,000

Source: © 2014 OnCourse Learning

Investor A is shown on the last line ($234,000). The $66,000 gain on the old property has been subtracted from the new property's $300,000 value. Although this lowers the property's depreciable basis, Investor A has more cash. Plus Investor A has achieved his or her goals of disposing of the old property while deferring the tax on the gain and acquiring a property worth more value than the old one.

INSTALLMENT SALE FINANCING

When a property is sold, it is treated as an outright sale if the seller pays income tax on the full capital gain in the year of sale. An alternative method of sale is the **installment sale**, which occurs when the seller takes back a promissory loan from the buyer. Ordinarily the IRS would consider the receipt of a promissory note as taxable income, the same as cash. This would require payment of taxes in the year of sale. However, there is a section in the tax code that allows different treatment for a qualified installment sale. Installment sale can be elected only under the cash method of accounting. Under the accrual method the sale must be treated as an outright sale.

To qualify as an installment sale, the seller must receive at least one payment after the year of sale. The typical scenario would have the seller receiving a down payment in the year of sale followed by a series of payments over the installment period. The installment method can be used only when a gain results from the sale. Losses incurred on the sale of business assets must be deducted in the year of sale, and losses from property held for personal use are not tax deductible. Installment sales are used most frequently on income properties to postpone taxes. The financing provided by the seller may take a first, second, and so on mortgage position. The result is a series of payments on which the seller is taxed only on the portion of capital gain received with each payment. The major task in an installment sale is distinguishing with each payment the portions of taxable profit and the return of original investment. The capital gains percentage is called the **gross profit percentage**. It is calculated as a percentage of the contract price. Once the gross profit percentage is determined, it stays constant and is applied to each payment as received to determine the taxable portion of the payment.

Previously, if payments were to be received by the seller, the installment method had to be elected if desired. Currently, however, under these circumstances the installment method is required and the seller must elect out if he or she wants the sale to be treated as an outright sale. Interestingly, a sale can be treated as an outright sale where taxes are paid on the full capital gain in the year of sale even though the seller receives the proceeds from the sale over future periods. Other tax rules include the **related persons rule**, which says that if an installment sale is made to a related person (defined as spouse, children, parents, and grandparents; brothers and sisters do not qualify) who, in turn, sells the property within a 2-year period, the original seller must recognize the balance of his or her gain at the time the related person makes the sale. Exceptions to this rule include involuntary conversion by the related person.

Installment sales are also subject to the imputed interest rate rules. A seller might have an incentive to set an interest rate below the market rate and raise the contract price to capture the lost interest. This transforms income from interest to capital gains, which may have more favorable tax treatment. To avoid this, the IRS instituted the imputed interest rule. This rule is addressed in the system of applicable federal rates that was established by Congress in 1985. This is not designed to be a form of credit control or the setting of interest rates.

EXAMPLE:
INSTALLMENT SALE

Suppose that Smith sells property to Jones for $150,000 in a 2-year installment agreement with 40 percent down payment and the balance financed at 10 percent. The adjusted basis of the property is $80,000 with accumulated depreciation of $45,500. Smith has selling expenses of $5,000 and is in a 28 percent marginal tax bracket. The property has been depreciated on a straight-line basis and the buyer will make annual debt service payments. What are the seller's ATCF in the year of sale and ATCFs from the installment receipts?

These cash flows are calculated in Table 16-8. The calculation in the upper left corner shows the ATCF in the year of sale. It is the down payment minus selling expenses and taxes. The tax liability in the year of sale is shown in the middle left side. The entry excess of mortgage over adjusted basis and selling expenses is applicable if the transaction includes the assumption of a loan by Jones from Smith. If the loan is not assumed, this entry is zero. If the loan is assumed, the sum of adjusted basis plus selling expenses is subtracted from the balance of the assumed mortgage. A positive difference is entered in the table. If this difference is negative or zero, then the entry is zero. Calculating the tax also requires the profit percentage, which is shown in the table in the bottom left side. The profit percentage is the total gain (selling price minus selling expenses minus adjusted basis) divided by the contract price.

The tables on the right side show the ATCFs for the installment receipts and the corresponding tax liabilities. The principal portion of the payment must be distinguished from the interest portion to determine the portion of the principal that is taxable in a given year.

TABLE 16-8
After-Tax Cash Flows from Installment Sale Agreement

A. ATCF in Year of Sale			D. ATCF from Installments		
Down payment	$60,000			Yr. 1	Yr. 2
− Selling expenses	− 5,000				
− Taxes	− 5,720		Debt service payment	$51,857	$51,857
= ATCF	$49,280		+ Balloon payment	+ 0	+ 0
			− Tax on installment	− 6,605	− 5.814
			= ATCF	$45,252	$46,043
B. Tax in Year of Sale					
Down payment	$60,000		E. Taxes on Installments		
+ Excess of mortgage over			Repayment of principal	$42,857	$47,143
Adj. basis and selling expenses	+ 0		+ Balloon payment	+ 0	+ 0
= Total payment in year of sale	$60,000		= Principal portion	42,857	47,143
× Profit percentage	0.4333		× Profit percentage	× 0.4333	× 0.4333
= Taxable portion of gain	$25,998		= Taxable principal	18,570	20,427
× Tax rate on gain	× 0.22[a]		× Tax rate on principal	× 0.22[a]	× 0.22[a]
= Taxes in year of sale	$5,720		= Tax on principal	4,085	4,494
			Interest earned	9,000	4,714
C. Profit Percentage			× Marginal tax rate	× 0.28	× 0.28
Sale price	$150,000		= Tax on interest	2,520	1,320
− Selling expenses	− 5,000		Tax on principal	4,085	4,494
− Adjusted basis	− 80,000		+ Tax on interest	2,520	1,320
= Total capital gain	$ 65,000		Tax on installment	$6,605	$5,814
Sale price	$150,000				
− Mortgage balance assumed	− 0				
+ Excess of mortgage over					
Adj. basis and selling expenses	+ 0				
= Contract price	$150,000				
Total gain/contract price = profit percentage 65,000/150,000 = 0.4333					

[a]*Tax rate on gain = (0.70) (0.25) + (0.30) (0.15) = 0.22. The depreciation recapture is 70% of the total gain and is prorated equally across the installment period.*

Source: © 2014 OnCourse Learning

Other Considerations in an Installment Sale

Note that in the above example the debt is fully amortized over the installment period of 2 years. In some cases, however, the note may be amortized over a longer period than the installment agreement. This results in a balloon payment in the last year of installment receipts. An amortization period longer than the installment period is usually done to make the debt service payments more affordable. This would have the effect of rearranging the cash flows from the installment receipts. Also, if a sale is greater than $150,000 and the seller has a large amount of other debt, the seller may have to recognize additional gain through the allowable installment indebtedness rule.

Summary

Historically, tax rules and regulations have favored real estate as an investment. Prior to 1986, the rules allowed real estate to be depreciated over a relatively short period. These noncash expenses reduced taxes and, given their ability to offset paper losses against other income, actually increased the after-tax cash flows over the before-tax cash flows. The lower tax rate on capital gains income allowed real estate investors to transfer ordinary income to capital gains through the depreciation write-off. Also, interest payments on debt were tax deductible. Depreciation and interest expenses combined to produce losses that could be used to offset other income. The high tax rates at the time meant that the rebate substantially increased the amount of after-tax cash flows.

Certain limitations were placed on losses to avoid abusive practices, however. Such limitations included those on the amount of interest that could be deducted for nonoperating real estate investments (land) and those on the rate of interest that could be charged on loans, especially seller-supplied, nonrecourse loans. Reported losses also were limited to the amount the investor had at risk. Finally, investors who used too many tax preferences were subject to an AMT. Despite these limitations, the preponderance of favorable rules caused real estate to become the tax shelter of choice.

This situation changed with the Tax Reform Act of 1986. Four major changes reduced the value of real estate as a tax shelter. First, the depreciation period was extended, substantially reducing the amount of depreciation in the early life of the investment. Second, the preferable tax rate on capital gains was eliminated, removing the incentive to use real estate to transform ordinary income into capital gains income. Third, with minor exceptions, losses on real estate activity could not be used to offset income from non-real estate activities. Fourth, the top tax rate was reduced. This diminished the value of tax losses. The investment income, OID, and at-risk limitation rules were retained. The combined effect of these changes was to remove real estate as a favored tax shelter and cause investment in real estate projects to be based more on their economic feasibility and less on their ability to generate tax losses. About the only remaining tax shelters involve investment in historic structures or low-income housing. Even here, though, the tax credits are limited to the $25,000 exemption amount. The Tax Act of 1993 raised marginal tax rates and extended depreciation to 39 years straight-line for nonresidential income properties. It did ease to some extent the passive loss limitation rules for real estate professionals. The 1997 Tax Act reintroduced capital gains.

Tax-deferred exchanges of real estate property represent an excellent way in which property owners can alter their real estate investment portfolio without having its value reduced by tax payments. The owner of the relinquished property must receive another property in exchange within 180 days of relinquishing the property. The basis of the acquired property is generally that of the relinquished property. The installment sales agreement is an alternative to the outright sale and allows the seller to defer payment of taxes on capital gains by electing to receive a series of installment payments.

Key Terms

Accelerated cost recovery system (ACRS)

Active income

Adequacy-of-interest test

After-tax cash flow

After-tax discount rate

Alternative minimum taxes (AMTs)

At-risk limitations

Before-tax discount rate

Boot

Capital loss limitation

Certified historic structure (CHSs)

Depreciation tax shield

Double-declining method

Gross profit percentage

Imputed interest rule

Installment sale

Investment interest limitation

Low-income housing credit

Modified accelerated cost recovery system (MACRS)

Net leased investment

Nonrecourse debt

Original issue discount (OID)

Passive income

Passive losses

Passive loss limitation

Portfolio income

Portfolio losses

Property held as principal residence

Property held for investment

Property held for resale

Property held for use in trade or business

Recourse debt

Related persons rule

Straight-line method

Sum-of-the-years' digits method

Suspended passive losses

Tax-deferred exchange rule

Tax preference items

Tax Reform Act of 1986

Tax shelter

Time-value-of-money test

Review Questions

16-1.   Explain what a tax shelter is, and indicate at least three different tax rules that favor an investment as a tax shelter.

16-2.   Explain, in general, the following tax "limitations" in the present tax code:
a. Investment interest limitation
b. Capital loss limitation
c. Passive loss limitation

16-3.   Explain why the tax code "imputes" interest rates on loans under the original issue discount (OID) rules.

16-4.   Discuss, in general terms, the recent three tax regimes, insofar as the treatment of depreciation expense is concerned: pre-1981, 1981 to 1986, and post-1986.

Which was the most and which the least favorable for real estate investment and why?

16-5. Explain the use of tax credits to encourage investment in certain types of real estate properties.

16-6. Explain how the $25,000 exemption under the passive loss limitation rules works.

16-7. How are passive losses treated when real estate is held under the corporate form versus the limited partnership form?

16-8. Explain the at-risk limitation rule and why it was introduced.

16-9. Why is a nonrecourse loan provided by the seller of a property not considered to be at risk?

16-10. Indicate the way in which you believe the Tax Reform Act of 1986 has affected investment in real estate. Indicate specific facets of the act.

16-11. What is the purpose of allowing like-kind exchanges of real estate properties?

16-12. Indicate two main criteria that must be met so that a like-kind exchange of real estate property will satisfy the rules of a tax-deferred exchange.

16-13. List the major differences between the four tax categories of real estate.

16-14. What is the profit percentage in an installment sale, and why is it important?

16-15. Explain the treatment of an assumed mortgage in an installment sale.

Problems

For Problems 16-1 and 16-2, assume a real estate investor is considering the purchase of an office building and knows the following information:

- The purchase price is $800,000 with acquisition costs of $25,000.
- The project is two 2-story office buildings containing a total of 42,000 leasable square feet.
- The rents are expected to be $6.00 per square foot per year and are expected to increase 5 percent per year.
- The vacancy rate is expected to be 8 percent each year.
- The project has concession vendors that generate other income in the amount of 8 percent of gross revenue.
- Operating expenses are estimated at 45 percent of the gross revenue each year.
- Eighty percent of the purchase price can be borrowed with a 20-year, annual payment mortgage at an interest rate of 12 percent plus 2 percent financing costs. The loan has a prepayment penalty of 4 percent of the outstanding balance.
- Of the total cost, 85 percent is depreciable.
- The value of the investment is expected to increase 5 percent per year. Selling expenses are expected to be 8 percent of the selling price.
- The investor plans to hold the project for 5 years, is in a 28 percent marginal tax bracket, and requires a 14 percent equity return.

16-1. Compute the after-tax cash flows from operations and the after-tax equity reversion for the investor's holding period.

16-2. Calculate the net present value (NPV) and the internal rate of return (IRR) for the investment.

16-3.   Assume the following data related to the purchase of raw land and calculate the amount of the interest charge that must be deferred under the investment interest limitation rules.

Purchase price	$1,500,000
Loan amount	$1,100,000
Interest rate	12%
First-year income royalties	$150,000
First-year expenses property tax	$55,000

16-4.   Determine the amount an investor is at risk at the end of year 1 for the following investment:

Asset	Limited partnership interest
Initial cost	$100,000
Financed as follows:	
	$5,000 cash down payment
	$25,000 promissory recourse note
	$40,000 seller-financed, nonrecourse note
	$30,000 land (tax basis)
Year 1 payments from partnership to investor	$10,000

16-5.   Given a $500,000 building (land valued separately), determine the present value of the tax shield, assuming a 12 percent discount rate for the tax rules in effect from 1981 through 1986 and for the tax rules in effect after 1986. What accounts for the difference?

16-6.   Under OID rules, what rate of interest will the IRS apply to determine the interest expense on a loan under the following conditions:

STATED RETE (%)	APPLICABLE FEDERAL RATE (%)	IMPUTED OR ALLOWABLE RATE (%)
10	10	
12	10	
11	10	

16-7.   Determine the tax due for the following investors. Assume the investment is real estate for which passive loss limitations apply.

	INVESTOR A	INVESTOR B	INVESTOR C
Participates in management	Yes	Yes	No
Other taxable income ($)	90,000	120,000	200,00
Marginal and average tax rate (%)	28	28	28
Income for real estate ($)	(100,000)	(100,000)	(100,000)
Taxable income	_____	_____	_____
Tax due	_____	_____	_____

16-8.   Seller sells property to buyer for $250,000 on a 3-year installment basis. Buyer will pay 30 percent down payment and the balance will be financed over a 5-year period at 8 percent interest, annual payments. Seller's original purchase price was $160,000 with acquisition costs of $10,000. He has made no capital improvements, and his accumulated depreciation is $37,000 on a straight-line basis. Seller also has selling expenses of $8,000 and is in a 28 percent tax bracket. Calculate seller's ATCF in the year of sale and the ATCFs from the installment receipts.

Notes

1. For incomes between $71,901 and $180,850, the marginal rate was actually 33 percent. Beyond that the marginal rate is 28 percent. We will use the convention of referring to 28 percent (and not the 33 percent "bubble rate") as the highest rate, since it applies to the highest income categories.

2. Note that the value of depreciation has increased since 1986 as marginal tax rates have gradually increased even though the depreciation schedule has not changed. For example, with the maximum tax rate of 39.6 percent in 1994, the value of depreciation goes to $13,300 from $9,405.

3. George Lentz and Jeffrey Fisher. Tax reform and organizational forms for holding investment real estate: Corporation vs. partnership. *AREUEA Journal* 17(3) (Fall 1989), 314–337.

4. Susan Nelson and Tom Petska. Partnerships, passive losses, and tax reform. *Statistics of Income Bulletin, Internal Revenue Service* 9(3) (Winter 1989–1990), 31–39.

5. Partnerships report income on their own form even though they do not pay taxes. Individual partners pay taxes on the gain or loss passed through to them.

Web Sites

http://www.taxsites.com
  Tax, accounting, and law site

http://realestate.about.com/od/knowthemath/ht/cashflow_after.htm
  Real estate investing after-tax cash flow

APPENDIX 16-A   Tax Preference Items for Alternative Minimum Tax

Certain deductions are allowed when determining regular income. The following items must be added back to regular income in the process of determining the alternative minimum tax:

- For taxpayers using a 27.5- or 31.5-year life under the Tax Reform Act of 1986, the difference between the depreciation under those lives and that of straight-line for a 40-year life.

- Losses of passive (no material participation) farming activity. (Losses from one passive farming activity cannot be used to offset income from another passive farming activity.)

- The amount of capital gains on an appreciated real estate property that has been donated to a qualified charity. The additional income realized by the taxpayer by using the percentage of completion method for accounting for real estate developments.

- Tax-exempt interest for certain private activity bonds.

- Intangible drilling costs to the extent they exceed 65 percent of net income from oil and gas properties.
- Excess of depreciation of pollution control facilities (amortized over 60 months as opposed to regular life).
- The excess of percentage depletion over the property's adjusted basis.
- The excess of research and development expenditures over that which would result from a 10-year amortization.
- Income deferred by installment sales.

SOURCES OF FUNDS FOR COMMERCIAL REAL ESTATE PROPERTIES

LEARNING OBJECTIVES

Chapter 17 describes debt financing and equity financing—the major sources of investment funds for real estate. The chapter is short and descriptive. After reading it, you should be familiar with these sources of funds that support the development and purchase of real estate. You also should understand the difference between debt and equity sources of funds and understand how different institutions specialize in either debt or equity financing or in financing various types of real estate. You should know how government regulations affect the real estate investment decisions of financial institutions.

INTRODUCTION

The current estimated value of America's real estate structures is approximately $29.249 trillion: $17.561 trillion in residential structures and $11.688 in non-residential stuctures.[1] The ownership of this property is financed by both debt and equity. While much of the property is financed with mortgage debt, significant amounts are predominantly or entirely financed with equity. In 2012, nearly $11 trillion of all residential real estate was financed by mortgage debt. Some institutions supply debt financing only, others equity financing only, and others a combination of the two. Some institutional lenders that preferred one type of financing in the past have redirected their priorities and now prefer another type of financing. Also, the type of financing that a particular institution prefers is determined by its liquidity needs—its short-term and long-term cash flow requirements. Finally, with the exception of a slowdown as a result of the 2008 real estate downturn a tremendous increase has been seen in the last 20 years in the securitization of debt and equity. This securitization has provided real estate with greater access to the capital markets. Examples of securities that have increased in popularity during the last several years are real estate investment trusts (REITs), commercial mortgage-backed securities (CMBSs), and credit tenant leases (CTLs).

DEBT FINANCING OF REAL ESTATE PROPERTIES

Estimates of the Stock of Residential Debt

The Federal Reserve System estimated that $10.8 trillion in residential (both single-family and multifamily properties) mortgage debt was outstanding in America at the end of 2012. Several types of institutional lenders held that debt. Table 17-1 shows the residential mortgage debt (both one-family and multifamily) of these institutional lenders. The data in Table 17-1 reveal the following about the various institutional lenders:

- Depository institutions were the largest private institutional holders of residential mortgage debt, holding 26 percent of all debt.

TABLE 17-1

Mortgage Debt Outstanding: 2007–2012[a] (Billions of dollars)

**PART A
HOME MORTGAGES**

	DEPOSITORY INSTITUTIONS	CREDIT UNIONS	INSURANCE COMPANIES	PENSION FUNDS	GSE's	AGENCY & GSE POOLS	ABS ISSUERS	OTHER	TOTAL
2007	3,068.0	280.2	9.4	1.2	447.9	4,371.8	2,200.3	816.0	11,194.8
2008	2,883.6	312.2	8.6	1.3	456.6	4,864.0	1,885.3	671.2	11,082.8
2009	2,686.6	316.9	6.4	2.0	445.3	5,266.5	1,564.6	592.4	10,880.7
2010	2,612.0	317.0	5.6	1.9	4,699.3	1,068.8	1,290.8	417.7	10,413.1
2011	2,535.0	320.5	6.4	1.6	4,595.9	1,216.8	1,098.7	383.1	10,158.0
2012	2,554.3	325.7	6.8	2.2	4,508.3	1,301.7	961.0	265.9	9,925.9

**PART B
MULTI-FAMILY MORTGAGES**

	DEPOSITORY INSTITUTIONS	CREDIT UNIONS	INSURANCE COMPANIES	PENSION FUNDS	GSE's	AGENCY & GSE POOLS	ABS ISSUERS	OTHER	TOTAL
2007	261.1		51.8	2.1	147.7	88.1	124.0	115.5	790.3
2008	276.0		51.8	2.4	190.2	92.8	113.2	113.1	839.5
2009	267.0		48.5	2.7	204.4	105.7	107.4	111.4	847.1
2010	254.9		47.5	3.1	256.5	66.9	98.7	107.8	835.4
2011	248.3		49.4	2.9	259.2	86.4	81.3	102.7	830.2
2012	248.2		51.0	3.4	264.6	104.3	74.3	100.9	846.7

**PART C
TOTALS**

	DEPOSITORY INSTITUTIONS	CREDIT UNIONS	INSURANCE COMPANIES	PENSION FUNDS	GSE's	AGENCY & GSE POOLS	ABS ISSUERS	OTHER	TOTAL
2007	3,329.1	280.2	61.2	3.3	595.6	4,459.9	2,324.3	931.5	11,985.1
2008	3,159.6	312.2	60.4	3.7	646.8	4,956.8	1,998.5	784.3	11,922.3
2009	2,953.6	316.9	54.9	4.7	649.7	5,372.2	1,672.0	703.8	11,727.8
2010	2,866.9	317.0	53.1	5.0	4,955.8	1,135.7	1,389.5	525.5	11,248.5
2011	2,783.3	320.5	55.8	4.5	4,855.1	1,303.2	1,180.0	485.8	10,988.2
2012	2,802.5	325.7	57.8	5.6	4,772.9	1,406.0	1,035.3	366.8	10,772.6

[a]A balance in 2012 are as of September, 2012

Source: Federal Reserve Board

- The government-sponsored enterprises (GSEs) held 43 percent of all residential mortgages directly in their own portfolios.
- Mortgage pools, including the off-balance sheet pools of the GSEs held 13 percent of all mortgages.
- In 2010 some mortgage pools of the GSEs were reclassified as portfolio holdings, thus accounting for the apparent discontinuities in each series.

Flow of Debt Funds

Institutions invest in real estate debt securities by either lending funds directly or by purchasing debt obligations from another originator. The holder of the securities, either by origination or by purchase, is the ultimate source of funds. Nonetheless, originators who may sell off much of their debt are important players in directing the funds from their source to their use. The data in Table 17-2 show the net investment of the same major institutional lenders listed in Table 17-1. For a particular institution, the net investment in its end-of-year holding of debt securities will equal its **originations** plus its purchases less sales and less repayment of the debt outstanding at the end of the previous year. The origination plus purchases less sales is referred to as **net acquisitions**. These relationships may be presented as:

$$\text{Originations} + \text{Purchases} = \text{Gross acquisitions} - \text{Sales}$$
$$= \text{Net acquisitions} - \text{Repayments}$$
$$= \text{Net change in holdings}$$

Several important features of the flow of funds in Table 17-2 stand out. First, in regards to single family properties (Part A) the total column shows a continual

TABLE 17-2

Net Investment in Mortgage Debt Outstanding: 2007–2012 (billions of dollars)

**PART A
HOME MORTGAGES**

	DEPOSITORY INSTITUTIONS	CREDIT UNIONS	INSURANCE COMPANIES	PENSION FUNDS	GSEs	AGENCY & GSE POOLS	ABS ISSUERS	OTHER	TOTAL
2008	(184.4)	32.0	(0.8)	0.1	8.7	492.2	(315.0)	(144.8)	(112.0)
2009	(197.0)	4.7	(2.2)	0.7	(11.3)	402.5	(320.7)	(78.8)	(202.1)
2010	(74.6)	0.1	(0.8)	(0.1)	4,254.0	(4,197.7)	(273.8)	(174.7)	(467.6)
2011	(77.0)	3.5	0.8	(0.3)	(103.4)	148.0	(192.1)	(34.6)	(255.1)
2012	19.3	5.2	0.4	0.6	(87.6)	84.9	(137.7)	(117.2)	(232.1)

**PART B
MULTIFAMILY MORTGAGES**

	DEPOSITORY INSTITUTIONS	CREDIT UNIONS	INSURANCE COMPANIES	PENSION FUNDS	GSEs	AGENCY & GSE POOLS	ABS ISSUERS	OTHER	TOTAL
2008	14.9		–	0.3	42.5	4.7	(10.8)	(2.4)	49.2
2009	(9.0)		(3.3)	0.3	14.2	12.9	(5.8)	(1.7)	7.6
2010	(12.1)		(1.0)	0.4	52.1	(38.8)	(8.7)	(3.6)	(11.7)
2011	(6.6)		1.9	(0.2)	2.7	19.5	(17.4)	(5.1)	(5.2)
2012	(0.1)		1.6	0.5	5.4	17.9	(7.0)	(1.8)	16.5

Source: Federal Reserve Board

decline in holdings. This decline is due to two factors. One factor is the drop in GSEs holdings due to government mandates that they reduce their role in the secondary mortgage market. The second factor is the decline in the "value" of existing mortgages for all holders, including the GSEs, because of defaults, foreclosures, and REOs. This trend should reverse itself beyond 2012 as the housing market continues to recover.

Commercial Debt

There are a great number of sources of commercial debt, including life insurance companies, commercial banks, and savings institutions. Increasingly, one important recent source of debt financing for commercial properties has come through the use of **commercial mortgage-backed securities (CMBSs).** Table 17-3 shows the amount of commercial mortgages outstanding and the net changes from 2008 through the third quarter, 2012. In 2012 depository institutions held about 54 percent of all commercial mortgages. CMBSs accounted for about 22 percent. This was up from only about 8 percent in 1997. In Table 17-3 CMBSs are identified by the more general term, Asset-Backed Security (ABS) Issuers.

A Closer Look at Commercial Mortgage-Backed Securities

CMBSs are becoming an important source of debt financing for commercial properties. Like their counterpart in residential financing, these are securities backed by commercial mortgages. The first CMBSs were securities backed by a mortgage on a single, large property, such as an office building in a large metropolitan area. Later, mortgages on different and smaller property types were packaged and collateralized. Currently, many CMBSs are backed by a mix of mortgages on different

TABLE 17-3

Commercial Mortgage Debt: 2007–2012 (billions of dollars)

	DEPOSITORY INSTITUTIONS	INSURANCE COMPANIES	PENSION FUNDS	ABS ISSUERS	OTHER	TOTAL
PART A OUTSTANDING						
2007	1,286.8	252.2	6.8	633.6	269.6	2,449.0
2008	1,404.4	267.1	7.4	604.7	283.2	2,566.8
2009	1,367.4	257.7	8.9	563.3	280.8	2,478.1
2010	1,273.2	251.3	10.4	518.3	269.5	2,322.7
2011	1,210.3	263.2	10.5	509.9	255.8	2,249.7
2012	1,184.9	271.9	9.1	488.0	243.0	2,196.9
PART B NET CHANGE						
2008	117.6	14.9	0.6	(28.9)	13.6	117.8
2009	(37.0)	(9.4)	1.5	(41.4)	(2.4)	(88.7)
2010	(94.2)	(6.4)	1.5	(45.0)	(11.3)	(155.4)
2011	(62.9)	11.9	0.1	(8.4)	(13.7)	(73.0)
2012	(25.4)	8.7	(1.4)	(21.9)	(12.8)	(52.8)

Source: Federal Reserve Board

property types in different geographical locations. Commercial CMBSs were introduced for the same reason as residential MBSs—to provide liquidity through a secondary market mechanism. Unlike residential MBSs, commercial CMBSs may be more risky for several reasons. First, they may lack the mortgage insurance that is nearly always present in residential mortgages (such as Federal Housing Administration [FHA] and Veterans Administration [VA] insurance). Second, the mix of mortgages on various properties may prevent a thorough analysis of the risk of the underlying properties. Third, even for CMBSs backed by a single mortgage, the risk of the under lying property may be difficult to ascertain for the average investor.

For these reasons, most commercial CMBSs, unlike their residential counterparts (except for residuals), are rated by rating agencies such as Moody's and Standard and Poor's. The rating provides investors with a snapshot, as it were, of the risk of the CMBS. For example, the Structured Finance Division of Moody's Investors Service considers many variables and factors when rating a particular commercial CMBS. First, they assign a **quality rating** (QR) of A, B, C, D, or E to the CMBS by considering financial factors of the mortgage and property, such as the loan-to-value ratio, debt-to-service coverage, and current loan balance per square foot. They also consider qualitative factors, such as the state of repair of the property, the trend in the economic stability of the neighborhood, and the financial strengths of the tenant of the property. They will also consider the type of property because, historically, some types such as hotels and health care facilities have had higher default rates than other types. Table 17-4 summarizes the mortgage characteristics used by Moody's in their quality rating of CMBSs.

After Moody's assigns a quality rating, it makes a final rating based on the regional market strength of the state and city in which the property is situated. In

TABLE 17-4

Summary of Mortgage Characteristics Used in the QR System

QUALITY RATINGS:	A	B	C	D	E
Loan-to-value ratio	<65%	<70%	<75%	<80%	>85%
Debt-service coverage	>1.35x	>1.25x	>1.15x	>1.05x	<1.05x
Number of 30-day delinquencies/months	0/36	0/24	1/24; 0/12	1/12; 0/6	1/6
Mortgage seasoning (months)	>36	>24	>24	<12	—
Balloon risk	Minor	Minor	Average	Substantial	Substantial
Occupancy level	>95%	>90%	>90%	>85%	<85%
Property age (years)	<10	<15	<20	<25	>25
Deferred maintenance	None	Minor	Average	Excessive	Substantial
Construction quality	Excellent	Good	Average	Fair	Poor
Neighborhood					
Trends	Stable/impr	Stable/impr	Stable	Stable/decl	Declining
Current status	Excellent	Good	Average	Below average	Poor
Property size					
Multifamily (units)	>200	>150	>75	>10	<10
Office, industrial & retail (sq. ft.)	>100,000	>75,000	>50,000	>25,000	<25,000
Retail	Credit anchor	Credit anchor	Credit anchor	Anchor anchor	No
Owner/tenant credit	Excellent	Good	Average	Fair	Poor

Source: Moody's Structured Finance

TABLE 17-5

Benchmark Credit Support Levels[a]

REGIONAL MARKET STRENGTH														
STRONG					AVERAGE					WEAK				
QR:	AAA	AA	A	BAA	QR:	AAA	AA	A	BAA	QR:	AAA	AA	A	BAA
A	8	4	2	1	A	12	8	6	5	A	18	14	12	11
B	9	5	3	2	B	13	9	7	6	B	19	15	13	12
C	11	7	5	4	C	15	11	9	8	C	21	17	15	14
D	14	10	8	7	D	18	15	12	11	D	24	20	18	17
E[b]	—	—	—	—	E[b]	—	—	—	—	E[b]	—	—	—	—

[a]*These benchmarks are offered as a guideline only. The actual level of credit enhancement will reflect the specifics of each rated transaction and therefore may diverge significantly.*

[b]*Credit enhancement of mortgages with a QR of E must be determined on a case-by-case basis because of the large variance in credit risk for these mortgages.*

Source: Moody's Structured Finance

the late 1980s, for example, California was rated as a strong regional economy, Michigan an average regional economy, and Texas a weak regional economy. Table 17-5 shows how the strength of the regional economy is used with the quality rating to assist rating agencies in arriving at a final rating assignment. The benchmark figures show the relative change in credit enhancement or support that must occur to obtain a given rating.

Appendix 17-A shows that the market classification for Boston was relatively low risk in 1987. We chose this example to demonstrate how risk can change. Even though Moody's rated Boston a low-risk region in 1987, property values subsequently suffered, and defaults and foreclosures rose for awhile. Since 1992, however, the Boston real estate market has revived. Thus, the Boston experience demonstrates that investors in commercial CMBSs must be aware of the cyclical nature of regional economies. Since real estate investments typically have a long investment horizon, current market conditions must be tempered with the reality that regional economies can change quickly.

CMBSs with Tranches

Just as with residential MBSs, their commercial counterpart can have various tranches with different levels of risk. The risk can result from different maturities or different credit risk, or both. Figure 17-1 shows how a conduit will set up a CMBS. The conduit will purchase commercial mortgages from originators such as commercial banks and mortgage brokers. They will then issue CMBSs with several tranches. The various tranches (securities) will have different maturities and credit risk. The risk of default, for example, may go first to the residual class and then to the last security, then to the next-to-last security, and so forth. The less risky class of security (security one in this example) will be rated highest by the rating agencies and will, therefore, carry the lowest interest rate. In addition, the conduit may obtain pool insurance to help cover any losses from default. The conduit will make a "profit" as long as the weighted average of rates paid in the securities (and premiums for pool insurance, if any) is less than the interest received on the mortgages and as long as there is not a significant amount of defaults accruing to the residual class.

FIGURE 17-1 **CMBS—The Securitization Process**

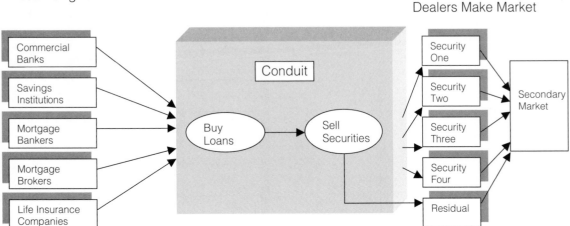

Loan Originators

Securities Brokers and
Dealers Make Market

Buy Side
1. Analyze and underwrite loans
2. Commit to purchase loans
3. Buy loans
4. Manage loans until securities issued

Sell Side
1. Along with investment banker structures securities
2. Arrange for trustee to hold assets
3. Arrange for master servicer
4. Arrange for credit support (pool insurance)
5. Arrange legal support for all areas

Source: © 2014 OnCourse Learning

Figure 17-2 shows how interest rates may be structured. Here we have $100 million in commercial mortgages that pay the conduit an average of 8 percent annually. The weighted average of the rates paid on the six classes is 6.755 percent. The amount received from the commercial mortgages is 8 percent, producing an average margin of 1.245 percent. Notice that the last three classes carry a rate higher than that on the mortgages. Because these classes absorb most, if not all, of the default risk, the conduit can pay a lower rate on the first three classes that make up the bulk of the CMBS.

In 2001 office buildings represented about one-third of the properties financed by CMBSs, followed by retail properties (one-fourth), and then multifamily properties (one-fifth). A key to the future growth of this source of real estate financing is the standardization of the assets backing the commercial CMBSs. To obtain the best ratings from rating agencies, CMBSs at a minimum will have to

- Standardize loan documents.
- Extend amortization beyond the popular "bullet" loans of 5 to 7 years.
- Establish minimum debt service and loan-to-value ratios.
- Establish a prohibition against any prepayments for some standard initial number of years.

Given the diversity of terms and conditions in commercial loans, it will be difficult to achieve full standardization of these loans.

Table 17-6 shows the total amount of CMBS issues from 2004 through year-end 2012. The peak year of issues was 2007, the year prior to the beginning of the real estate downturn. During the real estate downturn beginning in 2008 the

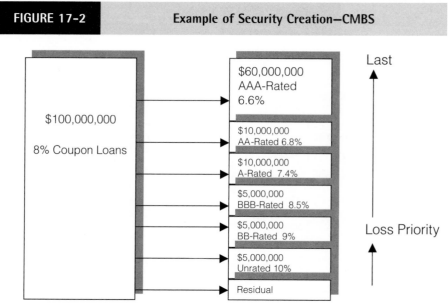

FIGURE 17-2   **Example of Security Creation—CMBS**

Excess interest = 0.08− (0.6×0.066)− (0.1×0.068)− (0.1× 0.074)− (0.05×0.085)
− (0.05× 0.09)− (0.05× 0.1) = 0.08− 0.06755 = 0.01245

Source: © 2014 OnCourse Learning

TABLE 17-6

CMBS Issues, U.S.: 2004–2011 (millions of dollars)

2004	95,495
2005	166,502
2006	198,383
2007	228,556
2008	12,146
2009	2,744
2010	11,633
2011	32,706
2012	42,021

Source: Commercial Mortgage Alert

default rate on CMBSs increased significantly. This led to a reluctance of investment bankers to issue and investors purchase, new CMBSs. The 60-day plus default rate on all CMBSs was 28 percent (less than one-half of 1 percent) in 2007. By mid-2010 the default rate had increased to 7.41 percent.

Table 17-7 shows the holders of all commercial and multifamily loans from 2005 through year-end 2010. CMBS holders represented 22 percent of the total commercial real estate loans in 2010. Again, as the real estate market continues to recover it is expected that the role of CMBSs in financing commercial properties will continue to increase.

Institutional Investors

As indicated in Table 17-7, one important class of institutional investors in equity real estate is life insurance companies. Another increasingly important class, (in the other category) is pension funds. We now look at these two sources in detail.

Life Insurance Companies

Mortgages by far represent the majority of real estate asset holdings of life insurance companies, with equity representing a smaller proportion. The proportion of their total equity real estate assets has held steady at approximately 3 percent for

TABLE 17-7

Holders of Commercial and Multi-family loans, 2005–2010 (billions of dollars)

	COMMERCIAL BANKS	CMBS ISSUERS	INSURANCE COMPANIES	SAVINGS INSTITUTIONS	GSE's	OTHER	TOTAL
2005	1,128.1	643.3	266.7	198.4	93.0		2,621.8
2006	1,280.8	752.5	281.5	205.4	105.4	324.7	2,950.3
2007	1,396.9	919.1	304.0	215.4	147.7	343.9	3,327.0
2008	1,548.1	895.6	315.5	192.9	189.4	357.1	3,498.6
2009	1,506.3	855.3	307.4	183.8	197.8	332.4	3,383.0
2010	1,428.0	705.9	298.6	180.1	251.3	338.6	3,202.5

Source: Commercial Mortgage Alert

the last 2 decades. In contrast, they held $343,500 million in mortgages in the third quarter of 2012, about 20 percent of their total assets. Life insurance companies have held about one-third of their equity real estate in separate accounts. A separate account is a fund established by a life insurance company and held separately from other assets. State laws provide that assets in separate accounts may be invested without regard to restrictions that are normally placed on other investments. The separate account may be comprised of only stocks, only mortgages, or only equity real estate. The role of life insurance companies in financing equity real estate has been limited because of concern about the liquidity of equity real estate. Their primary role remains in providing debt financing.

Pension Funds

The growth of **pension funds** has been phenomenal. In 1970 they held only $135 billion in assets. In 2011 their assets had skyrocketed to $16.08 trillion. Their interest in real estate as an investment has been recent. In 1980 pension funds held a negligible amount of equity real estate, but their interest in real estate grew throughout the decade. By the late 1980s dozens of investment advisors managed real estate investments for pension funds and by 1990, their holdings of real estate had grown modestly to represent about 5 percent of their assets.

Tables 17-8 and 17-9 show the percentage of real estate holdings by a sample of pension funds by the Pension Real Estate Association. The survey also indicates that pension funds hold about 4 percent of their assets in real estate. The percentage is greater for funds that hold real estate, about 7 percent to 8 percent.

Pension plans can be categorized into two classes: **defined-contribution plans** and **defined-benefit plans.** In short, the former specifies a certain contribution made during the working years of the employee. Retirement benefits are based on

TABLE 17-8

Percentage Allocation of All Plan Sponsors-Sample By Pension Real Estate Association

	EQUITIES	BONDS	REAL ESTATE	OTHER	TOTAL
2007	55.10%	24.50%	4.40%	16.00%	100.00%
2008	54.60%	25.40%	4.40%	15.60%	100.00%
2009	51.10%	28.70%	4.60%	15.60%	100.00%
2010	51.60%	27.30%	3.70%	17.40%	100.00%
2011	50.30%	25.20%	3.90%	20.60%	100.00%

Source: Pension Real Estate Association, Investort Report, August 2012

TABLE 17–9

Percentage Allocation of All Plan Sponsors With Real Estate Holdings–Sample By Pension Real Estate Association

	EQUITIES	BONDS	REAL ESTATE	OTHER	TOTAL
2007	57.80%	23.60%	7.70%	10.90%	100.00%
2008	58.00%	24.90%	8.00%	9.10%	100.00%
2009	56.50%	26.40%	8.10%	9.00%	100.00%
2010	57.10%	25.40%	7.00%	10.50%	100.00%
2011	57.50%	23.00%	7.30%	12.20%	100.00%

Source: Pension Real Estate Association, Investort Report, August 2012

the accumulation of the fund at the time of retirement. Defined-benefit plans specify a certain pension payment. Employees contribute sufficient funds to guarantee the defined payment when they retire. The amount they contribute may vary with the investment performance of the fund.

Defined-contribution plans are by far the largest of the pension plans, both in the amount and in number. Their administrators have been reluctant, until recently, to invest in equity real estate. As late as 1988, the largest defined-contribution plan held only 0.7 percent of its assets in real estate. The largest 200 funds held only 4.3 percent of their assets in real estate.[2] Participants in defined-contribution plans usually have a say in how the funds are invested. They may prefer not to invest in real estate for several reasons. They may not understand that adding real estate to a portfolio of assets significantly affects portfolio diversification. Second, they may have been unimpressed with the generally weak returns generated by real estate securities in the 1970s and early 1980s. Even today, real estate returns are weak in certain areas of the United States. Finally, participants may value liquidity and the option to quickly sell and buy assets for the fund.

A survey by Elebash and Yost revealed that most pension fund managers believe that diversification is the most attractive feature of equity real estate investment. On the other hand, 64 percent of managers of corporate pension funds and 47 percent of managers of public pension funds cited lack of liquidity as an unattractive feature of real estate as an investment.[3] Indeed, lack of liquidity can be a significant problem for defined-contribution pension funds because many of the funds allow their participants to switch from one investment option to another. Essentially, the liquidity problem would require that real estate be packaged similarly to mutual funds or in REITs.

Restrictions on Pension Fund Investments

Pension fund investments can be affected in at least three ways—by rules and regulations established under the Employee Retirement Income Security Act, by tax regulations concerning unrelated business income, and by generally accepted accounting principles. In 1974, Congress passed the **Employee Retirement Income Security Act (ERISA)**. It was designed to protect the integrity of pension funds and, thus, the retirement benefits of workers covered by retirement plans. ERISA regulations can affect the real estate investments of pension funds in several ways. First, the stipulations of a retirement plan must be adhered to only to the extent that they do not conflict with ERISA rules. Second, pension funds must invest as "a prudent man" would invest his own funds. Third, pension funds must undertake to diversify their respective portfolios.

ERISA does not restrict the types of real estate properties that pension funds can purchase. However, it discourages a pension fund from purchasing the property of the company that funds the plan, because the company may be tempted to sell property of low value to the fund at an inflated price. Apart from this minor restriction, ERISA places no constraints on real estate investment by pension funds. However, tax rules may affect the types of real estate in which pension funds can invest.

Pension funds are exempt from paying federal taxes. This does not mean that pension funds can take advantage of the tax exemption to compete unfairly for debt financing as a source of investment funds. For this reason, tax regulations prohibit pension funds from engaging in any business that is not related to their primary purpose. If a pension fund does earn unrelated business income by engaging in a business unrelated to its purpose, it is subject to a tax on that income. The tax is referred to as **unrelated business income tax (UBIT)**.

Until 1981 a pension fund that purchased real estate that was in part financed by a mortgage had to treat a portion of the income (rents, for example) as unrelated business income and pay taxes on it. This discouraged pension fund investment in real estate, except for an occasional all-equity investment. In 1980 the tax law was changed to allow investment in debt-financed properties without the burden of UBIT. Even here, there are some restrictions. The purchase price of the property must be fixed in amount and not be contingent on future revenues or profits from the property. The property cannot be leased to the seller (sale-leaseback), and the financing must be standard (no nonrecourse purchase money mortgage or below-market-rate financing). In addition, pension funds must comply with the **fractions rule** in leveraged real estate through a partnership in which at least one of the other partners is not an organization that qualifies for tax-exempt status (qualifying organization [QO]). The fractions rule was established to prevent such a partnership from allocating a disproportionate amount of annual expenses to the taxable partner in the early years of the partnership and a similar disproportionate amount of revenues to the tax-exempt pension fund in the later years of the partnership (remember the time value of money). The rule states that revenue and expenses allocated to a QO partner for any taxable year cannot exceed the partner's fraction rule percentage. That percentage, in turn, is its percentage share of overall partnership loss for the taxable year for which that partner's percentage loss share will be the smallest. This rule prevents a pension fund or other QO from "lending" its tax-exempt status to a taxable partner. Pension funds must be very careful not to violate the fractions rule since any violation is incurably fatal. Once a partnership flunks the fractions rule, it does so for all remaining taxable years of the partnership. Also, a violation of the fractions rule can be highly contagious. Compliance with the rule is tested at the partnership level and not at the partner level. Thus, when numerous partners are QOs, a bad allocation to one of them taints all of the QOs in the partnership, including those in compliance with the fractions rule. Although the fractions rule can be complicated and difficult to adhere to, the Department of Treasury established regulations in May 1994 that clarify exactly what can and cannot be done under the rules. The permitted and excluded activities are beyond the scope of this text, but in general they allow "preferred returns" to a QO to compensate for cash equity investments, distribution of the proceeds of subsequently obtained nonrecourse debt to the partners, and a *di minimus* rule that allows QOs with very small interests in a partnership to avoid the fractions rule entirely.

As you can see from this very casual discussion, the rules governing UBIT, as they relate to real estate securities, are extremely complex and beyond the scope of this discussion. In brief, income from or the gain on the sale of RELPs is generally considered UBIT for pension funds. Because of potential tax problems, many pension funds do not invest in limited partnerships. Partnerships with other taxable entities require careful compliance with the fractions rule. Income from real estate investment trusts, however, generally is not considered UBIT. Thus, many pension funds that invest in real estate securities avoid RELPs and invest in REITs.

The Future of Pension Fund Investment in Real Estate

Although lack of liquidity is a problem for defined-contribution plans, the outlook for increased pension fund investment in real estate is bright, because plan managers better understand portfolio theory and the need to diversify investments and because Financial Accounting Standards Board Statement Number 87 (FASB-87) made changes, effective in 1990, for the reporting of pension liabilities. These changes will encourage pension funds to invest in equity real estate, because FASB-87 limits the range in the discount rate that companies can use to determine their pension liability and requires unfunded portions of the liability to be recorded on the company's balance sheet. Here's how it works.

Under FASB-87, companies report as a liability on their respective balance sheets the present value of future retirement benefits that they are expected to incur, based on the number, ages, salaries, and so forth, of their employees. The annual pension expense that is reported in the income statement is the change in the liability (present value) reported on the balance sheet from year to year. Prior to FASB-87, companies had a wide latitude in the selection of the discount rate. If their profits for any one year were low, they could increase the discount rate. This would reduce the amount of the pension liability at year end and, therefore, the change in the pension liability, which was reported as an expense. It was this abuse that led FASB-87 to restrict a company's choice of discount rates.

A financially distressed company would fear a fall in interest rates. A large drop in rates, given the lack of choice of discount rate, would require a company to record a large increase in its pension liability. This would appear on the income statement as a large pension expense, which would reduce the company's net profit. It also would cause pension liability to exceed the value of the assets placed in the pension fund, unless the assets also rose with the drop in interest rates.

FASB-87, therefore, has caused many firms to invest in noncallable bonds that rise with a fall in rates. Many professional pension plan managers offer such "immunization" from changes in rates, but as some companies have learned, investing a large proportion of a pension plan's assets in bonds provides lower yields and little protection from inflation. Investment in real estate, on the other hand, may solve some of the problems for pension funding. Real estate values tend to rise when interest rates drop, which would give funds some immunization against a large drop in rates. Real estate investments are also less volatile than bonds or stocks and appear to offer better protection from unanticipated inflation than does a bond portfolio.

Public/Private Partnerships

Public funds are also a source for real estate investment and development. In a public/private partnership, the local government provides land, money, or both, and the developer provides the skill. In such partnerships, the land or funds provided by the government can make some projects feasible that otherwise would not be undertaken on a purely economic basis. The most common government subsidies include contributions of land (or the sale of land at below-market prices), cash, grants, subsidies, or outright investments in the real estate, with the expectation of below-market rates-of-return, low-interest loans (often from funds obtained through the issue of tax-free bonds), and credit enhancement.

In addition to government financial support, the real estate developer may benefit from community support and from visibility arising from the public/private partnership. Such partnerships also mean that the developer can move more quickly through the otherwise lengthy approval process. However, the accelerated approval process may be offset by a more lengthy planning process. Divided votes within the local governing body could stall the project, and the developer also may face restrictions from local ordinances that must be dealt with. Examples include conflict of interest laws, public hearing requirements, minority employment and affirmative action requirements, environmental regulations, wage requirements, and land use limitations.

The local government may benefit from projects that serve a community need. Often the development will improve the appearance of blighted locations, reduce crime, and improve nearby property values (and, therefore, property taxes). Some developments may involve more risk than the local government is willing or legally able to assume. Although most states have prohibitions of some sort against local governments selling land at reduced values or lending funds to private enterprises, the courts in many of these states have allowed public/private partnerships where a public benefit from the project is clearly demonstrated, even though there may be an incidental private benefit.

Public/private partnership developments are restricted by federal tax regulations if they are financed by the sale of tax-free municipal bonds. Under current federal laws, the interest on such bonds will not be tax exempt if more than 10 percent of the project financed with the proceeds of the bonds is used by a private business and more than 10 percent of the interest payments on the bonds are paid from private business sources. Limited exceptions to the rules allow specifically for the development of airports, public water facilities, sewage facilities, solid-waste-disposal facilities, structures for charitable organizations, mass transportation facilities, and docks and wharves.

Summary

Sources of commercial real estate financing can be divided into debt sources and equity sources. The bulk of debt financing for commercial real estate is provided by three institutional lenders: commercial banks, thrifts, and life insurance companies. These three lenders hold approximately 85 percent of all commercial real estate debt. Commercial banks are generally very close to, and knowledgeable about, local economic conditions. For this reason, they advance the most debt for construction and purchase of real estate developments. Their lending follows the local economic cycle closely.

Commercial banks and thrifts are active in the purchase and sale of mortgages backing multifamily residential properties. Life insurance companies, on the other hand, originate more than 97 percent of their total acquisition of real estate debt.

Recently, there has been a trend to collateralize commercial property debt or mortgages. Some private financial institutions have created CMBSs that are the counterpart to residential CMOs. Since the risks of investing in commercial CMBSs are different from those of residential CMOs, the former are likely to be rated by the rating agencies. The rating agencies will take into account characteristics of the property and loan, such as the loan-to-value ratio, debt-to-service ratio, and current loan balance per square foot, as well as the local economy in which the property is located. Some complex CMBSs are created by packaging mortgages for different types of properties in different locations. Although the real estate downturn of 2008 reduced the amount of CMBSs that were issued, recent developments point to a recovery of this market for the near future.

Investors can provide equity financing by direct purchase of commercial properties or by purchasing securities that represent an equity interest. Two examples of the latter form of investment are real estate limited partnerships and real estate investment trusts. Limited partnerships are declining in importance as a result of the Tax Reform Act of 1986, which limited the pass-through of passive losses to partners. In the late 1980s and early 1990s, real estate investment trusts gained in market share to fill the gap left by the decline in real estate limited partnerships. Life insurance companies and pension funds also invest directly in commercial real estate. Pension funds, in particular, have increased their investment in recent years. The desire to diversify their portfolios and accounting regulations make real estate more attractive for pension funds now than in the past. The major problem faced by pension funds to date has been the lack of liquidity. This is particularly true for defined contribution plans, where the participants have a say and an inclination to determine the investment vehicles for their contributions.

Key Terms

Commercial mortgage-backed securities (CMBSs)	Net acquisitions
	Originations
Defined-benefit plans	Pension funds
Defined-contribution plans	Quality rating
Employee Retirement Income Security Act (ERISA)	Unrelated business income tax (UBIT)
Fractions rule	

Review Questions

17-1. What are the three major financial institutions that provide debt financing of commercial properties?

17-2. Discuss the role that life insurance companies play in financing commercial real estate.

17-3. Which institutions specialize in originating and selling commercial mortgage debt?

17-4. Which institutions purchase much of the commercial mortgage debt they hold?

17-5. How do commercial CMBSs differ from residential CMOs?

17-6. What factors do the rating agencies consider when rating a commercial CMBS?

17-7. How did FIRREA affect the sources of acquisition, development, and construction loans?

17-8. Why have pension funds become interested in acquiring equity real estate? What is the major drawback of real estate investment for pension funds?

17-9. What is unrelated business income, and how does it affect pension fund investments in real estate?

17-10. Give a general explanation of the fractions rule for pension fund investment in real estate partnerships.

17-11. Explain how accounting rules may affect the assets that pension funds acquire.

17-12. How do risk-based capital requirements affect the real estate investment decisions of life insurance companies?

Notes

1. United States Department of Commerce, Bureau of Economic Analysis estimates for structures only.
2. Real estate assets up 26%. *Pensions and Investment Age* (January 23, 1989), 69–71.
3. C. Elebash and G. Yost. Real estate attitudes differ greatly. *Pension and Investment Age* (August 7, 1989), 35.

Web Sites

http://www.c-lender.com
Information on commercial loans

http://www.pionline.com
Site for the periodical *Pension and Investments*

APPENDIX 17-A   A Moody's Market Classification

MARKET ANALYSIS   March 1987

Boston   Market Classification: **I**

Compound Employment Growth[1] (1981 – 1985) :	2.9%		Vacancy Rate [2] :	8%
Export base size[1]:	24%		New Construction Rental Range[2] : $19.00–26.00 per sq. ft.	
Key Industries[1] : Health Services, Educational Services, Insurance, Business Services, Banking.			New Construction [2] 1987: 2.7 1988: 2.0	
			Years of Supply [2] 1987: 3.0 1988: 3.8	

Source: [1]Wharton Econometric Forecasting Associates. [2] Cushman & Wakefield, New Construction in mil. sq. ft.

Summary Opinion

Boston's office market falls within the lowest risk classification because of its low vulnerability to a decrease in demand for office space and strong controls on commercial development. Office space demand in Boston should be relatively less vulnerable to a downturn because of above-average industrial diversity, improving trends in employment growth, and high representation of less volatile industries. On the supply side, Boston's development process is highly controlled as a result of both a lack of readily developable sites and a strict approval process. In addition, commercial development in the areas surrounding the central business district tends to be complementary rather than competitive in nature.

Market Fundamentals

Employment Growth: The city of Boston has benefited in recent years from strong economic growth in the surrounding region. More specifically, the finance, insurance, and service sectors that the city specializes in have expanded significantly. The metropolitan area has recently experienced excellent growth in "high tech" and other manufacturing industries. This growth, combined with subsequent increased growth in nonmanufacturing sectors, has given the region a growth rate equal to or higher than the nation's since 1976. Boston itself has also participated in this upsurge in growth, moving from substantial declines in the pre-1976 period to substantial positive growth since the late 1970s, at about 1 percentage point below national rates.

Employment Volatility: The mix of industries in Boston heavily favors the less volatile nonmanufacturing sectors, with a notable de-emphasis on the more volatile durable manufacturing, construction, and mining sectors. Some of the industries which dominate in Boston (such as insurance, educational services, and health services) are among the least volatile sectors.

Industry Diversification: The industries in which Boston is relatively specialized form a diverse economic base for trade outside the local economy. The "extra" employment in these industries is distributed in significant amounts across enough different industries to indicate a high amount of economic diversity in the export base. This export base is also large relative to the rest of the local economy, with total "extra" employment in export-base industries accounting for about 24 percent of employment in the city. This indicates good connections to the rest of the world and less dependence on purely local factors.

Commercial Development Controls: The Boston Redevelopment Authority (BRA) strictly controls commercial development through one of the most comprehensive planning processes in the United States. These controls should continue to limit Boston's vulnerability to overbuilding in the furure as the BRA gains additional community support. Boston's progressive linkage program, which requires the developer to pay certain fees to the community in order to gain the right to build, also adds significantly to the cost of development and therefore slows the pace of new construction. Additionally, the lack of readily available quality locations for new development will further restrict the rate of future commercial building.

CBD/Suburban Dynamics: Boston's central business district has only limited vulnerability to out-migration of tenants to the suburbs. This is because the service firms located there have exhibited a strong preference for a dowtown location. In fact, the strong performance of the metropolitan area's economy has supported the service firms located in the central business district. In addition, Boston's downtown tenants tend to maintain contiguous space for all levels of employees, in contrast with long-standing trends in other major cities.

Moody's Structured Transactions Group Newsletter

Source: Moody's Market Report, 1991

ACQUISITION, DEVELOPMENT, AND CONSTRUCTION FINANCING

LEARNING OBJECTIVES

In this chapter, you will read about financing commercial developments from the land-acquisition stage through the construction stage. While most of the chapter is descriptive, one concept permeates the relationship of the lender, the developer, and the contractor—that of the agency cost problem. You should understand that a large proportion of the covenants and restrictions contained in loans to finance the acquisition and development of commercial properties are directed at agency problems. Several parties may be involved in one project: the developer, the contractor, and two or more different lenders. Each has an incentive to act in his or her own interest. Agency costs are those costs necessary to prevent parties from acting in their own interest to the detriment of others. You should view many of the loan covenants and restrictions as methods to avoid agency costs. On the factual side, you should understand those loan provisions that are common to commercial developments and how they may differ from residential loans. You also should understand the basic mechanics involved in determining the loan amount and periodic disbursements.

INTRODUCTION

Commercial real estate financing is covered in this and the following chapter. The subject matter is divided between the two chapters according to the time sequence involved in the financing of commercial properties. In this chapter, we discuss the financing associated with the purchase of raw land, the development of the raw land to ready it for construction, and the construction of the facility. In the following chapter, we discuss the forms that the permanent, long-run financing of commercial properties takes. Permanent financing takes over once the real estate project is completed and ready to generate operating income.

We divide the nonpermanent financing discussed in this chapter into three stages: acquisition, development, and construction (ADC). In the trade, this type of financing is referred to as ADC financing. We will proceed as if the financing of the acquisition of the property, development for construction, and construction itself is done in stages and involves different sources from different lenders. While this is often the case in practice, there is no reason why the total financing of acquisition through construction cannot be done at one time, through one source, and with one set of loan package documentation. In fact, it can be accomplished in both ways.

When the ADC process is financed in stages, the separate lenders often require that a detailed set of provisions be met by the other lenders. For example, a lender that finances the development of a property may require that a commitment from another to finance the construction of the facility be in place at the time of the development loan. The development loan lender often will stipulate the terms of the construction loan. Likewise, the construction lender often will require that there be a permanent lender, sometimes referred to as a "takeout" lender, ready to commit to a permanent loan when the facility is completed and ready for operation. It would appear that lenders involved in the various stages of the acquisition, development, construction, and permanent-lending process could simplify matters and avoid agency problems (not to mention litigation expenses) by financing the project from the initial land-acquisition stage through the operation of the completed facility.

Although such full-scale financing has occurred, the more popular method involves different lenders financing distinctly different stages of the development process. The most likely reason for the persistence of this practice is the specialization developed by various types of lenders. Some lenders have developed an expertise in, for example, construction financing. They can monitor the construction process and make sure that loan proceeds are disbursed only according to the development of the project. They also make sure that the project is developed at or under the original cost projections. They may have little expertise in determining the economic viability of the completed project, however. Other lenders, on the other hand, may have an expertise in determining the economic worth of the completed project but cannot monitor the disbursement of the proceeds (perhaps because they are not located in the community where the project is constructed). In this case, the construction lender will require that a permanent takeout lender be secured before it will agree to finance construction of the project. The permanent lender will have judged the economic viability of the project and determined that, if completed as designed, the project could support the payments on the permanent loan. Such specialization appears to be the only rational reason for the separation of the financing by the stages of acquisition and development.

In this chapter, we will review the stages of acquisition and development and indicate how these stages are financed. We also will indicate where agency problems arise between the various lenders in the acquisition and development process and how those agency problems are handled. Finally, we will review the mechanics of how the total amount of the loan and its disbursements are determined.

ACQUISITION

The Land Loan

The first stage of the process involves the acquisition of the raw land to be developed. Raw land is acquired by two types of investors, the speculator and the developer. The **speculator** has no particular development plans for the land. The speculator sees an opportunity for price appreciation because of growth constraints, new transportation facilities, zoning changes, and other economic or institutional changes that will cause the value of the property to appreciate over the near term. The developer, on the other hand, has definite plans for the property. The **developer** is likely to be a specialist in a particular type of development, such as housing, shopping centers, or industrial facilities. Developers may specialize even further within these categories, so that some developers may develop only low-income housing or upscale housing. Some shopping center developers may specialize in malls, others in strip shopping centers. Whatever the specialization, the developer has immediate plans for the land and likely will proceed as quickly as possible to complete the project.

WAREHOUSING

Large developers, especially those that specialize in large residential developments, may desire to warehouse substantial amounts of property. **Warehousing** refers to the holding of large parcels of properties in advance of the development process. As one residential development is completed, the next has housing units under construction, the next has housing construction started, and the next has the land being prepared for development (roads, utilities, and so on being installed). In this way, the developer creates residential developments in a continual process. As part of the process, the developer is continually looking for additional parcels to purchase to begin a new development process, even as he is completing the latest development. Here, financing becomes very important because the developer desires to tie up as little equity as possible in large parcels of land. That is, since assets must be financed, the developer that holds large quantities of land will seek out the lowest cost financing possible. There are several sources of such financing.

Institutional Lenders

One source of land-acquisition financing is the traditional financial institution. We saw in the previous chapter that commercial banks and thrifts were the dominant sources of land financing. These local lenders are in the best position to judge the risks (underwrite) involved in a land loan. **Land acquisition loans** are risky for several reasons. First, raw land usually does not provide any operating income, so that the proceeds of the loan must be repaid either from appreciation in the value of the land or from subsequent loans made for the purpose of development and construction. Also, few tax benefits accrue from holding raw land. Land cannot be depreciated, and there are limitations on the deductibility of interest costs. If the land falls in value and is not developed, the owner may default on the loan, putting the property to the lender. Second, the raw land may not be physically suited for its ultimate highest and best use, and the cost of preparing land for that use is uncertain. The cost of preparing land for development may be unexpectedly high, or development may even be impossible if certain geological formations are discovered that preclude development as planned. Also, there may be no guarantees that the legal factors, such as zoning changes, necessary for development will be forthcoming. Many developments have been approved by local planning commissions only to have further legal objections raised by local citizens opposed to the project. In short, unforeseen physical and legal problems may raise the cost of development of the land to prohibitively high amounts. In such cases, the lender would be stuck with a lien on a nearly valueless piece of land. Because of these risks, land loans will seldom exceed 50 percent or 60 percent of the appraised value of the land.

A financial institution that makes a loan on raw land will have a lien on the property as collateral for the loan. If the land is to be used for a residential development, provisions will have to be made for a release of a portion of the land from the lien, the so-called **release provision**. For example, assume that a residential developer purchases 1,000 acres of land on which he desires to develop and sell 2,000 residences. It is unlikely the developer will be able to build and sell the houses over a very short period of time. The "absorption" (sales) rate for the development may take several years in some cases. The developer will want to sell the first houses in the development long before the final houses are even constructed. However, the land lender will have a lien on the entire acreage of the development. The potential home buyers of the initial houses will demand unencumbered, or free, title to their property, subject only to their own mortgage. To accommodate the sale of the initial phase of the development, the land loan will contain a **partial release provision** of the lien on those portions of the development that are sold. As the properties are sold, the developer will use the sales proceeds to pay off a portion of the land loan in exchange for a release of the lien on that portion of the development that is sold.

The provisions detailing the partial release will be included in the original loan documents and must be carefully thought out. Specifically, the lender must make sure that after a significant portion of the development has been sold, the value of the remaining land (on which the lender still has a lien) is greater than the remaining amount of indebtedness. The indebtedness can exceed the value of the land if the developer was not required to reduce the debt sufficiently as each parcel was sold. This would be the case if the partial release provision required the developer to only pay off 10 percent of the debt when 10 percent of the land was sold. Here, the developer may sell off the more valuable parcels first, leaving less valuable parcels to secure the remainder of the debt. In this regard, the release provision may establish a "release pattern" that describes the order in which various parcels will be developed and sold. This ensures that the developer will not develop and sell the more desirable parcels without adequately reimbursing the lender.

The mechanics of the partial release are handled in escrow. When the developer sells the property, a new lien (buyer's mortgagee) will be substituted for the developer's lien.

Seller Accommodation

Another source of land acquisition financing is the seller of the property. Often the seller of the property will be asked to accommodate the developer in financing the sale. This can be done in several ways, including option financing, seller financing, and subdivision trusts.

Options

Rather than purchasing land outright, many developers will prefer to purchase an option to buy the land at a future time. The terms of a **land purchase option** will include the purchase price, the expiration date of the option, and the premium or cost of the option. In this way, the developer can secure the land that he wishes to develop without securing immediate financing or tying up equity in land. If, at a later time, the development of the property is not economically feasible, the developer can let his option lapse. His loss will be the option premium, which may very well be less than the loss of the equity investment in the land.

The cost of the option will depend on several factors. The longer the term of the option, the higher the premium. This is especially true where the purchase price of the land is set in the option contract. The longer the period of exercise, the greater the chance that the market value of the land will rise substantially above the contract price in the option agreement. In essence, the seller has agreed to hold the land for the developer until the last day of the option period. The seller incurs the carrying costs of the property (such as property taxes), while the developer receives the benefits from appreciation in the value of the property over the exercise period. Thus, the longer the exercise period, the higher the premium demanded by the seller. Second, the option price will depend on the volatility of land prices. If land prices have been or are expected to be very stable, then the premium price for the option will be low. Stable prices reduce the probability that at the time of exercise the value of the land will be substantially above the contract price. Third, the option premium will be smaller if the contract price of the land is allowed to float with some sort of index. This reduces the chance that the market value of the land will be substantially above the contract sales price when the option is exercised.

In some cases, the seller of the land will inflate the cost of the land but then give a credit for the option premium. In other cases, the seller will give a declining portion of the option premium as a credit as time elapses. This provision will encourage an earlier exercise of the option than otherwise.

Rolling Options

Some developers will contract for **rolling options**. Rolling options give the developer additional options on more land as the existing options are exercised. Residential developers in particular use rolling options. As they purchase land and develop it with housing, they want to be in a position of having options on other parcels. They often will have a rolling option agreement to purchase land that is contiguous with the land already purchased.

Seller Financing

In some cases, the seller of the land will agree to finance the purchase by taking back a note from the buyer. In this way, the seller becomes a lender as well. The sales price of the land under such arrangements is higher than otherwise. The reason is that the seller almost always will provide nonrecourse financing. Since the seller is granting the developer a put option should the project fail, the seller will be compensated with a higher selling price for the property. Seller financing can complicate the development process, because the seller will have a lien on the property. Lenders will advance funds for development and construction only if they can have a priority lien, however. In cases of seller financing, there is nearly always a provision in the loan documents that allows the seller's lien to become subordinated to a subsequent construction loan. The seller's note is subject to an increase in risk through the **subordination** process. This is another reason the sales price of the property will be higher than if seller financing were not used.

Where a subordination clause exists, it is likely to be quite detailed. There is a severe agency problem here. Once the seller's note is subordinated to a construction lender, there is no one to look after the interests of the seller. The developer has an incentive to maintain as much flexibility as possible in the development process. The construction lender will stand ahead of the land seller through the subordination process, concerned only that the value of the property exceed the amount of the construction loan and not the entire amount of indebtedness (construction loan plus seller's note). Thus, after the seller's note is subordinated, the remaining parties will act on their own behalf and not in the seller's interest.

Because of these agency costs, the seller will insist on as many restrictive covenants as possible. The seller must act like a construction lender in this case.

The subordination provision often will spell out the terms of the construction loan, such as the amount of the loan, its maturity, the interest rate (as in 2 percent over prime at the time of the loan, and so on), and loan-to-value ratio. The subordination agreement also will give the seller the right to make payments on the construction loan and supervise the disbursement of the loan as construction takes place, should the developer default. In short, the terms of the subordination agreement will, as much as possible, ensure that the total value of the property as it is developed always exceeds the total amount of indebtedness as the construction loan is paid out. The total amount of indebtedness, of course, will include the seller's note.

When a construction loan is made and the subordination of the seller's note takes place, the construction lender will have the senior position (**senior financing**) in case of default. Although the construction lender will have no interest in the land seller's now junior lien (**junior financing**), the construction lender will have to be sure not to recklessly jeopardize the position of the junior lien holder. If the construction lender inappropriately endangers the collateral of the junior lien holder, it may be held legally responsible and have its position moved behind that of the land seller. The construction lender can follow certain procedures to ensure that it does not open itself to litigation and damages from a junior lien holder.

First, it should ascertain that there is a specific subordination agreement with the original sale documents. A general statement that the land seller "agrees to at some point in the future consider a subordination of the security" is too vague to be enforceable. The subordination agreement should be as specific as possible. Second, the construction lender must make sure that the disbursement of the proceeds of the construction loan are used as intended and not misappropriated by the developer. If the funds are not used as intended, the value of the property may not rise in step with the indebtedness, placing the junior lien holder in an increasingly disadvantageous position. Third, in regard to the disbursement of the construction funds, the construction lender should clarify the difference between those disbursements that are optional and those that are obligatory. Fourth, the construction lender should acquire from the junior lien holder a specific waiver for disbursing any funds that are not in strict accordance with the construction loan and/or subordination agreement. Finally, the construction lender should avoid any oral commitments to the junior lien holder, such as an agreement to continue to advance more funds to the developer.

Subdivision Trusts

Under a **subdivision trust**, the developer puts up only a portion of the sales price and agrees to pay the balance when the property is developed and sold. The seller of the land transfers title to a trust and is designated the first beneficiary of the trust. As the developer, designated the second beneficiary, sells off parcels of the developed property, he or she is entitled to have portions of the lien released by the trustee. Under the typical subdivision trust, the developer will have the right to develop the property as he or she sees fit. This arrangement avoids the vesting of the title to the property in the hands of the developer, and this provides certain safeguards in the event of developer default and bankruptcy.

DEVELOPMENT

Once the land is acquired, the next stage of the development process involves making the site ready for construction. This involves several steps, including:

1. *Zoning.* If necessary, the proper application and legal procedures must be taken to ensure that the area is zoned in accordance with the intended development.

2. *Engineering and surveying.* Engineers and other experts must work out the details of grading, drainage, removal of natural obstacles, and preparing accurate maps of the area. This must all be done before any physical work can be done on the project.

3. *Subdividing.* If applicable, a subdivision of the land into smaller sections may be necessary. This is particularly so for residential developments.

4. *Physical work.* The final stage of preparation will involve the physical work of grading the land and putting in streets, utilities, landscaping, and so forth.

All of these elements of site preparation are costly. In fact, it is not unusual for the expenses associated with the first three steps to be greater than those of the actual physical work. Even though no physical changes in the land occur in the first three steps, value is added through the expenditures made in these efforts. The land development lender, just as the construction loan lender discussed later in this chapter, will want to make sure that value is added to the project as the **land development loan** proceeds are disbursed. The loan documents generally will state that in the event of default, the lender will have the right to the work materials produced by the various experts and technicians involved in the site-preparation process. Such work materials will include maps, surveys, engineers' reports, and so forth. In the event of default, the lender may wish to proceed with the development as planned. These work papers will be invaluable in that case. Also, the engineers, surveyors, planners, and architects will have a lien on the property for any work performed but not paid for.

Lenders of funds for land development are specialized in that they can judge how the development of the land will increase its value and if the loan proceeds plus the developer's equity will be less than or equal to the value of the land when it is ready for construction. They are also aware of local land use regulations and required governmental approvals for developing the land. The lender will make sure that the loan documentation provides for deadlines for obtaining the necessary government approvals.

Some of the more important government approvals concern subdivision control ordinances and impact fees. **Subdivision control ordinances** usually relate to residential developments and require the developer to construct a minimum infrastructure. The ordinances exist in every state and nearly every locality and are designed to protect the consumer from the unkept promises of developers. Before such ordinances were introduced, it was not unusual for a developer to sell residential lots with a promise to install the necessary roadways, utilities, drainage, and such after a sufficient number of lots had been sold and ready for construction. Then, after many of the lots were sold, the developer would refuse to make the promised improvements, leaving the consumers with buildable lots but no utilities or roads.

Subdivision control ordinances take two forms. Under one form, the developer is required to construct the infrastructure prior to building residences or selling lots. The infrastructure must be built to minimum specifications. Under another method, the builder must post a performance bond, place cash in escrow, or obtain a letter of credit. This is where the land development lender comes into play. The developer often will ask this lender to lend the funds to be placed in escrow or issue a letter of credit to secure the bond.

Impact fees are fees placed on developers by municipalities to cover the added costs of the burden to the infrastructure that results from the new development. Municipalities argue that new developments increase the local population and therefore require additional highways, schools, libraries, firehouses, wastewater and sewer treatment facilities, and so forth.

There are two popular types of impact fees: dollar-based fees and non-dollar-based fees. **Dollar-based fees** are payments made to municipalities or other local governments. An example is a fee imposed on the developer for new construction (usually based on a formula) that may or may not be paid over a period of years. Another dollar-based fee is the **cost recovery fee**, paid by the developer to help recover the cost of the infrastructure built by the local government.

Non-dollar-based fees are contributions in lieu of cash payments. An example is an **exaction**, whereby a developer agrees to construct and donate a public facility such as a park, school, or firehouse. Sometimes developers will be allowed to construct more houses per acre than usually provided for by zoning regulations if the exaction is valuable. This is called a **density bonus**. Another example of a non-dollar-based fee is **inclusionary zoning**, whereby the developer agrees to build low-income housing, either on site or off site, in return for a right to develop the property or for a density bonus. Finally, there is **tax increment financing**. Here, improvements in the infrastructure are financed by additional property taxes applied to properties in the geographical area of the development.

As discussed earlier, the lender must consider partial release clauses. The land developer may desire to sell off some of the developed lots rather than proceed with construction. The usual approach is to set the release price at a fraction of the sales proceeds so that the developer can pay the expenses associated with the sale (such as a broker's commission) and make a reasonable profit for his efforts. The partial release clause also will likely set a minimum sales price to ensure that sufficient funds are given to the lender in exchange for the partial release of the lien.

CONSTRUCTION

The **construction loan** is the final type of financing for a project prior to the permanent or "takeout" loan, when the project is completed and set for operation. Most construction loans have the following characteristics:

1. They are short term and cover the length or period of construction only.
2. The interest rate is variable and usually set at a given number of percentage points over the prime rate of the lender.
3. Since the project provides no operating revenues during the construction stage, interest payments are deferred and "financed" by the lender.
4. Loan-to-value ratios are generally in the 70 percent to 80 percent range for commercial projects built for sale and 60 percent to 70 percent for speculative projects.

Underwriting Construction Loans

As in the case with land development lenders, construction lenders tend to be very knowledgeable, both about local policies and about the risks involved in construction lending. They are specialists in assessing and controlling the risks that result from the construction process itself and from local conditions. The risks involved in construction lending include the following:

- The collateral for the loan includes unfinished or partially completed projects.
- Unknown construction risks, such as unexpected increases in material costs, strikes, poor weather, and financial difficulties of subcontractors, can arise.
- The intervening rights of third parties, such as mechanic's liens or claims for personal injury by construction workers, can present a risk.
- If the permanent lender fails to honor a commitment, permanent financing may be lost.

- Failure to meet with building codes may result in a denial of certificate of occupancy.

For these reasons, the construction lender usually will be a specialist in assessing and controlling the risks of the construction phase of the project. In assessing and controlling the risk, the construction lender will do all of the following:

1. The lender will request an appraisal of the finished project based on generally accepted appraisal methods. The lender should make sure that the appraiser is independent of the developer. Federally related lenders must ensure that key federally mandated requirements of the appraisal are met. The appraisal should be based on a financial analysis of the finished project. If a financial analysis is missing or inadequate, then the lender should have its own analysis performed.

2. The lender will have its staff review all construction plans, engineer's reports, applications for government permits, applications for zoning changes, and so forth, to determine if the project can be built for the amount estimated and in the time frame indicated. The lender will make sure the loan documents indicate which parties are responsible for cost overruns or failure to meet the deadlines set for completion.

3. The lender will make sure that the proceeds of the loan are disbursed only for approved expenditures and made to the parties responsible for the construction. This has a twofold impact. First, it ensures that the work has been done so that the collateral for the loan increases step by step with the increase in the loan balance outstanding. Second, it ensures that no mechanic's liens will be placed by parties who performed work on the project but were not paid. By law, mechanic's liens can be given priority over the lender's lien.

4. The lender will monitor *holdbacks*. A holdback is a reserve of funds held back from payment to subcontractors until the work of the subcontractor has been inspected and accepted by the general contractor.

5. The lender will make sure there is a takeout commitment from the permanent lender and will analyze that commitment. The financial stability and reputation of the takeout lender are important in this analysis.

The Construction Loan Commitment

As part of the planning process for a real estate project, the developer at some point will desire to have a lender commit to make a construction loan. A **construction loan commitment** is a separate agreement whereby a lender makes a commitment to make a loan in exchange for a fee. Even though the construction loan commitment is a separate agreement, it will provide extremely detailed information about the construction loan itself. In fact, to be enforceable (in court), the commitment will have to be as specific as possible and contain no vague language. The following are among the more important terms of the construction loan itself that should be covered in a commitment: (1) the loan amount, and when the proceeds of the loan are to be disbursed; (2) the interest rate, which can be fixed or floating and may include a floor and ceiling for the protection of both parties; (3) a description of the collateral; (4) a commitment for a permanent loan and the details of the permanent loan; (5) the amount of equity that the developer is required to contribute to the construction phase; (6) a statement indicating that the project will comply with legal restrictions, such as environmental laws and zoning regulations; (7) a requirement that rental agreements with major tenants of the project have been completed; (8) statements of personal liability in the event of default; and (9) a statement to the effect that the commitment is not assignable to another party.

The commitment fee paid by the developer is intended to ensure the availability of the construction loan. When the construction loan calls for a fixed interest rate at the time the commitment is made, the developer may have an option. The developer can exercise the option and take the construction loan if the market rate is at or above the commitment rate. If the market rate is below the commitment rate, the developer will have an incentive to seek alternative financing. In many cases, the commitment is two sided, however. That is, even if market rates fall below the commitment rate, the developer may be obligated under the commitment to finance the project at the higher commitment rate. Thus, commitment fees tend to be higher if the developer has the option to seek alternative financing. Stated differently, the commitment fee will be lower if the developer is obligated to take the construction loan at the rate indicated in the loan commitment, regardless of the market rate at the time of the funding. If the market rate does drop and the developer is obligated to the higher rate stated in the commitment, this may lead to some interesting legal procedures.

First, if the developer fails to initiate construction, he or she generally will have no right to a return of the commitment fee. The fee would be refundable only if the developer fails to initiate the project for any reason specifically allowed in the loan commitment documents, or because he or she is prevented by some legal restriction from developing the project.

Second, in the event that the lender fails to make the construction loan as committed (perhaps because interest rates have risen above that in the commitment), the developer may be able to recover the costs of development that were expended prior to the loan commitment date. The developer also can recover for any alternative financing costs that are greater than those indicated in the loan commitment. Recovery for future profits on the project is more speculative and is generally not available.

Construction Loan Provisions

An example of a building loan agreement is shown in Exhibit 18-1 at the end of this chapter. The agreement sets out the rights and obligations of the lender and the developer. The agreement accomplishes several general things. First, the agreement refers to the promissory note (the collateral that serves as security to the note) and the deed-of-trust (the instrument that actually secures the collateral). The note and deed are separate documents from the loan agreement. They are, however, executed simultaneously with the agreement. Second, the agreement spells out the details of how the construction is to proceed and how the loan proceeds are to be disbursed. By these details, the lender attempts to cover every contingency that may impair the security of the loan. Essentially, the details are designed to ensure that the facility is constructed as expeditiously as possible, within the designed budget, and without additional liens intervening in priority to that of the lender. It is not our intent here to describe each of the details in all of the items included in the agreement. However, we will explore certain important provisions that stand out and should be given attention.

First, the essential terms of the note and reference to the security for the note are included in item 3 of the exhibit. Items 4 and 5 describe the security for the loan. These items make certain that, in addition to the land and building, equipment, furnishings, and the like also serve as collateral for the loan. Also, the lender may require written statements from subcontractors and vendors that they have no cause for a lien on the property. Item 6 requires the borrower to obtain a title insurance policy on the property. This is designed to protect the collateral for the lender. The title company must meet with the approval of the lender (that is, it has to be a financially strong title company). Also, the lender must approve any exceptions in the policy. (Exceptions are liens and claims against the property by others that the title company specifically mentions in the title policy as not being covered under the policy.) Items 7 through 10 relate to the disbursement of the loan funds. These provisions ensure that the proceeds are used as intended and lead to an increase in the value of the property in step with the disbursement of the loan. Item 7 indicates that the lender may use an agent (often referred to as a voucher control agent) to monitor the disbursement of the loan proceeds. Item 8 assures the lender that the actual cost of each of the stages of development will not exceed the cost established in the loan agreement. Item 10 is a detailed description of the mechanics of disbursement to the contractor and subcontractors. It also names an architect to ensure that the facility is being constructed as indicated in the preapproved plans. Item 13 provides the details of how the physical work on the construction of the facility will be carried out. Here, the lender wants to make sure that the work is carried out expeditiously, in conformity with local construction codes, and in accordance with the authorized architectural plans.

Item 15 indicates that before the lender will make the final disbursement, the designated architect will verify that the facility has been constructed as planned and that all contractors have been paid and given releases from any mechanic's liens. Sometimes this item will include a reference to a verification by an engineer that the construction meets the required specifications. Items 17 and 18 indicate that it is the responsibility of the borrower to make sure there are no mechanic's or tax liens on the property that may have priority over the lender's security interest. Item 21 identifies those actions that constitute a default by the borrower. They include the failure to pay interest or a deposit of principal as called for in the loan amortization schedule, bankruptcy or insolvency of the borrower, delay in the construction of the project, and allowing items of security to be transferred to another party. Item 22 indicates the lender's remedies in the event the borrower breaches the agreement. One of the more important of the remedies is the right to accelerate (demand immediate payment of the entire balance) the loan. The next important item is Item 27, which states that the loan agreement is part of the deed-of-trust (security) and that if there appears to be any conflict between terms in the deed and terms in the loan agreement, then the latter will control. The reason for this provision is that the loan agreement is usually much more detailed and explicit in many of the terms and conditions of the construction loan.

What happens if the state takes the property under an eminent domain action before the project is completed? Who is entitled to the proceeds from the state, the property owner (borrower) or the lender? Item 29 protects the interest of the lender by stating that the proceeds will be applied to the loan balance at the time. This prevents the developer from taking the proceeds and defaulting on the loan, leaving the lender with no collateral. Items 32 and 33 together prevent the developer from assigning (selling) rights under the loan agreement to another party, but allow the lender to assign (sell) the loan to another lender.

Item 37 is very important in light of recent court cases on the liability of lenders for the costs of cleaning up hazardous waste found on properties that serve as loan collateral. If there is a loan default and the lender forecloses on the property, the lender will own the property. Under certain interpretations of the Comprehensive Environmental Response, Compensation, and Liability Act of 1980 (CERCLA), the courts have held lenders (as owners) liable for the cost of cleaning up any hazardous waste on the sites that they own through a foreclosure. To escape liability, the lender must prove that it was unaware of the presence of hazardous waste and that it took all necessary steps to ensure that no hazardous process was undertaken. This provision is one step the lender takes in this regard. Other steps will include what is called an **environmental audit**. The lender may require that the borrower hire a specialist to explore the property, including its history of use and its current physical condition.

A loan will be made only if there is a clean audit. Issues of lender liability under CERCLA are explored more fully in Chapter 22. Item 37 is an attempt by the lender to insulate itself from liability under CERCLA.

Item 38 requires that the borrower waive the right to a jury trial in the event of a dispute over the terms of the loan agreement. Basically, lenders feel that juries can come up with some pretty weird decisions. They would rather trust the knowledge of a judge if there is a dispute. This makes sense, given the detailed and exhaustive nature of the terms of the loan agreement.

Finally, Item 41 allows the borrower to prepay the loan at any time without a prepayment penalty. Since construction loans have short maturities, the lender does not worry about the risk of prepayment in a falling interest rate environment. Long-term, permanent, commercial (takeout) loans generally have prepayment penalties to protect the lender in the event that interest rates fall subsequent to loan origination.

Construction Loan Administration

After a construction loan has been made, the lender must monitor the construction process and oversee the disbursements of the loan to the contractors. **Construction loan administration** involves these steps:

1. Making sure that construction proceeds as scheduled. A delay in the construction process means that the amount of the outstanding debt, which includes accrued interest, is becoming larger and larger. The lender does not want the amount of the indebtedness to exceed the value of the completed project.

2. Making sure that the construction work conforms to all specifications. The lender does not want a finished project that will require additional expenditures to cure defects in workmanship.

3. Making sure that the cost of the project does not exceed the original estimates. This ensures that at all times the remaining portion of the loan exceeds the cost to complete the project.

4. Making sure that no other liens intervene ahead of the lender's. The best way to accomplish this is to make sure that the contractors are paid for the work as done, so that no mechanic's liens will be placed on the property.

5. Making sure that none of the conditions of the permanent lenders are violated. The construction lender does not want to give the permanent lender any excuse for not financing the finished project.

Usually, a loan administrator is placed in charge of the administration of the loan. The loan administrator will make sure that all the requirements of the loan agreement are met as the project is constructed. The developer will make periodic applications for payment to the contractors and subcontractors involved in the construction of the facility. The loan administrator will make sure that the request for the disbursement includes an indication of the value (or percentage) of the work done and that which remains to be done. The loan administrator will request that an architect verify that the work is being done according to the approved specifications.

Also, many lenders use the services of voucher control agents. A **voucher control agent** is an independent third party who specializes in monitoring the disbursement of the loan to the proper contractors. These agents also regularly inspect the job site to ensure that construction is proceeding as indicated and that materials paid for have been delivered. They also collect material and labor releases (to guard against mechanic's liens) when the funds are paid.

Determination of Loan Amount and Disbursements

In this section we outline the "mechanics" of the determination of the loan amount, payments (disbursements), and repayment. The determination of these amounts will hinge on the cost and the timing of the construction of the project. In this regard, there are several general considerations.

First, the lender will require that the developer put some equity into the project. When the project is completed, the loan-to-value ratio of the ADC loan should reflect the lender's perception of the risk of the project. An 80 percent loan-to-value ratio for a typical commercial project is not uncommon. Second, the developer will want to borrow the funds only as needed to complete the project. By borrowing funds only to finance the construction, the developer will minimize the interest cost of the loan. Third, since the project will generate no cash flows until completed, the developer will not be in a position to make interest payments on the loan until permanent financing is secured. In other words, each advance by the lender will continue to accrue interest until the project is completed. At the time of completion, a permanent loan will be used to repay the construction loan.

Fourth, as with many types of real estate financing, the lender will charge a contract rate of interest and also assess loan fees or points. In the case of an ADC loan, the points may be determined at the time the loan is paid off when the actual balance is known. Fifth, even though the actual balance of the loan will not be known until the project is complete and the loan is to be repaid, a reliable estimate of the amount must be made. For one thing, the lender must be assured that the final loan amount will not be so large as to exceed a desirable loan-to-value ratio. Finally, several risks are associated with ADC loans, for both the lender and the borrower. We will address these risks following a review of a sample ADC loan.

ADC LOAN EXAMPLE

Table 18-1 shows the basic cost data for a multifamily project similar to the example used throughout the text. The ultimate investment in the project will be approximately $2.8 million. The amount that is invested, or "put into," the project will not determine its final value, however. A value based on anticipated cash flows will be used to justify the expenditures for development of the project. Thus, for simplicity, we assume that the value of the project upon completion is approximately the amount invested in it, in terms of the cost of developing it, including interest costs associated with the ADC loan. The cost of the land is $300,000 (5 acres at $60,000 each). The project is estimated to take 18 months to complete, once funding is approved by the lender. Site-preparation expenses total $195,000, hard costs total $1,940,000, and soft costs, $55,000. Total costs, excluding acquisition of the land, are $2,190,000. For now, we will assume that the developer purchases the land with cash as a portion of his equity interest in the property and the lender funds the remaining development costs.

Table 18-2 shows the construction schedule as agreed on by the developer and the lender. It shows the disbursement of the $2,190,000 in development expenses over the 18-month period. In this example, the lender charges a 12 percent (annual, 1 percent monthly) contract rate, with two percentage points at the termination of the loan. Table 18-3 shows the "mechanics" of the loan disbursement and repayment.

Disbursements are assumed to be made at the beginning of each month. At the beginning of the first month, the lender advances the developer $105,000 as indicated by the construction cost schedule. At the end of the month, the balance due reflects this first disbursement and the 1 percent monthly interest rate on the loan. At this time, the lender advances the second month's disbursement, $95,000. The balance due at this point is $106,050 + $95,000, or $201,050. This

TABLE 18-1
Project Data

Basic data	
Site area 5 acres	$60,000/acre
Units	35
Square footage	42,000 rentable
	52,500 total
Development period	18 months
Cost information	
Site acquisition	
(including settlement costs)	$300,000
Site preparation	
Sewer and water	$ 60,000
Paving and curbs	100,000
Landscaping	35,000
Total	$195,000
Construction costs	
Hard costs	
Structure	$1,025,000
Heating and air conditioning	100,000
Electrical	85,000
Plumbing	70,000
Finish work	660,000
Total	$1,940,000
Soft costs	
Architect fees	$40,000
Legal fees	15,000
Loan costs	$55,000
Interest	$199,143
Fees	47,783
Contingency	60,000

Source: © 2014 OnCourse Learning

sum, likewise, accrues interest at the 1 percent monthly rate, so that the balance due at the end of the second month is $201,050 × 1.01, or $203,061. This process continues, so that if the construction proceeds as planned, the balance of the loan at the end of the 18 months will be $2,389,143.

Another way to arrive at this figure is to compute, for each disbursement, its future value at the end of the 18 months (column 5) and sum those values. For example, the future sum of $105,000 compounded at a 1 percent monthly rate for 18 months is $125,595 ($105,000 × $[1.01]^{18}$ = $125,595). The future value of the second month's disbursement is $95,000 × $[1.01]^{17}$, or $112,509. The sum of the future values in column 5 of Table 18-3 is $2,389,143 (neglecting the $47,783 charge for points). The lender will add 2 percent of this amount ($47,783) to arrive at the balance due, $2,436,926.

Recall, that in order to simplify this example, we have assumed that the developer contributes the value of the land and the lender funds the construction of the project. Also, we assume that the developer is responsible for any contingencies or overruns (which we have assumed will equal $60,000). In the end, the capitalized value of the property will be $2,436,926 + $300,000, or $2,736,926, if there are no contingencies or overruns. If the overrun occurs as estimated ($60,000), then the total cost of the project will be near the $2.8 million assumed value used throughout the text. In this case, the loan-to-value ratio at the end of the 18 months will be $2,436,926/$2,800,000, or 87 percent, a rather high amount. Most likely, the lender would not fund the full amount of the development costs as portrayed in this simplified example. To reduce risk, the lender would require the developer to add equity to the project by funding a portion of the development costs.

TABLE 18-2
Construction Cost Schedule

MONTH	SEWER AND WATER	PAVING AND CURBS	LANDSCAPING	STRUCTURE	HEATING AND AIR CONDITIONING	ELECTRICAL EXPENSES	PLUMBING EXPENSES	FINISHING EXPENSES	ARCHITECT	LEGAL EXPENSES	TOTAL (%)
1	$30,000	$25,000							$40,000	$10,000	$ 105,000 (4.8)
2	30,000	50,000	$15,000								95,000 (4.3)
3		25,000	20,000								45,000 (2.1)
4				$ 20,000							20,000 (1.9)
5				50,000							50,000 (2.3)
6				100,000							100,000 (4.6)
7				100,000							100,000 (4.6)
8				125,000							125,000 (5.7)
9				125,000							125,000 (5.7)
10				300,000							300,000 (13.7)
11				125,000	$ 20,000		$30,000				175,000 (8.0)
12				80,000	40,000	$40,000	20,000	$ 80,000			260,000 (11.9)
13					20,000	30,000	15,000	100,000			165,000 (7.5)
14					20,000	10,000	5,000	100,000			135,000 (6.2)
15						5,000		100,000			105,000 (4.8)
16								100,000			100,000 (4.6)
17								100,000			100,000 (4.6)
18								80,000		5,000	85,000 (3.9)
TOTAL	$60,000	$100,000	$35,000	$1,025,000	$100,000	$85,000	$70,000	$660,000	$40,000	$15,000	$2,190,000

TABLE 18–3
Construction Loan Disbursement

MONTH	LOAN AMOUNT	CONTRACT RATE = 12% OF TOTAL	BALANCE DUE	FUTURE VALUE
1	$ 105,000	4.79%	$ 106,050	$ 125,595
2	95,000	4.34	203,061	112,509
3	45,000	2.05	250,541	52,766
4	20,000	0.91	273,247	23,219
5	50,000	2.28	326,479	57,474
6	100,000	4.57	430,744	113,809
7	100,000	4.57	536,051	112,683
8	125,000	5.71	667,662	139,459
9	125,000	5.71	800,588	138,078
10	300,000	13.70	1,111,594	328,106
11	175,000	7.99	1,299,460	189,500
12	260,000	11.87	1,575,055	278,755
13	165,000	7.53	1,757,455	175,151
14	135,000	6.16	1,911,380	141,886
15	105,000	4.79	2,036,544	109,263
16	100,000	4.57	2,157,909	103,030
17	100,000	4.57	2,280,488	102,010
18	85,000	3.88	2,389,143	85,850
Loan fees				47,783
Total	$2,190,000			$2,436,926
Yield: 1.23% monthly, 14.71% annually				
P.V. Disbursements	$1,957,035 at 0.0123			
P.V. Repayment	$1,957,035 at 0.0123			

Source: © 2014 OnCourse Learning

YIELD CALCULATION

The lender's yield can be determined by finding that rate that equates the present value of the disbursements to the present value of the loan repayment. The lender's yield in this example is r, such that:

$$\$105,000 + \$95,000/(1+r)^1 + \$45,000/(1+r)^2 + \cdots + \$85,000/(1+r)^{17}$$
$$= \$2,436,926/(1+r)^{18}$$

The rate that solves the equation is 1.23 percent monthly, or 14.71 percent annually.

Risks of ADC Loans

Several risks are associated with ADC loans for both developers and lenders. From the lender's perspective, the major risk involves a failure of the value of the property (collateral) to increase in proportion to the expenditures for construction. Some development expenditures may not increase the value of the property. Costs to obtain the proper government permits, legal expenses, and other soft costs may not improve the value of the property at all. For this reason, the lender may require the developer to incur the soft costs as an equity contribution. Also, as indicated earlier, the lender will monitor all aspects of the development to make certain that the loan disbursements are used to develop the property in conformity with architectural and engineering plans.

The lender also will be concerned that the project be completed on time. Delays in construction will result in a larger balance due on the ADC loan at completion. If the project is delayed too long, the amount due on the ADC loan may begin to approach or exceed the value of the property. In this regard, the risks of bad weather, worker strikes, or material shortages affect the riskiness of the loan. Many ADC lenders will require the developer to incur some of the development costs if the project is delayed beyond the agreed-on schedule.

The lender also will require that permanent financing be approved prior to formalizing the ADC loan. The amount of the permanent financing must be sufficient to cover the expected balance of the ADC loan when the project is terminated.

The developer also faces risks. A delay in construction can cause losses for the developer. The developer will incur greater interest charges as a result of a delay and may have to put more equity into the project. An increase in materials costs also will expose the developer to risk. For short-term projects, this risk can be reduced by contracting for a fixed price on materials at the commencement of the project.

Also, some ADC loans carry a floating interest rate. The lender may charge a monthly interest rate equal to the prime rate plus a margin. A rise in the rate of interest during construction will increase the developer's interest costs. (Very-short-term ADC loans may be made at a fixed rate, the floating rate occurring more frequently on lengthy ADC loans.) Small developers likely will not have the incentive or the resources to hedge this interest rate risk with sophisticated financial instruments.

Summary

The three stages in the construction of a real estate project are acquisition of the land, development or preparation of the land, and construction of the facility. Loans for these stages are referred to collectively as acquisition, development, and construction (ADC) loans. There is no reason why one lender could not finance all stages of the construction process, and some in fact do. In many cases, however, lenders specialize in financing one or two stages. Definite specialization is seen between ADC lenders and lenders that finance the completed project—the so-called takeout or permanent lenders. The reason that various stages of the development process are financed by different lenders lies in specialization. Local lenders, especially, know the legal and institutional parameters of the construction process in their area. They are in a better position to underwrite (analyze) the risks involved in the development and construction process.

Two types of buyers acquire raw land: speculators and developers. Speculators rely on an increase in the value of the land to make a return on investment. Developers intend to create a commercial real estate project on the land. Residential developers have a need to warehouse large amounts of land to ensure that the development and sale of residential properties flows at an even pace and in step with the demand (absorption) of the houses. Institutional lenders, such as commercial banks and thrifts, are by far the largest of the land acquisition lenders. For residential developments, it is necessary for the developer and the lender to work out a well-designed, partial release program that allows a release of the lender's lien on those portions of the land that the developer desires to sell when construction is completed.

Landowners often will finance the sale by taking back a note on the property. The seller will almost always have to agree to a subordination of a lien to a construction lender at some time in the future. The risk of default by the developer and the eventual subordination of the seller's lien increase the risk for the seller. For these reasons, the price of the property with seller financing is generally greater than a third-party-financed sale.

When land is prepared for construction, the developer often will have to meet the provisions of subdivision control ordinances. These ordinances require that the developer put in place an adequate infrastructure before selling off any of the property. Alternatively, the developer can post a bond or letter of credit guaranteeing that the infrastructure will be put in place prior to sale of the finished development. The lender that finances the developer often will be called on to provide the financing to meet the provisions of the subdivision control ordinances.

Construction lenders are specialists in analyzing and managing the risks of the construction process. The major risk factor is that loan disbursements are made as the construction takes place and value is added to the site. The loan administrator must make sure that the proper payments (collateral) increase step by step with the loan balance. The loan administrator also must make sure that no additional items of indebtedness intervene to jeopardize the security of the construction lender. This means that the administrator must verify that the payments have been made to the proper parties, so as to avoid mechanic's liens and the like. Some construction lenders use the services of voucher control agents to handle all of the verification necessary to protect the collateral of the lender.

Key Terms

Construction loan	Land development loan
Construction loan administration	Land purchase option
Construction loan commitment	Partial release provision
Cost recovery fee	Release provision
Density bonus	Rolling option
Developer	Senior financing
Dollar-based fees	Speculator
Environmental audit	Subdivision control ordinances
Exaction	Subdivision trust
Impact fees	Subordination
Inclusionary zoning	Tax increment financing
Junior financing	Voucher control agent
Land acquisition loans	Warehousing

Review Questions

18-1.   Discuss the differences in the motives of the land speculator and the land developer.

18-2.   Discuss the advantages of the arrangement whereby each of the stages of acquisition, development, and construction are financed separately by different lenders.

18-3.   What is the purpose of partial release provisions? What are the dangers of an improperly designed partial release provision for the lender?

18-4.   Explain why a developer would purchase an option to buy land rather than purchase the land outright and immediately.

18-5.   Indicate two reasons the sales price of a parcel of land will be higher if the seller provides some of the financing.

18-6.   Explain what a subordination agreement is and why it is necessary in the presence of seller financing.

18-7.   Indicate the steps involved in land development—that is, the development of the land in preparation for construction.

18-8. What are subdivision control ordinances, and why have they been enacted?

18-9. Indicate at least four areas of risk that construction lenders must analyze and control when designing a loan package.

18-10. Indicate at least four control measures that a construction lender will implement to monitor and manage the risk involved in construction lending.

18-11. What are the benefits to both the developer and the lender of a construction loan commitment?

18-12. Indicate at least four procedures involved in construction loan administration.

18-13. What is a voucher control agent, and what are the agent's duties?

Problems

Use the following project cost schedule data to answer Problems 18-1 and 18-2.

MONTH	UTILITIES AND LANDSCAPING	STRUCTURE	HEATING AND AIR CONDITIONING	ELECTRICAL AND PLUMBING	FINISHING	SOFT COSTS
1	$75,000	0	0	0	0	$40,000
2	125,000	0	0	0	0	8,000
3	52,000	$14,000	0	0	0	0
4	0	126,000	0	0	0	0
5	0	452,000	0	0	0	0
6	0	318,000	0	0	0	0
7	0	200,000	0	0	0	0
8	0	125,000	0	0	0	0
9	0	52,000	$40,000	0	0	0
10	0	4,000	72,000	$48,000	0	0
11	0	0	115,000	152,000	0	0
12	0	0	0	26,000	$122,000	0
13	0	0	0	0	216,000	0
14	0	0	0	0	146,000	22,000
Total	$252,000	$1,291,000	$227,000	$226,000	$484,000	$70,000

Land value (cost) $750,000

All Files ADC Example

18-1. Assume a lender agrees to finance all costs (except for the acquisition of the land) at 14 percent interest and 2 points.
a. What will be the final payment due the lender at the end of month 14?
b. What will be the yield on the loan to the lender?
c. What will be the loan-to-value ratio at the end of month 14?

All Files ADC Example

18-2. Assume the lender reviews the above loan and decides to reduce the risk by requiring the developer to pay all costs associated with installing utilities and landscaping.
a. What will be the final payment due at the end of month 14?
b. What will be the loan-to-value ratio?

Web Site

http://www.boma.org

Information on Building Owners and Managers Association, a trade group that collects data on revenues and expenses of operating commercial real estate.

APPENDIX 18-A   Building Loan Agreement

BUILDING LOAN AGREEMENT

THIS AGREEMENT is made and entered into at

County,   , on the
day of   , 20   by and between

a   ("**BORROWER**"),
qualified to do business in the County of   ,
State of   , and
("**LENDER**").

R E C I T A L S:
WHEREAS, BORROWER is the owner and holder of fee simple title estate in that property ("**SECURITY**") situated in
, described
in legal description attached hereto as Exhibit A and made a part hereof; and

WHEREAS, BORROWER has applied to **LENDER** for a construction loan in the total aggregate principal amount of
DOLLARS
($ U.S.) ("**LOAN**") for a loan term
ending no later than   ,   at an interest
rate on the daily outstanding balance as hereinafter provided and

WHEREAS, the **LOAN** shall be advanced as hereinafter provided, said advances being evidenced by a Promissory Note ("**NOTE**")
payable to the order of **LENDER** for the principal sum as above stated; and

WHEREAS, the **NOTE** shall be secured by a first lien on the **SECURITY** evidenced by Deed of Trust ("**DEED**"); and

WHEREAS, BORROWER has represented to **LENDER** that the **SECURITY** is to be improved (the "**IMPROVEMENT**") in the
manner set forth in plans and specifications and/or other documents heretofore made available to **LENDER** by **BORROWER**, a description or copy of which plans and specifications and/or documents are attached hereto; and

WHEREAS, BORROWER has represented to **LENDER** that the **LOAN** funds are to be used solely for the purposes set forth herein
and for no other purpose;

NOW, THEREFORE, in consideration of the sum of One Dollar ($1.00) and other good and valuable consideration, the receipt and
sufficiency of which is hereby acknowledged, it is stipulated and agreed as follows:

1. **RECITALS:** The foregoing recitals are true and correct.

2. **DEFINITIONS:** Wherever used herein, the following words shall be considered in the context of these definitions:

    (a) **DEED:** The Deed of Trust, Assignment of Rents and Security Agreement, used to establish the first priority lien of **LENDER**
    against the **SECURITY**;

    (b) **NOTE:** The Promissory Note or Notes or other evidence of the indebtedness created by the **LOAN**;

    (c) **LOAN:** The **LOAN** which is the subject matter of this Agreement and the other documents to which this Agreement refers;

    (d) **LENDER:** The named party to this Agreement, and any subsequent owner and holder of the rights and obligations established
    under this Agreement, the **NOTE** and **DEED**;

    (e) **BORROWER:** The named **BORROWER** in this Agreement and any successor in interest to **BORROWER** whose
    designation as such shall be previously consented to in writing by **LENDER**;

    (f) **SECURITY:** The real property described in legal description and the improvements thereon upon which the lien of the
    DEED attaches, including all fixtures and other personal property identified in Paragraph 4 hereinbelow;

    (g) **IMPROVEMENT:** The improvements, or any portion therof, contemplated by this Agreement to be constructed on
    the **SECURITY**;

    (h) **AGENT:** Any person or entity, other than a **LENDER**, acting as disburser of the **LOAN** funds, or any portion thereof,
    under the terms of this Agreement; and

3. **NOTE: LENDER** shall make to **BORROWER** and **BORROWER** shall accept from **LENDER** a **LOAN** in the aggregate
    principal sum of   **DOLLARS**
    ($ U.S.) for a term ending   which
    LOAN shall be evidenced by **BORROWER'S NOTE** and **DEED**. The **NOTE** and **DEED** are to be simultaneously executed
    with this Agreement. The interest rate payable under the **NOTE** may be increased or decreased   by
    LENDER based on the increase or decrease in

    referred to in **NOTE** as "Index", plus a margin of   percentage points as defined in the **NOTE**.
    Although the **NOTE** evidencing the indebtedness of **BORROWER** to **LENDER** may provide that it shall bear interest
    from a specific date therein, the parties herein agree that the **NOTE** shall bear interest, which shall be payable monthly, from
    the date of each advance and on the sum outstanding from time to time under this Agreement. Said interest shall be computed
    on a per diem basis on a   -day year.

    It is the intention of the parties that under no circumstances shall **BORROWER** be charged more than the highest lawful
    rate of interest under the applicable law, and notwithstanding anything contained herein to the contrary, the amount of interest
    payable under the terms of the **NOTE** shall in no event exceed the maximum amount of interest permitted to be charged by
    law at the date hereof. Interest shall be computed and accrued on the daily outstanding principal balance after each advancement or disbursement under the **LOAN** from the date thereof until the **LOAN** is fully paid. In the event that **BORROWER**
    fails to make any interest payments when due, then all such outstanding amounts may be deducted by **LENDER** from any
    subsequent advance or disbursement without notice to **BORROWER**. All interest as well as principal due under the **NOTE**
    shall be secured by the lien created by the **DEED**.

—1—

4. **SECURITY:** The **LOAN** shall be secured by a first lien in the form of a **DEED** encumbering the **SECURITY** set forth and described in legal description. Such lien shall be subject only to those encumbrances, limitations, restrictions, or easements which are listed in the Preliminary Title Report or are approved by Counsel designated by **LENDER** as more fully provided hereinbelow in Paragraph 6.

5. **ADDITIONAL SECURITY: BORROWER** shall contemporaneously with the execution and delivery of this Agreement, execute in favor of **LENDER** any Security or Collateral Agreement creating a security interest in personal property or any assignment or pledge of other property, all as may be required hereunder by **LENDER,** which additional security shall include, but not be limited to, the following:

(a) the Note to evidence the Loan;

(b) the Deed of Trust encumbering the Real Property and the Project;

(c) a Security Agreement granting **LENDER** a Security Interest in all building materials, equipment, fittings, furniture, furnishings, fixtures and all other articles of personal property of every kind or character now owned, or hereafter acquired by **BORROWER** in connection with or for use in constructing, equipping, furnishing, operating or maintaining the Project;

(d) a Security Agreement granting a Security Interest in and an assignment of all Leases ("**LEASES**") between **BORROWER** and Lessees of space in the Project, whether now, or hereafter, in existence, together with the rents, issues, proceeds and profits therefrom; and

(e) a Title Policy insuring **LENDER'S** lien under the Mortgage as a first lien upon the Real Property.

6. **TITLE INSURANCE: BORROWER** shall provide, at its own expense, title insurance in form satisfactory to **LENDER** and issued by a title insurance company acceptable to **LENDER.** The title policy is to be issued without exceptions, except for those exceptions which are acceptable to Counsel for **LENDER,** insuring the **DEED** required hereunder as a first, valid, and paramount lien against the **SECURITY** and insuring against loss or change in priority as a result of the filing of any lien or special assessment for any materials and/or work either under construction or completed.

Designation by **BORROWER** of the title insurer shall be subject to **LENDER'S** approval of the financial ability of said insurer to pay the face amount of the new policy and all of its other policies insuring **LENDER** in the event of loss.

The designated title insurer shall also provide at **BORROWER'S** expense, on **LENDER'S** demand and at an appropriate time, an endorsement that the foundations and/or pad of the premises do not violate setback requirements of the appropriate municipal agencies and copies of all easements and restrictions of record, as shown on the report of binder. If for any reason the title insurer does not or cannot provide this endorsement as to any of the aforesaid information, then **BORROWER** shall provide **LENDER** with such other certifications or documentation as may be required by **LENDER** at **LENDER'S** discretion.

Prior to making any disbursement under the **LOAN, LENDER** shall receive evidence satisfactory to it that the title insurance company is prepared to issue its title insurance endorsement insuring the amount being disbursed and that the **MORTGAGE,** as of said date, remains a first, valid and permanent lien on the **SECURITY,** free and clear of any and all Mechanics', Materialmen's and/or Laborer's Liens and subject only to such exceptions as **LENDER** may approve, as more specifically set forth in Paragraph 11 below.

7. **DISBURSING AGENT: LENDER** may, at its election and at **BORROWER'S** cost, disburse the **LOAN** proceeds to **BORROWER** through a title insurance company, mortgage company, or other third party ("**AGENT**") selected by **LENDER** or directly to the sub-contractors, materialmen and laborers. Such election, however, except as required by agreements with the title insurance company insuring the **LOAN,** does not prevent **LENDER** from making subsequent disbursements in a different manner and through a different party.

The account of any selected **AGENT** for **LENDER,** maintained with **LENDER** for **BORROWER,** as may be referred to herein, shall be deemed a direct account of **BORROWER** with **LENDER** and shall be maintained at **BORROWER'S** expense. Any disbursements to be paid by **AGENT** to **BORROWER** shall be payable in accordance with the provisions of this Agreement.

In no event shall **AGENT** be construed as the **AGENT** of **BORROWER,** nor shall said **AGENT** be construed as assuming **BOR-ROWER'S** responsibility for proper payments. Said **AGENT** shall at all times be entitled, and is hereby authorized by **BORROWER,** to rely upon representations of **BORROWER.** This latter provision shall in no way alter **AGENT'S** liability to **LENDER** as its disbursing **AGENT** pursuant to the terms hereof.

8. **CONDITIONS PRECEDENT TO DISBURSEMENT: LENDER** shall incur no obligations hereunder, nor shall it deposit any monies in **AGENT'S** account for **BORROWER** or to the account of **BORROWER** maintained with **LENDER,** until all of the following are completed:

(a) **BORROWER** has, if required by **LENDER,** either deposited with **AGENT** or to **BORROWER'S** account with **LENDER,** as the case may be, an amount equal to the difference, if any, between the **LOAN** and the estimated cost of construction, or has expended **BORROWER'S** own funds in an amount equal to said difference. The deposit to be made by **BORROWER** under the provisions of this subsection, together with the proceeds of the **LOAN,** shall constitute the total fund to be disbursed hereunder. If such a deposit is not required by **LENDER,** then **BORROWER** shall provide **LENDER** or **AGENT,** whichever may be applicable, with paid bills and waivers of lien to the extent of the difference between the amount of the **LOAN** and the estimated cost of construction of the **IMPROVEMENT** before the disbursement of any of the proceeds of the **LOAN;**

(b) **BORROWER** has recorded the **DEED** in the office of the Recorder of the County in which the **SECURITY** is located; and

(c) **BORROWER'S** condition title, as certified by the title insurer, by issuance of a form of title insurance as acceptable to the **LENDER.**

(d) After the initial recording draw for purposes other than construction and upon **LENDER'S** request, **BORROWER** shall supply to **LENDER** executed subcontracts with assignments to the **LENDER.**

LENDER may, at its election, require that **BORROWER** furnish, in addition to the foregoing, executed construction contracts between **BORROWER** and all contractors, executed copies of all subcontracts between the general contractor or contractors and all of their subcontractors and suppliers, including contracts, subcontracts, and purchase orders for all fixtures and equipment required to be installed for the operation of the premises. **LENDER** may require executed copies of firm bids or estimates of costs from any or all of the contractors and subcontractors.

The amounts called for under any of the aforesaid contracts shall not be in excess of the total amount allocated for the purpose in the schedule entitled "Use of Funds" set forth below.

LENDER, at its election, may verify the correctness of the amount of any contract, subcontract, estimate or bid furnished pursuant to the terms hereof.

USE OF FUNDS

Subject to the provisions herein set forth, **LOAN** funds contemplated in this Agreement have been allocated as follows and shall only be disbursed in accordance therewith:

A.	Land Acquisition consisting of	$
B.	Acquisition and Development consisting of	$
C.	Acquisition of Developed Lots consisting of	$
D.	Construction consisting of	$

ML23 (4/88)

9.　**ADDITIONAL DEPOSIT BY BORROWER:** If, at any time pending or during the disbursement of the **LOAN** proceeds or any portion thereof, it appears that the amount remaining undisbursed will be insufficient to complete the construction of the **IMPROVEMENT** in accordance with the plans and specifications and/or to pay for any of the necessary labor, material, and costs, **BORROWER** shall, within ten (10) banking days of **LENDER'S** demand, deposit with the **LENDER** or assign or hypothecate to **LENDER** in a form acceptable to **LENDER** additional monies which shall, when added to the undisbursed proceeds of the **LOAN,** be sufficient to pay for the cost of completion of the **IMPROVEMENT** and the costs and expenses in connection therewith. The amount so deposited shall be disbursed to pay for the cost of completion of the **IMPROVEMENT** before any additional **LOAN** proceeds will be disbursed.

10.　**DISBURSEMENT OF LOAN FUNDS:** Upon recordation of the **DEED** and delivery to **LENDER** of all items required and specified hereunder or herein by **LENDER, LENDER** shall periodically disburse the **LOAN** funds to **BORROWER** in accordance with the Cost Breakdown, and in the following manner:

(a)　Each request for disbursement shall be made on a Construction Loan Requisition form (**"VOUCHER"**) furnished to **BORROWER** by **LENDER** or **AGENT,** which shall, if applicable, be accompanied by a contractor's cost breakdown and request for partial payment form, which shall be executed by **BORROWER** and Contractor, the contents of which must meet the approval of **LENDER** or **AGENT.** At no time shall **LENDER** or **AGENT** disburse any monies from the proceeds of the **LOAN** when the total of such disbursement would be in excess of twenty percent (20%) of the value of the **SECURITY** and the **IMPROVEMENT** at the time of the request. No funds shall be disbursed prior to an inspection by such persons designated by the **LENDER** ("Inspector"). Said Inspector's function is solely for the purpose of verifying the voucher and not for the inspection of the quality of the work or compliance with any applicable building codes.

(b)　Upon the application for the first disbursement and each subsequent disbursement thereafter, **BORROWER** shall furnish **LENDER** or **AGENT** with waivers of lien, receipted bills and such other items as may be required by them or either one of them pursuant to subsection (d) below, evidencing the payment of all sub-portions of construction paid out of the last preceding disbursement. It is the intention and agreement of the parties that no disbursement shall be applied for or made at any time when the waivers of lien and receipted bills, when added to the balance of undisbursed portion of the **LOAN,** equal an amount in excess of the amount shown in the Contractor's Cost Breakdown spread sheet as necessary for completion of the construction of the **IMPROVEMENT.** However, in any event, **BORROWER** shall only be entitled to payment in the specific amount approved by **LENDER** as to each requisition or application for disbursements under this Agreement;

(c)　If required by **LENDER,** an architect (**"ARCHITECT"**) shall be designated to verify with each requisition of **LOAN** proceeds that all construction to the date requisition has been completed to the extent indicated in the Contractor's requisition form and in accordance with the final plans and specifications previously submitted to **LENDER. ARCHITECT** shall be subject to **LENDER'S** approval. Any fees incurred in connection with this subsection shall be paid by **BORROWER;**

(d)　**LENDER** or **AGENT** shall make disbursements for contract items to **BORROWER'S** Contractor or to **BORROWER,** if **BORROWER** is the Contractor, in accordance with the Contractor's Cost Breakdown spread sheet, and shall impose such additional conditions to this approval of requisitions and to disbursements of advances by way of sworn statements, waivers, partial waivers or releases of lien, proof of paid bills, inspection of payroll vouchers and submission of **ARCHITECT'S** certificates and progress surveys as it may deem necessary to protect the priority of the **DEED** and comply with the provisions of this Agreement;

(e)　Ten percent (10%) of all disbursements shall be withheld until **BORROWER** has complied with the provisions of Paragraph 15 below;

(f)　**BORROWER** (or **AGENT**) shall utilize all portions of the Mechanics' Lien Law which will shorten the time in which such liens can be filed, and shall comply with all applicable laws, as a prerequisite to any requested disbursements;

(g)　**LENDER** shall not be obligated to make disbursements hereunder until **BORROWER** has delivered to it all requisitions and other proofs as may be required. Tendered requisitions and other proofs shall be deemed acceptable to **LENDER** unless, within ten (10) days after delivery, **LENDER** notifies **BORROWER** of the deficiencies;

(h)　Each request shall be submitted in sufficient time prior to **BORROWER'S** requested date for an advance hereunder to enable **LENDER** or **AGENT** to process such request. Funds shall be characterized as disbursed to **BORROWER** when disbursed by **LENDER,** irrespective of instruction by **BORROWER** to disburse to another entity. **LENDER** shall disburse within ten (10) days of receipt of all necessary documentation for a draw request; and

(i)　**LENDER** may deduct from any disbursements, where necessary and in addition to the amount withheld pursuant to subsection (e) of this Paragraph, the amount of any retainage, fees, expenses, reserves, advances or deposits specified in the Cost Breakdown. **BORROWER** shall advance in cash any sums not provided in said Exhibit to pay premiums on casualty and title insurance, taxes, assessments, recording expenses, filing fees, or such other sums as **LENDER** may deem necessary for the protection and preservation of the **SECURITY,** and payment of the premiums for insurance required by **LENDER** during the life of this **LOAN.** In the event **BORROWER** does not make timely payment of any of the aforesaid sums, **LENDER** is hereby authorized, if **LENDER** so elects, to advance out of **LOAN** proceeds and at **BORROWER'S** expense, after thirty (30) days' notice or such lesser time as allotted by an insurer, etc., any sums necessary to make such payments.

11.　**ENDORSEMENTS TO TITLE INSURANCE POLICIES:** Periodically, at the **LENDER'S** discretion, the **LENDER** may request the title insurance company to issue a title certificate to **LENDER** which shall certify that there are no changes in the condition of title of the **SECURITY** from the condition thereof as set forth in the original title policy. In the event said title certificate indicates an objection, defect in, or cloud upon the title to the **SECURITY** which arose subsequent to the issuance of the original title policy, **BORROWER** shall pay such monies, take such action or do whatever else may be necessary in the opinion of **LENDER** to cure any such objection, defect or cloud, and **LENDER** shall not be required to disburse any monies until the title insurance company is able to certify to **LENDER** that such objection, defect or cloud has been cured.

Any surveys delivered to **LENDER** to support advances shall be accompanied by a certificate from the title company listing the legal description of the **SECURITY** and certifying that such survey has been inspected by the title company and no condition has been found to exist thereon which will in any way affect the original title policy.

12.　**MISREPRESENTATION BY BORROWER:** Unless otherwise specified herein, if any representation contained in this Agreement, or in any agreement, report, or statement given to **LENDER** regarding any transaction hereunder or submitted in support thereto, is untrue and incorrect in any material respect, or in the event of any breach on the part of **BORROWER** of any of the terms contained in this Agreement, or in the **NOTE** or other instrument given by **BORROWER** to **LENDER,** then, in any such event, **LENDER** shall have all of the rights and remedies provided in this Agreement as well as those provided for by applicable law and, in addition to such rights and remedies, all obligations hereunder of **BORROWER** to **LENDER** shall become immediately due and payable without demand or notice and shall forthwith be paid and discharged by **BORROWER** notwithstanding any time or credit otherwise allowed. Upon the failure of **BORROWER** to pay or discharge all such liabilities and obligations forthwith, or upon the failure of **BORROWER** to pay the **NOTE** or other obligation to **LENDER** on demand, or at the expressed or declared maturity thereof, **LENDER** may proceed to exercise all of its rights and remedies as provided herein. Every term contained in the **NOTE** or other obligation shall be deemed incorporated into this Agreement. All rights, remedies, and powers granted to **LENDER** herein, or in the **NOTE** or other instruments, or implied in law, shall be cumulative and may be exercised separately or concurrently with such other rights as **LENDER** may have and shall include, among other rights, the right to apply to a court of equity for an injunction to restrain a breach or threatened breach by **BORROWER** of this Agreement. **LENDER** may exercise such rights from time to time as to all or part of the **SECURITY** as **LENDER**, in its sole discretion, may determine.

13. **WORK:**

(a) **Development Work Criteria:** The development of the subject property shall be in accordance with the proposed plans and specifications submitted as the basis for this **LOAN** and in compliance with all restrictions, conditions, ordinances, codes, regulations and laws of governmental departments and agencies having direction or jurisdiction over, or an interest in, said premises and improvements. No extra work nor change in plans and specifications shall be authorized by **BORROWER** without the prior express written consent of **LENDER**. **LENDER** shall respond to all such requests within five (5) Banking days of receipt. If **LENDER** shall consent to any such extra work or change in plans and specifications, **BORROWER** shall immediately deposit the amount of the cost thereof with **LENDER** (or **AGENT**), such deposit to be held in an interest bearing account and disbursed by **LENDER** or **AGENT** in accordance with normal disbursement procedures;

(b) **Commencement and Continuity of Work:** Development of the property shall commence within one (1) month of recording the Deed of Trust and shall be carried on diligently, continuously and with dispatch until completed. **BORROWER** agrees to devote its full effort and energy to the immediate development, construction and completion of the **IMPROVEMENT** without any abandonment thereof;

(c) **Construction Costs:** No development work may commence or continue under this **LOAN** until (i) engineering cost estimates have been provided to **LENDER** and such cost estimates have been reviewed and found acceptable by **LENDER**, and (ii) firm construction contracts have been provided to and approved by **LENDER**;

(d) Not withstanding the above, the improvements shall be completed on or before twelve (12) months from the date of the **DEED'S** being recorded; and

(e) **Use of First Class Materials: BORROWER** shall use first class materials in construction of the project. Such material shall be owned by the **BORROWER** and not subject to any liens or liabilities.

14. **REPRESENTATIONS AND WARRANTIES OF BORROWER: BORROWER,** based upon its best knowledge and belief, makes the following warranties and representations:

(a) **Correctness of Documents:** The documents furnished in support of the **LOAN** and those documents listed in the Opinion of Counsel are true and correct and accurately set out the facts contained therein.

(b) **Absence of Proceedings and Actions:** There are no actions, suits, or proceedings pending or, to the knowledge of **BORROWER**, threatened against or affecting **BORROWER** except as set forth in the Credit Report which is attached hereto.

(c) **BORROWER'S Powers, Status of Authority and Compensation of Employees:** There is a true, complete, and correct statement with respect to **BORROWER'S** powers, and status of authority contained in the Credit Report attached hereto.

(d) **Absence of Judgments and/or Awards and/or Orders:** There are no outstanding and unpaid judgments or arbitration awards against **BORROWER** except as are set forth in the Credit Report. **BORROWER** is not in default or violation with respect to any valid regulation, order, writ, judgment or decree or any court or other governmental or municipal department, commission, board, bureau, agency or instrumentality.

(e) **Non-Default of BORROWER Contractually: BORROWER** is not in default under and has not breached in any material respect any agreement or instrument to which it is a party or by which it may be bound. The execution and delivery of this Agreement, the **NOTE** and **DEED**, and the consummation of the other transactions contemplated by this Agreement do not and will not conflict with or result in violation of any valid regulations, order, writ, judgment, injunction or decree of any court or governmental or municipal instrumentality or in the breach of or default under any indenture, contract, agreement, or other instrument to which **BORROWER** is a party or by which it is bound, except where the amount of all such liability is, in the aggregate less than $ and no one item exceeds $ provided all such items are bonded. Neither the execution and delivery of this Agreement, nor the **DEED**, nor the issuance of the **NOTE** will result in the creation or imposition of, or be any cause for imposing, any lien, charge or encumbrance of any nature whatsoever upon any of the **SECURITY** or assets of **BORROWER** other than those created, imposed or required by this Agreement or the **DEED**.

(f) **Marketable Title in BORROWER Without Liens:** Except as stated in the Preliminary Title Report, **BORROWER** has, and at all times until payment of this **LOAN** in full will have, good and marketable title in fee simple to the **SECURITY**. The **SECURITY** is subject to no liens, charges or encumbrances except as shown on the Preliminary Title Report or as may be acceptable to counsel designated by **LENDER**.

(g) **Use of Proceeds:** The proceeds of this **LOAN** will be used solely for the purposes specified herein and in supporting documents.

(h) **Licenses: BORROWER** has, or has applied for, all necessary licenses to effect the use of the **SECURITY**, but not limited to, business licenses.

15. **FINAL DISBURSEMENT:** The obligation of **LENDER** hereunder to make the final disbursement to **BORROWER** shall be conditioned upon the following in a form and substance acceptable to **LENDER**:

(a) Receipt of evidence of approval by all applicable authorities for permanent occupancy of the **IMPROVEMENT** in its entirety by issuance of a certificate of occupancy;

(b) Written notice from an **ARCHITECT** approved by **LENDER** to the effect that the **IMPROVEMENT** has been completed in accordance with plans and specifications;

(c) A final survey showing the completed **IMPROVEMENT**;

(d) The Contractor's final affidavit pursuant to the   Statutes, final waivers and releases of liens from all subcontractors and suppliers as well as any parties that have served a notice to owner's affidavit in accordance with the   Statutes; and

(e) Final signoff by the title insurer.

16. **INSURANCE POLICIES AND CERTIFICATES: BORROWER** at its expense shall maintain with insurers acceptable to **LENDER** and furnish **LENDER** certificates from the insurance carrier evidencing the following: (i) insurance against loss from fire, windstorm, theft, vandalism and other perils generally included in "extended coverage" policies, and for such other hazards as may be reasonably required by **LENDER**; (ii) public liability and property damage insurance; (iii) Workmen's Compensation Insurance; and, (iv) such other insurance coverage as **LENDER** may reasonably require and which is usually obtained for ownership and use of property similar to the use contemplated of the **SECURITY**. As to the insurance described in (i) of the preceding sentence, said policy shall contain a Mortgagee's "Loss Payable" clause (Form CF-1219 or its equivalent) providing for payment to **LENDER** and its successors and/or

assigns to the extent of its interest in the event of loss. Said policy may, during construction, be in ''Builder's Risk'' form so far as the same relates to the **IMPROVEMENT**. In the event said policy is cancelled, **BORROWER** shall notify **LENDER** in writing within five (5) days of receipt of notice of such cancellation, and shall advise insurer to forward any and all refunds resulting from such cancellation to **LENDER** for the account of **BORROWER**. All such insurance shall be in amounts acceptable to **LENDER**, and in such form and amounts as will comply with applicable law; and said insurance shall, where necessary or permissible, name **LENDER** as an additional insured as its interest may appear. The aforesaid public liability insurance shall be carried during the full course of construction work on the premises, naming **LENDER** and its successor and/or assigns as an additional insured, and with minimum limits of coverage for death of or injury to persons of not less than $300,000.00/$500,000.00 and for damage to property of not less than $ unless otherwise agreed to in writing by **LENDER**. Copies of such policies shall be delivered to **LENDER** at, or before, disbursement of the **LOAN** proceeds with proof of premium payment. At the election of **LENDER** any proceeds of such insurance in excess of   **DOLLARS** ($ U.S.) shall be paid to **LENDER** and its successors and/or assigns and shall be applied first to payment of accrued interest and then to reduction of principal or, at **LENDER'S** option, said excess proceeds may be made available under usual disbursing procedures to rebuild the project. In the event **LENDER** must place coverage in order to protect **LENDER'S** security interest, the premium for such coverage shall be disbursed from the loan proceeds and will accrue interest at the **NOTE** rate.

17.   **REMOVAL OF MECHANICS' LIENS: BORROWER** specifically agrees to have any and all Mechanic's and/or Materialmen's Liens which may be filed against the **SECURITY** released or bonded within twenty (20) calendar days of the date **BORROWER** receives notice of the same, time being of the essence. **BORROWER** need not secure the release of a Mechanic's Lien against the **SECURITY** within such period, if, and so long as, the priority of **LENDER'S** lien as against such Mechanic's Lien is affirmatively insured by the title insurance policy. **BORROWER'S** failure to promptly insure **LENDER'S** priority or promptly remove such liens shall constitute an act of Default.

18.   **PAYMENT OF TAXES: BORROWER** agrees to promptly pay and discharge any taxes, assessments, charges, levies or indebtedness upon the **SECURITY**, which may become due or payable during the existence of this **LOAN.** At least ten (10) days before delinquency, **BORROWER** shall furnish to **LENDER** evidence satisfactory to **LENDER** that taxes and assessments have been paid. **LENDER** may pay such sums as may become due out of undisbursed **LOAN** proceeds in the event **BORROWER** fails to promptly pay as aforesaid.

19.   **ACCESS TO BORROWER'S BOOKS AND RECORDS: LENDER**, or its agents, shall at all reasonable times have unrestricted access to the records, accounting books, contracts, subcontracts, bills and statements of **BORROWER,** including any supporting or related vouchers or other instruments as relate in any manner to the **IMPROVEMENT** contemplated to be constructed by the funds disbursed under this Agreement, and shall have the right to make copies of the same. If **LENDER** so requires, the records, books, vouchers, or other instruments shall be made available to an accountant of **LENDER'S** choice for audit, examination, inspection, and photocopying or other type of duplication; such audit to be done at **BORROWER'S** office.

20.   **FINANCIAL STATEMENTS: BORROWER** shall furnish to **LENDER** signed monthly Profit and Loss statements, including current leasing data, quarterly un-audited statements of financial condition; and, **BORROWER** shall also furnish **LENDER** with a signed and audited or un-audited annual statement acceptable to **LENDER**. The quarterly statements shall be delivered by **BORROWER** to **LENDER** within thirty (30) days of the end of each quarter and the annual audited statement within ninety (90) days after close of the fiscal year. Upon the event of any default, **LENDER** may choose to request any reasonable financial data.

21.   **EVENTS OF DEFAULT:** The happening of any one, or more, of the following events shall constitute a default under this Agreement, the **NOTE**, and **DEED:**

(a)   **Nonpayment of Interest: BORROWER** failing to make the required interest payments on any due date;

(b)   **Non-Deposit of Principal: BORROWER** failing to make any required deposit of principal, or any portion thereof, on any due date;

(c)   **Breach of Condition: BORROWER** violating any material term, condition or representation contained in this Agreement, the **NOTE,** or **DEED**, or the determination by **LENDER** of the existence of a material mispresentation of fact as set forth in Paragraph 15 not cured after thirty (30) days' notice;

(d)   **Bankruptcy or Insolvency: BORROWER** being insolvent by being unable to pay its debts when they become due or by having the amount of its liabilities exceed the amount of its assets; or **BORROWER** committing an act of bankruptcy, making a general assignment for the benefit of creditors; or if there is filed by or against **BORROWER** a voluntary or involuntary Petition in Bankruptcy or for the appointment of a receiver; or if **BORROWER** admits in writing to a creditor that he is financially unable to pay such creditor any indebtedness due him; or if there commences under any law relating to bankruptcy, insolvency, reorganization or relief of debtors proceedings for **BORROWER'S** relief or for the composition, extension, arrangement or adjustment of any of **BORROWER'S** obligation's or affecting the **SECURITY**, which is not withdrawn or dismissed within thirty (30) days after the filing of, or the entry into, the same; or if **BORROWER'S** business is discontinued as a going concern; or if there is a suspension of **BORROWER'S** business or if **BORROWER** defaults on any other obligation it may have to **LENDER**; or if a Writ of Attachment, execution, or any similar process is issued or levied against any significant part of **BORROWER'S** property which is not released, stayed, bonded or vacated within a reasonable time after its issue or levy;

(e)   **Liens or Foreclosures:** The institution of foreclosure action against the **SECURITY** or the filing of a valid lien against the **SECURITY**, which is not removed of record, bonded, vacated, released or dismissed within thirty (30) days after **BORROWER** receives notice of such filing, except as provided above in Paragraph 18;

(f)   **Substantial Discontinuance of Construction or Development:** The substantial discontinuance of construction or development work for a period of ten (10) days which discontinuance is, in the sole determination of **LENDER**, without cause;

(g)   **Transfer of Security:** The sale, assignment, pledge, transfer hypothecation or other disposition of the **SECURITY** by **BORROWER** to some other person or entity without the prior express written consent of **LENDER** as proscribed in the **DEED** unless as provided under the release agreement, Section 14 hereof and Opinion of Counsel;

(h)   **Ability of BORROWER to Perform:** The sale, assignment, pledge, transfer, hypothecation, or other disposition of any proprietary or beneficial interest in **BORROWER** or its property by the owner thereof, or, any change in the executive management or operating control of **BORROWER** unless, in **LENDER'S** sole judgment, such sale, assignment, pledge, transfer, hypothecation, other disposition or change does not materially and adversely affect the ability of **BORROWER** to perform in accordance with the terms of this Agreement;

(i)   **Impairment of Security:** Any condition or situation which, in the sole determination of **LENDER**, constitutes a danger to, or impairment of, the **SECURITY** or repayment of the **LOAN**, where such condition or situation is not remedied within thirty (30) days after written notice to **BORROWER** to remedy such condition or situation, or, where it is not possible to fully remedy such condition or situation within thirty (30) days and no action has yet been commenced to remedy such condition or situation. **LENDER** agrees that it will not exercise this right in an unreasonable manner.

(j) **Failure to Pay Taxes:** Should **BORROWER** fail to pay taxes as they become due or fail to make such payment within ten (10) days after written notice that such payments are due.

(k) **Cross Default:** Any default on this Agreement or the **NOTE** is a default on any other **NOTES** to the **LENDER** executed by the **BORROWER**, successors or assigns in any capacity. Conversely, any default on any other Agreement or **NOTE** to the **LENDER** executed by the **BORROWER**, successors or assigns in any capacity, is a default on this Agreement or **NOTE**. Further, in the event of any default on this Agreement or **NOTE**, or any other Agreements or **NOTES** to the **LENDER** executed by the **BORROWER**, successors or assigns in any capacity, the **LENDER** may, at its option, declare the remainder of any and all said debts due and payable and any failure to exercise that option shall not constitute a waiver or a right to exercise the same at any other time, nor shall such failure to exercise the option be construed as any form of acceptance of said default. Notice of the exercise of said option is hereby waived. Upon exercise of said option, interest shall accrue at the then prevailing rate of the **NOTE**.

22. **LENDER'S REMEDIES:** Upon the occurrence of any event of default hereunder, **LENDER** shall have the absolute right to refuse to disburse any funds provided in the Cost Breakdown hereof. If said default is not remedied by **BORROWER** within the time periods as may be elsewhere herein provided, if any, **LENDER**, at its option and election and in its sole discretion, shall have the absolute right to do any of the following, singly or in combination:

(a) **Cancellation:** Cancel this Agreement by written notice to **BORROWER**;

(b) **Specific Performance:** Institute appropriate proceedings to specifically enforce performance of the terms and conditions of this Agreement;

(c) **Withhold Advances:** Withhold further advances hereunder;

(d) **Taking of Possession:** Take immediate possession of the **SECURITY** encumbered by the **DEED**, as well as all other **SECURITY** given hereunder, as is necessary to fully complete all on-site and off-site **IMPROVEMENTS** contemplated to be developed and/or constructed under this Agreement;

(e) **Receivership:** Appoint a Receiver, as a matter of strict right without regard to the solvency of **BORROWER**, for the purpose of preserving the **SECURITY**, preventing waste and protecting all rights accruing to **LENDER** by virtue of this Agreement and of the **DEED** executed in connection with this Agreement, and expressly to make any and all further improvements, whether on-site or off-site, as may be determined solely by **LENDER** to be necessary to complete the development and construction in accordance with this Agreement. All expenses, including attorney's fees, incurred in connection with the appointment of said Receiver, or in protecting, preserving, or improving the **SECURITY**, shall be chargeable against **BORROWER** and shall be enforced as a lien against the **SECURITY**, any statutes or judicial decisions to the contrary notwithstanding;

(f) **Acceleration:** Accelerate maturity of said **DEED** and **NOTE** and demand payment of the principal sums due thereunder, with interest, advances, costs and attorneys' fees, and in default of said payment or any part thereof, to enforce collection of such payment by foreclosure of the said **DEED** and/or other appropriate action in any court of competent jurisdiction;

(g) **Other:** Exercise any other right, privilege, or remedy available to **LENDER** as may be provided by applicable law and/or any other document executed in connection herewith.

In addition to the rights hereinabove granted, in the event of default by **BORROWER**, **LENDER** may, at its option, enter into and upon the **SECURITY** and the **IMPROVEMENT** and complete the construction thereof, **BORROWER** hereby giving to **LENDER** full power and authority to make such entry and to enter into such contracts or arrangements as may be necessary to complete the construction of the **IMPROVEMENT**. If **LENDER** does not enter upon the **SECURITY** and undertakes the completion of construction of the **IMPROVEMENT**, **LENDER** shall be entitled to have any funds then on deposit with the **AGENT** or in the account of **BORROWER** maintained with **LENDER** disbursed to it or, under its direction, disbursed in the payment of bills theretofore or thereafter contracted in connection with the construction of the **IMPROVEMENT**. In addition, **LENDER** may, at its option, expend money in completing the construction of the **IMPROVEMENT** which shall be over and above the amount of the **NOTE**; and, any such monies, when so expended, shall be added to the principal of the **LOAN** and the same, together with interest thereon at the rate specified in the **NOTE**, shall be secured by the lien of the **DEED**.

The said remedies and rights of **LENDER** shall be cumulative and not mutually exclusive. **LENDER** shall have the absolute right to resort to any one, or more, or all, of said remedies, neither to the limited exclusion of the other.

Further, in the event of any such default or breach of this Agreement, the **NOTE** or **DEED** by **BORROWER**, **LENDER** shall have the absolute right to refuse to disburse the balance of the **LOAN** funds, as aforesaid, and no other party, whether contractor, materialmen, laborer, subcontractor, or supplier, shall have any interest in **LOAN** funds so applied and, further, shall not have any right to garnish, require, or compel payment thereof to be applied toward discharge or satisfaction of any claim or lien which they or any of them have, or may have, for work performed or materials supplied for the development and/or construction work. Any additional funds advanced by **LENDER** to complete development and/or construction shall be secured by the lien of said **DEED** and considered a part of the **LOAN** as though initially included therein.

23. **ASSIGNMENT OF PLANS AND SPECIFICATIONS:** In the event **BORROWER** fails to construct and complete the **IMPROVEMENT** in accordance with the terms and provisions of this Agreement, **BORROWER** hereby assigns to **LENDER** the right to possess and use the architectural plans and specifications and engineering drawings for the purpose of completing the **IMPROVEMENT**.

ARCHITECT and **ENGINEER** shall agree to continue his or their services on behalf of **LENDER** in such an event and if so requested, and shall further agree that **LENDER** shall, without cost, be entitled to use all plans, specifications, and drawings with all modifications thereof, prepared for use in the construction of the **IMPROVEMENT** and the Contractor shall agree to continue its services for **LENDER**, pursuant to its agreement with **BORROWER**.

24. **UNLIMITED ACCESS TO PROPERTY:** Until the **LOAN** has been repaid in full, **LENDER**, **ARCHITECT** and/or **AGENT** and their agents shall, at all reasonable times, have the right of entry and free access to the **SECURITY** and the right to inspect all work done, labor performed, and material furnished on, or about, the **SECURITY**.

25. **WAIVER OF DEFAULTS:** The waiver by **LENDER** of any breach or default by **BORROWER** under any of the terms of the **NOTE**, **DEED** or this Agreement, shall not be deemed, nor shall the same constitute, a waiver of any subsequent breach or default on the part of **BORROWER**.

26. **LENDER'S RIGHT TO APPEAR IN LITIGATION:** **LENDER** shall have the right to commence, to appear in, or to defend any action or preceding purporting to affect the rights or duties of the parties hereunder and, in connection therewith, to pay out of the **LOAN** all necessary expenses and reasonable attorney's fees. **BORROWER** hereby agrees to repay all of the foregoing to **LENDER** upon demand, and all **SECURITY** given hereunder shall secure any such sums.

27. **THIS AGREEMENT PART OF DEED:** The **DEED** and other Security Agreements provided for herein shall specifically incorporate this Agreement by reference and, in the event that the same and the **NOTE** are duly assigned, this Agreement shall be considered assigned in like manner. In the event of a conflict between any of the provisions of the **NOTE**, **DEED**, or this Agreement, then the provisions of this Agreement shall control. A breach or default by **BORROWER** of any term or condition of this Agreement shall constitute a default under the **NOTE** and **DEED**.

28. **EXCLUSIVE OF AGREEMENT:** This Agreement, and the **NOTE** and **DEED** are made for the sole protection of **BORROWER**, **LENDER**, and **LENDER'S** successors and assigns, and no other person or entity shall have any right of action pursuant to, or because of, any of the terms hereof.

29. **CONDEMNATION:** All of the right, title, and interest which **BORROWER** and its successors or assigns have, or shall have, to any award or awards as a result of the taking of, or damage to, the **SECURITY** or any part thereof, including any award or awards for any change or changes of grade or route of streets affecting said **SECURITY**, by reason of condemnation proceedings under the power of eminent domain, is hereby assigned to **LENDER** to be applied to the indebtedness secured by the **DEED**. **LENDER** is hereby authorized, directed, and empowered, at its option, to collect and receive the proceeds of all awards from the authorities making same and to give proper receipts and acquittances therefore and to apply the same toward the payment of the amount owing on account of the **NOTE** and **DEED**, notwithstanding the fact that such amount may not then be due and payable. **BORROWER** agrees to make, execute and deliver any and all assignments and other instruments sufficient for the purpose of assigning the aforesaid awards to the holder of the **NOTE** and **DEED** free, clear and discharged of any and all encumbrances of any kind or nature whatsoever. Any sums received by **LENDER** pursuant to the terms of this Paragraph in excess of the sum of the outstanding amount owed by **BORROWER** to **LENDER**, and the additional interests, if any, shall be remitted to **BORROWER**.

30. **NOTICE TO PARTIES:** All notices provided for herein shall be mailed by Certified or Registered Mail—Return Receipt Request—addressed to the appropriate party as follows:

BORROWER:

LENDER:

or such other address as the party who is to receive such notice may designate in writing. Notice shall be completed by depositing the same in a letter box or other means provided by the United States Post Office for the posting of mail and shall have the proper amount of postage affixed thereto. Actual receipt of notice shall not be required to affect notice hereunder.

31. **LOAN FUND:** **LENDER** shall not be required to segregate the **LOAN** funds or to earmark such funds in any manner. The sole obligation of **LENDER** shall be to disburse the funds as set forth herein, provided there exists no default under this Agreement, the **NOTE** or **DEED** at the time of any request for disbursement.

32. **NON-ASSIGNABLE BY BORROWER:** **BORROWER** shall not assign this Agreement or any part of any advance to be made hereunder, nor convey, nor encumber the **SECURITY** by mortgage or other lien, without the prior written consent of **LENDER**. Any Assignment, conveyance or encumbrance made without such consent of **LENDER** shall constitute an immediate default under this Agreement, the **NOTE** and **MORTGAGE**. Consent of **LENDER** hereunder shall not be unreasonably withheld.

33. **LENDER'S RIGHT TO ASSIGN:** The rights of **LENDER** under this Agreement are assignable, wholly or in part, and any assignee of **LENDER** shall succeed to and be possessed of the rights of **LENDER** hereunder to the extent of any such assignment, including the right to make advances to **BORROWER** or any approved assignee of **BORROWER** in accordance with this Agreement.

34. **BROKER'S COMMISSIONS:** **LENDER** shall be furnished with a statement in writing signed by **BORROWER**, fully disclosing all fees and commissions paid or to be paid to any licensed mortgage broker or other in connection with the obtaining of the **LOAN**, including an affirmative statement indemnifying and holding **LENDER** harmless from any and all claims for any such fees and commissions.

35. **CLOSING COSTS:** All expenses incurred in connection with the making, closing, servicing and/or modification of the **LOAN** shall be paid by **BORROWER**, including, but not limited to, charges for title examination and title insurance, recording and filing fees, mortgage and documentary taxes, all other applicable excise and intangible property taxes and fees of all appraisers, architects, attorneys, engineers, escrow agents and surveyors incurred in connection with the **LOAN**. Where there are funds provided in the **LOAN** for the payment of any of the foregoing costs, fees, expenses or other charges, **LENDER** is hereby authorized to disburse those funds directly in payment thereof.

Any fees and expenses of **LENDER** paid at the time of closing by **BORROWER** are for services rendered and expenses incurred to date of closing only.

36. **NO AGENCY RELATIONSHIP:** **BORROWER** understands and agrees that **LENDER** is not the agent or representative of **BORROWER**, and this Agreement shall not be construed to make **LENDER** liable to materialmen, contractors, craftsmen, laborers, or others for goods delivered to or services performed by them upon the **SECURITY**, or for debts or claims accruing to said parties against **BORROWER**, and it is further understood and agreed that there is not a contractual relationship, either expressed or implied, between **LENDER** and any materialmen, subcontractors, craftsmen, laborers or any other person supplying any work, labor, or materials for the **IMPROVEMENT** of the **SECURITY**.

37. **HAZARDOUS WASTE:** Neither the **BORROWER** nor, to the best knowledge of the **BORROWER**, any other person has ever caused or permitted any Hazardous Material to be placed, held, located or disposed of on, under or at the Premises or the Land or any part thereof or into the atmosphere or any watercourse, body of water or wetlands or any other real property legally or beneficially owned (or any interest or estate in which is owned) by the **BORROWER** (including, without limitation, any property owned by a land trust the beneficial interest in which is owned, in whole or in part, by the **BORROWER**), and neither the Premises, the Land, any part of either thereof, nor any other real property legally or beneficially owned (or any interest or estate in which is owned) by the **BORROWER** (including, without limitation, any property owned by a land trust the beneficial interest in which is owned, in whole or in part, by the **BORROWER**) has ever been used (whether by the **BORROWER** or, to the best knowledge of the **BORROWER**, by any other person) as a treatment, storage or disposal (whether permanent or temporary) site for any Hazardous Material. For purposes of this Agreement, "Hazardous Material" means and includes any hazardous substance or any pollutant or contaminant defined as such in (or for purposes of) the Comprehensive Environmental Response, Compensation, and Liability Act, any so-called "Superfund" or "Superlien" law, the Toxic Substances Control Act, or any other Federal, state or local statute, law, ordinance, code, rule, regulation, order or decree regulating, relating to, or imposing liability or standards of conduct concerning, any hazardous, toxic or dangerous waste, substance or material, as now or at any time hereafter in effect, asbestos or any substance or compound containing asbestos, or any other hazardous, toxic or dangerous, waste, substance or material.

BORROWER hereby indemnifies the **LENDER** and agrees to hold the **LENDER** harmless from and against any and all losses, liabilities, damages, injuries, costs, expenses and claims of any and every kind whatsoever, including reasonable attorney's fees, paid, incurred or suffered by, or asserted against, the **LENDER** for, with respect to, or as a direct or indirect result of, the presence on or under, or the escape, seepage, leakage, spillage, discharge, emission, discharging or release from, the Premises or into or upon the land, the atmosphere, or any watercourse, body of water or wetland or any Hazardous Material (including, without limitation, any losses, liabilities, damages, injuries, costs, expenses or claims asserted or arising under the Comprehensive Environmental Response, Compensation and Liability Act, any so-called "Superfund" or "Superlien" law, or any other Federal, state or local statute, law, ordinance, code, rule, regulation, order or decree regulating, relating to or imposing liability or standards of conduct concerning any Hazardous Material.

38. **WAIVER OF JURY TRIAL:** BORROWER hereby expressly waives any right to trial by jury in any action or proceeding to enforce any right under this Agreement, the Promissory Notes or Deeds of Trust, or under any amendment, instrument, document, or other Note(s) delivered (or which may in the future be delivered) in connection with any banking relationship existing in connection with this Agreement. BORROWER agrees that any such action or proceedings shall not be tried before a jury. To the extent permitted by law, any dispute by and between the parties shall be resolved by arbitration. Any arbitration for which provision is made herein shall be conducted in accordance with the Uniform Arbitration Act, as provided in the Nevada Revised Statutes, 38.015 et seq, as it may be amended from time to time. The fees and expenses of the arbitrator(s) shall be divided equally between the parties. LENDER and BORROWER shall each bear their own expenses (including, but not necessarily limited to, attorney's fees and expenses of witnesses) in any arbitration proceedings. The arbitration proceedings shall be held in the County of _____ , State of _____ . Judgment upon the award rendered by the arbitrator(s) may be entered in any court having jurisdiction thereof.

_____ (initials)   _____ (initials)

39. **MISCELLANEOUS PROVISIONS:** All inspections and other services rendered by, or on behalf of, LENDER, whether or not paid for by BORROWER or its successors in title, shall be rendered solely for the protection and the benefit of LENDER. BORROWER or its successors in interest, shall not be entitled to claim any loss or damage against LENDER, or against its agents or employees for failure to properly discharge their duties to LENDER.

This Agreement, the NOTE and DEED, are executed and delivered in the State of _____ . The laws of the State of Nevada shall govern in the interpretation, enforcement and all other aspects of the obligations and duties created under this LOAN.

BORROWER and LENDER agree that, by mutual consent evidenced by a written instrument, this Agreement, NOTE and DEED, from time to time, may be extended or renewed in whole or in part or the rate of interest thereon may be changed or fees in consideration of LOAN extensions imposed. Any related right to security therefore waived, exchanged, surrendered or otherwise dealt with any of the acts mentioned in the NOTE may be done, all without affecting, limiting, or negating the liability of the BORROWER and all other obligors, endorsers, and guarantors under this Agreement, the NOTE and DEED.

The release of any party liable upon the NOTE shall not release any other such party who may be liable. BORROWER hereby waives presentment, demand of payment, protest and notice of non-payment and protest, and any and all other notices and demands whatsoever except as may be elsewhere provided herein.

Nothing contained in this Agreement, the NOTE and DEED shall impose upon LENDER any obligation to see to the proper application of any disbursements and advances of funds made pursuant to this LOAN.

No provisions of this Agreement shall be amended, waived, or modified except by an instrument in writing signed by the parties hereto.

All covenants, agreements, representations and warranties made herein and in documents delivered in support of the LOAN request shall be deemed to have been material and relied on by LENDER and shall survive the execution and delivery to LENDER of the NOTE and DEED hereunder and the disbursements and advances of funds made pursuant to this LOAN. Title Instructions, attached hereto, identify, but are not an exclusive list of, such documents.

All sections and descriptive headings of paragraphs in this Agreement are inserted for convenience only and shall not affect the construction or interpretation hereof.

This Agreement may be executed in any number of counterparts, each of which, when executed and delivered, shall be an original; but such counterparts shall, together, constitute one and the same instrument.

If any provision of this Agreement, NOTE or DEED is deemed unenforceable or illegal by a court competent to so rule, then the offending words will be stricken and all remaining provisions shall remain in full force and effect.

40. **LOAN PROCEEDS LIMITATION:** BORROWER shall, under no circumstances, use any of the LOAN proceeds disbursed by LENDER hereunder for the payment of any item, purchase, or obligation not directly connected with the IMPROVEMENT being financed under this LOAN program or shown on the Cost Breakdown. All LOAN proceeds are to be utilized solely in connection with the IMPROVEMENT and for no other purpose as shown on the Cost Breakdown and the letter of commitment.

41. **PREPAYMENT:** BORROWER shall have the right to prepay without penalty the monies provided for under the terms and conditions of this Agreement and the NOTE and DEED.

42. The use of the masculine form shall be inclusive of the feminine form and the singular inclusive of the plural.

43. **ATTORNEY'S FEES:** LENDER shall be entitled to recover attorney's fees, cost and expenses should lawsuit be instituted to enforce this Agreement.

BORROWER

By_____

CO-BORROWER

By_____

STATE OF _____
          ss:
COUNTY OF _____
   On _____ , 20 ___ ,
before me, the undersigned Notary Public in and for said County and State, personally appeared

_____ ,
proven to me on the basis of satisfactory evidence to be the person who executed the within

instrument on behalf of the
therein named, and acknowledged to me that such

executed the within instrument pursuant to its

_____
          NOTARY PUBLIC

LENDER

By_____

STATE OF _____
          ss:
COUNTY OF _____
   On _____ , 20 ___ ,
before me, the undersigned Notary Public in and for said County and State, personally appeared

_____ ,
proven to me on the basis of satisfactory evidence to be the person who executed the within

instrument on behalf of the
therein named, and acknowledged to me that such

executed the within instrument pursuant to its

_____
          NOTARY PUBLIC

PERMANENT FINANCING OF COMMERCIAL REAL ESTATE PROPERTIES

LEARNING OBJECTIVES

By now you have solid information about the principles of real estate finance. Many of the concepts that you have learned can be applied to standard long-term commercial real estate finance. Therefore, after reading this chapter, you should be able to show how concepts such as agency problems, interest rate risk, and leverage apply to permanent commercial property financing. In addition, you should understand the differences between permanent commercial property finance covered in this chapter and residential or acquisition, development, and construction finance covered in earlier chapters. Specifically, you should know the terms and conditions that are standard to and characteristic of long-term, fixed-rate financing of commercial properties.

After reading this chapter, you also should understand how equity participation loans are structured and what the benefits of such loans are to property investors and lenders. You should understand the arguments on each side of the issue of the lease-versus-own decision. In this regard, you should understand what factors influence an owner of commercial real estate to sell the property and lease it back from the new owner. Finally, you should know the mechanics of a sale-leaseback and the accounting rules that govern the reporting of such transactions on the seller's financial statements.

INTRODUCTION

In this chapter, we discuss the permanent financing of commercial real estate properties. Permanent financing is the long-term financing of existing properties. Financing commercial real estate ownership refers simply to the alternative of all-equity ownership. First, we consider a standard, long-term, fixed-rate loan. This type of loan is very similar to a standard, fixed-rate, residential loan. Some differences would include a provision for a prepayment penalty and more vigorous underwriting. Second, we look at two variations in long-term financing. One is the equity-participation loan, where the lender shares in the income or cash flows from the property. Next we look at leasing as an alternative.

In particular, we investigate the economics of and accounting for sale-leaseback transactions.

Historically, commercial banks have been the largest originators of debt on income-producing real estate. Also, life insurance companies have been a major source of funds for commercial real estate. They hold the largest concentration of commercial loans. Some institutions such as life insurance companies and pension funds provide funds for real estate indirectly by purchasing mortgage-related securities. These commercial mortgage-backed securities (CMBs) are considered riskier than residential mortgage-backed securities because they lack mortgage insurance and the mix of mortgages on various properties may prevent a complete analysis of the risk of the underlying properties.

LONG-TERM, FIXED-RATE LOANS

A long-term, fixed-rate loan is a common instrument used to finance commercial real estate. Most of these loans are originated by financial institutions such as commercial banks and life insurance companies. Pension funds also purchase some of these loans, and some collateralization exists in the secondary mortgage market. These loans are very similar to long-term, fixed-rate loans on residential properties, with several exceptions.

First, long-term commercial loans involve a more intricate underwriting process. With a residential loan, the value of the property is determined primarily with reference to sales of comparable properties. Although this method also is used to appraise commercial properties, underwriting here relies more heavily on the income capitalization approach. For commercial properties, the lender is very concerned with the value of the collateral, as determined by its income-earning capacity. Lenders realize that changes in the marketplace, including competition from newly added properties, can quickly alter the earnings picture of existing properties. For this reason, lenders are cautious with these types of loans, in the sense that they generally lend a smaller portion of the value. While residential properties may have loan-to-value ratios over 90, commercial properties carry much lower loan-to-value ratios in the neighborhood of 60 to 70 percent. There is also less prevalence on mortgage insurance in the commercial loan market than in the residential loan arena.

A second major difference between long-term commercial and residential loans is the ability of the borrower to prepay. Residential mortgages typically grant the borrower the option to prepay the loan without penalty because of the lack of **prepayment penalties**. This is not the case for commercial loans. Most long-term loans on commercial properties have prepayment penalties, which are usually set at an amount related to the spread between the market rate and the contract rate. The larger the spread between the market rate and the contract rate, the larger the prepayment penalty on a commercial loan. A properly constructed prepayment penalty will reduce or eliminate the value of the refinancing option. It is called a **yield maintenance prepayment penalty**.

A third difference between residential and commercial loans relates to the nature of the collateral. Since the lender has a security interest in a commercial property, the note is likely to have an **assignment of rents** clause. This clause allows the lender to step in and collect lease payments directly from the tenants in the event the borrower defaults (becomes delinquent) on the loan.

Some examples of basic loan parameters for commercial loans are as follows: (1) first mortgages secured by fee simple ownership, (2) loan maturities generally between 5 years and 20 years with a maximum amortization of 30 years,

(3) fixed-rate loans at a spread over U.S. Treasury issues, (4) required yield maintenance on prepayment, (5) nonrecourse loans except under special circumstances such as hazardous waste or borrower bankruptcy, (6) borrower's financial position sufficient to cover potential operating deficits, and (7) management must have some stipulated minimum experience.

ALTERNATIVES TO STANDARD LONG-TERM, FIXED-RATE LOANS

The two popular alternatives to the standard, fixed-rate commercial loans are equity-participation loans and sale-leaseback agreements.

Equity-Participation Loans

Equity-participation, or equity "kicker," refers to the participation by the lender in the property's income. They are sometimes referred to simply as participation loans. However, you should be aware that the term *participation loan* may have another meaning. The term may refer to a situation where more than one financial institution agrees to participate in a loan by each advancing a portion of the total loan amount. Here, however, a participation loan refers to the participation in the income of the property by a sole lender. With an **equity-participation loan**, the lender offers a lower interest rate on the loan in return for a share of the income from the property and/or a share of the price appreciation of the property. In most cases, the share of the income is a portion that exceeds a specified minimum amount. Essentially, a portion of the loan can be viewed as an equity interest in the property, because of the nature of equity as a claim on residual income. With an equity-participation loan, the lender has a claim to a portion of the income if it exceeds a certain amount—that is, a residual amount. This means that, in addition to some agreed-upon debt service payment, the lenders earns a share of the income or price appreciation that would normally be reserved for the equity investor.

Basic Principles

Before we present an example of an equity-participation loan, we should consider some basic principles of such an arrangement. First, the arrangement represents a trade-off between the owner/ borrower and the lender. The lender gives up some interest for a right to share in a residual. The owner gives up some of the rights to income for a reduction in the interest rate. In one respect, it is difficult to see how the arrangement can create new value. One would expect that in an efficient market, with full knowledge of the expected cash flows by each party, the trade-off would be priced appropriately. That is, under the "no free lunch" theory, neither party could gain or lose at the expense of the other. Or, the value of the property would be determined by its expected cash flows, and the riskiness of those cash flows, and not how those cash flows would be divided between the investor and the lender.

Second, there appears to be no value creation from a tax savings. If the loan arrangement is structured properly, the share of income paid to the lender qualifies as an interest deduction for the borrower. In other words, the borrower obtains a lower interest payment on the loan in return for a portion of the income, both of which are deductible for tax purposes.

Third, given that the parties to the trade-off will attempt to determine the terms of the loan, they will use certain considerations to do so. In a participating loan, the lender is exposed to an increase in risk since the lender gives up a portion of the interest payments associated with a conventional loan for a residual interest in the income from the property. Essentially, the lender advances funds that are part debt and part equity. For a conventional loan, the lender would discount the interest payments by the contractual interest rate to arrive at the present value of the payment stream. Once the payment stream includes a participation in the income of the property, the risk is increased. So, the discount rate necessary to value the payment stream will be greater than that on an interest-only loan. Even though the lender's risk is increased by the share in the equity position, the standard arrangement calls for the lender to share in the positive cash flows. Although risk is increased, it is nonetheless limited.

Likewise, the risk to the owner is reduced by the participation agreement. In return for a portion of the income, the borrower receives a lower interest obligation. For a loan of a given size, the debt-to-coverage ratio will increase and the probability of insolvency and default will be reduced. Therefore, the discount rate used to value the cash flows to equity will be lower by virtue of the participation agreement. In short, an equity-participation agreement increases the total equity component and reduces the debt component of financing. But, the larger equity component is shared by the owner and the lender. The result increases the risk position of the lender and decreases the risk position of the property owner. Commensurate changes in their respective discount rates used to value their expected cash flows are justified.

These considerations taken together imply that the trade-off in terms of participation should be priced efficiently and that the discount rates used by the lender and owner should reflect the value of the trade-off.

The Popular View of Equity-Participation Loans

Some of the published finance literature points out the advantages of equity-participation agreements for the borrower. The question of the efficient pricing of the terms of the loans is not addressed, however. Nonetheless, they bear repeating here. One argument is that borrowers benefit because they give up a portion of the equity without giving up ownership of the property. This gives the borrower control over the property and the right to the depreciation write-off. Also, the agreement will lower the debt service costs and reduce the break-even point. The cost of reducing the break-even point is the share of the profits and property appreciation that is traded to the lender. Another advantage mentioned is the increase in leverage. Since the owner shares a portion of the equity, the equity base is lower than would occur otherwise, leading to the increase in leverage.

None of these so-called advantages address the question of any increase in value for the borrower. Logically, knowledgeable lenders should extract the value of the lower interest payment in terms of the share of profits and property appreciation such that, when efficiently priced, the borrower would be neither better nor worse off under the participation agreement. After we present an example of an equity-participation loan, we suggest one reason why these loans exist and how value can be created by the agreement.

Equity-Participation Loan Example

Next, we explore the nature of the trade-off of terms of an equity-participation loan through an example of a familiar, standard loan discussed earlier in the text. Consider a long-term (30 years), fixed-rate (12 percent) loan for approximately 70 percent of the value of the property. Data on the operating revenues and expenses, as well as the growth rates in key variables of this example, are shown in Table 19-1. Table 19-2 shows the before- and after-tax cash flows for a 5-year holding period. The property has positive income each year, so there are no passive losses to be suspended. The debt ratio (net operating income [NOI]/payment) rises from 1.66 in year 1 to 2.28 in year 5. Table 19-3 shows the cash flows from reversion (sale) of the property at the end of the fifth year. Finally, Table 19-4 pulls the example

TABLE 19-1

Analysis of Commercial Real Estate Project

Project cost	
Land	$300,000
Building	2,500,000
Total	$2,800,000
Project financing	
Loan amount	$2,000,000
Interest rate	12%
Amortization period	30 years
Initial-equity investment	$800,000
Gross rent	
[Year 1]	$522,100
Vacancy rate	5%
Operating expense	
[Year 1]	$83,536 (16% of gross revenue)
Growth rates	
Gross rent	8%
Operating expense	7%
Resale price	6%
Resale expense rate	5%
Investor's marginal tax rate	28%

Source: © 2014 OnCourse Learning

TABLE 19-2

Cash Flows from Operations

	Before-Tax Cash Flows				
	YEAR 1	**YEAR 2**	**YEAR 3**	**YEAR 4**	**YEAR 5**
Gross rent	$522,100	$563,868	$608,977	$657,696	$710,311
Vacancy	26,105	28,193	30,449	32,885	35,516
Effective gross income	495,995	535,675	578,529	624,811	674,796
Operating expense	83,536	89,384	95,640	102,335	109,499
NOI	412,459	446,291	482,888	522,476	565,297
Mortgage payment	248,287	248,287	248,287	248,287	248,287
Before-tax cash flow	164,172	198,004	234,601	274,188	317,010
Debt coverage ratio	1.66	1.80	1.94	2.10	2.28

	After-Tax Cash Flows				
	YEAR 1	**YEAR 2**	**YEAR 3**	**YEAR 4**	**YEAR 5**
NOI	$412,459	$446,291	$482,888	$522,476	$565,297
Depreciation	87,000	91,000	91,000	91,000	87,000
Interest	240,000	239,006	237,892	236,644	235,247
Taxable income	85,459	116,286	153,996	194,831	243,050
Loss carry forward	0	0	0	0	0
Net carry forward	0	0	0	0	0
Net taxable income	85,459	116,286	153,996	194,831	243,050
Tax due	23,929	32,560	43,119	54,523	68,054
Before-tax cash flow	164,172	198,004	234,601	274,188	317,010
After-tax cash flow	140,243	165,444	191,482	219,636	248,956

Source: © 2014 OnCourse Learning

TABLE 19-3

Cash Flows from Sale of Property, Year 5

Sale price	$3,747,032
Less sales expense	187,352
Less mortgage balance	1,947,352
Less tax	225,649[a]
	$1,386,679

[a]*Tax rate = 0.187 = (0.37)(0.25) + (0.63)(0.15). Total gain = $1,206,680 of which $447,000 (37%) is depreciation recapture. Adjusted basis = $2,353,000.*

Source: © 2014 OnCourse Learning

TABLE 19-4

Present Value and Yield Calculations

	YEAR 0	YEAR 1	YEAR 2	YEAR 3	YEAR 4	YEAR 5
Cash flows	−$800,000	$140,243	$165,444	$191,482	$219,636	$1,635,635
Discount rate:						
15%						
Net present value:						
$511,730						
IRR, 30.44%						

Source: © 2014 OnCourse Learning

together and summarizes the cash flows and net present value of the equity position of the investor. Assuming a discount rate of 15 percent, the net present value of the equity position is $511,730. The cash flows to the lender are not shown. Be aware, though, that assuming the lender charges a rate reflective of the risk of the loan, then the net present value would, of course, be zero, and the internal rate of return would be the loan contract rate, 12 percent.

Now, let's consider an equity-participation loan. Note that we have constructed the following participation loan to demonstrate a point. We purposely have chosen the terms of the trade-off and the discount rates to show no increase in value to either the investor (borrower) or the lender.

Table 19-5 shows the terms of the participating mortgage. Several items should be noted. First, the interest rate on the loan is 10 percent, less than the 12 percent rate on the standard loan. The loan amount remains the same. Next, note the terms of the participation. In this example, the lender receives the right to 15 percent of any net operating income over $280,000, and 10 percent of the appreciation in the value of the property. The appreciation in the value of the property will be measured as the difference between the gross selling price in year 5 and the current value ($2.8 million). Both participation amounts are deductible for tax purposes.

An infinite combination of participation terms can be arranged. In addition to alternative percentages, the participation terms can specify a proportion of either cash flows or net income. Also, the terms of the equity participation loan may indicate that the participation in income begins only after a given period of time. All the combinations will have a common theme, however. The lender will receive a right to some sort of residual in return for reducing the rate on the loan. Although the investor and the lender will bargain for the best terms possible, the investor will not wish to give up participating cash flows that are significantly greater than the reduction of interest payments. Obviously, the greater the discount in the rate on the loan, the greater the share of the cash flows that the investor will be willing to give up.

TABLE 19-5

Analysis of Commercial Real Estate Project with Lender Participation

Project cost	
Land	$300,000
Building	$2,500,000
Total	$2,800,000
Project financing	
Loan amount	$2,000,000
Interest rate	10%
Amortization	30 Years
Participation terms	
Share of NOI	
Over $280,000	15%
Share of appreciation	10%
Initial equity investment	$800,000
Gross rent: Year 1	$522,100
Vacancy rate	5%
Operating expense: Year 1	$83,536
Growth rates	
Gross rent	8%
Operating expense	7%
Resale price	6%
Resale expense rate	5%
Investor's marginal tax rate	28%

Source: © 2014 OnCourse Learning

Remember that risk as well as cash flows is shifted between the parties of the participation agreement. The investor is in a lower risk position, while the lender is in a higher risk position. This means that the investor's discount rate should fall, while the lender's will rise.

Table 19-6 shows the before- and after-tax cash flows of the equity-participation loan. Table 19-7 shows the calculation of the after-tax cash flow from the sale of the property, including the revisionary participation. The data in Tables 19-6 and 19-7 can be used to determine the returns to the investor and the lender. Table 19-8 summarizes the present value and yield calculations for the investor and the lender. The cash flows that accrue to the investor are not significantly different from those in Table 19-4. This is because the lender has given up a portion of the net operating income in return for a reduction in the interest expense. If one assumes that there has been a slight decrease in the investor's discount rate because of the reduction in risk (for example, from 15 to 14.75 percent), then the net present value of the investment is virtually the same as with a standard, fixed-rate loan.

The annual cash flows that accrue to the lender include the mortgage and participation payments. Because of the slight increase in risk, the lender's discount rate is raised (for example, from 12 percent to 12.25 percent). The result is a net present value of the loan of zero, the same as in the case of the standard loan. Thus, neither the investor nor the lender obtains an increase in value under the terms and assumptions of this participation loan. If one accepts the changes in the discount rates as reflective of the changes (sharing) of the risk of the equity to each party, it appears as though the terms of the participation loan have been priced efficiently. In other words, given the changes in the discount rates, the trade-off of the lower interest payments for a portion of the returns to equity leaves neither party better off.

Of course, if the changes in the discount rates do not reflect the sharing of the risk, these results are not valid. If, for example, the lender's discount rate does not rise as much as indicated in the example, the lender would be better off with the participating loan. If this is the case, one would expect the lender to be in

TABLE 19-6
Equity Participation Loan

	Before-Tax Cash Flows				
	YEAR 1	YEAR 2	YEAR 3	YEAR 4	YEAR 5
Gross rent	$522,100	$563,868	$608,977	$657,696	$710,311
Vacancy	26,105	28,193	30,449	32,885	35,516
Effective gross income	495,995	535,675	578,529	624,811	674,796
Operating expense	83,536	89,384	95,640	102,335	109,499
NOI	412,459	446,291	482,888	522,476	565,297
Mortgage payment	212,158	212,158	212,158	212,158	212,158
Cash flow before participation	200,301	234,133	270,730	310,317	353,139
Participation	19,869[a]	24,944	30,433	36,371	42,795
Before-tax cash flow	180,432	209,189	240,296	273,946	310,344
Debt coverage ratio	1.94	2.10	2.28	2.46	2.66

	After-Tax Cash Flows				
	YEAR 1	YEAR 2	YEAR 3	YEAR 4	YEAR 5
NOI	$412,459	$446,291	$482,888	$522,476	$565,297
Depreciation	87,000	91,000	91,000	91,000	87,000
Interest	200,000	198,784	197,447	195,976	194,357
Participation	19,869	24,944	30,433	36,371	42,795
Taxable income	105,590	131,563	164,008	199,129	241,145
Loss carried forward	0	0	0	0	0
Net carry forward	0	0	0	0	0
Net taxable income	105,590	131,563	164,008	199,129	241,145
Tax due	29,569	36,838	45,922	55,756	67,521
Before-tax cash flow	180,432	209,189	240,296	273,946	310,344
After-tax cash flow	150,866	172,351	194,374	218,190	242,823

[a][$412,459 − $280,000] × 0.15

Source: © 2014 OnCourse Learning

TABLE 19-7
Sale of Property: Year 5

Sale price	$3,747,032
Less sales expense	187,352
Less mortgage balance	1,925,771
Less participation	94,703[a]
Less tax	211,276[b]
	$1,327,930

[a]10% × ($3,747,032 − $2,800,000)

[b]19% × ($3,747,032 − $187,352 − $94,703 − $2,353,000).
Depreciation recapture is 40 percent of total gain.

Source: © 2014 OnCourse Learning

a position to offer the investor an even better participation agreement (other things being equal, a lower interest rate). Accordingly, creation of value would seem to result simply by a rearrangement of the terms of the participation loan.

We suggest that this may be the case for lenders that do not experience a significant increase in the required discount rate as a result of the equity-participation agreement. A couple of reasons may account for this result. First, the lender may

TABLE 19-8

Present Values and Yield Calculations

	YEAR 0	YEAR 1	YEAR 2	YEAR 3	YEAR 4	YEAR 5
Owner						
Cash flows	−$800,000	$150,866	$172,351	$194,374	$218,190	$1,570,753
Discount rate, 14.75%						
Net present value, $506,333						
IRR, 30.26%						
	YEAR 0	YEAR 1	YEAR 2	YEAR 3	YEAR 4	YEAR 5
Lender						
Cash flows	−$2,000,000	$232,027[a]	$237,102	$242,592	$248,530	$2,275,427[b]
Discount rate, 12.25%						
Net present value, $0						
IRR, 12.25%						

[a]$212,158 + $19,869

[b]$212,158 + $1,925,771 + $94,703 + $42,795

Source: © 2014 OnCourse Learning

not perceive the participation loan as more risky than a standard loan because of its hedging qualities. If the lender has a particular need to hedge against inflation risk and views real estate as a particularly useful investment for this purpose, the project cost equity-participation loan may appear to offer no additional risk. Indeed, it may offer risk-reduction benefits because of the inflation-hedging qualities of this type of loan. Second, some lenders may not view a participation loan as more risky because they may, at the time, have negative net worth. This concept was discussed earlier in the text as it relates to thrifts. An operating thrift with a negative net worth has an incentive to take on risky investments. If the investments fail, the thrift occupies worse position, and if the investments succeed, the thrift may extricate itself from insolvency.

During the mid- to late 1980s many thrifts entered into participation loan arrangements. In those sections of the country that experienced falling real estate values in the late 1980s and early 1990s, the gamble by thrifts was unsuccessful, and their losses were much greater than they would have been had they not sought the equity-participation loans.

The key is that there may be reasons why a participating loan for a lender does not warrant a significant (or any) increase in the discount rate used to value the loan. If this is the case, then the risk sharing created by an equity-participation loan can be beneficial to both parties.

Lease versus Own Analysis

An alternative to owning for the real estate investor who needs to occupy space is to lease the property. If the property is purchased, the investor would most likely incur debt to pay the purchase price and would have to make the down payment. In this case, the interest paid on the debt would be tax deductible. Additionally, the investor could depreciate the property and would receive any price appreciation. On the other hand, by leasing the property, the investor avoids having to make a down payment, avoids the expense of incurring debt, and can fully tax deduct the lease payments. However, the investor does not enjoy any price appreciation that may accrue to the property. The preferable option depends on the after-tax return and risk of each alternative. Certain cautions, however, must be considered. For example, if the lease payments are not reasonable and an option to purchase is allowed, the IRS may consider the lease to actually be a financing arrangement.

| E X A M P L E | Suppose that Mr. Max A. Million, a small businessman, needs to occupy office space for 5 years. He is considering buying an office building but that would also entail buying equipment and furniture, incurring acquisition costs to make the purchase, and paying financing costs to acquire the mortgage. His thoughts turn to leasing. |

Mr. Million has found a building for sale that suits his needs. The purchase price is $225,000 of which $180,000 is the building value and $45,000 is the value of the land. He can purchase the building with a $175,000 interest-only mortgage at a rate of 10 percent. The loan would be due and payable at the end of year 5. Mr. Million expects to sell the property at the end of year 5 for $280,000. He is in a 28 percent marginal tax bracket and requires a 12 percent equity return.

Alternatively, Mr. Million can lease this same building for 5 years at $20,000 per year. In either case, there will be no cash inflow (since it is owner-occupied) and Mr. Million will pay property taxes, insurance, and maintenance. Thus, interest and depreciation are the only factors if he buys the property and the lease payment is the only factor to be considered if he leases. Table 19-9 shows the after-tax cash flows from owning the property. This produces a net present value of −$39,122. Alternatively, Table 19-10 gives the after-tax cash flows from leasing the same property and the net present value is −$51,909. In this case, the least cost alternative is to own the property. At a lease payment of $16,453, Mr. Million would be indifferent between the two options. In this case, the two alternatives would have the same net present value. At any lease payment less than $16,453, he would prefer to lease the property.

TABLE 19-9
After-Tax Cash Flow from Owning the Property

	Year					
	0	1	2	3	4	5
Net operating income	-	0	0	0	0	0
− Mortgage payment	-	− 17,500	− 17,500	− 17,500	− 17,500	− 17,500
= Before-tax cash flow	-	− 17,500	− 17,500	− 17,500	− 17,500	− 17,500
− Taxes	-	+ 6,138	+ 6,192	+ 6,192	+ 6,192	+ 6,138
= After-tax cash flow	− $50,000	− 11,362	− 11,308	− 11,308	− 11,308	− 11,308
After-tax equity reversion		91,093				

NPV at 12%: − $39,122

ATER	= Sales price	$280,000
	− Mortgage balance	− 175,000
	− Tax	− 13,907
	= After-tax equity reversion	= 91,093
TX	= Sales price	280,000
	− Adjusted basis	− 202,309
	= Gain	= 77,691
	× Tax rate	× 0.179
	= Tax	= 13,907

Tax rate = (0.29)(0.25) + (0.71)(0.15) = 0.179

(Depreciation recovery is 29 percent of total gain.)

Source: © 2014 OnCourse Learning

TABLE 19-10

After-Tax Cash Flow from Leasing

			Year			
	0	**1**	**2**	**3**	**4**	**5**
Net operating income	–	0	0	0	0	0
– Lease	–	– 20,000	– 20,000	– 20,000	– 20,000	– 20,000
– Taxes	–	+ 5,600	+ 5,600	+ 5,600	+ 5,600	+ 5,600
= After-tax cash flow	0	– 14,400	– 14,400	– 14,400	– 14,400	– 14,400
NPV at 12% = – $51,909						

After-tax cost of lease = 20,000 (1 − t) = 20,000 (0.72) = $14,400.

Source: © 2014 OnCourse Learning

Leases and Sale-Leaseback Agreements

Consider an all-equity owner (individual or corporation) of a commercial property that is fully depreciated. The owner wants to finance the property because he or she has an immediate need for cash. Two alternatives, as outlined in Table 19-11, may accomplish this task. As you can see, the two alternatives are essentially identical. One alternative is to take out a loan on the property. The other, a **sale-leaseback**, is to sell the property and lease it from the new owner with an option to repurchase. In either case, the current owner will retain use of the facility.

In our example, the value of the property is $10 million. If the owner obtains a loan for 80 percent of its value ($8 million) at 10 percent for 20 years, the annual (interest-only) payments will be $800,000. With an interest-only loan, the balance at the end of 20 years will be $8 million. On the other hand, the owner can sell the property for $8 million and enter into a 20-year lease with annual payments of $800,000. The sale-leaseback arrangement also will provide that the seller has the right (option) to repurchase the property at the end of the lease term for $8 million. For each alternative, the cash flows are the same and the current owner is guaranteed use of the property. Interest payments and lease payments are both deductible for tax purposes. Therefore, from the standpoint of the cash flows, there is essentially no difference between the two alternatives. For this reason, leasing property can be viewed as a method of financing.

One might argue that the lease alternative is superior, since it involves the same cash flows and grants the current owner the option to purchase the property at the end of the lease term. If property values fall, the current owner will not

TABLE 19-11

Comparison of Financing Methods[a]

DEBT			SALE-LEASEBACK		
Borrow	$8,000,000	Cash inflow	Sale	$8,000,000	Cash inflow
Interest payments	800,000	Cash outflow	Lease payments	800,000	Cash outflow
Repayment of loan	8,000,000	Cash outflow	Repurchase	8,000,000	Cash outflow

[a]*Value of property: $10,000,000.*

Source: © 2014 OnCourse Learning

exercise that option and is in a better position than if the property were owned. However, many sale-leaseback agreements provide for the seller to guarantee a certain value of the property at the end of the lease and agree to indemnify the buyer in the event property prices fall and the option to repurchase is not exercised. To the extent such an agreement is included in the sale-leaseback, both of the alternatives are identical.

The Economics of Lease versus Ownership of Assets

Before we look at an example of a real estate sale-leaseback agreement, it may be useful to discuss the economics of leasing versus ownership of assets in general. This will help us to focus on the advantages and disadvantages of sale-leasebacks of real estate. An argument can be made that a firm should never lease an asset that it anticipates using for a long period of time. The reason is that leasing an asset requires that a separate structure be created to own the asset. This separate ownership structure requires the expenditure of resources (management, secretarial personnel, and so on), but does not affect the productivity of the asset; that is, the asset's productivity is not influenced by the entity that has legal title to it. If a separate entity is established to own the asset and lease it to the firm that uses it, some of the cash flows produced by the asset must be diverted to the resources necessary to establish that entity. If one also considers that the selling firm may have to pay tax on any appreciation in the asset, it becomes even more uneconomical to enter into a sale-leaseback arrangement.

One may be quick to point out that one advantage of leasing rather than owning an asset is the probability that the asset may become obsolete before the end of its physical life. However, if one assumes that knowledge of the probability of obsolescence is available to all market participants, there is still no advantage to leasing. Although the risk and cost of obsolescence is shifted to the lessor, the lessor will charge for the risk in the lease payments. Thus, the firm that uses the asset cannot shift the risk of obsolescence to another firm without paying for it.

There are some reasonable arguments why leasing may have its advantages. First, leasing is advantageous if the firm expects to use only a portion of the asset (which is indivisible), or if the firm expects to use the asset for only a relatively short period of time. Ownership involves transaction costs. It may not be feasible to incur transaction costs in the purchase and sale of an asset if the firm intends to use the asset for a short period of time. The firm is better off leasing, even at relatively high lease payments, if it anticipates using the asset only briefly. Since firms often require use of only a portion of a real estate property, or use for only a short period of time, leasing of real estate is common. However, this argument cannot be used to justify the sale-leaseback of a property that will be used for a lengthy period of time.

Second, there is the tax argument. A firm may benefit more from leasing than from owning if the lessor can use the tax benefits from depreciation more than the property user. Thus, an owner of a real estate property that cannot use the depreciation benefits (because of no other income with which to offset passive losses) may be better off selling it to a firm that can use the depreciation write-off and then leasing the facility from the new owner. Since the new owner of the property can use the tax benefits, the lease terms may be more favorable than the terms (interest) on a loan on the property.

Also in this regard, a property may have been fully or nearly fully depreciated on the books of the owner. A sale of the property is the only way to obtain a **stepped-up basis** to its current market value. Once the new book value of the property is stepped up to its market value, a larger amount of depreciation can be taken. If that depreciation is taken by the new owner, he or she in turn can provide favorable lease terms to the seller. In this way, both parties to the sale-leaseback transaction will benefit at the expense of the U.S. Treasury.

Third, there is the **window dressing** argument for the firm's financial statements. Consider a firm that sells a property and leases it for lease payments that are similar to interest payments it would make if it incurred debt. In such a case, the total assets on the firm's balance sheet are less, so that the return on assets will be greater. There is also less debt (mortgage) on the balance sheet. So the firm's rate-of-return on assets increases, and its debt-to-equity ratio declines if it sells and then leases back the property. In an efficient market, the window dressing ploy may have no value. After all, financial analysts would recognize the present value of the future lease obligations as an implicit debt for the firm. Regardless of these arguments, current accounting rules prohibit these window dressing techniques.

In short, sale-leaseback transactions that are structured to reduce taxes or improve the financial statements of the property owner may not be entirely successful in accomplishing these goals.

Tax regulations state that any transaction that is designed for the express purpose of avoiding taxes can be voided by the Internal Revenue Service. And, accounting rules require that the firm's financial statements reflect the substance of a transaction and not the form.

EXAMPLE
SUBSTANCE
VERSUS FORM

A perspective on the advantages and disadvantages of a sale-leaseback transaction can be gained by considering an example. Table 19-12 shows the data on a commercial real estate property owned by a noncorporate investor. The investor has owned the property for some time because the book value (undepreciated) of the property is very low. The remaining annual depreciation deduction and the amount of debt on the property are low. For simplicity, we will assume that there is no expected growth in the revenue, expenses, net operating income, or value of the property for the next 10 years. If the investor retains the property for 10 years, the annual cash flows will appear as given in Table 19-13.

The before-tax cash flow calculations begin with the NOI. From NOI, the mortgage payment is deducted to arrive at the before-tax cash flow. The after-tax cash flows are determined by calculating the tax charge for each year. From NOI, interest and depreciation are deducted to determine taxable income. Note that the tax charge each year is substantial, due to the low interest and depreciation expense. We will return to an analysis of the cash flows in this table shortly. For now, let's analyze the cash flows that would result from a sale-leaseback of the property.

TABLE 19-12
Property Characteristics

Original cost	$2,000,000
Book value	$60,000
Market value	$2,000,000
Debt balance	$100,000
Rate	12%
Remaining term	10 years
Payment	$17,698
Investor's tax rate	28%
Annual depreciation	$6,000
Growth rates	0%

Source: © 2014 OnCourse Learning

TABLE 19-13
Retention of Property

	Before-Tax Cash Flows					
	YEAR 1	YEAR 2	YEAR 3	YEAR 4	. . .	YEAR 10
Net operating income	$338,900	$338,900	$338,900	$338,900		$338,900
Mortgage payment	17,698	17,698	17,698	17,698		17,698
Cash flow	321,202	321,202	321,202	321,202		321,202
	After-Tax Cash Flows					
Net operating income	$338,900	$338,900	$338,900	$338,900		$338,900
Interest	12,000	11,316	10,550	9,693		1,896
Depreciation	6,000	6,000	6,000	6,000		6,000
Taxable income	320,900	321,584	322,350	323,207		331,004
Tax	89,852	90,043	90,258	90,498		92,681
Cash flow	231,350	231,158	230,944	230,703		228,521

Source: © 2014 OnCourse Learning

Terms of Sale-Leaseback

For ease of comparison, assume that the investor enters into a sale with a leaseback of 10 years. The sale price is $2 million. The investor agrees to repurchase the property at the end of 10 years for the same amount. The annual lease payments are set at $275,000. You should note three things. First, after the 10-year period, the investor owns the property. Second, we assume for simplicity that there are no taxes due on the sale of the property. Third, the annual lease payment is close to what the payment would be on a loan for $2 million for 10 years. Taken together, you can see how the sale-leaseback agreement has all of the characteristics of a loan. With the sale-leaseback, the buyer advances $2 million to the investor, receives lease payments that behave as loan payments, and gets a return of the $2 million at the end of the 10-year period (repurchase of the property). It is for this reason that accounting rules have been developed that force property owners to treat sale-leaseback agreements on their financial statements just as if they were loan arrangements; that is, taxpayers must carry the property on the books as an asset, record the lease obligation as a liability, and treat lease payments as interest expense. Such accounting rules are discussed further below.

Table 19-14 shows the cash flows to the investor from the sale-leaseback agreement. The seller receives $2 million from the buyer at the outset. The cash flow in year 10 reflects the $2 million repurchase price. Table 19-15 compares the cash flows associated with owning the property for the next 10 years (from Table 19-13) and from a 10-year sale-leaseback agreement (Table 19-14). In both cases, a 15 percent discount rate is used to value the cash flows. (The risks associated with ownership are not transferred with the sale-leaseback, since the seller agrees to repurchase the property at an agreed-on price. Typically in sale-leasebacks, the owner agrees to insulate the buyer from a decline in the market value of the property.) Note that the present value of the cash flows from the sale-leaseback agreement is greater than that of the continued ownership.

The first thought is that the increase in value for the owner has come at the expense of the buyer. However, we can show that this is not the case. Table 19-16

TABLE 19-14
Sale-Leaseback Cash Flows[a]

	YEAR 0	YEAR 1	YEAR 2	YEAR 3	YEAR 4	. . .	YEAR 10
Net operating income		$338,900	$338,900	$338,900	$338,900		$ 338,900
Lease expense		275,000	275,000	275,000	275,000		275,000
Taxable income		63,900	63,900	63,900	63,900		63,900
Tax		17,892	17,892	17,892	17,892		17,892
Cash flow	2,000,000	46,008	46,008	46,008	46,008		(1,953,992)

[a]Sale price, $2,000,000; lease payment; $275,000.

Source: © 2014 OnCourse Learning

TABLE 19-15
Net Present Value: Own vs. Lease[a]

		Own					
		YEAR 1	YEAR 2	YEAR 3	YEAR 4	. . .	YEAR 10
Net present value = $1,156,744		$231,350	$231,158	$230,944	$230,703		$228,521
		Lease					
	YEAR 0	YEAR 1	YEAR 2	YEAR 3	YEAR 4	. . .	YEAR 10
Net present value = $1,736,534	$2,000,000	$46,008	$46,008	$46,008	$46,008		$(1,953,992)

[a]Cash flow discount rate 15%.

Source: © 2014 OnCourse Learning

TABLE 19-16
Cash Flows for Buyer-Lessor

	YEAR 0	YEAR 1	YEAR 2	YEAR 3	YEAR 4	. . .	YEAR 10
Lease income	0	$275,000	$275,000	$275,000	$275,000		$ 275,000
Depreciation	0	150,000	150,000	150,000	150,000		150,000
Tax	0	35,000	35,000	35,000	35,000		35,000
Cash flow	(2,000,000)	240,000	240,000	240,000	240,000		2,240,000
Discount rate = 12%							
Net present value = $0							

Source: © 2014 OnCourse Learning

shows the cash flows accruing to the new owner (lessor). The first year's cash flow includes the cash outflow of the purchase price, while the last year's cash flow reflects the cash inflow from the repurchase. We also have assumed that the new owner can take a larger amount of depreciation because of the higher sales price of the property. In this example, the discount rate for the new owner is lower than the rate for the original investor. Recall that the original investor has retained all of the risks of ownership, including the possibility of a decline in the property's market value. The new owner is really in the position of a lender. The present value of the cash flows discounted at (a lender's) discount rate is zero, which is to say that the lease payments replace the 12 percent loan payments of a lender. One of the factors that makes the sale-leaseback arrangement work is the larger depreciation deductions resulting from the stepped-up basis of the property.

A few considerations might mitigate the value of a sale-leaseback, however. First, we have not considered the impact of any taxes due on the gain on the sale of the property. Consideration of capital gains taxes will reduce the value of the sale-leaseback. Second, the original owner may have been able to accomplish much the same result by borrowing against the property. Although it is likely the investor could not borrow as much as the sales price, any additional debt (at a 12 percent rate) may have the same impact as the sale-leaseback, since interest payments would replace lease payments and both are tax deductible. In other words, the leveraging effect can occur by incurring new debt at 12 percent or by a sale-leaseback with a new owner with a similar discount rate. Next, if the amount of depreciation does not increase significantly, one of the main elements driving this type of transaction would be missing. Our example allows for significantly more depreciation than would be allowed for under current tax regulations. In fact, the volume of sale-leasebacks has fallen since the Tax Reform Act of 1986, which lowered the depreciation allowance on commercial real estate.

Further evidence of the effect of the Tax Reform Act of 1986 can be seen from looking at the effect on a firm's stock price as a result of announcing a sale-leaseback of all or part of its real estate holdings. If a sale-leaseback would be financially advantageous to a firm then the value if its stock on the market should reflect that advantage on or about the time the firm announces an intention to enter into such an arrangement. Alvayay, Rutherford, and Smith researched this issue.[1] They looked at the stock market reaction to an announcement of a sale-leaseback for 28 deals announced prior to January 1, 1987 (effective date of the Tax Reform Act [TRA] of 1986) and 17 deals announced after this date. For each set of announcements they calculated the daily return (in percent) on the stocks for 30 days prior to and 30 days subsequent to the announcement. They then calculated the daily "abnormal" rate of return as the difference between the actual return on the stocks and their expected return based on the return of the entire stock market. Finally, they added the daily abnormal returns to form a "cumulative abnormal rate of return." For the 28 announcements prior to January 1, 1987 they found little evidence for abnormal returns in the 30 days prior to the announcements but did find a 6 percent cumulative abnormal return in the 30 days after the announcement. This abnormal return was statistically significant. For the 17 sale-leaseback announcements after January 1, 1987 they found no abnormal returns either before or after the announcement. They concluded that the TRA of 1986 had a negative impact on the equity value of a seller/lessee in a sale-leaseback transaction.

Finally, if accounting rules require that sale-leasebacks be treated as debt financing on the financial statements of the original owner, the impact of window dressing will be lost. It is instructive to look briefly at the accounting rules for sale-leasebacks and see how they often view such arrangements as alternatives to debt financing.

Leases and Accounting Regulations

The accounting treatment for leases in general, and real estate sale-leasebacks in particular, are very detailed and complicated. In establishing accounting rules, the

Financial Accounting Standards Board (FASB) has attempted to cover virtually every type of sale-leaseback arrangement imaginable. It is not our purpose here to give you thorough training in the rules of real estate sale-leaseback accounting. Instead, we will provide an overview and an example or two to show the nature and intent of the accounting regulations. If you are interested in an exhaustive analysis of accounting for real estate sale-leasebacks, you may consult authoritative accounting sources for that material.[2]

Accounting for Leases in General. Accounting standards attempt to distinguish between a normal business lease and a lease that is a substitute for debt financing. The former types of leases are termed **operating leases**, and the latter are called **capital leases**. In general, if it appears that a lease is a substitute or alternative for debt financing, the accounting rules will require that the leased property and the present value of the future lease payments be carried on the balance sheet as an asset and liability, respectively. Lease payments are accordingly treated as interest expense. A lease will be considered a capital lease if the risks and rewards of ownership are basically retained by the firm that uses the asset. Specifically, a lease is a capital lease if it meets any one of the following criteria:

1. The lease terms provide for the transfer of the ownership (title) of the property to the lessee at the end of the lease term.
2. The lease contains an option to purchase the asset at a bargain price.
3. The lease term is equal to or greater than 75 percent of the estimated economic life of the asset.
4. The present value of the minimum lease payments is equal to or greater than 90 percent of the current fair market value of the asset (less any investment tax credit retained by the lessor).

As you can see, each of these criteria establishes some sort of ownership position for the lessee.

Accounting for Real Estate Sale-Leasebacks. The primary accounting rules that govern the sale-leaseback transaction are set out in the following Statement of Financial Accounting Standards (SFAS):

1. SFAS No. 13, accounting for leases;
2. SFAS No. 28, accounting for sales with leasebacks;
3. SFAS No. 66, accounting for sale of real estate; and
4. SFAS No. 98, accounting for leases: sale-leaseback transactions involving real estate, sales-type loans of real estate, definition of lease term, initial direct costs of direct financing leases.

The last statement, issued in May 1988, encapsulates the rules of the earlier statements for all sale-leaseback transactions involving real estate. **SFAS 98** amends Paragraph 40 of SFAS 66, which previously directed the accountant to SFAS 13 for guidance in recognizing gain in sale-leaseback transactions. SFAS 13 had less stringent requirements for sale recognition than did SFAS 66. In particular, Paragraph 28 of SFAS 66 prohibits a seller from recognizing a sale in a sale-leaseback transaction, because lease payments were interpreted as a guarantee of return to the buyer. Some accountants, therefore, relied on Paragraph 40, which directed them to the more liberal rules of SFAS 13. Now, SFAS 98 clears any confusion and establishes rather strict rules before a sale leaseback transaction can be treated as a sale.

Under SFAS 98 rules, not all sale-leaseback arrangements will be considered capital leases, however. An owner of a commercial real estate property can sell it and lease it back, yet treat the transaction as a sale. That is, the property will be removed from the balance sheet, and lease expenses will not be treated as interest expense. If this is done, then the accounting rules indicate the sale can be treated as a sale-leaseback. However, if certain very strict criteria are met, then the owner may not treat the sale-leaseback as such, but must treat the arrangement as a capital lease and retain the asset on the balance sheet, along with a liability for the lease payments. In general, to be treated as a sale-leaseback (and not as a capital lease), the arrangement must transfer the risks and rewards of ownership to the new owner. There are two very widely used features of sale-leasebacks that do not transfer risk and returns and that prohibit accounting for the transfer as a sale. First, the seller-lessee either has an obligation or an option to repurchase the property. Often it is an obligation to repurchase the property at a given price, so as to insulate the buyer from the risk of depreciation. A right of first refusal on an offer from a third party ordinarily is not considered as an option or an obligation to repurchase the property. Second, the seller-lessee guarantees the buyer-lessor's return on the investment for either a limited or extended period of time.

Each of these two provisions indicates that the **risks and returns of ownership** are not transferred to the buyer-lessor and, therefore, treating the transaction as a sale would not be warranted. There are several additional commonly-used terms of sale-leaseback agreements that indicate that the risk and rewards of ownership are not transferred or that, subsequent to sale, the seller-lessee has some continued involvement with the property in an ownership capacity. A third term is that the seller-lessee is required to compensate the buyer-lessor for a decline in the fair market value of the property at the end of the lease term (except for a decline resulting from normal wear and tear). Fourth, the seller-lessee provides nonrecourse financing for all or a portion of the sales price. Fifth, the seller-lessee is not relieved of any existing debt on the property that may be assumed by the buyer-lessor. Sixth, the seller-lessee lease payment is contingent on the economic performance of the property. Seventh, the buyer-lessor is obligated to share with the seller-lessee a portion of the appreciation in the value of the property over the term of the lease.

If any of these (or other criteria outlined in SFAS 98) are met, the seller-lessee cannot account for the transaction as a sale of the property. The seller-lessee will have to carry the asset on the balance sheet, will report sales proceeds as a liability (called a finance obligation), will report all or a portion of the lease payments as interest expense, and will defer the recognition of any gain or loss on the sale until such a time that the transaction can be considered a sale. Sometimes the terms of a sale-leaseback will indicate that, for example, the seller-lessee has an option to repurchase the property within 5 years of a 10-year lease. After the fifth year, if the option is not exercised, then the transaction may qualify for sales treatment. At that time, the accounting statements will be adjusted to reflect the sale, including the recognition of any gain or loss on the property.

Examples of Sale-Leaseback Accounting. It will be instructive at this point to provide a couple of examples of **sale-leaseback accounting** for transactions. The examples show how certain arrangements must be treated as though the property is retained by the seller and financed with debt.

EXAMPLE 1

Investor B (the seller-lessee) sells a building to a buyer-lessor for $1 million and enters into an agreement to lease the building for 5 years at $120,000 annually. The lease agreement includes an option to repurchase the property, and the seller guarantees that

TABLE 19-17

Calculation of Gain on Sale of Property Example 1

Sales price	$1,000,000
Basis	475,000[a]
Gain to be recognized	525,000

[a]$1,300,000 − $450,000 − [5 × $75,000]

Source: © 2014 OnCourse Learning

TABLE 19-18

Journal Entries for Example 1

	DEBIT	CREDIT
Year 1		
Cash	$1,000,000	
Finance obligation		$1,000,000
Annual Journal Entries: Years 1 through 5		
Depreciation expense	$75,000	
Accumulated depreciation		$75,000
Interest expense	120,000	
Cash		120,000
Year 5		
Recognition of gain on sale:		
Accumulation depreciation	$825,000	
Finance lease obligation	1,000,000	
Property		$1,300,000
Cash		35,000
Gain on sale		490,000[a]

[a]$525,000 gain less $35,000 payment or guarantee.

Source: © 2014 OnCourse Learning

the residual value of the property will be at least $1 million at the end of the lease term. The historical cost of the property is $1.3 million and the accumulated depreciation is $450,000. Annual depreciation is $75,000. After the initial lease term is up, the seller-lessee decides not to exercise the option to repurchase the property but instead purchases another, unrelated property. The fair market value of the property at the time is $965,000, so the seller-lessee pays the buyer-lessor $35,000 to honor the guarantee of residual value.

At the time of the sale-leaseback, the transaction cannot be accounted for as a sale because of the option to repurchase and the guarantee of the residual value. At the end of the 5-year lease term, the seller-lessee has no further involvement with the property. It qualifies for treatment as a sale at that time.

Table 19-17 shows the calculation of the gain on the sale of the property. Recall that the gain will be recognized only in year 5 after the purchase option has expired. The gain is calculated with reference to the accumulated depreciation at the end of the lease term. Table 19-18 shows the journal entries associated with the sale-leaseback transaction. The sale of the property in year 1 establishes a liability called a **finance obligation**. Annual entries for the lease payments are recorded as interest expense. After the lease term expires and the repurchase option expires, the property and finance obligation are removed from the books of the seller-lessee. Also at this time, the gain on the sale of the property is recognized.

This first example illustrates a relatively simple transaction. The following example illustrates a somewhat more complicated arrangement.

EXAMPLE 2

In this example, we assume the same set of circumstances as in the first example, with the following changes: (1) There is no guarantee of the residual value of the property at the end of the lease term, and (2) the seller-lessee finances a portion of the sales price by making a nonrecourse note for $950,000.

The option to purchase expires unexercised at the end of the 5-year lease term. There are two consequences of the nonrecourse seller financing. First, the transaction cannot be accounted for as a sale, but must be treated as a financed lease. Second, the note complicates the accounting for the finance obligation. Recall that the finance obligation is set up as a liability on the balance sheet of the seller-lessee. This is part of the arrangement establishing the transaction as a financing and not a sale. Lease payments to the new owner are treated just as payments on a debt would be—part interest expense and part reduction in the "debt" liability (finance obligation). However, in this case, the transaction involves annual payments by the buyer on the seller's note. A portion of these expenses will be considered interest income, and a portion will be considered an increase in the finance obligation (not a reduction in an asset, called a note receivable, because no such asset is recorded). Thus, things are happening with the finance obligation: Lease payments by the seller-lessee reduce this liability item, and note payments by the buyer-lessor increase it.

Also, at the time that the transaction can be recognized as a sale, the effects of the interest expense and income over the 5-year term of the lease must be adjusted (reversed). The adjustment is made to the retained earnings of Investor B but through the recognition of the gain on the sale. The calculation of the gain is shown in Table 19-19. The adjustments reflect the reversal of the interest charges and credits on the lease and note payments, respectively. The supporting schedules for the items in Table 19-19 are included in Appendix 19-A. Table 19-20 shows the journal entries for this transaction. The interest expense portion of the lease payment is established assuming a 10 percent rate. The actual rate used must be computed using the so-called interest method, a discussion of which is beyond the scope here. For simplicity, we assume a 10 percent rate. Because the sale is recognized at the end of the lease term, the finance obligation is removed as a liability and the balance of the note receivable is established as an asset. Also, the property, along with its accumulated depreciation, is removed from the balance sheet, and the gain is recognized.

The essence of the accounting rules is to treat the sale-leaseback transaction as a financing until the criteria used to determine sales status are met. This generally occurs when all of the risks and rewards have been transferred to the buyer and the lender has no involvement with the property from the perspective of ownership. A virtually limitless number of variations of sale-leaseback agreements can be constructed. Each will involve variations as to the magnitude and timing of the transfer of the risks and rewards to the buyer. You should be aware that the accounting rules on the more complex transactions can be very complicated. The accounting rules and regulations are designed to cause the financial statements of the seller-lessee to reflect the substance of the sale-leaseback transaction and not the form.

TABLE 19-19

Calculation of Gain on Sale of Property Example 2

	Sale price	$1,000,000
	Basis	475,000
		$525,000
Adjustments		
Lease expense charged to finance obligation; Years 1–5		$(600,000)
Interest expense charged to income; Years 1–5		76,178
Interest income credited to finance obligation; Years 1–5		452,748
Gain to be recognized		453,926

Source: © 2014 OnCourse Learning

TABLE 19-20
Journal Entries for Example 2

DESCRIPTION	DEBIT	CREDIT
Year 1		
Cash	$50,000	
Finance obligation		$1,050,000
Annual Journal Entries: Years 1–5		
Cash	$161,311	
Finance obligation		$161,311
(Collection of payment on $900,000 note)		
Depreciation expense	75,000	
Accumulation depreciation		75,000
Nonrecurring Journal Entries; Years 1–5		
Year 1		
Finance obligation	$115,000	
Interest expense	5,000	
Cash		$1,120,000
Year 2		
Finance obligation	$110,369	
Interest expense	9,631	
Cash		$1,120,000
Year 3		
Finance obligation	$105,275	
Interest expense	14,725	
Cash		$1,120,000
Year 4		
Finance obligation	$99,671	
Interest expense	20,329	
Cash		$1,120,000
Year 5		
Finance obligation	$93,507	
Interest expense	26,493	
Cash		$1,120,000
Year 5		
Finance obligation	$332,733[a]	
Note receivable	596,193[a]	
Accumulation depreciation	875,000	
Property		$1,300,000
Gain on sale		453,926

[a]*From Appendix A.*

Source: © 2014 OnCourse Learning

GROUND LEASE MORTGAGES

Sometimes lenders will write a loan against a ground lease.[3] A **ground lease mortgage** is unusual because the borrower does not own the land. The land is leased from the owner/developer for construction of improvements. These arrangements are most common in densely populated areas. Long a staple in syndicated partnership transactions, ground leases have also been used in low-income housing tax credit transactions and multi-use development projects involving separate retail, entertainment, office, and/or residential components. Usually the terms of the lease call for ownership of the improvement to pass to the land owner at expiration of the lease. Sometimes the lease will give the tenant an option to purchase. Ground leases are written for long terms (50 years is not uncommon) and are generally structured as triple-net leases.

The treatment of ground lease loans can vary. In some states loans made to the owner-developer secured by the lease are viewed as real property and treated the same as a mortgage loan. In other states the lease is viewed legally as personalty and is secured under the Uniform Commercial Code Financing Statement. In either case, the lender can foreclose on the lease if the borrower defaults. The Bankruptcy Reform Act enacted in 1994 provided some clarification of lenders' rights to collateralize leases. It also provided some protection for lenders in the event of landowner bankruptcy.

CREDIT-BASED FINANCING

Credit-based financing uses the tenant's good credit rather than the real estate asset itself as the basis for financing. This type of financing may be useful when the tenant has stronger credit than the landlord. Two formats are available for credit-based financing.[4] Both require a direct financing agreement with the tenant. In either case, credit-based financing falls outside the traditional real estate financing areas of mortgage and general obligation bond financing.

In the first format, **multisite securitization**, a pool of facilities is net leased to the tenant. A third-party entity is established to build the facilities and repay debt backed by the properties and the rental receivables. Securitized debt in this fashion may be more desirable by the tenant than having the developer finance each site separately if the funds are less costly. Also, securitization would allow the tenant to pool a number of small and/or scattered facilities. Various types of lease arrangements may allow the tenant to repay the debt and purchase the facilities.

The second format is **tenant improvements financing**. In this case tenant improvements are financed in a personal property lease. The tenant improvements financing—but not the real estate—is conveyed to the third-party financier. The accounting treatment of this arrangement is acceptable to the tenant since it is the same as if the tenant improvements were included in rents paid to the landlord. Both tenants and landlords may have incentives to use credit-based financing. For a tenant these may be financing an expensive new facility or financing a group of facilities. Other advantages for the tenant are off-balance-sheet accounting, 100 percent financing, and the flexibility to take real estate as is (thereby obtaining a better economic deal). For landlords the incentives may be the ability to deliver substantial allowances, thereby attracting more and/or new tenants and enhancing their property values.

Summary

In this chapter, we discussed the different ways of financing existing income-producing properties. One common method is by a standard, long-term loan not much different from a loan on a residential property. These permanent loans do not reflect the nature of the collateral, however. Generally, the underwriting criteria are more strict than with residential loans. The riskiness of the cash flows of commercial properties requires a careful analysis of the property and generally leads to lower loan-to-value ratios than on residential properties. The risk of commercial loans also is reduced by an assignment of rent provision in the note. Prepayment penalties are also common with these loans. The prepayment penalties, which may be determined with reference to market interest rates, reduce the interest rate risk exposure for the lender.

Alternative loan arrangements include equity-participation loans and sale-leaseback transactions. Equity-participation loans grant a share of the income of the property or a share of the property's appreciation to the lender in return for a lower interest rate. Essentially, this type of loan increases the amount of equity in the deal and gives a portion of the equity to the lender. The risk for the lender is increased, and the risk for the investor is decreased. In an efficient market, one would expect that the investor could not gain from the trade-off, since its terms should be priced to reflect the transfer of risk. There are no tax benefits to either party for equity-participation loans; both the interest and the participation payments are tax deductible to the investor and are also taxable income to the lender.

There may be some benefit to the arrangement for both parties if the discount rate used to value the cash flows does not change commensurate with the transfer of risk. Briefly, the lender may not view the increase in risk as warranting an increase in the discount rate. This may be true for lenders seeking an inflation hedge or for lenders with negative net worth seeking more risky investments to extricate themselves from their insolvency.

Sale-leaseback transactions can be viewed as an alternative to debt financing. It can be shown that the cash flows from such a transaction are identical to those of a debt financing. Sale-leaseback transactions appear to have little advantage compared to more traditional debt financing of the property. At one time, such a transaction might have led to fewer taxes because of the greater depreciation allowed by a stepped-up basis. With the new tax laws in place, there may be little tax relief from a larger basis generated by a sale. Window dressing advantages (where the financial statements reflect a greater return on assets and a smaller debt-to-equity ratio) have been frustrated by accounting regulations that require the transaction be recorded on the financial statements as a debt financing. SAFS 98 requires that, if certain criteria are met, the property be carried on the books as an asset and a liability be established for the debt. This is so even if title to the property has been transferred to the buyer. The criteria that require this type of financial reporting hinge on whether or not the risks and returns of property ownership have been transferred to the buyer. If not, then the transaction cannot be reported as a sale but must be reported as a financing.

Key Terms

Assignment of rents	Risks and returns of ownership
Capital leases	Sale-leaseback
Credit-based financing	Sale-leaseback accounting
Equity-participation loan	SFAS 98
Finance obligation	Stepped-up basis
Ground lease mortgage	Tenant improvements financing
Multisite securitization	Window dressing
Operating leases	Yield maintenance prepayment penalty
Prepayment penalties	

Review Questions

19-1.   Compare long-term commercial property loans with their residential counterparts. Explain the reasons for any differences.

19-2.   a. Define an equity-participation loan.
          b. Give an example of the terms of an equity-participation loan.

19-3. Concerning an equity-participation loan:
a. What are the advantages for a property investor?
b. What are the advantages for a lender?
c. How can both parties benefit from this type of loan?

19-4. Compare a sale-leaseback transaction to the alternative of standard debt financing by noting the similarities and differences between the two.

19-5. Indicate the factors that would have made sale-leaseback transactions attractive in earlier times. Indicate the recent tax and accounting changes that have reduced the attractiveness of sale-leasebacks.

19-6. Distinguish, by definition, between operating and capital leases in general. Indicate the criteria that establish a lease as a capital lease.

19-7. List five terms of a sale-leaseback transaction that would require accounting as a financing rather than as a sale.

19-8. If a sale-leaseback must be treated as a financing, generally describe how the financial statements reflect the transaction.

Problems   All Files
Equity
Participation

19-1. An investor can purchase a property for which the net present value of the expected cash flows to equity (15 percent discount rate) is $400,000 for a 5-year holding period. The purchase can be made with a standard, long-term, fixed-rate loan. Now, consider the following alternative equity-participation loan.

BASIC TERMS

Project cost	
Land	$300,000
Building	$2,500,000[a]
Total	$2,800,000
Project financing	
Loan amount	$2,000,000
Interest rate	9%
Amortization	30 years
Participation terms	
Share of NOI	20% over $250,000
Share of appreciation	15%
Discount rates	
Investor	14.75%
Lender	12.25%
Holding period	5 years
Operating data	
Gross rent, year 1	$522,100
Vacancy rate	5%
Operating expense, year 1	$83,536 (16% of gross rent)
Growth rates	
Gross rent	8%
Operating expense	7%
Resale value	6%
Resale expense rate	5%
Investor's marginal tax rate	28%

[a]*Depreciation years 1 and 5 = $87,000; other years = $91,000.*

a. Determine the after-tax cash flows from operations for the 5-year holding period. (Check figure: Year 3 value is $194,578.)

b. Determine the after-tax cash flow from the sale of the property in year 5. (Check figure: Share of participation to the lender upon sale is $142,055.)

c. Determine the net present value of expected after-tax cash flows to the investor.

All Files
Equity
Participation

19-2.   For the loan in Problem 19-1:

a. Determine the cash flows to the lender for the 5-year holding period. (Check figure: Year 2 value is $233,931.)

b. Determine the total cash flow to the lender in the year of the sale of the property. (Check figure: share of NOI in year 5 is $63,059.)

c. Determine the net present value of the expected cash flows to the lender.

All Files
Equity
Participation

19-3.   Compare the net present values of the equity-participation loan in the above problems to a standard loan. Should the investor agree to the loan? Should the lender agree to the loan?

19-4.   You are trying to decide whether to lease or buy warehouse space for the next 5 years. Since you will pay property taxes, insurance, and maintenance in either case (a triple-net lease), the major factors to consider are the debt service and depreciation versus the cost of the lease. The property that suits your needs has the following characteristics:

Purchase price	$300,000
Building value	$240,000
Land value	$60,000
Selling price EOY5	$400,000
Interest-only mortgage	$225,000 at 9%, balance paid end of year 5
Marginal tax rate	28%
Required equity yield	14%
Lease payment if leased	$22,000 per year

a. Which alternative is preferable?

b. What is the break-even point at which you would be indifferent between the two options?

19-5.   Assume the following information about a commercial warehouse facility.

Original cost	$1,500,000
Book value	0
Market value	$1,800,000
Value of building	$1,500,000
Value of land	$300,000
Annual depreciation	0
Debt	$100,000
Rate	12%
Term	10 years
Payment	$17,698
Investor's tax rate	28%
Year 1 NOI	$338,900
Growth in NOI	0%

a. Calculate the after-tax cash flows from operations for the next 10 years. (Check figure: Year 3 value is $229,264.)

b. Assuming the investor has a 15 percent required rate of return (discount rate), calculate the present value of the after-tax cash flows from operations for the 10-year period.

c. Calculate the after-tax cash flows from a sale-leaseback assuming (1) annual lease expense of $275,000, (2) the property is sold and repurchased for $1,800,000, and (3) repurchased in year 10.

d. Calculate the cash flows to the buyer-lessor. (Assume the buyer-lessor is in the 28 percent tax bracket.)

e. Assuming the buyer-lessor has a discount rate of 12 percent, calculate the present value of the cash flows.

f. Assuming no objections to the arrangement from the IRS, should the sale-leaseback be undertaken? Why or why not?

Notes

1. Jaime R. Alvayay, Ronald C. Rutherford, and William S. Smith. Tax rules and the sale and leaseback of corporate real estate, *Real Estate Economics* 23(2) (1995), 207–238.

2. A good source is Financial Accounting Standards Board. *Accounting Standards, General Standards.* Homewood, IL: Irwin Publishing Co., 1991.

3. T. Cornwell. Ground lease mortgages easier now. *National Mortgage News* 19 (December 5, 1994), 2.

4. A good discussion of credit-based financing is found in Miller Blew. Credit-based financing: New tools for tenants and landlords. *Corporate Real Estate Executive.* Boston: Greyfield Finance, 1993.

Web Sites

http://www.loanuniverse.com/realestate.html
Real estate commercial financing

http://www.iirealestate.com
Real estate financing and investment

APPENDIX 19-A

Supporting Schedules for Example 2

CALCULATION OF FINANCE OBLIGATION ACCOUNT; YEARS 1–5

	YEAR 1	YEAR 2	YEAR 3	YEAR 4	YEAR 5
Beginning balance	$ 50,000[a]	$ 96,311	$147,253	$203,289	$264,929
Plus note payment	161,311	161,311	161,311	161,311	161,311
Less lease payment	(115,000)	(110,369)	(105,275)	(99,671)	(93,507)
Ending balance	$ 96,311	$147,253	$203,289	$264,929	$332,733

AMORTIZATION OF NOTE; YEARS 1–5

	YEAR 1	YEAR 2	YEAR 3	YEAR 4	YEAR 5
Beginning balance	$950,000	$893,189	$830,129	$760,132	$682,436
Plus note payment	104,500	98,251	91,314	83,615	75,068
Less lease payment	(161,311)	(161,311)	(161,311)	(161,311)	(161,311)
Ending balance	$893,189	$830,129	$760,132	$682,436	$596,193

Sum of interest portion = $452,748

[a]*Initial deposit.*

OWNERSHIP STRUCTURES FOR FINANCING AND HOLDING REAL ESTATE

CHAPTER

20

LEARNING OBJECTIVES

Real estate properties can be held in several forms of ownership, including individual, corporate, partnership, and trust ownership. After reading this chapter, you should understand that the ownership form is defined by legal considerations, but that the choice of ownership form is driven by institutional and economic considerations. You should know the three main determinants of the form in which real estate is held: the federal tax environment, issues of personal liability, and access to equity capital markets. In addition, investors will be concerned with issues related to control and transfer of the property, as well as the continuity of the ownership structure. Unless there are overriding considerations, real estate will be held by that structure that tends to pass on to the owners the most after-tax dollars. You also will understand that investors are averse to incurring liability beyond the amount of their investment. You will see that the illiquid nature of individual real estate properties affects the choice of ownership form. Next, you should understand the basic tax regulations and legal considerations that govern each type of ownership form. Finally, you should be able to compare the risks and returns of various ownership forms.

INTRODUCTION

Several alternative ownership structures can be used to hold real estate properties. Properties can be held by an individual, a corporation (both chapter C and chapter S), a partnership (private or publicly traded), or a trust. The choice of ownership is driven by tax considerations and institutional constraints in accessing large equity markets. The federal government has played an active role in determining the ownership form of real estate by passing legislation affecting how the various ownership forms are taxed. Investors will choose that ownership form that provides them with the most after-tax cash flows. The intrinsic value of a property is determined by its expected cash flows and the risk of those cash flows.

Beyond that, the ownership form is determined primarily by tax regulations. Investors typically wish to minimize their income tax liability. In general, the corporate form of organization is not well suited for this, whereas the partnership form is.

Of course, other considerations come into play. Legal factors, such as personal liability, will affect the ownership form. Investors desire to be insulated from personal liability. For example, in the event of bankruptcy, investors want to be liable only for the amount they have invested. As expected, in an efficient market, insulation from liability has a price. Some ownership forms shift liability from certain investors to others. The trade-off is priced in terms of return on the various interests: those accepting more personal liability obtain a greater return. Both the corporate form and the real estate limited partnership (RELP) form insulate investors from personal liability beyond the amount invested.

Also, economic factors such as access to capital markets affect the ownership form. Access to large, efficient capital markets lowers liquidity risk. Real estate properties are not liquid. Liquidity can be enhanced by virtue of the form of ownership, however. Although a corporation can purchase real estate, and the shares of a sufficiently large corporation can be exchanged in the large, efficient equity market, the double taxation associated with the corporate form of organization presents a major deterrent to the use of this structure. Fortunately, tax rules allow a certain specially designed form of corporation to avoid the double taxation. This form, called a real estate investment trust (REIT),[1] provides liquidity by providing access to large capital markets without the burdensome double taxation. It is not surprising that increasing amounts of real estate have been securitized, or held in the form of REITs. Tax regulations have, in fact, pushed this structure to the forefront.

In summary, access to large, efficient capital markets lowers the financing cost through the reduction in liquidity risk. Also, flotation costs of securities, relative to the size of the investment, are lower when they are issued in large capital markets. Other ownership forms remain because of the special advantages they may provide investors.

In the next section, we present the various ownership forms that can be used to hold real estate and give a brief description of each. Then we will make a more detailed examination of two forms of ownership structure: the real estate limited partnership and the real estate investment trust.

FORMS OF REAL ESTATE OWNERSHIP

Table 20-1 outlines the various forms by which real estate properties can be owned. Each of these forms is discussed briefly here.

Sole Ownership

This form of ownership is exactly as the term implies. Real estate can be owned at the individual investor level. Usually, sole owners will have modest portfolios of properties. They may hold several residential properties, occasionally a small apartment complex or small strip shopping center. Such investors will have to rely heavily on debt to secure any sizable portfolios because of their limited equity. Individual owners do not have access to the large equity markets. In such cases, the property will secure the debt, which is likely to take the form of a recourse note. If the note is recourse, the investor is personally liable for any loss. Thus, if the value of the property falls below the amount of the indebtedness and the investor defaults on the loan, the lender can seek a judgment for the deficiency.

TABLE 20-1

Ownership Forms for Real Estate

FORM	MAJOR CHARACTERISTICS
Sole ownership	Low liquidity, control over property
Corporations:	
C corporation	Double taxation
S corporation	No double taxation, limited number of shareholders
Partnerships:	
General	Unlimited liability, control over property
Limited	Limited liability, centralized management
Publicly traded partnership	Limited liability, access to capital markets
Real estate investment trusts	No double taxation, access to capital markets, high liquidity

Source: © 2014 OnCourse Learning

Antideficiency statutes in some states usually do not apply to investor-owned (commercial) properties. There is no double taxation as with the corporate form of ownership. Losses sustained by the individual owner can be used to offset other positive income, but only if the owner actively participates in the management of the properties. Annual operating losses that can be used in this manner are limited to the $25,000 exemption. For all of these reasons there is little investor-owned (as opposed to owner-occupied housing) real estate at the personal level.

CHARACTERISTICS OF SOLE OWNERSHIP

Tax environment	Fair to moderate
Personal liability	Significant
Access to capital markets	Poor
Overall	Poor to moderate

Corporate Form of Ownership

Legally, corporations have identities separate from that of their stockholders. There are two types of corporate structure: the regular **C corporation** and the **S corporation**. They are named after different chapters in the tax code that set forth how each is treated from the tax standpoint. Since a regular C corporation is the standard corporation and is recognized as having a legal identity separate from its stockholders, it earns income and incurs liabilities; the stockholders do not. Taxes must be paid on the corporate income. The corporation also distributes dividends to the stockholders from any excess after-tax earnings. Because the corporation pays a tax on its income and then the stockholders pay a tax on their dividends, the term **double taxation** applies to this form of ownership. The impact of double taxation can be onerous.

Consider a small real estate investment. Assume that a strip shopping center produces $100,000 annually after operating expenses and after interest payments on debt. If the shopping center is owned by an individual, the owner will pay federal income taxes based on the individual's tax rate—for example, 28 percent. The cash flow after tax is $72,000 for this investor. On the other hand, if the shopping center is owned by a corporation, the sole shareholder of which is the same hypothetical investor, then the after-tax cash flows will be somewhat less. If the corporate tax rate is 35 percent, then the corporation will have a $65,000 after-tax cash flow to distribute to the stockholder in the form of a dividend. The stockholder must then pay personal taxes, equal to $18,000 ($65,000 × 28%), on this amount. The after-tax cash flow to the stockholder is now only $46,800, much less than the $72,000 owed as a sole owner.

Regular C corporations exist and endure the double taxation because they provide limited liability to the stockholders, allow access to large equity markets, and often invest in unique assets. There are better vehicles for holding real estate, however—vehicles that provide **limited liability** but avoid double taxation. For these reasons, C corporations are not a desirable ownership structure for investments that are purely or mostly real estate.

CHARACTERISTICS OF CORPORATE OWNERSHIP (C CORPORATIONS)

Tax environment	Poor
Personal liability	None
Access to capital markets	Good
Overall	Poor to moderate

An S corporation derives its name from the Subchapter S section of the IRS (Internal Revenue Service) Code and provides for the same limited liability as the C corporation, but it does not have the double taxation problem since it is a pass-through entity. Tax regulations allow the income (and losses) to be passed through to each stockholder and reported on their individual income tax returns. The major drawback of the S corporation as a real estate ownership form is the limitation on the number of shareholders; an S corporation is limited to no more than 100 shareholders and shareholders must be U.S. citizens/residents. Also S corporations can have only one class of stock, whereas C corporations can have multiple. These restrictions can severely limit the ability of an S corporation to raise substantial amounts of equity, which may be needed for many large real estate investments. Prior to 1983, S corporations were not allowed to receive more than 20 percent of their gross revenue from what is now referred to as passive investment income (for example, rents from commercial real estate properties). However, the Subchapter S Revision Act of 1982 eliminated this restriction, so that S corporations can now invest in real estate properties.

CHARACTERISTICS OF CORPORATE OWNERSHIP (S CORPORATIONS)

Tax environment	Good
Personal liability	None
Access to capital markets	Poor
Overall	Moderate

Partnerships

A *partnership* is an association made up of individuals who pool their resources to carry out an enterprise. Two types of partnerships are defined by law: general and limited. Neither type is taxed at the partnership level, so double taxation is avoided for each. The partners of a general partnership may be held personally liable for the debts of the partnership, however. For those seeking limited liability, the general partnership is not a recommended ownership vehicle. For this reason, general partnerships, where they exist, tend to have only a few partners. The affairs of the enterprise can be attended to by those who may incur potential liabilities. Also, because investors do not wish to expose themselves to unlimited liability, few would even consider becoming a partner in a general partnership. For this reason, general partnerships have little, if any, access to the capital markets. **General partnerships** usually carry out endeavors for which human rather than money capital is required: law firms, accounting firms, and the like.

A **limited partnership** allows for some of the "investing" partners to avoid liability beyond the amount of their investment. A limited partnership must have at least one general partner with unlimited liability. Because of the limited liability, investors are more likely to purchase "interests" in a limited partnership than in a general partnership. There is, likewise, no double taxation. Profits and losses are passed through to the limited partners. Prior to the Tax Reform Act of 1986, when partners' losses could be used to offset other positive income, limited partnerships were one of the dominant ownership forms of real estate. Limited partnerships can be small, private placement partnerships or large publicly traded partnerships (PTPs). We will look more closely at real estate limited partnerships in the next section.

CHARACTERISTICS OF PARTNERSHIP OWNERSHIP

Tax environment	Good
Personal liability	None
Access to capital markets	Good (for PTPs)
Overall	Good

Real Estate Investment Trusts

REITs must be structured as a corporation, trust, or association and be managed by a board of directors or trustees. The REIT must have transferable shares or certificates of interest and must not be a financial institution or an insurance company. Prior to 1960 some real estate was held in trust form to avoid the double taxation associated with the corporate structure. Beneficial interests in the trusts were then sold in the capital markets. In 1960 Congress passed the Real Estate Investment Trust Act. The act authorizes the corporate form of real estate ownership, but with no double taxation as long as certain restrictive conditions are met. The restrictions, described later in this chapter, relate primarily to the form of assets that a REIT can invest in and the type of income it can generate. There are also restrictive conditions relating to the distribution of income to shareholders. Now, virtually all REITs have a corporate form of ownership. Their limited liability, favorable tax status, and access to capital markets make them a favored vehicle for ownership of large portfolios of properties.

CHARACTERISTICS OF REITs

Tax environment	Good
Personal liability	None
Access to capital markets	Good
Overall	Excellent

Because tax regulations, liability issues, and access to capital markets are important in the determination of the ownership structure of real estate, we will take a closer look at two forms of ownership that successfully meet investment criteria in these areas. Both real estate limited partnerships and real estate investment trusts are important investment vehicles and sources of financing for real estate properties.

| A CLOSER LOOK AT REAL ESTATE LIMITED PARTNERSHIPS AND REAL ESTATE INVESTMENT TRUSTS | ## Real Estate Limited Partnerships |

A CLOSER LOOK AT REAL ESTATE LIMITED PARTNERSHIPS AND REAL ESTATE INVESTMENT TRUSTS

Real Estate Limited Partnerships

Real estate limited partnerships (RELPs) are associations of individuals that form a "partnership" for the purpose of investing in real estate properties. There must be at least one general partner who is liable for the debts of the partnership. The remaining limited partners have no liability beyond their actual or promised contribution to the partnership. The structure and financial arrangements of limited partnerships are governed by the **Uniform Limited Partnership Act (ULPA)**, promulgated in 1916, and the **Revised Uniform Limited Partnership Act**, published in 1976 (more about this revision shortly). The acts establish rules for the determination of when a partnership exists and the relationship among the partners, and between the partners and outside creditors of the partnership. Under the ULPA a limited partnership is one formed by two or more limited partners. The general partners administer the affairs of the partnership and are personally liable for the partnership's debts. As such, the general partners must have sufficient personal financial resources to meet any expected liabilities. As previously stated, the limited partners have no liability beyond their investment and are prohibited from managing the affairs of the partnership or even having their name appear in the partnership name.

All limited partners stand on an equal footing regarding the right to distribution of the partnership assets. Although they are not liable for partnership debts beyond their contribution, they may be required to give the partnership a sum equal to a promised but unpaid contribution or, in some cases, a return of any amounts given to them in the past that may have rightfully belonged to a creator of the partnership. The 1976 revision (adopted by about 70 percent of the states) made it easier for limited partnerships to raise needed capital. Prior to the revision, certain restrictions of the original ULPA had hindered the ability of partnerships to attract investors. For one, the original act prohibited a limited partner from obtaining a security interest on any partnership property in exchange for a loan. Thus, limited partners were not willing to loan the partnership additional capital, since they could not get a security interest. Such rules certainly would discourage large financial institutions from issuing a mortgage on a partnership property and simultaneously being a limited partner. The revision allows any partner to lend money or transact business with the partnership on the same basis as any other person who may not be a partner.

The original act also prevented limited partners from taking part in the control of the partnership without risking their limited-liability status. Many potential investors did not like this provision, since they wanted to have some say in the management of the partnership's assets. Under the revision limited partners may consult with and advise the general partner; approve or disapprove amendments to the partnership agreement; vote on the dissolution of the partnership; vote on the sale, exchange, mortgage, or transfer of substantially all of the assets of the partnership (other than in the ordinary course of business); and vote on the removal of a general partner. Also prior to the revision, ULPA allowed disgruntled partners to sue for the dissolution of the partnership to obtain a return of their contribution. The revision now protects the integrity of the partnership by requiring a disgruntled partner to sue for the contribution just as any general creditor must. In short, the 1976 revision liberalizes the participation of limited partners in the partnership, gives the partnership greater access to additional funds (loans from partners), and protects its integrity from injurious dissolution by dissenting partners.

Limited partnerships experienced their greatest popularity from 1983 through 1989. Limited partnerships were attractive to investors because they could offer benefits of direct ownership without the burden of management responsibility and personal liability. The limited partnerships of the early 1980s were tax-driven mainly due to the accelerated depreciation provided in the Economic Tax Recovery Act of 1981. By the end of the 1980s, however, tax law changes and increased scrutiny had caused limited partnerships to lose favor with investors. The Tax Reform Act of 1986, which instituted the passive loss limitation and extended the "at-risk" limitations to real estate tax shelters, was the biggest factor.

For a time in the mid-1980s master limited partnerships (MLPs) were formed to deal with the Tax Reform Act of 1986. These were designed to produce income so that passive losses could be used to offset the passive income. Favorable income tax rates gave MLPs an advantage over corporations. However, the Revenue Act of 1987 eliminated the tax advantages of MLPs. The consequences in the 1990s for investors already holding limited partnerships were not good due to tax reform and falling real estate prices. The choices have been to continue to own or to sell in the secondary market at deep discounts. Limited partnerships have clearly lost their luster.

Distinguishing a Partnership from a Corporation

A partnership offers significant advantages over the corporate form of ownership, notably the absence of double taxation. However, the Internal Revenue Service requires that certain tests be made to determine if a partnership is indeed a partnership and not a corporation. Actually the tests were designed at a previous time when many professional partnerships (such as medical firms established by a small number of physicians) wanted to be considered corporations for liability purposes. A partnership must pass four tests. In order not to be considered a corporation, the partnership must meet no more than two of the following tests.

Continuity of Life. Because corporations are considered to have a perpetual life, an indication that the partnership will have a termination date points to a partnership and not a corporation. This test is easy to meet. If the partnership has a termination date, even 50 years in the future, it has not passed the first test. Also, if the partnership indicates that the retirement, death, or insanity of the general partner constitutes grounds for the termination and dissolution of the partnership, then it is considered to have a finite life.

Centralized Management. Corporations have a centralized management, as do limited partners. The general partners make the major decisions for the limited partners, with the exceptions discussed earlier. This test would indicate that a limited partnership was a corporation.

Limited Liability. This, of course, is a hallmark of corporations. Limited partnerships must make at least one (general) partner liable for the debts of the partnership. The general partner also must have sufficient assets to meet any contingent liabilities.

Free Transferability of Interest. Stocks of corporations are freely transferable from one owner to another. If there is any doubt about failing to meet two of the first three tests, the limited partnership agreement should specify that interests in the partnership are not transferable without the consent of the general partner. A condition that allowed a transfer of the rights to share in the profits of the partnership but not the management would probably be considered a restriction of **free transferability of interest**. Of course, restrictions on the transferability of interests will lead to a reduction in access to capital markets. Thus, most limited partnerships that contain restrictions on the transferability of interest tend to be small, often intrastate, offerings designed for a small real estate investment. Limited partnerships that desire access to the capital markets will be large, PTPs, sometimes referred to as master limited partnerships.

Master Limited Partnerships

Master limited partnerships (MLPs) or **publicly traded partnerships (PTPs)** had their origin in the need to make the interests in small limited partnerships more liquid. Essentially, one who creates an MLP issues partnership interests in the new, larger partnership in exchange for those in the smaller, less liquid partnerships. Thus, an investor that previously had an interest in a small partnership equal to, for example, 5 percent of the partnership may end up having an interest in the new MLP equal to a much smaller percentage. This MLP "roll-up," as it is called, creates one large partnership out of many smaller ones.[2] The newly formed MLP will have greater liquidity. In fact, interests in MLPs trade on the New York, American, and NASDAQ markets. They were first listed on the New York Stock Exchange in March 1987.

MLPs got their start in February 1981 in the petroleum industry when Apache Petroleum rolled up the interests of many small oil and gas partnerships into a single large one. In all, 33 separate limited partnerships were rolled into one large limited partnership. If the partnership is structured to fail to meet the test for corporate designation, then interests can be traded freely. Notice the use of the term *interest*. What is really transferred is not the ownership in the partnership but rather an assignment of the beneficial interest (units), beneficial assignment certificates (BACs), or depository unit receipts (DURs). These terms indicate that rather than the ownership in the partnership being traded, what is traded is the right to share in the profits and cash distribution of the partnership. Although MLPs got their start in the petroleum industry, virtually all MLPs today are real estate-related. The Omnibus Budget Reconciliation Act of 1987 provided that all MLPs would be treated as corporations for the purpose of taxation. However, certain MLPs were made exempt from this rule—namely, those that derived at least 90 percent of gross income from qualifying income. Qualifying income includes interest, dividends, real property rents, gain on sale of real property, and other items of less interest here. As you can see, the exemptions allow an MLP to be treated as a partnership if it invests heavily in real estate properties. The 1987 act went further, however. It reclassified income from an MLP from passive to portfolio income and indicated that losses could not be offset until the MLP had sufficient positive income in subsequent years. A loss from an MLP cannot be used to offset any other income from another MLP or any other passive income. Neither can MLP partners use their $25,000 exemption for passive activities. About the only tax relief MLP partners receive is an allowance for low-income housing and rehabilitation tax credits. Given this reclassification of income and the restriction on losses, it became apparent that real estate property could be held more effectively by the REIT structure.

REAL ESTATE INVESTMENT TRUSTS

A **real estate investment trust (REIT)** in the United States is a corporate form of organization structured under the rules of the Real Estate Investment Trust Act of 1960 and designed as an investment in real estate properties, the income from which is not taxed at the corporate level. Besides the United States, REITs now exist in a number of other countries. Some examples and the year REITs were introduced include Australia (1971), Bulgaria (2003), Canada (1993), Germany (2007), Hong Kong (2005), Japan (2001), and the United Kingdom (2007).

One intent of the U.S. Congress in creating REITs was to enable small investors to invest in real estate through professionally managed companies. To qualify as a REIT, the organization must meet certain requirements. For decades REITs played a limited role in real estate investment. However, since 1992, the REIT marketplace has increased dramatically. In 2007, nearly 200 REITs were actively traded on the New York Stock Exchange and other markets.

The Internal Revenue Code lists a number of criteria for a REIT to qualify as a tax-free intermediary:

1. It must distribute at least 90 percent of its net annual income (net cash flow) to its shareholders.
2. At least 75 percent of its assets must be real estate, loans secured by real estate, mortgages, shares of other REITs, cash, or government securities.
3. It must derive at least 75 percent of gross income from its real-estate-related investments.
4. It must have 95 percent of its income derived from dividends, interest, and property income.
5. It must have no more than 50 percent of the shares held by five or fewer individuals during the last half of each taxable year.
6. It must have no more than 25 percent of its assets invested in taxable REIT subsidiaries.
7. It must be jointly owned by 100 persons or more.
8. It must be managed by one or more trustees or directors who may be individuals or corporations.
9. It must engage independent advisory and management firms to manage its real estate properties.
10. It must issue transferable shares.
11. It may not be a financial institution or insurance company.

The Tax Reform Act of 1986 changed the investment environment for REITs by reducing dramatically the opportunity for tax shelters in real estate investment. The tax act limited interest deductions, increased depreciation recovery periods, and instituted the passive/active rule. The restriction on passive losses made REITs more attractive as real estate investments. REITs could now own, operate, and manage most types of income-producing real estate by providing the services that were customary with real estate ownership.

The Taxpayer Relief Act of 1997 included the following provisions affecting REITs. A REIT may earn up to 1 percent of its gross income on a property-by-property basis from nominal services to customers. An example would be occasionally helping a tenant move in or out. Also, the 30 percent gross income test was repealed allowing greater sales of properties held for less than 4 years. In addition, hedging rules were relaxed so that income from all types of derivatives is considered qualifying income for purposes of the 90 percent gross income test.

The REIT Modernization Act of 1999 allows REITs to own up to 100 percent of "taxable REIT subsidiaries" (TRS). These are entities that provide services to tenants. Examples include cleaning services, maid service, moving assistance, clerical services, and concierge services. Also, the bill requires a 10 percent or more shareholder of a closely held REIT (when five or fewer persons own 50 percent or more of the REIT) to annualize the dividends for purposes of computing estimated taxes.

The REIT Improvement Act of 2003 favored REITs by removing uncertainties in applying REIT rules, by removing restrictions against foreign investors in REITs, and by imposing monetary penalties for minor violations instead of more damaging REIT disqualification. The three main goals of the act were to: (1) amend REIT tax rules, especially to correct an unintended problem caused by the REIT Modernization Act of 1999 that caused a loss of REIT status by holding commercially ordinary debt such as a loan to a tenant for tenant improvements; (2) align the tax treatment of foreign institutional investors in publicly traded REITs to that of similar investment in other publicly traded companies and to align the tax treatment of REIT capital gains distributions to foreign institutional investors to that of ordinary REIT distributions; and (3) empower the IRS to impose monetary penalties for reasonable cause violations of REIT tests rather than revoke REIT status.

Rules were established to ensure that REITs operate basically as mutual funds for the purpose of holding real estate-related assets. The first three rules ensure that the REIT invests in and engages in real estate activities. Shareholders in the REIT may be individuals, corporations, partnerships, trusts, and estates. Depending on whether the REIT is a trust or corporation, it is run by either a board of trustees or a board of directors. Next, the board must employ an outside advisor to manage the assets of the REIT. The advisor can be a bank, real estate advisory company, life insurance company, or even an individual. The advisor is paid an annual management fee, usually equal to a percentage of the assets managed or the income and gains realized during the year. The advisory fees are not subject to any federal limits, but may be subject to restrictions set by the North American Securities Administration Association (NASAA) in conjunction with state securities regulators. The advisors often can use the REIT as a source of financing. Thus, if the advisor is a mortgage banker, it can use the REIT as a short-term source of financing (warehousing) to originate loans. An advisor who is in real estate development may use the REIT to provide short-term acquisitions, development, and construction (ADC) loans. Finally, there is a provision that prevents the REIT from engaging in short-term speculative real estate transactions. A REIT cannot hold real estate property primarily for sale (in the ordinary course of business). It can sell a property only under certain conditions:

1. It must have held the property for at least 4 years.
2. During the 4-year period prior to sale, it must not have incurred capital expenditures on the property in excess of 30 percent of its sales price.
3. It must not have sold more than seven properties during the same year or the fair market value of all properties sold during the year does not exceed 10 percent of the fair market value of all the REIT's assets as of the beginning of the year.
4. It must not have acquired the property through a foreclosure.

As you can see, REITs must meet a highly restrictive set of conditions to retain favorable tax treatment. The avoidance of double taxation and access to capital markets are sufficient incentives for REITs to meet these conditions. Since the

Tax Reform Act of 1986 placed limits on the pass-through of losses to real estate partnerships, REITs have gained a dominant share of the real estate securities market. In the early 1990s REITs increased their use of joint venture partnerships based on complementary strengths and economies of scale. In 2002 about 24 percent of REIT property acquisitions involved joint ventures.

Because of their nature, measuring the operating performance of REITs has historically been a problem. In 1991 the National Association of REITs (NAR-EITs) developed a definition of **funds from operations (FFO)** to provide a more accurate measure of operating performance of REITs. Industry analysts have generally felt that basing performance on historical cost-accounting approaches could be misleading. In addition, REIT analysts agree that company prices of REIT stocks in terms of conventional price/earnings (P/E) ratios are not meaningful. FFO is net income, excluding gains or losses from debt restructuring and sales of property, plus depreciation and amortization, and after adjustments for unconsolidated partnerships and joint ventures. It can be written as:

$$FFO = \text{net income (GAAP)}$$
$$+ \text{Depreciation (real property)}$$
$$+ \text{Amortization of leasing expenses}$$
$$+ \text{Amortization of tenant improvements}$$
$$+ \text{Gains (losses) from infrequent and unusual events}$$

FFO is not a deviation from generally accepted accounting principles (GAAPs). However, it was designed to not have some of the drawbacks associated with net income under GAAPs. Since its introduction in 1991, this supplemental measurement to net income has significantly benefited the REIT industry by providing an "industry standard" measurement of operating performance. The net asset value (NAV) is the net market value of all of the company's assets minus its liabilities.

A computation to measure the cash available for distribution to shareholders is adjusted FFO (AFFO). AFFO is calculated as FFO minus normalized recurring expenditures (new carpet, tenant improvement allowances, etc.) and straight-lining of rents. This calculation is also called cash available for distribution (CAD) or funds available for distribution (FAD). Straight-lining of rents averages the tenant's rent payments over the life of the lease.

Types of REITs

There are several types of REITs. **Equity REITs** invest in and operate properties. As you will see below, equity REITs can be subclassified if they specialize in the acquisition and operation of certain types of properties. **Mortgage REITs** acquire mortgages, primarily commercial. Here again, some mortgage REITs may specialize in certain types of mortgages just as equity REITs may specialize in certain types of properties. A third type of REIT is a **hybrid REIT**. These REITs invest in both mortgages and properties. Regardless of the type of REIT, equity or mortgage, a given REIT can have its own preferred capital structure. For example, a REIT can issue stock and debt and use the proceeds to purchase only equity properties. It would be an equity REIT, even though it had debt in its capital structure. A fourth type of REIT is a **finite-life**, or **self-liquidating**, REIT. This type is established to purchase and operate properties for a limited and defined period of time. At the expiration of the time frame for the finite-life REIT, the board of directors will sell off the properties, pay off any liabilities, and distribute the remainder to the stockholders. Equity REITs generally liquidate their assets in 5 to 10 years, whereas mortgage REITs may establish a 12-year horizon. As the liquidation date approaches, the market value of the shares will approximate the market value of the properties held by the REIT. For this reason, market values of self-liquidating REITs track the values of the underlying assets much better than is the case for perpetual REITs. The self-liquidating REIT was established, in part, to compete with limited partnerships that almost universally establish liquidation dates. They have several advantages over partnerships, however. The minimum purchase price is generally lower, and the shares can be traded on a liquid market. Shareholders may have more control over the management decisions of the REIT, because the managers must be independent and elected by the stockholders.

REITs can be either open or closed. An **open-end REIT** fund continually offers new stock for sale to investors and uses the proceeds to purchase additional real estate assets. When new stock is issued, the existing assets must be valued so that a price can be set on it. Continuous valuation may prove difficult, especially for REITs that invest in equity properties. For this reason, most REITs are not open-end funds. Rather, they are **closed-end REIT** funds. This means that after the initial stock is issued and assets purchased, no further stock is issued. The value of the existing stock will depend on the performance of the assets in the REIT's portfolio. A closed-end REIT can purchase additional properties from the small amount of earnings (5 percent) it is allowed to retain or from the cash flow afforded by depreciation of existing properties.

A REIT may be an UPREIT or DownREIT. In a DownREIT the REIT owns and operates properties other than its interests in a controlled partnership. In a typical UPREIT, the partners of an existing partnership and a newly formed REIT form a new partnership called the operating partnership. The partners contribute the real estate and the REIT contributes proceeds from its public offering. The REIT is usually the general partner.

REIT Specialization

Many REITs specialize in certain types of real estate. Some REITs invest in hotel/motel properties only, while others may be formed to purchase distressed real estate in recession-hit portions of the country. As of October 31, 1997, the approximate composition of the equity REIT market was retail (24 percent), residential (18 percent), health care (6 percent), office (10 percent), industrial (5 percent), self-storage (3 percent), hotel (7 percent), manufactured homes (2 percent), diversified (13 percent), mortgage-backed securities (7 percent), and other (5 percent). REITs may specialize because of the expertise of their management or advisory group. For example, a REIT may purchase only shopping centers. In fact, specialization can be carried even further; the REIT may invest only in smaller shopping centers in rural areas of the mid-Atlantic states. Some REITs are good at finding somewhat distressed properties, restoring the facility, and finding anchor tenants. Some REITs focus on properties only in particular geographic regions. There is no reason why REITs should consider diversification as essential. We know that potential shareholders of REITs can diversify their portfolio by purchasing shares in numerous REITs. If investors can diversify at the personal level, there will be no reward to the individual REIT for diversifying. In fact, because of particular expertise in certain areas of real estate, it may be worthwhile for a REIT to specialize.

Some REITs specialize in residential mortgages. They may purchase Federal Housing Administration- and Veterans Administration- (FHA- and VA-) insured loans and hold them for investments. By doing this they are really replicating some of the secondary mortgage market agencies. It is not unusual to find REITs specializing in derivative mortgage securities, such as (residential) commercial mortgage obligation (CMO) residuals. Investors may buy the shares of such

REITs as an interest hedging device. Recall from Chapter 11 that the returns on CMO residuals rise when interest rates increase. Thus, if an investor, such as a bank, has a heavy portion of its portfolio in traditional bonds, it may wish to invest in derivative securities that increase in value when rates rise. One way to accomplish this is to invest in REITs that hold the residuals.

REIT Advisors

REIT legislation requires that the assets of the REIT be managed by an independent advisor. Most advisors are financial institutions or firms that specialize in real estate advisory services. Some, such as mortgage bankers and developers, may use the REIT as a short-term source of financing for their non-REIT business. The performance (rate of return) of a REIT will be a function of the quality of its investments, the managerial ability of the advisor, and the fees that the advisor charges. Theoretically, the performance of a REIT should not be affected by the type of advisor. However, at least one study showed that there was an effect. In a study of 105 REITs, Howe and Shilling found that the rate of return on REITs advised by mortgage bankers was significantly less than those on others.[3] The return on REITs advised by life insurance companies and real estate advisor firms performed the best. Thus, there appears to be some evidence that the selection of advisors for a REIT is important.

Development of REITs in the United States

A perspective on the performance of REITs can be gained by looking at Table 20-2. The table shows the total annual return on all equity, mortgage, and hybrid REITs for the period 1972 to 2012. As seen, returns on REITs have been somewhat volatile. For example, in 1974 REITs overall earned a negative 42 percent, while the return was 36 percent and 49 percent for the 2 years following, respectively. In general, returns were lower for REITs in the 1980s, whereas they rebounded in the 1990s. Returns in the late 1990s were dismal with an overall return in 1998 of −19 percent. Returns rebounded somewhat in the 2000s, with a high overall return of 38 percent in 2003. Although the overall return in 2006 was 34 percent, returns plummeted in 2007 to −18 percent. As of 2009, REIT returns have remained generally positive.

Subsequent to moderate initial growth in the early 1970s, the growth of REITs declined in the mid-1970s. After the decline in the importance of REITs in the mid-1970s, REITs made a comeback in the 1980s, the major growth occurring in the late 1980s after the 1986 Tax Reform Act. On the asset side, REITs have significantly reduced their holdings of acquisition, development, and construction loans. On the liability side, REITs have reduced their short-term borrowing. The reasons for the shift in asset and liability position, is the widespread failure and losses attributed to REITs in the mid-1970s. REIT values fell precipitously in the early and mid-1970s. Share value did not reach its 1972 value until 1983. The decline in share values depressed the access of REITs to the capital markets. Investors, aware of the sharp drop, were wary of investing in REITs. Offerings were moderate in the 1980s and then accelerated in the 1990s, especially secondary offerings, until 1998. After a slight lull in the early 2000s, offerings (again secondary offerings) were robust until 2006. Offerings dropped substantially in 2007. Table 20-3 shows the volume of public offerings from 1970 through 2011. Offerings increased in 2008 and have remained at a relatively constant level through 2011.

The widespread failure of REITs in the 1970s gave a black eye to this type of ownership form, and REITs did not recover until the late 1980s. There were two primary reasons for the decline in the number, assets, and value of REITs. One was the maturity mismatch problem that occurred about the same time for thrifts

TABLE 20-2
Annual Total Return for REITs

YEAR	ALL	EQUITY	MORTGAGE
1972	11.19%	8.01%	12.17%
1973	−27.22	−15.52	−36.26
1974	−42.23	−1.40	−45.32
1975	36.34	19.30	40.79
1976	48.97	47.59	51.71
1977	19.08	22.42	17.82
1978	−1.64	10.34	−9.97
1979	30.53	35.86	16.56
1980	28.02	24.47	16.80
1981	8.58	6.00	7.07
1982	31.64	21.60	48.64
1983	25.47	30.64	16.90
1984	14.82	20.93	7.26
1985	5.92	19.10	−5.20
1986	19.18	19.16	19.21
1987	−10.67	−3.64	−15.67
1988	11.36	13.49	7.30
1989	−1.81	8.84	−15.90
1990	−17.35	−15.35	−18.37
1991	35.68	35.70	31.83
1992	12.18	14.59	1.92
1993	18.55	19.65	14.55
1994	0.81	3.17	−24.30
1995	18.31	15.27	63.41
1996	35.75	35.27	50.86
1997	18.86	20.26	3.83
1998	−18.82	−17.50	−29.22
1999	−6.48	−4.62	−33.22
2000	25.89	26.37	15.96
2001	15.50	13.93	77.34
2002	5.22	3.82	31.08
2003	38.47	37.13	57.39
2004	30.41	31.58	18.43
2005	8.29	12.16	−23.19
2006	34.35	35.08	19.32
2007	−17.83	−15.69	−42.35
2008	−37.34%	−37.73%	−31.31
2009	27.45	27.99	24.63
2010	27.58	27.96	22.60
2011	7.28	8.29	−2.42
2012	16.42	15.49	21.50

Source: NAREIT web page (http://www.NAREIT.com).

and was discussed earlier in the text. Essentially, the structure of some of the REITs was almost exactly that of a thrift. In 1974, for example, 34 percent of the assets of all REITs consisted of long-term (other) loans, while nearly half of their sources of funds were in short-term loans (bank borrowings and commercial paper). As interest rates ratcheted upward in the 1970s, REITs had to refinance their borrowing at increasingly higher rates while the return on their assets remained stable. As the market value of REIT assets fell relative to their liability, their equity was eroded. A second reason that many REITs failed was related to an agency problem. In 1974, 47 percent of REIT assets were in land, construction, and development loans. These types of loans can be risky, since they are made to develop a property

TABLE 20-3
Public Offerings of Securities by REITs (millions of dollars)

YEAR	ALL OFFERINGS		INITIAL OFFERINGS		SECONDARY OFFERINGS	
	NUMBER	TOTAL	NUMBER	TOTAL	NUMBER	TOTAL
1970	72	1,687	41	1,358	31	329
1971	78	1,987	32	1,183	46	804
1972	67	1,223	29	563	38	660
1973	68	852	18	157	50	695
1974	17	24	5	2	12	22
1975	5	0.4	1	0.0	4	0.4
1976	8	20	0	0.0	8	19.7
1977	8	92	0	0.0	8	92
1978	12	92	3	8	9	83
1979	18	111	4	0.0	14	111
1980	20	264	4	30	16	234
1981	22	245	5	100	17	145
1982	12	454	3	315	9	139
1983	23	741	4	159	19	582
1984	34	2,730	9	379	25	2,351
1985	59	4,271	29	2,792	30	1,479
1986	63	4,669	20	1,204	43	3,465
1987	50	2,929	12	634	38	2,295
1988	37	3,069	13	1,374	23	1,695
1989	34	2,441	11	1,075	23	1,366
1990	24	1,765	10	882	14	883
1991	35	2,289	8	808	27	1,480
1992	58	6,616	8	919	50	5,698
1993	141	18,327	50	9,335	91	8,991
1994	146	14,771	45	7,176	101	7,596
1995	195	12,435	8	922	187	11,513
1996	221	17,063	6	1,108	215	15,955
1997	463	45,271	26	6,297	437	38,974
1998	474	38,382	17	2,129	457	36,252
1999	205	17,214	2	292	203	16,921
2000	114	10,376	0	0	114	10,376
2001	127	18,752	0	0	127	18,753
2002	187	19,768	3	608	184	19,159
2003	228	25,562	8	2,646	220	22,915
2004	266	38,773	29	7,980	237	30,502
2005	259	38,179	11	3,789	248	33,704
2006	204	49,018	5	2,271	199	46,746
2007	129	36,031	4	1,820	125	34,211
2008	82	17,991	2	491	80	17,500
2009	130	34,656	9	2,990	121	31,366
2010	173	47,450	9	1,975	164	45,476
2011	164	51,280	8	2,307	156	48,973

Source: NAREIT web page (http://www.NAREIT.com).

rather than purchase an existing property. With a development loan, the cash flows are speculative. The interest rate on development loans is higher than for loans for purchase because of the added risk.

The agency problem that arose in the 1970s had to do with originators of development loans selling them to REITs at their face value, when in fact they may have declined in value. Thus, a commercial bank that may be an advisor to a

REIT might cause the REIT to purchase development loans that it has originated and subsequently determined to be very speculative. If a bank (also the REIT advisor) sells the loan to the REIT at face value, it captures a wealth premium at the expense of the stockholders in the REIT. This sort of activity, where REIT advisors sold real estate assets to REITs, caused investors to take a cautious view of REITs. The data in Table 20-3 indicate the public offerings of REITs fell to a trickle in the mid- to late 1970s. Today, land development and construction loans represent only a small percentage of the assets of all REITs. Agency problems can also arise from the type of REIT management: whether it is internally or externally managed. Under external management, agency problems can occur between shareholders and REIT managers. The transformation from external management to self-management in the 1990s helped eliminate the agency problem to some extent. Self-management should promote more responsible managerial behavior.

REITs: A Laboratory for Analyzing Capital Structure Decisions

Regardless of the form of assets held by REITs (equity, mortgage, or hybrid), they may choose to finance a portion of their acquisitions by issuing debt. Those REITs that choose to issue debt are leveraged REITs. They may represent an interesting case. As you know, REITs are not taxed at the entity level. They do not benefit from the tax deductibility of interest payments as do regular corporations. Thus, the tax reasons for leverage are absent in the case of REITs. In this sense, they present an opportunity to view the effect of leverage in a "no-tax world."

Arguments can be presented on either side of the issue of whether or not the use of leverage should increase the value of a REIT. That is, should a REIT use debt to finance its asset acquisitions? Here are some arguments. First, there is the personal tax issue. Even though the REIT entity is not taxed, the bondholders and stockholders of the REIT are. If the personal tax rate on equity is lower than that on interest, then more equity should be used. Fewer dollars will go to the U.S. Treasury. The tax shelter nature of real estate suggests that the tax rate on equity is less than on debt and the use of leverage would negatively impact the value of REITs. Second, if the use of debt increases the probability of bankruptcy and default, a negative impact should result from the use of debt. Third, REITs that borrow funds must compete with taxable firms, for which a portion of their interest payments represents a tax savings. This implies they are at a disadvantage in the marketplace in bidding for debt. The rate they pay will be too high. All of these arguments weigh against the use of debt for REITs.

On the other hand, real estate assets are immovable and readily identifiable. From this standpoint, they generally represent excellent collateral for debt. There is also the argument that firm managers may have better information about the value of the firm than does the marketplace. If management believes that the equity of the REIT is undervalued, they will prefer to issue debt to finance asset acquisitions. (Why issue equity if the firm is not going to receive the full value for the new shares?) This may be a signal to the marketplace that the value of the REIT is greater than that set by the marketplace. We also know that some REIT investors are institutional investors such as pension funds. Pension funds are prohibited from borrowing money to invest in assets. They cannot leverage themselves. Even if they purchase mortgage properties, they may run the risk of incurring the unrelated business income tax (UBIT) discussed earlier in the text. However, REIT investments are specifically exempt from the UBIT provisions. Thus, purchasing leveraged REITs may be a way for such institutional investors to obtain leverage they cannot obtain for themselves. As you can see, the theoretical arguments for the use of debt by REITs are mixed.

The evidence on the effectiveness of REIT leverage is also mixed. Maris and Elayan looked at the cost of capital for 61 REITs in the 1980s.[4] They found there was a slight increase in the cost of capital as a result of the use of leverage. This would imply that the value of the REITs should fall if debt is used. Additional debt raises the average cost of acquiring funds. On the other hand, Howe and Shilling found that the value of a large sample of REITs increased concurrently with the announcement of a debt offering.[5] Conversely, the value of REITs that announced new equity issues fell. In neither study were the changes substantial, however. This indicates that the use of leverage by REITs likely has offsetting impacts.

A Closer Look at Corporate versus Partnership Forms of Ownership

We conclude this chapter with another, more in-depth comparison between the corporate and partnership forms of ownership of real estate. These two ownership forms are alternatives when the REIT form is not a candidate for holding real estate; for example, if the scale of the investment is moderate, if there is the need or desire to retain earnings for reinvestment, or if there is no need for access to large capital markets. Depending on the characteristics of the real estate investment, one or the other form will yield superior returns. Here, we will assume that limited liability is not an issue, since limited partnerships can be used to hold real estate in the partnership form.

The form of ownership that dominates is the one that provides the highest present value of after tax cash flows to the investor. Several items are important. First, it is the present value of the cash flows that matters, not the total income over time. Second, it is after-tax dollars that are measured, not before-tax returns. Thus, tax laws have an important impact on the most advantageous form by which to hold real estate. Finally, it is the return to the investor that matters, not the holding entity. If real estate is held by a corporation, the proper measure of value is the return to the shareholder, not the return at the corporate level.

Prior to the Tax Reform Act of 1986, it was almost always advantageous to hold real estate in the partnership form because of the double taxation of corporations and the pass-through of losses for partnership. If income and cash flows were positive, they would be subject to double taxation under the corporate form of ownership, but only at the investor level under the partnership form. If income was negative (regardless of the cash flows), the losses could not be passed-through with corporate ownership as they could be with partnership ownership. Thus, prior to 1986, the partnership form dominated. The 1986 Tax Reform Act removed this dominance. Recall that the main provision of the 1986 Act was the restriction on the availability of passive losses to offset other income. Although investors in a partnership cannot use passive losses (except to offset passive income), the corporation can use such losses to offset other income. This reduces the sting of the double taxation and gives some advantage to the corporate form. The major disadvantage of the corporate form, however, remains the double taxation of income. Given the tax environment, several factors will determine the best ownership form of real estate.

Amount of Depreciation. Depreciation is a noncash expense that is deductible for tax purposes. Given sufficient depreciation, the net operating income (NOI) of the real estate investment may be near zero (but with positive cash flows). If the NOI of the real estate investment is near zero for a significant portion of the holding period, the double taxation problem nearly disappears. Thus, high levels of depreciation expense will favor the corporate form of ownership. Lower levels of depreciation will result in positive levels of (taxable) NOI, which will favor the partnership form of ownership.

Holding Period. If an investor anticipates a long holding period, this will favor the corporate form of ownership. Any cash flows that are retained by the corporation will not be taxed until distributed. With a long holding period, the cash flows can be reinvested and the longer reinvested cash flows escape the double taxation. The taxes are eventually paid but at a future date, reducing their present value (cost). A shorter holding period favors the partnership form, especially if there are suspended passive losses in the early years of the investment. The suspended losses are available to offset other income only when the property is sold. Thus, a short holding period will result in the use of the suspended loss and the associated tax benefits at an earlier date.

Amount of Retained Earnings. If the investor desires to reinvest a large portion of the cash flows back into the real estate investment, then the corporate form of ownership will be beneficial. Again, the reason is the double taxation. If a large portion of the cash flows is to be retained, the corporation can do so and avoid taxes at the individual investor level. With a partnership, any income flows through to the partner (investor) and is taxed at that level.

Tax Credits. If low-income or rehabilitation tax credits are available for the property, the partnership form may be the best of the two alternatives. With the corporate form, the tax credit accrues at the corporate level. The corporation pays less tax than otherwise, but this means that the investor will eventually receive more cash flows (by virtue of the tax saving at the corporate level) on which taxes must be paid at the personal level. Under a partnership, the tax credits are passed-through directly to the investor.

Use of Debt Financing. In the case where the property is well suited as collateral for debt and equity sources of funding are scarce, the use of a large amount of debt to finance the property may be desirable. This will favor the corporate form of ownership because of the tax shield nature of the interest payments. This argument is the same as the one used above for large depreciation expenses. Thus, for properties that have both large depreciation and interest expenses, the corporate form of ownership may be the most advantageous.

Passive Loss Limitations. An investor may have positive passive income with which to offset passive losses. In such a case, the passive loss limitation is going to be less binding and the partnership form of ownership will be preferred. If the investor has no passive income to offset, this would favor the corporate form since only the corporation can use the passive losses to offset nonpassive income.

Table 20-4 presents a summary of the characteristics of real estate investments that affect the choice of type of ownership—corporate or the partnership form. In general, the double taxation of corporate income places this form of ownership at a

TABLE 20-4

Factors Affecting Optimal Holding Form for Real Estate

FAVORS CORPORATE OWNERSHIP	FAVORS PARTNERSHIP OWNERSHIP
1. Large depreciable base	1. Small depreciable base
2. Long holding period	2. Short holding period
3. Need to retain cash flows	3. Need to distribute cash flows
4. No tax credits available	4. Tax credit available
5. Financed by debts	5. Financed by equity
6. No passive income available	6. Passive income available to be offset by passive losses

Source: © 2014 OnCourse Learning

distinct disadvantage relative to the partnership form. It may take several factors to cause the corporate form of ownership to dominate the partnership form, even with the limitation of passive losses. Yet, for properties that (1) have large amounts of depreciation, (2) are expected to be held for a long period of time, (3) have a need for reinvested cash flows, (4) are not eligible for tax credits, and (5) are debt financed, the corporate form may dominate for the reasons stated here.

The final determination of the best form of ownership can be made by finding the present value of the after-tax cash flows that accrue at the investor (not holding entity) level. The after-tax cash flows will take into effect the lack or presence of double taxation, the deductibility of depreciation and interest expenses, reinvestment of cash flows, and the use of passive losses to offset other income. The present value will take into account the timing of the after-tax cash flows. The preceding discussion is summarized in Table 20-5. There is no perfect ownership vehicle for real estate. Even a sole ownership may be warranted for investors interested in small acquisitions, which they can manage by themselves. However, if one considers the effect of tax legislation, access to capital marketing (liquidity), and the large scale of many real estate investments, then a form of ownership such as a RELP or REIT is likely to be the overall best ownership form.

TABLE 20-5
Summary of Real Estate Ownership Forms

ATTRIBUTE	SOLE OWNERSHIP	C CORPORATION	S CORPORATION	PRIVATE LIMITED PARTNERSHIP	PUBLICLY TRADED PARTNERSHIP	REAL ESTATE INVESTMENT TRUST
Personal liability	Unlimited	Limited	Limited	Limited	Unlimited	Limited
Tax treatment:						
Double taxation	No	Yes	No	None	None	None
Pass-through of losses	Up to $25,000	Offset active business and portfolio	Offset active business loss only	None	None	None
Liquidity	Low	Low	Low	Low	Good	Excellent
Access to equity capital markets	None	Moderate	None	Limited	Good	Excellent
Minimum investment requirement	Burdensome	Moderate	Moderate	Moderate	Moderate	Minimum
Scale of asset acquisition	Small	Medium	Medium	Medium	Medium to large	Large
Government restrictions of financial decisions	None	None	None	None	None	Substantial
Participation in management decisions	Great	Moderate	Great	Moderate	None	None
Overall	Poor to moderate	Poor to moderate	Poor to moderate	Moderate	Moderate to good	Good to excellent
Comments	Good for small investors seeking small properties, ability to diversify limited.	Good for real estate investments with no income but positive cash flow to reinvest.	Mimics a partnership but with limits on number of shareholders.	Useful for small-scale investments. Relatively large cost of raising funds.	Similar to REITs. Since passive losses cannot be used, REITs may be better vehicle.	Tax regulation makes this a good choice for large investments.

Source: © 2014 OnCourse Learning

Summary

Three major factors influence the ownership form for real estate investments: tax regulations, personal (investor) liability, and access to capital markets. Tax regulations affect the investor's after-tax cash flow from the real estate acquisition. Other things being equal, those ownership forms that allow greater (and sooner) after-tax cash flows will be the preferred ownership vehicle. The double taxation of the corporation puts this form at an immediate disadvantage. But the restriction on the pass-through or losses (1986 Tax Reform Act) also has diminished the value of the partnership form. Investors also value limited liability. Leveraged real estate can be especially risky. Should the value of the property fall below that of the indebtedness, the lender will seek judgments to recover the difference. Investors do not desire to become liable for any such amounts beyond their initial investment. Sole ownership will expose investors to this risk. Most other forms of ownership, including corporate, limited partnership, and REIT structures, afford limited liability. For large real estate investments, access to capital markets may be important. Here, the ownership form will have to involve shares or interests that trade on large, efficient, capital markets. Large MLPs and REITs offer much better access to capital markets than do the private limited partnership, S corporation, or sole ownership forms.

Real estate limited partnerships were very popular prior to the Tax Reform Act of 1986. Losses could be passed-through to the limited partners at that time. In many cases, investors in highly leveraged limited partnerships would often receive tax deductions over the first few years at least equal to their initial investment. The restrictions on the use of passive losses introduced by the act have diminished the value of this form of ownership. Unless the partnership has access to large capital markets (MLPs), this form may not be the preferred one.

The REIT structure was created by Congress in 1960. The act that created REITs eliminated the double taxation that is usually present for the corporate form of ownership. REITs did poorly in the 1970s, however, because of maturity mismatch and investment in risky and speculative ADC loans. Rising market interest rates in the 1970s increased the cost of short-term funds for REITs at the same time that the yield on their mortgage portfolio remained low. While their equity was being eroded by the squeeze play from interest rates, many of their speculative ADC loans were going bad. The combination led to widespread failure of REITs, a loss of confidence in this form of real estate ownership, and a drought in new public offerings. REITs made a comeback in the mid- to late 1980s. The maturity of the assets and liabilities was structured better, and the Tax Reform Act of 1986 diminished the value of the partnership form of investment.

The best forms of ownership for large-scale investments remain the large, publicly traded partnership and the REIT. For smaller-scale investments, the corporate form may offer some benefits despite the double taxation. The corporate form of investment may prove prudent (1) if the real estate property is intended to be held for a long period of time, (2) if it is financed with debt, (3) if it has a significant depreciable base, and (4) if the corporation has other income with which to offset losses from the property. Otherwise, for moderate-size investments, the private limited partnership may dominate simply because of the absence of double taxation. All ownership forms of real estate exist because of the wide variety of investors' needs and desires. Even the sole ownership form may be preferred by small investors who desire to have maximum control over the management of the property and can use the $25,000 exemption of pass-through losses allowed to active manager-investors.

Key Terms

C Corporation

Closed-end REIT

Continuity of life

Double taxation

Equity REIT

Finite-life REIT

Free transferability of interest

Funds from operations (FFO)

General partnerships

Hybrid REIT

Limited liability

Limited partnership

Master limited partnerships (MLPs)

Mortgage REIT

Open-end REIT

Publicly traded partnerships (PTPs)

Real estate investment trust (REIT)

Revised Uniform Limited Partnership Act

S Corporation

Self-liquidating REIT

Uniform Limited Partnership Act (ULPA)

Review Questions

20-1. Three general factors affect the form in which investors choose to hold real estate. List each and explain how they affect the ownership form.

20-2. List each ownership form by which investors can hold real estate. List at least one advantage and one disadvantage of each form.

20-3. Explain what is meant by double taxation of corporation income.

20-4. Why would a limited partnership be a better ownership form for real estate than an S corporation?

20-5. How is a limited partnership different from a general partnership?

20-6. List the four IRS tests that distinguish a partnership from a corporation. Indicate which of the four differentiate a partnership from a corporation.

20-7. What is a master limited partnership, and how does it differ from a regular limited partnership?

20-8. List at least six requirements for an association of investors to qualify as a real estate investment trust.

20-9. List and define four types of REITs.

20-10. Explain why large numbers of REITs failed in the 1970s.

20-11. What characteristics of a real estate property investment would favor the corporate form of ownership over the partnership form? What characteristics would favor the partnership form? Explain each answer.

Notes

1. Originally, to avoid taxation, real estate investment trusts were established whereby the real estate was held in trust form, and beneficial interests in the trust were sold in the capital markets. Later, in 1960, the U.S. Treasury allowed real estate to be held in the corporate form and still avoid the double taxation as long as certain restrictive conditions were met. Today, what is still referred to as a real estate investment trust is most probably a corporate form of organization that holds real estate assets.

2. There are other ways of creating MLPs that are beyond the scope of this text.

3. J. Howe and J. Shilling. REIT advisor performance. *AREUEA Journal* 18(4) (Winter 1990), 479–500.

4. B. Maris and F. Elayan. Capital structure and the cost of capital for untaxed firms: The case of REITs. *AREUEA Journal* 18(1) (Spring 1990), 22–39.

5. J. Howe and J. Shilling. Capital structure theory and REIT security offerings. *Journal of Finance* 43(4) (September 1988), 983–993.

Web Sites

http://www.nareit.com
  Web page for the National Association of Real Estate Investment Trusts

http://www.404.gov/answers/reits.htm
  Real estate investment trusts

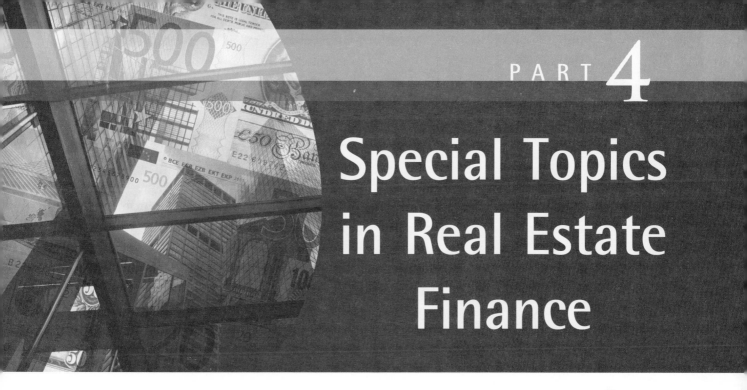

PART 4

Special Topics in Real Estate Finance

*T*he two chapters in this section deal with topics tangential to financing real estate properties. Here, we look at portfolio construction and the role of diversification in reducing the risk of investment in real estate. We also look at issues of lenders' legal liabilities and fraud and ethics in real estate lending.

REAL ESTATE IN A
PORTFOLIO CONTEXT

LEARNING OBJECTIVES

In this chapter, we discuss the relevance of real estate investments in constructing portfolios of assets. A **portfolio** is a set or combination of assets. Although a portfolio can consist of only one asset, it is generally viewed as a mixture of different types of assets. After you have read this chapter, you should understand how the risk and return of a portfolio of assets can differ from that of the individual assets that make up the portfolio. You should understand how diversification, the process of forming portfolios consisting of different types of assets, affects the risk of a portfolio. You also will understand what characteristics of assets are important insofar as constructing "efficient" portfolios. Efficient portfolios are those that maximize expected return for a given level of risk, or minimize risk for a given level of expected return. You will see what characteristics of real estate investments contribute to the construction of efficient portfolios. Finally, you will see that diversification of real estate assets can be achieved in several ways, including by property type and by location.

INTRODUCTION

In this chapter, we explore the role of real estate investment in the context of a portfolio of assets. The discussion begins with the nature of diversification and the effect of diversification on the risk and return of a portfolio of assets. You will come to understand the difference between the risk of an asset held in isolation and the risk of a portfolio of assets. We will then discuss asset-pricing theories that incorporate the concept of portfolio risk. Here you will view the risk of an asset only in terms of its relationship to a portfolio of other assets.

In the following section of this chapter, we will consider the role of real estate in a **mixed-asset portfolio**—that is, one that includes different types of assets. Finally, we will analyze the diversification of a portfolio that consists only of real estate assets. Here, **diversification** means different property types in different geographical locations.

THE NATURE OF DIVERSIFICATION

Investors are concerned with both the expected return and the risk of an asset. Return and risk cannot be considered in isolation. A basic premise of finance theory states that investors must be rewarded with higher expected returns for taking on added risk. This is the reason that more risky investments, say, technology stocks, have initially higher yields than riskless investments, such as U.S. Treasury obligations. Fortunately, investors need not invest in assets in isolation: They can form portfolios that are mixtures of different assets with different expected returns and risks. The main thrust of portfolio diversification is the disproportionate reduction of risk compared to return.

Risk can be defined as the possibility (and probability) that the actual return on an investment will be different from the expected return. It can be measured as the volatility of an asset's returns. There are two implicit elements in this definition of risk. First, there is the notion of the absolute difference that can occur between the actual return and the expected return. Second, there is the consideration that the probability of the actual return will be different from the expected return. Consider the following simple example. Table 21-1 shows the expected and possible returns on two assets for the coming year. The possible returns for Asset A differ from the expected returns by a substantial amount, while those for Asset B are close to the expected return. At first glance, one is tempted to view Asset A as the more risky of the two. However, note the probabilities that have been assigned to the possible and expected returns in each case. Very low probabilities are associated with the possible returns of Asset A (other than the expected). It is possible to assign such small probabilities to the alternative returns as to make Asset A virtually riskless. The probabilities associated with the different returns for Asset B indicate it may be more risky. Shortly, we will review the formulas for determining the risk of an asset held in isolation. If that formula is applied to the data in Table 21-1, it would indicate that the risk of Asset B is indeed greater than that of Asset A.

To understand the risk reduction that is possible through diversification, consider the following simple example. Table 21-2 shows the expected and possible returns on two assets, X and Y. The expected return $E(R)$ for an asset is calculated by considering the possible returns and their probabilities $(P.R., P_2R_2, ..., PR)$ with the following formula:

$$E(R) = P_1R_1 + P_2R_2 + \cdots + P_nR_n = \sum_{i=1}^{n} P_1R_1 \qquad \text{(Equation 21-1)}$$

where i represents each asset. For both assets X and Y the expected return is

$$E(R) = (0.06 \times 0.2) + (0.07 \times 0.2) + (0.08 \times 0.2) + (0.09 \times 0.2) + (0.10 \times 0.2) = 0.08$$

Likewise, the formula for risk takes into account not only the difference between the expected return and the possible returns but also their probabilities. That is, the

TABLE 21-1

Distribution of Returns for Upcoming Year

	Asset A		Asset B	
	POSSIBLE RETURN	PROBABILITY	POSSIBLE RETURN	PROBABILITY
	2%	0.02	7%	0.30
	9	0.96	9	0.40
	16	0.02	11	0.30
Expected return	9%		9%	

Source: © 2014 OnCourse Learning

TABLE 21-2

Distribution of Returns for Upcoming Year

	Asset X		Asset Y	
	POSSIBLE RETURN	PROBABILITY	POSSIBLE RETURN	PROBABILITY
	6%	0.2	6%	0.2
	7	0.2	7	0.2
	8	0.2	8	0.2
	9	0.2	9	0.2
	10	0.2	10	0.2
Expected return	8%		8%	
Variance	0.00020		0.00020	
Standard deviation	0.01414		0.01414	

Source: © 2014 OnCourse Learning

(squared) differential between each possible return and the expected return $[R_1 - E(R)]_2$ is multiplied by the probability P of the possible return as follows:

$$\sigma^2 = [R_1 = E(R)]^2 \times P_1 + [R_2 - E(R)]^2 \times P_2 + \cdots + [R_n - E(R)]^2 \times P_n$$
$$= \sum_{i=1}^{n}[R_i - E(R)]^2 P_i \qquad \text{(Equation 21-2)}$$

In this equation, σ is the standard deviation or risk and n is the number of assets. Thus, for the example in Table 21-2, the risk of each asset can be computed as

$$\sigma^2 = (0.06 - 0.08)^2 \times 0.2 + (0.07 - 0.08)^2 \times 0.2 + (0.08 - 0.08)^2$$
$$\times 0.2 + (0.09 - 0.08)^2 \times 0.2 + (0.10 - 0.08)^2 \times 0.2$$

The statistical measure of risk derived in Equation 21-2 is called the **variance**. Its square root σ is called the standard deviation.

The expected return and the risk of each asset in Table 21-2 have been made identical for the purpose of illustration. It is obvious that the two assets are identical insofar as their risk/return structure is concerned. Each has the same expected return, 8 percent, and the same risk, $\sigma = 0.01414$. The probability distribution of returns for either asset is shown in Figure 21-1.

A rational investor should be indifferent between the two assets if he or she is to hold either one in isolation, because both provide the same expected return and

FIGURE 21-1   **Distribution of Returns for an Individual Asset**

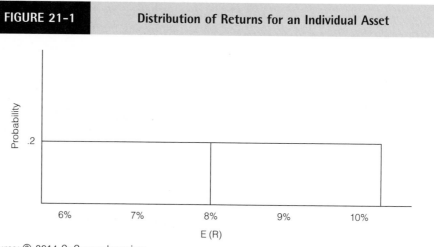

Source: © 2014 OnCourse Learning

the same risk. But what if the investor chooses to invest half of his or her wealth in each asset? What would be the expected return and risk of a portfolio so divided? One may be tempted to conclude that the risk and the return of a portfolio of two identical assets would be the same as that of the assets held in isolation. However, this is likely not to be the case.

To see why, assume that the returns on assets X and Y are completely independent of one another. (In statistical terms, the correlation between the returns of the two assets is zero.) This means that the return on one asset will have no influence on the return on the other asset. A more precise way of stating the relationship of independence of returns is to say that knowledge of the actual return on one asset will be useless in predicting the return on the other. In other words, if someone were to tell you that the actual return on Asset X for the past year was 7 percent, that information would be useless for you to predict the return on Asset Y. If the returns on the two assets are completely independent, the expected return and the risk of a portfolio consisting of an equal share of X and Y will be as indicated in Table 21-3.

The values in Table 21-3 are derived as follows. Note that the first listed possible return on the portfolio is 6 percent. For this to occur, however, both assets would have to have a return of 6 percent. From probability theory, we know that the probability of two independent events occurring simultaneously is equal to the product of their separate probabilities. Thus, the probability that both assets (and, therefore, the portfolio) will return 6 percent is $0.2 \times 0.2 = 0.04$. The next listed possible return is 6.5 percent. This portfolio return can occur two ways: if Asset X has a return of 6 percent and Asset Y a return of 7 percent, or the reverse. Since each of these two possibilities has a probability of 0.04, their combined probability is 0.08.

The same thinking applies to the other listed probabilities. For example, a portfolio return of 8 percent can occur in five different ways (X and Y returns of 6 and 10 percent, 7 and 9 percent, 8 and 8 percent, 9 and 7 percent, and 10 and 6 percent, respectively), so that the probability here is 20 percent (5×0.04). The entire probability distribution is shown in Figure 21-2, where you should notice two things. First, the probabilities of the extreme rates of return, 6 percent and 10 percent, have been reduced significantly—from 20 percent to 4 percent.

TABLE 21-3
Distribution of Returns for Upcoming Years

Portfolio of Assets X and Y		
POSSIBLE RETURN		**PROBABILITY**
6.0%		0.04
6.5		0.08
7.0		0.12
7.5		0.16
8.0		0.20
8.5		0.16
9.0		0.12
9.5		0.08
10.0		0.04
Sum	1.00	
Expected	8%	
Variance	0.0001	
Standard deviation	0.01	

Source: © 2014 OnCourse Learning

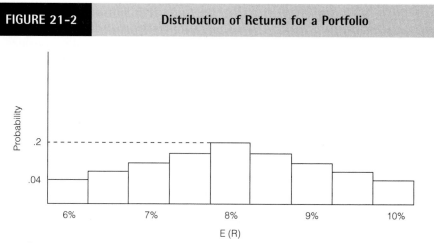

Second, the expected value (and its probability) has remained the same. Taken together, this indicates that the risk of the portfolio is less than that of either asset held in isolation. However, the expected return is not less. The standard deviation for this simple two-asset portfolio is 0.01, less than that of either asset held in isolation. In fact, if 100 assets identical to X or Y could be combined into a portfolio, the expected return would remain 8 percent but the risk, as indicated by the standard deviation, would be negligible. It would be extremely unlikely that the return on such a portfolio would be much less than 7.9 or more than 8.1 percent. Given a sufficient number of assets all identical to X or Y, it would be possible to construct a portfolio for which an 8 percent return would be virtually assured.

The amount of risk reduction that takes place through diversification is determined by the extent to which the returns of the assets are correlated. For example, if the returns of X and Y are perfectly correlated, then there would be no benefit from diversification. If the return on Asset X is 6 percent and the return on Y is also 6 percent, there is no benefit from diversification. The portfolio will behave precisely as either asset held alone. On the other hand, if the returns of the two assets are perfectly negatively correlated, diversification can reduce the risk of the portfolio to zero.

The (historic) **correlation** in the returns of two assets can be determined from a statistical sample of past returns and is indicated by the **correlation coefficient** r_{xy}:

$$r_{xy} = \frac{\displaystyle\sum_{t=1}^{n}(R_{x,t} - \overline{R}_x)(R_{y,t} - \overline{R}_y)/N}{\sigma_x \sigma_y} \qquad \text{(Equation 21-3)}$$

where N is the number of time periods in the sample, $\overline{R}_x$ and $\overline{R}_y$ are the average returns on Assets X and Y, $R_{x,t}$ and $R_{y,t}$ are the actual returns on Assets X and Y in each time period t, and σ_x and σ_y are the standard deviations of the returns of Assets X and Y, respectively.

Note that whenever R_x and R_y are both above their respective average return, the numerator in Equation 21-3 is positive. When both are below their respective average, then the numerator is also positive. Thus, if the returns vary together in a positive manner (rising together and falling together), the correlation coefficient is positive. It is negative if the return on one rises as the other falls. Of course, if there is no relationship at all between the returns, the correlation coefficient is zero. From these relationships, you can see that the risk of a portfolio of two (or more) assets will depend, in part, on the correlation coefficient(s) between their returns. For a two-asset *(x, y)* portfolio, the standard deviation in the return on the portfolio σ_p can be given by

$$\sigma_p = \sqrt{(\alpha \cdot \sigma_x)^2 + [(1-\alpha) \cdot \sigma_y]^2 + 2\alpha \cdot \sigma_x[(1-\alpha) \cdot \sigma_y r_{xy}]} \quad \textbf{(Equation 21-4)}$$

where α is the weight of the portfolio represented by Asset X.

This formula was developed in the late 1950s by Harry Markowitz and is referred to as the Markowitz diversification.[1] Note that the smaller r_{xy} is the smaller will be the risk of the portfolio. In fact, if r_{xy} is sufficiently negative, the standard deviation in the returns of the portfolio can be zero. The returns in Table 21-3 were constructed under the premise that the correlation in the returns of Assets X and Y was zero. Employing Equation 21-4 and the standard deviation from Table 21-2, one can confirm that the standard deviation is 0.01.

$$0.01 = \sqrt{(0.5 \times 0.01414)^2 + (0.5 \times 0.01414)^2 + 0}$$

Although the risk of a portfolio may be reduced by diversification, this is not necessarily so for its return. The return on a portfolio of assets will be equal to an average of the individual returns weighted by the relative proportion that each asset represents in the portfolio. Thus, the return on a portfolio can be expressed as:

$$R = \alpha R_x + (1-\alpha)R_y \quad \textbf{(Equation 21-5)}$$

Benefits of Diversification

Diversification derives its value from the reduction in risk that occurs when assets are combined into portfolios. Even where the returns on assets are independent (not correlated), portfolio construction reduces risk associated with holding assets in isolation. Furthermore, the reduction in risk comes at no cost to the investor. Aside from slightly higher (and in some cases no higher) transaction costs, the diversification achieves a costless reduction in risk. Yet, diversification does not reduce the return. Equation 21-5 indicates that the return on a portfolio is the weighted average of the return on the individual assets. These relationships are shown in Figure 21-3. There we consider the expected risks and returns of two assets in isolation and in a portfolio. Points X and Y represent the expected risk and return of two separate assets. Asset Y is more risky and has a higher expected return than Asset X. A rational investor may be indifferent between the two, since the asset with the higher risk also has the larger expected return. But what if the two assets are combined into a portfolio? Equation 21-4 indicates that the risk (standard deviation) of the portfolio will depend on the risk of the individual assets, the correlation of their returns, and their weights in the portfolio. Equation 21-5 indicates that the expected return on the portfolio will depend on the expected returns of the individual assets and their relative weights in the portfolio.

Here we consider three cases, each with a different correlation coefficient: perfect positive correlation (+1), no correlation (0), and perfect negative correlation (−1). In Figure 21-3 the straight-line segment between points X and Y corresponds to the assumption that the returns are perfectly positively correlated. There are no benefits from diversification. Portfolios constructed with more of Asset Y will have a larger return but also a larger risk, giving no benefits to the investor beyond investing in a single asset. The curved-line segment shows the risk/return tradeoff when the correlation coefficient is assumed to be zero. Risk can be reduced (to a theoretical minimum of σ'). Including some of the Y asset in a portfolio that begins with a concentration of the X asset has two benefits: Return is increased

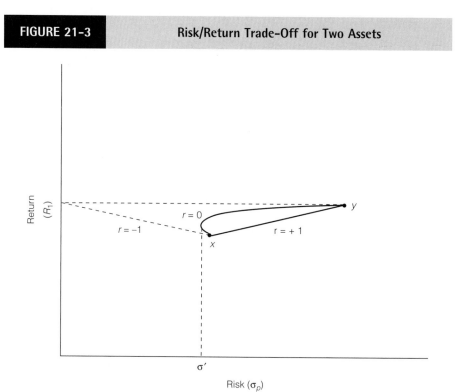

FIGURE 21-3   **Risk/Return Trade-Off for Two Assets**

Source: © 2014 OnCourse Learning

and risk is reduced. No rational investor would ever invest totally in Asset A, since he or she can increase the return and reduce risk through diversification. The kinked-line segment associated with a correlation coefficient of 21 shows that the proper proportion of X and Y can yield a zero risk. That proper proportion will depend on the risk of the individual assets. From here we will assume that most assets have a zero correlation coefficient, so that the risk/return trade-off can be characterized by curved-line segments such as that shown in Figure 21-3. A rational investor will choose a portfolio with a risk/return trade-off in the upper portion of the curve, say, at point B.

Next, we can consider the results from introducing a third, fourth, and other assets into the portfolio. Figure 21-4 shows how other assets can be considered. If we introduce a third asset, Z, we can think of a portfolio that can be formed by adding Asset Z to a portfolio already consisting of X and Y at point B. Thus, the new risk/return trade-off will appear as the line segment designated by the points Z, B, and Y. Adding more assets in such a fashion will introduce new curves, and eventually the risk/return trade-off of an almost infinite number of possible portfolios will appear as in Figure 21-5.

The dark, heavy line represents all those portfolios that have the greatest expected return for a given amount of risk or have the lowest risk for a given expected return. This portion of the curve is called the *efficiency frontier,* and all rational investors will choose a portfolio with a risk/return trade-off on this curve. Portfolios located on the efficiency frontier are often referred to as mean variance efficient, because they have the greatest return for the risk or the lowest risk for the return. Investors will choose their portfolio from among those on the frontier according to their risk preferences. More risk-averse investors will locate to the left portion of the curve, while less risk-averse investors will seek the higher returns on the rightward, more risky portion of the curve.

FIGURE 21-4	Risk/Return Trade-Off for Multiple Assets

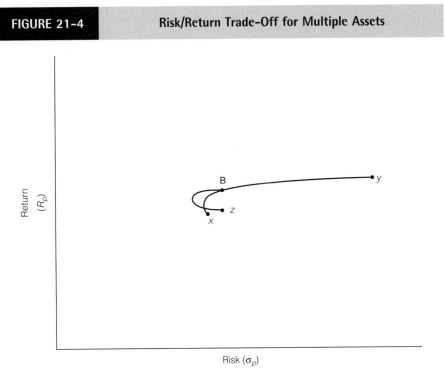

Source: © 2014 OnCourse Learning

FIGURE 21-5	Efficiency Frontier

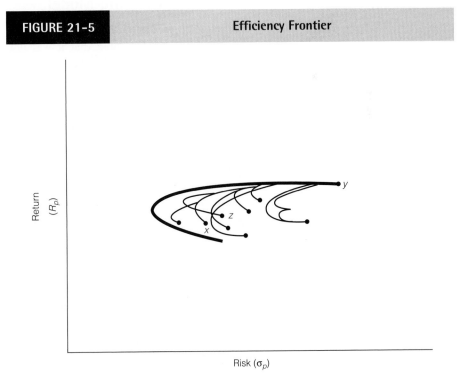

Source: © 2014 OnCourse Learning

The important thing to remember from this discussion is that assets that have little, no, or negatively correlated returns with each other can be combined to create efficient portfolios. The efficient portfolios reduce risk without reducing return at nearly no cost. The key to portfolio construction is the search for assets with negatively correlated returns.

Theories of Asset Pricing

A formula such as Equation 21-4 is useful to determine the risk of a portfolio of a few or several assets. The formula can be used to determine the impact of an additional asset on the risk of a portfolio. The relevant risk of an asset then becomes that associated with its contribution to the risk of the portfolio. Assets with returns that are negatively correlated to assets in the existing portfolio are excellent candidates for inclusion in the portfolio. One can use the formula to judge how much risk is reduced by adding another asset. Unfortunately, the formula has some drawbacks.

The major shortcoming of using such a formula to determine the contribution to the risk of a portfolio from including an asset is the large number of terms and calculations that must be made. Even with modern computers the data collection, data entry, and calculations can be a monumental task for portfolios with more than a few assets. The formula for portfolio risk must consider not only the risk (standard deviation) of each asset but also the correlation coefficient between each asset and every other asset in the portfolio. As the number of assets included in the portfolio increases, the number of terms required to determine the new portfolio risk (and thus the contribution of the added assets to portfolio risk) explodes geometrically until the task is unmanageable. For this reason, the Markowitz formula was of limited use to practitioners who desired to create efficiently diversified portfolios.

Capital Asset Pricing Model

An alternative to the Markowitz methodology was offered about a decade later by William Sharpe,[2] who noted that it was not necessary to relate the correlation of returns of each asset to each other but only to an overall index (or portfolio). The mathematical demonstration of this model is shown in Appendix 21-A. Here, however, we opt for an intuitive explanation of Sharpe's model by considering the following example in the context of the stock market.

Assume that the only market for assets of interest is the stock market, and that the portfolio managers of larger institutional investors seek to eliminate as much risk as possible. Since diversification is costless, they begin by diversifying their portfolios as much as possible. A naive diversification process occurs at first, with portfolio managers simply adding stock without regard to the stock's individual risk or its contribution to the risk of the portfolio. Now, every stock that exists will be held by someone. After all, if no one desired a stock to be held in a portfolio, the demand would fall and so too would the price until it was attractive for someone to hold. The result of this naive process is that all portfolio managers would end up with a portfolio of all stocks. Their portfolios would be small representations of the large overall stock market. By definition, they would have eliminated all the risk that can possibly be eliminated through the diversification process. They would have eliminated all **diversifiable risk**. Does this mean that none of the portfolios would contain any risk? Not at all. They would each represent a portfolio of the stock market and, therefore, each would have a risk associated with the market. Investing in the stock market is not riskless. The return on the market fluctuates from year to year.

Now imagine that each of the portfolio managers attempts to reduce the risk of his or her portfolio further. How can this be done? There is no more diversifiable risk left to eliminate, only the **nondiversifiable risk** of the market as a whole.

Assume that each manager identifies stocks that appear to move with the market but by more than the market. When the market returns increase, the returns on these stocks increase more, and conversely when the returns decrease. In other words, the return on a portfolio is the average of the returns on the assets in the portfolio. If the return on the market portfolio increases, it must be because the returns on some stocks increase more than the average, while the returns on other stocks increase less than the average. The same can be said about decreases in the return on the market.

The optimal strategy of the managers would appear to be to sell off those stocks whose returns fluctuate more than the market. In this way, they not only get rid of all the diversifiable risk, they eliminate some of the nondiversifiable market risk. Thus, the Sharpe method concentrates on the relationship between the return of a stock (or other asset) and the return on a portfolio (market index). To continue the example, imagine that each portfolio manager has identified the stocks that fluctuate more than the market. This is not a difficult task, given the quantity of price data that is available. Each will attempt to sell those stocks and purchase stocks that fluctuate less than the market. But in the process of doing so, the price of the former type stock will fall and the price of the latter will rise. Falling prices imply, other things being equal, a higher expected return. Rising prices imply a lower expected return. In this simple way, stocks that fluctuate more than the market and represent added risk to a portfolio must have a higher expected return to be candidates for investment. The relationship expressed mathematically by Sharpe is called the **capital asset pricing model (CAPM)** or:

$$R_J = R_f + \beta(R_m - R_f) \qquad \text{(Equation 21-6)}$$

where R_J is the return on stock J, R_f is the risk-free rate, and R_m is the return on the market. In the CAPM, β (beta) represents the relationship between the return on a stock and the return on the market portfolio. Assets with a β greater than 1 will command an expected return greater than the return on the market and vice versa. Note that the CAPM formula implies assets with a β of 1 will have an expected return equal to the return on the market, which is reasonable since the returns on the asset behave like those on the market.

The same result can be obtained by noting that investors also will hold risk-free assets, notably U.S. Treasury obligations. When risk-free assets are added to a portfolio, the efficiency frontier changes shape. If we consider adding a risk-free investment to a portfolio represented by point B in Figure 21-6, then the new efficiency frontier appears as the line segment R_fBC, a straight line.

The new frontier, also called the capital market line, is straight because adding a risk-free asset affects the return on the new portfolio but does not affect the risk from a diversification standpoint (risk-free assets have no variance in return). Note that the new frontier as drawn will contain a set of portfolios that dominate all others in terms of higher returns and less risk. Thus, point B represents the optimal mix of assets with some risk. Investors will, according to their risk preference, locate their portfolios along this capital market line.

Some may invest only in risk-free securities (point R_f), others only in portfolios of assets with some degree of risk (point B), and others in a combination of the two. It is easy to develop an equation for the capital market line. Linear equations take the form:

$$Y = A + BX \qquad \text{(Equation 21-7)}$$

where A is the intercept on the vertical axis and B is the slope of the line. The slope of the line is equal to the rise over the run. If in Figure 21-6 the market

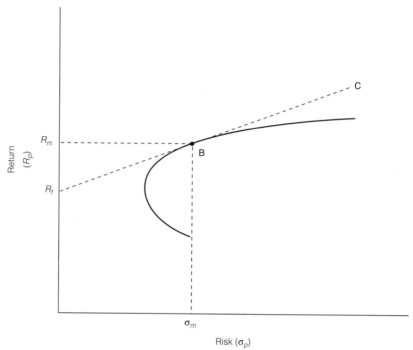

FIGURE 21-6   **Portfolio Construction with a Risk-Free Asset**

Source: © 2014 OnCourse Learning

portfolio is point B, its expected return and its risk will be those of the market: $E(R_m)$ and d_m, respectively. Beginning at point R_f the slope (rise over run) of the capital market line is

$$\frac{R_m - R_f}{\sigma_m - 0} = \frac{R_m - R_f}{\sigma_m} \qquad \textbf{(Equation 21-8)}$$

The equation for the capital market line can be expressed as

$$R_p = R_f + \frac{R_m - R_f}{\sigma_m}\sigma_p = R_f + (R_m - R_f)\frac{\sigma_p}{\sigma_m} \qquad \textbf{(Equation 21-9)}$$

which is similar to the CAPM for individual securities.

Subsequent to the development of the CAPM, many empirical studies were conducted to determine its validity as a pricing model. Most of these studies were confined to the returns on stocks alone. The form of the tests was simple. Historical data up to a cutoff point were employed to determine the β of a stock. Then, using the β and the risk-free rate, predictions were made for the return on the stock subsequent to the cutoff date. Predicted returns were then compared to actual returns. The predictability of the model met with limited success. Most studies confirmed the basic relationship but with less than ideal accuracy. In general, the tests showed the following:

- A positive and linear relationship exists between a stock's beta and its return in excess of the market.
- The slope of the capital market line was generally less than predicted.
- The overall predictive results were disappointing.

The two main reasons given for the disappointing empirical results were the use of historical β to predict future returns and the choice of assets to test the model. Most tests of the model utilized stock returns when, in fact, a proper portfolio should consist of every possible asset that can be held, including bonds, real estate, and human capital.

Arbitrage Pricing Theory

Following a critique of the CAPM by Roll[34] in the late 1970s, Roll and Ross proposed the **arbitrage pricing theory (APT)**. The central theme of this model was that the return on an asset is likely to be a function of more than one index (return on the market). The CAPM is a special case of the APT in the sense that the former only includes one factor, the return on the market. The APT model does not rely on a mean-variance efficient portfolio, but rather on asset pricing such that no arbitrage profits exist. Tests of the APT suggest that several factors affect assets' returns, including the return on the market, inflation, industrial production, and the return on the industry within which a company is located. Tests of the APT have been generally restricted to the stock market, however.

Both the CAPM and the APT indicate that diversification can reduce some risk with no sacrifice of expected return. The sole condition necessary for this result is that the mix of assets has returns that are not perfectly correlated with each other. Furthermore, the smaller the correlation, the greater the risk reduction that can be accomplished through diversification. In the next portion of this chapter, we look at the role of real estate in a mixed-asset portfolio. That is, does the addition of real estate to a portfolio consisting of non-real estate assets have diversification benefits?

REAL ESTATE IN A MIXED-ASSET PORTFOLIO

Here we discuss the advantages of adding real estate investments to a portfolio of mixed assets. A 1999 study by Seiler, Webb, and Myer provides a review of the research regarding real estate diversification in the United States.[5] They conclude that a real estate factor premium does indeed exist in addition to stocks and bonds. This implies that portfolios should contain some real estate. In addition to the real estate factor premium, the real estate's inflation hedgeability would warrant its inclusion in an optimal portfolio. Seiler, Webb, and Myer also examine the question of how much real estate is appropriate. Published studies have shown the amount to range from zero to two-thirds of the portfolio. A 1997 study by Ziobrowski and Ziobrowski finds 20 percent to 30 percent to be the optimal proportion.[6] Waggle and Johnson, in a 2004 study, find optimal portfolio allocations for real estate investment trusts (REITs) to be between 10 percent and 20 percent for individual investors.[7] Furthermore, a 1999 study by Chua concludes that international real estate has a viable role in global mixed-asset portfolios.[8] He finds that the optimal allocations range from about 4 percent to 21 percent depending on the investor's risk preferences. Bulan, Mayer, and Somerville, in a 2009 study, examine the extent to which risk and uncertainty delays real estate investment.[9] Using a sample of condominiums in Vancouver, Canada the authors find that both idiosyncratic and systematic risk cause developers to delay new real estate investments. Their results support the notion of using a real options framework over a simple risk aversion framework in real estate investing.

The crucial test is the extent to which the returns on real estate investments are correlated with a wide variety of other assets such as stocks, bonds, human capital, and collectibles. One of the difficult tasks in this determination has been an accurate measurement of the returns on real estate properties. Stocks and bonds are traded frequently in large, efficient markets. Their market prices and, therefore, their returns over time can be determined with ease and accuracy. As Norman,

Sirmans, and Benjamin discuss, however, real estate investments are traded infrequently, and their prices are not reported to some centralized market as is the case for stocks and bonds.[10] The prices of real estate properties that are traded relatively frequently, such as single-family homes, also are not reported to a centralized market. An additional problem concerns capital improvements to real estate properties. Even where traded prices for a particular property on two different dates may be available, lack of information on any capital improvements made in the interim can lead to a miscalculation of the return.

The Problem with Appraised Values

Much of the data that are available on real estate property values are based on periodic appraisal and not on actual sales. This is so because many properties are held by one owner for long periods of time. Many properties held for investment by institutions such as pension funds and insurance companies must be appraised regularly so that the institutions can file financial statements with their regulators. Often, the institutions may make an "inside" appraisal on a quarterly basis but will have an outside independent appraisal made at least annually. The appraisal data can be used to estimate the value of the properties at various dates, but the estimates of value will not be transaction prices. Measures of return based on appraised values rather than transaction prices will show less variation through time. In other words, the return series based on appraised values is "smoothed" and does not exhibit the fluctuations that would result from returns based on transaction prices.

A primary reason for this smoothing process lies in the method of appraising properties—the income method. This method, combined with what Geltner calls the "lack of confidence" factor, causes the smoothing.[11] Lack of confidence refers to the subjective nature of the appraisal process and the tendency for appraisers to rely too much on the most recent past appraisals of the property in forming a new opinion of value. Often, new appraisals may be simply past appraisals adjusted upward for inflation. Inside appraisals may be made much in this fashion—an adjustment of the latest outside appraisal for whatever inflation has occurred.

A 1993 study by Myer and Webb seems to substantiate this problem with smoothing.[12] They found that the return on properties of securitized real estate (REITs) appears to be much more like the returns on common stocks and closed-end funds than like the returns on unsecuritized commercial real estate. They attribute this to the fact that REITs, common stocks, and closed-end funds are all traded in the same markets and the returns on unsecuritized real estate are appraisal/accounting based rather than market/transaction based. Alvayay and Kuhle, in 2000 study, find a significant level of price inefficiency in the equity REIT market.[13] They attribute this to limited information.

Follain and Calhoun, in a 1997 study, provide some insight into the multifamily housing market by examining price movements during the 1980s and early 1990s.[14] By developing price indices, they draw several conclusions about the national multifamily housing market. First, various methods of creating indexes yield similar patterns of price movement. Second, regional variation in price movements seems to be great. Third, the impact of the Tax Reform Act of 1986 does not appear to have been as dramatic as some have suggested given that price declines do not appear in either the 1986 or 1987 indices. Before we further explore the relationship between the return on real estate and other assets, we will look briefly at some typical sources of data that can be used to estimate real estate returns.

Sources of Real Estate Data

When one speaks of the returns to real estate and their role in a mixed-asset portfolio, one is generally concerned with the return to the equity portion of real estate and not debt or mortgage returns. The ideal source of data of such a return series would be the transaction prices of all equity properties adjusted for any capital improvements. Such clean data are difficult, if not impossible, to obtain. There are, however, some sources that allow estimates of returns to equity real estate to be made. These sources have been used in various studies of real estate portfolios.

The Russell–NCREIF. The **Russell–NCREIF Property Index** measures the historical performance of all-equity, income-producing properties owned by commingled funds on behalf of qualified pension and profit-sharing trusts, or owned directly by these trusts and managed on a separate account basis. The index gets its name from the Frank Russell Company, which computes the index on the basis of the value of properties held by members of the National Council of Real Estate Investment Fiduciaries. The index began in 1977 and calculations are based on quarterly returns of individual investment-grade properties. In 1987, Russell-NCREIF began tracking a separate index for apartments. It is the most widely quoted index of property values. The net income of the properties and their values are used to construct a quarterly return series divided into two components: income and appreciation. The Russell-NCREIF Property Index contains performance data on five different property types: apartments, office buildings, retail properties (including regional community and neighborhood shopping centers), research and development facilities, and warehouses.

National Association of Real Estate Investment Trusts. REITs are trusts that invest in real estate properties and issue shares of stock. The REITs invest in mortgages on real estate, real estate equity, or a combination of the two (hybrid REITs). The advantage of return data based on REIT performance derives from the fact that prices of REIT stock are market transaction prices and not appraisals. The disadvantage is that, except for a few very large REITs, most are not traded in large, efficient markets. The return on nontraded REITs will reflect a lack of liquidity. Studies that have employed data on REIT prices have taken the information from the major stock exchanges or have obtained data from the National Association of Real Estate Investment Trusts (NAREITs), a trade organization that collects and maintains data on REIT transactions. From the transaction data, this organization publishes the **NAREIT Equity Index**, based on the return to equity REITs.

Commingled Real Estate Funds. Commingled real estate funds (CREFs) are managed by large financial institutions for investors such as pension funds. The funds are referred to as *commingled* because they combine funds from several investors and purchase real estate properties. Some of these funds track their return record. An example is the Prudential Property Investment Separate Account (PRISA), managed by Prudential Realty Group.

National Association of REALTORS®. This trade organization for the nation's real estate salespeople and brokers surveys its members periodically to determine selling prices of residential properties. The data are released on a quarterly basis and indicate the median selling prices in four geographical areas of the country. A limitation is that data are not adjusted for any changes in the quality of the houses sold. Other sources of data on residential properties include Finnegan's Financial Green Sheet Rates of Return and the U.S. Department of Commerce series on prices for constant quality houses. The main problem with all such data on residential properties is the lack of transaction data on identified properties—that is, so-called repeat sales. The transaction data in the time series are, for the most part, on different properties.

U.S. Department of Agriculture. The U.S. Department of Agriculture publishes a series called *Farm Real Estate Market Developments: Outlook and Situation*, based on recent transactions. The data suffer from the same problem as the data for residential sales—lack of data on repeat transactions. It is one of the more widely used sources for data on farmland values.

R. G. Ibbotson Associates. Under the direction of Roger Ibbotson, this company annually publishes rates of return on various investments including real estate. The real estate component is a combination of residential, commercial, and farm properties. It is a good source for comparing rates of return and risk (variance in rates of return) on various investments.

The Diversification Benefits of Real Estate

Using these and other sources of data on real estate returns, many researchers have attempted to judge the diversification value of real estate. The results overwhelmingly support the notion that real estate offers substantial diversification benefits while at the same time offering protection against unanticipated inflation. An early 1980s study by Ibbotson and Siegel indicated that the average annual return on real estate from 1947 to 1982 was 8.27 percent.[15] This return compared to 3.98 percent on U.S. government securities and 3.56 percent on corporate debt. Only corporate stock had a higher annual rate of return—11 percent. The standard deviation in the annual returns was very low for real estate, 3.71 percent. It was moderately higher for U.S. government securities, 4.92 percent, and corporate debt, 6.47 percent, and substantially higher for corporate stock, 17.52 percent. Over this period, the risk/return trade-off for real estate indicated that it was a superior investment to any other asset. The diversification benefits of real estate were also substantial. Table 21-4 shows the correlation coefficients between real estate and other assets from 1947 to 1982. The returns on real estate are a composite of those on residential, farm, and commercial real estate. The return series was based on appraised values, so it suffered from the smoothing problem discussed earlier. The conclusion reached by Ibbotson and Siegel was that real estate offered superior returns if held as an asset in isolation, and excellent diversification benefits if held in a mixed-asset portfolio.

TABLE 21-4

Selected Cross Correlations of Asset Returns 1947–1982, Ibbotson and Siegel

	REAL ESTATE	S&P COMMON STOCK	SMALL COMPANY STOCK	LONG-TERM CORPORATE BONDS	LONG-TERM GOVERNMENT BONDS	U.S. TREASURY BILLS
Real estate	1.0					
S & P common stock	−0.06	1.0				
Small company stock	0.04	0.79	1.0			
Long-term corp. bonds	−0.06	0.14	0.05	1.0		
Long-term gov't bonds	−0.08	0.01	−0.06	0.95	1.0	
U.S. Treasury bills	0.44	−0.25	0	0.15	0.21	1.0

Source: Ibbotson and Siegel, "Real Estate Returns: A Comparison with Other Investments," AREUEA Journal Vol. 12, No. 3, 1984, Table 3, p. 231.

Benjamin, Sirmans, and Zietz provide a review of the literature on real estate returns and risk.[16] They find, when adjusting for risk, that real estate has a higher return per unit of risk than bonds or common stocks. Bajtelsmit and Worzala examined the decision-making process used by pension plans in either their mixed-asset portfolio allocations or within asset class.[17] The most interesting result was that most are making the between-class allocations before and independently of within-class allocations. The primary diversification techniques used by pension managers were not surprising. The mixed-asset portfolio was diversified by risk and return and by asset class, whereas the individual asset classes were most often diversified by asset type. They also found that pension funds' portfolio allocations to real estate were substantially less than the theoretically derived allocations suggested by research.

Zietz, Worzala, and Sirmans examined investment decisions and allocation patterns for large insurance companies and found evidence that larger companies are more likely to have direct real estate, mortgage, and mortgage-backed security investments.[18]

New Equilibrium Theory. The superior returns to real estate outlined in the Ibbotson and Siegel paper led them to introduce the **new equilibrium theory**. Returns to real estate appeared to be greater than that predicted by either the CAPM or the APT. The new equilibrium theory suggests that the apparent excess returns to real estate are a reward for some of the unique risk characteristics of that asset. While there appears to be a small stock β for real estate (the correlation between real estate returns and stock market returns), the major risk elements are residual risk, marketability costs, and information costs. **Residual risk** refers to the difficulty for other than very large investors to diversify real estate holdings. Most real estate assets are very large relative to the portfolio of the typical investor. In other words, for the typical investor, it is not possible to own only a small portion of a particular real estate asset, making diversification difficult. **Marketability risk** refers to the liquidity of real estate. Again, because real estate is not divisible and does not trade frequently in large, efficient markets as does corporate stock, liquidity risk can be a problem for the average investor. **Information risk** refers to the cost of obtaining all the information sufficient to make an informed and rational investment in real estate. Information such as proposed zoning changes, changes in the infrastructure, and changes in the local economy is costly to obtain. Yet, these factors will play an important role in the returns of a real estate asset. In short, these risks, unique to real estate, are the source of the apparent excess returns to real estate relative to its risk.

Webb and Rubens also investigated the role of real estate in a mixed-asset portfolio.[19] They constructed a "restricted" portfolio and included two types of real estate: farm and residential properties. A **restricted portfolio** includes only those assets that are eligible by law for investment by large institutional investors such as pension plans. Some of the correlation coefficients from their study are presented in Table 21-5. The farm and residential real estate returns data were taken from Finnegan's Financial Green Sheet Rates of Return. Once again, the negative correlations attest to the diversification benefits of real estate. When optimal portfolios were constructed based on the return and risk data, they were dominated by real estate. Webb and Rubens found that the optimal portfolios would consist of nearly 75 percent real estate, approximately 15 percent small corporate stock, and only 5 percent common stock. Government bonds represented a negligible part of the optimal portfolio. The dominance of real estate in the optimal portfolio persisted, even when the returns on real estate were held to their historic levels but the risk (standard deviation in returns) was arbitrarily increased fivefold.

TABLE 21-5

Selected Cross Correlations of Asset Returns 1967–1986, Webb and Rubens

	FARM	RESIDENTIAL	COMMON STOCK	SMALL STOCK	CORPORATE BONDS	GOVERNMENT BONDS
Farm	1.0					
Residential	−0.37	1.0				
Common stock	−0.36	−0.37	1.0			
Small stock	0.01	−0.23	0.73	1.0		
Corporate bonds	−0.57	−0.47	0.32	−0.07	1.0	
Government bonds	−0.55	−0.55	0.42	0.04	0.96	1.0

Source: James Webb and Jack Rubens, "The Effect of Alternative Return Measures on Restricted Mixed Asset Portfolios," AREUEA Journal Vol. 16, No. 2, 1988, Exhibit 5, p. 132.

Geltner used return data from the Russell-NCREIF, PRISA, and NAREIT indexes to judge the value of real estate in mixed-asset portfolios.[20] Geltner used a statistical technique to "de-smooth," so to speak, the return series. That is, he estimated return series after adjusting for the smoothing effects of appraised values in the series. The adjusted series naturally exhibited more risk (variance) than that based strictly on appraised values. As a result, real estate taken in isolation did not exhibit excess returns for the risk involved. However, it did present solid diversification benefits. Geltner computed the correlation coefficient between the various real estate indexes and the stock market over a period of time from the early 1970s to the late 1980s. He found no coefficients that were significantly different from zero.

Pagliari, Webb, and Del Casino also used the Russell-NCREIF data to compare ex ante (before the fact) and ex post (after the fact) portfolios.[21] Their goal was to point out the problems of using ex post historical to build ex ante portfolios. In fact, their results showed that using data from previous periods may yield suboptimal ex ante allocations when examined historically since, for none of the subperiods examined, did the ex ante strategies generate portfolios that were on the ex post efficient frontier.

In summary, most of the studies of real estate in a mixed-asset portfolio find that the returns of real estate are high relative to the risk and offer substantial risk reduction through diversification. Most studies imply that real estate should occupy a larger role in the portfolios of large institutional investors. They indicate that lack of liquidity is one of the primary reasons why large institutional investors have not increased their investment in real estate to portions that would appear to be optimal.

Next, we look at the advantages of diversifying within real estate—that is, taking a portfolio of real estate assets only and diversifying by such characteristics as property type and geographical location.

WITHIN-REAL-ESTATE DIVERSIFICATION

For various reasons, some portfolios may be constructed entirely or mostly out of real estate properties or real estate–related investments. This may be the case, for example, for institutions that because of regulation or by choice invest in real estate or real estate securities (such as mortgages). Other funds, such as CREFs, have been established for the primary purpose of investing in real estate. Here, we discuss the advantages of diversification within a real estate portfolio. Within-real-estate diversification can take place in any of several ways. One is by property type, in which the portfolio is constructed with investments in various property types such as hotels, warehouses, office buildings, and apartment complexes. The idea here is, of course, that even within one local area, all property types may not prosper or fail together. Often, office buildings may do well at a time when apartment complexes are doing poorly. However, there certainly are cases where all property types may do well or poorly together, depending on the state of the local economy.

Another method of diversification is geography. This involves constructing a portfolio from properties in various parts of the country or the world. This strategy can involve a single property type or a mix of properties. The strategy can be accomplished in a naive way, selecting properties in the East, West, South, and Northeast, for example, or in a more sophisticated way by looking closely at the economies of the various regions. These more sophisticated types of diversification can be accomplished by analyzing the correlation of the economies of the various regions or by looking at the extent to which the local economies are themselves economically diversified.

Diversification by Property Type

It should not be surprising to see that **property diversification** by type is beneficial in terms of risk reduction. In a 1982 study, Miles and McCue tested diversification strategies that consisted of dividing the country into four geographic regions versus a strategy that diversified the portfolio by property type.[22] They found that diversification by property type showed better risk/return characteristics than a four-region geographic strategy. They looked at the returns of REITs that specialized in investment of property types from 1972 through 1978 and found the correlation in returns between REITs that held office facilities and those that held retail properties to be 0.48. The correlation coefficient between REITs involved in the acquisition of residential properties and those with office properties was −0.49. The retail to residential coefficient was only 0.0806. The negative coefficient between residential and office properties indicates that the addition of residential properties to an existing real estate portfolio would provide risk-reduction benefits. This corresponds to the heavy emphasis on residential properties in the efficient portfolios analyzed by Webb and Rubens.

More recently, Firstenberg, Ross, and Zisler analyzed the quarterly performance of nearly 600 individual properties from 1974 through 1987.[23] The authors divided the properties into four types: office, retail, industrial, and apartments. The returns were used to create mean-variance efficient portfolios (those that would lie on the efficiency frontier) that would return at least 10.5 percent to 11.5 percent annually. Their results indicated that the efficient trade-off between risk and return depended crucially on the property types included in the portfolio. As an example, the authors demonstrated the beneficial impact of adding a fourth property type to one with the other three. Table 21-6 shows decline in risk (for selected levels of return) accomplished by adding apartments to a portfolio of office, industrial, and retail properties. In a 2007 study, Danielsen and Harrison[24] examined the degree to which property type diversification affects REIT market liquidity. They found that underlying property type affects liquidity measures and more volatile underlying property types are reflected in larger spreads, and adverse selection measures.

Geographic Diversification

There is strong evidence that diversification of real estate investments by geographic area can have substantial risk-reduction benefits. Miles and McCue

TABLE 21-6

Impact of Adding Apartments on Portfolio Risk/Return Relationship

EXPECTED RETURN	STANDARD DEVIATION OF THREE-PROPERTY PORTFOLIO	STANDARD DEVIATION OF PORTFOLIOS WITH APARTMENTS	BASIS POINT DECLINE IN RISK (%)
10.8	3.41	3.29	0.12
10.9	3.59	3.33	0.19
11.0	3.88	3.45	0.43
11.1	4.24	3.63	0.61
11.2	4.67	3.87	0.80

Source: *Managing Portfolio and Reward, Paul Firstenberg and Charles Wurtzebach,* Real Estate Review, *Vol. 19, No. 2, Summer 1989, Exhibit 2, p. 64.*

calculated a reward-to-variability ratio (excess return divided by the standard deviation in returns) for the REITs in their study.[25] With the calculated value as the dependent variable, they regressed it against the number of types of properties held by each REIT and the number of states in which the properties were located. Both variables had a positive impact on the reward-to-variability ratio, indicating that in addition to property diversification, **geographic diversification** had positive benefits. However, the statistical significance of the geographic diversification variable was much weaker than that of the property diversification variable. In another paper, Hartzell, Hekman, and Miles analyzed the returns to CREFs from 1973 to 1983 and concluded that geographic diversification was not nearly as important as diversification by property type.[26] However, their geographic diversification was based on placing properties into one of four broad regional classifications: East, West, South, and Midwest. It is suggested that if investors construct portfolios on the basis of such naive geographic diversification, little benefit will derive from the effort. Thus diversification of real estate portfolios historically has been accomplished by using either a geographic- or property-type strategy.

A new direction was taken in a 1987 paper by Hartzell, Shulman, and Wurtzebach.[27] They divided the United States into eight sections based on a commonality of their regional economies. State borders were ignored in the partitioning. As an example, southern California was joined with southern Nevada but both were separate from northern California. As much as possible, the regions were based on local economies. Montana and Wyoming were considered to be mineral-extraction states and placed in the same section as Texas and Louisiana. Some Midwestern states were split, because that area was partitioned into two segments: an industrial sector and a farming sector. The authors used the same database as did Hartzell, Hekman, and Miles but expanded the data to include returns through mid-1987.

A 1993 study by Mueller reexamined the efficiency of the existing geographic and geographic/ economic strategies against an economically based diversification strategy using government groupings.[28] His study found that the addition of the economic aspect to a geographically constrained model creates a higher risk and return efficient frontier than the purely geographical diversification model. Table 21-7 shows the correlation coefficients for the four major and the eight geographic regions. As you can see, the correlation coefficients based on the more sophisticated diversification are smaller than those based on a naive four-section identification of property location. This is evidence that geographic diversification can yield substantial risk-reduction benefits, if it is done with respect to the regional economies and not strictly physical location. The importance of this study is that geographic diversification has been resurrected and given more importance than indicated by earlier studies. Along

TABLE 21-7

Correlation Coefficients Based on Geographic Diversification

Four Region 1973 IV–1990 IV				
	EAST	MIDWEST	WEST	SOUTH
East	1.0			
Midwest	0.308	1.0		
West	0.282	0.459	1.0	
South	−0.038	0.076	0.199	1.0

Eight Region Diversification 1973 IV–1990 IV								
	NEW ENGLAND	MID-ATLANTIC	OLD SOUTH	INDUSTRIAL	FARM BELT	MINERAL	SO. CALIF.	NO. CALIF.
New England	1.0							
Mid-Atlantic	−0.212	1.0						
Old South	−0.170	−0.077	1.0					
Industrial	−0.042	0.306	0.025	1.0				
Farm Belt	−0.013	0.125	0.167	0.323	1.0			
Mineral	−0.238	0.070	0.136	0.177	0.205	1.0		
So. Calif.	−0.045	0.378	0.085	0.473	0.361	0.102	1.0	
No. Calif.	−0.007	0.095	0.139	0.207	0.139	0.145	0.371	1.0

Source: GlennMueller, "Refining Economic Diversification Strategies for Real Estate Portfolios" Journal of Real Estate Research, Vol. 8 (Winter, 1993), pp. 55–68.

with geographic/economic strategies, Mueller also argues that the benefits of real estate investing can be maximized by recognizing the real estate market follows both a physical and financial cycle.[29] The physical cycle is based on the demand and supply of the physical space, whereas the financial cycle revolves around the flow of capital into real estate. The validity of the latter cycle was observed with the fallout of the subprime mortgage crisis beginning in 2007 as lenders became more restrictive in providing funds for real estate.

A 2003 study by Nelson and Nelson examined geographic diversification based on economic factors, particularly employment-related measures.[30] They were interested in measuring broad economic cycles. They used NCREIF property returns data to show that superior diversification benefits can be achieved by using a "capacity clusters" approach. Capacity clusters were areas with economic and development capacity.

International Real Estate Diversification

Globalization has increased investment opportunities and changed the way investments are made. Real estate investing has achieved an international orientation. Some reasons for international diversification are higher yields/lower risk, lack of opportunity in domestic markets, and illiquidity. Some studies have examined the benefits of international diversification in real estate. Asabere, Kleiman, and McGowan in 1991 concluded that international real estate could improve portfolio efficiency for U.S. investors.[31] In 1998 Liu and Mei found that international real estate provided additional diversification benefits beyond investing in international stocks.[32] Ling and Naranjo in a 2002 study found that international diversification opportunities existed even after controlling for worldwide systematic risk.[33]

A 2002 study by Conover, Friday, and Sirmans compared the risk and return for publicly traded foreign real estate to that for U.S. stocks, U.S. real estate, and foreign stock investments.[34] Using data encompassing the stock market crash of 1987, they found that foreign real estate had a lower correlation with U.S. stocks than foreign stocks for five of the six countries examined. This lower correlation was shown to be stable over time, implying that not including foreign real estate reduces the return relative to risk for the U.S. investor. A 2003 study by Wilson and Zuibruegg provides a literature review on the benefits of international diversification and find no consensus on the benefit level of diversifying internationally.[35] They did find mixed outcomes of direct or indirect property investment. Hoesli, Lekander, and Witkiewicz, in a 2004 study, provide a comparison of the international benefits of real estate in a mixed-asset portfolio.[36] They find real estate to be an effective diversification tool, especially when both domestic and international investments are considered. The optimal allocation to real estate is 15 percent to 25 percent. They find that allocations between domestic and international real estate varied greatly across countries.

Lim, McGreal, and Webb in a 2006 study examine the potential investment appeal of Africa and Central/South America as they have improved their economic and political structures. Their results show that investors' lack of familiarity and knowledge of these markets make investments seem to be very risk and create psychological barriers for investors.[37]

Other Methods of Diversification

Investment managers can diversify their real estate portfolios in other ways. Corgel and Gay studied the correlations of employment between large U.S. cities in the context of investing in mortgages.[38] Their thinking was that employment reflects the economies of the cities, and investment managers should construct real estate mortgage portfolios based on such correlations, investing in mortgages in cities with low or negative employment correlations. Of course, their implications can be extended to investment in real estate equity as well. They used monthly rates of change in employment levels for the 30 largest metropolitan areas from 1969 through 1984, and demonstrated that there was no large systematic component. That is, sufficient independence of employment rates existed to allow portfolio managers to exploit geographic diversification. Furthermore, the geographic diversification based on correlation in employment rates is superior to naive geographic diversification (North, South, and so on).

Clauretie suggested that substantial diversification benefits can be achieved by managers of small portfolios by investing in properties in locations that are themselves economically diversified.[39] He considered several measures of economic diversification. He showed that foreclosure rates on residential mortgages were related to the economic diversification of the region. Localities with greater economic diversification had fewer foreclosure rates than areas that were economically specialized. The conclusion here is that managers of small portfolios that cannot achieve substantial diversification by investing in properties in many diverse locations can achieve some of the benefits of diversification by investing in a few properties that are in locations where the economy is itself economically diversified.

Ziobrowski and Curcio addressed the issue of international diversification by combining the notions that international diversification enhances portfolio performance and that adding real estate to financial asset portfolios improves yield.[40]

They hypothesized that the greatest gains should be available from international mixed-asset portfolios. They investigated this hypothesis as an explanation for investment in U.S. real estate by foreign investors. Their results showed that U.S. real estate does not improve foreign portfolio performance. The evidence suggests that volatile exchange rates induce a level of risk that offsets potential diversification benefits. Mueller and Mueller, in a 2003 study, show that inclusion of both public and private real estate in a mixed-asset portfolio increases the performance of the overall portfolio by producing a more efficient frontier, low volatility, and strong returns.[41]

Addae-Dapaah, Wee, and Ebrahim found that, in relation to real estate, the contrarian strategy implied that properties with high running yield (value properties) could outperform properties with low running yield (growth properties).[42] They found a strong association of both the cash flow concentration level and the diversification index to the portfolio performance index, implying that diversification by sources of return could improve real estate portfolio performance.

Newell and Peng point out that, although investors have traditionally invested in mainstream real estate, an increase in investment in nontraditional real estate has been observed.[43] Nontraditional types of real estate include self-storage, health care, and retirement facilities. Strong returns and low correlation with the traditional real estate sectors make nontraditional real estate attractive to investors in REIT portfolios.

Summary

The diversification of a portfolio into several or many assets can have a significant effect on reducing the risk of the portfolio while maintaining or even increasing the expected yield. Furthermore, the cost of the diversification is negligible. For this reason, rational investors take advantage of the opportunity to diversify. The size of the risk reduction due to the diversification depends on the correlation in the returns of the added assets with the existing portfolio. The correlation of the returns of the assets to be included in a portfolio with that of the portfolio is the relevant risk that must be priced and is the basis of the capital asset pricing model (CAPM).

The returns on equity real estate investments indicate that those investments should be included in all portfolios of any size. The historic returns to real estate have been far in excess of their risk, and they appear to have no or negative correlation with other assets. This is particularly true of residential properties. The apparent excess returns to real estate have been the basis of the new equilibrium theory, which states that those returns must be due to the peculiar risk characteristics of real estate, such as liquidity, residual, and information cost risks. Nonetheless, many large institutional investors have responded by increasing their real estate holdings. Within-real-estate diversification also appears to have risk-reduction benefits. At one time, it was thought that only diversification by property type produced benefits. Recent evidence suggests that if regions are defined in terms of their economies and not by state boundaries, then geographic diversification also can produce risk-reduction benefits. Investors with small- to medium-size portfolios also can take advantage of other methods of diversification. They can invest in properties in metropolitan areas that exhibit negative employment correlations, or they can invest in localities where the regional economy is itself diversified.

Key Terms

Arbitrage pricing theory (APT)

Capital asset pricing model (CAPM)

Correlation

Correlation coefficient

Diversifiable risk

Diversification

Geographic diversification

Information risk

Marketability risk

Mixed-asset portfolio

NAREIT Equity Index

New equilibrium theory

Nondiversifiable risk

Portfolio

Property diversification

Residual risk

Restricted portfolio

Risk

Russell-NCREIF Property Index

Variance

Review Questions

21-1.   Explain how diversification can reduce the risk of a portfolio of assets.

21-2.   Provide a definition of an efficiency frontier.

21-3.   Define β and explain why it is the only risk of an asset that is relevant to investors.

21-4.   Why is it difficult to measure historical returns on real estate investments?

21-5.   Explain the new equilibrium theory with regard to the historical returns to real estate.

21-6.   Do the historical returns on real estate suggest it should be included in a mixed-asset portfolio? Explain.

21-7.   Describe several methods to accomplish within-real-estate diversification.

21-8.   Describe a successful geographic diversification program for a real estate portfolio.

Notes

1. H. Markowitz. *Portfolio Selection: Efficient Diversification of Investments.* New York: John Wiley, 1959.

2. W. Sharpe. *Portfolio Theory and Capital Markets.* New York: McGraw-Hill, 1970.

3. R. Roll. A critique of the asset pricing theory's tests. *Journal of Financial Economics* 5 (May 1977), 129–176.

4. R. Roll and S. Ross. An empirical investigation of the arbitrage pricing theory. *Journal of Finance* 35 (December 1980), 1073–1103.

5. M. Seiler, J. Webb, and F. Myer. Diversification issues in real estate investment. *Journal of Real Estate Literature* 7 (1999), 163–179.

6. B. Ziobrowski and A. Ziobrowski. Higher real estate risk and mixed-asset portfolio performance. *Journal of Real Estate Portfolio Management* 3(2) (1997), 107–115.

7. D. Waggle and D. Johnson. Home ownership and the decision to invest in REITs. *Journal of Real Estate Portfolio Management* 10 (2004), 129–144.

8. A. Chua. The role of international real estate in global mixed-asset investment portfolios. *Journal of Real Estate Portfolio Management* 5(2) (1999), 129–137.

9. L. Bulan, C. Mayer, and C. T. Somerville. Irreversible Investment, Real Options, and Competition: Evidence from Real Estate Development. *Journal of Urban Economics* 65:3 (2009), 237–251.

10. For a review of the literature showing returns and risk on real estate relative to other assets see E.J. Norman, G. Stacy Sirmans, and J.D. Benjamin. The historical environment of real estate returns. *Journal of Real Estate Portfolio Management* 1 (1995), 1–24.

11. D. Geltner. Estimating real estate's systematic risk from aggregate level appraisal-based returns. *AREUEA Journal* 17 (Winter 1989), 463–481. See also D. Geltner. Smoothing in appraisal-based returns. *Journal of Real Estate Finance and Economics* 4 (September 1991), 327–345.

12. C. Neil Myer and J.R. Webb. Return properties of equity REITs, common stocks, and commercial real estate: A comparison. *Journal of Real Estate Research* 8 (Winter 1993), 87–106.

13. R. Alvayay and J.L. Kuhle. The efficiency of equity REIT prices. *Journal of Real Estate Portfolio Management* 6 (2000), 349–354.

14. J.R. Follain and C.A. Calhoun. Constructing indices of the price of multifamily properties using the 1991 residential finance survey. *Journal of Real Estate Finance and Economics* 14 (1997), 235–255.

15. R. Ibbotson and L. Siegel. Real estate returns: Comparison with other investments. *AREUEA Journal* 12 (Fall 1984), 219–242.

16. See J.D. Benjamin, G.S. Sirmans, and E.N. Zietz. Returns and risk on real estate and other investments: More evidence. *Journal of Real Estate Portfolio Management* 7(3) (2001), 183–214; and E. Norman, G. Stacy Sirmans, and J.D. Benjamin. The historical environment of real estate returns. *Journal of Real Estate Portfolio Management* 1 (1995), 1–24.

17. V. L. Bajtelsmit and E.M. Worzala. Portfolio decision-making by pension fund managers: A survey of corporate, public, and union plans. Paper presented at the American Real Estate and Urban Economics Association meeting, January 6, 1995.

18. E. Norman Zietz, E. Worzala, and G. Stacy Sirmans. Insurer portfolio allocations: An exploration of investment decision-making techniques. Paper presented at the American Real Estate Society Meeting, March 1996.

19. J.R. Webb and J. Rubens. The effect of alternative return measures on restricted mixed-asset portfolios. *AREUEA Journal* 16 (Summer 1988), 123–137.

20. D. Geltner. Estimating real estate's systematic risk from aggregate level appraisal-based returns. *AREUEA Journal* 17 (Winter 1989), 463–481.

21. J.L. Pagliari, Jr., J.R. Webb, and J.J. Del Casino. Applying MPT to institutional real estate portfolios: The good, the bad and the uncertain. *Journal of Real Estate Management*, 1995.

22. M. Miles and T. McCue. Historic returns and institutional real estate portfolios. *AREUEA Journal* 10 (1982), 184–197.

23. P. Firstenberg, S.A. Ross, and R.C. Zisler. Managing real estate portfolios. Goldman Sachs & Co. (November 1987).

24. B.R. Danielsen and D.M. Harrison. The impact of property type diversification on REIT liquidity. *Journal of Real Estate Portfolio Management* 13 (2007), 329–344.

25. Miles and McCue. Historic returns and institutional real estate portfolios.

26. D. Hartzell, J. Hekman, and M. Miles. Diversification categories in investment real estate. *AREUEA Journal* 14 (Summer 1986), 230–259.

27. D. Hartzell, D. Shulman, and C. Wurtzebach. Refining the analysis of regional diversification of income-producing real estate. *Journal of Real Estate Research* 2 (Winter 1987), 85–95.

28. G. Mueller. Refining economic diversification strategies for real estate portfolios. *Journal of Real Estate Research* 8 (Winter 1993), 55–68.

29. G.R. Mueller. What will the next real estate cycle look like? *Journal of Real Estate Portfolio Management* 8 (2002), 115–125.

30. T.R. Nelson and S.L. Nelson. Regional models for portfolio diversification. *Journal of Real Estate Portfolio Management* 9(1) (2003), 71–88.

31. P.K. Asabere, R.T. Kleiman, and C.B. McGowan, Jr. The risk-return attributes of international real estate equities. *Journal of Real Estate Research* 6 (1991), 143–152.

32. C. Liu and J. Mei. The predictability of international real estate markets, exchange risks, and diversification consequences. *Real Estate Economics* 26 (1998), 3–39.

33. D. Ling and A. Naranjo. Commercial real estate return performance: A cross-country analysis. *Journal of Real Estate Finance and Economics* 24 (2002), 119–142.

34. C.M. Conover, H.S. Friday, and G.S. Sirmans. Diversification benefits from foreign real estate investments. *Journal of Real Estate Portfolio Management* 8(1) (2002), 17–25.

35. Wilson and Zurbruegg. International Diversification of Real Estate Assets: Is It Worth It? Evidence from the Literature. *Journal of Real Estate Literature.* 11:3 (2003), 257–278.

36. M. Hoesli, J. Lekander, and W. Witkiewicz. International Evidence of Real Estate as a Portfolio Diversifier. *Journal of Real Estate Research* 26:2 (2004), 161–206.

37. C.L. Lim, S. McGreal, and J.R. Webb. Perception of Real Estate Investment Opportunities in Central/South America and Africa. *Journal of Real Estate Portfolio Management* 12 (2006), 250–285.

38. J.B. Corgel and G. Gay. Local economic base, geographic diversification, and risk management of mortgage portfolios. *AREUEA Journal* 15 (Fall 1987), 256–267.

39. T.M. Clauretie. Regional economic diversification and the residential default rate. *Journal of Real Estate Research* 3 (Spring 1988), 87–97.

40. A.J. Ziobrowski and R.J. Curcio. Diversification benefits of U.S. real estate to foreign investors. *Journal of Real Estate Research* 6 (Summer 1991), 119–142.

41. A.G. Mueller and G.R Mueller. Public and private real estate in a mixed-asset portfolio. *Journal of Real Estate Portfolio Management* 9 (2003), 193–203.

42. K. Addae-Dapaah, S.G. Wee, and M.S. Ebrahim. Real estate portfolio diversification by sources of return. *Journal of Real Estate Portfolio Management* 8(1) (2002), 1–15.

43. G. Newell and H.W. Peng. The role of non-traditional real estate sectors in REIT portfolios. *Journal of Real Estate Portfolio Management* 12 (2006), 120–135.

Web Sites

http://www.nareit.com

National Association of Real Estate Investment Trusts provides overall returns on REITs plus returns on equity, mortgage, and hybrid REITs.

http://www.ncreif.com

National Council of Real Estate Investment Fiduciaries provides an unleveraged index of returns on equity and leveraged properties.

http://realestateinvesting.com/blog/2012/05/18/build-your-real-estate-investing-portfolio/

Real estate portfolio investing

APPENDIX 21-A

The Capital Asset Pricing Model Derived from Combining an Asset with the Existing Market Portfolio

If an Asset X is added to the market portfolio, the expected return and risk on the new portfolio can be given as

$$E(R_p) = \alpha E(R_y) + 1 - \alpha E(R_m) \qquad \text{(Equation A21-1)}$$

and

$$\sigma_p = \sqrt{\alpha^2 \sigma_x 2 + (1 - \alpha)^2 \sigma_m 2 + 2\alpha(1 - \alpha)\sigma_x \sigma_m r_{xm}} \qquad \text{(Equation A21-2)}$$

But, if X already exists in the portfolio in its optimal ratio, the excess demand for X must be 0, or

$$\frac{\partial E(R_p)}{\partial \alpha} \Big| = E(R_x) - (R_m) \qquad \text{(Equation A21-3)}$$

$$\frac{\partial \sigma_p}{\partial \sigma} \Big| = r_{ym}\sigma_x - \sigma_m$$

$$\frac{E(R_m) - R_f}{\sigma_m} = \frac{E(R_m) - E(R_x)}{\sigma_m - r_{xm}\sigma_x} \qquad \text{(Equation A21-4)}$$

rearranging,

$$E(R_x) = R_f + \frac{r_{xm}\sigma_x\sigma_m}{\sigma_m^2}\left(E(R_m) - R_f\right)$$

or

$$E(R_y) = R_f + \beta[E(R_m) - R_f]$$

where

$$\beta = \frac{r_{xm}\sigma_x\sigma_m}{\sigma_m^2}$$

LIABILITY, AGENCY PROBLEMS, FRAUD, AND ETHICS IN REAL ESTATE FINANCE

LEARNING OBJECTIVES

In this chapter, we review several topics related to the legal environment of real estate finance. After reading this chapter, you should understand how parties to real estate finance transactions can be held liable for their actions, including fraud, misrepresentation, negligence, and, in some cases, violation of state and federal laws. You should also understand the structure of agency relationships within real estate finance and how those relationships can create incentives for parties to behave in their own interest and against the interest of others. Such behavior may include fraud or unethical practices. You also should see that there are costs—agency costs—associated with preventing parties from acting solely in their own interest and against the interests of others. You will see how insufficient agency monitoring costs lead to agency problems. The failure of many federally insured savings and loans is an example where some parties used fraud and unethical practices to enrich themselves at the expense of others, mainly the general taxpayers. You should understand how insufficient agency costs allowed this wealth transfer.

INTRODUCTION

The central topic of this chapter is the legal environment that surrounds those involved in real estate finance. We also are concerned here with agency relationships, agency costs, fraud, and ethics—both within and outside of the legal system.

In terms of the legal environment, one focus is on the contractual relationships among the parties to real estate finance transactions, the duties that such contractual relationships impose on the parties, and the liabilities faced by the parties for failure to fulfill those duties. Another focus concerns liabilities that arise from violations of state and federal laws. Whether by failure to abide by contractual obligations or by violation of state and federal law, the liabilities faced by lenders, borrowers, and property owners can be substantial. Here, we concentrate on the liabilities faced by lenders, although other parties such as real estate developers and brokers also may incur liabilities. Lenders face liability that may arise from many areas, including enforcement of laws related to the disposal of hazardous waste, laws related to drug enforcement, misrepresentation or fraud in a contract to loan funds, abrupt termination of loan arrangements, or the exercise of undue influence in managing the affairs of a delinquent borrower.

In the remainder of the chapter, we discuss agency relationships between the parties to real estate finance transactions and the role that fraud and ethics plays in those relationships.

LENDERS' LEGAL LIABILITY

In this section, we discuss the legal liability of lenders and other parties involved in financing real estate transactions. The greatest focus over the last several years has been on the liability for a variety of acts or omissions, and the awards have been substantial. Lenders who are not vigilant to the legal environment may find themselves in the role of the debtor. Others, such as real estate developers, brokers, and property owners, must also be aware of the legal environment of real estate finance. To repeat, lenders may be subject to liability in two broad areas. The first occurs when lenders are found liable under state or federal laws regulating certain activities. An example is the liability that results from the improper disposal of hazardous waste on a property for which the lender has a secured interest. The second occurs when lenders have been found to violate contractual obligations involving loan arrangements. Recently, lenders have been held increasingly liable under actions in both arenas.

Hazardous Waste Disposal

As a result of the growing problem associated with the improper disposal of hazardous and toxic waste, the federal government passed the Comprehensive Environmental Response, Compensation, and Liability Act of 1980 (**CERCLA**) and its companion legislation, the Superfund Amendments and Reauthorization Act of 1986 (**SARA**). Then, after much debate, Congress again modified CERCLA in 2002, with the Small Business Liability Relief and Brownfields Revitalization Acts (Brownfields Act). A central purpose of the acts was to pass the cost of cleaning up contaminated sites to those parties that had benefited from the generation and disposal of the waste materials. In 1986 the Environmental Protection Agency (EPA) estimated that the American industry generated about 266 million metric tons of hazardous waste annually, of which 68 percent came from the chemical industry.[1] The EPA currently estimates that there are approximately 27,000 sites in need of cleanup at a cost of more than $300 billion. The cost of cleaning up the most contaminated sites can be overwhelming. In 1986 Union Carbide Corporation agreed to pay at least $40 million to clean up a hazardous waste site in Colorado.[2] CERCLA and SARA attempt to make the parties responsible for the problem bear these large cleanup costs. The Brownfields Act was intended to lessen the CERCLA liability on small businesses, promote and provide financial assistance for the redevelopment of brownfields, and aid efforts by the states to cleanup sites. Lenders may be involved in the process because of the language of the acts and because of recent court decisions that have interpreted that language.

Liability under CERCLA is strict, retroactive, and joint and several. **Strict liability** means that a charged party may not offer as a defense a claim that its actions were not in violation of any law prior to CERCLA. Parties can act in good faith, adhere to a standard of care of a reasonable manufacturer in a similar situation, and still be liable. If they discharged hazardous waste and contaminated a site, they are liable for the cost of cleanup even though they may not have violated previous laws. Retroactive means that parties may be held responsible for previous discharges even though they may no longer own the contaminated property. **Joint and several liability** means that each potentially liable party can be made to bear the entire cost of cleanup even though several parties may have been responsible for the contamination. Also, one or more liable parties may force contribution from other potentially liable parties. Section 113(f) of the act provides that any person may seek contribution from any other person who is liable. Congress wrote the act in this way so as to include as many potentially liable parties as possible, making cleanup more expeditious and less costly to the taxpayer. This feature of the legislation is particularly dangerous for lenders, since the government and other parties to the contamination may look for so-called deep pockets in the cleanup effort.

If a facility is found to be contaminated by hazardous waste, the act defines **potentially responsible parties (PRPs)** as

1. Current owner(s) and operator(s) of the facility.
2. Owner(s) or operator(s) at the time of discharge.
3. Generator(s) of the hazardous substance or the party or parties who arranged for its disposal and treatment.
4. Transporter(s) of the hazardous substance.

By facility the law means "any site or area where a hazardous substance has been deposited, stored, disposed of, or otherwise come to be located." [3] This definition includes a parcel of raw land. Hazardous waste disposal includes any inadvertent leaking and spilling. Under CERCLA, PRPs can be held for damages defined as the cost to remove or mitigate the effect of the hazardous waste as well as injury to any natural resources, and the costs of any studies necessary to determine the effect of the contamination of public health. In writing the law, Congress did not intend to extend liability to lenders in their capacity as lenders. The law excludes from the category of an owner or operator "a person, who, without participating in the management of a vessel or facility, holds an indicia of ownership primarily to protect his security interest in the vessel or facility."[4] This is termed the **secured-lender exemption** and means that a PRP owner or operator does not include a lender that holds a mortgage or deed-of-trust on a property as security for a note.

Lenders may lose this exemption, however, if they foreclose on the contaminated property (and through a foreclosure sale become an owner) or if, in an effort to avoid foreclosure, they become involved in the operations of a contaminated facility. When a company is losing money and cannot make its loan payments, a lender frequently becomes involved in the firm's operations. The lender would like to restore profitability so that the company can resume loan payments and costly foreclosure can be avoided. It is likely Congress did not foresee issues related to liability under the act when lenders foreclose or influence the operations of contaminated facilities. The lack of congressional guidance in the act for such circumstances left a void to be filled by the judiciary. As you will see shortly, interpretive court decisions have not been kind to lenders.

Lender Defenses

Several defenses are available to a lender who may be a PRP, through either a foreclosure or a loan workout whereby the lender influences the business operations of the borrower. Under the first defense, the lender simply claims not to be a PRP. Under a second defense, the lender claims the contamination resulted solely from an act of God, an act of war, or the act or omission of a third party being neither an employee or agent nor having a contractual relationship with the lender. This is the "Hey, how did that happen?" defense. For this defense to hold, the actual contaminator cannot have any contractual relationship with the lender. CERCLA broadly defines a contractual relationship as "including but ... not limited to land contracts, deeds, or other instruments transferring title or possession."[5] A third defense is the innocent landowner (or innocent purchaser) defense. Here, the lender claims to have had no knowledge of the contamination when it foreclosed and obtained title to the property. Under this defense, there is no liability if the lender can demonstrate that it acquired the property after the disposal or placement of the hazardous waste and did not know or have any reason to know that there was hazardous waste on the property. There is a "Catch 22" to this defense, however. Courts have ruled that in order not to have any reason to know of the contamination, the lender would have had to make the "all appropriate inquiry" into the previous ownership and use of the property. Furthermore, the discovery of hazardous waste at a site is sufficient evidence that the lender failed to make the necessary inquiry to discover its existence. In any event, it is likely that lenders for commercial real estate will be held to a higher standard of inquiry than lenders for residential real estate, since hazardous waste is much more likely to occur on commercial and industrial sites. An owner that discovers the hazardous waste and then sells the property also loses this defense. A fourth defense is the secured-lender exemption discussed above.

Furthermore, a responsible party may avoid CERCLA liability through an indemnity or hold harmless agreement entered into before filing of a lawsuit. Most courts have held these contracts valid, since they do not excuse the fundamental liability. The agreements only change who will pay for the cleanup and the administration efforts. Accordingly, a responsible party may transfer any potential loss from a CERCLA action to someone else through a contractual relationship.

Finally, in Section 113 of CERCLA, a contribution suit may allow responsible parties to recoup financial losses from others after assuming a disproportionate share of the response costs. Initially, the U.S. Supreme Court held that a responsible party may not sue for contribution under Section 113 if they have not been a party to prior action under Section 106 or 107(a) of CERCLA; however, on July 2, 2007, in *United States v. Atlantic Research Corp.* 127 S. Ct. 2331 (2007), the court unanimously reinstated the right of private parties who cleanup another's mess either voluntarily or by coercion to bring a lawsuit for strict liability under CERCLA that may impose joint and several liability on the defendants. Historically, the courts choose to evaluate one to many factors in determining the totality of the circumstances when allocating response costs among liable parties.

Moreover, parties with very little or negligible contributions or firms that discharged only municipal waste to the site may receive a *de micromis* exemption from the government. The EPA receives broad latitude in making these decisions, which is peculiarly exempt from judicial review.

Initial Judicial Decisions

Several early court cases have addressed each of the above defenses. We review the important cases.

United States v. Mirable.[6] This 1985 case involved three lenders that had a secured interest in a property. Anna and Thomas Mirable obtained title to the property from American Bank and Trust (ABT) after the latter had foreclosed on its loan to Turco Coatings Inc., the former owner. Of the three lenders, ABT was the high bidder at the foreclosure sale. ABT did not immediately accept the deed to the property from the sheriff but instead secured the property against vandalism, showed the property to prospective buyers, and made some inquiries about disposing of some drums containing hazardous waste. It was about 4 months after the foreclosure sale that ABT assigned its right to the deed to the Mirables. Then, about a year later, the EPA discovered the drums, ordered a cleanup, and sued the Mirables for recovery of the cleanup costs, $249,702.52. The Mirables then joined the three lenders as defendants.

The federal district court found that ABT was not liable, since it had simply foreclosed on the property and taken steps to secure it against further depreciation. A second lender, the Small Business Administration (SBA), also was held not liable under CERCLA. Although SBA regulations called for extensive management assistance when borrowers faced default, no such assistance was ever provided by the SBA. Their failure to follow their own administrative procedures may have saved the SBA from liability.

A third lender was not so fortunate. One of the loan officers attended advisory meetings with the borrower. The purpose of the meetings was to improve the management of the financial and marketing affairs of the company. A second loan officer was even more involved with the running of the company's business affairs. Testimony indicated that he was always at the plant site and was in "control" of the day-to-day operations of the facility. He reassigned personnel, determined which orders were to be filled, and made changes in the manufacturing process. As a result, the court held that the third lender exercised sufficient control over the operations of the business and facility as to make it a responsible party.

United States v. Maryland Bank and Trust Company.[7] This 1986 case involved a secured lender that foreclosed on a property and took title through a sheriff's sale. The lender, Maryland Bank and Trust (MBT), still had title to the property 4 years later when the EPA inspected the site and discovered that hazardous waste had been improperly disposed of on the site in the 1970s. After MBT refused to clean up the site, the EPA had the job done and then sued MBT to recover the costs. MBT pleaded the secured-lender exemption defense. The court rejected this defense, however. It stated that the law grants the exemption if the PRP "holds" (present tense emphasized) an indicia of ownership. The foreclosure, the court noted, changed the indicia of ownership to actual ownership at the time of the cleanup. Because of the foreclosure, the security interest did not exist at the time of the cleanup; rather, actual ownership existed. Furthermore, it interpreted the phrase "owner and operator" in the CERCLA legislation in the disjunctive—that is, a PRP need not be both an owner and an operator but only one or the other. The court also was concerned that granting MBT a secured-lender exemption would allow it to benefit from the government's cleanup of the wastes. If the bank were held to be unaccountable, it could purchase the contaminated property cheaply at a foreclosure sale, wait for the government to clean it up, and sell the property at a profit. This would simply "convert CERCLA into an insurance scheme for financial institutions by protecting them against possible losses due to the security of loans with polluted properties."[8] We will return to this issue when we discuss the next case.

The MBT ruling seems a little harsh and for reasons discussed below would likely lead lenders to think twice before foreclosing on delinquent loans. It could even have more extended effects. As a result of the ruling, lenders may be reluctant to loan funds where the security is any property on which there is even the remote possibility that hazardous waste could have been disposed in the past or even subsequent to the loan. Funding for industrial and commercial developments may be severely reduced. Fortunately, the court gave hope that not all foreclosures on contaminated properties would result in lender liability for cleanup costs. In the MBT decision, the court added that the lender had owned the property for nearly

4 years before the EPA cleanup. The court emphasized that it was not considering the issue of the exemption when applied to a lender who quickly resells the property after a foreclosure, although the court gave no indication why the length of time that a lender holds ownership is important in determining liability for cleanup costs.

Guidice v. BFG Electroplating Co.[9] This 1989 case is interesting for the court's recognition of option values related to the CERCLA legislation first hinted at in the *Maryland Bank* case. To set the scene, imagine a parcel of real estate with great market value, except for the presence of hazardous waste. Its value with waste present will be its value with no waste less the cost of cleanup. It could have negative value if the cost of cleanup is substantial. Now, consider what may occur if secured lenders could never be held responsible for the cost of cleaning up hazardous waste. They would have a call option on contaminated properties. The strike price would be the value of the property with the waste present, and the market value would be the value with no waste. To see how this works, assume the value of a property is $1 million without waste present and $100,000 with waste present (the cost of cleanup is therefore $900,000). The owner of the property is unable to sell it in the marketplace for more than $100,000. If the amount of the loan securing the property is more than $100,000, the owner may default and give the property to the lender by default (exercise the put option). The lender need only bid $100,000 at the sheriff's sale to acquire the property. If the lender cannot be held responsible for the cleanup, the lender can sell the property for its higher market value, $1 million. A wealth redistribution from the party occurs that pays for the cleanup (taxpayers, in this example) to the lender.

In *Guidice v. BFG Electroplating Co.* the court recognized this problem. In this case, the owner of a metal polishing company defaulted on his loan from National Bank. The lender did not immediately foreclose but preferred to work toward solving the borrower's financial problems. For about a year, representatives of the lender met with company officials to discuss management affairs such as work shifts, customer accounts, and so forth. The lender also attempted to find buyers for the business. Despite these efforts, the company failed and defaulted on its loan. The borrower owned the property for 9 months subsequent to a foreclosure sale, before selling it to members of the family of the former owner. During this time, the lender arranged for the removal of drums of hazardous materials inherited at the foreclosure sale. Two years after resale of the property, nearby residents claimed damage from toxic waste and sued several parties. National Bank was named as a PRP because it was an owner and operator for 9 months. National Bank claimed a secured lender exemption.

The court found no excessive involvement in the management of the business by the lender prior to foreclosure and certainly no involvement in the disposal of waste materials. However, citing the *Maryland Bank and Trust* case, the court held that once National Bank foreclosed and held title to the property, it lost its secured-lender exemption. There was no reference to the period of time that National Bank held the property, however. Recall that the length of time of ownership appeared to be a crucial element in the *Maryland Bank and Trust* case. In this case, the court noted that there was leaking and dripping of hazardous waste during the 9 months that National Bank owned the property. This was sufficient to find the lender liable as an owner or operator that allowed contamination during its tenure as owner. Additionally, the court noted another concern. It stated that all prospective buyers at a foreclosure sale would have to factor in the cost of cleaning up hazardous waste in their bids. Moreover, they would not have secured-lender exemptions. This would give the secured lender a comparative advantage and allow it to obtain the property for a very low amount. The court added that the lender could then hold the property while the government cleaned it up. The lender then could sell the property at a substantial profit, putting the cleanup cost to the taxpayers.

The court was clearly influenced by this option value in making its decision. Note, however, that in this case, the lender sold the property before any cleanup was attempted. The court appears to have been concerned with a general situation of enhancement rather than any enrichment in this particular case. As a result of the *Maryland Bank* and *Guidice* decisions, the optimal policy for lenders may be to avoid foreclosing on contaminated properties. Foreclosure may be optimal only after the EPA has cleaned up the property. Although the EPA can obtain a lien for the cost of cleaning up the property, it is a judgment lien and would not have priority over the lender's secured lien, since the secured lien was recorded first. In this way, the lender never becomes an owner and would not become a PRP, providing that the lender also avoided controlling the facility. As we see in the following case, the exercise of control over a facility can cause a lender to become a PRP.

Fleet Factors Corporation.[10] Lender liability may have been extended even further by this 1990 case. Here, the focus returned to lender involvement with management decisions in a case where the lender did not foreclose on the real estate. Fleet Factors Corporation advanced funds to Swainsboro Print Works and secured the loan principally with Swainsboro's accounts receivable, but also with equipment and real estate. After the business encountered some difficulties, it filed for bankruptcy and continued operations under the supervision of the bankruptcy court. Things did not get better, and Swainsboro eventually ceased operations and began selling off its inventory and collecting accounts receivable. Before any inventory was sold, Fleet Factors checked the credit of the buyer before authorizing shipment. Any factor would do this, since the inventory and accounts receivable are collateral for the loan.

Several months after Swainsboro ceased operations, Fleet Factors foreclosed on its loans, taking title to the equipment but not the real estate. Fleet Factors then auctioned off a portion of the equipment and removed the remainder and washed its hands of the affair. Two months later the EPA discovered 700 leaking drums of hazardous waste and damaged asbestos on the premises. The defunct Swainsboro still owned the real estate. However, it was revealed that the auctioneers that sold the equipment for Fleet Factors had moved the leaking drums, and the contractor that removed the unsold equipment damaged the asbestos, making it hazardous. Both the auctioneer and the contractor would have had a contractual relationship with the lender, Fleet Factors. The EPA sued Fleet Factors as a PRP.

The federal district court found that financial advice and actions as a factor did not involve or influence the day-to-day operations of the facility and thus, Fleet Factors was not liable on this account. On the question of whether Fleet Factors should be held liable for the actions of the auctioneer and the contractor, the district court noted that there was a dispute about the facts. It suggested that the parties allow the appellate court to rule on this issue. Fleet Factors took the district court's invitation and appealed the case (even though it was not liable under the management of the business issue). The appellate court took another look at all the issues and facts. The result was remarkable. First, the court rejected the distinction between influencing the financial decisions of a firm and influencing or controlling its day-to-day operations. It concluded that influencing a firm's financial decisions can affect the day-to-day operations. The court noted that "a secured creditor may incur CERCLA liability, without being an operator, by participating in the financial management of the facility to a degree indicating a capacity to influence the (borrower's) treatment of hazardous wastes."[11] Thus, under this interpretation, a secured lender can incur liability if its involvement with the financial management of the business is sufficiently broad to conclude that it may affect how the firm disposes of its hazardous waste. It should be added that Fleet Factors had somewhat more control of the company than indicated by the testimony at the district court trial. The appellate court pointed out that Fleet Factors required Swainsboro to obtain permission before shipping products, established prices on excess inventory, determined when employees should be laid off, processed the firm's employment and tax forms, and even controlled access to the facility. This was sufficient involvement in the management of the firm to warrant liability under CERCLA. The court was also quick to point out that nothing in its decision gutted the secured-lender exemption. Lenders simply must be careful to restrict their involvement in the debtor's business to only the purely financial aspects.

Although the holding of Fleet Factors to be liable for the cleanup costs appears to be harsh, there are several considerations of this decision that blunt its impact on lenders. The nature of the liability established by this decision is that any participation by the lender must have the capacity to influence the manner in which hazardous wastes are treated. The simple fact that a lender may have influence with a borrower by virtue of the loan arrangement does not expose the lender to CERCLA liability. Even agreements in the loan document that give the lender the right to control the business in the event of delinquency or default may not establish liability. Only lender actions that influence or have the capacity to influence disposal of hazardous waste will create a potential CERCLA liability. Also, because the case was on appeal for a summary judgment, the facts as indicated by the EPA were accepted as true. The case was remanded back to the district court for a hearing on the merits of the case. Finally, in this case, two principals of Fleet Factors were also principals of Swainsboro Paint Works. The appellate court may have been influenced by the close relationship of the parties. That is, the court may have considered Fleet Factors and Swainsboro Paint Works to be the same entity.

Bergsoe Metal Corporation.[12] This is another 1990 case that addressed the issue of lender control of business activities. This decision backed away somewhat from the broad sweep of the *Fleet Factors* decision. The case involved a municipal corporation in Oregon, the Port of St. Helens that had issued industrial revenue bonds and advanced the proceeds to various industrial firms to locate in the port. After Bergsoe purchased the property in question, it entered into a sale-leaseback agreement with Port of St. Helens Authority. Thus, legal title vested with the authority. As owner of the property and as lender, the authority gave some financial advice to Bergsoe. When the plant site was found to be contaminated, the authority was declared to be the owner for the purpose of CERCLA liability. It claimed secured-lender exemption.

The court ruled in the authority's favor in this case. The court recognized that the focus was on the extent of lender control over management. The court stated that under any reasonable standard there must be "some actual management of the facility" before CERCLA liability can be established. This opinion appeared to retreat somewhat from the *Fleet Factors* decision in terms of establishing liability in cases where lenders may exercise some control over the strictly financial decisions of the borrower.

APRIL 1992 EPA REGULATION

As a result of the uncertainty surrounding the liability of lenders caused by these various court cases, many lenders lobbied the EPA to clarify the rules under which they could foreclose on a property and escape liability under CERCLA. In April 1992, the EPA responded by promulgating such rules. The new rules gave guidance by categorically providing examples of management activity that a lender can participate in and not incur a liability for cleanup costs. Specifically, the rules are as follows:

1. any and all actions that occur prior to the creation of the security interest;
2. periodic monitoring and/or inspection of the property;
3. ongoing involvement that results from an inspection of the property;
4. requiring the borrower to clean up any contamination;
5. requiring the borrower to comply with any laws;
6. restructuring the loan arrangement;
7. requiring the payment of more rent or interest;
8. exercising the right the lender may have under the law or under any warranties, covenants, conditions, or promises of the borrower; and
9. providing specific or general financial or administrative advice, suggestions, or even control.

BUT THEN A COURT DECISION

If lenders thought that the new EPA regulation would clarify the risk faced under foreclosure proceedings, they were wrong. In 1994 an appeals court invalidated the 1992 EPA regulation. In *Chemical Manufacturers Association v. Environmental Protection Agency,*[13] a federal appeals court ruled that the EPA regulation exceeded its authority. In its decision the court said that "it cannot be argued that Congress intended EPA, one of many potential plaintiffs, to have authority to, by regulation, define liability for a class of potential defendants." Thus, it appeared that any relief of the sort intended by the 1992 EPA regulation would have to occur in Congress.

CONGRESS ACTS

On September 9, 1996, President Clinton signed into law an omnibus spending bill for fiscal year 1997. Contained in this budget bill was a provision that codified the 1992 EPA rule Asset Conservation, Lender Liability and Deposit Insurance Protection Act of 1996). Under the act, the term *participating in the management* now includes actually participating in the operations but not merely having the capacity to influence or the unexercised right to control operations. Under the act, the lender can engage in the following activities and still retain the secured lender exemption: (a) hold, abandon, or release a security interest; (b) include in the loan documents, covenants, warranties; or other conditions relating to environmental compliance; (c) monitor or enforce loan documents; (d) inspect the property; (e) require the borrower to remediate the property; (f) provide financial services to cure a default; (g) renegotiate the terms of a loan; and (h) exercise remedies allowed under the law for a breach of the terms of the loan. Finally, the act allows a lender to foreclose on a property and thereafter sell, maintain business activities, wind up operations, and undertake a response action under CERCLA without losing its exemption.

The EPA rule essentially provides that a lender is defined to participate in management or decision-making control over a borrower's handling of hazardous waste when it takes responsibility for the day-to-day operations regarding environmental compliance or exercises control over the business as a whole. Under these circumstances the lender may be held liable under CERCLA.

Summary

As a result of case law, it is clear that lenders face increased exposure to liability for the cleanup costs of improperly disposed hazardous waste. The exposure becomes greater when lenders foreclose on and participate in the management of the firm that owns the contaminated facility. This increased exposure to liability may have an effect on real estate finance that was hinted at by the court in the Fleet Factors decision. If lenders become increasingly liable for the risk posed by hazardous wastes (beyond the risk of a decline in the market value of property that serves as collateral), they will, in an efficient market, incorporate the higher expected risk into loan terms, say, the interest rate. Firms that are likely to produce hazardous waste will find financing more expensive. Such firms will either be unable to obtain financing (eliminating the hazardous waste at the source) or will behave in a fashion that reduces the risk of contamination. For example, a firm may incur added costs of safety measures to avoid contamination. These added costs may be more than offset by lower interest costs imposed by lenders. In this way, contamination risks are reduced through terms in the real estate finance market.

Risk Management for Lender Liability

Lenders can mitigate their exposure to liability for the cleanup costs of hazardous wastes in any of several ways. First, they can avoid taking a security interest in any industrial facility that is likely to be used in such a fashion as to produce hazardous waste as a by-product. Second, they can make sure that any site is absolutely free of contamination before making a loan. Third, the lender should avoid any loan covenants that may negatively impact the borrower's ability to properly dispose of wastes. Subsequent to a loan, a borrower may need to obtain additional financing to install equipment to eliminate wastes. Covenants in the original note that prevent such additional financing may be considered an action that affects the borrower's ability to treat waste. The same may be true if the lender finances the borrower with a continuing line of credit and then refuses to advance funds for a waste prevention or cleanup program. Recall that under the appeal in *Fleet Factors*, the standard for the court was the lender's capacity to influence the borrower's treatment of toxic wastes.

Fourth, lenders may seek a separate indemnity agreement from the borrower. A typical indemnity agreement would provide for the borrower to reimburse the lender for any liability that the lender incurs as a result of an improper disposal of hazardous materials. Such indemnities are not disallowed under CERCLA. Recall that Section 113(f) of CERCLA provides that "any person may seek contribution from any other person who is liable or potentially liable under Section 107(a) (and) … such claims … shall be governed by Federal law." Despite this wording, there is some question as to whether an indemnity agreement may be enforceable after a foreclosure where state laws preclude deficiency judgments. That is, although federal law allows for actions that seek contribution, the act does not provide any guidance as to where state laws may affect the indemnity agreements. Some lenders in California, the largest antideficiency judgment state, have executed separate nonsecured indemnity agreements to cover environmental claims. They are nonsecured so as to place them outside of the antideficiency judgment statutes.

Even if a state court were to deny a judgment on an indemnity contract because it violated antideficiency statutes designed to prevent double recovery, the lender may proceed on other grounds. The lender could seek recovery, for example, for bad faith waste of the property. That is, most deeds of trust that secure a property contain provisions that preclude the borrower from taking actions that destroy the market value of the collateral. Improperly disposing of hazardous waste on the property would certainly qualify as bad faith waste. Also, if the borrower did not divulge the true nature of the anticipated use of the facility on the loan application, the lender may recover by alleging fraud.

The area of lender liability for hazardous waste costs is a developing area of the law. Certainly, lenders are exposed to greater risks as a result of CERCLA, SARA, and recent court cases. Securedlender exemption and innocent-owner defenses are not as solid as one may think. In an effort to solve the huge hazardous waste cleanup problem, the judicial arena in which many of these issues are played out is disposed toward finding as many responsible parties with adequate resources (deep pockets) as possible.

Lenders may find themselves on the losing end of real estate transactions for other reasons. Another area fraught with dangers for lenders is the war on drugs.

Lenders and the Drug War

As a result of a growing drug problem in this country, Congress passed the Comprehensive Drug Abuse Prevention and Control Act in 1970. This act authorizes the federal government to confiscate property used to manufacture, transport, store, and dispense illicit drugs. The original focus of the act was on personal property, such as cars and boats. Real estate could be confiscated only if purchased with the proceeds of drug sales. In 1984 the act was amended to include real estate. Now, all rights and interests in real estate property are subject to forfeiture if the real estate is used in any way to facilitate the drug trade. This means that real estate may be confiscated from an owner, even if the owner rented the property to someone who used it to carry out drug transactions. It also means that a lender who forecloses on a property may lose it under the same circumstances. The 1984 amendment did include an innocent-property owner defense that said "that no property shall be forfeited under this paragraph, to the extent of an interest of an owner by reason of any act or omission established by that owner to have been committed or omitted without the knowledge or consent of the owner." Lenders run the risk of losing property held as collateral for the loan because of several features of this federal legislation.

First, the seizure of the property is a civil, not a criminal, proceeding. The property, not the owner, is charged with the offense. This means that the owner need not be convicted or even charged with a drug-related offense. Second, the federal government claims a right to the property interests at the moment the property is used for illegal drug transactions. This means that if a lender obtains title to a property previously used for drug sales (for example, by way of a foreclosure), the lender may lose it even though it is no longer used for such purposes. Third, all of the owner's real estate may be confiscated, even though only a portion has been used for illegal purposes. Fourth, property of great value may be seized, even if the illegal activity involved minor amounts of drugs. The amount of drugs involved need only be sufficient to be punishable by at least 1 year in jail. (In *Calero-Toledo v. Pearson Yacht Leasing Co.*,[14] the U.S. Supreme Court upheld the seizure of a $19,800 yacht after authorities discovered two marijuana cigarettes on board.) Fifth, the owner or mortgagee of the property may be completely innocent. Someone who leases the property and conducts an illegal drug trade will expose the property to forfeiture. Finally, the owner or mortgagee does not have any rights to the income from the property after it has been seized. In *U.S. v. Property Known as 708-710 West 9th St., Erie, Pa.*,[15] the owner-mortgagor defaulted on a loan after he was arrested for selling drugs. The government seized the rental property and began collecting rents but paid nothing to the mortgagee. The court held that the mortgagee was not entitled to any income from the property, despite an assignment-of-rents provision in the deed-of-trust. The court did allow the mortgagee to collect the balance of the mortgage when the government disposed of the property, however.

The danger for the lender is greatest when it forecloses on property that has previously been used to support illegal drug transactions. The lender may lose the property to the government if it fails in an innocent-owner defense. To establish this defense, the owner (lender) must prove more than simple ignorance that the property was used for drug sales. The owner must demonstrate that all reasonable measures to investigate the use of the property were taken. This is called a **due diligence defense** and may be an enormously difficult task for some lenders, especially those that advance many loans on properties in diverse geographical locations. Furthermore, the lender may run into trouble if it attempts to avoid this risk by denying loans in areas of known drug activity. It runs the risk of violating the Home Mortgage Disclosure Act (1975) and the Community Reinvestment Act (1978). In Chapter 7, we saw that these antiredlining acts impose penalties on lenders who identify neighborhoods within which they will not make loans.

Liability from Lender/Borrower Relationship

Lenders and borrowers enter into contractual relationships. These relationships are governed by both statutory law and the interpretation of that law by the courts. Since real estate loans are considered commercial transactions, the applicable law governing the lender/borrower relationship is the **Uniform Commercial Code (UCC)**. The code specifies the rights and obligations of contracting parties. The courts interpret the meaning and intent of the code, assess or absolve liability, and fix judgments (monetary damages or awards). Often the decision of the trial court may be reversed by an appeals court. Judicial law is determined ultimately at the appeals level.

There are two primary and several minor areas of lender behavior that can give rise to liability. The two primary areas involve nonperformance of oral commitments and failure to extend credit beyond a certain date. In the latter case, a common cause of legal action is the calling of a demand note by the lender without notification. We discuss these two problem areas first and then consider other sources of lender liability.

Oral Commitments for Extension of Credit

First, consider how most real estate projects are developed. A developer will have a plan to construct a commercial real estate project. The plans may call for the acquisition of the land, the development of the property (roads, utilities, and so on), and the construction of the facility. In most cases, the developer will sell the property when completed. The developer's financing need is limited to the acquisition, development, and construction (ADC) phase of the investment. Since few developers have the means or the desire to finance the ADC stage from their own equity, they seek lenders for this purpose. The typical ADC loan will be for only the period through completion of the project, at which time the loan will be repaid from the proceeds of the sale of the facility by the developer. To see how a lawsuit may result, consider the following scenario. A real estate developer desires to purchase a piece of raw land for $1 million and build a $7 million office building on the site. The seller of the land requires an earnest money deposit of $50,000 before signing a sales contract. Before the developer gives the seller of the land the $50,000, he requests a loan from a loan officer, who is also his friend, at a local bank. He has done business with this loan officer for many years. The loan officer assures the developer that, based on his past credit history, there will be no problem in obtaining a loan for the acquisition and development of the property. Based on this **oral commitment** the developer, unwisely, gives the seller of the land a $50,000 deposit and signs a contract to purchase the land in 1 month hence. Two weeks later, when the developer arranges for the loan to purchase the property, the bank, concerned with a recent reversal in the local real estate market, refuses to make the loan. The developer loses not only the $50,000 deposit but also any profits that he would have made on the deal. He may attempt to seek compensation through the court system on the basis that an oral commitment to make a loan was breached.

Consider a second example. Assume that the developer had been successful in arranging the ADC loan. Also, assume that the bank was concerned with some cost overruns in previous projects developed by the borrower. If the bank lends the developer several million dollars to construct a project, it does not wish to see those funds exhausted when the facility is only half-completed. It would have only a half completed facility as collateral for the loan. Thus, the bank puts in a demand feature to the line-of-credit. The developer can "take down" as needed as the project is developed, but if the bank's construction auditors (experts in the field of construction costs) determine that there are insufficient safeguards to prevent cost overruns, the bank can freeze the remaining line-of-credit and call the amount due on the note immediately. Demand notes (payable upon the demand of the lender at any time) are common in commercial transactions. By their terms, they do not require prior notification before payment is demanded.

In this example, if the bank were to determine that its collateral was in danger when the project was half-completed and decide to call the note, the developer would be unable to make the payment on short notice. The developer can neither quickly sell a half-completed real estate project nor arrange for a substitute loan. If the bank forecloses on the note and sells the property at a foreclosure sale, the developer loses not only the original deposit but also the profits on the development. Again, the developer may attempt to seek relief from the court system.

In the one case, there is a failure to make a loan based on an oral commitment. In the other case, there is a failure to make a loan extension (extend an existing loan) beyond the demand date. In both cases, it would appear that the developer has little hope of success in court. As explained later in this chapter, contracts for real estate financing must be in writing to be enforced. Also, the UCC allows parties to contract for loans that are payable on demand without notice. But, suppose you were a member of a jury in a case brought by the developer and were made aware of the following facts: that the developer had always received oral commitments in the past and had come to rely on this method of doing business; that in the case where the demand note was called, the bank had no reason to believe that the collateral was in jeopardy; that the loan was called because a new loan officer was hired who simply "didn't like" the developer. In whose favor would you decide? In many such cases, jurors have sided with the developer. But, before we review some actual lender liability cases, consider the following arguments that suggest the lender in our example might, or should, prevail.

Oral Commitments by Lenders

Lenders may orally commit to make a loan. At first, one might think that there would be little room for liability in cases of oral commitments, since contracts to borrow funds to finance real estate are always in writing and usually quite detailed. In fact, the statute of frauds requires such contracts to be in writing. Specifically, the statute of frauds says that the following contracts must be in writing in order to be enforced:

- Agreements that cannot be performed within 1 year.
- Promises to answer for the debts of another (surety contracts).
- Promises made in consideration of marriage.
- Agreements relating to real property.
- Contracts exceeding $500 for the sale of goods.
- Contracts by executors.

If the agreement is not in writing, then the provisions of the agreement will not be binding on either party (unless some exception, not discussed here, may apply). It is obvious that nearly every real estate loan will fall under the provisions of the statute of frauds. Yet, several successful suits have been brought by borrowers against lenders for oral statements or commitments related to a real estate loan. Lenders have been increasingly subject to suits concerning items in the contractual relationship of a real estate loan that have not been part of some written agreement. In their suits, borrowers generally do not claim that the lender violated any technical terms of a written loan agreement, only that it reneged on oral commitments or violated long-standing practices.

As a result of the moderate success that borrowers have had in such suits in the past, lenders in many states have sought legislation implementing one of two types of modification—**statute of fraud** amendments or **credit agreement statutes**. Statute of fraud amendments would invalidate any oral commitment for granting or extending credit. These relate primarily to loans made by financial institutions for other than personal, family, or household extension of an existing line of credit and typically consist of three main sections. The first section defines certain terms such as creditor, debtor, credit agreement, and financial institution. The second section requires extensions of credit to be in writing and signed by both parties. The third section generally contains what are known as safe harbors for lenders. Safe harbors are actions that the lender can take that cannot be interpreted as implying an extension of credit. Examples include giving financial advice to the borrower, agreeing with the borrower not to take certain actions under the existing loan contract such as accelerating the loan, and so forth. Statute of fraud amendments and credit extension agreements are similar in that they both give added support to lenders by explicitly requiring modification of loan contracts to be in writing before either party can enforce them.

Termination of Demand Notes without Notification

As you can imagine, a call of a demand note without notification can be financially distressing to a cash-short real estate developer or other business that depends on the line of credit for its day-to-day operations. Many lawsuits have resulted from a short notice call of a demand note. The damages often may include the value of a business that has failed because of the call of the demand note by the lender. The plaintiff (borrower) will assert that the lender failed to act in "good faith" as required by law. Although the requirement to act in good faith is a well-accepted legal concept, it is not clear if it should apply to situations where the terms of contracts are spelled out, such as with demand notes and other types of real estate financing.

Section 1-203 of the UCC provides that "every contract or duty within this chapter imposes an obligation of good faith in its performance or enforcement," while Section 1-201 defines **good faith** as "honesty in fact in the conduct or transaction concerned."[16] Most of the concern in the code about good faith centered on commercial sales (and not loans) where one or more of the terms of a contract may have been left open ended. This is to say that the framers of the code were concerned that one party to an open-ended sales contract might be disadvantaged if the other were not required to bargain in good faith. As an example, assume that a buyer of a product signs a contract to purchase an item for a given price plus an unstipulated charge for shipping and handling.

When the item is delivered, the bill reflects an outrageously high shipping and handling charge. The courts would probably not require the buyer to pay for the charges.

Yet, the code does address good faith in loan contracts as well. In Section 1-208, it states that when the terms of a note allow the lender to "accelerate payment or performance ... 'at will' or 'when he deems himself insecure' ... he shall have the power to do so only if he in good faith believes that the prospect of payment or performance is impaired."[17] This remark is aimed more at term notes (those with a specific maturity date) that can be accelerated than at demand notes. The Official Commentary to Section 1-208 states that the section has no application to demand notes because their nature permits call at any time with or without good reason. The difference between calling a term note "at will" and a demand note is confusing, to say the least. Some court decisions have required good faith practices for demand notes, even though it is clear from the Official Commentary that good faith should be applicable only to term notes that have acceleration clauses. Other court decisions, on the other hand, have held the opposite view and have refused to consider whether the lender has acted in good faith in calling a demand note.

Oral Commitments and Credit Termination: Court Cases

Lenders generally have been successful in defending themselves against liability on these issues, but the success has occurred primarily at the appeals level. In *Kruse v. Bank of America*[18] an apple grower in California claimed damage as a result of the lender's failure to make a loan after making an oral commitment. Although the jury at the trial level awarded the apple grower almost $47 million, the appeals court overturned the decision based on the fact that the commitment was not in writing. The results in this case are typical of many suits brought against lenders for failure to advance funds for which there is no written agreement. The results of suits are more mixed when an existing loan is accelerated (terminated), either before its maturity date or, if a demand note, without any notification.

In *Centerre Bank of Kansas City v. Distributors, Inc.*,[19] the lender extended a line of credit to the sole shareholder of Distributors, Inc., in return for a $900,000 demand note, a security interest in the firm's inventory and accounts receivable, and the personal guarantee of the owner. In the early 1980s, the owner had sold 20 percent of the stock to the firm's general manager, who desired to purchase the remainder. The general manager was concerned that the lender might not continue the financing arrangement under new management. The loan officer at Centerre assured the general manager that the financing arrangement would continue as long as the original owner continued to provide a personal guarantee. After the general manager purchased the firm, the loan officer informed him that his personal guarantee also would be required, in addition to that of the former owner. These additional guarantees would assure the continued financing, according to the loan officer. Three days after the guarantees were delivered, the bank gave 60 days notice that it was calling the demand note. During this time, the bank extended funds and received payments on the line of credit. To no avail, it also helped the new owners seek alternative financing. Ultimately, the new owners were forced to turn over the assets of the business and cease operations.

Evidence at the trial suggested that the bank knew that the call of the demand note would put Distributors out of business, but the president of the bank did not think that the new owner could manage the business and, in fact, did not like the new owner personally.

Although the jury found for the plaintiff in this case (undoubtedly as a result of the behavior of the lender), the appellate court held that a good faith obligation does not apply to the decision of a lender to call a demand note.[20] Citing the appellate court in another case,[21] it stated that the application of Section 1-203 of the UCC would add another term to the loan arrangement that was not intended by either party.

The lender in similar case did not fare as well. In *K.M.C. Co., Inc. v. Irving Trust Co.*[22] the lender called a demand note on a line of credit without any notification. The jury found for the debtor, K.M.C., and the appeals court affirmed, undoubtedly because of the apparently callous nature of the lender's actions. The evidence indicated that the lender called the demand note without prior notice despite the fact that the bank had a policy of notification in such events. Also in the past, the bank had covered previous K.M.C. overdrafts via a line of credit. The evidence demonstrated that the bank knew that calling the note would lead to financial ruin for the firm. Finally, the call of the demand note was motivated by a personality conflict between a bank officer and the president of K.M.C.

Given this scenario, one can see why the case focused on the "good faith" concept. In its decision, the trial court stated that the lender had a good faith obligation to notify K.M.C. prior to discontinuing the line-of-credit arrangement, this despite the express written provisions of the line-of-credit agreement that did not call for notification. The demand provision, it said, is like a general insecurity or default clause and is therefore subject to the good faith standard outlined in Section 1-208 of the UCC. Although that section allows acceleration on default, it requires that the lender feel that the security is jeopardized. That, according to the *K.M.C.* court, was not the motivation in the call of the line of credit. This decision was made in spite of the Official Commentary on this section that stated that such good faith standards did not apply to demand notes whose very nature permitted a call at any time and for any reason. It is clear that the *K.M.C.* court was confused between the acceleration clause of a loan with a maturity date and the acceleration of a demand note or line of credit. The court justified its decision by way of analogy to another section of the UCC that addresses contracts for sales of goods [Sec. 2-309(3)], stating that "the application of principles of good faith and sound commercial practice normally call for such notification of the termination of a going contract relationship as will give the other party reasonable time to seek a substitute arrangement."

The court in this case likely failed to understand the nature of a demand note. Demand notes have the provision of call at the will of the lender precisely because notification may give the debtor an opportunity to waste more of the secured assets or take other actions that may be injurious to the lender. If lenders have the ability to call a demand note or line of credit at will, they will have greater protection and less risk. For the reduced risk, lenders will require a lower initial interest rate. Both the lender and the borrower profit from the arrangement. This is stating the obvious, since demand notes or lines of credit are very popular loan instruments sought out by borrowers because of these favorable terms. The very fact that borrowers and lenders freely enter into such loan arrangements indicates that the terms are advantageous to both parties.

The decision in *K.M.C.* is likely to be an anomaly. In cases where a line of credit is called by a lender, most courts have held that the demand note is callable by definition at the will of the lender and is outside the scope of good faith requirements. The requirements that contracts for loans be in writing and that the call of demand notes be exempt from good faith restrictions both provide relief for lenders from liability in these areas. However, there are other areas where lenders may be held liable; these include loans with fixed termination dates, such as many real estate loans.

Other Theories of Lender Liability

There are several other legal theories of actions that may give rise to lender liability. They are not addressed as frequently as breach of oral commitments or a lack of good faith, but they do arise and should be mentioned.

Prima Facie Tort

A **tort** is a breach of a duty created by law, whereby the injured party seeks compensation from the wrongdoer. **Prima facie tort** is described in Section 870 of Restatement (Second) of Torts thus: "One who intentionally causes injury to another is subject to liability to the other for that injury, if his or her conduct is generally culpable and not justifiable under the circumstances. This liability may be imposed even though the actor's conduct does not come within the traditional category of tort liability." Although an act may be lawful, it becomes a tort if it is done with the intent to cause injury, it results in an injury, and there is no justification for the act. The wrongdoer's state of mind and intention transform a lawful act into one that is unlawful. It may be insufficient that the person performing the act knew that the consequence would be injurious. What may be required is that the actor desired to bring about the outcome. Since the thrust of a *prima facie* tort goes to the intention of the wrongdoer, it is particularly difficult to establish liability without the wrongdoer admitting to his frame of mind.

Promissory Fraud

Fraud is an intentional misrepresentation intended to deceive, whether by misstating or concealing the truth. It can also be a statement made with reckless disregard for whether it is true or not. **Promissory fraud** involves the making of a promise with no intention of fulfilling it. Promissory fraud may be difficult to prove, because proof of the fraud requires that the wrongdoer intended not to perform at the time when the promise was made. The failure to perform is not sufficient proof to demonstrate promissory fraud.

Promissory fraud was one of the principal foundations in a $19 million verdict in the *State National Bank of El Paso v. Farah Manufacturing Co.*[23] In this case, the lender did not approve of the new management proposed by the firm. The provisions of its loan to the company allowed it to declare default at its option if there was a change of management. The lender induced the company not to install Mr. Farah as president and chief executive officer by stating it would not declare a default if someone else were selected. The evidence showed that the lender, in fact, had not determined what its action would have been if Mr. Farah had been installed as CEO. The company failed under the alternative management, which was shown to be inexperienced and to have divided loyalty. The failure of the company was the damage claimed in this case.

Contrary to a claim for a **breach of contract**, a claim for fraud can include punitive damages. For this reason, if there is any hint that promissory fraud may be involved, the plaintiff will include it as part of the claim.

Nondisclosure Fraud and Breach of Fiduciary Duty

Fiduciary means "characterized by trust." **Nondisclosure fraud** involves not only a misrepresentation but also the duty of one party to make a disclosure to another based on a fiduciary duty. Many relationships involve a fiduciary duty. The managers of a company have a fiduciary duty to act in the interests of the stockholders. The rules of agency require that **agents** have a fiduciary duty to act in the interests of the principal. There are numerous other examples of the relationship. In terms of lender liability, the issue centers on whether or not a lender has a fiduciary duty with the borrower.

Consider the following example. Assume that a real estate developer approaches a lender to obtain a loan to purchase a property. The purchase price is above its true value because of facts known to the lender but not to the buyer. To thicken the plot, also assume that the lender has a secured interest in the property, having made a nonrecourse loan to the present owner. In the event of default, the lender may look only to the property as collateral. The lender also knows that the current owner is delinquent. The lender would like to make a loan to the prospective buyer for the amount of the purchase price for the following reason: The amount of the new loan will be equal to that of the existing delinquent loan, and the lender can require that the buyer assume personal liability for the loan. The sale and loan would benefit the lender because of the additional security interest. It would disadvantage the buyer because the true value is much less than the purchase price. If the lender makes the loan and the buyer eventually defaults and makes up any deficiency out of personal funds, is the lender liable for nondisclosure fraud? That is, does the lender have a duty to disclose to the buyer the facts that make the true value of the property less than the purchase price?

Generally, to be liable under this theory, the lender should have a duty to disclose information only if there exists an inequality of position, a fiduciary relationship, or knowledge by one of the parties of facts that are not within the reasonable reach of the other. It is not clear how the courts would rule in the above example. In *Hill v. Securities Investment Co. of St. Louis*,[24] the court ruled that a lender did not have an obligation to tell a borrower who desired a loan to invest in a company that the lender had refused financing for the company. Also, in *Denison State Bank v. Madeira*,[25] the court held that the bank did not have to disclose to a potential borrower that a company in which the borrower had plans to invest had overdrafts at the bank. In many such cases, the courts generally have found that there is no fiduciary relationship between the lender—for example, a bank—and customers and depositors.

Breach of Contract

Plaintiffs may attempt to establish liability under the assertion that a lender failed to extend the existing financing after an oral agreement to do so. Generally, this attempt will run head on against the **parole evidence rule**, which states that the terms of a written contract cannot be contradicted by any prior or contemporaneous oral agreement. The reasons for the parole evidence rule are as follows:

1. There can be no contract without a meeting of the minds of the parties.
2. There can be no meeting of the minds unless the terms of the contract are certain and ascertainable—in other words, definite.

Generally, oral agreements to extend credit are not sufficiently definite to create a contract. One needs to state the interest rate, date of maturity, default provisions, and many other terms to be definite. As an example, the court in *Labor Discount Center, Inc. v. State Bank and Trust Co. of Wellston*[26] held that an oral agreement to continue interim financing is insufficiently definite to be enforceable. Many other cases have confirmed that lenders do not incur liability for breaching alleged oral commitments to extend credit.

Duress and Lender Control

It is difficult for many start-up firms and emerging real estate development companies to obtain pure equity financing. Even if they could, the owners frequently do not wish to give up control of the firm through large stock issues. These firms will seek out debt financing but with an equity complexion. They will attract funds from lenders interested in financing the operations of new and emerging start-up real estate firms because of the potential for excess returns. The loan arrangements will, in many respects, have the complexion of equity. The lender will insist on an exclusive lending arrangement, cutting off competition from other lenders. The lender also will be rewarded in some fashion according to the success of the firm. Equity-participation loans whose terms are tied to the performance of the firm are not uncommon. Examples include arrangements for participating in the annual operating profits of the firm or sharing in the appreciation of the value of the property.

Many of these loan agreements stipulate that, in the case of financial difficulties, the lender has the right to take over certain operations of the borrowing company. Such **lender control** arrangements are designed to reduce the risk of the lender. If the management of the borrowing company does a poor job, then the lender has the opportunity to substitute management. In this case, it is difficult to deny that the lender is, in reality, an equity holder. It has a "loan" with equity characteristics and can take over management of the firm in the event it perceives financial mismanagement.

If a lender exercises a right of control under such an agreement, it will run the risk of incurring some liability. If the business ultimately fails despite the control of the lender, several parties may wish to seek compensation from the lender. Those parties would include, in addition to the stockholders of the corporation, such third parties as creditors of the corporation, including suppliers, and the government, if taxes are unpaid. The magnitude of the liability will be a function of the extent and character of the actual control. There are several legal areas in which lenders may be liable for control. For third parties, two areas are bankruptcy and agency law. Lenders may be liable to the debtor (owner of the firm) under tort or fiduciary law.

Liability to Third Parties: Bankruptcy and Agency Law

The legal rules that are followed in bankruptcy can be complex. Of interest here are the so-called voidable preference rules. Generally, if a debtor transfers assets to a preferred creditor within 90 days of filing for bankruptcy, the trustee in bankruptcy may require that those assets be returned to the debtor for the satisfaction of the general creditors. The voidable preference period of 90 days can be extended to 1 year if the creditor to which the assets are transferred is an insider. An insider is one who owns a certain amount of stock in the company or controls the operations of the company. You can see where problems might arise in this area. If a lender takes over control of a company, it will have an incentive to make payments on its own debt to the detriment of other creditors. Thus, a lender could be held liable by the trustee in bankruptcy for all payments made to itself within 1 year of filing for bankruptcy if it takes over control. If the lender does not take over control but simply forecloses on its loan, then only payments made within the 90-day period may be considered a preference item.

A second area of the law where lenders may become liable to third parties is **agency law**. Restatement (Second) of Agency states that "Agency is the fiduciary relationship which results from the manifestation of consent by one person to another such that the other shall act on his behalf and subject to his control, and consent by the other so to act."[27] Three essential elements are necessary for an agency relationship to exist. First, both parties must consent to the relationship. Second, the agent must act in the interest of the principal. Third, the agent must be subject to the direction and control of the principal.

Agency law comes into play with lender control in this way: If the lender undertakes sufficient control of the operations of the creditor's business, then the debtor becomes an agent of the lender. Suppose, for example, that a lender takes control of the development of a real estate project in the belief that the developer is mismanaging the project. The lender may be within its rights to do so by the terms of the loan agreement. But now, the lender may have assumed the role of a **principal**. The lender takes over control and directs the operations of the business. Assume, further, that in the role of managing the business, the lender has the business order some construction material. If the developer (business) fails prior to paying for the material and declares bankruptcy, who is responsible for paying for the material? Under the laws of agency, the lender may be. The material supplier likely will claim that the business was acting as an agent on behalf of a principal, not the (failed) business. Section 140 of the Restatement (Second) of Agency states that "A creditor who assumes control of his debtor's business for the mutual benefit of himself and his debtor may become a principal, with liability for the acts and transactions of the debtor in connection with the business."[28] The extent of liability in such cases depends on the amount of control. If, in the above example, the lender did not control an aspect of ordering materials, it would not likely be found to be a principal in this regard and therefore would not be liable for payment.

Finally, a lender may be liable for the unpaid payroll taxes of a debtor. This would be the case where lender control extended to hiring, firing, and other payroll decisions or the lender made a loan for the purpose of paying the payroll taxes and was aware that the debtor firm did not use the funds to pay the taxes.

The greatest exposure to liability is undoubtedly harm done to debtors when a lender exercises control over the business operations. As indicated above, many loan agreements call for the lender to take various actions when a loan becomes troubled. The actions may range from giving management advice to suggesting a new management consulting team to actually controlling the affairs of the business. When a lender takes some control over the day-to-day affairs of the debtor's business, the lender may have a fiduciary duty to act in the interest of the firm's owners. A breach of that duty may expose the lender to liability. The greater the degree of control that a lender exercises, the larger the potential liability may be if the business ultimately fails. Not all cases of lender control will lead to liability, however. The fiduciary duty of the lender does not require that the lender abandon its self-interest. The controlling factor would be the extent to which the lender operates outside of a contract and its fiduciary duty to act in the interest of the borrower.

In summary, lenders can be liable for damages anytime they exercise some control over a borrower. The liability will be minimized if the control that is exercised is within the scope of the loan agreement and if the lender does not operate capriciously and in bad faith against the interest of the debtor. In many cases where juries have found lenders to be liable, the verdict has been reversed at the appellate level. Liability will result generally in cases of extreme lender misbehavior.

In cases where lenders have intervened in real estate developments, the lender likely will avoid liability if the developer has acted in violation of the loan agreement. Examples of the latter scenario include the use of project funds or materials for other developments or projects, appropriation of funds from an operating account for personal uses, and failure to exercise proper project supervision and cost controls.

BANKRUPTCY AND AGENCY COSTS

Lenders must be aware that the bankruptcy laws can be used by creditors to serve their own interest against that of the lender. Although bankruptcy laws have been formulated and designed primarily for ongoing business enterprises, they can and have been used in the context of the development of real estate projects. The usual scenario involves a real estate developer that borrows funds, contributes a small amount of equity, and develops a real estate project that is not economically feasible. In this situation, the value of the completed development is often less than the amount of debt secured by that property. Faced with the loss of the property through a foreclosure, the developer/debtor may attempt to use the bankruptcy laws to salvage an interest in the property. If successful, the developer may be able to reduce the amount of debt that is owed the lender.

Bankruptcy Law and the "Cramdown" Process

Potentially bankrupt debtors have access to what is referred to as a Chapter 11 bankruptcy. The purpose of this type of bankruptcy is to allow the troubled "firm" to continue operations in the hope that eventually economic success will allow it to pay its debts and continue operation. From a social policy standpoint, the government views this as preferable to an immediate liquidation of the firm and its assets. Since a real estate development can be considered a firm with business operations, developers have employed the provisions of Chapter 11 bankruptcy to fight off an immediate foreclosure by a lender and in some cases, to reduce the amount owed by the developer to the lender. The term **cramdown** refers to the ability, under the law, to force a restructuring of the debt owed by the developer. The types of restructuring that occur include extending the maturity date of the loan, reducing the interest rate on the loan, or even reducing the principal balance of the loan.

A simple example will demonstrate the value of the cramdown to the developer and the danger to the lender. If a property with a market value of $4 million is secured by a $6 million loan, the loss of the property through foreclosure will leave the developer with no equity and, most likely, a deficiency judgment of $2 million. If the developer can use bankruptcy laws to cram down the loan principal to $4 million, an immediate capture of $2 million in wealth results. Should the market value of the property increase subsequent to the cramdown—to $5 million, for example—then the developer gains $1 million in positive equity in the property that would not have existed without the cramdown. Obviously, lenders would prefer to foreclose if there is the possibility of obtaining a valuable deficiency judgment against the developer's other assets.

To be successful in a cramdown, the developer must obtain a confirmation of a bankruptcy plan in federal court. In such a reorganization plan, the developer/debtor must segregate the claims of all creditors into various classes, each of which receives a special treatment under the plan. For a real estate developer, other creditors might include subcontractors, tenants of the facility, and others. All the claims in a class must be similar in nature, but not all similar claims need to be placed in the same class. Thus, the developer/debtor may form two classes of creditors, all with similar characteristics. A class of creditors is considered "impaired" if the plan alters equitable or contractual rights of the creditors in a class, fails to cure prebankruptcy arrearages and damages, or does not pay the claims of the debtors in cash for the full amount of the debt owed. Obviously, a lender with a secured interest in the real estate property will be impaired under a plan that attempts to reduce the principal amount of the debt. For any impaired class of creditors, if two-thirds by amount or one-half by number agree to the bankruptcy plan, it is considered approved by the class. The lender has a choice of how to be classified. Using the above example, the lender may elect to be placed in two classes: a secured class with a debt of $4 million (the value of the real estate collateral) and an unsecured class for the remaining $2 million (a deficiency claim). Alternatively, the lender may elect to be placed only in one class, a secured class, where the entire claim is treated as secured. This selection is important because of the cramdown rules. Those rules address the treatment of the claims in each class and the approval of the plan by all classes.

Insofar as the treatment of the creditors in each class, the cramdown rules require that a secured creditor must receive deferred cash payments that both total and have a present value at a minimum equal to the value of the security and some treatment of the unsecured deficiency. In effect, this rule states that since through foreclosure the lender is likely to recover only the value of the collateral, he is in no worse position after the reorganization than before. Thus, in our example, the lender would have to be assured of future payments with a total and a present value of $4 million and some payment of the $2 million residual. In most situations, the creditor will offer a very small fraction of the dollar claim of the residual.

If all classes of debtors approve of the reorganization plan, then it will be binding on all creditors, even those minority debtors in classes that did not approve of the plan. If one impaired class does not approve the plan, it will not be binding unless the court feels that the plan is equitable and fair to all parties, in which case the plan is "crammed down" on that dissenting impaired class.

The developer/debtor who wishes to salvage value from the uneconomic real estate investment will attempt to establish several classes of debtors. Some will consist of a small number of unsecured creditors with small claims, and the remaining class will be made up of the secured lender. The developer hopes that the acceptance of the plan by the classes of the unsecured creditors will be sufficient to cram down a reduction in the principal amount of the loan of the secured creditor. Here is where the lender must choose into which class(es) to place the claim. If the lender places all of the claim into the secured class, then he will be entitled to future payments with a total equal to the amount of the loan and a present value equal to the value of the collateral. In our example, the lender would be entitled to deferred payments that total at least $6 million and have a present value of $4 million.

The lender is in a better position financially under this election. But if this choice is made, then the lender is represented in only one class and may be forced to have its claim crammed down by the other classes that may approve the plan. Strategy is the key in this regard.

Practical Considerations

From the above discussion, you can see that the real estate lender must be concerned with agency relationships. If the value of a completed real estate project fails to meet projections, the lender may not feel secure in the foreclosure process, which gives him the property and a deficiency judgment. The developer/debtor may be able to use the bankruptcy laws to reduce the amount of the debt to the value of the property. If successful, any subsequent increase in value will accrue to the developer and not the lender. For this reason, lenders will have to pursue the strategy that has the greatest probability of defeating the plan.

Although it is in the interest of the creditor to put forth a successful plan that will result in a reduction of the principal due the lender, it may not be an easy task. First, the plan must show that it is likely that the future cash flows from the project will be sufficient to meet the new debt payments under the plan. Second, all classes of creditors must approve the plan. Third, the courts are not likely to approve a plan designed solely to reduce the amount of debt owed the lender.

In the case where a loan is secured by a single real estate asset, the above criteria may be difficult to meet. A severely distressed property may not show sufficient cash flows to meet even the reduced amount of debt. Second, creating several classes of creditors to cram down the plan on the lender may be difficult if there are very few other creditors. Even if such classes can be "manufactured," it is likely the court will view the plan as being unfair to the lender.

An excellent example of such a situation is the case of *In re Meadow Glen, Ltd.*[29] where the debtor created four classes of unsecured creditors, including the tenants (total, $2000), unsecured creditors with claims less than $100 (total, $500), unsecured creditors with claims more than $100 (total, $23,000), and the deficiency claim of the lender ($5.5 million). The bankruptcy plan proposed to pay the claims as follows: tenants, 90 percent of allowed claims; unsecured claims less than $100, also 90 percent; unsecured claims more than $100, 75 percent of claims; and the deficiency claim, 10 percent equity interest in the property. The court reasoned that the plan was unfair to the lender. It stated there was no justification for distinguishing between the unsecured creditors. Also, it noted the high payoff to the small classes, and that the payment to the lender of a 10 percent equity interest was a dubious value at best. The court found that since the amount of the nondeficiency claims was so small, the impairment of these classes produced no material benefit for the secured lender. It ruled that the creation of the classes was done solely to produce impaired classes for the purpose of the cramdown in the debt owed the secured lender.

In short, the lender needs to be aware of the possibility that bankruptcy laws may be used to reduce the amount of principal owed, but that plans created for this sole purpose are unlikely to be approved by the courts. It should prove very difficult for developer/debtors of single properties to effectively reduce indebtedness and retain the property through bankruptcy proceedings. It may be more likely that developers of many properties under one firm name may succeed in such a strategy, however, because it may be easier to create multiple impaired classes for the purpose of effectuating the cramdown.

ETHICS, FRAUD, AND AGENCY COSTS

In many circumstances ethics, fraud, and agency costs are all related. **Ethics** deals with the moral duties and obligations that individuals have to deal justly with each other. In a real estate finance text, we prefer to leave it to the philosophers to discuss the meanings of such terms as *just*, *fair*, and *moral*. Here, it is sufficient to say that there is no scientific manner in which to determine if a particular action is moral or not. No standard can be applied to measure how moral or how ethical an action may be. We will state simply here that it is to the benefit of society if individuals deal with each other in a fair and just way. One should not confuse ethical actions with legal actions. Some actions can be legal but not ethical, and vice versa. However, many laws are passed with ethical standards in mind. That is, many laws reflect the desire to have people treat others fairly and justly. We saw a good example of this earlier in the chapter. The UCC specifically requires that parties to a contract deal in good faith with one another. Other examples of such laws are those that make it illegal for individuals to trade in securities based on inside information. Laws also restrict the dealings of public officials who may have inside information or whose actions can affect their private well-being through legislation.

Finally, agency relationships have legal and ethical implications. As explained earlier, an agency relationship exists when an agent is held to act on behalf of, or for the interests of, another. Often, but not always, the agent is compensated by the principal, so that the agent has a legal and ethical obligation to act on behalf of the principal only. Numerous situations arise, however, where the nature of the relationship provides an incentive for the agent to act on his own (or another's) behalf, rather than for the benefit of the principal. In these cases, the principal must expend resources to make sure that the agent acts only in the principal's interest. These resource expenditures are referred to as **agency costs**. An example will clarify these comments.

When a real estate developer requests a loan to finance a new project, the lender will require an appraisal of the property (in its completed form). The appraised value of the property will serve as a guide to the amount of financing the lender is willing to advance. To avoid default risk, the lender may agree to finance only 80 percent of the appraised value. To obtain an appraisal of value, the lender will hire an appraiser. The appraiser is, therefore, an agent of, and is required to act on behalf of, the lender. But the appraiser may wish to obtain other appraisal assignments from the developer. If numerous appraisers are competing for assignments, the appraiser may have an incentive to make sure the loan is approved. In this way, he gains the favor of a real estate developer, who may be able to give him additional assignments.

Let's assume that the value of the completed project is $1 million but that the developer does not desire to risk an equity position of $200,000. He may ask the appraiser to value the property at $1.3 million so that the lender will feel comfortable in advancing $1 million or so. Many areas of an appraisal report call for a judgment to be made. The appraiser may have to make a judgment as to the value of a proposed new highway intersection near the property. Also, it is possible for the appraiser to make out-and-out false statements. The appraiser has a conflict of interest between providing a fair report for the lender or an exaggerated or falsified one for the borrower. Ethically, the appraiser must be unbiased where any judgment is called for in the appraisal report. Legally, the appraiser is liable if he makes a false statement in the appraisal report. If the appraiser makes a biased judgment in favor of the developer, but it does not involve a false statement, the issue becomes clouded. While ethically wrong, the appraiser may escape legal liability, because it would be difficult to prove that the appraiser acted in his own interest against that of the lender.

Where do agency costs come in? Most large commercial real estate lenders employ a staff of review appraisers. It is their function to review the appraisal reports done by outside appraisers for inaccuracies and mistakes. Review appraisers are retained because lenders recognize that appraisers may act against the interests of the lender. The cost of maintaining a review appraiser staff can be considered an agency cost.

The following examples illustrate agency relationships in real estate finance. Two examples involve mortgage insurance, and one discusses the failure of many thrifts in the late 1980s and early 1990s.

Agency Relationships and Mortgage Insurance

Government (Federal Housing Administration [FHA], Veterans Administration [VA]) and private mortgage insurance protects the lender against losses on defaulted loans. The major element in the loss on many defaulted loans is the carrying costs of the property during and after the foreclosure process. The lender pays these costs and is then reimbursed by the insurer. (FHA pays the full costs, while private mortgage insurers pay only a portion over a minimum amount.) These costs include property taxes, hazard insurance, maintenance costs, and foregone interest on the loan. Foregone interest is reimbursed at a rate equal to the contract rate on the loan. Although the premium is paid by the borrower, the agency relationship is between the lender and the insurer. In the event of a default, the lender will have two basic options: Forebear and seek an arrangement to restructure the loan with the borrower, or foreclose on the loan and file a claim with the insurer for any loss. If the lender chooses the second option, it faces several other decisions. One would be the method of foreclosure in a state where a choice is allowed between a judicial and power-of-sale procedure. As indicated in Chapter 14, the judicial procedure is the more time-consuming and expensive method. Another decision would be whether or not to monitor the property and make repairs. From these decisions, two different agency relationships arise. Consider first the agency relationship between the lender and the FHA. Here, foregone interest is reimbursed at the contract rate on the loan. How would the current level of interest rates affect the decision of the lender in its choice of foreclosure method? If the current market rate is above the rate on the loan, the lender will have an incentive to foreclose as quickly as possible, so as to obtain the insurance funds and lend them at the higher rate. If, on the other hand, the current market rate is below that on the loan, the lender will have an incentive to slow the foreclosure process. This is so because the lender is being reimbursed for foregone interest during the foreclosure process at the higher (loan) rate. In this second case, the lender's incentive is contrary to that of the FHA. A drawn-out foreclosure process causes the carrying costs, borne entirely by the FHA, to increase. There is evidence to suggest that some lenders do, in fact, behave in this fashion.[30]

Note that the FHA is an agent of U.S. taxpayers and should act on their behalf to reduce claim costs. The agency relationship among government departments, government employees, and taxpayers is beyond the scope of this example, however.

A second example of an incentive conflict between lenders and insurers involves maintenance costs of foreclosed properties. Lenders generally have no incentive to make repairs on a property, since such repairs would require managerial resources and any loss on the value of the property is covered by insurance.[31] Here, the private mortgage insurer may have to expend resources (agency costs) to make sure the lender makes the repairs on the property. The insurer may require that the lender make repairs to bring the property up to the condition at the time the policy was taken out before a claim can be filed. The lender would have to inspect the property to see that the repairs had in fact been made. All of these efforts are costly procedures required to control the incentive conflicts between agents (lenders) and principals (mortgage insurers).

Agency Relationships and Thrift Failures

A final example of the relationship among the law, ethics, and fraud involves the recent failure of many thrifts. To set the stage, consider the environment of thrifts after the deregulation legislation in the early 1980s. Also assume that you are an enterprising person bent on exploiting the agency relationships that exist in such an environment, and that you have no regard for ethics. You only want to create as much wealth for yourself as possible. Here is how you might proceed.

First, you would identify a target savings and loan to purchase. You would look for a small- to medium-size thrift that had financial difficulties: Perhaps its assets had declined in value because of rising interest rates. The value of the thrift's stock might be very low or even near zero. You can purchase the stock in the thrift for next to nothing. After you purchase the thrift, you place an ad in all the leading national newspapers offering extremely high rates of interest on large ($100,000) deposits. The rate you offer on the deposits is irrelevant because you have no intention that the thrift will ever make a profit. Let's say that $100 million arrives shortly from around the country. Since the deposits are guaranteed by the government, there is no concern on the part of the depositors that the thrift is near insolvency. Next, with all the deposit funds arriving, you seek out some real estate developers who have perhaps been turned down for loans by other lenders. You do not care if their developments are risky. You lend $10 million to one developer for a project worth only $8 million. The developer is so happy, he agrees to pay a loan commitment fee (not points) of $1 million. If you make several such loans, your thrift will earn millions in commitment fees. The earnings of the thrift look impressive. But the assets are all bad loans, loans for values greater than the property. At the end of the year, you report that the thrift made record earnings under the new ownership. In fact, you as the major stockholder take a $5 million bonus in your salary. You continue to do this year after year. If depositors want their money back, you issue new deposits in a continuing "Ponzi" scheme. After several years, the loans eventually default, the thrift is insolvent, and you hand the operation over to the Federal Savings and Loan Insurance Corporation (FSLIC). All of your bonuses are personal pay, and you get to keep that.

Dozens of similar actual stories played themselves out in the late 1980s and early 1990s as a result of a regulatory situation that permitted such activities. Although different in detail, many such stories have been reported in the press. One story involved a sleepy little Texas thrift that was purchased in 1982, moved to Dallas, and opened up dozens of branches.[32] The thrift then sold millions of dollars in "jumbo" certificates of deposits ($100,000) in a "boiler room" type operation. At times, $20 to $25 million a day was pouring into the thrift through this operation. The thrift then made dozens of bad loans on which it charged a 6 percent loan fee. The fees, in turn, went to the bottom line of its income statement. Often the borrower was not even required to submit any supporting paperwork for the loan. Less than 4 percent of the thrift's loans in the first 2 years were to homeowners. The same article reported that the new owner of the thrift took more than $3 million in dividends over a 2-year period. The ultimate cost to the FSLIC (taxpayers) was more than $1 billion.

The thrift actions described in this particular article may or may not be within the letter of the law. The loosened regulation of the early 1980s created the environment that allowed these agency problems to evolve. Nonetheless, the Financial Institutions Reform, Recovery, and Enforcement Act (FIRREA) of 1990 authorized $75 million annually from 1990 through 1992 for U.S. Department of Justice investigations and prosecutions involving fraud at financial institutions. Additionally, the Dallas Bank Fraud Task Force was established in 1987 to investigate and prosecute fraud connected with thrift failures in Texas. At least one thrift CEO has been sentenced to 30 years of imprisonment as a result of the efforts of the task force.

A final note: Some actions involve out-and-out and blatant fraud that victims must be on the lookout for. A common example is the sale of bogus mortgages—notes that have been fabricated. It is not too difficult for a seller of mortgages to make up fictitious home buyers and place their names and other information on bogus mortgage notes. The seller may intend to pay only the first several installment payments on the mortgage before defaulting, just so as to stay in business. Or the seller may plan to disappear with the sale proceeds. In 1991 the former president of the American Mortgage Company, a Milwaukee mortgage banking firm, pleaded guilty to selling 92 fictitious mortgages worth $10.7 million to a secondary mortgage

TABLE 22-1
Fraudulent Information Appearing on Mortgage Applications: through 1998 (percent)

INFORMATION					
	Pre-1994	1995	1996	1997	1998
Application information	71%	80%	72%	74%	71%
Incorrect employment	45	48	41	41	47
Tax returns and financial statements	39	35	35	36	40
Verification of deposits	28	28	21	19	32
Appraisal/valuation	7	5	4	4	5
Credit history	4	4	4	12	9

Source: Mortgage Asset Research Institute.

market agency. In the same year, the president of a Detroit mortgage company forged 99 mortgage loan notes worth approximately $10 million and promptly left the country. In another scam, a Washington, D.C., mortgage broker set up a bogus loan operation and siphoned off an estimated $3 million in fraudulent loan proceeds. He was arrested in 1996 and in 1997 sentenced to 51 months in prison. (In 1990 the federal sentencing guidelines were changed by a congressional mandate to require a 51-month minimum sentence for fraud convictions where the perpetrator stole more than $1 million or jeopardized the financial soundness of a federally insured financial institution. Estimates place the number of bogus mortgages at about 1 percent of those held by the secondary mortgage market agencies.)

Often, the fraud involves loan application information by potential borrowers. Table 22-1 shows the percentage of fraudulent information by type that appeared on mortgages through 1998. Incorrect application information such as income and employment data head the list of false information provided on loan applications. Appendix A lists and describes a sample of mortgage fraud convictions in 2013.

Summary

It is clear that there is more to real estate finance than the simple notion of lenders advancing loans to developers and investors and then collecting interest and principal. Legal issues and agency relationships complicate what otherwise might be such a simple relationship. Lenders may face liability from a variety of circumstances. The court's interpretation of PRPs under CERCLA may make lenders liable for hazardous waste cleanup costs, despite the secured-lender exemption, when lenders obtain ownership or exercise some control over the day-to-day operations of the debtor. Lenders also risk the loss of their security if the property has been used in any aspect of the illegal drug trade.

Lenders may be liable for their actions in their contractual relationship with borrowers. Secured loans come under the provisions of the UCC. One provision of the code requires parties to contract to act and bargain in good faith. Several lenders have been found liable for failure to act in good faith, although in many cases the decisions have been reversed on appeal. Even if lenders do act in good faith, they may be liable for other reasons. Typical causes of action by borrowers include a breach of an oral agreement, promissory fraud, misrepresentation, and undue control over the business affairs of the debtor. The likelihood of liability from a breach of an oral agreement is mitigated by the Statute of Fraud and Credit Agreement Statutes. However, liability from promissory fraud and undue control is greater, however.

Agency problems and costs permeate the real estate finance market. Parties to real estate finance arrangements that are also agents have an incentive to act in their own behalf and against the interests of the principal. Lenders may act in their own interest and against that of the government mortgage insurer or the government deposit insurer. The problem is compounded when one considers that the government programs are also agents of the general taxpayers. Government bureaucrats may prefer to act in their own interest and not that of the taxpayers. This "layering" of agency relationships has resulted in large losses sustained by the agencies and/or the taxpayers. Many of the self-serving activities of lenders, developers, and appraisers may have been technically legal, but certainly not ethical. Other activities may have involved fraud and were therefore illegal.

Key Terms

Agency costs	Nondisclosure fraud
Agency law	Oral commitment
Agents	Parole evidence rule
Breach of contract	Potentially responsible parties (PRPs)
CERCLA	*Prima facie* tort
Cramdown	Principal
Credit agreement statutes	Promissory fraud
Due diligence defense	SARA
Ethics	Secured-lender exemption
Fiduciary	Statute of fraud
Fraud	Strict liability
Good faith	Tort
Joint and several liability	Uniform Commercial Code (UCC)
Lender control	

Review Questions

22-1. Explain how a lender is likely to become liable as a potentially responsible party for hazardous waste cleanup costs.

22-2. How can lenders avoid liability for cleanup costs under CERCLA?

22-3. Explain the reasoning by the court in the *Mirables* case for assigning liability to the lender for hazardous waste cleanup costs.

22-4. What is meant by joint and several liability under CERCLA?

22-5. How does the statutory law protect lenders from liability for breach of oral commitments?

22-6. List a lender's four defenses from liability under CERCLA.

22-7. Explain the major risk that lenders face from enforcement of laws against trading in illicit drugs.

22-8. Explain the term *good faith* and the requirement of parties to a contract to deal in good faith.

22-9. Are demand loans covered by the good faith requirement to provide notification of the demand feature?

22-10.   Define each of the following and give an example of how a lender might be liable under each action.
a. *Prima facie* tort
b. Promissory fraud
c. Nondisclosure fraud
d. Breach of fiduciary duty
e. Lender control

22-11.   Give an example whereby a lender might become liable as a principal under agency law.

22-12.   Give an original real estate finance example (not one from the text) of an agency relationship that invokes a conflict of interest and involves agency costs.

22-13.   Distinguish between illegal and unethical acts.

22-14.   What is a contribution lawsuit under CERCLA?

Notes

1. *Wall Street Journal.* October 31, 1986, p. 48.
2. *Wall Street Journal.* November 3, 1986, p. 47.
3. 42 U.S.C. 9601(9).
4. 42 U.S.C. 9607(a)(1).
5. 42 U.S.C. 1906 (35)(A).
6. 15 Envtl. L. Reg. 20, 992 (E.D. Pa. Sept. 4, 1985).
7. *United States v. Maryland Bank and Trust Co.*, 632 F. Supp. 573 (D. Md. 1986).
8. Id. at 580.
9. *Guidice v. BFG Electroplating Co.*, 732 F. Supp. 556 (W.D. Pa. 1989).
10. *Fleet Factors Corp.*, 724 F. Supp. at 955. (S.D. Ga. 1988).
11. *Fleet Factors*, 901 F. 2d at 1557. (11th Cir. 1990).
12. *In re Bergsoe Metal Corporation*, 1990 U.S. App. Lexis 13541 (9th Cir., Aug. 9, 1990).
13. 15 F. 3d 1100 (D.C. Cir. 1994).
14. *Calero-Toledo v. Pearson Yacht Leasing Co.*, 416 U.S. 663.
15. *U.S. v. Property Known as 708-710 West 9th St., Erie, Pa.* (715 F. Supp. 1323).
16. U.C.C. 1-203, 1-201(19).
17. U.C.C. Sec 1-208.
18. *Kruse v. Bank of America* 202 Ca. 3rd 38 (1st Dist, 1988).
19. *Centerre Bank of Kansas City v. Distributors, Inc.*, 705 S.W. 2d 42 (Mo. Ct. App. 1985).
20. As a technical note, the court did not cite the Official Commentary to the UCC that states a demand note is callable by its nature but, rather, said that a call of a demand note was not related to the "performance or enforcement" of a contract mentioned in Sec. 1-203.
21. *Fulton National Bank v. Willis Denny Ford, Inc.*, 154 Ga. App. 8416, 269 S.E. 2nd 916 (1980).
22. *K.M.C. Co., Inc. v. Irving Trust Co.*, 757 F. 2d 752 (6th Cir. 1985).
23. *State National Bank of El Paso v. Farah Manufacturing Co.*, 678 S.W. 2d 661 (Tex. Ct. App. 1984).

24. *Hill v. Securities Investment Co. of St Louis*, 423 S.W. 2d 836, 842 (Mo. 1968).

25. *Denison State Bank v. Madeira*, 230 Kan. 684, 640 P2d. 1235 (1982).

26. *Labor Discount Center, Inc. v. State Bank and Trust Co. of Wellston*, 526 S.W. 2d 407, 425 (Mo. App. 1975).

27. Restatement (Second) of Agency 1(1958).

28. Restatement (Second) of Agency 140 (1958).

29. *In re Meadow Glen, Ltd.*, 87 Banker, 421, 424–425 (Banker, W.C. Tex. 1988).

30. Terrence M. Clauretie and Mel Jameson. Interest rates and the foreclosure process: An agency problem in FHA mortgage insurance. *Journal of Risk and Insurance* 47 (December 1990), 701–711.

31. J. Harold Mulherin and Walter J. Muller. Resolution of incentive conflicts in the mortgage industry. *Journal of Real Estate Finance and Economics* 2 (February 1989), 35–46.

32. How Texas S&L Grew into a Lending Giant and Lost $1.4 Billion. *Wall Street Journal* (April 27, 1989), 1.

Web Site

http://www.eli.org
Environmental law information

A Refresher on the Time Value of Money and Related Concepts

The material presented in this appendix is intended to be a refresher on the important concepts involved with what is known as the time value of money. Here, we reacquaint you with the mechanics of the time value of money, including the process of discounting and compounding. We strongly recommend that you understand the concepts in this appendix before you attempt to read the main body of the text. For those of you who have had several courses in finance, this material will be repetitive and you may skip this section. For those of you who may not come to this course with a strong background in finance, we recommend that you learn this material.

DISCOUNTING AND COMPOUNDING (COMING AND GOING)

Compounding: Finding a Future Value of an Investment

To set the stage for what follows, consider this situation. Assume that someone offers you an "investment": If you will give him $10,000 now, he will return to you a sum of $16,000 at the end of 5 years. To make the example simple, assume that there is no default risk whatsoever. That is, you are certain to receive the $16,000 at the end of 5 years. Also, assume that interest rates are not expected to change in the next 5 years and that you are content to tie up your investment for the entire period. These assumptions are made so that we can concentrate on the value of this investment in terms of its rate-of-return without consideration of risk.

In this example you are in the position of being the lender, and the seller of the investment is the borrower. You are lending money to the borrower in return for the promise to return a greater sum in the future. The "interest" that you will earn over the 5-year period is the difference between the amount you lend today and the amount returned at the end of the term. What we want to do at this point is determine if this is a "good" investment for you. One way to determine the worth of this investment is to consider what other alternatives are out there in the "market." If there are investments with the same risk characteristics that offer superior returns, you will not want to take this deal. What we do at this point is to consider an alternative market investment—for example, putting your money in the bank.

Assume that your local banker is willing to give you 10 percent interest at the end of each and any year on the amount of funds you have in an account at the beginning of that year. This is termed **annual compounding.** Furthermore, assume that the banker is willing to guarantee this 10 percent rate for the next 5 years. You are now in a position to judge the value of the above investment by comparing the results to the alternative of placing your funds in the local bank.

If you put the $10,000 in the bank, we can ask several questions. For example, how much will the account be worth at the end of the first year? The end of the second year? The third year? And, most important, the end of the fifth year?

The answer to the first question is easy. At the end of the first year, the amount in the account will equal the initial fund plus 10 percent, or

$$\text{Year 1 balance} = \$10,000 + (0.1 \times \$10,000)$$
$$= \$10,000 \times (1 + 0.1) \qquad \textbf{(Equation A-1)}$$
$$= \$11,000$$

Since the year-end balance for the first year is the beginning balance for the second year, the year-end balance for the second year will be

$$\text{Year 2 balance} = \$11,000 \times (1 + 0.1)$$
$$= \$10,000 \times (1 + 0.1) \times (1 + 0.1)$$
$$= \$10,000 \times (1 + 0.1)^2 \qquad \textbf{(Equation A-2)}$$
$$= \$12,100$$

Similarly the year-end balance for the third year will be

$$\text{Year 3 balance} = \$12,100 \times (1 + 0.1)$$
$$= \$10,000 \times (1 + 0.1) \times (1 + 0.1) \times (1 + 0.1) \textbf{ (Equation A-3)}$$
$$= \$10,000 \times (1 + 0.1)^3$$

As you might guess, continuing this process will produce an end-of-year balance for the fifth year equal to

$$\text{Year 5 balance} = \$10,000 \times (1 + 0.1)^5 \qquad \textbf{(Equation A-4)}$$

To generalize for any present value amount compounded at a given interest rate over a given time period, the equation can be written as

$$FV_n = PV(1+i)^n$$

where

FV_n = the future (compounded value at time n),
PV = present value amount (initial investment),
i = periodic interest rate, and
n = the number of compounding periods

The $(1 + i)^n$ portion of the equation is called the **future value interest factor** (FVIF). There are two easy ways to compute this value. One way is to use a table that provides a factor for the future amount of each one dollar invested in the present. An example of such a table is Table A-1, which can be found at www. oncourselearning.com, along with the other Tables mentioned below. This table includes the FVIF of one dollar for a large number of combinations of years and interest rates. The value in Table A-1 for a 10 percent interest for 5 years is 1.611. This means that each dollar invested now at 10 percent annual compounding will return $1.611 at the end of 5 years. So, $10,000 invested now will return $16,110 at the end of 5 years. Can you confirm from Table A-1 that $10,000 invested today will result in a future value of $19,740 if invested for 6 years and compounded annually at 12 percent?

A second way to find the terminal or future value is to use a financial calculator. An equation such as A-4 involves four elements: the present amount of the investment ($10,000), the interest rate (10 percent), the term of the investment (5 years), and the amount to be returned at the end of the term (the future value). Given any three of the four terms, the fourth can be determined with the use of a financial calculator. Most financial calculators will have (at least) four buttons representing the terms of an equation such as A-4. Generally, the buttons will be marked as:

Beginning amount (present value)	PV
Interest rate	% or I/YR
Term	N
Future value	FV
Payment (or cash flow)	PMT

By entering values for any of three elements in an equation, the fourth can be determined. For a Hewlett-Packard 10-B, the keystroke entries would appear as follows:

10000	/PV
10	I/YR
5	N

Then press the FV key. The calculator will display $16,105.10, which is different, but more accurate, than the answer from the table because the factor in the table is rounded off. Other types of financial calculators may have somewhat different notation or keystroke entries. However, they will come with an operator's manual that will include many typical examples. Note that the HP 10-B should be set to one payment per year to account for annual compounding.

Since you can accumulate a larger end-of-year-5 endowment by placing your funds in the bank than by purchasing this investment, it makes sense that you would do the former and not purchase the investment. Recall that the investments are identical in all respects except the future value. You should select the one with the largest future value.

DISCOUNTING: FINDING THE PRESENT VALUE OF A FUTURE SUM

Now that you have rejected the investment, the seller of this investment may turn to you and say, "Well, if you will not give me $10,000 for the promise to return $16,000 at the end of 5 years, how much will you give me for it?" You know that the investment is not worth $10,000, but it must be worth something. How can you find out what it is worth? Since the investment is similar to placing your funds in the bank, you simply ask, "How much would I have to put in the bank to have $16,000 at the end of 5 years?" This question in equation form is

$$X(1 + 0.1)^5 = \$16,000 \qquad \text{(Equation A-5)}$$

What is the value of X? Rearranging Equation A-5 we find the value of X to be

$$\begin{aligned} X &= \$16,000/(1 + 0.1)^5 \\ &= \$9,934.74 \end{aligned} \qquad \text{(Equation A-6)}$$

That is, if you were to put $9,934.74 in the bank and it earned 10 percent annually, it would grow to an amount equal to $16,000 at the end of the fifth year. This is the present value of the investment opportunity. Again, there are two ways in which the value can be determined.

First, you can utilize a table of factors that shows the present value of one dollar for a large set of interest rates and terms. Table A-3 shows that the present value interest factor of one dollar to be received in 5 years and discounted at 10 percent is 0.621. Or, 0.621 $16,000 $9,936 (the difference is due, again, to rounding). Can you show that the present value of the $16,000 payment to be received at the end of the fifth year is worth only $9,072 if the discount rate is 12 percent? Can you explain why it is less?

Alternatively, the financial calculator can be used. The following entries would accomplish the purpose:

16000	FV
10	I/YR
5	N

Then press the PV key. The answer should be $9,934.74.

The general equation for the present value of a future lump sum is

$$PV = FV_n[1/(1 + i)^n]$$

where the terms are as described earlier. The portion of the equation in brackets is the **present value interest factor** (PVIF).

DISCOUNTING AND COMPOUNDING ANNUITIES

The same principles noted here can be applied to a series of payments rather than just one. A series of payments, all of which are identical, is called an annuity. When the payments are identical, it becomes easy to calculate factors and place them in tables just as in the earlier examples.

DISCOUNTING

First, let's work backward. Assume that someone offers you the following investment opportunity. In return for you giving him $10,000 now, he would return to you $2,500 at the end of each of the next 5 years. The cash flows look like this:

END OF YEAR	YEAR 1	YEAR 2	YEAR 3	YEAR 4	YEAR 5
Cash Flow	$2500	$2500	$2500	$2500	$2500

To find out if this is a good deal, proceed as follows. Envision putting a sum of money in the bank (again at 10 percent annual interest) that would provide you with these exact cash flows. What sum would accomplish this goal? To make the calculation simple, consider opening five different accounts in the bank. The entire contents of account #1 will be removed at the end of the first year. The entire contents of account #2 will be removed at the end of the second year. The entire contents of account #3 will be removed at the end of the third year, and so forth.

The amount that must be deposited in account #1 is simply

$$\$2500/(1 + 0.1) = \$2272.73 \qquad \text{(Equation A-7)}$$

The amount to be deposited in account #2 is

$$\$2500/(1 + 0.1)^2 = \$2066.11 \qquad \text{(Equation A-8)}$$

This amount also can be determined by applying the present value interest factor for 10 percent for the second year from Table A-2, 0.826. That is, 0.826 $2,500 $2,065. Continuing, the amount needed to be deposited in the remaining accounts would be

$$\$2500/(1 + 0.1)^3 = \$1878.28$$
$$\$2500/(1 + 0.1)^4 = \$1707.53$$

and

$$\$2500/(1 + 0.1)^5 = \$1552.30$$

Thus, the total to be deposited will be

$$\$2272.73 + \$2066.11 + \$1878.28 + \$1707.53 + \$1552.30 + \$9476.97$$

Depositing $9,476.97 at the outset will allow you to withdraw $2,500 at the end of each of the next 5 years and have no money remaining in the bank. This is equivalent to

$$\$9476.97 = \$2500/(1+0.1) + \$2500/(1+0.1)^2$$
$$+\$2500/(1+0.1)^3 \cdots \$2500/(1+0.1)^5$$

(Equation A-9)

This formula can be rewritten as

$$\$9476.67 = \$2500 \times [1/(1+0.1) + 1/(1+0.1)^2 + 1/(1+0.1)^3 \cdots + 1/(1+0.1)^5]$$

This can be generalized to

$$PV_a = PMT\left[\frac{(1+i)^n - 1}{i(1+i)^n}\right]$$

where:

$$PV_a = \text{present value of an annuity}$$

and

$$PMT = \text{the annuity payment}$$

The term in brackets is called the **present value interest factor of an annuity** (PVIFA). Again, a table can be constructed that will show the factors for a large array of discount rates and time periods. Table A-4 is an example. Note the entry under the 10 percent column and row five:

3.791. If one multiplies this factor times the amount of the annuity payment, the result will be the present value of the annuity. That is,

$$3.791 \times \$2500 = \$9477$$ **(Equation A-10)**

Can you demonstrate that the present value of an annuity of $4,400 for 6 years at 9 percent is $19,738.40?

Another way to determine the present value of an annuity is by using the financial calculator. For our example the entries would appear as follows:

2500	PMT
5	N
10	I/YR

Then press PV. The display should show $9,476.97.

You should pay no more than $9,476.97 for this investment since you can replicate its cash flows by placing this sum in the bank. Of course, you need not set up five different accounts; one will do. We only set the problem up in this fashion to draw a clear picture of the cash flows.

One can always verify the answer by setting up an amortization schedule of the funds placed in, and withdrawn from, the bank as follows:

YEAR	BEGINNING BALANCE	+	END OF YEAR INTEREST EARNED	−	ENDING WITHDRAWAL	=	BALANCE
1	$9476.97		$947.70		$2500		$7924.67
2	7924.67		792.47		2500		6217.13
3	6217.13		621.71		2500		4338.85
4	4338.85		433.88		2500		2272.73
5	2272.73		227.27		2500		0

COMPOUNDING ANNUITIES

One also can ask, "If I place $2,500 in a bank account at the end of each of 5 years, beginning with a deposit 1 year from today, how much will I have in the account at the end of the fifth year?" The answer, called the **future value of an annuity,** can be determined by considering the amount to which each of the deposits will accumulate. That is, one can "decompose" the annuity into a series of deposits and solve the problem by considering the future value of each of the payments. For example, the first cash flow will be deposited 1 year from the present and will, thus, accumulate interest for 4 years by the time of the end of the fifth year. The future value will be

$$\$2500 \times (1 + 0.1)^4 = \$3660.25 \qquad \text{(Equation A-11)}$$

(The future value interest factor from Table A-1 for 10 percent and 4 years is 1.464 and 1.464 $2,500=$3,660.)

Likewise, the future value of the second payment at the end of the fifth year will be

$$\$2500 \times (1 + 0.1)^3 = \$3327.27 \qquad \text{(Equation A-12)}$$

Continuing the future values of the remaining three payments will be

$$\$2500 \times (1 + 0.1)^2 = \$3024.79$$
$$\$2500 \times (1 + 0.1)^1 = \$2749.81$$
$$\$2500 \times 1 = \$2500.00$$

The sum of these five values is $15,262.12. This sum is equivalent to

$$\$2500 \times [(1.1)^4 + (1.1)^3 + (1.1)^2 + (1.1)^1 + 1]$$
$$FV_a = PMT \left[\frac{(1 + i)^n - 1}{i} \right] \qquad \text{(Equation A-13)}$$

The term in brackets is called the **future value interest factor of an annuity** (FVIFA). As you might expect by now, the future value interest factor of an annuity can be determined for a large combination of interest rates and number of payments. The value for this case is included in Table A-2 under the 10 percent column and the fifth row, 6.105. So, 6.105 × $2,500 is equal to $15,262.

Can you confirm that the future value of a $1,000 annuity deposited at the end of each of the next 11 years will be worth $17,560 if the funds earn 9 percent interest?

The financial calculator can be used to solve these types of problems as well. For our example the entries would appear as follows:

2500	PMT
5	N
10	I/YR

Then press FV. The display should show $15,262.75.

DISCOUNTING AND COMPOUNDING AT INTERVALS OTHER THAN ONE YEAR

In the examples used thus far, we assumed that the relevant interval for compounding and discounting was 1 year. It is a simple step to consider intervals of other lengths. For example, how do the calculations change if one assumes that the relevant interval is 6 months? That is, assume that the bank in the above examples credits the account with interest at the end of 6 months based on the amount in the account at the beginning of the period. Consider the initial deposit of \$10,000. At the end of the first 6 months, the bank will credit the account with 6 months worth of interest at the 10 percent annual rate, or 5 percent of the beginning balance. The amount in the account at the end of the first 6 months will be

$$\$10,000 \times (1 + 0.05) = \$10,500 \qquad \text{(Equation A-14)}$$

This is the beginning balance for the next 6-month period. Thus at the end of the second 6-month period, the amount in the account will be

$$\begin{aligned} \$10,500 \times (1 + 0.05) &= \\ \$10,000 \times (1 + 0.05)^2 &= \$11,025 \end{aligned} \qquad \text{(Equation A-15)}$$

Note that when the bank credited the account with interest only at the end of the year, the amount (from the first example) in the account at the end of the first year was \$11,000. The extra \$25 in this example results from interest being paid in the second 6 months on the interest earned in the first 6 months. That is,

$$0.05 \times \$500 = \$25$$

The amount in the account at the end of 5 years will be

$$\$10,000 \times (1 + 0.05)^{10} = \$16,288.94 \qquad \text{(Equation A-16)}$$

which is greater than the amount when the compounding was done annually. When interest is compounded semiannually rather than annually, the formula is changed by halving the interest rate and doubling the number of time periods. To find the future value interest factor in Table A-1 simply find the factor in the column for 5 percent and the row for 10 periods. There you will see that the factor is 1.629. Alternatively, the financial calculator can be used as follows:

Enter	then	Press
10000		PV
5		%
10		N

Then press FV. If using an HP 10-B, the calculator should be set to one payment per year.

More frequent compounding leads to a larger future value in this case. If the compounding is accomplished monthly, the future value will be

$$\$10,000 \times (1 + 0.1/12)^{60} = \$16,453.09 \qquad \text{(Equation A-17)}$$

More frequent compounding will lead to yet higher future values. The future value at the end of 5 years will not increase without limit, however. If the compounding is accomplished every day, minute, or second, the future value will reach a limit. Indeed, if the compounding is accomplished over an infinitesimal interval, called continuous compounding, the future value will be given by the following:

$$\$10,000 \times e^{rt} = \$16,487.21 \qquad \text{(Equation A-18)}$$

Here e is the base of the natural logarithm and is equal to 2.7182818, r is the rate of interest, and t is the term of the investment.

When we reverse the process and find the present value of a future cash flow, more frequent compounding leads to a smaller present value. Thus, the present value of \$10,000 to be received at the end of the second year when discounted at 10 percent annually is

$$\$10,000/(1.1)^2 = \$8264.46$$

When discounted semiannually, the present value is

$$\$10,000/(1.05)^4 = \$8227.03$$

When discounted continuously, the present value is

$$\$10,000/e^{rt} = \$8187.31 \qquad \text{(Equation A-19)}$$

ANNUITY DUE

An annuity sometimes is received at times other than the end of each period. When an annuity payment falls at the beginning of a time period, it is known as an **annuity due.** To account for this situation, the PVIFA and the FVIFA can be revised in the following manner:

$$\text{PVIFA}_{ad} = \left[\frac{(1-i)^n - 1}{i(1+i)^n} \right](1+i)$$

$$\text{PVIFA}_{ad} = \left[\frac{(1+i)^n - 1}{i} \right](1+i)$$

In each case the ordinary annuity factor is multiplied by the payment to determine the annuity due. For our earlier example, the present value of an annuity due is $10,245, and the future value of an annuity due is $16,789.

CONCLUDING REMARKS

The equations that show the present value of a future (stream of) cash flows(s) can be referred to as a basic valuation equation. Such an equation essentially capitalizes future cash flows into a present value. These equations all have one thing in common. They consist of four elements: the present value, the amount of the cash flows(s), the interest or discount rate, and the term over which the cash flows are to be received. Given any three of the elements in the equation, the fourth can be determined. Furthermore, different situations in real estate finance will call for the determination of the various elements in the equation. This concept is developed further in the Appendix to Chapter 4. You are encouraged to read this Appendix.

ACRONYM LIST

APPENDIX 2

ACRS—Accelerated cost recovery system

ADC loan—Acquisition, development, and construction loan

ALTA—American Land Title Association

AMT—Alternative minimum tax

APR—Annual percentage rate

ARC—Accelerated remittance cycle

ARM—Adjustable rate mortgage loan

BCFP—Bureau of Consumer Financial Protection

BSPRA—Builder/sponsor profit and risk allowance

CDO—Collateralized Debt Obligation

CDS—Credit default swap

CERCLA—Comprehensive Environmental Response, Compensation, and Liability Act

CLO—Computerized loan origination systems

CMB—Certified mortgage banker

CMBS—Commercial mortgage-backed security

CMO—Collateralized mortgage obligation

COFI—Cost of funds index

CPM—Certified property manager

CPR—Constant prepayment rate

CRV—Certificate of reasonable value

CTL—Credit tenant lease

ECOA—Equal Credit Opportunity Act

EPA—Equity–participation agreement

ERISA—Employee Retirement Income Security Act

FASB—Financial Accounting Standards Board

FDIC—Federal Deposit Insurance Corporation

FFIEC—Federal Financial Institutions Examination Council

FHA—Federal Housing Administration

FHFA—Federal Housing Finance Agency

FHLMC—Federal Home Loan Mortgage Corporation

FIDA—Financial Institutions Deregulation Act

FIRREA—Financial Institutions, Reform, Recovery, and Enforcement Act

FIRSTS—Floating interest rate short-tranche securities

FmHA—Farmers Home Administration

FNMA—Federal National Mortgage Association

FRM—Fixed-rate mortgage

FSOC—Financial Stability Oversight Council

GAAP—Generally accepted accounting principles

GEM—Growing equity mortgage

GMC—Guaranteed mortgage certificate

GNMA—Government National Mortgage Association

GPAM—Graduated-payment adjustable mortgage

GPM—Graduated-payment mortgage

GSE—Government–sponsored enterprise

HMDA—Home Mortgage Disclosure Act

HOLC—Home Owners Loan Corporation

HTG yield—"Honest to God" yield

HUD—Department of Housing and Urban Development

ILSFDA—Interstate Land Sales Full Disclosure Act

IOs—Interest-only bonds

IRB—Industrial revenue bond

IRS—Internal Revenue Service

LIBOR—London Inter-Bank Offer Rate

MACRS—Modified accelerated cost recovery system

MAI—Member, Appraisal Institute

MBS—Mortgage–backed securities

MCA—Financial Institutions Deregulation and Monetary Control Act

MCF—Mortgage cash flow obligation

MIP—Mortgage insurance premium

MLO—Mortgage Loan Originator

MLP—Master limited partnership

NCUS—National Credit Union Administration

NOD—Notice of default

NOI—Net operating income

NOO—Nonowner-occupied

OCC—Office of the Comptroller of Currency

OID—Original issue discount

OILSR—Office of Interstate Land Sales Registration

OTS—Office of Thrift Supervision

PAC bond—Planned amortization class bond

PAM—Pledged-account mortgage

589

PC—Participating certificate

PITI—Principal, interest, taxes, and insurance

PLAM—Price level adjusted mortgage

PMI—Private mortgage insurance

POs—Principal-only bonds

PSA—Public Securities Association

PUD—Planned unit development

PV—Present value

QMI—Qualified monthly income

RAM—Reverse annuity mortgage

RAP—Regulatory accounting principles

REIT—Real estate investment trust

REMIC—Real estate mortgage investment conduit

REO—Real estate owned

RESPA—Real Estate Settlement Procedures Act

RFC—Residential Funding Corporation

RTC—Resolution Trust Corporation

SAFE—Secure and Fair Enforcement for Mortgage Licensing Act

SAM—Shared appreciation mortgage

SARA—Superfund Amendments and Reauthorization Act

SEC—Securities and Exchange Commission

SF—Single family

SMM—Single monthly mortality

SMM—Secondary mortgage market

SMMEA—Secondary Mortgage Market Enhancement Act

SREA—Senior real estate analyst

TARP—Troubled Assets Relief Program

TRA—Tax Reform Act

UCC—Uniform Commercial Code

VA—Veterans Administration

VRM—Variable-rate mortgage

WAC—Weighted average coupon

WAL—Weighted average life

WAM—Weighted average maturity

GLOSSARY

Ability-to-pay theory of default The theory that mortgage defaults occur because the mortgagor is unable to meet the monthly payment (see **equity theory of default**).

Abusive practices Practices that are consistent and in substantial violation of a particular law.

Accelerated cost recovery system (ACRS) A system of depreciation in existence from 1981 through 1986 in which assets were placed into several classes with various expected useful lives and depreciated under an accelerated rate (see **modified accelerated cost recovery system**).

Acquisition costs The F HA-appraised value or purchase price (whichever is less) plus closing costs, such as origination fees, appraisal fees, and attorney fees.

Active income A category of income established by TRA 1986. Refers to income from working in a trade, profession, or business.

Adaptations model of inflationary expectations The forecast of future inflation based on the most recent past price behavior.

Adequacy-of-interest test An IRS rule inputs the rate of interest on a loan if the contract rate is less than 110 percent of the applicable federal rate.

Adjustment rate cap A cap (usually one or two percent) on the change in the interest rate on an adjustable rate mortgage.

Adjustable-rate mortgage (ARM) A type of mortgage in which the interest rate adjusts periodically according to a preselected index, such as Treasury Bill rates, and a margin. This adjustment results in the mortgage payment either increasing or decreasing. Limits can be set on the amount by which interest rates or payments can change.

Advantageous (creative) financing Generally a loan with a contract rate of interest below the current market rate.

Affordability index An index of housing cost which uses the cost of housing, interest rates, and familiar income to track the affordability of housing over time.

Affordability problem The effect of an increase in interest rates on the ability of a borrower to purchase a house.

After-tax cash flow The cash flow from an investment after all applicable taxes have been paid.

After-tax discount rate The required rate of return on a commercial project after taxes are considered.

Agency costs Costs incurred by a principal to ensure that his or her agent operates in the interest of the principal. They include bonding, monitoring, and structuring costs.

Agency law Laws related to the agent-principal relationship.

Agency theory A model of the conflict in interest between an agent and a principal.

Agent One who legally represents another, called a principal, from whom authority has been granted.

Alternative minimum taxes (AMTs) The minimum federal taxes that a taxpayer must pay if there are substantial tax preference items that would otherwise result in low or no taxes due.

Alternative mortgage instruments (AMIs) Various mortgage loans differing from a traditional, fixed-rate, 30-year amortizing mortgage because the monthly payment, interest rate, term, or other provisions are changed.

American Land Title Association (ALTA) A national association, founded in 1907, representing 2,100 title abstractors, title insurance companies, title insurance agents, and associate members. It is the role and responsibility of the title industry and its ALTA members to guarantee the safe, efficient transfer of real property and to provide protection for consumers and lenders alike. The association speaks for the title industry and establishes standard procedures and title policy forms.

Amortization schedule A schedule of the payment of principal and interest on a loan.

Annual percentage rate (APR) The actual annual cost of credit which represents the relationship of the total finance charge (interest, loan fees, points) to the amount of the loan.

Appraisal An estimate or opinion of value supported by factual data by a qualified person. Also, the process by which this estimate is obtained.

Arbitrage pricing theory The theory that an investor could simultaneously buy and sell an asset in different markets and make a profit (riskless).

Asset valuation Techniques to place a market value on an asset.

Assignment of rents clause An agreement between a property owner and lender which gives the lender rights to the rents of the property if the owner defaults.

Assumable loan A loan on a property that can be assumed (taken over) by the buyer of the property.

At-risk limitations An IRS rule that limits the losses on an investment to the amount the taxpayer has at risk in the investment.

Bankruptcy costs Costs, such as court costs, associated with going bankrupt.

Basel Accords An international framework for adequate capital (equity) standards for financial institutions.

Before-tax discount rate The required rate of return on an investment before considering taxes.

Blockbusting The illegal practice of inducing panic selling in a neighborhood for financial gain.

Boot Property in addition to cash used in exchange to purchase another property.

Breach of contract Violating a term of a contract.

Building and loan associations Precursors to the modern savings and loan association.

Bureau of Consumer and Financial protection (BCFP) Created by the Dodd-Frank Act this federal agency creates protection for consumer financing such as credit cards, automobile loans, and residential mortgages.

Buydown mortgage A mortgage made by a lender with a below-market interest rate for a certain period of time in return for money received from a builder or seller.

Call An option to purchase an asset (usually a security) at a pre-determined price for a specific length of time.

Callability risk The risk that a debt instrument, including a mortgage, will be paid off prior to maturity if the market rate of interest falls.

Capital asset pricing model (CAPM) A model that relates the rate of return on an asset (usually a stock) to its volatility in relationship to the entire market.

Capital gains tax A tax on the appreciation in the value of an asset.

Capitalization The process of determining the present value of a series of future payments or cash flows by discounting them into a present worth using an appropriate discount rate (or rate-of-return).

Capital leases Leases of assets that are treated as ownership on the balance sheet with an entry for the present value of the lease payments as a liability (see **property lease**).

Capital loss limitation An IRS rule that limits the tax deductibility of a loss on a capital investment to the amount of gains on other capital investments plus $3,000 of ordinary income.

Capital markets Markets for long-term (usually more than a year) securities.

Carryback financing Financing arranged by the seller of the property.

Cash-equivalent value The value of a property when purchased either with all cash or with financing at market rate of interest.

Cash settlement In a credit default swap, a payment by the insurer to the insured equal to the drop in value of a security.

C Corporation A corporation that is taxed at the corporate level as opposed to the personal level (an S-Corporation, for example).

CDO-squared A collateralized debt obligation that is issued to finance the purchase of another CDO.

CERCLA The Comprehensive Environmental Response, Compensation, and Liability Act. A federal act passed in 1980 that requires owners of properties to bear the cost of cleaning up toxic or hazardous waste found on the properties.

Certified historic structures (CHSs) A designation given by the Department of Interior to structures that meet certain age and/or site conditions. Designation may be important for a taxpayer to claim a credit for restoring such a structure.

Closing costs Expenses incidental to a sale of real estate, such as loan origination fees, title fees, appraisal fees, mortgage insurance premiums, termite inspection fees, attorney fees, and so forth.

Co-insurance A sharing of insurance risk between insurer and owner depending on the relation of the amount of the policy and a specified percentage of the actual value of the property insured at the time of loss.

Collateralized Debt Obligation (CDO) A mortgage derivative security (debt obligation) backed by mortgage backed securities.

Collateralized mortgage obligations (CMOs) Multiple-class, pay-through bonds, first issued by the FHLMC in June 1983. They are secured by a pool of mortgages or a portfolio of pass-through securities. The CMO provides a type of call protection and pays principal and interest semiannually rather than monthly, as a pass-through security does.

Commercial banks Financial institutions that specialize in commercial, industrial, and agricultural loans.

Commercial mortgage-backed security (CMBS) A debt instrument backed by mortgages on commercial properties.

Community Development Block Grants Grants from the Department of Housing and Urban Development to allow communities to *carry* out a wide range of community development projects.

Community Reinvestment Act (CRA) An act passed by Congress in 1978 that requires federally insured thrifts to adopt a community reinvestment statement that defines the community in which the institution makes loans and maintains a file of loans for public inspection.

Comptroller of the Currency A federal regulatory agency with oversight duties for national banks and federally chartered thrifts.

Computer loan origination systems (CLO) Computerized networks that offer information or process loans of various lenders that participate in the network.

Constant prepayment rate (CPR) The rate at which the principal balance on a pool of mortgages is being paid, stated on an annualized basis.

Construction loan A short-term loan for financing the cost of construction. The lender makes payments to the builder at periodic intervals after he is assured that work on the project is progressing on schedule.

Construction loan administration The process of supervising the construction process by the ADC lender.

Construction loan committment A committment by an ADC lender to a developer to fund a construction project.

Cost approach An appraisal technique used to establish value by first estimating the cost to reproduce the facility, then deducting for depreciation and finally adding the value of the land.

Cost of Funds Index (COFI) Index for an adjustable rate mortgage based on the average of interest rates paid by thrifts to their depositors (their cost of funds).

Counterparty risk The risk that either party to a contract may default on the agreement.

Coverage ratio For private mortgage insurance, that portion of the exposure (potential loss) that is covered by the insurance and for which the lender will be indemnified.

Cramdown The process of reducing the debt of a company down to the values of the assets that collateralize the debt. This typically occurs in a bankruptcy.

Creative financing Any method of financing the purchase of (usually) a residence with a loan that is other than that offered by traditional mortgage lenders. These include loans with rates below the current market rate, such as assumable loans, owner financed loans, and interest rate buy-downs.

Credit default swap An instrument that insures a bondholder against a loss in the value of those bonds.

Credit enhancement The process whereby the issuer of a mortgage-related security adds support to the underlying assets by contributing capital or overcollateralizing the assets.

Credit event Any event that results in the loss in value of debt obligations (bonds).

Credit report A detailed financial history of a person or company used by a lender in determining whether to extend credit.

Credit risk The risk that a bond or other obligation will lose value.

Credit tenant lease (CTL) security A debt security issued by a developer of a commercial project and backed not only by the property but also by the rents from the tenants of the building.

Deed-of-trust A type of security instrument conveying title (in trust) to a third party (trustee). It is used to secure the payment of a note. A conveyance of the title land to a trustee as collateral security for the payment of a debt with the condition that the trustee shall re-convey the title to the borrower (trustor) upon the payment of the debt. The trustee has the power to sell the real estate and pay the debt in the event of a default on the part of the debtor.

Default risk The risk of incurring a loss on a loan as a result of a default by the issuer.

Deficiency judgment A judgment levied against the borrower personally (personal assets) for the difference between the mortgage debt (including payments in arrears) and the liquidation value of the property.

Defined-benefit plans Retirement plans that promise a certain sum (payment) of money upon retirement.

Defined-contribution plans A retirement plan that states a certain amount of money to be placed in the plan when a worker is employed. The retirement plan will pay whatever the accumulated amount will earn upon retirement.

Density bonus A waiver of regular limits on the density of housing in a development in return for the developer paying the local government in-kind or dollar-based impact fees.

Depository Institutions Deregulation and Monetary Control Act (MCA) A 1980 bill that authorized deregulation of all depository financial institutions and the phaseout of most deposit interest rate ceilings by 1986.

Depreciation recapture The amount by which a commercial property has been depreciated on the books over its life. This amount is subject to tax upon sale of the property.

Direct endorsement program An FHA program whereby qualified lenders are authorized to approve borrowers prior to all information being provided to the FHA.

Discount points Fees charged by a lender at closing or settlement that results in increasing the lender's effective yield on the money borrowed. An amount equal to 1 percent of a loan's principal.

Discounted cash flow (DCF) model A model of valuation for an asset that discounts to present value future expected cash flows. The discount rate reflects the riskiness of the asset.

Discrimination, economic theories of discrimination Two prevalent theories of discrimination are the "taste" for discrimination and the "cost of information" theory. The first attributes discrimination to the irrational decision by the discriminator who receives pleasure from discrimination. The second attributes discrimination to the prohibitive cost of obtaining sufficient information to avoid the discrimination.

Disintermediation The flow of funds out of savings institutions into short-term investments in which interest rates are higher. It occurred primarily when short-term money market rates rose above institutional deposit rates.

Diversifiable risk Risk that can be reduced by combining several assets into one portfolio (see **non-diversifiable risk**).

Diversification The process of constructing a portfolio of different assets where returns are not expected to be perfectly correlated with each other. A method of risk reduction.

Dodd-Frank Act Passed in 2009 the act established a new regulatory system for financial institutions and established the Financial Stability Oversight Council (FSOC).

Dollar-based fees Fees charged to developers by local governments that are denominated in dollars.

Double-declining balance A depreciation method allowed prior to 1981 where the depreciation of an asset in the early years was double the straight-line amount on whatever the nondepreciable difference was.

Double-declining method A former method of depreciation that accelerates depreciation in the early years of the life of an asset.

Double taxation Refers to the taxation of a C-corporation at the corporate level and then taxation of the dividends and capital gains to the stockholders of the same corporation.

Duration A measure of the extent to which the cash flows of a security are "pushed back" in time. It is found by taking a weighted average of the present values of the cash flows. Similar to maturity of a security.

Econometric prepayment models Models that predict the prepayment of mortgages based on demographic data.

Effective (implied) duration The duration of an interest contingent security found by observing the percentage price change in the market as a result of a change in interest rates.

Efficient market (theory) The theory that asset markets are efficient in that assets prices reflect all known and available information. No excess returns can be gained by trading on information known to market participants.

11th District Cost of Funds Index The cost of financial institutions in the 11th district to obtain funds from depositors. An example would be the rate of interest financial institution pay on one year certificates of deposit.

Emergency Economic Stabilization Act of 2008 An act passed by Congress to provide economic stability as a result of the financial downturn in 2007 and 2008 due to the collapse of the housing market.

Employee Retirement Income Security Act (ERISA) A federal law that regulates the investments that pension and profit-sharing plans can make, and the conduct of their fiduciaries.

Environmental audit A test of soils for toxic waste and/or contamination, usually before a commercial real estate project commences.

Equal Credit Opportunity Act (ECOA) A federal law that requires lenders to make credit equally available without discrimination based on race, color, religion, national origin, age, sex, marital status, or receipt of income from public assistance programs. Also known as Regulation B.

Equation of exchange An economic equation which states that the total amount of money spent (money times velocity, MV) equals the total amount received (prices time number of transactions, PT).

Equitable (right of) redemption The common law right to redeem property during the foreclosure period by paying past due amounts. In some states the mortgagor has a statutory right to redeem property after a foreclosure sale. This is limited to several months or a year.

Equity In real estate, equity is the difference between the fair market value of the property and the amount of debt.

Equity-participation loan A loan whereby the lender agrees to a reduced interest rate in exchange for a participation in the cash flows of a commercial project and or the appreciation in the project.

Equity REIT A real estate investment trust that invests in the equity of real estate (see **mortgage REIT**).

Equity theory of default A theory that states that mortgage defaults only occur if there is negative equity in the property (see **ability-to-pay theory of default**).

Eviction The lawful expulsion of an occupant from real property.

Expectations theory A theory that says the structure of the yield curve incorporates the market's expectations of future interest rates.

Federal credit agencies Federally sponsored and/or supported agencies that support various activities such as housing or agriculture through credit availability.

Federal Deposit Insurance Corporation (FDIC) An organization originally established by the Banking Act of 1933 to insure the deposits of banks.

Federal Home Loan Bank Board The federal government's supervisory agency for insured savings and loans and mutual savings banks.

Federal Home Loan Mortgage Corporation (FHLMC) A private corporation authorized by Congress with an independent board of directors to provide secondary mortgage market support for conventional mortgages. It also sells participation certificates secured by pools of conventional mortgage loans. Popularly known as Freddie Mac, it is under the regulation of HUD.

Federal Housing Administration (FHA) A federal agency whose main activity is the insuring of residential mortgage loans made by private lenders. FHA is a division of HUD which sets standards for construction and underwriting and charges a fee, generally 3.8 percent of loan amount.

Federal Housing Finance Agency A federal regulatory agency with oversight duties for the government sponsored agencies (GSE's).

Federal Financial Institutions Examination Council (FFIEC) established in 1979 this agency makes regulations of financial institutions uniform and harmonious.

Federal National Mortgage Association (FNMA) A privately owned corporation created by Congress to support the secondary mortgage market. It purchases and sells residential mortgages insured by FHA or guaranteed by VA, as well as conventional home mortgages. Popularly known as Fannie Mae, it is under the regulation of HUD.

FHAing The practice by lenders of making only FHA loans in certain risky or transition neighborhoods. Lenders suffer no loss with FHA insurance as they may with private mortgage insurance.

FHA prepayment experience The historical rate of the annual prepayment of FHA loans over an extended period of time.

Fiduciary A person in a position of trust and confidence for another.

Financial Accounting Standards Board (FASB) An independent, private entity that establishes standards for financial accounting and reporting and derives its authority from the SEC.

Financial Institutions Reform, Recovery, and Enforcement Act (FIRREA) An act passed in 1989 to help bail out the failing savings and loan industries. It established the Resolution Trust Corporation (RTC) and changed the regulatory structure of financial institutions.

Financial intermediary An institution that accepts funds from surplus income units and lends them to deficit income units.

Financial leverage The use of some debt (rather than all equity) to finance the acquisition of an asset.

Financing costs The total of all payments on a loan (through payoff) less the original amount of the principal.

Fisher equation Named after economist Irving Fisher, an equation that indicates that the nominal rate of interest is equal to the real rate plus anticipated inflation.

Floaters Financial instruments whose rate of interest varies directly with a market rate.

Forbearance The act of refraining from taking legal action despite the fact that a mortgage is in arrears. It is usually granted only when a mortgagor makes a satisfactory arrangement by which the arrears will be paid at a future date.

Foreclosure A legal procedure taken by a mortgagee or lender under the terms of a mortgage or deed of trust for the purpose of having the property sold and the proceeds applied to the payment of a defaulted debt.

Fractions rule A rule for pension funds that participate in an investment with other QOs (qualified organizations) such as partnerships which requires that the expenses associated with each entity be allocated in proportion to the ownership percentages.

Frequency of rate change How often the rate of interest on an adjustable rate mortgage can change.

Full coverage A mortgage insurance program where all losses to the lender under a default are covered. FHA is an example of full coverage.

Fully indexed rate The rate of interest on an adjustable rate mortgage when no discount or "teaser" rate applies.

Garn-St. Germain Act An act passed in 1982 to place savings and loans on a more equal footing with commercial banks.

Generally accepted accounting principles (GAAP) Accounting principles established by the accounting profession which are intended to produce a uniform and consistent set of accounting rules and practices.

Geographic diversification In real estate investment, the process of adding properties to a portfolio from different areas of the country. An area may be defined in terms of a commonality of its economy.

Gibson paradox An apparent paradox that recognizes that interest rates move in the same (not opposite) direction from changes in the money supply.

Government National Mortgage Association (GNMA) Nicknamed Ginnie Mae, this HUD agency operates as a participant in the secondary mortgage market. It is involved with special government financing programs for urban renewal projects, elderly housing, and other high-risk mortgages. GNMA also carries out the liquidation and special assistance functions performed by the Federal National Mortgage Association prior to its reorganization in 1968. The association is involved with the mortgage securities pool and the tandem plan.

Government-sponsored enterprise (GSE) Examples are Freddie Mac, Fannie Mae, and Ginnie Mae.

Graduated-payment mortgage (GPM) A residential mortgage designed to overcome the "tilt" effect. The monthly mortgage payments that start at a level below that on a FRM and increase at a predetermined rate with later payments above that on a FRM. They may level off at some predetermined point.

Guaranteed mortgage certificates (GMCs) A bond-like instrument issued by Freddie Mac that represents ownership in a large pool of residential mortgages. Principal is returned annually and interest is paid semiannually.

Guarantor A person or entity that guarantees the performance of a loan taken out by another party.

Hedonic price equation Usually refers to an equation that allocates the price of a residential property to its component characteristics such as the square feet, number of rooms, etc.

Historic rehabilitation credit A credit for federal taxes computed as a percent of the amount of funds used to restore historic properties.

Home Mortgage Disclosure Act (HMDA) A federal act passed in 1975 that requires disclosure of an institution's loans by census tract or by zip code.

Home Owners Loan Corporation (HOLC) An agency formed in 1933 to help stabilize the economy. HOLC issued government-guaranteed bonds to lenders for delinquent mortgages and then refinanced homeowner indebtedness.

Homeowners Protection Act An act passed by Congress in 1998 that sets rules for the elimination of mortgage insurance as a function of the paydown in the principal of the loan.

Housing and Urban Development Act An act passed by congress in 1968 that established the Government National Mortgage Association (Ginnie Mae) within the Department of HUD and privatized the Federal National Mortgage Association (Freddie Mac).

Hybrid REIT A REIT that invests in mortgages as well as equity real estate.

Impact fees Fees charged a developer by a local government to cover the added government expenditures (fire, police protection, etc.) necessitated by the development.

Index A rate of interest, such as a T-bill rate, used to measure periodic interest rate adjustments for an adjustable rate mortgage.

Installment sale The selling of an appreciated property on terms rather than for cash so as to postpone the payment of capital gains taxes on the profits.

Intent approach A rule by the Federal Reserve System that attempts to measure potential discrimination in mortgage lending by the "intent" of the lender.

Interest-only (IO) strip A security that represents the receipt of all interest payments and interest payments only from a pool of mortgages.

Interest rate caps A provision in an adjustable rate mortgage that limits the increase in the rate of interest at each anniversary date of the rate change.

Interest rate contingent securities Securities (usually mortgage-related securities) for which the amount and timing of the cash flows are dependent on (changes in) market rates.

Interest rate risk The risk that, subsequent to the purchase of a debt security, interest rates will change, thereby affecting the value of the security.

Internal rate of return (IRR) The rate of return that is particular to a specific asset.

Interstate Land Sales Full Disclosure Act (ILSFDA) A federal act passed in 1968 that requires a developer to provide complete disclosure of all relevant facts concerning the interstate sale of undeveloped land.

Inverse floater A security for which the interest rate varies inversely with a particular market rate of return (such as the LIBOR).

Investment interest limitation An IRS rule that limits the amount of interest on debt used to finance the acquisition of an asset (usually raw land) that a taxpayer can deduct to determine taxable income.

IOs Interest only securities. The owner receives the right to receive all of the interest payments from a pool of mortgages.

Joint and several liability A situation in which a creditor may sue one or more of the parties separately, or all of them together. For example, partners are jointly and separately liable for all debts and obligations incurred by the partnership.

Judicial procedure (foreclosure) A foreclosure process that involves a court proceeding (as opposed to a power-of-sale foreclosure that avoids a court proceeding).

Land contracts Contracts ordinarily used in connection with the sale of property in cases where the seller does not convey title until all or a substantial portion of the purchase price is paid by the buyer. Often used to avoid a due-on-sale clause.

Land development loan A loan for the purpose of developing land so as to ready it for construction.

Leverage The use of borrowed money to increase the return on a cash investment. For leverage to be profitable, the rate of return on the investment must be higher than the cost of borrowed funds.

Lien A legally recognized hold or claim of one person on the property of another as security for a debt, duty, or obligation.

Life-of-loan rate cap The maximum rate of interest allowed under the terms of an adjustable rate mortgage.

Liquidity effect A short-term effect on interest rates resulting from a change in the growth rate of the money supply. Generally, when the money supply is increased, there is a short-term drop in interest rates.

Liquidity premium theory The theory that short term and readily marketable securities *carry* a lower rate of interest because investors perceive them as having less risk.

Liquidity risk The risk that an asset may not be easily and rapidly sold for cash at its current value.

London Inter-Bank Offered Rate (LIBOR) An average of daily lending rates from several major London banks, used as a common international interest rate index.

Low-income housing credit A credit against federal taxes for investing in low-income housing.

Margin The number of basis points a lender adds to an index to determine the interest rate of an adjustable rate mortgage.

Marketing rate difference The difference between the amount a mortgage banker sells a loan for and the amount originated. A source of revenue for mortgage bankers.

Market segmentation theory The theory that different investors prefer one end of the maturity spectrum of bonds to the other.

Mark-to-market A procedure where an asset (or liability, but usually an asset) is revalued periodically (can be as frequently as daily) on the books of the holder.

Master limited partnerships (MLPs) Large limited partnerships usually holding multiple projections either directly or through ownership of subsidiary partnerships.

Maturity mismatch A difference in the maturity of the assets and liabilities of a financial institution. Usually refers to assets with a longer maturity than liabilities.

Maturity risk The increase in risk due to the increase in the maturity of a debt obligation due to possible changes in interest rates or inflation rates.

Mixed-asset portfolio A portfolio of assets with distinctly different characteristics (a portfolio of real estate investments that consists of many different property types in different areas of the country or globe).

Modified accelerated cost recovery system (MACRS) A system of depreciation in effect since 1986 whereby the expected lives of assets under the previous ACRS system were lengthened.

Modigliani—Miller hypothesis In regard to capital structure, the hypothesis that the mix of debt and equity has no effect on the value of the company.

Monetary control act (MCA) The short title of the Financial Institutions Deregulation and Monetary Control Act of 1980 which deregulated commercial banks and savings and loans especially in regards to eliminating Regulation Q.

Monetary theory of inflation The theory that inflation is a monetary phenomenon in the sense that it results from a growth in the money supply in excess of the growth in productivity.

Money markets Markets where short-term (less than one year) debt obligations are exchanged.

Mortgage-backed bonds (MBBs) A "bond" or debt instrument which is backed by a pool (large group) of mortgages and for which the cash flow of the mortgages serves as the source of repayment.

Mortgage-backed security (MBS) A security purchased by investors that are secured by mortgages. Such securities are also known as pass-through securities since the debt service paid by the borrower is passed through to the purchaser of the security.

Mortgage banking The packaging of mortgage loans to be sold to a permanent investor or to be packaged into mortgage-backed securities with servicing retained for the life of the loan for a fee. Mortgage banking includes the origination, sale, and servicing of mortgage loans by a firm or individual. The investor-correspondent system is the foundation of the mortgage banking industry.

Mortgage derivative security A debt obligation for which the cash flows derive from those of the underlying assets which are mortgages.

Mortgage insurance premium (MIP) The charge paid by a mortgagor for mortgage insurance either to FHA or to a private mortgage insurance (PMI) company. On an FHA loan, the payment is 3.8 percent of the loan balance.

Mortgage REIT A real estate investment trust that invests in mortgages on real estate properties (see **equity REIT**).

Mortgage revenue bonds A bond issued by a public entity payable from revenues derived from repayments of principal and interest on mortgage loans that were financed from the proceeds of the bonds.

NAREIT Equity Index An index of the value of REITs that invest only in equity properties, not mortgages.

National Credit Union Administration The federal supervisory agency for the nation's credit unions.

National Housing Act Passed by Congress in 1934, it created the Federal Housing Administration and the Federal Savings and Loan Insurance Corporation. The FSLIC was merged into the Federal Deposit Insurance Corporation.

Negative amortization A loan payment schedule in which the outstanding principal balance goes up, rather than down, because the payments do not cover the full amount of interest due. The unpaid interest is added to the principal.

Negative duration Refers to a security whose value varies positively with a change in interest rates. An example is an interest-only strip of a mortgage pool.

Negative leverage This occurs when an asset is financed with debt and the interest rate on the debt is more than the return on the asset.

Net present value (NPV) The excess of the present value of an asset's future cash flows over its current cost. A positive net present value indicates an asset should be acquired.

Nondisclosure fraud Involves a misrepresentation or a failure to disclose important information by an agent that has a fiduciary responsibility to a principal.

Nondiversifiable risk Risk that remains in a well-diversified portfolio of assets and thus cannot be reduced through further diversification (see **diversifiable risk**).

Nonrecourse debt A loan for which the lender may have a claim or lien on the property financed by the loan but not on assets such as the borrower's personal assets.

Office of Thrift Supervision (OTS) The Financial Institutions Reform, Recovery, and Enforcement Act created the OTS to replace the Federal Home Loan Bank Board and place the OTS in the Department of the Treasury so as to separate a regulatory agency from the insurance fund that insured S&Ls.

Operating leases Leases for which the assets are not carried on the balance sheet of the user. Lease payments are treated as an operating expense (see **capital lease**).

Optimal capital structure That ratio of debt and equity which maximizes the value of the two components. Refers primarily to corporate finance but can be used in reference to financing real estate properties.

Options Rights, given for consideration to a party (optionee) by a property owner (optionor), to purchase or lease within a specific time at a specific price and terms.

Oral commitment A commitment to fund a loan that is oral and not in writing.

Ordinary Income Tax Tax ordinary income as opposed to capital gains.

Original issue discount (OID) A tax concept that requires investors to pay taxes on the effective yield of an investment rather than on the coupon rate of the cash flows when debt is issued at a below-market coupon.

Origination fee A fee or charge for the work involved in the evaluation, preparation, and submission of a proposed mortgage loan.

Originations The processes of making mortgage loans.

Owner-second financing A loan made by the owner/seller of a property to the buyer to help finance the sale.

Partial coverage Refers, usually, to mortgage insurance where the insurer will reimburse the lender for only a portion of the debt. VA insurance is an example.

Participation certificate (PC) Mortgage-backed security issued by FHLMC which is backed by mortgages purchased from eligible sellers. Called PC because seller retains some interest (5 or 10 percent) in the mortgages sold to FHLMC.

Passive income One of three classifications of income under TRA 1986. Most real estate and all limited partnerships are placed in this class of income.

Passive losses A loss (negative income) on a real estate property or any limited partnership (such as an oil & gas limited partnership).

Passive loss limitation A limitation on the amount of a loss that may be available to reduce taxes. Generally passive losses are limited to offset only passive gains.

Pass-through securities Securities issued by the Government National Mortgage Association which provides for the interest and principal to pass through to the holder of the security.

Pension funds Financial and other institutions that receive workers contributions to retirement and invest them in interest earning assets.

Physical settlement In a credit default swap whereby the insured delivers the (now less valuable) bond to the insurer for a payment equal to the insured value.

Pledged-account mortgage A graduated payment mortgage in which part of the buyer's down payment is deposited in a savings account. Funds are drawn from the account to supplement the buyer's monthly payments during the early years of the loan.

Pool insurance Mortgage default insurance on an entire pool of mortgages. Generally only a certain percent of the pool is insured.

Portfolio A combination of distinct assets into one group, often for the purpose of diversification.

Portfolio income One of three classes of income under TRA 1986. Income from stocks and bonds is the primary type of income in this class.

Portfolio losses A decline in value of a portfolio of stocks, bonds, and other investments.

Portfolio theory The theory that the risk of individual assets can be reduced by combining them into a portfolio and that there need be no reduction in expected return.

Positive leverage This occurs when an asset is financed with debt and the rate of interest on the debt is less than the return on the asset.

POs Principal only strips. The buyer of the PO receives the right to receive all the principal payments (including prepayments) fro a pool of mortgages.

Potentially responsible parties (PRPs) Under CERCLA, parties that will be considered legally responsible for the cost of cleaning up hazardous or toxic waste found on a property.

Power of sale procedure A process of foreclosure that allows the lender to avoid court costs by presenting evidence to a trustee who holds the title to the property and receives title in return.

Prepayment (or call) option The option a borrower has to prepay his or her mortgage in its entirety prior to the maturity date. It is termed a call option because the borrower is "calling in" the old mortgage.

Price-anticipation effect A change in the market rate of interest in the same direction as recent inflation. Market investors incorporate expectations of future inflation in their required yield.

Price compression The tendency for increasingly higher coupon rate pass-throughs to not experience a significant increase in price. This is because the pass-throughs are more and more likely to be called (prepaid).

Price-level adjusted mortgage (PLAM) An alternative mortgage instrument that provides the lender with a real rate of interest in the form of a contract rate and inflation premium through an adjustment of the mortgage balance by the most recent amount of inflation.

Pricing ARMs The process of determining the effect of value and other factors such as interest rate risk of an ARM by changing one or more of its terms.

***Prima facia* tort** Concept that one who causes injury to another is subject to liability to the other for that injury.

Primary market The market where financial securities are first originated.

Principal The face value of a note or mortgage. In a real estate transaction, the principal is the person who hires a real estate broker to sell his or her property.

Principal only (PO) strip Gives the investor the right to receive all the principal payments whenever they are received.

Private debt Debt that is not comprised of public securities.

Private mortgage insurance (PMI) Insurance written by a private (nongovernmental) company protecting the mortgage lender against loss caused by a mortgage default or foreclosure.

Promissory fraud Making a promise with no intention of fulfilling it.

Promissory note The portion of a residential financing arrangement that contains the important provisions of a loan.

Property diversification Investing in different types of real properties to achieve maximum return for a given level of risk.

Property held as principal residence Income tax classification for a property that is owned and occupied as a primary residence.

Property held for investment Income tax classification for a property that is held strictly for income or investment and the owner has no participation in the operations of the investment.

Property held for resale Income tax classification for a property held as inventory for resale.

Property held for use in trade or business Income tax classification for a property, referred to as a Section 1231 asset, that is owned and operated for the purpose of deriving rental income.

Property risk Inherent risk of a property usually based on the riskiness of its cash flows.

Public debt Debt available through publicly traded securities.

Public Securities Association (PSA) prepayment rate A widely used model of mortgage prepayment rates established by the PSA.

Publicly traded partnerships (PTPs) Large partnerships, the interests of which are traded on the major security exchanges.

Purchase money mortgages Mortgages given by the purchaser of real property to the seller as part of the sales price.

Purchasing power risk Risk of investor loss in purchasing power based on positive inflation.

Qualified thrift investments (QTIs) Investments in which thrifts are allowed to acquire under the 1989 FIRREA act.

Quality rating Rating by a rating agency such as Moody's or Standard and Poor's of the quality of a mortgage-backed security.

Rate cap A limit on the contract rate of interest (for a particular adjustment period) on an adjustable rate mortgage.

Rating Agency An agency such as Standard and Poors or Moodys that rates the financial safety of debt obligations of private companies, as well as state and federal issues.

Real estate investment trust (REIT) An organized association whereby individual investors pool their funds for the purpose of investing in real estate. A REIT is created in the form of a business trust. If the tax requirements are met, it provides for a pass-through of income without double taxation.

Real estate limited partnerships (RELPs) Partnerships formed to invest in real estate where limited partners have limited liability.

Real Estate Mortgage Investment Conduit (REMIC) A type of mortgage-backed security that allows for income to be taxed only to the holders of the bond and not to the entity holding the mortgages.

Real Estate Settlement Procedures Act (RESPA) A federal law that deals with procedures to be followed in certain types of real estate closings. RESPA requires lenders to provide loan applicants with pertinent information so that the borrower can make an informed decision as to which lender to use in financing the purchase.

Real estate synthetic investment securities (RESI) Bonds structured such that all default losses are passed to the lowest rated classes first.

Real rate of interest The nominal rate of interest adjusted for inflation.

Reasonable accommodations Accommodations that would be considered reasonable to the typical renter.

Reconciliation phase Portion of the appraisal where the appraiser considers all the estimates of value and arrives at a final estimate.

Reconstruction Finance Corporation (RFC) Agency established in 1932 to make loans to savings and loan associations to help them survive their liquidity crisis.

Recourse debt A debt in which the lender in a default can pursue borrower assets other than the named collateral.

Recourse note A note attached to a mortgage that allows the lender in a default to seek attachment of other assets owned by the borrower.

Redlining The practice by lenders of refusing to make loans in certain risky or transitional neighborhoods.

Refinancing Repaying one or more existing mortgage loans by simultaneously borrowing funds through another mortgage loan.

Regulation and negative amortization Regulations that address whether a mortage can incur negative amortization.

Regulation Z (Truth-in-Lending) A regulation issued by the Federal Reserve System to implement the Truth-in-Lending Act.

Regulatory accounting principles (RAP) The accounting principles required by regulation that allow savings institutions to elect annually to defer gains or losses on the sale of assets and amortize these deferrals over the average life of each loan group or the stated life of each security sold.

Related persons rule A rule in an installment sale that says if the sale is made to a related person, who in turn sells the property within a two-year period, the original seller must recognize the balance of the gain at the time the related person makes the sale.

Release provision A provision in a land development loan that allows parcels to be released from the lien of the lender so that they may be sold.

Rental Rehabilitation Program Program to provide grants to cities and states to encourage rehabilitation of rental properties.

Replacement reserve Requirement by investors that the owner of a property set aside funds to make replacements in items such as air conditioners, appliances, etc.

Residual method One of two income ratio tests applied by the VA for loan qualifications. The method concentrates on the residual income after housing payments sufficient to meet other living expenses, such as food and clothing.

Resolution Trust Corporation (RTC) A government organization set up by the 1989 FIRREA act to dispose of property acquired by the federal government when it acquired the assets of failed savings and loans.

Return on equity The ratio of cash flow after debt service to the difference between the value of property and total financing (see **cash-on-cash return**).

Reverse annuity mortgage (RAM) A financing arrangement whereby a lender pays the borrower a fixed annuity or periodic payment based on a percentage of the property's value.

Reverse mortgage Refers to a mortgage with falling equity, rising debt, in which the lender makes payments to the borrower for a stipulated time.

Review appraiser A lender's appraiser who reviews an appraisal for acceptability.

Revised Uniform Limited Partnership Act 1976 act that established rules for the existence of a partnership and the relationship between the partners.

Right of rescission The right to rescind (undo) a contract if certain legal requirements are not fulfilled.

Risk The possibility combined with the probability that the actual future outcome will differ from the expected outcome.

Risk-based capital guidelines Rules established by the Office of Thrift Supervision (OTS) which determine the amount of capital a thrift must have as a function of the riskiness of its assets.

Risks and returns of ownership Provision in a sale-leaseback that defines whether a sale is actually a sale or not.

Rolling options Options to purchase more land to be developed as the existing development is completed.

Sale-leaseback A technique in which a seller deeds property to a buyer for a consideration and the buyer simultaneously leases the property back to the seller, usually on a long-term basis.

Sale-leaseback accounting Rules that define the tax treatment of a property in a sale-leaseback arrangement.

SARA Superfund Amendments and Reauthorization Act of 1986.

Savings-investment cycles An identity in which the amount of savings equals the total amount invested in an economy.

S corporation Corporate form that eliminates double taxation by having stockholders report income on their individual tax returns.

Secondary market The market where existing securities are exchanged.

Secondary mortgage market A market where existing mortgages are bought and sold. It contrasts with the primary mortgage market, where mortgages are originated.

Secured lender exemption Under CERCLA, an exemption from responsibility for cleanup costs given to lenders with a security interest in a property (collateral) on which toxic or hazardous waste is found.

Secure and fair Enforcement for Mortgage Licensing Act (S.A.F.E. Act) passed in 2008 this act requires states to set up requirements for licensing and oversight of mortgage originators, especially mortgage brokers.

Securitization The process of creating new securities backed (collateralized) by a package of other securities or assets.

Self-Help Homeownership Opportunity Program (SHOP) Provides funds for eligible nonprofit organizations to establish an infrastructure to help low-income persons gain homeownership.

Self-insurance Process of the individual providing personal insurance against losses.

Self-liquidating REIT REIT that is established for a definite time period after which the assets are liquidated.

Semi-strong firm Form of market efficiency that states that an individual cannot earn excess returns by utilizing publicly available information.

Senior financing Financing that is superior in claim to earning and assets to other debt issues.

Senior/subordinated securities A mortgage passthrough security issued in two classes. The subordinated class absorbs payment risk for both classes.

Senior tranche The tranche in a CMO that has superior claim to earnings and assets.

Servicing rights The provision that gives the mortgage lender the right to collect the monthly payments and other cash flows on a mortgage.

Settlement charges Charges by the lender to the borrower for originating a mortgage.

Settlement services Services provided by the participants in a loan settlement: attorneys, lenders, title companies, escrow companies, and others.

SFAS 98 Rule providing guidance for recognizing gain in sale—leasebacks.

Shared appreciation mortgage (SAM) A mortgage in which a borrower receives a below-market interest rate in return for which the lender receives a portion of the future appreciation in the value of the property.

Shorter term wrap A wrap-around mortgage that is written for a shorter term than the remaining term of the original mortgage.

Simulation model Model that provides outcomes for various scenarios or random changes in explanatory variables.

Simultaneous term, full amortized wrap A wrap-around mortgage that is written for a fully amortizing term equal to the remaining term of the original mortgage.

Speculator Spread (price) Asset price spread created by speculators.

Statute of fraud A state law requiring that certain contracts be in writing and contain certain essential elements to be enforceable. A contract for the sale of real estate must be in writing to be enforceable.

Statutory (right of) redemption The right of a borrower after a foreclosure sale to reclaim his property by repaying his defaulted loan.

Stepped-up basis An increase in the depreciable basis of an asset usually brought about by its sale.

Straight-line depreciation Depreciation based on dividing the depreciable basis of an asset by the number of years of its remaining useful life.

Straight-line method Method of depreciation requiring a constant recovery rate over the recovery period.

Streamline Refinance Plan (SRP) Method to promote more rapid refinancing of FHA loans.

Strips (IO and PO) A mortgage pass-through security created by separating and reassembling the principal and interest payments on a pool of long-term mortgages.

Strong form Form of efficiency (that does not hold true) stipulating that an individual investor cannot earn excess returns from using private or inside information.

Structured finance CDOs Collateralized debt obligations created by using mortgage-backed securities as security for the debt.

Subdivision control ordinances Local government ordinances that require developers to put in place the necessary infrastructure before development may take place. Alternatively, the developer may place funds in a trust for this purpose.

Subdivision trust Arrangement in which the developer provides a portion of the sales price and agrees to pay the balance when the property is developed and sold.

Subordinated tranche A CMO tranche which has an inferior claim behind other tranches in terms of claim to income and assets.

Subordination A clause that may be included in a written recorded instrument in which the mortgagee (lender) agrees to permit a later-acquired debt to have priority. Subordination may apply not only to mortgages but also to leases, real estate rights, and any other types of debt instruments.

Subprime loan A mortgage loan originated for a riskier borrower under terms different than those for a prime borrower.

Sum-of-the-years' digits method Method of depreciation in which the numerator is the number of years remaining and the denominator is the sum of the years in the depreciable life.

Suspended passive losses Losses remaining after the disposition of an income property that can be used to offset outside income.

Swap The selling of mortgages in exchange for PCs representing interests in those same mortgages under the Guarantor program.

Systematic Risk Risk that affects many institutions simultaneously due to widespread economic developments such as a recession in the economy or real estate downturn.

Tandem plan A mortgage assistance program in which a federal agency agrees to purchase below-market interest rate mortgages at near par prices. The mortgages purchased are accumulated and periodically sold at auction as either mortgage-backed securities or whole mortgages. As the subsidy cost of the program, the agency absorbs the difference between the price it paid for the loan and the market price paid by the investor.

Tax-deferred exchange rule Section 1031 rule defining a tax-deferred exchange.

Tax increment financing Exists where the infrastructure for a new development is paid for by property taxes on properties within the development.

Tax preference items Items added to regular taxable income when determining alternative minimum tax.

Tax Reform Act of 1986 Tax act that compressed marginal tax rates for individuals, created straight-line depreciation only for real estate, and eliminated favorable treatment of capital gains among other things.

Tax shelter An asset whose value is partially created by its favorable tax treatment.

Teaser rate A below-market rate of interest for an initial period of time only on an adjustable rate mortgage.

Tilt effect The effect of a rise in interest rates whereby the real payments on a standard fixed rate mortgage (FRM) are much greater at the beginning of the loan than at the end.

Time-value-of-money test Requires that interest be imputed and reported as revenue or expense annually.

Title plant A duplicate set of public records maintained by a title company.

Title search A search of the public records to discover any liens or other impediments to a transfer of an unencumbered title.

Total mortgage payment (TMP) The total monthly mortgage payment for the borrower that may consist of principal, interest, and escrow for payment of property taxes and insurance.

Tranches A class of securities in a multi-class securities offering.

Truth-in-lending disclosure Disclosure to the borrower that must contain the major financial terms of the loan.

Uniform Commercial Code (UCC) A comprehensive law regulating commercial transactions. It has been adopted, with modification, by all states.

Uniform Limited Partnership Act (ULPA) 1916 act regulating structure and financial arrangements of limited partnerships.

Uniform Settlement Statement A standard form required by HUD that stipulates the fees and charges to be paid by the buyer and seller at a loan closing.

Unrelated business income tax (UBIT) A tax law that requires otherwise tax-exempt organizations (such as pension funds) to pay tax on income earned from any business endeavor not related to its main purpose.

Usury Charging a higher interest rate than allowed by law.

Value Price attached to an asset by investors.

Value creation The process of implementing characteristics that increase the value of an asset, such as tax shelter value.

Variance The extent that an asset price deviates from the mean.

Velocity of circulation The average number of times the money supply "turns over" in one year. Measured by dividing the gross national product by the supply of money.

Voucher control agent An independent company that verifies that all monies advanced by a lender on an ADC loan have been used to construct the facility and that there are no mechanic's or other liens on the property being developed.

Warehousing The holding of a mortgage on a short-term basis pending either a sale to an investor or other long-term financing. These mortgages may be used as a collateral security with a bank to borrow additional funds. A builder "warehouses" mortgages when he takes back a mortgage from a home buyer and holds the mortgage for a time period. A mortgage banker "warehouses" mortgages until a sufficient number is accumulated to package into a mortgage-backed security.

Warehousing loans Short term loans from commercial banks.

Warehousing rate difference The difference between the interest rate on a mortgage (revenue) and the rate on a warehouse loan (cost) for a mortgage banker. A source of funds for a mortgage banker.

Weak form A form of efficiency stating that an individual investor cannot earn excess returns by following past price changes.

Wellenkamp **case** A famous court case in California that established the right of a borrower to assume a mortgage even though it had a due-on-sale clause.

Window dressing Creation of a firm's financial statements so that they are presented in the best possible light.

Yield curve Graph depicting the relationship between assets' returns and term to maturity.

Yield maintenance prepayment penalty Prepayment penalty in a mortgage designed to allow the lender to maintain a certain rate of return.

Yield on tax-free bonds The rate of return on tax-free bonds.

"Zombie" theory of thrift failure Theory that insolvency leads to risk-taking which in turn leads to further insolvency.

INDEX

equity-participation loans, 477–482

importance of, 3

Modigliani-Miller argument, 387–389

pass-throughs, 269–271

risk of, 29

sale-leasebacks, 487–489

structure of, 379–381

timing of, 28–29

value of, 384–389

cash settlements, 232

CBO (Congressional Budget Office), 165

C corporations, 503

CDOs (collateralized debt obligations), 152, 301

CDO-squared, 152, 301

CDSs (credit default swaps), 232–234

Centerre Bank of Kansas City v. Distributors, Inc., 564

CERCLA (Comprehensive Environmental Response, Compensation, and Liability Act of 1980), 457–458, 551–560

certified historic structures (CHSs), 417

CFR (Code of Federal Regulations), 147

Chancery Court, 50

Chandler, G. G., 182–184, 203–204

CHAP (comprehensive homeless assistance plan), 162

Chemical Manufacturers Association v. Environmental Protection Agency, 558

Cherry v. Home Savings and Loan Association, 80

Chicago Mercantile Exchange (CME Group), 37

Chicago Mercantile Exchange Clearing House (CMECH), 151

Chomsisengphet, S., 361

CHSs (certified historic structures), 417

Citicorp Mortgage Power Program, 182

Clauretie, Terrence M., 366

CLOs (computer loan origination systems), 180–183

closed corporations, 415

closed-end REITs, 512

closing, 343–344

closing costs, 392

CMBSs (commercial mortgage-backed securities)

overview, 230–231

risk of cash flows, 31

with tranches, 436–438

CME Group (Chicago Mercantile Exchange), 37

CMOs (collateralized mortgage obligations)

FHA, 241–242

first issued, 247

overview, 228–229, 280–287

risk of cash flows, 31

CMT (Constant Maturity Treasury) Indexes, 104

Coast Bank v. Minderhout, 80

Code of Federal Regulations (CFR), 147

COFI (Cost of Funds Index), 105

co-insurance, 349

collateralized, 221

collateralized debt obligations (CDOs), 152, 301

collateralized mortgage obligations. *see* CMOs

commercial banks, 7

commercial mortgage-backed securities. *see* CMBSs

commingled real estate funds (CREFs), 537

commitment fees, 456

Commodity Futures Modernization Act of 2000, 232–233

Community Development Bank Bill, 218

Community Development Block Grants, 162

Community Reinvestment Act (CRA) of 1978, 126, 197, 205–210

Competitive Equity Banking Act, 217

Comprehensive Drug Abuse Prevention and Control Act of 1970, 560

Comprehensive Environmental Response, Compensation, and Liability Act of 1980 (CERCLA), 457–458, 551–560

comprehensive homeless assistance plan (CHAP), 162

computer loan origination systems (CLOs), 180–183

Congressional Budget Office (CBO), 165

Consolidated Farmers Home Administration Act, 215

Constant Maturity Treasury (CMT) Indexes, 104

constant prepayment rate (CPR), 264–265

construction cost schedule, 459

construction financing. *see* ADC financing

construction loan administration, 458–459

construction loan commitment, 455–456

construction loan provisions, 456–458

construction-to-permanent loans, 351, 354

Consumer Credit Protection Act, 150, 169–175, 216

consumer durable goods, 5

continuity of life, 507

contract for deed, 79

contract interest rate, 89

contractual relationships

deed-of-trust, 331–332

promissory notes, 326–330

convertible ARMs, 106

corporate form of ownership, 418, 419, 503–504, 507–508, 517–519

correlation, 528

correlation coefficient, 528

cost approach, 339

Cost of Funds Index (COFI), 105

cost recovery fee, 454

counterparty risk, 232

Countrywide Financial Corp., 71

covenants, 332

coverage ratio, 355

CPR (constant prepayment rate), 264–265

cramdown, 71, 570–571

Cranston-Gonzalez National Affordability Housing Act of 1990, 161, 164, 217–218

CRA (Community Reinvestment Act) of 1978, 126, 197, 205–210

creative financing, 77–79

credit agreement statutes, 563

credit-based financing, 495

credit default swaps (CDSs), 232–234

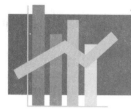

Exhibit 11. Housing Affordability Index: 1974–Present

Period	United States				Affordability Indexes[*]		
	Median Price Existing Single-Family ($)	Mortgage Rate[1]	Median Family Income ($)	Income To Qualify ($)	Composite	Fixed	ARM
Annual Data							
1974	32,000	9.02	12,902	9,905	130.3	130.3	130.3
1975	35,300	9.21	13,719	11,112	123.5	123.5	123.5
1976	38,100	9.11	14,958	11,888	125.8	125.8	125.8
1977	42,900	9.02	16,010	13,279	120.6	120.6	120.6
1978	48,700	9.58	17,640	15,834	111.4	111.4	111.4
1979	55,700	10.92	19,680	20,240	97.2	97.2	97.2
1980	62,200	12.95	21,023	26,328	79.9	79.9	79.9
1981	66,400	15.12	22,388	32,485	68.9	68.9	68.9
1982	67,800	15.38	23,433	33,713	69.5	69.4	69.7
1983	70,300	12.85	24,580	29,546	83.2	81.7	85.2
1984	72,400	12.49	26,433	29,650	89.1	84.6	92.1
1985	75,500	11.74	27,735	29,243	94.8	89.6	100.6
1986	80,300	10.25	29,458	27,047	108.9	105.7	116.3
1987	85,600	9.28	30,970	27,113	114.2	107.6	122.4
1988	89,300	9.31	32,191	28,360	113.5	103.6	122.0
1989	94,600	10.11	34,218	30,432	112.4	105.9	116.8
1990	97,300	10.04	35,353	31,104	113.7	110.6	122.8
1991	102,700	9.30	35,940	30,816	116.6	113.5	128.3
1992	105,500	8.11	36,573	28,368	128.9	124.9	150.8
1993	109,100	7.16	36,959	26,784	138.0	133.0	160.4
1994	113,500	7.47	38,790	28,704	135.1	125.2	153.3
1995	117,000	7.85	40,612	30,672	132.4	126.6	143.3
1996	122,600	7.71	42,305	31,728	133.3	129.6	142.9
1997	129,000	7.68	44,573	35,232	126.5	123.6	137.2
1998	136,000	7.10	46,740	35,088	133.2	131.9	142.6
1999	141,200	7.33	48,955	37,296	131.3	128.8	142.0
2000	147,300	8.03	50,733	41,616	121.9	120.5	133.3
2001	156,600	7.03	51,407	40,128	128.1	128.1	137.3
2002	167,600	6.55	51,680	40,896	126.4	124.2	138.7
2003	180,200	5.74	52,680	40,320	130.7	128.2	141.8
2004	195,200	5.73	54,061	43,632	123.9	120.3	132.2
2005	219,000	5.91	56,914	49,920	112.6	110.9	116.4
2006	221,900	6.58	58,407	54,288	107.6	107.1	109.6
2007	217,900	6.52	61,173	52,992	115.4	115.3	117.6
2008[2]	196,600	6.15	63,366	45,984	137.8	137.4	143.0
2009	172,100	5.14	61,082	36,048	169.4	169.2	NA
2010	173,200	4.89	61,313	35,232	174.0	169.0	NA
2011	166,200	4.67	60,831	32,976	184.5	174.6	NA
Monthly Data							
2011							
Jan	158,500	4.82	60,743	32,016	189.7	188.6	NA
Feb	156,900	4.91	60,769	32,016	189.8	188.4	NA
Mar	160,600	4.98	60,792	33,024	184.1	181.7	NA
Apr	161,300	4.93	60,813	32,976	184.4	182.0	NA
May	169,800	4.87	60,823	34,464	176.5	174.1	NA
Jun	176,100	4.75	60,831	35,280	172.4	170.3	NA
Jul	171,700	4.70	60,850	34,176	178.0	176.1	NA
Aug	171,200	4.69	60,845	34,080	178.5	177.5	NA
Sep	165,400	4.51	60,851	32,208	188.9	185.1	NA
Oct	161,100	4.32	60,873	30,672	198.5	194.2	NA
Nov	164,000	4.33	60,876	31,296	194.5	190.1	NA
Dec	162,600	4.27	60,901	30,768	197.9	192.5	NA
2012							
Jan	154,600	4.37	60,944	29,616	205.8	201.2	NA
Feb	156,100	4.21	60,974	29,328	207.9	200.4	NA
Mar	165,100	3.96	60,999	30,144	202.4	199.5	NA

[*]The composite affordability index is the ratio of median family income to qualifying income. Values over 100 indicate that the typical (median) family has more than sufficient income to purchase the median-priced home.

ARM = Adjustable-rate mortgage. NA = Data not available.

[1] The Federal Housing Finance Agency's monthly effective mortgage rate amortizes points over 10 years. Annual data are averages of the monthly rates.

[2] Beginning in December 2008, the Adjustable-Rate Mortgage Affordability Index could not be derived because the rates for ARMs were no longer available.

Source: NATIONAL ASSOCIATION OF REALTORS®   **http://www.realtor.org/research/research/housinginx**

Historical Data